Contemporary Media
Structures, Functions, Issues and Ethics

Fourth Edition

K. Tim Wulfemeyer

KENDALL/HUNT PUBLISHING COMPANY
4050 Westmark Drive   Dubuque, Iowa 52002

Table of Contents

Introduction v

Chapter 1: Converging Communications 1

Chapter 2: The Process of Communication..37

Chapter 3: Mass Media Economics...55

Chapter 4: The History of Mass Media..73

Chapter 5: Newspapers 109

Chapter 6: Magazines 131

Chapter 7: Books..151

Chapter 8: Radio 171

Chapter 9: Television...205

Chapter 10: The Recording Industry 225

Chapter 11: The Motion Picture Industry 237

Chapter 12: Public Relations..255

Chapter 13: Advertising...275

Chapter 14: Legal Rights and Limitations...311

Chapter 15: Ethics 337

Learning Opportunities 363

Feedback 399

Introduction

Welcome to the latest edition of *Contemporary Media: Structures, Functions, Issues and Ethics.* The book will help you become more knowledgeable about the mass media. You'll find information about the past, present and future of the mass media. You'll find information about newspapers, magazines, book publishing, the Internet, radio, television, the recording industry, movies, public relations and advertising. You'll find information about structures, functions, theories, roles, responsibilities and ethics. You'll find information about issues and problems. You'll find information about laws and regulations. You'll find information about jobs and careers.

You won't find much information about the technological aspects of the mass media. The concentration is on the content, structures and issues associated with the mass media. The impacts that technology, especially emerging technologies, have on the mass media are addressed, of course, but the science of television, radio, movies and the other mass media is not included.

Special emphasis is placed on news in the mass media, because it is critical that you develop an understanding of how news is gathered, processed and distributed. Every person needs to know how journalists think and work so that the news can be put in its proper perspective. Journalists help us learn about the world around us, so it is imperative that we develop the skills and knowledge necessary to be able to evaluate how effective journalists are in bringing us accurate, complete, meaningful, useful and balanced information about the important people, events and issues that affect our lives.

Contemporary Media: Structures, Functions, Issues and Ethics forces you to take an active role in your quest to develop such skills and knowledge. The book is designed to engage you as much as possible in the learning process. To maximize the learning potential from the book, you'll need to read carefully, think critically about what you read and write cogently about your views concerning the critical issues facing the mass media.

Included in each chapter are sections called **YOUR THOUGHTS**. These sections ask you to stop reading, think about an issue or problem, and write briefly about it. Don't skip over these sections. Take the time to respond to each question. It will help you gain insights and a deeper understanding of the significant aspects, issues, problems and dilemmas associated with the mass media.

At the end of each chapter, are features called **THINK BACK** to give you a chance to test yourself to see how much you've learned from the chapter. If you can answer such questions without much trouble, you'll likely do well on tests, quizzes and exams.

At the end of the book, several exercises and learning opportunities are included. Be sure to look them over. Even if your instructor doesn't assign any of them, do some on your own. They'll help you find examples of many of the things covered in *Contemporary Media: Structures, Functions, Issues and Ethics.*

A new feature has been added to this fourth edition of *Contemporary Media: Structures, Functions, Issues and Ethics.* A special web site contains updated information about the people, events and issues associated with contemporary media. Included are links to media-related web sites, study guides, sample test questions, behind-the-scenes looks at media-related organizations, course-management aspects and much more. Check with your instructor to find out how to access and maximize the benefits associated with the web site.

A special thanks to James K. Buckalew, coauthor of the first three editions of *Contemporary Media: Structures, Functions, Issues and*

Ethics (Formerly titled *Mass Media in the New Millennium: Structures, Functions, Issues and Ethics*). Dr. Buckalew, a professor emeritus at San Diego State University, decided not to participate in the latest revision and web site development of this edition in order to pursue other interests. Many of his contributions to this book remain, however. Dr. Buckalew has been my teacher, colleague, mentor and friend for almost 40 years. His insights, perspectives, critical thinking abilities and sense of humor, developed over a period of about 50 years as a professional journalist and journalism educator, provide the foundation for much of the content of this book.

Another special thanks to my wife, Dr. Lori McFadden Wulfemeyer. She has served as a sounding board for many of the ideas featured in this book, assisted with the organization of the content and helped edit several of the chapters. Dr. Wulfemeyer has worked as a journalist, high-school teacher, university professor and assistant dean of communications at a law school.

Finally, I encourage you to be an active consumer of the various mass media. If you read newspapers and magazines regularly, watch television and television news every day, listen to the radio a couple of hours a day, listen to digital music and CDs every day, read for pleasure as much as possible, surf the Internet and attend a movie or two per month, you'll get a lot more out of this book. Be a critical reader, listener and viewer, though. Think about why things are done the way they're done. Think about the issues associated with the mass media messages. Think about the ethics associated with the mass media messages. If you think critically about the mass media, you'll gain a greater appreciation and understanding of the mass media. Such knowledge will help you make sense of the issues and problems associated with the mass media and it will help you get more out of life in the 21st Century.

K. Tim Wulfemeyer
San Diego, California
June, 2008

Converging Communications

Many of the traditional mass media—newspapers, magazines, books, radio, television, the recording industry and the film industry—are experiencing tough times. The traditional revenue streams of advertising and use fees (subscriptions, sales, tickets) are not as robust and dependable as they once were. Competition from new media technologies and content-delivery methods have eroded the economic base on which mass media organizations have depended for years. As a result, both old and new media continue to explore creative ways to create, deliver, pay for and profit by content. It makes for exciting and interesting times for those who make their living via contemporary media and for those who hope to make their living via one or more of the various contemporary media, for those of us who depend on the various contemporary media to provide the news and information we use to make the important decisions in our lives and for those of us who simply enjoy consuming the products produced by the various contemporary media. And that's just about all of us—right?

Many Americans believe that we possess the world's freest and most open media, which provide all the news in a fair and honest manner. Many of us are so confident in this trust that we pay no attention to foreign or alternative media, although they are readily available.

We are so conditioned to believing that our media are accurate and fair that it might take some time for us to notice even drastic changes in the fulfillment of this trust. Even in times when Americans condemn the media, we depend on the same media to report accurately. After all, it was the media that informed us when the American media lost credibility.

Ownership and control of the U.S. media are now undergoing extensive consolidation. The change is accelerated by a number of economic and social conditions. It is not possible to predict how media ownership and control will alter the effectiveness of the mass media or their credibility in the eyes of the public, but it is important for citizens in democratic societies to take note of what is happening and to find ways to evaluate its impact.

History's media giants did not necessarily endorse competition. In many cases they went to great lengths to defeat or destroy their competitors. However, technology, times and economic conditions were such that competition flourished. The competition forced media owners to strive for excellence, because that was one efficient way to beat the competition.

By the early years of the 21st century, many changes had caused the media to consolidate into bigger organizations, competition to lessen, and the media business to become more and more like other businesses. A number of newspapers grouped under one organization is usually called a chain or group, a number of broadcast stations grouped under one organization is usually called a group, meshing several types of media in one organization is known as cross-ownership, and ownership of media organizations by a corporation that also owns other, nonmedia businesses is called a conglomerate. We are now witnessing all of these actions at an increasing rate, for a number of reasons.

One obvious reason is the cost of new and necessary equipment. No matter the cost of adjusting to new technology in the digital age, the media cannot resist for long because of the likelihood that they will quickly lose out to the competition. That takes capital that most small organizations cannot raise.

New and more specialized equipment requires better-trained and more specialized workers to maintain and operate it. Media writers, broadcasters, producers, and technicians must be better qualified than ever before to keep pace with digitalization. Most communication professionals these days are college graduates who merit and demand better pay than their predecessors. This encourages media owners to consolidate and make maximum use of each employee and manager.

Laws and government agency directives affecting the media make it profitable to combine, buy, or sell. About one-third of all present laws in the United States affect communications in some way. Many of the requirements for safety and employee welfare can best be met by large media organizations.

The production and distribution of media products has become big business. The weight of investment needed to compete on a yearly basis tends to encourage media organizations to expand their capital bases.

Finally, the basic urge for power also enters the equation. As governmental agencies have relaxed controls, media capable of doing so have moved to maximize power and profits.

As a result of these and many other pressures, communication organizations are getting larger. Because stock in a public corporation is publicly traded, in theory, media corporations could be owned by small middle-class stockholders. In practice, however, a small number of individuals usually own enough shares to control the organization's operation. That has powerful implications in the consideration of media control.

Most Americans seem to believe that so long as there is real competition for their attention between media, they will be well served. So long as media operators know that the public has a choice, they reason, the media will provide high-quality information and entertainment at the lowest profitable costs. However, American confidence in competition has not always been substantiated.

Most Americans expect that a condition of near monopoly in the media would bring prompt government action. It is the government's charge, after all, to protect the rights of each person. But others decry wholesale government intervention. Beginning in the 1980s and continuing well into the years that opened the new millennium, government had lessened restrictions on businesses generally and on media specifically. A concept called deregulation evolved, which essentially meant less regulation.

In the early years of the 21st century, our news content seemed to be devoted to the prospect of, or the completion of, the sale of one vast telecommunications empire to another. Editorialists whined that concentration of ownership of media through mergers and consolidations was constricting access and limiting diversity. Decisions anticipated by the Federal Communications Commission were as newsworthy as the eventual determinations made by the commission. Media ownership reforms—expected, feared or actual—were apparently as newsworthy as celebrity murders and sex scandals.

Relaxed limits on media ownership were enhancing the economic prospects of companies such as News Corp., Viacom Inc., and Tribune Corp. by boosting their ability to conglomerate further with the biggest media conglomerates. Critics asked whether loosening restraints on the broadcast industry would allow too much control of information and entertainment to the highest bidder. At the core of the criticism was the opportunity for broadcasters not only to grow but also to merge with the biggest newspapers. Local broadcast-newspaper and local TV-radio cross-ownership limits have been relaxed to allow, in larger markets, a company to own a newspaper, a television station and several radio stations.

A few decades ago, the Justice Department's Anti-Trust Division would have been asked to look at any or all of these media empires as possible illegal monopolies. Now that is not a concern for the Justice Department. The Anti-Trust Division waits until there is proof of some obvious and serious price-fixing in the media marketplace before even considering any possible action. Media critics, however, argue that restraints on competition aren't the problem so much as closing off public access to the media, as well as sameness of media content. Critics point to one voice emanating from the Gannett Corporation, which owns several newspapers, including *USA Today,* as well as radio and television stations. Hearst Corporation owns magazines, newspapers, publishing houses and broadcast properties. Do they echo the corporate line? Does each part of the Hearst or Gannett chain speak independently of the others?

As restraints on media growth were being lifted, readers, viewers and listeners of those media were already well into the age of digital communication. The Internet had become mainstream. Americans embraced digital media with ease, demonstrating that the Internet had taken its place alongside traditional businesses. Commerce had transformed the culture of the Internet and had made the World Wide Web a mainstream phenomenon. The millennium ushered in the post-revolutionary age for digital communication, with the Internet adopted eagerly by traditional businesses including media-related businesses.

With the breakneck pace of technology, media and their audiences are changing dramatically. The new millennium brought a convergence of traditional conduits for information, entertainment and persuasion with computers, the Internet and e-commerce, a collision of powerful forces that has already delivered much of its promise. An early sign of the convergence was when audience studies revealed that more people increasingly surf the Internet while watching television. Another study found that roughly 20% of American households have both the computer and the TV on at the same time. Television is seeing audience defections to new channels that sign on daily. Research is reported indicating that Americans who spend a lot of time on the Web spend less time with television, radio, newspapers, and have even less time in face-to-face interaction with other humans. Television screens are growing bigger, clearer and are incorporating features such as Internet data links to data streams that augment whatever program or movie happens to be on. Hundreds of channels are expected to supplement the 200 broadcast and cable services available at the turn of the century through interactive delivery systems that allow users to create personal viewing experiences.

Online radio gives listeners more choices than 20th century radio offered. As online radio grows, much of its promise lies in its ability to reach audiences by crossing time zones and geographic boundaries, and in the fact that more and more Americans are getting comfortable with the idea of radio that you listen to through your computer.

Another trend involves the emergence of "information entrepreneurs." Technological advances, especially digital information transmission, have made it possible for many more voices to enter the marketplace of ideas than perhaps ever before. People can produce their own "newspapers" and "magazines" online or on paper much more easily and inexpensively now. People can distribute their own musical creations online without having to be "signed" by a record company. People can create and distribute their own e-movies and video clips online without having to find a great deal of financial support. People can become radio programmers and performers without having to leave the front of their computer screens. People can also publish online books without having to get an agent and be picked up by a publishing house.

If all of the possibilities associated with convergence within the traditional industries of mass media, digital transmission capabilities and the political will to empower all segments of society with the ability to join the Information Age are developed fully, we might actually reach most of the goals set by many media experts. We might more fully democratize information gathering, creation, distribution and consumption. We might also achieve the 4 As of the Internet:

1. Anyone will have access to and be able to use the Internet
2. Anywhere you are, you will be able to use the Internet—home, car, work, play, etc.
3. Any time you want to use the Internet, you will be able to.
4. Any device will be Internet-compatible—cell phone, TV set, etc.

The Media as Wasteland

It isn't only the professor, the communications students, editors, reporters, station managers, and publishers who are attentive to the inquiries into public attitudes toward the media. Much has been written about the Roper organization's frequent polling of a cross section of the American adult population and the resultant assumption that people increasingly say that they usually get most of their information about what's going on in the world from television. In addition, when asked if conflicting reports were heard which source would be believed, respondents most often pick television as the nation's most credible news source.

Other research has supported, contradicted, explained, refuted, agreed with, disagreed with, examined, or revised the Roper findings. Newspaper trade groups and broadcast associations have battled over which medium is the public's favorite and which is most believable. A consensus from the variety of studies into audience attitudes toward media reveals that for some purposes radio is ideal, for other uses newspapers are desired, for others magazines are preferred.

There is also research indicating that when questions are made more specific, the results show newspapers are preferred for local news and for political news while television is a favorite source for news farther from home. The more local the news the more support the public gives to radio.

The debate has been heated at times with each medium offering evidence to support its claim to the title of the "public's choice." It is fair to say that different questioning techniques can produce different responses from the sample. It is also fair to all of the media to say that attitudes expressed about a medium are not the same as actual patterns of use. The newspaper publishers have noted that their surveys show that even those who say that television is their first choice will also read a newspaper, saying that they do it to get even more information. It has also been learned that respondents discussing one issue say they learn about it from television, but when dealing with a greater number of issues they turn to newspapers. Better informed persons indicate both a preference for and greater use of newspapers as news sources.

We learn from conflicting claims and the research upon which they are based that the media do not really compete for the audience in the same way they compete for advertisers or for access to sources or story information. In fact, some readership studies suggest that exposure to an event by radio and television tends to increase newspaper and magazine readership about that same event. When readers have already heard of items over the air before looking them up in print, it tends to support a hypothesis that exposure to an event by one medium tends to stimulate further exposure through another medium.

Many years ago cries of "Extra! Extra! Read All About It!" were heard in the streets of our cities as hawkers of newspapers aggressively heralded the arrival of each edition. These newshawks have been replaced by coin-operated boxes and an increasing dependence on home delivery or sedate displays in stores and newsstands. Perhaps their hawking function, or their vocal announcements of further promise from loudly proclaimed headlines, has been taken over by the newer media.

How many times have we heard a brief, headline-style item on a radio newscast that made us curious enough to actively seek out more about the story later in a newspaper? How often have we watched the sights and sounds, although sketchily done, on a late night television newscast and then turned to the same story in the next morning's newspaper? One assumption that we can make that explains the contradictory claims of the various media trade associations is that they tend to complement each other while competing.

Each medium at a given moment might supply the same service to a different audience, or different services to the same audience. Various media at a given moment might supply the same service to one or more audiences, but in a different length, style or format. One medium, or several media, at different times might supply the same or different services to an audience or audiences in the same or different lengths, styles or formats. Studies of news diffusion reveal multi-media habits. Readers of newspapers tend to be television news watchers. Those who hear of fast-breaking events by word-of-mouth tend to go to radio news for more information and for confirmation. Radio's brief treatment tends to send us toward television and newspapers for more than confirmation.

It is not uncommon for us to attend sporting events with portable radios tuned to the games we are watching. Afterwards we race through heavy traffic to get home in time to see televised snippets of the key plays from those same contests. Of course, we check the newspaper sports section first thing the next morning and read about what we witnessed. A week later in a sports magazine we peruse the detailed follow-up to that event.

Note that each medium gives us something different about the game. The radio gives us immediacy. Television gives us a capsule version of the highlights, a not-so-instant replay of our favorite moments, and with both sight and sound. But the details and the first real background we get come hours later from a medium, the newspaper, that is simply physically able to give us so much more detail. Sometimes it takes even longer for the significance of events to be realized and for opinion to crystallize. That means it takes the special nature of the magazine to give us perspective, coupled with the additional time for gathering behind-the-scenes data and opinion, generating the final link in a media chain. It takes print to give us detail and it takes time to sort out the relevant detail.

A good exercise in learning how the media relate to each other and how they perform different and complementary functions is found in the attempt to take the written copy for a radio or television newscast and place it in a newspaper format or in a magazine setting. The typical 30-minute television newscast will generate enough copy for less than one newspaper page. Copy from a typical radio newscast wouldn't even fill one column in a newspaper.

An overview from studies of news diffusion, from readership and listening and viewing data, from research into audience attitudes and use patterns, can explain away the arguments and lay to rest the individual claims to media supremacy by displaying an overlapping, multi-media, complementary relationship. The media sound like adversaries in their attempts to point out where they are in public favor and yet they apparently combine in the presentation of a nexus of information and entertainment. Therefore, it is not a contradiction when television's leaders say two-thirds of American adults get most of their news from television at the same time that others point out that less than one adult in five watches television news on the average weekday, but four out of five read newspapers. Each is right. It simply takes an understanding of the complexity of inter-media relationships and of the habits of media users. We have to remember that some

of the survey questions have been too general, others have called for multiple answers, others required the expression of attitudes, and some asked for diaries to be kept documenting media use. The result is a picture of a mass public of individual consumers of a variety of media products, some of them consuming different content at the same time in varying forms, others consuming the same content at different moments and in different packaging.

For example, college-educated respondents in surveys are likely to say their favorite pastimes are attending movies, dining out, entertaining or going to the theater. Those with less formal education tend to cite watching television as the preferred way to spend an evening. The level of education is related to the type of program selected for viewing and to the decision about whether to read a newspaper or magazine. The higher the education level, the more likely the individual will be a reader not only of newspapers and magazines but also of books. Also, those who say they read newspapers also watch television news. There is an obvious overlap of media habits when a summary of all of the

Your Thoughts

Which medium do you turn to most for news about what's going on in the world outside the United States? Why?

Which medium do you turn to most for news about what's going on in the United States? Why?

Which medium do you turn to most for news about what's going on in your state? Why?

Which medium do you turn to most for news about what's going on in your local community? Why?

Do you agree or disagree that media tend to complement each other more than they compete with each other? Why?

research shows four out of five reading a newspaper on an average day, more than half listening to radio and nearly two-thirds of adults saying they turn to television for their news. This means when Americans want news and information, they don't make exclusive choices among media. They use them all.

Misdeeds and Mistrust

The publisher of the prestigious *New York Times* described it as "a day of deep sadness" when the paper's management accepted Pulitzer Prize-winning reporter Rick Bragg's resignation after suspending him over a story that carried his byline but was reported largely by a freelancer. That and other revelations resulted in resignations from the paper's top two editors. Earlier, reporter Jayson Blair resigned when an internal investigation revealed fraud, plagiarism and inaccuracies in 36 of 73 articles written by Blair. As an outgrowth of five weeks of turmoil, including a story in the *Times* detailing Blair's serial plagiarism and fraud, the newspaper said it would review newsroom policies, including hiring practices, the use of unidentified sources and freelancers and byline and dateline practices. Bragg's suspension resulted from relying almost exclusively on an unpaid (and uncredited) freelancer's work. Blair was brought to the attention of top management first when the *San Antonio Express-News* sent an e-mail to the *Times* accusing Blair of plagiarizing one of its stories. Subsequent inquiries into several of Blair's stories also revealed that many of his unnamed sources could not be located and were quite probably non-existent.

Perhaps the most unpardonable offense in the practice of journalism is the fabrication of quotations or of complete stories. A staff writer for *The New Republic* seemed to be nearing the peak of his young career and was much sought after as a freelance writer when his deceptions put him and the integrity of his profession into question. He had written for *Harper's, George* and *Rolling Stone,* among others, when subjects of some of his stories challenged their accuracy. It quickly became evident that many of his articles were figments of his imagination. The scandal was reminiscent of earlier revelations about *Washington Post* reporter Janet Cooke, who wrote a phony account of an 8-year-old heroin addict. The newspaper returned a Pulitzer Prize for feature writ-

ing when the fabrication was discovered. Investigation revealed that there was no "Jimmy," as the fictitious boy had been named by Cooke, who had insisted for weeks that her story was accurate in the face of challenge after challenge by other reporters, editors and Washington law enforcement who never believed her. When it was learned that her job application and résumé had been fabricated, claiming for example schooling and degrees that she did not have, she could no longer sustain her defense of the fraud.

The media themselves often carry analyses of their problems, their rapidly declining reputation and a growing distrust among their readers, viewers and listeners. A *Los Angeles Times* poll found that 40% of those surveyed said they had less confidence in the news media than when they first became news consumers. The report on the distrustful public concluded that credibility of the media has declined and that members of the public feel a growing disenfranchisement from the news media.

A survey by the Pew Center for the People and the Press found that even journalists themselves were greatly concerned about declining public trust in the news media. Print, TV, radio and Internet journalists seemed to agree that reporting was often sloppy, there was too much speculation and opinion by reporters, financial pressures hampered news coverage and there was too much blurring of the line between news and entertainment. More specifically, more than half the journalists surveyed expressed concerns about sensationalism, lack of objectivity and inaccuracies. About 40% expressed concerns about too much emphasis on the bottom line, competition with other news organizations and declining audiences. About 33% expressed concerns about the general loss of public trust, confidence and credibility.

If the credibility of the media is frequently being challenged, it is imperative that efforts be made to restore public confidence. There have been instances of challenges to media practices from Spiro Agnew to Rush Limbaugh, from Jane Fonda to Jesse Jackson. From every direction, from critics and complainers, from opinion leaders to officialdom, have come attacks that center on perceptions of bias and a view of ethical mistakes.

A new wave of sensationalism, reminiscent of the penny press of the 1830s, yellow journalism of the 1890s, and the tabloids of the 1920s, has resulted from the proliferation of television's pseudo news. Crossing the line between news and show business is so prevalent that the credibility crisis is understandable.

The recent sensationalism differs from earlier such periods of excessive attention to the trivial in that it is not, for the most part, being presented by the print media. *USA Today* gets criticism for its superficial approach to news, a coverage that rarely provides any depth, but it is only one newspaper. The *National Enquirer* and others of its tawdry ilk are complained about as major exponents of sex, violence, trivia and human interest rather than conduits of news of significance, but they are not representative of the newspaper industry. There is nothing in the newspapering of today to compare with the *New York Herald* of James Gordon Bennett, nor of the circulation wars later between William Randolph Hearst and Joseph Pulitzer. The extremes of New York newspapers in the 1920s, especially Bernarr Macfadden's *Graphic* and Joseph Patterson's *Daily News,* were major entities reflecting a period of American life, the Jazz Age, in which sensational coverage could dominate.

Early in the 21st century, newspapers were content to leave the banal and the breathless, as well as the gory and grimy, to the newer media, especially television and the Internet. Perhaps it began with the "happy talk" formats and the "Ken and Barbie" news anchors of the local TV stations. Network news departments resisted the "showtime" aspects of their affiliates until the early 1990s, but network programming departments and independent production companies, working with syndicators, made entertainment inroads into journalistic areas and a crisis was created. Public acceptance of infotainment and docudramas resulted in a blurring of the classical distinction that set broadcast journalism apart from the rest of the broadcast programming. The crisis was one of lowered credibility and a loss of public esteem for all of broadcasting, perhaps for all of the media.

To advocate ethical practices is to advocate for an increased credibility. To strive for ethical decisions in determining all media content is to seek more esteem from the public for the carriers of entertainment, advertising and information.

When media people do wrong things, when they insult their audiences or pander to baser instincts, they do it in a very visible setting. Their mistakes are obvious. Their ethical errors are presented to the public, often resulting in an outcry of public disappointment or even outrage. If students of journalism, broadcasting, public relations, advertising and related disciplines are to avoid inflaming such negative reactions during their eventual careers, they are going to need to address ethics early on. If today's media decision-makers are to gain public acceptance, they must consider ethical pressures not, just ratings, circulation figures, profit margins, and competition from peers. It can be argued that the greatest departure from ethics is when someone decides to compromise another person's welfare to acquire something that is wanted very badly. The support for this decision is usually referred to as a need to commit an act that is permitted because it is not illegal. Ethicists, and affected individuals, would point out that just because it is not illegal does not make it right nor even acceptable. There are consequences to the choices we make and those consequences can be harmful.

The media decision-makers can improve the image of themselves and their peers by doing no harm when choosing from alternatives. That sounds too easy to say until one considers that the harm in the long run could be to your profession. A faulty ethical decision that appears to help in your career in the short run may so diminish your profession that it will not be worth it in the long run. The ethical practice of news gathering and of news presentation is in itself a goal. Ethical behavior is good for the profession and benefits the individual in that profession.

Even in 19th century America there were newspapers that broke sharply from the sensationalism of the Penny Press and the political partisanship of the viewspapers. We went from Federalist Party newspapers and the Kitchen Cabinet of the Andrew Jackson administration to organs of political leadership independent of political party. As we moved toward the 20th century, despite the era of yellow journalism, our newspapers often looked toward striving for civic betterment and actively seeking coverage that would contribute to the community welfare. E.W. Scripps and Joseph Pulitzer earned reputations as crusaders for the common man and were appreciated for their altruism. Later, Henry Grady and William Allen White demonstrated that through newspapering they could offer programs of social change at a time when sober voices were needed and society was being torn by divisive forces.

Eventually, broadcasting developed its own corps of highly respected journalists, chief among them, of course, the commentators and analysts of the 1930s and 1940s. The early leadership of Paul White and the emergence later of Edward R. Murrow and Walter Cronkite, among others, made CBS a prestigious

What are your views concerning the credibility of the news media?

Why do you feel the way you do?

Which medium do you think is the most credible? Why?

organization known for standards of excellence; however, now even the network that gave us Edward R. Murrow, "the conscience of broadcast journalism," has fallen into some disrepute and is no longer the acknowledged leader in broadcast credibility.

The Internet has opened new areas of concern about media content. With few restrictions associated with who can become an information provider and what kind of information can be made available, rumors, lies, half-truths and bogus information abound. Studies have found that many web sites, especially those dealing with health-related issues, contain inaccurate, undocumented and unconfirmed information. In addition, many examples of Internet "payola" have been found. Creators of web sites have taken money or other inducements in exchange for favorable reviews of certain products, people and services.

The Credibility Chasm

Instances of ethical lapses that fostered outcries against the media included two separate actions by NBC, one in a story on the NBC Nightly News and the other on the program, "Dateline NBC." NBC eventually apologized for errors in the news story because of what was described as inadvertently misused videotaped footage about federal forest management in Idaho. The story had claimed that overcutting of forests by federal employees had caused fouled streams and endangered fish. Anchorman Tom Brokaw, in the network's apol-

ogy, admitted that inaccurate videotape was used in two instances, including one tape that showed fish that appeared to be dead but actually had simply been stunned for testing purposes. The other footage showed dead fish from a forest farther south of the one that was being discussed in the NBC report.

If the media are already mistrusted by many, such mistakes in judgment, such ethical lapses, contribute to further erosion of credibility. It was unfortunate for NBC that the botched federal forest management story followed closely the other faulty decision that put the network before the public as one willing to insult and dupe its viewers. "Dateline NBC" crossed the ethical line when it failed to tell audiences that its footage demonstrating a test of vehicle safety was misleading. An NBC crew arranged to have a General Motors pickup truck rigged with remote-controlled ignition devices to make sure that its gas tank would explode during a collision. The crash was staged as if it were a test conducted for the network's news crew to demonstrate that such trucks were built by GM with dangerously unsafe gas tanks. NBC news producers must have determined that getting such a visually dramatic display of the point to the story was worth the risk of violating journalistic ethics, but it turned out to be an embarrassment for the network specifically and to broadcast journalism generally.

Another embarrassment for broadcast journalism came when a television station in Seattle announced that it had spent $3 million to change the look of news programs, without investing any dollars to augment its staff of writers, reporters, photojournalists, or newsroom technicians. The station said it was spending the money on promoting the new format and on the set itself, which was designed by a former set designer from Industrial Light and Magic and the co-artistic director of the Seattle Ballet, indicating less interest in journalistic improvements than in glitzy packaging.

A different Seattle station was criticized at about the same time for airing a special report on the area's transit system when that report was partially funded by the transit agencies. Some of the money for the program came from a public relations agency doing promotion for the Seattle Metro Transit Agency. All told, three transit agencies defrayed costs of the special report that focused on more than $9 million in proposed improvements in transit operations. The program's host told a Seattle newspaper that the program was subsidized in part, but was not actually paid for.

A San Diego television station once breathlessly promoted an upcoming report on local gang members hiring out as contract killers as an "exclusive," then simply reiterated the information about the gang members' possible involvement in the killing of a Roman Catholic Cardinal that all of the other San Diego media had conveyed over the previous three days.

At about the same time, CBS was being sued by a man who was pictured by a camera crew while his car was being repossessed. The suit charged the network with fraud and invasion of privacy, saying the camera crew went into his back yard, his private property, and followed the repossession specialist as he went about his task. The plaintiff charged that the field producer never identified himself.

Print media also embarrassed themselves with decisions that disappointed fellow journalists and possibly widened the gap between public and press. *USA Today* took what was called significant disciplinary action against a reporter for his role in arranging a misleading photograph in a story about gang violence in Los Angeles. An executive with the newspaper admitted that the picture was set up under false pretenses, that the reporter staged the setting that created the impression of five angry-looking young black men with guns. The men actually were gathered to turn in the weapons under a guns-for-jobs program and originally had shown up at the site without any guns. The reporter had even driven one of them to his mother's house to get a rifle so it could be used for the photograph. None of the circumstances were mentioned in the caption nor in the story.

Hyping and Hoaxing

No airplanes fell from the sky. No automobiles suddenly stopped running because of computer

Your Thoughts

What could/should the news media do to rebuild some of their lost credibility? Be specific. Suggest at least FIVE improvements.

What sanctions, if any, do you think there should be for journalists who violate ethics code guidelines and/or the public trust?

Who should monitor journalistic performance and invoke appropriate sanctions for unprofessional conduct?

malfunction. No supermarkets or drug stores were forced to close. Gas pumps continued to fill tanks and ATM machines continued to dispense money and issue receipts. Some overly concerned purchasers of gas-powered generators and other survivalist equipment ended up seeking refunds from retailers who sold such items. The Federal Reserve Board opened the new millennium by collecting the unneeded extra $10 billion that it had distributed to banks in case of a cash panic. Any Y2K problems reported were from firms that suffered only minor glitches.

It was a surprise to many in a media-saturated public that Y2K was greeted with a yawn rather than a groan, relief rather than terror. Newspaper readers and radio and television audiences had survived the most over-hyped non-event yet.

Did the government over-react when round-the-clock monitoring of the potential problem was set up at considerable cost to taxpayers, then shut down earlier than planned when nothing seemed to be happening?

Despite all of the media attention and subsequent public concern, we entered the 21st century calmly. It was, for the most part, business as usual. The calendar shift affected some computers in retail stores, but in those instances, purchases and exchanges were handled by employees manually with no serious problems.

The most obvious glitch was one not blamed on the Y2K bug. Wal-Mart chose the weekend of the move into a new century to launch a re-designed Web site and learned how perilous e-commerce can be when it inadvertently featured explicit sex books among its family-oriented fare. Wal-Mart promotes a clean image and marks potentially offensive music with "sanitized for your protection." Yet, inappropriate paperbacks with content inconsistent with the Wal-Mart image slipped through because a data base of titles from a third-party supplier was downloaded. Human error, said Wal-Mart officials, not the Millennium bug.

Was the bug a hoax? Probably not. Were the predicted disasters averted because businesses and industries conducted extensive analyses and installed critical upgrades to internal systems? Possibly. Was it because it was always likely that only a smattering of minor problems, if any, could have ever occurred from what had been called the year 2000 computer bug? Possibly. Was the bug squashed? Probably. Was the computer bug actually a media creation? Probably not. Did the media overwork and overplay the

potential for cash shortages, hoarding of food and water, a societal breakdown, and even an Armageddon-like panic? Apparently so.

In the calm after the media storm, there were sighs of relief from those who believed the media predictions and projections. There were cries of "I told you so" from many who said journalists were hyping and sensationalizing what should have been a relatively insignificant, unlikely possibility. Even with the media frenzy and the possible waste of $300–500 billion spent worldwide to forestall something that likely was not going to happen, there were major benefits. Sensationalized or not, the billions spent on technology upgrades helped boost long-term productivity and helped American business maintain cutting-edge positions. Within a few months after the turn of the century, economists were saying that Y2K was turning out to be a large net plus for the United States economy.

Jitters about computer disruptions prompted American businesses to open their checkbooks and replace aging computer systems with sleek, modern ones, resulting in an historic push to modernize. Anxieties over a feared computer chaos at the shift to a new century, whether well founded or not, stimulated United States industry to leap into a 21st century of technology.

Was the media hype all bad? Probably not. Was the journalistic sensationalism typical? Certainly. More than 150 years ago, the *New York Sun* printed a brief story about a large telescope that had been invented, employing new magnification principles, by the son of the man who had discovered the planet Uranus. A few days later, the *Sun* carried a longer, front-page story about new discoveries made by this unusual telescope. The story said that planets had been discovered in other solar systems and objects on earth's moon had been noted as clearly as if seen by the unaided eye from only 100 yards. The article added that the telescope settled the question of whether the moon was inhabited and by what kinds of beings. The third appearance of news about the telescope gave specifics about strange amphibious creatures living on the moon and resulted in republication of the information in other newspapers. A fourth article described creatures that resembled both humans and bats and the *Sun*'s circulation increased greatly. The concluding article told of irreparable damage to the telescope which caused a suspension of observations of the moon or any other bodies in this solar system or others. Eventually, a reporter could hold it back no longer and admitted that the stories were concocted out of whole cloth.

That moon hoax may have been the greatest fraud ever perpetrated by a news organization but it was not the only one. Edgar Allan Poe contributed a piece of fiction designed as a news story for a literary magazine. Newspapers of the so-called penny press era were quick to invent news if it could fit their sensational approach, stimulate their readers, and result in a competitive advantage in the circulation wars of the 1830s. In the late 19th and early 20th century, newspapers of the yellow journalism type were often charged with manufacturing news to help increase their circulations. Today, supermarket sleazepapers, the tabloids of the ilk of the *National Enquirer,* carry stories of babies weighing 40 pounds at birth or of mothers delivering babies at the age of seven after first making visits to space creatures aboard their intergalactic vessels.

One of the biggest hoaxes ever carried by the mainstream media did not originate with a creative reporter, a publisher intent on circulation increases, nor a television talk show host trying to create higher ratings. This hoax originated in the public where so much legitimate news begins. It was covered virtually unquestioningly by all of the media and accepted as fact by millions of Americans.

It finally ended when the federal Food and Drug Administration concluded that its investigators were never able to find a single instance of a syringe being placed in a Pepsi Cola can, despite news media accounts of such tampering. It had started with an 82-year-old man in Tacoma, Washington, who claimed that he found a syringe in a Diet Pepsi can. Apparently, the mistake was caused by the elderly man not realizing that a relative had followed a measure recommended by the American Diabetes Association and disposed of her syringe in a soda can. Although the man's daughter's mother-in-law was diabetic and knew of the protective measure for disposing of her needles, the man was not aware of the practice and believed that the can had been tampered with. Before the mistaken notion could be countered by investigators' findings, the news of the man's complaint to authorities began to appear and was followed by additional reports of tampering. Pepsi drinkers in nearly half the states reported finding needles and syringes in their Pepsi cans. As word of the first case spread through the media, additional reports were bred by the media accounts. Not a single one of these reported tamperings was ever substantiated.

Officials with the Food and Drug Administration went to the media with their contention that all of the reports were hoaxes and that such false reports of tampering would be prosecuted. Making a false report to federal officials is a crime. Immediately, a man in Pennsylvania was arrested after FDA investigators concluded that his story about finding a needle in a Pepsi can was untrue. Then, local officials in Rantoul, Illinois, and Branson, Missouri, took into custody men who were charged with making false police reports. Federal charges were filed against a woman in Ohio and a woman in Michigan. A woman in Covina, California, admitted to federal officials that she falsified a story about finding a plastic syringe and a needle in a can of Diet Crystal Pepsi. Other people in various parts of the country admitted to investigators that they made up their claims. In California, a woman said that she just wanted to get on television. Others simply said they were mistaken. One said that a needle that she at first thought was in a Pepsi can probably had just fallen from an article of her clothing. As others reneged on their stories, they admitted to being prompted by media stories to get some of the media attention for themselves.

The FDA eventually concluded that it could cite no actual cases of tampering and that there was nothing to link the nationwide claims of tampering because of the variety of products and containers involved. The FDA also noted the large number of geographical locations of bottling plants and the fact that production dates were months apart. Pepsico officials were glad to receive the final conclusion that an initial mistake reported by news media had resulted in a series of false claims by people wanting media attention, which eventually caused a giant hoax.

Federal officials, among others, blamed news accounts for creating and then spreading the wave of phony Pepsi tamperings nationwide. Journalists themselves re-examined their role in this and other cases where they were taken in by contrived pseudo-stories. Journalists will have to search their own motives in determining how they can warn the public about health threats without encouraging hoaxes.

Reporters and editors must be concerned about the impact of their stories.

The Pepsi tampering hoax was just a new trap for the media. They had fallen into other pitfalls before. In the 1980s there were instances of phony tamperings that were reported by the media and were then followed immediately by more reported tamperings. Halloween is the time of year when media jump all over stories about possible tamperings with candies and other treats that are given to children. It has been nearly impossible for anyone to verify reports of Halloween treat tampering, but year after year all of the media, national and local, resurrect such stories. No doubt the justification is that if it happens even once it is important to warn youngsters and their parents of the potential danger. No matter how remote the possibility, the media decision-makers feel that they are performing a public service by awakening their viewers, listeners and readers to the chance that there will be pins and needles in Girl Scout cookies. These rarely real and frequently imagined product-tampering incidents are reported faithfully in a pattern that is quite repetitive, despite the evidence that most are hoaxes.

The media lose public confidence when such hoaxes are revealed for what they are. Media credibility is at risk when reporters are too quick to accept information from sources without adequate verification. Perhaps too many reporters and editors justify not confirming their information by saying that they are attributing it to the source and if the source is wrong it is not the fault of the news people. Attribution may not always be sufficient. How many times do news organizations have to get burned by their sources before they realize they have problems with credibility and with their ethical stature?

The Big Seven

Generally, the mass media in the United States have been assigned and/or have adopted seven major roles and responsibilities. These are:

1. To inform
2. To educate
3. To entertain
4. To serve as a watchdog over big business and big government
5. To help establish public policies
6. To help bring about social change
7. To serve as a vehicle for advertising

Information

Most of us depend on the media, especially the news media, to provide us with information about what is going on in our community, state, country and world. Most of us want to know about the major events, developments and issues of the day. We need such information to help us make the important decisions in our lives. In addition, most of us like to be knowledgeable about local, national and international happenings so that we can discuss such things with friends, family, co-workers and acquaintances.

Education

Sometimes it's difficult to see much of a difference between information and education; however, information can be defined as mostly "short-term" knowledge—traffic accidents, crimes, legislative actions, court decisions, sports scores, etc. It's not really something that you can usually use directly to improve the quality of your life or the lives of the people you care about. Education involves mostly "long-term" knowledge. It deals more with information that people can use directly to help them live better lives.

A good example of the difference between "informing" and "educating" would be how a house fire might be covered by the news media. An "information-only" story would give us the standard details about the fire—the five Ws and the H (Who, What, Where, When, Why and How). An "education-oriented" story would include the 5Ws & the H, plus provide advice from experts on how to prevent house fires—things to watch out for, fire safety tips, advice for how best to avoid injuries, etc.

Entertainment

The mass media do a pretty good job of providing entertainment. Movies, newspapers, magazines, books, the Internet, broadcast television, cable television, radio, iPods and CDs all help us to enjoy our limited leisure time and to forget, at least for a short while, some of our problems.

Some people argue that the news media take the role/responsibility of entertaining much too seriously and exercise it much too often. Television news is especially criticized for having too few real "news" stories and too many meaningless, "fluff" stories about off-beat people, animals or places. Entertainment has its place, though, even in the most news-oriented publications and radio-TV newscasts.

Amusing, diverting, exciting, titillating or relaxing media content helps take the edge off a tough day at the office, at school or at home. When such content is included in news media products, it can help lessen the effect of the "doom and gloom" stories that normally dominate the day's news.

Providing entertaining stories and features can help a newspaper, newsmagazine, radio newscast or television newscast compete with other forms of leisure-time activities for the attention of the public. People have a great many choices when it comes to deciding how to spend their free time. Most people have many television and radio stations to choose from, maybe three daily/weekly newspapers, at least three major newsmagazines and about 15,000 other magazines. Of course, they can also read books, listen to iPods or CDs, play video games, watch videos, participate in a variety of sports, talk with family members or friends, putter in the yard or workshop, go on a picnic or just hang out.

In short, the competition for the attention of readers, listeners and viewers is intense, not only between direct competitors—one newspaper vs. another or one TV station vs. the other TV stations in a city—but also among the various media and among all of the other things people can do besides being an active news consumer.

Providing some entertaining stories and features along with the more traditional "hard news" of the day probably does encourage some people to read, listen to or watch news rather than read, listen to, watch or do something else, but there might be other, better ways to accomplish the same thing. Some people argue that news media organizations should leave the "entertaining" to the BIG boys and girls—film makers, authors, comedians, singers, etc.—and concentrate on doing a better job of informing, educating and watchdogging.

Some of the typical "entertaining" aspects of daily newspapers include comic strips and panels; movie, television program, drama, concert and book reviews; feature stories about interesting people and places, sports coverage; etc. Such things can take up quite a bit of the newspaper each day, especially when you consider that the vast majority of space—at least 60% and up to 70%+ in some cases—is already taken up by advertising. With so much space being devoted to advertising and entertaining, how much is left for the significant news of the day?

Television newscasts are usually filled with "entertaining" elements. Profiles of off-beat people, animals and places are common. Reviews of movies, restaurants and concerts regularly appear. Weathercasters and sportscasters often try to be comedians or impish pranksters. Newscasters occasionally even try their hand at comedy, puns or putdowns when they chat among themselves or with a reporter, the weathercaster or the sportscaster.

Such "fun-filled frolics" cut into the time available for news, of course. In the average half-hour TV newscast, at best only about 22 minutes are available for news, weather and sports. The other eight minutes are devoted to commercials. So, if about four minutes of "news" time are devoted to sports, about three minutes to weathercaster fun, about one minute to chit-chat and maybe about three minutes to features, that leaves only about 11 minutes for the "real news" of the day! That's not a lot of time to do an adequate job of covering the significant events and issues of the day.

Watchdogging

The media, especially the news media, play a very important role in helping us to monitor the performance of our elected and appointed government officials plus people involved in big and small business. Most of us don't have enough time to attend all the public hearings we'd like to and we certainly can't sort through the thousands of pages of public documents available to find out what's happening in Washington, DC and the other power centers in the country. We rely on the news media to keep an eye on the important power brokers to prevent them from abusing the power and trust we've given them.

Most major daily newspapers publish investigative reports. The three major newsmagazines, *Time, Newsweek* and *U.S. News & World Report*, devote most of their space to investigative reports. Radio is not known for its commitment to investigative journalism, but we still find some in-depth reporting on radio, especially on all-news radio and public broadcasting radio stations. The television networks have their weekly investigative journalism programs—60 Minutes, 20/20, Dateline, 48 Hours, etc.—plus on the nightly news programs, we often get one or two "in-depth" stories. Local television stations also do occasional investigative stories, especially during ratings periods. Some independent, TV-related and newspaper-related web sites feature in-depth investigative stories that often include multimedia features, interactive elements and even opportunities for the public to comment on issues and attempts to remedy problems.

Public Policy

The mass media help establish public policy essentially by living up to their responsibilities to provide information, to educate and to serve as a watchdog. By providing information about an important issue facing our community, state, nation or world, the media help give us the background we need to make decisions about how we, as individuals and as a community or country, should act. We can decide to start referendums, sign petitions, vote for certain candidates or propositions, lobby legislators, support the passage or defeat of legislation or participate in protest marches or boycotts.

The news media also can help establish public policy by endorsing candidates and propositions. Research evidence is a bit mixed on the effect of endorsements, but such partisanship can be a factor in swaying public opinion.

Social Change

The mass media's role in helping to bring about social change is the same as their role in helping to establish

public policies. By providing information about both what is good and what is bad in a society, the media help people make up their minds concerning what laws, rules, regulations, processes, procedures, policies and traditions need to be changed. Recent examples include media coverage of affirmative action, immigration issues, the homeless, anti-drug campaigns, anti-smoking campaigns, anti-drinking and driving campaigns and the abortion issue.

Advertising

Advertising is usually the main way that most mass media organizations make money. Advertisements are almost everywhere we go and everywhere we look. They're on billboards, park benches and the sides of busses. We get ads in theaters before movies start. We're even seeing ads in books and on the Internet. It's clear that the mass media are certainly living up to their responsibility of serving as a vehicle for advertising. With at least 60% of most daily newspapers and magazines devoted to ads and about 30% of radio and television newscasts devoted to commercials, product placements in movies and television programs, perhaps the media have embraced this responsibility too well.

The Commission on Freedom of the Press

Criticism of the mass media for abusing their power and not living up to their roles and responsibilities is not a new phenomenon, of course. Critics and criticism have been around since the beginnings of the mass media. The news media are often the targets of the most vocal critics. In the late 1940s, a commission of scholars, businesspeople and community leaders who were tired of sensational and irresponsible news reporting got together and developed some suggested guidelines for the news media. The guidelines were designed to ensure that in a society where not everyone really had an equal chance to share their views with the masses, the people who did have the opportunity through their control of the vehicles of mass communication would conduct themselves and operate their organizations in a "socially responsible" manner.

The guidelines include:

1. To provide factual, comprehensive and intelligent stories about the day's events/issues in a context that gives them meaning and helps people understand them.
2. To provide a representative, factual picture of the main groups in our society.
3. To provide a way for people to exchange comments and criticisms.
4. To provide coverage of significant ideas even though such ideas may be contrary to those of the owners, editors and reporters of the news organization.
5. To provide a forum for the discussion of the goals and values of society.
6. To keep a close watch on governmental activities and to provide vigorous criticism when it's warranted.
7. To provide fair and balanced coverage of the news that is reported.

Meaningful Information

This responsibility is basically the same as "to inform," but it adds a bit of complexity to the formula. Journalists are expected to provide information in a FACTUAL (accurate, objective, honest, trustworthy), COMPREHENSIVE (exhaustive, thorough, complete, never-ending, ever-vigilant) and INTELLIGENT (smart, wise, insightful, creative, innovative) way. In addition, reporters and editors are expected to explain what events and issues MEAN to people's lives. How will our lives be changed? Why should we care? What can we do?

Finally, we count on journalists to help us UNDERSTAND complex issues and events. Why are we faced with such problems? Who's to blame? Who are the major players? What are the major factors at work? How do issues and events relate to one another?

Representative Picture

Again, this responsibility simply extends the general prescription "to inform." The REPRESENTATIVE part means that journalists are expected to do more than just take a "snapshot" of reality at any given time. To provide a truly factual, accurate and representative picture of the dominant groups in a society, journalists clearly need to spend a great deal of time getting to know the members of the various groups. They need to get a handle on the beliefs, attitudes, values and behavior patterns of the members. They also need to find out about the history, goals, objectives, philosophies and procedures of the groups. Sadly, all too often, journalists simply can't or don't choose to invest such time and effort in really trying to obtain a "representative" picture of the dominant groups in a society.

Forum for Comment and Criticism

At first, this responsibility perhaps does not appear to be as critical as some of the others, but even though we all could certainly make it through the day without being exposed to the opinions, feelings, compliments and complaints of our fellow human beings, the world would not be as interesting a place. Most of us kind of enjoy finding out how other people feel about the major events and issues of the day. It's kind of fun to compare our own opinions and views with those of other people. In addition, we can learn things and improve ourselves by being exposed to the opinions of others.

Providing a forum for the exchange of comment and criticism is especially important in a society like ours where everybody really does not have an equal opportunity to own a newspaper, magazine, radio station or television station. We depend on those people and corporations that can afford to operate a news organization to be socially responsible enough to allow people and organizations with various points of view to have their say so we can be exposed to as many points of view as possible. Without such socially responsible behavior, most of the viewpoints we'd get would be limited to those of the wealthy, privileged, usually conservative people who normally own newspapers, magazines, radio stations and television stations.

Coverage of Significant Ideas

Providing a forum for the exchange of comment and criticism is often a somewhat passive responsibility. Journalists can simply let it be known that space or time is available and if qualified people want to take advantage of such space and time, fine. If nobody takes advantage of the opportunity, that's fine, too.

The responsibility to provide coverage of significant ideas even though such ideas may be contrary to those of reporters, editors and owners involves a much more "proactive" component. It is also further recognition of the fact that most people have limited opportunities to publish or broadcast their ideas and opinions, so journalists are expected to actively seek out significant ideas and opinions and share them with all of us.

Clarifying Goals and Values

Few of us have the time to do all of the research that we'd like to do into the pros and cons of all of the important political, economic and social issues that are part of our everyday lives. In addition, it's almost impossible for most of us to arrange personal interviews with major political and business leaders and other experts to find out how they feel about things.

We need such information, however, to help us decide what's important and what's not, what candidates and causes to support, how to conduct ourselves, what societal changes to lobby for, etc. So, once again,

the burden falls on the socially responsible journalists and journalism organizations. We expect them to present the goals and values of society and to clarify the ideals toward which society should strive.

Watch and Criticize

The news media are expected to keep an ever-vigilant watch on people in power, especially elected and appointed government officials. We entrust journalists with the responsibility of monitoring the goings on of government to keep us informed about how the people who are supposed to be looking out for our best interests are doing.

If abuse of power or neglect of duty is detected, we need to be told. In addition, we expect the news media not only to simply point out such things, but also to vigorously criticize poor performance. Such criticism should be fair and justified, of course, but a reasonably respectful "adversarial" attitude between power brokers and journalists is usually a healthy thing.

Fair and Balanced Coverage

Journalists can play a major role in helping to shape how people think and act. With that ability comes the responsibility to be as fair and balanced as possible. We expect journalists to be objective most of the time. We expect them to report the "truth" as best they know it. We expect them to avoid embellishing, exaggerating and distorting facts. We expect them to avoid slanting stories, lying or fabricating information. We expect them to do a thorough job of gathering and reporting the news. We expect them to seek

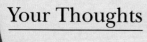 Your Thoughts

How good of a job do you think journalists are doing in living up to their roles and responsibilities? Why do you feel the way you do? Cite specific examples.

What solutions can you offer to the most critical problems you've identified?

out the important players from all of the competing camps in connection with events and issues and to allow such players to speak their minds.

Armed with the information we need about the ideas and opinions of others, we can begin the process of forming our own opinions and deciding on courses of action. It's a long, winding road, but journalists can help smooth out many of the bumps and turns if they live up to their many roles and responsibilities.

Journalistic Problems

Journalists face a number of problems as they attempt to fulfill their roles and live up to their responsibilities. These include:

1. Selectivity vs. objectivity
2. Fairness and balance
3. Thorough reporting
4. Proactive vs. reactive reporting
5. Fear of "investigating"
6. Serving the public vs. making money
7. Ratings/circulation wars
8. Legal entanglements
9. Ethical dilemmas

Selectivity vs. Objectivity

Journalism is a highly subjective process. Journalists decide what "news" is. They evaluate the events and issues they know about, select what they feel are the most significant, interesting, amusing, stimulating and thought-provoking and share them with us. There is plenty of opportunity for personal, institutional and/or organizational biases to play a significant role in the process of determining what is and what is not "news."

Reporters choose what sources they're going to interview, what documents they're going to read and what events they're going to attend. Then they choose what "facts" and comments to include in their stories. Finally, journalists choose how long to make their stories and where to place them in the newspaper, magazine, on-line report, radio newscast or television newscast. Again, there's plenty of room for individual likes, dislikes, attitudes and values to come into play. In short, even though the goal of most journalists is to report the "truth," with so many choices, whose TRUTH is being reported?

Many news media critics believe it's ridiculous to expect journalists to be truly "objective" in their reporting of the news. The whole process is too fraught with subjectivity. Even the best intentioned journalists have to make choices about what events and issues to cover, what sources to consult and what information to include in stories. And, when so many choices exist, "objectivity" becomes more of a dream than a reality.

Fairness and Balance

True objectivity might be impossible in journalism, but journalists can and should be fair and balanced in their reporting of events and issues. Such things are often missing, though. Many factors can contribute to real or perceived unfairness and imbalance. At the top of the list come biases of journalists, news sources and news consumers. We all tend to see the world through the filters of our heredity, upbringing and experiences. Most of our windows to the world are somewhat clouded as a result. Other factors include deadline pressure, ratings/circulation pressure, a desire to build or maintain a reputation, missed appointments, unreturned telephone calls, misunderstandings and malfunctioning equipment.

Thorough Reporting

Journalists, especially broadcast journalists, are often criticized for not providing "complete" stories. Journalists often provide sketchy bits of information about even the most significant events and issues. It's pretty difficult to cover a complex issue or event in just 90 seconds, yet that's often the MAXIMUM length that a television news story is permitted to be.

Proactive vs. Reactive Reporting

Should journalists simply hang around the newsroom waiting for something to happen, rush out and report on it, come back and write it up and then wait for something else to happen OR should they attempt to anticipate problems and developments and try to stay one step ahead of events, developing trends and emerging issues?

Most people expect journalists to be ever-vigilant. They need to warn us and our elected officials ahead of time if something bad is coming. We want to know how to prevent plane, car, train and stock market crashes. We want to know how to prevent crimes from happening. We want to know how to protect our families and how best to provide for them. We want to know how we can humanely reduce the budget deficit in the United States. We want to know about upcoming events so we can decide if we want to attend them or prepare ourselves for the likely outcomes of such events.

Most of us don't want to read or hear about things only after it's really too late to do much, if anything, about them. Unfortunately, too often that's exactly what happens. Journalists simply do not do a good enough job of anticipating events and issues. They are much too passive and reactive. They need to be much more proactive.

Investigative Reporting

In many parts of the country, journalists don't do a very good job of "investigative" reporting. There are several reasons for this:

1. Fear of offending readers, listeners or viewers
2. Fear of offending government officials and other power brokers
3. Fear of offending advertisers
4. Fear of "rocking the boat"
5. Fear of lawsuits
6. Lack of resources—people, time, money, etc.
7. Lack of support from owners—no commitment or policies

None of the reasons seems very convincing, do they? Frankly, too many journalists are simply too incompetent, too fearful, too lazy and too wimpy to do the kind of regular, hard-hitting, necessary investigative reporting that they should be doing.

Public Service vs. Making Money

Many people view journalism as a form of public service. It certainly is that, but it is also a business, a public service-oriented business, but still a business. Most of the owners of journalistic organizations expect to make a profit just like owners of other types of businesses. Most of the time, the public-service nature and the business nature of journalism co-exist with few problems. Serving the public well usually pays off in large circulations or high ratings and those numbers translate into dollars. Every so often, however, conflicts arise between the dual goals of serving readers, listeners and

viewers AND making money. For example, what about exposing some "less-than-ethical," and/or "less-than-legal" practices of your newspaper's biggest advertiser? What about laying off several veteran reporters in an effort to keep the profit margin in double figures? Sure, the public might not be served quite as well, but a buck's a buck, right?

Ratings/Circulation Wars

The desire to be "Number One" in the ratings or to have the largest possible circulation too often results in good journalism taking a backseat to ratings/circulation boosting journalism. During ratings periods, local television stations almost always fill their newscasts with sex, crime, violence, perversion, oddity and "investigative" reports. Stories are sensationalized, dramatized, exaggerated, hyped and even embellished. Newspapers have their own methods for trying to boost circulation. They run bigger headlines. Sex-oriented stories find their way onto the front page more often. Oddities are stressed. Color photos appear more regularly. The writing style becomes "breezier." More human-interest stories about off-beat people and exotic locales are featured.

Such manipulations aren't always bad, of course. It's just that too often such things are done at the expense of quality journalism. Again, when so much time, energy and effort are spent trying to ATTRACT an audience, there's a good chance that efforts to INFORM, EDUCATE and UPLIFT an audience will suffer.

Legal Entanglements

Libel, invasion of privacy, infringing on someone's right to a fair trial and violating copyright are among the legal entanglements that sometimes rise up and bite journalists. In addition, journalists have been known to do a little "breaking and entering," stealing and speeding in their efforts to gather information.

Ethical Dilemmas

Even if journalists manage to stay within the letter of the law, ethical transgressions quite often rear their ugly heads. Breaking promises, lying, cheating, misusing anonymous sources, distorting, embellishing and exaggerating are among the most common of these. Research has found that growing numbers of news consumers are unhappy with journalists and are especially skeptical about the integrity and credibility of journalists.

Media Aims and Standards

Pressures are directed at media decision-makers from several sources, including some that are self-generated. An individual's mood, or physical state, can alter responses to the same situation at different times. A particularly sweet dessert gets a different reception from a diner who has eaten heavily beforehand than from someone who is still hungry. A personal code of conduct can influence what is supposed to be an objective consideration. One's internalized religious, familial and experiential background will create a highly individualized decision-making potential. Self-esteem, or lack of it, can influence perceptions of how best to proceed when confronted with options.

Job-related pressures, or career-enhancing or career-threatening possibilities, can affect the outcome. Is there an obvious or implied policy in the newsroom? Does everyone know the bias of the publisher? Is this an award-winning prospect? Will a decision to cut expenses be more valued than one to increase circulation or ratings? Is the increased readership from sensationalism worth the loss of prestige or credibility?

Advertisers, politicians, special interest groups, social scientists, and other media critics attempt to influence decision-making. Typically, they offer their own self interest as the public interest. They argue that the media have an obligation to provide service to their audiences, to provide more than news and entertainment. A major complaint is that it takes a lot of advertising income to keep the media operating and the news and entertainment are merely there to justify all of those paid messages. That justification, therefore, dictates that media provide a responsible and comprehensive account of the news and an entertainment approach that is responsive to the best interests of the audiences.

It is often expressed that the media are and always have been affected with a public interest, but are they any different from other industries or enterprises in that obligation? Do we expect journalists to adhere to a higher standard of accountability to the consumers of the news than we do of automobile manufacturers or supermarket operators? Certainly there is no legal requirement that a newspaper or magazine follow a duty to the public, although broadcasters are given their licenses to serve the public interest.

The Communications Act of 1934 dictated a public service responsibility for licensees but the commission created by that act has never been able to enforce that provision very strongly, no doubt partly because of the First Amendment. Nevertheless, many broadcast executives fear the loss of their licenses and are sensitive to the convenience of the public, although much less so since the so-called deregulation of broadcasting in the 1980s.

The print media, with no federal commission looking on, would be engaged in public service as an assumed duty or as an opportunity to receive commendation from society generally or their readers specifically. Such a practice could prove beneficial to the effort to acquire the public support needed for any business. Serving the public could be good for business in the view of many publishers. However, many others might suggest that operating a private enterprise results in financial risk-taking that they would not jeopardize by any perceived civic duty. A newspaper can be considered a business proposition and nothing more, with nothing owed to its readers but everything owed to its stockholders. A publishing firm supplies a manufactured product and has no legal obligation to those who buy the product. Of course, anti-trust laws and Federal Trade Commission regulations regarding false advertising impact publishers, just as the laws that regulate any other industries apply to them. Inevitably, print or broadcast, the media are responsible to their audiences in much the same way any capitalistic enterprise is responsible to and responsive to consumers.

Our media can be thought of as feeding at the public trough. They are dependent upon public acceptance of products that are intangible and somewhat service-oriented—entertainment, information and involvement. They involve listeners, viewers and readers, not only in awareness of issues and related responses to them, but also in consumer goods and services and reactions to them, as well as in the escapism and pleasure of the fun and frivolity inherent in movies, situation comedies, music, crossword puzzles, astrology columns and other light fare. The media do not so much tell their consumers what to think as what to think about. Many scholars have noted that the media set our agenda, both personal and public.

Even the persuasive messages of advertising and public relations are packaged in entertaining and informative vehicles. The owners and operators of radio and television stations and print media claim a status far different from other businesses based on their argument that they perform public service. The First Amendment may not be absolute, but it is used as justification for a special relationship with the public. An argument results that certain rights are guaranteed to publishers and broadcasters, or film-makers, that do not accrue to shoe manufacturers or automobile dealers. If there are responsibilities for the media to bear, are they self-determined or based on societal pressures? If government is limited in enforcing any media responsibility, where does such responsibility come from?

Our media are influential, informative, entertaining, and persuasive. Some individuals have said, perhaps in a complaint, that the media are powerful. That is not so. Government can exercise power. The media can only influence. An old adage that fits is the one that says you only have power if you have the key to the jail house door. The expression, "the power of the press," is inaccurate. One should always substitute the word influence for power.

The influence of the media comes primarily from the editorial pages, op-ed pages, commentaries and analyses, columnists, and letters to the editor of newspapers and magazines, as well as in the commentators, editorialists and documentaries in broadcasting. The presentation of opinion in clearly labeled opinion or editorial sections of print media and direct attempts at influencing audiences by broadcasters can be called the major part of the influence function, if they are totally separate from advertising. Informative content and entertaining material may overlap into influence at times.

There can always be an underlying effect from news coverage that creates an image or reaction that tends to influence readers, listeners and viewers. There can be inherent messages even in televised dramas or lyrics of music played on radio. Any attempt to define the influence function, or any other function of the media, too narrowly must be arbitrary and must depend upon the specifically stated primary intent. Therefore, our definition of what is influential is meant to include primarily the presentation of the viewpoints of the management of the medium or the commentator or analyst offered to the public by the medium, including editorial cartoonists and writers of letters to the editor columns.

Information is defined as anything covered in the news sections of print media and the newscasts over radio and television stations, as well as cable. It includes coverage of politics, the economy, business, education, social unrest, civil strife, fires, disasters, earthquakes, accidents, wars, labor unions, taxes, overseas events, legislatures, courts, and many other reports of the unusual and the significant.

This definition is relatively clear for newspaper and television, less clear for magazines, and often cloudy when applied to some radio stations. Magazines vary greatly in their approaches to content and at times they integrate advertising with content. Many magazines are journals of opinion or offer background on items that were covered in the news days or weeks earlier. The real hybrid, however, is the so-called news and information radio format, with its telephone call-in programming. The overlap with influence and entertainment is considerable in radio talk shows that are labeled informational by station management. Because so many of them demand opinion both from callers and their hosts they should properly be called part of the influence function with overtones of information and entertainment.

Obviously, entertainment can indirectly, perhaps even directly in some cases, impart information and exert a degree of influence. For most of us, however, it is understood to be, in newspapers and magazines for example, the crossword puzzles, games and quizzes, horoscopes, advice-to-the-lovelorn columns, and comic strips. For television, entertainment is provided by the music and variety shows, westerns, situation comedies, soap operas, game shows and the like. For radio, it is primarily the disc jockey and the recorded music.

Persuasive communication through the media is defined as advertisements in print and commercials over the air. These include any messages from an identified sponsor bought and paid for and intended to sell a product or service, or create an image about a product or service. Persuasion can also be seen in promotional pieces for the newspapers and magazines designed to increase circulation or to generate interest among advertisers. Persuasion is also noted in so-called public service messages on radio and television, as well as in those spots that promote the station's programs or personalities.

Despite the word news in its title, a newspaper is made up primarily of advertising. On average, a newspaper is 65% advertising and only 20% news. About 10% is entertainment, such as comic strips, crossword puzzles and other light features. The remaining 5% is devoted to editorials and clearly-labeled opinions. Some papers, especially weeklies, have an even higher percentage of advertising. Publications that are usually referred to as "shoppers," or "throwaways," are usually 100% advertising. Other weekly publications quite similar to them will include two or three reprinted public relations puff pieces designed to look like news, thereby reducing their percentage of advertising into the 90s. Excluding such "shoppers," one finds that advertising income brings in 75% of the money earned by newspapers and more than half of the income for magazines. In other words, subscription income represents only 25% of the income for the newspaper publishing firm, and less than half for the magazine ownership. It often seems like a lot more, but about 55% of a magazine's content is devoted to advertising.

Depending on the time of day and the type of program, radio and television stations carry from 12 to 18 minutes of commercials each hour. That comes out to about 25% of the broadcast day turned over to persuasive messages. In recent years, television stations have expanded the time given to information, largely because they found that newscasts give them an opportunity to sell even more local commercials.

Most radio stations, on the other hand, have cut back on the amount of their news programming, with program directors and station managers pointing out that the deregulation of broadcasting during the Reagan administration lifted that obligation from them.

The nation's radio stations, on average, allot about 10% of their time to news. That average is almost meaningless when you consider the variety of formats and the vast difference in attitude toward news between FM stations and AM stations. Those on the AM band are more likely to produce more and longer newscasts and AM is where you find the all-news stations and the news and information stations, or talk-radio operations.

It is obvious that the major part of the broadcast day is devoted to entertainment, but it is no doubt surprising to many that so much of what appears in newspapers can be defined as entertainment, about 10%. The typical newspaper allots 5% of its space to influential material, defined earlier as editorials, commentaries and letters to the editor, as well as other opinion pieces. After 65% is given to persuasion, or advertising, that leaves the news hole at 20%.

With the exception resulting from the AM stations that carry telephone call-in programming, radio and television stations give only about 1% of their time to influence, with some stations carrying no editorials or commentaries at all.

Magazines are severely specialized, aiming at narrowly defined target audiences, resulting in a

Your Thoughts

If you could assign content percentages to the media, how would you do it? Your totals for each medium should be 100%.

	Newspapers	Magazines	TV	Radio
News				
Ads				
Opinions				
Entertainment				

Why did you assign such percentages to each medium?

major difficulty in trying to estimate the typical allotments to opinion, news or entertainment, although the 55% advertising ratio is a consistent estimate. Magazines are greatly varied in content because they aim for mostly small audiences of demographically identified sub-audiences appealing to specific types of advertisers. This keeps the production and circulation costs down so that the rates charged to advertisers will be competitive with other media.

High Sounding Phrases

The controlled society of feudal Europe functioned from the top down, with tight controls by authority on what the masses could know. In modern Western society, the people are free of constraints and have a free marketplace of ideas and information to allow them to govern themselves. Representative government, of the people, by the people and for the people, needs an informed citizenry, an electorate that selects its governors from its own constituency. Western thought assumes that the people have personal liberty and political freedom, as well as the right to govern themselves, with a concomitant opportunity to use the ballot box to return their representatives to the masses when disappointed with them.

The freedom to publish without prior restraint, freedom of speech, and the right to criticize government are fundamental to a society exercising democratic processes. This libertarian concept of communication has its roots in the 17th century and has been dominant since the 19th century. The English poet John Milton in 1644 wrote an essay advocating a right of discussion, stressing a free marketplace of thought necessary for a public liberty. When the United States was being founded, Thomas Jefferson and others believed that the people should be censors of their governors and used as support Milton's contention that the masses can discern between truth and falsehood themselves. The Declaration of Independence and the U.S. Constitution carried statements from those who viewed Milton's ideas as essential to allowing the people to determine public policy. They also used John Locke's 17th century philosophy of the social good in the confrontation of ideas. John Locke had espoused the natural right of every person to life, liberty and property. Locke's argument for individual rights helped to rationalize Western

thought that open debate is necessary for sound public policy. Free expression then is held as essential for both the social and individual good. Widespread discussion, freely engaged in, brings about understanding and agreement.

Before glasnost and perestroika, and the eventual dissolution of the whole system, the USSR had a press system largely owned and operated by Communist party members. Dictators and military leaders in most nations impose prior restraint, as well as harsh punishment, on those few who have access to the media. Yet, in the United States newsworthiness is a solid defense if you are sued for invasion of privacy, the need for scrutiny of public officials can allow a news medium to win a libel suit when there has been an inadvertent publication of something false and defamatory, and the Constitution itself says Congress cannot make laws abridging a free press.

An oft-stated axiom says your right to swing your arm ends at the other guy's nose. Our right to drive our vehicles through certain intersections ends when a light turns to red. Our individual rights are often in conflict with our collective rights.

Civil law in the United States is based on the assumption that individuals who do wrong to other individuals can be sued to redress those persons' grievances. Typically, a homeowner sues his neighbor because tree roots intrude across boundary lines and ruin a concrete driveway. Criminal law is based on the assumption that some rights belong to society, not simply to the individual. The state, on behalf of the people, brings charges against those who murder, maim, rob, rape, and steal, because, not just the victim, but all of us are injured by those wrongs.

Freedom of the Press

There are some constraints on United States media from the courts and government, but, for the most part, no prior restraint. The laws of libel, privacy and copyright come into the courts after publication or broadcast, not before. The right to speak out, the right to print or broadcast without censorship, is not absolute, but must compete with other rights. National security, when lives are in danger or troop positions revealed, could be balanced against the First Amendment. The Sixth Amendment, the right to an impartial jury, is often in conflict with the media's attempts at displaying extrajudicial, possibly prejudicial, information about a defendant.

Despite some conventions, conditions, and regulations, our media are free enough to serve the so-called watchdog function over government at all levels and to disseminate a variety of openness with virtually no official interference.

In the United States we talk about freedom of the press, but what we have is actually "liberty of the press," because liberty can be defined as freedom from all restraints except those justified by law.

An ancient Chinese proverb says there is no pleasure without commensurate pain. For American media, faced with primarily voluntary constraints, the analogy holds that there are no rights without commensurate responsibilities. Our carriers of news, entertainment and advertising are not totally unfettered by government, but do avoid the crush of laws common to media in other parts of the world.

Yet, much discussion in this country centers on the limits of press freedom. Is it limited or absolute? If freedom of the press is to be unlimited, doesn't that carry with it dangers related to recklessness and irresponsibility? Should there be limits when the public has a strong need for information to participate fully in a democratic and open society? If we assume that the media actually have qualified or limited access to information, does that mean that government bears a tremendous responsibility to define the limits and justify the qualifications?

When the Constitution was adopted, its framers did not say anything about limited freedom or anything about freedom for certain parts of press, nor did they indicate that access was available to certain types of information but not to others. At first glance, it would appear that the framers of the "law of the land" had to be assuming that there would be no limits on the press, at least the newspapers and magazines of that time.

A total freedom was anticipated by those who gave us the Constitution because they knew that a nation run by elected representatives would need an informed citizenry, with that information coming unfiltered to the electorate. No filtering by government was their hope. The press would be expected to observe the process of government and report such observations to the people, because of the people's need to scrutinize the actions of those who would choose to represent them. The people, in turn, could discuss their concerns among themselves, form a consensus on the issues and individually or through the press relay their wishes to government officials. For all of this to happen, the media, or printed press at that time, had to be free of the power and influence of elected and appointed officials.

Over many decades, there has been either an erosion of that concept of freedom or new interpretations of the First Amendment. Although there are still occasional voices to be heard saying that freedom of the press is absolute, generally we hear interpretations of the intent of the First Amendment that call for reasonable limits. A typical example of such limits is the idea that freedom of the press is extended only to information of genuine public concern and it is up to the courts to define what the public should genuinely be concerned about. That means invasion of privacy, defamation of character, and sexually-oriented material that would offend virtually all would be actionable without it being considered an infringement on our freedom.

Significantly, civil lawsuits for invasion of privacy and for libel or slander are not brought by government and appear in court only after the offending messages have appeared in the media. However, prior restraint is a concern for the media that carry sexually-explicit material that could lack serious artistic, literary, scientific, or educational merit. Censorship of obscene material, at least what a jury is likely to determine as obscene, is justified by labeling obscenity as something that wrongs all of society, not just the person who receives it. This means obscenity is a crime and the First Amendment cannot protect a criminal act. Freedom of the press is limited when criminal content could appear in a given medium.

You cannot find a "public right to know" expressed specifically in the Constitution. Instead, it is a phrase that has come into the language as some journalists have offered their interpretations of the freedom that the Constitution gives them. Unfortunately, such a phrase does not tell us what the public has a right to know, or how much the public has a right to know.

The Constitution doesn't tell us the limits a reasonable person might expect to impose on a reporter who is intrusive, reckless, rude, foul-mouthed, insensitive, slip-shod, untruthful or law-breaking. Does the right of the public to know about misdeeds in a private nursing home justify deception by reporters who sneak into the facility as if they were visiting relatives and then steal documents from private offices after illegally searching through desk drawers that had been closed to them? Does the public have a right to know the names of juveniles accused of crimes or of rape victims? In general, reporters cannot get such names because authorities guard them very carefully, but, with some exceptions, if the names are gained somehow there is nothing to stop the media from conveying that information.

It is too easy to overlook the fact that the media are the only private businesses in the United States whose right to exist is guaranteed by the Constitution. Although the media are private enterprises, they enjoy advantages that other businesses can only envy. The media do find that their advertising messages are not given the freedom that other content gets. Advertising is considered a business practice without the value to society that the information function is presumed to offer. The media are given latitude to keep an eye on the workings of government at all levels and to keep the public informed, but they are not assumed to be contributing to self-government or an informed electorate when they carry paid persuasive messages to support themselves financially so they can provide the public service that justifies their freedom otherwise.

Business practices, including advertising, bring up Constitutional questions that give the courts problems because they are not necessarily part of the media's role in observing, reporting or criticizing government. An example of a non-news aspect of the media that has faced the courts is the placement of newspaper racks. City and county governments in various parts of the country have tried to argue that they must be allowed to regulate newsracks on their sidewalks, alongside state highways or on any publicly owned property. They contend that they have an obligation to reduce congestion, to ensure public safety and even to guarantee aesthetics. The newspa-

per ownerships in these disputes have argued that any such regulation would be a violation of the First Amendment, saying that the Constitution guarantees a right of distribution. This contention holds that any effort to hinder a newspaper's circulation department goes right to the heart of the First Amendment, in that it interferes with the public's right to have access to the information in the newspapers.

Courts have come up with something called a public-forum analysis in an attempt to determine the constitutional status of any publicly-owned property. A public forum is a location where First Amendment freedoms are at their strongest and where government's power to regulate expression is at its weakest. Precedent holds that sidewalks and public parks are public forums and afford a high level of protection for free expression. Newspapers would like this concept extended to freeway rest areas, subway stations, airport terminals, and other areas that are open to the public. Arguments over coin-operated newspaper vending machines are expected to continue until more court cases are completed and a clearer definition evolves about what is or is not a public forum. Indications are that the First Amendment is not likely to apply when newspapers try to avoid having their newsracks regulated by government bodies that control airport terminals and maybe even subway stations, with the courts ruling that not all types of public property are meant for free expression, that they are not necessarily public forums.

The First Amendment is clearly not absolute when we have copyright laws, libel laws, newsrack regulations, a Federal Trade Commission regulating advertising, and a restriction that we cannot shout fire in a crowded theater when there is no fire. Another display of this fact is in the different inter-

Your Thoughts

How absolute do you think freedom of the press should be? Why?

List FIVE reasonable restrictions you'd place on the press. Why?

pretation the courts have given to the First Amendment protection afforded to broadcasters.

License versus Liberty

Frequently, pressure groups push for restrictions on print or broadcast media because of their own special agenda, with many believing that the presence of the 1934 Communications Act and the Federal Communication Commission will guarantee more government intervention in broadcasting than in print. A recent example was the effort by those who wanted to eliminate what they called hate speech, which they wanted to replace with their concept of what is politically correct speech.

How much liberty the people of a nation have in speaking and writing is more of a test of its freedom than its people's right to exercise self-government through the ballot. Our right to choose leaders from among our own to represent us temporarily at any level of government is grounded on our fundamental right to be intelligent or stupid, enlightened or racist, learned or ignorant, and the opportunity under law to express our stupidity or racism publicly.

The concept of politically correct speech is so patently un-American that it is distressing to realize its pervasiveness on university campuses. The American way has been to create a wide-open, uninhibited, robust public debate on issues and allow individual viewpoints to be freely expressed to make representative government work. When the people govern themselves, there is no basis for either minority views or majority views keeping their opposite number from being heard.

No one would argue with the statement that American mass media, especially broadcasting, are pervasive, and perhaps intrusive as well. Some complain that they are powerful. Others suggest that they are influential rather than powerful, that only a government can exercise true power, consistent with the adage that power exists only for those who have keys to the cells and dungeons. If the media are influential, how much so? Is it a problem, and, if so, for whom? Are they invited into our lives or do they intrude? Is the typical American's exposure to mass media voluntary or invasive, or a bit of both, and does it matter?

When the media are wrong, where does the punishment, if any, originate? Law is imposed in a few instances, very few, when juries find some media content to be obscene. Obscenity is not protected by freedom of the press because it is viewed as a harm to society, not to any given individual. Advertisers who practice out-and-out fraud, the basic bait-and-switch technique, are in violation of the law. Print advertisements and broadcast commercials, however, consistently offer subtle suggestions and sell the sizzle not the steak rather than practice clear-cut deception. Congress has banned cigarette advertising from broadcast stations on the assumption that they send those promotions for cancer over public property, the air waves. Print advertisement for those carcinogens could be considered just as dangerous to public health, but print media do not invade the public domain, at least as it is defined by law, and therefore are not limited by government.

Limits are placed on our media by themselves or by unenforceable codes of conduct created by various trade associations made up of individuals working within various levels of the media. Some newspapers and broadcast stations attempt to set standards for their employees stressing accuracy, completeness, objectivity, responsibility, or other rules of professional behavior. Where they exist, they are made known to staff members much as a dress code is, or a policy against drug use in the workplace. Trade associations, on the other hand, publicize their codes of conduct in their newsletters and other directives to members. A major problem with these rules of conduct is that so few media practitioners belong to such peer groups. An obvious problem is that there is no enforcement of the code provisions even for those who are members of such media organizations.

Colleges and universities offering courses in communication, journalism, broadcasting, mass communication or media study should be expected to address such issues. Students preparing for careers in the communications industry or learning how to be better consumers of the media's products are expected to learn about controversies over media excesses, conflict between media and government, media disregard for individual rights or societal concerns, and the individual and collective responsibility hoped for from those who work in the media.

Criticism of the media comes from the public generally, as well as from professional critics and scholars who view entertainment or journalism from their self-ordained role as authorities. Criticism also results from individuals and institutions directly affected by media content, such as those exposed to the spotlight of news coverage or other media attention.

The criticism often takes the form of complaints that the media offer gossip, trivia, human interest, sex and violence to the exclusion of news of significance or consequence, trash rather than information, or junk rather than substance. This criticism centers on sensationalism and catering to the lowest common denominator to increase ratings or to hype circulation through low-brow content. These complaints point to the profit motive as overcoming ethical standards and, as a result, creating a disservice to the public. It is too easy to point to the supermarket tabloids and say that they are the perpetrators of the sensational and titillating material complained about. Mainstream media are guilty of recklessness and carelessness, too,

Another common criticism is that the media are unfair and slanted in what coverage they give to politics and other issue-oriented material. Some contend that media owners are supporters of the Republican Party and of conservative positions on non-political issues, therefore their outlets are imbued with a right-leaning bias. Others insist that the reporters and writers are part of a liberal cabal of dissidents and advocacy journalists who oppose authority and favor the disenfranchised, the young, labor unions, minorities, political liberals and feminists. These so-called interpretive reporters are believed to be able to create media that support the Democratic Party and that come up with content that has a left-leaning bias.

Other criticisms have to do with the behavior of reporters rather than the content of their stories. So often we hear that reporters will do anything to sell newspapers or to increase ratings. One of the most famous examples of this is the "Janet Cooke" incident. Cooke was a reporter for *The Washington Post.* She wrote a touching and frightening story about an 8-year-old boy who was being injected with heroin by his mother and her boyfriend. The story won a Pulitzer Prize, but it turned out that Cooke made up the boy and many of the other details contained in the story. The Pulitzer Prize was returned.

Chicago Tribune editors once noticed that a story they carried from a correspondent in Israel was almost word-for-word in some places as the story that had run in the *Jerusalem Post* a few days earlier. The correspondent resigned.

A CBS news producer told an audience of journalists that some of his news crews had committed crimes that could be considered misdemeanors or felonies in the pursuit of stories. One example was the reporter who obtained a checking account by using a false social security card.

Reporters who are quick to attack the government for spying do not hesitate to use hidden cameras, hidden microphones and electronic eavesdropping techniques. They invade people's privacy in their quest of the "public's right to know" and to satisfy their perceived need to expose misconduct, malfeasance or illegal activity. They must believe that the ends justify the means.

Technology-Driven Changes

Digital video recorders (DVRs) and personal video recorders (PVRs) are good examples of converging media. Through the use of digital and computer technology, these devices blend the best of video cassette recorders (VCRs) and computer hard drives. TiVo, its retail competitors and many cable TV companies make it possible for consumers to record hours of TV programming, plus pause and rewind live programs. Through careful programming of a DVR, a consumer can easily record every appearance of a favorite actor or TV show, no matter when or where it airs. In some cases, a DVR "predicts" what a consumer might like based on past programming and can independently record shows and offer them to a consumer. What was science fiction only a few years ago is the reality of today.

Microsoft, Bell Canada and India's Research Alliance Intercomm have developed software to facilitate the delivery of standard television signals over Internet connections. Qualcomm and other companies have made it possible to receive TV signals via cell phones. It should not be too many more years until many American homes have a single device for traditional TV, radio, video games, telephone and computer use.

Concerns about the "information-haves" and the "information-have nots" seem to be fading a bit. Several studies in the early part of the 21st century indicated that the "digital divide" in the United States was closing. These days most households have online access and the majority have high-speed Internet access.

Sources of Information

An example of the dangers of limited, one-source mass media consumption can be found in the results of a study by the Program on International Policy Attitudes (PIPA). PIPA found that more than half of American adults had serious misperceptions about the Iraq War. About 52% believed evidence had been found linking Iraq to the September 11, 2001, attacks on the United States. About 56% believed most of the rest of the world supported the war. About 35% believed weapons of mass destruction had been found in Iraq. People who relied on Fox for most of their news had the most misperceptions and people who relied on public broadcasting, PBS and NPR had the fewest misperceptions. Clearly, a multimedia approach to news/information consumption helps guard against getting a distorted view of what's happening in the world.

A study by the Pew Research Center found that many Americans are using multiple sources to obtain information about political candidates, political campaigns and other election-related issues. In 2004, 42% of Americans said they regularly learned something about the political process from local TV news. Other sources included the following:

Cable TV news networks	38%
Network TV news	35%
Daily newspapers	31%
TV news magazines	25%
Morning TV news shows	20%
Talk radio	17%
National Public Radio	14%
Internet	13%
News magazines	10%
Comedy TV shows	8%

A somewhat unscientific Gannett study of more than 65,000 American teenagers in 2004 found that TV was the most important source for news and information. About 48% of the teenagers turned to TV first, followed by newspapers (18%), friends and family (14%), the Internet (9%), radio (7%) and magazines (4%). The teenagers rated newspapers as the most accurate news medium (52%), followed by TV (30%) and the Internet (10%). Newspapers were rated the most informative news medium, too (50%), followed by TV (23%) and the Internet (18%).

Surveys in mid-2004 found that about 63% of American adults go online. That works out to about 128 million people. Reading and sending e-mail was the most common activity, followed by searching for general information, obtaining a map for directions, researching a product or service, looking for information about a hobby, checking the weather, searching for news and looking for health and medical information.

In late 2004, Nielsen NetRatings found that the number of Americans who access the Internet via high-speed lines passed the number who use dial-up connections. Broadband use was highest among people under 35 years old and lowest among people older than 65.

The Terrorism of 9/11

The terrorist attacks on September 11, 2001, likely will have significant impacts on American media content and practices for years to come. In a highly unusual display of noncompetition and in an apparent desire to better serve the public, the TV networks and cable news channels agreed to share all video footage of the 9/11 attacks, at least for the first few days.

Many people turned to the Internet for information related to the 9/11 attacks. Experts pointed out that the Internet provided a different dimension of detail by permitting Americans to access web pages of foreign news organizations.

After 9/11, government officials turned to Hollywood in efforts to produce public service announcements to help in the recovery process. Among the themes suggested for the mass media products were the following:

- Encourage volunteerism
- Encourage support for U.S. troops and their families
- Clarify the point that the war was against terrorism, not Islam

Popular media faced some interesting dilemmas following the 9/11 attacks. Many organizations postponed "inappropriate" programs or stories. Several films with terrorism themes were "shelved," at least for a time. Video game manufacturers delayed the launch of particularly violent, "shoot-'em-up" games. Blockbuster Video put warning labels on movies and video games that featured terrorism. Recording companies asked artists to change lyrics, song titles and album content. Book publishers postponed the release of books about the airline industry and books that dealt with highly controversial subjects. Radio stations created lists of "inappropriate" songs. Many critics lamented the heightened "political correctness," but it flourished nonetheless.

Hindsight is always 20/20, but some media critics pointed out that had the American mass media done a better job of informing the public about the possibility of terrorist attacks, the World Trade Center might not have been destroyed. The critics complained that the media are too quick to cover gossip, deviance and sexy celebrities and too seldom devote enough time and space to the important events and issues of the day. Arianna Huffington blasted the media for being more concerned with the bottom line than guaranteeing that the public is fully informed. She noted that muckraking, the investigation of significant issues, has been replaced by smutraking, with the media too often opting for sensationalism at the expense of stories that are essential for maintaining freedom and democracy. She said the media play up fluff and too often shy away from issues of vital importance, because they fear that they'll lose consumers if they're too serious.

In the aftermath of 9/11, many media critics decried the lack of tolerance for dissenting opinions and some even feared additional limitations would be placed on First Amendment freedoms. Several journalists were suspended or fired for speaking out against government policies and actions. Critics warned that the damage done by the 9/11 terrorists could be enhanced if the owners of media organizations and the public turned the United States into a place where only officially sanctioned, popular opinions were allowed to be expressed in public. The critics suggested that offensive opinions are the ones that need the most protection and that the mass media should be the guardians of the right to express even the most heinous opinions.

Some media watchdogs became concerned about the outpouring of patriotism displayed by many TV newscasters following the 9/11 attacks. Lapel pins; buttons; hair ribbons; flags; and red, white and blue logos abounded. Critics worried about the apparent loss of "objectivity." Bob Steele, an ethics expert at the Poynter Institute for Media Studies, spoke for many when he said that journalists must take their role as independent observers seriously and avoid saying, doing or wearing anything that might compromise that role.

A group of university communication scholars became so concerned about the tone and substance of the news coverage of the 9/11 attacks that it created a list of "advised practices" to help guide journalists in covering the issues associated with the attacks. The list included the following six practices and policies:

1. Expand and balance the range of information sources beyond current and former U.S. military and government officials to include domestic and international academics, think tank analysts and civic leaders.
2. Seek diverse and contrasting perspectives regarding potential courses of action.
3. Incorporate more historical, cultural and religious dimensions into reports.
4. Provide information from scholars and practitioners of peace studies.
5. Select language and images carefully and describe events and conditions in a dispassionate and accurate manner.
6. Limit the repetition of extreme images of destruction, violence, pain and suffering and balance them with examples of cooperation, reconstruction and reconciliation.

Recent Research, Developments and Issues

A study released in mid-2008 found that more than 1,000 journalists had been killed while reporting the news since 1998. Most were murdered while investigating local criminal activity, corruption and other issues, *and* while reporting from various battlefields. The most dangerous countries for journalists are Iraq, Russia and Columbia.

Another 2008 survey found that the nature of a journalist's job is changing with the development of new media technologies and applications. Almost 60% of journalists surveyed said they were working more now and contributing to multiple media outlets more than ever before. More than two-thirds of the journalists surveyed expected to devote increased attention to the online products of their news organizations and more than 90% said their main role was to create content that was appealing to audience members. Almost 75% of the respondents said they relied on blogs to gather information for their stories. Finally, about 70% believed public opinion of journalists is declining.

A 2007 study found that only about 60% of Americans could name their favorite journalist. Katie Couric headed the list, followed by Bill O'Reilly, Charles Gibson, Dan Rather, Tom Brokaw, Brian Williams, Anderson Cooper and Jon Stewart. Jon Stewart?

The list of "favorite" journalists demonstrates the impact and popularity of television and television news. No wonder when a recent study found that the typical U.S. household has more TV sets than people—2.73 TVs vs. 2.55 people. On average, a TV is turned on for about 8.25 hours per day per household and the average person reportedly watches an average of 4.5 hours per day.

Not all is well among viewers, though. A study found that nearly two-thirds of Americans believe most TV programming and advertising is aimed at the 40-and-under crowd. About 80% of adults over 40 report they have a hard time finding TV programs that accurately reflect the happenings in their real lives.

Despite slipping ratings and low satisfaction numbers, TV remains as the most trusted news source, especially during tragedies and natural disasters. About 50% of people surveyed said they turn to TV first for news and information, followed by radio, local newspapers and cable TV. Internet sites of traditional media were mentioned by about 25%, followed by Internet user groups (6%), blogs (6%) and chat rooms (6%).

An earlier study found that Americans used about two sources for news each day. Local TV was used the most (59%), followed by national TV (47%), radio (44%), local newspaper (38%), Internet (23%) and national newspaper (12%).

The Internet and other "new media" sources of information are gaining in popularity. A survey found that voters in the 2008 elections picked the Internet as the best source for information about a candidate's positions and general election issues. About 26% intended to use the Internet for such information. TV came in second (22%), followed by newspapers (18%), radio (7%), magazines (5%) and direct mail (4%). With about half of the households nationwide wired for high-speed broadband Internet connections, the use of the Internet and all it offers in the areas of news, information and entertainment will continue to grow.

Even though the Internet and other new media applications are still trailing traditional media on most lists of preferred sources of information, the new media are challenging the economic models that have supported traditional media for more than 300 years. With audiences fracturing among multiple sources of information, traditional media continue to scramble to adapt and maintain their piece of the flattening-out advertising revenue. Compelling, high-quality content can now be found in a multitude of formats and those who can figure out how to convince advertisers to support and consumers to pay for such content will continue to survive in our increasingly competitive contemporary media marketplace.

A study in early 2008 found some gender-related differences in the types of news stories that interested people. Women were more interested than men in stories about weather, health, safety, natural disasters and celebrity gossip. Men were more interested than

Your Thoughts

Do you think the Internet will eventually replace television as the preferred source of news and information for most people? Why?

women in stories about international affairs, political news and sports. Sources of news differed, too. Women more than men preferred the network TV morning shows, network TV nightly newscasts and network TV news magazines, while men more than women preferred radio, the Internet and newspapers.

The American people seem to be concerned about the declining number of "competing" sources of information. While there may be more sources of information than ever before, the ownership of such sources is not as diverse and wide-ranging as some people think it should be. In keeping with the concern over a declining number of independent voices in the media marketplace, about 60% of people surveyed in late 2007 said they were opposed to laws and regulations making it possible for a single company to own both a newspaper and a TV station in the same city. About 70% believed media consolidation was a major problem. Critics pointed to the likelihood of fewer news voices, fewer news sources, less overall news and more biased reporting if consolidation continues.

Think Back

1. What is "convergence" in mass media? Give some specific examples.

2. List some of the major mergers in the mass media lately and list their impacts.

3. What is meant by the term "information entrepreneurs?"

4. List the arguments for and against the contention that the various media actually complement one another rather than compete with one another?

5. What can the media, especially the news media, do to improve their credibility?

6. What are the problems associated with hyping and hoaxing in the media?

7. What could/should the media do to reduce the hype and protect themselves and consumers from hoaxes?

8. List the SEVEN major roles and responsibilities of mass media organizations.

9. What was the Commission on Freedom of the Press and what did it do?

10. List the NINE major problems journalists face when attempting to live up to their roles and responsibilities.

11. What are some of the major problems and pressures facing the mass media?

12. Who regulates the mass media and what are the major regulations?

13. How do mass media influence people?

14. Define the following: news, information, entertainment, persuasive communication.

15. What are the percentages of news vs. advertising content for the major mass media?

16. What are the major problems associated with trying to balance the rights of the mass media with individual rights?

17. What are the major restrictions on freedom of speech and freedom of the press?

18. What are some of the major criticisms of mass media conduct and content? Who are the major critics?

19. What are DVRs and what do they do?

20. Why are concerns about the "digital divide" declining?

21. What are the major sources of political information for most Americans?

22. What source of news and information do teenagers use most often? How do they rate the accuracy of the various news media?

23. What are the statistics related to the online habits of American adults?

24. What were the major media-related impacts of the terrorist attacks on September 11, 2001?

25. How are the developments related to new media technologies and applications changing the roles and work habits of journalists?

26. What are some of the major findings in recent studies of the sources of news and information that people use and prefer?

27. What are some of the major findings in recent studies of the perceptions of people regarding media consolidation?

The Process of Communication

It is helpful in studying communication to attempt to identify the important components or parts of the process. One way to do that is by constructing a model. A model is a representation of something for the purpose of helping us to understand it.

One of the first models of the dynamic process of communication was developed by Harold Lasswell, a pioneer theorist in the field. It begins with the WHO, which many theorists call the source, communicator or encoder. Then, according to Lasswell, there is the WHAT, a message or content. Next is the WHOM, what other models call the receiver, decoder or audience. There has to be a CHANNEL, the carrier, conduit or medium. And there is expected to be some EFFECT. If there is no Effect, it must mean that no communication has taken place. The model simply is: WHO says WHAT to WHOM through a CHANNEL with usually some EFFECT.

The Lasswell model bears some resemblance to a model developed around the same time by Claude Shannon of Bell Telephone Laboratories and often referred to as the Shannon and Weaver model. Shannon's "mathematical model" was created primarily to clarify some problems of telephone engineering, but was general enough to apply to many other types of communication.

SOURCE in the Shannon model corresponds to WHO in the Lasswell model. MESSAGE in the Shannon model corresponds to WHAT in the Lasswell model. SIGNAL in the Shannon model corresponds to the CHANNEL in the Lasswell model. DESTINATION in the Shannon model corresponds to the WHOM in the Lasswell model.

The Shannon model also brings in the concept of NOISE, defined as anything added to the SIGNAL not intended by the SOURCE. NOISE applies directly to the problem of sending messages over telephone lines, but various kinds of noise occur in any communication situation. An article in a newspaper that you cannot read because of typographical errors is suffering from the problem of NOISE. So is a visual chart in a newspaper or a visual (called a graphic) on television that does not communicate because it is too cluttered. Shannon's model reminds us that one of our common problems in communicating is overcoming any interference.

The Shannon model describes communication as a linear, one-way process. It presents a picture in which messages move neatly from left to right and the message received on the right is essentially identical to the message sent from the left, allowing for any distortion caused by interference. The Shannon model does leave out some of the complexities of the continuous nature of communication as an ongoing process, with messages actually going both directions. Individuals in conversation and students listening to a professor in a large classroom are able to send feedback, even if only by body language, thereby making communication two-way.

SMCR Model

A simple, useful model to help explain how communication works is the SMCR Model—Sender, Message,

Channel, Receiver. Sometimes scholars add an encoder of the message and a decoder of the message, but the essential elements are covered by the initials, SMCR.

Sender—encoder—Message—Channel—decoder—Receiver

The sender in mass media often is a reporter, a news announcer, an author, a songwriter or an actor. The sender can be the source of the information, but often the sender is simply the organizer or transmitter of the information. Most of the time, in mass media communications, senders consult with a variety of sources prior to actually constructing and sending a message.

The message consists of the words, pictures and non-verbal language used to convey the information to an audience. How the message is organized, what is stressed, what is included and what is excluded can greatly influence how information is received and perceived by an audience.

The channel is what is used to transmit the information to an audience. In mass media, channels include newspapers, magazines, books, radio, television, recordings, films and on-line communications. Channels have qualities that can affect how a message is received. For example, some people retain more information when they receive both pictures and words while others do better when they have a written record of information that they can read at a time and place of their choosing.

The receiver is the person or persons who attend to the message. For the mass media, receivers range from a single person reading a book or listening to the radio to millions of people watching the same television program. The dynamics of how people receive information—time, place and circumstances—can affect how much and how well a message moves from sender to receiver.

Noise Gets in Your Eyes and Ears

Communication doesn't always move smoothly through the model. "Noise," or interference, often prevents a message from going from the sender to the receiver in the way the sender intends. Noise can be classified into three main categories: semantic, technical and situational.

Semantic noise involves problems related to definitions, meanings and understandings. When a receiver doesn't know the meaning of a word used by a sender, communication can be ineffective. When a receiver assigns a different meaning to a word used by a sender, communication can be ineffective. When a receiver doesn't understand or misunderstands a sender's message, communication can be ineffective.

Semantic noise can also be caused when a sender and a receiver do not have the same shared experiences. For example, a movie about growing up in the 1950s might not appeal to young people today, because they probably wouldn't be able to relate to what it was like to watch black-and-white television and get by without video games or computers.

Technical noise involves problems related to poor reception or mistakes. When a receiver can't adequately hear or see the sender's message because of static, low volume, small print or other mechanical problems, communication can be ineffective. When a sender makes a mistake or his/her channel fails in some way—typographical mistakes, factual errors, incorrect identification, distortions, misrepresentations, technical difficulties—the receiver will have difficulty receiving the message that was intended.

Situational noise involves problems related to aspects associated with the environments of both the sender and the receiver. If either the sender or the receiver is distracted during part of the communication process, communication can be ineffective. For example, a sender might be trying to use television to convey a message, but the receiver is playing with his/her dog while trying to watch the program. Some aspects of the message will likely be lost when the receiver tries to get Fido to fetch, sit or stay.

Situational noise can also occur if either the sender or the receiver is in a bad mood or is ill. If either the sender or the receiver isn't in a particularly receptive mood for effective communication, communication can be ineffective. For example, if a receiver doesn't feel good, a sender might have a difficult time getting the receiver to pay close attention to a complex message. The receiver's attention will likely be diverted and he/she might be preoccupied with thoughts of what needs to be done to feel better.

Noise   Noise

Sender-|-encoder—Message—Channel—decoder-|-Receiver

Feed Me Feedback

Some communication scholars believe the SMCR model should be drawn in a circle rather than a straight line. They believe communication is a continuous process with senders and receivers changing roles constantly. When a receiver turns into a sender, the information he/she sends is called "feedback." Feedback is important, because it gives a sender some idea of how well his/her message has been received.

While the circle SMCR model might be appropriate for interpersonal communication, the straight-line SMCR model better represents most mass communication episodes. When we communicate with someone face-to-face, over the phone or on the Internet, we can receive feedback immediately. The give and take of the communication process is dynamic, fluid, ever-changing. Feedback takes the form of head nods, smiles, frowns, "uh, huhs," quizzical looks and sighs. However, with the mass media, feedback rarely can be given immediately as the communication is being offered. Instead, feedback is delayed. We see something we like or don't like on television and we write a letter, send an email or make a phone call to complain or compliment. We read something we don't agree with in a newspaper or magazine and we dash off a letter to the editor, or send an email

```
        Noise                          Noise
Sender-|-encoder—Message—Channel—decoder-|-Receiver
       ←————————— Feedback ———————
```

Concerns

Among the many concerns associated with the SMCR model are determining the purpose of the sender, judging the credibility of the sender, analyzing the mechanics and content of the message and using feedback to evaluate the effectiveness of the message. Such concerns are important, because when consumers address them, they begin the critical thinking process that is necessary to put messages in their proper perspective and to improve the understanding of such messages.

It is important to try to figure out why a sender wants to send a message. What does he or she have to gain? It is equally important to judge the credibility of the sender. How objective, truthful, accurate, honest and fair has the sender been in the past?

The content of the message, its physical appearance/qualities and its elements need to be analyzed. What is being said and what is not being said? How has the message been constructed and why? Where is the message placed in the communication vehicle? Is it at the beginning, middle or end? How big or long is it?

Feedback should be used to let senders know that their messages have been received and analyzed. Senders need to know if receivers have paid attention to, processed and understood the messages.

The Process of Mass Communication

Mass communication is a much more complex process than interpersonal communication. Multiply several times over the problems and concerns associated with a relatively simple SMCR episode between two people and you can begin to understand why it is difficult for mass communicators to achieve maximum accuracy and effectiveness. Mass communication practitioners almost always must consult multiple sources of information BEFORE crafting the messages that are eventually sent to consumers. With each information-gathering opportunity comes the possibility of noise and feedback. In addition, in most cases, several "gatekeepers" get involved in the process and each one can change or misinterpret the original message, so by the time information reaches consumers, it is very possible that the original intent of the sources used by the writer/reporter and the intent of the writer/reporter have been slightly to significantly modified.

Mass communication likely involves all of the other basic forms of communication. Intrapersonal communication occurs when sources and writers/reporters have internal conversations, deciding what to say and how to say it. Interpersonal communication occurs when sources speak with or communicate to writers/reporters and when writer/reporters communicate with editors, producers, publishers and anyone else involved in the decision-making process associated with mass communication. Group communication occurs when practitioners get together to decide how to craft information for consumers. Editorial meetings, staff meetings, conference calls, teleconferences, chat rooms, and focus-group sessions are all examples of group communication situations. After all of the intrapersonal, interpersonal and group communication activities have been completed or when the production deadline approaches, mass communication begins.

Mass communication is a process in which communicators use media to disseminate messages widely, continually and rapidly in order to convey meanings to large, relatively diverse audiences in an effort to inform, educate, entertain or influence. If you break down this definition into its component parts, you get the following:

1. Communicators create messages
2. Messages distributed via media in constant, high-speed fashion
3. Messages received by large, diverse audiences
4. Audience members encouraged to interpret messages to obtain meaning
5. Audience members are influenced in varying ways, but effects are achieved

The Hub Model of Mass Communication

The HUB model of mass communication provides a good representation of the complex process of mass communication. The elements of the model include sources of information, communicators, codes/standards/traditions of professional organizations, ethics—personal and professional, the role of "gatekeepers," the role of government and other regulators, filters—personal and organizational, and audiences. The model is presented as a series of concentric circles, with communicators at the center and effects at the far edge. Feedback, noise and the constant impact of mediated communication cross all of the circles.

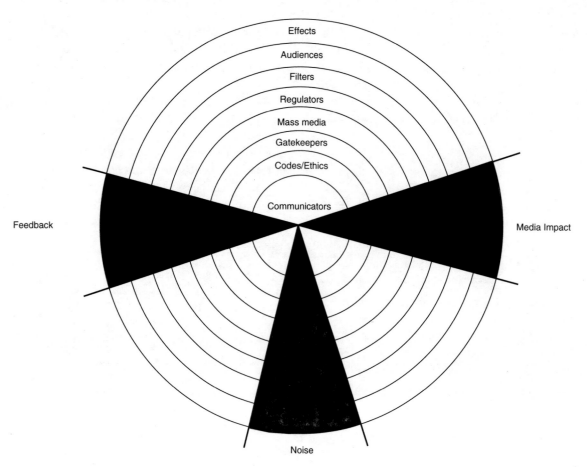

Hub Model of Mass Communication

Research to Improve Communications

In the study of mass communication, theories are developed, questions answered, problems solved and knowledge acquired by research. Communication research can be of two types: basic and applied. Basic research is usually aimed at building and testing theory. Basic research might be concerned with developing a theory of attitude change or the theory of agenda setting. Applied research is aimed more at solving immediate, practical problems. For instance, if you were editing a magazine, you might want to know whether a magazine article is written in a readable enough way to be understood by your intended readers. A readability study, a form of applied research, could help you answer your question.

Research can also be helpful in formulating communication policy. This is particularly important with new communications technologies. How can we ensure that some of the new information transmission systems will serve the public in the best possible way? Should certain regulations be put into effect to ensure public access to the media marketplace? The new digital media are creating a flood of information. What will people do with the information? How will they process it? What ways can be developed to involve users of newer media in the design of technologically advanced systems of message delivery and user interactivity? Communication research can offer us some help in answering these questions.

The goals of science are often said to be understanding, prediction and control. These are useful goals in the area of mass communication. If you were working in the field of mass communication, you would find it useful to understand communication better, to be able to predict outcomes of communication situations and to exert control over those outcomes.

Basically, communication research involves the use of the research methods of the social sciences to study human communication. These methods are the methods of science, and they are based on logic and careful observation. Scientific method depends to a large extent on the ability of several independent observers to agree about what they saw.

Mass communication has become a complicated and expensive endeavor, and people engaged in the practice of mass communication need to use techniques available to help them to save money and do the job better. Increasingly in recent years, research has found a place in the mass communication process.

The Research Process

Research typically begins with a problem or question. The question might be about possible bias in news coverage of a certain issue. It could be a question about the potential impact on the very presence of reporters covering a political campaign. Once you have a question, it must be narrowed down. This can be done by translating a question into a hypothesis. A hypothesis is a generalization that is tentative and testable. Since the purpose of scientific methodology is usually to explain things, the hypothesis most often suggests an explanation. A hypothesis could be that a certain candidate for public office phrases her answers to reporters' questions in sound bites, playing to television, rather than responding directly to questions.

Once a hypothesis has been formulated, it has to be tested by means of observations or experiment. A study has to be designed in which data can be gathered that will shed some light on the hypothesis. The four most common designs for studies in communication research are the case study, content analysis, the sample survey and the experiment.

The purpose of any research study is to gather data. Data can be either qualitative or quantitative. In a case study the data are typically qualitative. The researcher is involved in recording observations, but they are in the form of verbal notes rather than numbers. The other three research methods—content analysis, the sample survey and the experiment—are more likely to result in quantitative data, or data in the form of numbers.

Quantitative data have to be analyzed for the investigator to reach any conclusions, and this is usually done through various statistical methods. Analysis of data typically accomplishes two purposes. It brings about some data reduction, reducing many numbers to a few. It also produces some sorting and sifting of the evidence so that conclusions can be reached.

Once a research study is analyzed, the results must be written up in a report so that they can be used by others. The most common reports of research results are papers presented at scholarly conventions or articles published in scholarly journals. These reports are aimed primarily at the researcher's fellow scholars.

Case Study

A case study is an intensive examination of one person, institution or unit over an extended period of time. The case study is particularly useful for studying the workings of an organization or a person holding a specific job in a real-world setting. The case study is not very useful for testing hypotheses because it is limited to a sample of one. It can be useful for exploring a hypothesis in a general way, however, or for helping to generate new hypotheses.

Content Analysis

Content analysis is the systematic study of messages. We process a great number of mass communication messages every day; what makes scientific content analysis different is that it is systematic. The

sample of content material to be examined is carefully specified so that it is representative of the target population, and the content of interest is carefully defined. Steps are taken to make sure that the observation and categorizing of content are done objectively. This is accomplished primarily by having the content analysis done by several analysts separately.

Sample Survey

In a sample survey a carefully selected group of people, called respondents, is asked a standard set of questions, and their answers are recorded. The sample survey is useful for many kinds of research involving questions about the audiences of mass communication. Surveys also can be useful in planning communication. Survey research could be used to find out public attitudes toward various media or how people use their media, and perhaps even which medium is thought to be more believable. For example, a researcher could learn what issues concern most voters during an election campaign.

Quality survey research must have a representative sample of respondents that can be used to generalize findings to a larger target population. Below are some of the things that the American Association for Public Opinion Research believes consumers should expect to find in any report of a survey or public opinion poll to help ensure that the survey/poll actually measures what it purports to measure.

1. The identify of the sponsor of the poll or survey (the person or organization who paid for the project). Results can be spun to please he/she who pays for the information.
2. The exact wording of the questions. Pollsters aren't biased are they?
3. The exact population sampled. Who are these people?
4. The size of the sample. At least 400-500 (preferably more) should be sampled to represent large populations.
5. What's the sampling error? Usually, in most large samples, the statistical error that occurs in the process is anywhere from 2%-5%. What that means is the reported numbers could be off by an amount that is plus or

minus whatever the sampling error is. For example, if a reported number is 34% and the sampling error is 5%, the actual number could be anything from 29% to 39%.

6. The identification of any results that are based on sub-samples of the total sample. Any demographic breakdowns—gender, age, race, etc.—also should include a report of the new sampling error associated with the smaller sample.

7. A description of how the information was gathered—Internet, phone, mail, in-person, at a mall, etc. How the information was gathered can sometimes shape what is discovered.

8. When the poll/survey was conducted. Timing is everything.

Experiment

In an experiment, the researcher deliberately introduces a change to observe the effects of that change. The major strength of the experiment is demonstrating a causal relationship. The sample survey can explore a causal relationship but cannot provide conclusive evidence about what is causing what. The experiment does allow us to identify a cause. An experiment lets us pinpoint a causal relationship because it involves deliberately manipulating or changing a variable in a controlled situation. After manipulating the variable, the researcher carefully observes another variable that the first variable is thought to be influencing. If it changes, the evidence for a causal relationship becomes quite compelling.

Experiments can be used to determine if video in television news increases or decreases what viewers remember from newscast content. Experiments can help determine if people exposed to violent media content are more likely to commit violent acts compared to people who are not exposed to violent media content.

Theories of Message Effects

It is clear that mass media messages can affect people. Just what those effects are plus how and why they work is not as clear. A hierarchy of effects includes attention, comprehension, learning, attitude change and behavior change. The simplest effect is grabbing/focusing attention. The most complex effect is actually prompting people to change their behavior.

There is no shortage of theories of mass media effects. Among the most popular are the following:

1. Stimulation Theory
2. Modeling Theory
3. Conversion Theory
4. Reinforcement Theory
5. Activation/Crystallization Theory
6. Catharsis Theory
7. Agenda-Setting Theory
8. Cultivation Theory
9. Minimal Effects Theory
10. Trivialization Theory

Generally, the theories fall into three, broad categories—pronounced effects, moderate effects and limited effects. Supporters of the pronounced effects school believe mass media messages can move

Your Thoughts

How much faith do you have in the poll and survey reports that you read or hear about in the news media? Why?

mountains. They believe mass media messages can stimulate people to take action and change their opinions. True-believers of the moderate effects school think mass media messages simply reinforce and clarify already-held beliefs, attitudes and values. Limited effects school fans don't see the mass media as much more than a big entertainment system. They feel that people use a variety of sources to help them decide what to believe and how to act.

Stimulation

The "Stimulation Theory" suggests that people can be stimulated to believe things and even to do things because of mass media messages they see and/or hear. It is sort of like, "monkey see, monkey do." In its pure form, the theory suggests that perhaps "normal" people can be motivated to do something "abnormal" by a mass media message. For example, some average, middle-class person might be stimulated to commit a crime after seeing a crime depicted in a television drama, a reality program or a news report.

The "Stimulation Theory" doesn't suggest that everyone will be stimulated to act in an anti-social way if they're exposed to anti-social messages, but enough people likely will be to cause potential problems. Likewise, the theory does not suggest that everyone exposed to a pro-social message—doing something "good" for mankind—will act in a pro-social way. Perhaps not everybody will be stimulated and perhaps not everybody will be stimulated in the same way; however, stimulation will occur.

Not much support for the "Stimulation Theory" has been found by researchers. There are simply too many factors that can contribute to the motivation a person has to believe or act in a certain way. In addition, it seems counter-intuitive to think that reasonably normal people could be hyped up into taking some sort of action simply because they heard or saw something in the mass media.

Modeling

"Modeling Theory" is much like "Stimulation Theory." It suggests that people model their behavior after what they read, hear and see in the mass media. The theory does not really suggest that a mass media message can stimulate people to act in a way that is contrary to their normal behavior patterns, but it does

suggest that people who might be predisposed to act in certain ways find "models" in the mass media to help them decide how to conduct their own lives.

For example, a news media story about an airplane hijacking probably would not serve as a "model" for you, because you're not thinking about hijacking an airplane. But, for someone who is thinking about it, seeing such a story and finding out how the hijackers smuggled a gun onto the plane, might be useful as a "model."

Modeling is probably most influential in suggesting what kind of clothes to wear, cars to drive, foods to eat, beverages to drink, ways to talk and ways to deal with family, friends, lovers, co-workers and bosses. The theory has some validity. Many young people want to "be like Mike." They buy Michael Jordan shoes. They eat what Michael Jordan eats. They wear Michael Jordan underwear. Michael Jordan is their role model and they want to do what he does. They "model" their behavior after his.

Conversion

"Conversion Theory" doesn't have too many true believers. It suggests that mass media messages can actually change people's minds. Perhaps, over time and with many messages, a mass media organization could convert someone from one belief to another, but most research seems to indicate that if people believe something, they're unlikely to change their opinion simply based on any mass media messages they might read, hear or see.

When was the last time you changed one of your opinions or changed one of your behavior patterns based on some mass media message? If you don't support a candidate, will reading an endorsement of that candidate in your local newspaper convert you? It may cause you to THINK about your position, but it's unlikely to cause you to change your position.

Reinforcement

One of the reasons that mass media messages probably don't convert many people is that most people seem to seek out mostly those messages that reinforce already-held beliefs, attitudes and values. Most of us probably don't actively look for messages that contradict our preconceptions about people, issues, events and things. The old saying, "Don't confuse me with the facts; my mind is made up," rings too true too often.

We see a newspaper endorsement for a candidate we don't like and we probably won't read it. (What do those editors know anyway?) On the other hand, if we see an endorsement for a candidate we do like, we'll probably read it. (What a good newspaper!)

There's some pretty good research that seems to indicate that if people are predisposed to act in a certain way, mass media messages can help reinforce their convictions that such an action is proper. Most of us constantly seek information that will confirm our feelings that what we believe and what we do are the only "right, decent, humane and intelligent" ways to live our lives. Such reinforcement makes us feel better about ourselves.

Activation/Crystallization

Plenty of research seems to confirm that mass media messages can help crystallize foggy notions and encourage people to take action. In other words, reading, hearing or seeing something in the mass media can help people focus and clarify the component parts of their various beliefs, attitudes and values. In addition, mass media messages can act as a catalyst to prompt people to act on their convictions a bit sooner than they might otherwise have done had they not been exposed to such messages.

This theory makes pretty good sense. It incorporates facets from a number of other theories and suggests that mass media messages serve to motivate us to take action after helping us gain a clearer picture of why we believe what we believe and why we feel the way we feel.

Catharsis

Remember your studies of Greek tragic plays? Why were they so tragic? Why did people suffer so much pain and sorrow? Why are our mass media filled with so much sex, crime, violence, perversion and weird behavior? Why do the characters in daytime dramas have so many troubles?

The "Catharsis Theory" helps explain why. It suggests that by reading, hearing or watching sex, crime, violence, perversion, weirdness and/or tragedy, people are sort of "cleansed" of their hidden and maybe not-so-hidden desires to indulge in such activities themselves. In other words, being exposed to news stories or fictional accounts about mass murder, hostage taking, sexual assault, robbery, hijack-

ing, tax fraud, adultery, etc. serves as a kind of "deterrent" to such undesirable behavior.

What a wonderful world it would be for journalists and other people in the mass media, if this theory were correct. It would justify just about any report/depiction of horrendous, despicable or outlandish behavior. Journalists could feel good about making such reports, because they would be serving to prevent future occurrences of similar behaviors. Movie makers and magazine publishers could rejoice in their sleaziness and tout their public spirit in helping to reduce crime, violence and illicit sex. Sadly, there is not much research to support the "Catharsis Theory." Human beings are simply too complicated to be cleansed of their desires by simple mass media messages.

Agenda Setting

"Agenda Setting Theory" deals with the question of do the mass media tell people what to think and be concerned about or do the mass media simply deal with what people are thinking and are concerned about? It's a difficult question. Research is mixed on the subject, but generally it seems as if the mass media have some power to suggest things that people should think about and maybe even do something about. Sometimes the mass media simply focus on what people seem to think is important and what people are doing. At other times, the mass media, especially the news media, report what authors, producers, directors, reporters, editors and/or publishers think people should think about and take action on.

Sometimes the mass media help set the public agenda and sometimes the mass media simply deal with items and issues from a public agenda that has already been set. Clearly, many people and forces in our society have important agenda-setting roles to play. Parents, teachers, friends, religious leaders, political leaders, activists, pro athletes, movie stars and television stars all influence how we evaluate the importance of events and issues. Mass media messages are just part of the daily mosaic that helps us decide what to be interested in and what to care about.

Cultivation

"Cultivation Theory" has cultivated a great many believers. This theory suggests that people get many of their ideas, perceptions and understandings about their neighbors, community, nation and world from the mass media. What we see, hear and read about helps shape our perceptions of reality. We depend on the mass media to provide us with information about the millions of people, places and things that we can't experience for ourselves. This cultivation can be pervasive and powerful, especially in the absence of personal exposure to people, places and things.

Unfortunately, research has shown that too often people get a distorted picture of reality from the media. The news media have been especially criticized for emphasizing too much "bad" news and giving the wrong impression about neighborhoods, cultures, people and the likelihood of becoming a crime victim. In short, the world view that people get from the news media is too often not a valid representation of social reality.

Minimal Effects

Depending on your perspective, the "Minimal Effects Theory" is either comforting or discomforting for the mass media. Essentially, it suggests that mass media messages don't have much effect at all on the beliefs, attitudes, values or actions of people. The messages are basically just a form of "sound and fury signifying nothing."

The "Minimal Effects Theory" is based on the belief that mass media messages sort of "go in one ear and out the other." Some research tends to support this belief. Interpersonal relationships have been found to be more influential than mass media messages in shaping opinions and motivating actions.

If you don't like the idea of the mass media being able to manipulate information and con people into believing in certain things and acting in certain ways, the "Minimal Effects Theory" is comforting; however, if you like the idea of the mass media having some power to influence people's beliefs and actions, the theory is discomforting.

Trivialization

The "Trivialization Theory" seems to be growing in popularity. It suggests that most of the time, the mass media simply trivialize whatever it is they focus on. This criticism is often leveled at the news media. In their seemingly never-ending quest to be concise and report everything that's fit to report, the news media often report on the trivial and they certainly trivialize

important events and issues. Critics point to *USA Today*, *People* magazine, radio and television news stories that last just seconds and "image-only" advertisements as examples of the "Trivialization Theory" at work.

Talk shows, movies of the week, docudramas and television dramas tend to trivialize as often, and perhaps more often, than they illuminate. It's difficult to do justice to the truly significant problems of society—adequate health care, full employment, fair taxation, cutting the budget deficit, immigration, affirmative action, equal opportunity, 100% literacy, AIDS, drug abuse—and be entertaining at the same time.

Problems/Issues

Many problems and issues are associated with the theories of mass media message effects. Even if you don't believe the media are all-powerful, the potential effects that media messages might have on at least some people warrant at least some attention.

1. **Prompting action.** It's discomforting to think that people might actually be encouraged to commit anti-social acts if the mass media report on or dramatize such acts. In addition, it's disturbing to think that the mass media might have the power to persuade people to act in a way that might be contrary to their normal behavior patterns. What an opportunity for absolute power to corrupt absolutely!

2. **Inhibiting action.** It's equally discomforting to think that people might actually be dissuaded from taking pro-social actions by some mass media message. Even the dissuading of some usually anti-social behavior like destroying property or disrupting commerce could be a "bad" thing in some circumstances—legitimate boycotts, marches, strikes and protests.

3. **Providing poor models.** The specter of "copycatism" rears its ugly head whenever stories or programs about suicides, bombings, hostage taking, hijacking, mass murder, sexual assault or other sensational crimes are reported on or dramatized. "Monkey see, monkey do" is a cliché, because it is all too often true.

4. **Promoting poor values.** The encouragement of materialism, of cut-throat competi-

Your Thoughts

Which theories of mass media message effects make the most sense to you? Why?

What other problems and issues do you see associated with the possible effects of mass media messages on people? Why are you concerned about such problems and issues?

What do you suggest be done to deal with the problems and issues you identified?

tion, of illicit sex and of egotistical self-indulgence can have a deleterious effect on society. Mass media messages could encourage people to become too self-centered, too concerned with making a buck and too concerned with being Number One.

5. **Causing depression.** Research has shown that reading, hearing or watching "bad" news can cause people to become depressed. It can also cause them to be less altruistic—less willing to help their fellow human beings.

6. **Distorting reality.** The trivialization of important events and issues, abbreviated news reports and simplistic television dramas that seem to imply that significant problems can be quickly and easily solved could tend to give people a distorted picture of the real world. For example, if they can't resolve a problem themselves as quickly and easily as people on TV do, they might give up or come to incorrect conclusions.

7. **Adding little or no value.** It's depressing to think that all the hard work that goes into producing the various mass media messages every day might not have much of an effect on people. At the very least, you can wrap fish and train your dog with a newspaper, swat insects with a magazine and use radio and television to help lull you to sleep.

Theories of the Press

Philosophers have built ethical theories and ethicists have studied standards of conduct and classified such theories. Media scholars and practitioners have instead defined some operational systems and have, somewhat inaccurately, labeled them as theories.

The most common and most understood of these so-called theories resulted from a book written by Fred Siebert, Theodore Peterson, and Wilbur Schramm, *Four Theories of the Press*. The Authoritarian theory, as they outlined it, had private operation of the media, but with government control. Individuals or companies in sufficient favor with officials were the only ones given the opportunity to operate, probably through a licensing system. Censorship was common, as was review of content before publication or broadcast and severe punishments for any digressions from government policy.

In the Communist theory, the media were not in private hands, but were owned and operated by the Communist Party. In a one-party government that results in a state-run system, the closely controlled media function as an arm of the state. This system requires that media support the policies and aims of government. As a result, the media are part of the government structure.

The Libertarian theory was described as a reaction to the Authoritarian, with the individual expected to be rational. This system was based on the ideals of democracy, representative government, natural rights of the individual, and a freedom that would end only when the rights of others were abused.

The Libertarian model had its origins in the writings of John Milton, the philosophy of John Stuart Mill and John Locke, and the politics of Thomas Jefferson. In 1644, John Milton wrote *Areopagitica*, an appeal for freedom of expression, with a premise that truth could be determined by any peasant, serf, tradesman, artisan, etc., not just their leaders, as the prevailing thought held. Milton's England and the rest of Europe at the time were governed by those who believed that only they knew what was best for the masses. Those in power absolutely knew that only they had the ability to discern the true, good, and beautiful from the ideas available, some of which could be false or harmful. Milton argued, in effect, that if you put truth and falsehood in a wrestling match that truth would always win. Milton said that authorities had nothing to fear if they permitted freedom of expression. Milton's words, however, had very little effect until 100 or more years later.

By the 18th century in England and the American colonies, thought was turning to faith in man's reason as the foundation for government. A government of and by the people was now believed to be not only possible, but also desirable. Enlightenment led to ideas of self-government on the assumption that the people could choose their own leaders from their own ranks, leaders who would serve temporarily and be subject to review by the people. Much of this thought came from the theories of John Locke and John Stuart Mill. Locke believed that the masses turned over to their representatives the powers and rights necessary to protect the people in the enjoyment of their rights. Locke argued for individual rights as a natural right of every person to life, liberty and property. From Milton and from Locke, 50 years later, we get the notion that if the individual's right is strongly protected, rational individuals, allowing for some social control, will make choices for the benefit of all.

Disagreements between Thomas Jefferson and Alexander Hamilton over the direction to be taken by the new United States of America led to a compromise that resulted in the Bill of Rights. The cornerstone of American press freedom, the First Amendment, and the other nine of the original amendments have always been considered part of the U.S. Constitution. The Bill of Rights, including press liberty, can be credited to a great extent to the concessions made to Thomas Jefferson so that he and his followers would lend their support to ratification. Earlier, Thomas Jefferson was instrumental in the Declaration of Independence which has often been described as heavily dependent upon the thoughts and words of Milton and Locke. All in all, these events pointed to a major role for Thomas Jefferson in shaping these philosophies into practical application in the documents that created the legal basis for the Libertarian Theory underlying American print media initially and broadcast and film eventually.

The Social Responsibility theory developed as it became clear that the Libertarian theory simply was not working well in modern society. People did not have the time to read several newspapers and magazines, listen to numerous radio stations or watch a multitude of television stations. In addition, the control over media outlets was becoming more and more centralized. Few truly "independent" voices existed. So, the Social Responsibility theory encouraged media owners, operators and practitioners to be "socially responsible." Its cornerstone is providing fair and complete information even if it might be contrary to the views of media moguls.

Make-a-Buck Theory

In the 1970s, Jack Haberstroh stirred the academic waters and stimulated argument about the ethical posture of the media with his Make-a-Buck theory. Haberstroh used the term hogwash to describe his opinion of the Social Responsibility theory saying that the media were not safeguarding society, nor enlightening it. Haberstroh contended that the media, given our economic and political system, cannot operate in a socially responsible way, charging that the media are prostitutes to the purchasing units forming the American corporate state. Haberstroh's primary conflict with the idea of social responsibility centered on the advertising function of the media. He said advertising is responsible for inane programming on television, radio stations chasing big audience counts by giving listeners exactly what they want, and a slavish devotion to media consumers that lowers political and cultural standards.

Impacts of Media Messages

Research has found that news coverage of youth crime, especially violent crime, is not proportional to the incidence of such crime in reality. As a result, people have a distorted picture of the percentage of crimes committed by young people. In addition, news coverage tends to overrepresent the number of minority perpetrators and underrepresent the number of minority victims. According to an ABC news survey, about 75% of Americans report that they formulate their opinions about crime based on what they see, read or hear in the news media. So, with so many people using distorted information, it is easy to see why the "mean world" perception is so pervasive. It is clear that mass media messages can help cultivate public perceptions, so it is critical that the messages are mirrors of reality rather than distortions that reinforce stereotypes and inhibit effective public policy measures.

New concerns are being raised about the potential negative effects of playing violent video games. A summary of decades of research concluded that there is a link between media violence and real-life aggression. One expert estimated that as much as 10% of the juvenile violence in society can be blamed on aggressive acts portrayed in the entertainment media—movies, TV and music. Some scientists say the violence associated with video games may be the most problematic, because the violence is not just passive. In video games, players actually "rehearse" violent acts.

A study in the early 1990s found that the average American child will have seen more than 8,000 murders and more than 100,000 assaults, rapes and other acts of violence by the time he or she graduates from elementary school. Critics complain that all too often media violence is shown to be justified, heroic or even funny, so children get an unrealistic picture of real-world violence and are more likely to become violent themselves. A 17-year study that followed 700 children from age 6 to age 22 found that kids who watched more than three hours of TV per day were four times more likely to have acted aggressively by age 22 than were kids who watched TV less than one hour per day.

The American Academy of Pediatrics advises parents to limit their children's television viewing to no more than two hours per day. The group also suggests parents watch programs with their children and initiate discussions about program content. Some statistics on the television viewing habits of young people lend credence to the group's suggestions. For example, children ages 2 to 17 watch TV an average of almost 20 hours per week. That works out to more than 1,000 hours of TV viewing per year. By way of comparison, the average young person spends about 900 hours in school per year.

A recent example of modeling involved a 13-year-old Connecticut boy who tried to imitate a stunt he saw performed on the MTV program, "Jackass." On the show, a performer wore a fire-resistant suit covered with steaks and threw himself on a grill to cook the steaks. The boy, who wore no protective clothing, sprinkled gasoline on his legs in an attempt to recreate the stunt. He suffered second- and third-degree burns, but survived.

Another concern about the possible "modeling" influences of the mass media is associated with the portrayal of smoking in films. According to a 2001 study, cigarette products appeared an average of every three to five minutes in 1990s movies, compared to every 10 to 15 minutes in 1970s and 1980s movies. With so much on-camera inhaling by role models, is it any wonder that young people think smoking cigarettes is "cool?"

Recent Research, Developments and Issues

A study by two economists in early 2008 found that when violent films are screened on weekends, the incidents of real-world violent crime actually decrease. The researchers speculated that the reason for the decline in the crime rate likely was due to the fact that would-be criminals were in the theaters watching such films rather than drinking in bars and looking for trouble. The researchers analyzed a decade worth of statistics and discovered that assaults decreased by about 1,000 per weekend when violent films were screened. No increase in assault rates was found in the weeks following such screenings as well.

What concerns do you have with how much time people spend online and how they spend their online time?

What suggestions do you have to help people maximize the benefits of their online time?

The results and speculations from the study conducted by the economists was criticized by psychologists and others. Critics pointed to decades of research that has found that the brutality found in films, video games and television promotes aggressive behavior, especially among people predisposed to violent acts. Critics also complained that even if the screening of violent films might temporarily delay the commission of violent acts, the displays of violence in such films can only serve to increase the growing desensitization toward violence that pervades much of society.

Concerns and fears about the harmful effects of exposure to too much television viewing do not seem to be stopping parents from permitting their young children from becoming avid viewers. A study found that almost two-thirds of children one-year-old or younger watch more than one hour of TV every day. Most parents indicated they permitted TV viewing because it served as sort of an "electronic babysitter"

and made it possible for them to watch TV programs on other television sets.

As more and more people get easier, faster access to online communications, concerns have surfaced related to how much time people spend online and what kinds of activities occupy their time. A study in 2008 found that consumers spend about 43% of their online time visiting "content" sites. About 27% of their time is spent on "communication" sites, followed by "commerce" sites (16%), "community" sites (8%) and "search" sites (5%).

"Content" sites were defined as those providing basic news and information. "Communication" sites included email providers. "Commerce" sites included retail and wholesale operations. "Community" sites included the social-networking Facebook, MySpace and YouTube. "Search" sites included Yahoo and Google.

Think Back

1. What are the basic elements of the Lasswell Model and the Shannon Model of the communication process?

2. What is the SMCR model and what do each of the letters stand for?

3. What are the basic types of "noise" in the SMCR model that can inhibit effective communication? Give TWO examples of each type.

4. Why do some scholars believe the SMCR model should be written as a circle?

5. What are some of the major concerns related to the SMCR model?

6. What's the definition of mass communication?

7. What are the elements associated with the process of mass communication?

8. What are the elements associated with the HUB model of mass communication?

9. What are the basic elements of the communication research process and what are the basic types of research methodologies?

10. List and define the TEN theories of media effects.

11. What are the major problems and issues associated with the various theories of media effects?

12. List and define the FOUR major theories of the press.

13. What is the "Make-a-Buck Theory" of the press?

14. What are some of the negative impacts associated with media coverage and portrayal of crime and violence?

15. What are the eight aspects that should be included by news organizations in their reports of the results of public opinion polls and surveys?

16. What were the major findings of the study by economists on the effects of violent films on the rates of real-world assaults?

17. About how much television are babies watching and why do parents say they permit their children to become TV consumers?

18. What were the major findings of the study that examined how people spend their time online?

Mass Media Economics

3

Convergence, consolidations and mergers are having dramatic impacts on the economics associated with mass media organizations. It is clear that media companies believe that they cannot stand alone, that they must build up as much synergistic muscle as possible by finding ways to profit from combinations of old and new technologies and methods. Isolated, stand-alone, independent companies and organizations are finding it almost impossible to survive, much less succeed, in today's economic climate. Dominate or perish is the new technological imperative facing mass media companies as the worlds of entertainment and other forms of communication blend together in the hearts, minds and pocketbooks of advertisers and consumers. Traditional content providers are looking to partner with Internet access/service providers and vice versa. The costs of producing content and of delivering content to consumers via digital connections are not significantly different for 100,000 customers or 100,000,000 customers, so those companies that can find a way to maximize the number of their customers can sell their products more cheaply and dominate the marketplace. Just ask Bill Gates.

Legislation Paves the Way

The Telecommunications Act of 1996 paved the way for many of the recent economics-related developments in the mass media. It certainly made it easier for companies to merge and enter new and exciting areas. One of the major goals of the act was to free up the marketplace and make it more pro-competitive and less regulated. The hope was that greater freedom would lead to more research and development in telecommunications that would result in more and cheaper choices for consumers. More specifically, it was hoped that cable TV companies, telephone companies and Internet companies would begin to compete with one another by providing similar ranges of services and that the competition would lead to better and cheaper services or at least more choices for consumers.

The Telecommunications Act of 1996 ranged far and wide, but the following were among its most interesting economics-related components:

1. A company or network is permitted to own as many TV stations as it wants as long as the combined reach of the stations is no greater than 35% of viewers nationwide.
2. A company or network can own as many as eight radio stations in a given market.
3. A company or network can own a TV station and a cable TV system in the same area.
4. Cable TV systems can charge whatever they want for standard service.

As a result of enabling legislation and a general trend in business that "bigger is better," we've seen a decline in the number of major telecommunications-oriented companies. By most counts, we had 12 major companies in 1996, but now most experts agree there are just six. In addition, the mass media system is dominated by about 10 massive companies with about 15 lesser companies completing most of the rest of the mass media landscape. These super-colossal, transnational corporations have holdings in computing, telephony and traditional mass media.

The evolution of such companies can be tracked, in part, using the following timeline:

1. January, 1986—Capital Cities Communications purchases ABC for $3.5 billion to create Capital Cities/ABC.

2. June, 1986—General Electric buys RCA, parent company of NBC, for $6.4 billion.

3. November, 1989—Sony buys Columbia Pictures Entertainment for $3.4 billion.

4. January, 1990—Warner Communications merges with Time, Inc. in a $14.1 billion deal.

5. January, 1991—Matsushita Electric buys MCA, Inc. for $6.9 billion.

6. July, 1994—Viacom, Inc. buys Paramount Communications for $10 billion.

7. August, 1994—Viacom, Inc. buys Blockbuster Entertainment for $8 billion.

8. June, 1995—Seagram buys MCA, Inc. from Matsushita for $5.7 billion.

9. November, 1995—Westinghouse Electric buys CBS, Inc. for $5.4 billion.

10. February, 1996—Walt Disney Co. buys Capital Cities/ABC for $19 billion.

11. October, 1996—Time Warner merges with Turner Broadcasting System in a $7.6 billion deal.

12. December, 1996—Westinghouse Electric's CBS unit buys Infinity Broadcasting for $4.7 billion. A year later, Westinghouse Electric changes name of company to just CBS, Inc. and later to CBS, Corp.

13. December, 1998—Seagram buys Polygram records for $10.4 billion.

14. February, 1999—AT&T buys Tele-Communications, Inc., the country's second largest cable television company, for $44 billion.

15. April, 1999—AT&T buys MediaOne, the country's fourth largest cable TV company, for $58 billion.

16. April, 1999—CBS Corp. buys King World Productions for $2.5 billion.

17. September, 1999—Viacom buys CBS Corp. for $37 billion.

18. October, 1999—Clear Channel buys AMFM for $23.5 billion, creating the world's largest radio-focused company.

19. March, 2000—Clear Channel buys SFX, a concert producer and owner of 120 live entertainment venues, for $4.4 billion.

20. March, 2000—The Tribune Co. buys Times Mirror for $6.5 billion.

What Mergers and Buyouts Hath Wrought

In most of the acquisitions and mergers, content suppliers partnered with distributors, took over the operations of competitors and/or branched out into new areas of mass media. The end result, of course, is bigger, meaner, more diverse, more powerful, more profitable companies. For example, after Clear Channel completed its many deals, it owned about 1200 radio stations, 19 TV stations and 555,000 billboards. The CBS-Viacom marriage created the country's second largest media company, behind AOL-Time Warner. In addition to its TV station holdings, CBS-Viacom owned radio stations, Paramount Pictures, Blockbuster Video, Nickelodeon cable TV channel, MTV networks, Showtime and Simon & Schuster publishing company. CBS-Viacom also owns part of the CW TV network and the Comedy Central cable TV channel. The Tribune Co. acquisition of Times Mirror created a company with 11 daily newspapers, 22 TV stations, two cable TV channels, Internet properties, radio stations and the Chicago Cubs baseball club.

All of this multimedia, multichannel, highly diversified corporate structure means many more opportunities for cross-promotions, multiple uses of content, and discounted advertising rates for companies that agree to advertise across all of the outlets owned and operated by one of the new, super-colossal mass media giants. In short, it means money and plenty of it for those on the "inside." For those on the "outside," it may mean a fast-track trip to bankruptcy or a ride on the merger/buyout train. In addition, merger/buyout mania may also mean fewer voices reaching the American consumer and conflicts of interest associated with news coverage of co-owned baseball teams, movie studios, publishing houses, recording companies and other aspects of far-reaching media empires.

Recent Mergers

America Online and Time Warner merged in a $106 billion deal in early 2001. AOL-Time Warner struggled, so in mid-2004, AOL was dropped while Time Warner marched on.

NBC purchased the Bravo cable entertainment network from Cablevision Systems, Corp. for $1.25 billion in 2002. Analysts applauded the deal, because it gave NBC an alternative venue for its programming and allowed it to squeeze more profits out of its products via multiple airings. Quite a bit more money can be made when the same program is aired on more than one network. The second and subsequent airings are basically a way to rake in bonus advertising revenue.

NBC merged with Vivendi's Universal Entertainment in a $14 billion deal in late 2003. The new company, NBC Universal, included a TV network, the Universal movie and television studios, 14 local TV stations and a list of cable networks—USA, CNBC, MSNBC and Bravo.

A consortium headed by Sony Corp. of America bought Metro-Goldwyn-Mayer (MGM) in late 2004. Comcast joined Sony at the last moment in the $4.8 billion deal. Sony and its partners indicated they were most interested in MGM's library of more than 4,000 films. Tentative plans called for limiting original movie production, though.

Cable TV giants Comcast and Time Warner jointly bought out Adelphia for an estimated $17.5 billion in 2006. The deal added about 2 million customers for Comcast and about 3.5 million for Time Warner.

Also in 2006, the Walt Disney Company sold its 22 ABC Radio stations and its ABC network to Citadel Broadcasting for almost $3 billion. The deal left Citadel with 177 FM radio stations and 66 AM radio stations, making Citadel the third largest radio group in the United States.

At about the same time in 2006, Knight Ridder, the second-largest newspaper company in the United States, was sold to the McClatchy Company in a $4.5 million cash and stock deal. McClatchy also agreed to assume about $2 billion in Knight Ridder debt, so the deal was really worth about $6.5 billion. McClatchy acquired 32 daily newspapers in the transaction, but immediately sold 12 of the dailies because they didn't meet the company's goal of a minimum annual growth rate of 11%.

Two TV "netlets" merged in 2006 to create the CW. CBS and Warner Brothers Entertainment combined their UPN and WB networks to create the CW. The venture was designed to be a 50-50 ownership deal.

In 2007, the merger of the two major satellite radio companies, Sirius and XM, began. The almost $5 billion deal took a while before it received all the government-related okays it needed. The new company was expected to generate about $2 billion in revenue annually and have about 15 million subscribers.

Show Me the Money

Most mass media organizations are in business to make money. They make most of their money by charging advertisers a fee for placing sponsored messages in mass media products and/or charging consumers a fee for providing mass media products. Money can be made in other ways, of course. Sometimes companies pay a fee to have their products used or "placed" in films or television programs. Mass media organizations also sell copies of their products or portions of products to retailers, other mass media organizations or selected individuals. For example, retailers often pay for the right to use movie characters, especially cartoon characters, in their own marketing efforts. McDonald's, Wendy's and Burger King are well-known for this. Companies occasionally buy the rights to a song so they can use it in their advertising. Lawyers sometimes buy copies of television news stories to use in civil trials.

Advertising plays a major role in two of the four traditional economic support models for mass media organizations. The four are (1) consumer supported, (2) advertiser supported, (3) consumer and advertiser supported and (4) government/private subsidy supported.

Consumer Supported

In the consumer supported model, consumers pay most, if not all, of the costs associated with producing and distributing the product. Examples include the recording industry, film industry, "pay/premium" cable television—HBO, Cinemax, Showtime, pay-per-view, etc.—and the book publishing industry.

Advertiser Supported

In the advertiser supported model, advertisers pay most, if not all, of the costs associated with producing and distributing the product. Examples include radio, broadcast television, "freebie" newspapers and most web sites.

Advertiser and Consumer Supported

In the advertiser and audience supported model, advertisers pay for most of the costs associated with producing and distributing the product, but consumers contribute as well. Examples include newspapers, magazines and regular cable television.

Government/Private Subsidy Supported

In the government/private subsidy supported model, the government and/or foundations, organizations, groups or individuals contribute money to cover the costs of producing and distributing the product. Examples include public radio, public television and the in-house "newsletters" and other publications of corporations, businesses, agencies and organizations.

Creative Economics

Often two or more of the support systems can be blended together to form a more solid economic base for a mass media organization. For example, many public broadcasting stations have experimented with "low key, tasteful" commercials. A "company magazine" might sell advertising. A "consumer magazine" might refuse to sell advertising and combine audience support with subsidies from foundations or agencies. The producer of a film might approach various manufacturers and suggest that they pay a fee to have their products used in a film.

The point is, sometimes when money is tight, mass media organizations have to scramble a bit to make ends meet. Also, most of the owners of mass media organizations simply want to make as much money as they can so they look for ways to increase profits. They look for ways to increase their revenue streams.

Supply and Demand

The theory of supply and demand helps explain how the economics of the mass media play out. The supply side of the equation is the availability of specific

Your Thoughts

List the advantages and disadvantages of each of the four economic support models.

Consumer Supported—

Advertiser Supported—

Advertiser/Consumer Supported—

Government/Private Subsidy Supported—

space and time at a fair price. The demand side of the equation is the amount of the desire to purchase such space and time plus the ability to pay for it.

As long as mass media organizations can supply something that advertisers desire and advertisers are willing to pay what mass media organizations want to charge, everybody stays reasonably happy. Problems arise when the supply is not equal to the demand and/or the demand is not equal to the supply. When there is not enough time or space to accommodate all the requests for ads, costs to advertisers go up. Of course, that means costs to consumers go up, too. When there's not enough demand for advertising time or space, cuts have to be made in media operations. That usually means personnel cuts and/or salary reductions.

The shares of the advertising revenue pie have remained relatively constant among the various mass media for the past several years. In general, the breakdown has been similar to the following:

1. Daily Newspapers   22.1%
2. Broadcast Television   19.9%
3. Direct Mail   19.8%
4. Online   9.0%
5. Miscellaneous   7.8%
6. Radio   7.1%
7. Yellow Pages   6.2%
8. Magazines   5.3%
9. Cable TV   2.8%

The "miscellaneous" category includes weekly newspapers, free newspapers (shoppers and penny-savers), bus ads, and ads associated with movie theaters.

Issues and Problems

In general, the economics-related aspects of the various mass media are relatively similar, but there are some important differences. Each medium has its own set of economics-related issues and problems.

Daily Newspapers

The number of daily newspapers in the United States had been decreasing at a rather steady pace for several years. In the mid 1920s, we reached a peak at 2,650 dailies. In mid-2008, there were approximately 1,450 daily newspapers operating in the United States—about 820 morning newspapers and about 630 afternoon/evening newspapers.

Daily newspapers have many competitors for a relatively finite amount of advertising dollars. The Internet and other information providers give consumers many options for how to get the facts, figures and opinions they want.

Most daily newspapers do not have large circulations. Fewer than 10% sell more than 100,000 copies per day. More than half sell fewer than 25,000 copies per day.

About 85% of the daily newspapers are owned by "chains." A "chain" is defined as a person/company that owns more than one newspaper.

Few cities in the United States have true "competing" newspapers any more. Fewer than 50 cities have more than one newspaper and in about 25% of those cities, the "competitors" have entered into what is called a "Joint Operating Agreement." Such an agreement allows newspapers that are owned by different people/companies to "share" certain aspects of advertising, production and distribution. Most of the time, the news-editorial staffs of the newspapers remain separate, though.

Estimates vary, but advertising usually accounts for about 75% of a newspaper's annual revenue. For the most part, ad rates are determined by circulation figures. The more people who buy the newspaper, the more the newspaper can charge both classified and display advertisers.

Advertising revenues for daily newspapers are declining. Most "healthy" daily newspapers enjoy a profit margin of at least 15% and many reach or surpass the 20% level. For comparison, the normal profit margin for a successful business is about 13%.

Of course, these days, with advertising, street sales and subscription revenues declining, the only way for newspapers to retain such "healthy" profit margins is to cut costs. Such moves cause morale, news coverage and other problems for newspaper managers. Among the other issues and problems associated with the economics-related aspects of daily newspapers are the following:

1. **Loss of diversity.** As the number of newspapers declines and ownership becomes concentrated in the hands of just a few big companies, fewer independent voices get a

chance to be heard. Less competition might also mean higher advertising rates and higher ad rates usually means higher consumer costs.

2. **Loss of uniqueness.** Group ownership can lead to "homogenized" newspapers—a "by-the-numbers," formulized approach to news-papering.

3. **Absentee owners.** If the owners of a newspaper don't live in the community where it's published, perhaps they won't be as concerned about maintaining and/or improving the quality of life in that community. The public service aspect of a newspaper could suffer as a result.

4. **Bottom-line orientation.** Groups sometimes have a tendency to be more concerned about the "bottom line" than about the quality of content. As an example, sometimes staffs and/or salaries are reduced whenever a group buys a newspaper.

5. **High costs.** It costs quite a bit to start a daily newspaper from scratch. Estimates vary, but $15,000,000 is probably not too far off. That's high enough to dissuade most people from taking the risk. In addition, because the cost of buying a single copy of a newspaper or having a subscription continues to increase, fewer families can afford to subscribe to more than one paper and many people on fixed incomes have had to cancel subscriptions.

6. **Advertiser influence.** Since so many daily newspapers have such small circulations, advertisers can sometimes exert too much influence over content. In areas where there might be only a handful of major advertisers, some reporters and editors become fearful of offending a person/company who contributes a large percentage of the newspaper's revenue.

7. **Increased competition for ad revenues.** Weekly newspapers, shoppers' guides, Pennysaver-type freebies, the electronic yellow pages, computer data/shopping services, magazines, radio, TV, the Internet and now even the film industry are all after the same advertisers. Unethical or even illegal behavior can result from such a fiercely competitive quest for advertising.

Magazines

The average profit margin for most magazines is about 10%. In general, most magazines get about 50% of their revenue from advertising. Subscription sales account for about 33% and single-copy sales bring in about 17%.

"Shared revenue" is an important concept in the magazine business. Depending on contractual agreements, magazine publishers "share" subscription revenues with distributors, wholesalers and retailers. By the time everyone takes their share, a publisher usually ends up with about half of what he/she charged for a subscription.

Advertising revenue is often "shared" as well. Advertising agencies that place advertisements in magazines typically take about a 15% cut from what an advertiser paid to run an ad.

"Trends" in the magazine business include:

1. Subscription sales are up and single-copy sales are down.

2. The price of magazines continues to increase, but the number of copies sold is declining slowly.

3. The cost of producing a magazine is increasing.

4. Starting a new magazine is a risky enterprise. The failure rate is more than 50%.

5. Specialized magazines succeed more than generalized magazines. For example, a magazine designed for just insect collectors probably has a better chance of succeeding than a general "hobby" magazine. Specialization allows a publisher to charge more for his/her magazine—"fanatics" seem willing to pay the price to find out more about their particular hobby or area of interest. In addition, the publisher of a specialized magazine can charge advertisers more, because he/she can usually guarantee that almost all readers are likely buyers of specialized products.

Among the issues/problems associated with the economics-related aspects of the magazine industry are the following:

- **Too many mouths to feed.** Too many people "share" the revenue. Such sharing can deplete resources and drive up prices.

- **Production costs are too high.** The high cost of producing a magazine prevents would-be publishers from publishing and drives well-intentioned publishers out of business. That means fewer voices reach the public.
- **Specialization frenzy.** Things can get a bit ridiculous. Not every hobby or idiosyncratic aspect of life needs its own magazine.
- **Time constraints.** People don't seem to be spending as much time reading as they once did. Such declines could lead to less demand for magazines and fewer job opportunities for magazine journalists.
- **New technologies.** With electronic yellow pages, computerized data banks, the Internet, the World Wide Web, hypermedia, etc., etc., etc., competition for "readers" could drive many magazines out of business.
- **Dependence on "freelancers."** A large number of magazines depend almost exclusively on freelancers rather than staff writers and photographers to produce content. This can lead to a loss of control over the quality and accuracy of stories and photos. Decreased quality and/or accuracy could mean decreased revenues.

Radio

Radio, especially FM radio, did pretty well for many years. Now, however, advertising revenues are down and the average profit margin in radio is about 7%–10%.

A radio station generates advertising revenue in three ways:

1. Selling "spots" to local retailers—Valenzuela Ford, Eric's Pie Shop, San Diego Plumbing Supply, etc.
2. Selling "spots" directly to national advertisers who want to reach specific regions. For example, a manufacturer of snow tires probably would not want to advertise on radio stations in Southern California and Hawaii, but probably would want to run spots on stations in the Midwest.
3. Getting a percentage of the money paid to networks by advertisers. It doesn't happen too much in radio anymore, but when a local station runs a network program/segment, the

network pays the local station a small sum of money for airing the commercials that the network inserts within the program/segment.

In general, about 85% of a local station's revenue is generated by advertising that is sold to local retailers. Almost all the rest comes from spots sold directly to national advertisers. Only about 1% comes from networks.

For the most part, ratings determine what a radio station charges advertisers. The more listeners it has, the more it can charge. The demographic characteristics of listeners are factors, too, though. For example, if an advertiser wants to reach mostly teenagers, he/she might be willing to pay premium rates to a station that can deliver a large number of young buyers even though such a station might not have very high ratings over all age groups.

Radio advertising rates are fairly reasonable, especially compared to television rates. As a result, the demand for advertising time on radio is high. Since it's relatively inexpensive to produce an ad for and run an ad on radio, advertisers are returning to radio as a viable medium for helping them to sell their products.

Among the issues/problems associated with the economics-related aspects of radio stations are the following:

- **Salaries are low.** Some disc jockeys make decent money, but the salaries for most are not as high as you might think. Few make more than $100,000 per year. Salaries for radio newspeople are really low. Reporters average about $25,000 per year and newscasters average about $30,000 per year. Despite the meager salaries, many very good people continue to work in radio. How long this will continue is a real question, though.
- **Formula programming.** Tight money in radio often leads owners to use nationally syndicated programming services and/or to program "safe" music and/or talk. This results in a kind of "homogenization" of radio stations across the country and a reduction in the number of voices that get to be heard.
- **Group ownership.** Another threat to a diversity of voices is when one company owns several stations in the same market. Thanks

to recent federal legislation, this phenomenon is happening in many of the biggest cities in the United States.

- **"Shock" radio.** Competition among stations in some markets is fierce. With more than 30 radio stations in town, not everyone can succeed by programming country music or rock and roll classics, so some owners experiment with other formats. One that is used by some is "shock" radio. Talk show hosts insult and badger in-studio guests plus the people who call in. Sexy, emotional and exploitive topics are usually stressed and conscious efforts are made to anger and provoke people.

- **News linked to programming.** The type of programming—Top 40, Album Oriented Rock, Country, Shock Radio—can have an impact on how news is presented and/or how people perceive the news department. Journalists have enough image problems of their own without taking on those of the programming department, too.

- **Payola.** Occasionally, radio station personnel accept bribes from music promoters to give preferential treatment to certain artists. Such actions are illegal, of course, but it still happens.

- **Gimmicks.** Radio stations are infamous for running contests during rating periods to attract more listeners. Now that ratings are measured almost year-round in most areas, such giveaways are not as common, but they still occur. Examples include "$10,000 Thursdays," "Million Dollar Music," etc. Such gimmicks drain off resources that could be used for other purposes, including paying higher salaries and/or improving equipment.

- **Less news.** Radio stations are no longer required to air a minimum amount of news and information. Research has shown that the total amount of news aired has not declined much over the past few years, but in some parts of the country, less local news is being aired and it's being replaced by network or syndicated news. Less local news means fewer jobs for journalists and perhaps less public service to the local community.

Television

Local television stations receive revenue in the same ways as local radio stations. About 80% of a local TV station's revenue comes from advertising spots sold to local retailers. About 15% comes from spots sold to national advertisers who want selective placement for their ads and about 5% comes from the networks who pay local stations to run national ads during network programs.

As in radio, a TV station's ratings determine what it charges advertisers. Basically, the more people who watch, the more a station can charge. Having the "right" types of people watching helps, too, of course. For example, a station might be able to charge more for its time if it has a large number of young, upwardly mobile viewers.

Until the 1990s, local TV stations were very profitable, with average profit margins running about 20%. Times are changing a bit, though. Audience erosion due to video rentals, more cable channels and some dissatisfaction with programming plus more competition for advertising dollars have put an economic squeeze on some stations.

News departments are being especially hard hit, because at most stations, the news department generates at least half of the station's revenue. When revenues decline, budget cuts have to be made and there is great pressure to improve ratings.

The happenings at local stations include the following:

1. **Staff downsizing.** Some stations are laying off news staffers in an effort to save money. Cuts of 25% or more are not uncommon.

2. **Utility players.** People who can do more than one job in a station, especially in the newsroom, are more likely to get and keep a job. For example, newscasters might be expected to act as producers. Producers might be expected to act as assignment editors. Reporters might be expected to be able to shoot/edit video. Studio personnel might be called on to work in master control. Flexibility and adaptability will likely be the key to finding success in local television from now on.

3. **News increases.** Despite staff downsizing, most stations not only don't decrease the

number or length of newscasts, they often increase the number or length of newscasts. It is not uncommon for local television stations to program six or more hours of news per day. Some stations even have worked out agreements with local cable systems to program a 24-hour a day news channel. If you don't increase staff, but you do increase the number or length of newscasts, existing staffers have to either work a lot harder and/or other sources have to be called on to help fill news time—syndicated services, networks and freelancers. None is a particularly attractive option if you value local news content and quality.

4. **Concentration of ownership.** More and more TV stations are being purchased by "groups." Group ownership can mean loss of local control and a reduced "community-orientation."

5. **Local control.** Many network-affiliated stations are lobbying hard for more control over what goes out over their stations. Most don't want the network newscasts expanded and most want more time turned over to them to program as they see fit.

6. **Advertiser influence.** Reasonably regularly, advertisers threaten to boycott programs, stations and even networks if certain demands— less aggressive news reporting, less offensive story lines, less sexual innuendo—are not met. When money is tight, television executives might be more likely to give in to advertiser pressure concerning program and news content.

7. **Flash/Trash.** During ratings sweeps— usually November, February, May and July— many stations and networks turn to sleazy and titillating programming and news stories to try to attract viewers. Sex, crime, violence, perversion and extreme oddities are emphasized and sometimes squeeze out air time for more significant issues/events.

8. **Unreliable ratings.** The effort to determine how many people are watching a given program is fraught with problems. Research has found that sometimes Nielsen Media Research and the other ratings companies don't do a very good job of sampling certain groups. Among the groups that seem to be consistently overlooked are members of minority groups, college students, people staying in hotels and people who watch TV in bars. The viewing patterns of such groups could have pronounced effects on a station's ratings. Other problems with ratings include:

- **Accuracy of findings.** People might not tell the truth in their ratings diaries. They might forget what they watched. Audimeters can't record how many, if any, people are actually watching a program. Button fatigue might reduce the proper use of People Meters.

- **Poor samples.** Most local TV ratings are based on samples of between 500 and 2,000 people. National samples sometimes include up to 5,000 people. If the samples are drawn carefully, they should be reasonably representative of the total population being studied; however if sampling is not done correctly, the ratings could be almost meaningless. This concern is especially great now that People Meters are being used to measure audiences. Some critics believe that the people who agree to use People Meters are probably quite a bit different than many of the rest of the viewing public.

9. **Formula TV.** With so much at stake, few are willing to take risks when making programming or news content decisions. As a result, successful entertainment programs are "cloned," spun-off or ripped off. News formats, styles and philosophies are "borrowed." The result—stars, shows, plots, newscasts and newscasters all start to look and sound alike.

Recent Concerns

In 2001, the FCC voted to permit one company to own more than one TV network. The move opened the door for the major networks to purchase some of the upstart networks, and meant additional revenue streams for ABC, CBS, NBC and Fox. The commission did keep in place regulations that prohibited one of the big four TV networks from merging with another big four member.

A study of "clutter," the nonprogram material (commercials, public service announcements, promotional messages) on network TV, found that in 2002, the four major networks averaged about 14 minutes and 45 seconds of clutter per prime-time hour. ABC led with slightly more than 15 minutes of clutter per hour. CBS had the least clutter with a bit more than 14 minutes per hour. Networks run a risk devoting so much time to nonprogram material. For example, viewers can become annoyed and change channels. In addition, some research has shown that the more commercials a person sees in a row, the less likely it is that he or she will remember any particular one.

A study by the U.S. General Accounting Office in late 2003 found that the soaring cost of sports programming was pushing up cable TV rates. The average monthly bill for cable was $36.47 at the end of 2002, a 40% increase over the average bill in 1997. Overall inflation during that same period was just 12%. The report also showed that in the 2% of the United States where there is competition between cable companies, customers were charged 15% less than the national average.

In the wonderful world of sports, a tight advertising market and increasing rights fees hit the major TV networks, causing ABC, Fox and CBS to lose a combined $3 billion on their eight-year, $17.6 billion NFL contract. ABC and ESPN likely will lose a combined $2.2 billion on the six-year, $4.6 billion NBA contract.

A news organization's web site can have a positive impact on its traditional product. A study in 2001 found that 7% of the visitors to a newspaper's web site indicated they became subscribers of the hardcopy newspaper and 21% said they bought more single copies of the newspaper after visiting the web site. About 31% said they started reading more of the newspaper after checking out the web site.

Many cable TV systems introduced "video-on-demand" services in the early part of the 21st century. For a nominal fee, usually about $4, customers can download a movie and watch it at any time during a 24-hour period. Rewinding, fast-forwarding and pausing features are included. Cox Communications, Comcast Corp. and Time-Warner were among the first companies to offer video-on-demand. Soon after, Disney and other program providers started experimenting with similar services.

Recent Research, Developments and Issues

The tough economic times had experts predicting an ad revenue growth of less than 4% in the United States and about 6.5% worldwide in 2008. For specific media, the experts predicted the following for the rest of the decade: newspaper ad revenue down about 4% per year; television ad revenue up about 1.5% per year; Internet ad revenue up about 17% per year. Don't feel too bad for contemporary media, though. The experts estimate that while about $194 billion in ad revenue will be distributed among newspapers, magazines, radio, television, cinema, outdoor and the Internet in 2008, the amount will jump to about $203 billion in 2010.

In what perhaps is a glimpse into the future of U.S. advertising, experts are predicting that the Internet will surpass television as the biggest advertising medium in the United Kingdom by the end of 2009. The increase in Internet advertising has been attributed to improved access to online technologies, inexpensive computers, user control over various features and improved online content.

Newspapers

Newspapers are taking some of the hardest economic hits. In 2007, advertising revenue for newspapers dropped almost 8% overall. Interestingly, ad revenue from newspaper-related Internet sites increased almost 20% in 2007, but ad revenue from the "printed" newspapers dropped about 9.5%. Even with the impressive double-digit growth in Internet site ad revenue, such revenue accounted for less than 8% of the total revenue for U.S. newspapers. The inability to monetize the Internet more effectively, especially for newspapers, is among the greatest failures associated with contemporary media.

In an effort to increase ad revenue, many newspapers are breaking tradition and placing ads on the front pages of news, sports, entertainment, features and business sections. Such ads are normally relatively small and placed along the bottom of pages. Among the major newspapers trying such previously taboo advertising are *The Wall Street Journal*, *The New York Times* and the *San Diego Union-Tribune*.

Radio

Radio is losing ad revenue, too. Local radio stations suffered about a 3% drop in ad revenue in 2007, but network radio actually enjoyed a 4% increase in ad revenue. Experts attributed the network increase to a number of major retailers who shifted ad money to radio from other media. Good news for network radio, but bad news for the other media.

Commercials during radio programming apparently are not the big turn off that many experts had thought. A study found that about 92% of the audience stays with a station during commercials. The length of the commercial break period had an impact on audience retention, though. For a one-minute break, 99% of the audience remained. For a three-minute break, 90% stayed. For a six-minute break, 88% kept listening.

Commercial time on radio averages a bit less than 10 minutes per hour now. Clear Channel Communications enforces averages of a bit less than 8 minutes per hour. CCC stations charge a bit more for their air time, but based on the retention statistics for shorter commercial breaks, you probably can see how CCC stations can convince advertisers to buy time.

Arbitron is stepping up its use of Portable People Meters (sometimes also called Personal People Meters) to measure radio ratings. The devices, which automatically record the radio listening habits of the people selected to carry a PPM, have had mixed results in testing, but after experiments in Houston and Philadelphia, PPMs are starting to be used in many other markets. PPMs can also be used to track audio signals from television stations. Early statistics have shown that PPMs reveal lower overall ratings for most radio stations than do the numbers from diaries, but on a positive note, PPMs show that people actually listen to more radio stations than was indicated by data from diaries.

Television

Online advertising is helping local TV stations maintain decent profit margins. High double-digit increases in online ad revenue were common for most stations in 2006, 2007 and 2008.

Not all is rosy for TV advertising, though. The average cost of a prime-time, 30-second commercial dropped about 12% in 2008 to about $125,500. Popular programs like *American Idol, Dancing with the Stars* and *CSI* can still often command more than $500,000 for each 30-second commercial, but the gravy train of the 1990s and early 2000s appears to be grinding to a halt. The Super Bowl is the exception, of course. Every year, commercials cost a bit more. In 2008, 30-second commercials cost an average of $2.7 million.

To avoid the tuning out during commercials and the skipping of commercials by time-shifting viewers, some advertisers and program producers have turned to product placement as a way to enhance brand identification and exposure of products to potential consumers. A study in 2008 found that product placements were more "fully exposed" in TV comedies than in reality programs. In addition, products had more "dual-mode" placements—shown and discussed—in comedies than in reality programs.

Nielsen Media Research, in its continuing efforts to improve audience measurement, is rolling out use of Local People Meters. LPMs were in about 18 markets in 2008, but Nielsen planned to have LPMs in at least 56 markets by 2012. People Meters have been used to measure national ratings for more than 20 years, but the use of LPMs in local markets is relatively new. LPMs automatically record the stations that a TV set is tuned to, but people are required to enter data periodically as they watch programs.

Another thing Nielsen has promised to do is to increase the number of households/people for its national ratings data. Currently, Nielsen uses about 12,000 households and 35,000 people. Plans are to increase those numbers to 37,000 households and 100,000 people by 2011. In addition to increasing the number of households in ratings surveys, Nielsen has included Digital Video Recorder playback viewing in ratings, too.

Audience measurement is not always easy. A study in 2007 found that about 35% of viewers watch a TV program at a location other than their home at least once a week. Tracking such "out-of-home" viewing is problematic. Viewing locations included someone else's home, a restaurant, a bar, at work, at a hotel/motel, or at a vacation home. Sports (20%), a local newscast (19%) and an episode of a TV series (18%) were the most common out-of-home viewing experiences.

Nielsen started including college students living away from home in viewer surveys in 2007. The inclusion resulted in an increase of about 12% in the viewing of primetime programs by 18 to 24 year olds. Late night viewing rose in the demographic group by about 9% and daytime viewing increased by about 5%.

The Federal Communications Commission has endorsed the so-called "a la carte" pricing system for cable TV services. Under the system, customers would pay only for those channels they wanted to receive. They would not have to pay for a bundle of channels that they rarely or never watch. Consumer groups and members of Congress have lobbied for such a system for years. Cable TV industry leaders argue that such a system would result in higher costs for consumers, because they would have to increase prices greatly for popular programming to compensate for the lower demand for the less popular programming. A study in 2007 found that 52% of cable TV subscribers preferred some sort of a la carte pricing and 35% preferred the current "bulk" pricing system.

Cable TV is facing competition on a variety of fronts. In California in 2007, approval was granted to AT&T to provide video service. Permission was granted in an effort to increase competition among TV service providers and to give consumers an additional option to cable TV and satellite TV. The ability to receive TV programs via the Internet and via cell phones promises to challenge the dominance of cable TV, too.

The writers' strike of 2007–08 resulted in a great deal of soul-searching and viewing modifications. The strike cost the Los Angeles area about $21 million per day in lost wages and production-related revenue. The strike also forced viewers to find alternative ways to spend their media time. A study found that about 25% of the people surveyed said they were reading more, 13% said they were seeking out different forms of TV programming, 12% turned to DVDs and videos, 10% spent more time on the Internet and 2% went to the movies. In the end, the writers got most of what they wanted—an increased share of the profits from DVD sales and syndication deals in the United States and abroad.

Advertising is becoming ubiquitous in our lives. Ads show up at the gas pump, the supermarket, the doctor's office, in books and, of course, in the movie theater. Cinema ad revenue has increased for the past several years and is now more than $500 million.

Your Thoughts

What themes/trends do you see in the recent economics-related research, developments and issues?

What suggestions do you have for media executives to help them survive in tough economic times?

Think Back

1. What are some of the basic elements of the Telecommunications Act of 1996?

2. List TEN of the major mergers/buyouts in mass media.

3. What are the likely impacts associated with media mergers/buyouts?

4. What are the basic types of economic support systems for the mass media?

5. What are the average "profit margins" for the various news media organizations?

6. What techniques do news media organizations use to attract an audience?

7. What techniques do news media organizations use to attract advertisers?

8. How does the economic theory of "supply and demand" work in the mass media?

9. What are the economic trends in the daily newspaper business?

10. What are the problems associated with the economic aspects of the daily newspaper business?

11. What are the economic trends in the magazine business?

12. What is meant by "shared revenue" in the magazine business?

13. What are the problems associated with the economic aspects of the magazine business?

14. What are the THREE major ways that radio stations make money?

15. What are the economic trends in the radio business?

16. What are the problems associated with the economic aspects of the radio business?

17. Why are many local television news operations having economic problems?

18. What are the economic trends in the television business?

19. What are the problems associated with the economic aspects of the television business?

20. What is "clutter" and how much of it can be found on network television?

21. What are the recent trends in the world of televised sports?

22. What are the current trends associated with advertising revenue?

23. What impacts can a news organization's web site have on its traditional product?

24. What are the trends in ad revenue for the various contemporary media industries?

25. What are the trends and new developments associated with radio and television audience measurement?

26. What is "a la carte" pricing in the cable TV industry?

27. What activities did people turn to during the writers' strike of 2007–08?

The History of Mass Media

It is difficult to suggest that any one event was the beginning of journalism, or of mass-mediated messages. It no doubt took many varied and, at the time, unrelated steps to move us toward the inevitable techniques and technologies now in existence. Scholars of communication have described a continuum from an oral tradition to a print tradition to an electronic revolution in communication. There are no discrete points at which we move from one point on the continuum to another, but there are some notable inventions, events and personalities that strike our fancy.

Cave paintings discovered in France and Spain are thought of as the first attempts to represent ideas using pictures. Early man had nonverbal systems of communication dependent upon graphic representations; not only on cave walls, but also on pottery, clothing, and other available surfaces. Writing began when first a graphic symbol could be used to create a consistent system of linking ideas to combinations of those graphic representations of sound. Writing was useful for exchange of information when tribes or nations of similar people could attach the same or similar meanings to the graphic symbols that they all agreed to use.

Writing then led to printing, but only after centuries of book production by monks and scribes painstakingly using their knowledge of alphabetical writing to create handwritten manuscripts. Thousands of handwritten books, works of art complete with beautiful illustrations, were completed by monks during the Dark Ages. When the dark ages ended, commercial artists began to handcopy many of these books because of the demand for them in the home libraries of the wealthy. Almost all of these handwritten and/or handcopied books were in Latin, the language of the intellectuals, the most prosperous and most highly educated. By the 14th and 15th centuries, some of the commercial scribes were beginning to produce books in vernacular languages.

Block printing was next. A simple press was used to apply pressure to a sheet of paper that would pick up ink from a block of wood that had been carved with letters and words. Each carved block would constitute a page of a book and could never be used again for any other purpose.

Movable type was the invention that changed writing and printing so drastically that it made journalism possible and created the potential for media that would reach the masses rather than only the educated, prosperous landowners and aristocrats. The new technique was to use a separate piece of metal type for each letter of the alphabet and put them into and take them out of a wooden form that could be used over and over again. This led to the printing of handbills, pamphlets, broadsheets and other publications demanded by an increasingly literate middle class in the 15th and 16th centuries. Thus, news became a commodity and soon a fourth estate was identified in feudal Europe.

The term fourth estate is often used in reference to journalism, usually in the context of the government. When journalists are called members of the fourth estate, it typically means that they act on behalf of the people who need to be aware of how they are governed in a representative democracy.

The origin of the term is said to have been in the mid-1700s in feudal England when Edmund Burke was supposed to have pointed to the reporters' gallery in the English Parliament and labeled them a fourth estate. This was a direct reference to the three estates of the realm: the nobility, the clergy and the bourgeoisie, or commoners of the commercial or propertied class. Parliament could then be thought of informally as made up of four estates: the lords, bishops, commoners and the press. Perhaps, as much as anything, the belief was that only the three estates and the press had any influence on the monarchy. Certainly the peasants did not. As the media eventually developed, they could wield great influence, which is what Edmund Burke predicted in his use of the term.

The fourth estate today includes much more than a group of newspaper reporters. Newspapering was relatively new then, as was magazine publishing. Radio, television, film and the Internet, with its interactive communication, were in the distant future. Before all the media appeared, there were books. Some observers like to point to the significance of the Gutenberg printing press, but its significance is in making possible the development of newspapers and magazines. Thousands of books had been published before Gutenberg.

Prior to the 1450s, printing presses were operated by hand and could turn out only a few copies very slowly. Johann Gutenberg, from Mainz, Germany, was familiar with presses used to smash grapes in the wine-making regions of the Rhine valley. The presses at the wineries, with a hook and pulley arrangement, were more efficient than the presses used by printers at the time. So, Gutenberg modified a basic printing press to make it less cumbersome, less laborious, and more user-friendly. But Gutenberg's greatest contribution was the invention of movable type.

The improvements in printing credited to Gutenberg signified a threat to established order. Those who ruled by divine right, military strength, or raw force could see their power to govern jeopardized by an increasingly literate populace. Autocratic governments feared for their security as their subjects learned to process information themselves, instead of depending on their leaders. Their worry over the intrusion of popular thought into the affairs of government caused monarchs, priests, and military leaders to restrict the ever-increasing availability of information and ideas. Those who owned and operated printing presses were subject to censorship, usually through a licensing arrangement. This meant that censors would review material prior to publication, and that only printers willing to accept prior restraint would be given permission to operate their presses.

The first Gutenberg-style printing press in the English-speaking world appeared only 20 years after publication of the famous Gutenberg bible. In 1476, William Caxton imported one of the movable-type presses to London where he was a successful businessman engaged in commerce on the European continent. Caxton was a wealthy aristocrat who offered no threat to established order, thus he was not suppressed in his printing business. In fact, his ties to the British rulers were so strong he could easily have functioned as a censor.

By the middle of the 16th century, however, those Englishmen who followed Caxton in the printing trade found that difficult times were in store for them. The first formal licensing system in English law was set up in 1530, just one year after the crown produced a list of prohibited books. The Tudor dynasty was noted for its efforts at maintaining power, partly to stay strong enough to resist the growth of Protestantism. Among the Tudor weapons was the Privy Council, an agency of the crown that supervised administration of laws, regulated commerce, reviewed the system of courts, and tightly controlled printing. The Privy Council initiated proceedings against those who printed political commentary, seditious utterances and other publications that the council felt needed to be repressed.

Another control on thought and on the dissemination of ideas came from the Stationers Company, beginning in 1557. In another form, this association of writers, printers and illustrators had been in existence since late in the middle ages. In the middle of the 16th century, the monarchy began to use it as a monopoly of publishers and booksellers, thus making it a trust with its membership subject to government control. Members were subject to censorship and anyone not allowed to become a member was, in effect, an outlaw not sanctioned to print, publish or distribute written materials. For nearly 100 years, controls over the press were strengthened by the crown's active efforts at investigating possible abuses of the privilege of being part of the monopoly, which, of course, created an economic advantage to printers willing to accept prior restraint.

A well-known symbol of repression was the Star Chamber, with its harsh penalties against printers who defied authority. From the 1560s to the 1660s, this court would impose punishment against the press on the assumption that it was in the best interest of the general population to protect its leadership from criticism. The Star Chamber exercised harsh justice to protect established authority from the possibility that the government would be weakened by public awareness of dissent.

The first appearance in the English-speaking world of anything like a newspaper was in the 1620s. These forerunners to newspapers were called corantos and amounted to newssheets that were specialized in content. The corantos had their origins in Germany and the Netherlands where regional and local governments prevailed in the absence of any strong central authority. With government at the time noncentralized, there was little chance of strong interference with printing. English businessmen with commercial interests on the continent had a need for news of European developments that could affect their opportunities for cross-channel commerce. Foreign news then, especially news of European wars, was the content of the first corantos published in the English language in the Netherlands. These one-page specialized sheets eventually began to be produced by printers in London just a few years before another predecessor to the newspaper began to appear.

Another specialized publication, appearing around 1628, was a description of the decisions of Parliament. By the 1640s, these narrowly specialized accounts of local events began to be published rather frequently. They were called diurnals, indicating that daily local events were their content, even though diurnals were published weekly.

The melding of foreign news and news of local events was seen in the first English newspapers during the 1660s. Usually regarded as the first continuously published newspaper was the *Oxford Gazette*, in 1669. One year later, its founder, Henry Muddiman, moved to the big city and it became the *London Gazette.*

The crown continued to try to control the press until the 1690s when newly-emerging freedom led to the end of licensing laws. By 1694, Parliament was established firmly as a legislative body and the monarchy was already becoming something less than supreme. With the old controls diminishing, more and more printers found themselves interested in starting newspapers, not only in London but also in the provinces and in Scotland.

The American colonists were reading the contributions of notable essayists in London newspapers of the period from 1700 to 1720. These satirical newspapers had large circulations for the time and their content was often reprinted in the first colonial publications. On the American continent, the essays of Daniel Defoe, Joseph Addison, Sir Richard Steele, and Jonathan Swift were important to the success of the first continuously published American newspapers.

The first attempt at publishing a newspaper in the colonies was short-lived. An Englishman, Benjamin Harris, had to flee London after frequent difficulties with the authorities. Harris had earlier been convicted of printing criticism of the crown and sent to prison. Upon his release, unable to pay the fines assessed as part of his conviction, Harris set sail for the colonies. In North America, he also managed to acquire a reputation as a criminal, largely for defiance of religious authority. Harris was an anti-Catholic who was known primarily as a dealer in books until his ill-fated newspaper venture. In 1690, he created what was intended to be the first newspaper in North America. Harris, while operating a coffee house and bookstore in Boston, decided Massachusetts Bay colony was ready for a publication similar to those appearing in London. He believed that the British interest in public affairs was strong also in the colonies and that he would meet that interest with a newspaper to be filled with satire, strong viewpoints and gossip.

Unfortunately for Harris, the gossip in *Public Occurrences* got him into big trouble. That four-page newspaper lasted one issue, because it was unlicensed and because the gossip was about an alleged sex scandal involving the French king and the wife of a prince. Any attack on a monarch was considered a threat to public safety, even if it wasn't specifically the British monarchy. Harris was put out of business after only the one issue and eventually returned to England, where he failed again in a newspaper venture.

The first successful newspaper in America was produced by a postmaster in Boston, John Campbell, a sophisticated Scotsman. In 1704, Campbell started the *Boston News-Letter*, a weekly that was semi-official and approved of by the authorities. Campbell, of course, was a government official and he duly licensed the *News-Letter*, allowing it to become the first continuously published newspaper in the colonies. The *News-Letter* contained mostly reprints of items published first in London. It was dependent both on financial subsidies from the government and revenues from a few advertisements. Campbell was its publisher for 19 years. It continued to offer mostly foreign news to colonials under the direction of Bartholomew Green, who had been its printer from the beginning, then passed on to Green's son-in-law, John Draper. It passed through a few more hands until finally disappearing in the period of the Revolutionary War.

However, Campbell had started a tradition. After he left his duties as postmaster, he continued to publish the *News-Letter*, so the new postmaster, William Brooker, apparently believing that his duties required that he facilitate communication, founded the *Boston Gazette*, which was operated by a succession of five postmasters after Brooker. The *Gazette* eventually became an important organ during the Revolution. Significantly, Brooker used as his printer a feisty anti-establishment type, James Franklin, whose younger brother was to become the greatest printer and journalist of the time, among his many accomplishments.

In 1721, James Franklin started his own newspaper, the *New England Courant*. It was filled with essays and commentary from English authors, including the satire of Defoe, Addison and Steele. Younger brother Ben, using a pen name, also contributed satirical pieces while still a teenager.

It is worth noting that the first newspaper in the colonies appeared in Boston and that for a long time Boston was the only city with any newspapers. In the mid to late 1720s, newspapers began to appear in New York, Philadelphia and elsewhere; but Boston was, until the new country was founded, the center of newspaper activity. Many of the colonial newspapers, if not most, were started by postmasters or job printers. Postmasters must have assumed that spreading information by such publications was part of the job description. Much of the content of newspapers even through the Revolution was reprinted letters, often from overseas. Printing firms could be assured of printing contracts from business operators who saw the name of the printer on the masthead of the paper. It was a good way to make your service known to those who might need some ledgers, contracts, business forms, wedding announcements, or anything else printed.

Boston was the primary location for the first colonial newspapers for several reasons, perhaps primarily because for a long time that's where the presses were. The first press in the colonies was at Harvard University, then Harvard College, just outside Boston in Cambridge. In 1636, Harvard was starting to prepare the ministers who would go to the various colonies and preach the gospel. As early

as 1838, a press was installed to keep up with the demand for printed materials for the faculty and students, as well as for the new graduates and their parishioners. That first press and others to follow turned out bibles, hymn books, religious pamphlets, reprints of sermons, and essays on religious themes. The presses were heavy and transportation between colonies was quite difficult. The wilderness was being cleared, but there were no roads for decades to follow. Travel was by water, primarily sailing ships up and down the Atlantic coast. Some inland waterways helped the westward movement, but that was slow in coming. When the presses were taken off the ships at Boston harbor, they usually did not go much farther. Boston had a good harbor and it was the shortest trip from London.

Within 50 to 60 years of the first presses in Boston they began to appear more frequently in other colonial seaports. Still Boston was the primary location for newspapers. Boston was a religious center, as noted earlier, so the need continued for the printing of materials for ministers and their congregations. Boston was the first large population center in the colonies and continued to be until population grew in New York and Philadelphia. Boston was the first city in colonial America and the new United States to have public education. This meant that the literacy level was higher in Boston than elsewhere and created a stronger potential for readership.

Newspapering in New York, Philadelphia, Annapolis, Charleston and a few other cities was notable in the period leading up to the rebellion against the English, but Boston newspapers during the Revolution were still demonstrating their strength and influence to a degree not to be matched elsewhere until the United States was born. Newspapering in New York and Philadelphia followed parallel paths, partly because of the Bradford family. In 1719, Andrew Bradford established the first newspaper in Philadelphia, the *American Weekly Mercury*. Six years later, his father, William, launched the first newspaper in Manhattan, the *New York Gazette*.

William Bradford, in 1692, had set up the first printing press in New York before going to Philadelphia and operating a printshop there. He returned to New York after his son's newspaper venture. New York had the third largest population in the 1720s and was the third colonial city to have a newspaper. Father and son continued in the newspaper business as did Andrew's son, William III, who also made his mark as one of the best of the early magazine publishers.

Also in both newspaper and magazine publishing in the early to mid-18th century was Benjamin Franklin, who left his brother's employ and eventually made his way to Philadelphia. There, while still not much more than a boy, he became the manager of the *Pennsylvania Gazette* in 1728 and became its owner in 1729. Competing primarily with Andrew Bradford's *Mercury,* Franklin quickly became the leader not only in Philadelphia newspapering, but also in colonial journalism. He was known as a skilled printer, a literate and clever writer, and a highly successful businessman.

Ben Franklin was the ultimate publisher of the colonial era and the originator of the success factors in early United States newspaper and magazine practices. He was the first to see that the newspaper could be a vehicle for profit itself rather than a sideline for a job printer or a postmaster. Franklin was the first to recognize the value of advertising as the primary economic base of support for the publishing business rather than as a means of supplementing income. He was the first to show that millions of dollars could be made in newspapering. It turned out that because of political upheaval, a revolution, and partisan posturing about the direction the new country should take, Franklin's lessons were not learned very quickly by many newspaper operators until early in the 19th century. During that time, newspapers were actually "viewspapers," spreading dissent or supporting one side or another before, during and after the American Revolution.

Franklin had amassed his fortune entirely through his printing and publishing ventures before the revolution was underway. He was able to retire at the age of 42. It could be said that because of Ben Franklin, the success of other newspapers was assured. Franklin had sought advertising aggressively while job printers were printing newspapers to acquaint potential customers with their services. Franklin had more total pages and more advertising in them than any colonial publisher, and postmasters thought little of increasing their amount of advertising income while they collected government subsidies.

Franklin served as co-postmaster general for the colonies and later for the new United States. In each instance, he was able to generate favorable postal rates for those who would use the mails to distribute the newspapers and magazines that they produced. One not so obvious, but still beneficial aspect of this was that it aided publishers in guaranteeing content for their newspapers. Most colonial papers were filled with essays, religious thought, political diatribes, and philosophical offerings, with much of it reprinted from other publications, often English newspapers. The subsidized delivery of papers from other communities would arrive at the print shop with the very-welcomed store of new material to borrow and share with a new audience. Thus, printers had an inexpensive system for receiving more content to reprint while also able to distribute their own product at a rate lower than other businesses had to pay. It was a bonanza for a fledgling industry that helped to stimulate its growth.

It was, of course, a conflict of interest and benefited Franklin greatly because even in his retirement, he was owner and part-owner of newspapers. He was the first to see the value of chain ownership. The chain concept also stimulated newspaper growth. Franklin developed the chain approach by investing in the future of his former apprentices. He would choose the best of those who had learned their craft in his print shop and lend them the start-up capital, buy the initial printing equipment, and help with the first few rental payments. All of this under a contract guaranteeing eventual profitable return to the lender. This encouraged the growth of newspapering and increased Franklin's already vast fortune at a time when he no longer wore the printer's apron and no longer lingered over the type form. The fact that Franklin took on so many carefully selected apprentices and was able to go into business with the most promising of them has caused many historians to contend that Ben Franklin, in effect, started the first journalism school. Franklin is universally regarded as the father of the American newspaper for all of the accomplishments so far noted. There was to be no other journalist of such stature until the 1830s when James Gordon Bennett earned a reputation as a great innovator and became the second person to acquire a fortune from newspapering.

A stimulus to newspaper growth well ahead of Bennett's changes in the business was the foment and fervor associated with colonial discontent with the relationship with the mother country. Questions concerning British rule and colonial taxes supporting such rule became politicized in newspapers throughout the colonies, but most noticeably in Boston, the center of rebellion well before armed conflict ensued.

As revolution germinated in Boston and elsewhere, the pages of the newspapers became filled with viewpoints supporting either the existing system and the British crown or some modification of the relationship with Great Britain, if only for status as a more independent commonwealth, but still part of the empire. In Boston, however, the *Gazette* was the strident voice of complete rejection of British rule. Eventually, newspapers became so politicized that many were strongly pro-British and the others clearly supporting rebellion. It became difficult, if not impossible, for publishers to take the middle ground when feelings were so polarized that nonpartisanship was mistrusted and despised by each side.

Chief among the radical contingent even before the war was the *Boston Gazette*, operated by Benjamin Edes and John Gill as proprietors, but often directed in its editorial policy by Samuel Adams. The *Gazette* became the nerve center of the radical movement, an advocate for social reform. One of the most active advocacy journalists of the 18th century was Samuel Adams. Adams and his more cautious and reasonable cousin John were prominent among the contributors to the Gazette, although the writings of many famous Americans appeared in its pages. Samuel Adams started his newspaper career in 1748 with a Boston paper called the *Independent Advertiser,* a publication supported by a group of young radicals, but it was with the *Gazette* in the 1760s and 1770s that Adams became the highly effective leader of a group dedicated to the repudiation of everything British. His Committees of Correspondence gave Adams a group of agents throughout the colonies that could alert him to activities and sentiments that he could process and then transmit to readers of the *Gazette*. Other persuasive writers for the rebellious

Gazette included Joseph Warren, Josiah Quincy, James Otis, and, of course, cousin John Adams. Another contributor was Paul Revere, a silversmith and coppersmith whose craft resulted in engravings to give visual impact to the propagandistic prose of Samuel Adams and his followers.

To carry their messages beyond Boston, these radicals enlisted the help of the Sons of Liberty, an organization that seemed to be spontaneously created as a reaction by many colonials to the hated Stamp Act of 1765. The various chapters of the Sons of Liberty included members who were newspapermen in other major cities. William Bradford III was a member of the Philadelphia chapter, but was, like John Adams, much less strident than the core of the radical element. The most vociferous radical journalist outside Boston was John Holt of the New York chapter of the Sons of Liberty. Holt published the *New York Journal* and often ran material previously published in the *Boston Gazette*.

A prominent Boston member was the publisher and editor of the *Massachusetts Spy*, Isaiah Thomas, probably second only to Ben Franklin in journalistic reputation and financial success in the 18th century. Thomas ran a profitable business as a printer, book publisher, newspaper and magazine owner and operator, and, if not for his long-time full commitment to the revolution might have rivaled Franklin in terms of competence and value to the profession.

The events leading up to the war and the war itself commanded the attention of other prominent journalists, including those able to avoid the partisanship of the Boston group and its fellow travelers. An example of an influential writer of the period who was not a publisher and spent no time at the printing press was John Dickinson, who did not support a war for independence, but did believe in negotiating with the British for some change. Dickinson had economic concerns. He was not interested in the social reform espoused by the radicals. Dickinson refused to sign the Declaration of Independence and he never expressed in his writings a belief in complete independence. What he chose to write about was the need for men of property to be able to determine in their own colonial legislatures how their taxes should be spent. Dickinson opposed the imposition by Parliament of taxes on British subjects in the colonies and he opposed Parliamentary decisions that distributed money raised by colonial taxes without any input from those who paid the taxes. Dickinson wrote pamphlets to spread his taxation without representation concerns, but even more effective was a series that he wrote called "Letters from a Farmer in Pennsylvania."

Of the three dozen newspapers in existence in 1767 and 1768, all but three carried these letters; that included radical Tory and Whig publications. Dickinson's moderate approach is said to have influenced the propertied classes to deviate from their Tory sympathies to either support, to some extent, the radical elements that they would otherwise have regarded as rabble rousers or to, at least, not throw support to the king and Parliament as they might otherwise have tended to do. After all, who would be more likely to embrace government and its promise of law and order than the Whigs who prized their property rights? Yet, when the violence was inevitable and compromise not possible, the Whigs, even if reluctant, generally went along with the rebellion. Dickinson's writings are credited with bringing together disparate elements of colonial society into a cause that was perceived as serving both.

There were Americans loyal to their king and standing firm against the bloodshed that followed the protests heard in so many of the colonial papers. These Tories were heard from consistently in newspapers before the fighting began, but their voices were largely stilled once muskets were in hand and battles were fought on American soil. The Tory was the real Patriot when the colonials were British citizens, but was considered a traitor once there was a shooting war.

The most notable Tory newspaperman was James Rivington, a colorful, but quite capable journalist. Rivington was a new colonial, having arrived from London in 1762, when he opened the first chain of bookstores in America. Rivington's family had long been official publishers of religious books for the Church of England, giving him solid establishment credentials. Yet, when he embarked on his newspaper venture in 1773, he displayed an objectivity lacking in other papers of the time. Rivington published the *New York Gazetteer* and made it very profitable, striving much as Franklin and Thomas did, for a large amount of advertising. Rivington had a reputation for excellent writing and editing and for producing a skillfully printed newspaper. He also had a reputation as one who perhaps too much enjoyed making a wager on a contest, especially at the race tracks.

Despite his gambling losses, Rivington managed to live well on his bookstore profits and the success of his newspaper. His fair and accurate accounts of the conflict lasted until other Tory papers had been shut down by radicals and, in some cases, their editors either threatened by mobs or roughed up. Rivington then began to be just as partisan as his rivals. When the tide of war began to favor the revolutionaries, hard times came upon Rivington. Raiders stormed his printing facilities twice, causing major damage. He had renamed his paper the *Royal Gazette* to show his royalist sympathies. After the rebels' victory, Rivington continued to publish until 1783 when a mob stormed his offices and put his paper out of business for good. By that time he had again become conciliatory and fairly objective, but it did not matter to the radicals.

Early Magazines

Magazines, although already fairly successful in England, were slow to develop in America. There was no large population center like London. There was not a great deal of leisure time in a region where the wilderness still had to be tamed and urban centers created. Transportation was difficult, causing major distribution problems for such periodicals. Most transportation was by water, either rivers or canals inland and the sea for coastal residents. Colonists were busy building roads, footpaths, houses, and whole communities, so they did not have much time for the perusal of magazines.

Following Ben Franklin's *General Magazine* and Andrew Bradford's *American Magazine,* both monthlies, a weekly was started in Boston that proved to be more successful. Also in Boston, coinciding with an upsurge of interest in religion in the colonies, a magazine called *Christian Heritage* appeared and also lasted longer than the two Philadelphia-based magazines.

A magazine in Boston during the revolution that might have been the breakthrough publication for the struggling industry except for its publisher's involvement in the struggle for independence was the *Royal American Magazine* of Isaiah Thomas. It was, of course, noted for the quality of its protests against British rule, but also was remarkable for the rest of its content and the artistry of its typesetting and illustrations. The illustrator was Paul Revere. Thomas devoted so much energy to the rebel cause that perhaps the magazine never quite realized its full promise.

Another magazine achieving prominence during the war was Robert Aitken's *Pennsylvania Magazine,* often edited by Thomas Paine. It lasted 19 months, a long life for magazines of that era. Paine had already published in pamphlet form his "Common Sense," an essay that stirred many to embrace the spirit of independence that his writings eloquently expressed. In a few short weeks, his pamphlet had made virtually every literate American aware of the issue. Soon, however, Paine's "Crisis Papers" were to exceed "Common Sense" in popularity.

Paine was a regular contributor to Aitken's publication and thus could be considered a magazine journalist even though his most famous writings were expressed in pamphlets and reprinted in newspapers.

Few magazines were established before 1800 and none lasted long. Aitken's *Pennsylvania Magazine* and Isaiah Thomas' *Farmer's Weekly Museum,* of Walppole, New Hampshire, gave some indication that some day magazines might be self-supporting.

By the 1830s, magazines were increasing in number and had longer lives. The *Knickerbocker,* established in 1833, lasted until 1865. Women's magazines began to appear, with Godey's *Lady's Book,* the most notable of the period. It was founded in 1830 and by the 1850s had reached a circulation of 150,000. The circulation leader in the period before the Civil War was *Harper's* with 20,000 readers. *Harper's,* begun in 1850, introduced extensive woodcut illustrations and became a serious literary journal, although moving into public affairs and non-fiction in the 20th century.

Civil War era magazines of quality, largely because of artistic illustrations and literacy content, included, as well as *Harper's,* the *Century Scribner's* and the *Atlantic Monthly.* The most influential periodical was one of the growing number of weeklies, E.L. Godkin's *The Nation,* founded in 1865. Late in the century, competition for these quality publications came from *Munsey's* founded by Frank Munsey in 1889, and *McClure's,* started by S.S. McClure in 1893.

Magazine publishing was encouraged by lowered postal rates established by Congress in 1879, so a resurgence of magazine activity developed in the 1880s and 1890s. In particular, long-lived magazines devoted to hobbies, crafts, lifestyles, house and garden, and women's interests were to proliferate. These magazines with appeal to demographically clear special interests were so numerous and so successful that the turn of the century could be called a Golden Age for magazines.

Cyrus K. Curtis founded *Ladies' Home Journal* in 1883 and bought the *Saturday Evening Post* in 1897. Both competed for a mass readership with *Colliers,* which entered the field in 1888. These publications by 1900 were reaching circulations of one-half million. Also circulating extensively were *Cosmopolitan,* founded in 1886, and *Life,* which began in 1883. In the years immediately preceding the turn of the century, there was not only a surge of magazine activity, but also the creation of magazines that would have longer lives than those that preceded them. Many of the top circulation magazines of the 1880s and 1890s were to continue to be successful well into the 20th century.

The Political Press

As the United States came into being and struggled though partisan bickering about its direction in the formative years, newspapers flourished in a climate of dissension and polarized political communication. Many newspapers were created specifically to spread a single political party's message. Two distinct philosophies emerged and each had its proponents in the often vitriolic press of the period from 1780 to 1820. Thomas Jefferson and his followers wanted a loose federation of independent, strong states and a weak central government that encouraged the hopes of the agrarian southern and western states, a philosophy that would aid the poor and illiterate or barely literate. Alexander Hamilton and his followers, apparently fearing economic collapse and social unrest, offered instead a plan for a strong central government and federal support of banking and investing to assure a firm support for the new nation from the propertied classes, a platform that would support the urban centers of the northeastern states.

Jefferson and his supporters espoused the ideals of the French Revolution. Hamilton and his faction feared that the French upheaval would be brought to American shores. The Jefferson camp was enamored of the French radicals' cry for freedom, liberty and equality. Hamilton's legions were appalled by the excesses of violence and brutality, the notorious guillotine, that accompanied the French struggle for independence. Hamilton's political party newspapers stressed the concern that the recent rebellion in North America must not be repeated as its results were just then being implemented. Jefferson's papers scoffed at this fear, suggesting that it was generated by Anglophiles, who despised the French.

This is unfortunately an overly simple summary of incredibly complex issues facing the two political parties that evolved in the formative years of the United States, but it does demonstrate why each faction saw the need for publications that would be party organs. A series of articles that appeared in the *New York Independent Journal* in 1787 and 1788 were reprinted in other newspapers and in pamphlet form and gave voice to the political party led by Alexander Hamilton. This series, called *The Federalist*, was eventually published also in book form, with the inclusion of six new essays, and it resulted in the name that would be given to the political party. Hamilton wrote the largest number of the *Federalist* articles, establishing him as the leader of one of the two diverse political parties generated by legitimate differences of opinion about how the ship of state should be steered.

An early supporter of the Federalist party was the *Gazette of the United States*, published in New York starting in 1789. Its financial support came from Hamilton, but its content was largely dictated by Hamilton's choice as editor, John Fenno, one of the first newspapermen not to have come up through the ranks as a printer. Fenno was known as a journalist, a writer and editor, although his publication was as partisan as those produced earlier by revolutionaries or defenders of the status quo. The *Gazette of the United States* moved to Philadelphia when the nation's capital moved there in 1791.

Another early Federalist paper was the *Massachusetts Centinel*, published in Boston by Major Benjamin Russell, who had been a teenage combatant in the revolution. Russell had worked in Isaiah Thomas' printshop before founding the *Centinel*, which was not only a political party organ, but also a prosperous and well-edited paper generally. Russell eventually changed its name to *Columbian Centinel*.

A controversial Federalist organ was *Porcupine's Gazette* in Philadelphia. Its editor, William Cobbett, used the pseudonym Peter Porcupine and aimed his journalistic quills venomously toward any and all opponents of the Federalist doctrine. Cobbett expressed himself without restraint and was clearly the most argumentative of the Federalist editors.

The most reasoned and most literate of those editing Hamilton's party organ earned most of his fame as a lexicographer. However, Noah Webster did more than produce his famous dictionary. Webster had already demonstrated his skill as a lawyer, historian, teacher and economist before becoming a newspaper editor. Webster was an innovative and successful farmer who loved to study language. His passion for words led him to produce writings on grammar, spelling and word usage even before becoming a major voice for the Federalists. Webster's *American Minerva* in New York supported Hamilton fully until Webster became so consumed with his long-time interest in linguistic analysis that he left newspapering to work full-time on the dictionary that appeared in 1828.

Aligned against these and other papers that were edited as supporters of Hamilton's were publications that existed primarily to rally support for Thomas Jefferson and his anti-Federalists. In the George Washington cabinet, Hamilton as Secretary of the Treasury, and Jefferson as Secretary of State, were clearly antagonists. After Jefferson became president, following the Federalist administration of John Adams, the differences continued, but with Jefferson's newspapers no longer the outsiders seeking entry into the seat of power. Jefferson's supporters were just as severely critical of their opponents during his presidency as they were during the years that the Federalists had the upper hand.

The first of the Jeffersonian journalists was Philip Freneau, a Frenchman who took an active part in the American Revolution, even spending time as a prisoner of the British. After the war Freneau felt that the Federalists had British sympathies and were obstructing what he believed to be Jefferson's attempts to instill in the new government the original reasons for rebellion by the colonists.

Jefferson hired Freneau ostensibly as a translator for the State Department, but that job was available primarily as a subsidy for Freneau on the promise to Jefferson that he would produce an anti-Federalist newspaper. Freneau started the *National Gazette* in 1791, a publication so clearly articulating the anti-Federalist cause that many other newspapers quickly began to reprint its commentaries. This paper lasted only two years, with Freneau losing his subsidy when Jefferson left Washington's cabinet. Freneau then turned to the writing of poetry. The *National Gazette* had great influence during its short life and set the stage for other papers to take up the Jefferson cause.

The *Richmond Examiner*'s James Callender was such a contentious editor that Federalists put him on trial for seditious libel. Callender spent nine months in jail after being convicted of daring to criticize the president. The most contentious of the anti-Federalist organs was a Philadelphia newspaper that had a long and influential life. The *Aurora* was established in 1790 by Benjamin Franklin Bache, the grandson of Benjamin Franklin. After Bache's death, his widow married his assistant, William Duane, who also ran the *Aurora* as a partisan organ for Jefferson's ideas. Bache was a voice of opposition until the Jefferson presidency. Duane was a spokesman for the administration of the anti-Federalist president after 1880. Bache had made the Aurora a shrill and intemperate, even vicious spokesman for the cause. Bache filled the pages of the *Aurora* with personal attacks in an excess of violent partisanship. Duane's *Aurora* avoided the scurrilous tone of the attacks against Federalists and offered a reasonable and colorful display of justifications for the Jefferson ideals. Both Bache and Duane, like Callender, found themselves eventually under indictment as the Federalists tried to silence them.

Between 1810 and 1820, the platforms of both parties had pretty much disappeared as the ideas of each had more or less been accepted in part and rejected in part by members of Congress and the various state legislatures. The two factions merely disappeared or dissipated as their issues became moot.

Demonstrating this was the transformation of *The National Intelligencer*, founded in 1801 as a mouthpiece for President Jefferson. Samuel Harrison Smith was only 28 when Jefferson encouraged him to start a newspaper in the newly created city of Washington, D.C. *The Intelligencer* quickly became the semiofficial organ of the administration, but eventually began to display objective reporting of debates in Congress. As the presidencies of Madison and Monroe followed and the so-called era of good times resulted in the disappearance of the Federalist and anti-Federalist factions, the Intelligencer became an outstanding newspaper, reflecting the non-partisanship of the era that developed and effectively chronicling the activities of the federal government.

Another example was the *New York Evening Post,* founded in 1801, by Alexander Hamilton, who awarded its editorship to William Coleman, a Federalist lawyer. For four years, its editorials and other comments were prepared by Hamilton himself, but when Coleman split with Hamilton over the famous duel with Aaron Burr, the *Post* began to move away from its partisanship and took its place as a strong competitor in the growing number of newspapers in New York City that avoided political wrangling.

The period of polarization and politicization of the press was also notable for the emergence of daily newspapers. Until the advent of the steam driven press in 1811, there was not much impetus for attempting to produce more than a few hundred copies of a publication. Once power driven presses began to proliferate, daily production and mass circulation could be accomplished because it was cheaper and faster to print in increasingly larger quantities.

There had been occasional attempts at daily publication as early as the 1780s. By 1800 there were only 16 dailies in operation, most of them in New York and Philadelphia, which by then had passed Boston in population. The first two dailies in 1783 and 1784 were in Philadelphia. Even by 1820, of the more than 500 newspapers in the country, only 24 were dailies. There were some semi-weeklies and even tri-weeklies, but the majority still came out once a week. Circulations were not very impressive, with most people unwilling to pay for what was at the time an expensive product.

Newspapers before the 1830s were aimed at the more affluent classes with content that appealed to the most educated as well as the most prosperous. A circulation of 1,500 to 2,000 a week was quite common until newspapers directed toward businessmen in the 1820s began to reach 2,500 and 3,000 every day. Daily circulation worked for the business-oriented publications, although their cost was too great for the average person.

A pair of New York newspapers appealing to commercial interests were to open up possibilities, not only for the success of further daily publications, but also for the emergence of mass circulation ventures. Prior to the 1820s, news had been a minor part of American newspapers. They relied more on essays, commentaries, editorials, and similar efforts at expressing viewpoints. What news there was largely came from overseas, often in the form of reprinted letters. There were no reporters, unless you count the biased accounts of partisan witnesses to Revolutionary War battles or of biased observers of Congress during the Washington, Adams and Jefferson presidencies. This was to change after the War of 1812 when news seemed to be re-defined. Events happening on American shores began to be just as prominent in newspapers as overseas news had been earlier.

It was not until a few newspaper owners recognized the value to their subscribers of fresh information about ship arrivals in local seaports did anything like present day reporting evolve. Editors had used accounts of meetings or disasters like fires and floods only if someone had volunteered the information. To actively seek out information was a new concept when the *New York Courier and Enquirer* and the *New York Journal of Commerce* were competing for the favor of those desiring to read about circumstances related to commerce and industry. It was important to business operators to know what goods were arriving on which vessels and the value that might be placed on such goods. The *Journal of Commerce* and the *Courier and Enquirer* would publish the list of products imported as quickly as possible, because it was their subscribers who were buying, selling and trading in such commodities.

Both papers hired boats to run out to incoming vessels to get their manifests. David Hale and Gerard Hallock operated the *Journal of Commerce*. Both were journalists, but clearly also businessmen. Their paper strongly reflected their interest from its beginnings in 1827 on into the next two decades. The *Courier and Enquirer*, founded also in 1827, was published by Colonel James Watson Webb, a colorful, argumentative figure in New York society, well known beyond his newspaper accomplishments. Webb had a history of pugnacious confrontations

with those he disagreed with in print or in person and figured in public fights and duels. He was not the first nor the last colorful newspaperman. His *Courier and Enquirer* was successful from the outset and many years later was considered one of New York City's best. Because of the enterprise in newsgathering shown by these newspapers, news no longer would be something that arrived on an editor's desk by accident nor would news be something reprinted from other publications, probably from overseas.

The new era of actively seeking out events to mention in print and to do it on an ongoing basis with a newspaper's full resources actually came into full flower in the 1830s and largely through the genius of one man. This man, James Gordon Bennett, learned newspapering from James Watson Webb, but then became a great innovator, one who would change the newspaper's functions, structure, and operations so dramatically that it was like a new medium.

The newspaper patterned after Ben Franklin's model lasted until Bennett turned it into the kind of newspaper that we know today. Other than changes in technology, which have been considerable, little has changed in newspapering since James Gordon Bennett revolutionized the design, page format, layout, use of headlines, column widths, use of white space, jumping stories to inside pages, adding specialized sections for specific types of news, and many other techniques taken for granted in the look of and content of the 20th century newspaper. In the 19th century, specifically the 1830s, '40s and '50s, Bennett altered previous practices to ensure that the mass audience could be reached.

After Bennett, reporting was done aggressively and consistently, beat systems were set up, and the sectioning of the paper into departments resulted in the addition of section editors, copy editors, news editors, a managing editor, editor-in-chief, and a publisher. It was Bennett who was called responsible for setting up the current system where circulation, production, editorial, advertising and business office executives each run a separate division answerable to a publisher, who is answerable to the owner.

It has often been said that Bennett's greatest contribution was showing everybody how to go out and get news and how to display it, but that is only part of why he became the leading journalist of the 19th century. Bennett founded the *New York Herald* in 1835 and with a careful review of prospective advertisements, he gave himself a big advantage over his competitors. He not only refused to accept some ads, but also refused to run the same advertisement more than once, forcing advertisers to come up with fresh copy and fresh illustrations, thus making the ads more readable and more appealing to his audience. Soon other publishers had to follow suit. Prior to Bennett, the same ad might run for weeks or months.

Bennett's *Herald* became the circulation leader in New York City and the country, and stayed there through the 1850s. When Bennett left the *Courier and Enquirer* to strike out on his own, New York City's population was equal to that of the next three largest cities combined and a dozen papers were being printed, six of them dailies. Benjamin Day had already demonstrated by 1833 that a newspaper could reach the masses. Day's *New York Sun* used a press capable of printing thousands of copies a day operating at maximum capacity. Day was able to offer the first paper for huge audiences, because he believed that thousands of slum dwellers had never been offered a readable newspaper. Day came up with a paper written at a low level, aimed at a readership of farm workers just then moving into the cities to find employment and recent immigrants still not too well versed in their newly acquired language.

The former farmworkers, new into the urban setting, were just beginning to develop the literacy needed in a newly emerging industrial society, replacing the agrarian economy. Day's *Sun* was a broad appeal, something-for-everyone newspaper stressing both objectivity and sensationalism. The objectivity was needed to attract large numbers of readers on the assumption that opinions expressed in print would drive away potential readers who might disagree.

It was the cheap, lowbrow sensationalistic content that paid off for Day. The *Sun* circulated primarily in crowded tenements in low-rent districts with a huge population of barely literate immigrants and uneducated rural transplants. Stories about sex, human interest, gossip, violence and trivia were of universal appeal not requiring any special knowledge or education to appreciate. A new market had been found for the American newspaper—slum-dwellers and others not reached by the specialized content and literate writing style of other papers—and it was a huge market for advertisers who had never reached so many people before. Day sold his paper for 1¢ a copy on a daily basis, while other papers were still selling by six-month or one-

year subscriptions at a cost equivalent to seven or eight times more per issue than Day's. Newspapers of this type collectively became known as the "penny press," a label attached to the prevailing style of journalism of the 1830s and 1840s.

The *Sun* might have been the first of the breed, but it was eventually eclipsed by Bennett's *Herald*. Bennett embraced the sensationalism and objectivity that Day pioneered with an emphasis on local events and a breezy style, while also covering news of significance with a serious purpose that brought him a corps of readers denied to Day. An example was the excellent financial section in the *Herald*. Bennett's coverage of Wall Street was as good as the commercial papers. It should be noted that Bennett had been trained as an economist in Scotland and had been a professor of economics. He understood the banking system and made the *Herald* invaluable to businessmen while also of appeal to the wider audience sought by Day and other imitators who were quick to embrace sensationalism.

When one remembers all of Bennett's innovations and singular contributions, it becomes clear why the *Herald* stood out from the beginning and why by 1850 it reached a circulation of 40,000 daily. In the 1830s, Day and Bennett both produced 20,000 copies daily but even after the Herald raised its price to 2¢, its circulation continued to increase at the expense of other newspapers with sensational content. No publisher since Ben Franklin had affected the development of journalism as much as James Gordon Bennett.

A newspaper publisher whose fame spread beyond the journalistic reputation that he established was Horace Greeley, who founded the *New York Tribune* in 1841 as a fairly inexpensive paper that tended to avoid the excesses of sensationalism of its competitors. The *Tribune* was noted for its display of the personality of its feisty publisher. Greeley used his editorial page to vent his frequent frustrations and desires. Greeley was a personal journalist who placed himself prominently before his readers with opinion columns and signed editorials while also offering in the *Tribune* excellent news coverage. Greeley was opposed to slavery, to the use of alcohol and tobacco, and to deficit spending whether by government or the individual, among his many causes. Greeley was quick to display a zeal for his crusades and campaigns and the *Tribune*, as a result, circulated all over the country, an unusual circumstance for a newspaper of his time.

Entering the competition in 1851 was the *New York Times*, destined to become the most prestigious publication in the United States, our so-called newspaper of record. It began in 1851 as an attempt, like Greeley's *Tribune*, to be an inexpensive alternative to the sensational papers. The *Times* sold for 2¢ and was originated by three men who believed that there was an increasingly literate mass market that was ready for a well-written, well-edited, highly objective newspaper. The *Times* never reached the giant circulations of its sensational brethren, but it was attracting the type of reader who many advertisers wanted to reach. The *Times* was always, as it is now, able to project an image of completeness and accuracy, an image that generated sufficiently large circulation, but even better advertising revenues. Its founders, George Jones, E.B. Wesley and Henry J. Raymond, obviously had the right market in mind and the right product for the market. Raymond, in particular, distinguished himself as an outstanding journalist. Raymond led the *Times* to its greatness despite the cult of personality around Greeley and his *Tribune* and the continued aggressive reporting in the *Herald* under Bennett and, later, his son, James Gordon Bennett, Jr., who directed the fortunes of the *Herald* into the years just after the Civil War.

Civil War Journalism

Leading into the war between the states was the emergence of newspapers that devoted their pages to the issue of slavery. Chief among them was William Lloyd Garrison's *Liberator*, published in Boston from 1831 to 1865. This weekly took Garrison's anti-slavery views to the people and had as its sole purpose the effort to drum up support for the abolitionist movement.

An American journalist perhaps better known as an orator was Frederick Douglass, a former slave who had a long career in newspapering. Douglass edited the *North Star* in Rochester, New York, from 1847 to 1860, after starting his journalistic career in 1845 working for a black-owned newspaper in New York called the *Ram's Horn*. In 1851, the *North Star* was re-named *Frederick Douglass' Paper*. When the Civil War broke out, Douglass shut down his newspaper and tried a short-lived magazine before working as an editor for a pair of Washington, D.C. publications. Douglass was also renowned for his lengthy, three-volume autobiography.

The standard newspapers of the Civil War era were as divided on the slavery issue as they were on the matter of secession. Greeley's *Tribune* was the acknowledged leader of those opposed to slavery. The *New York Herald* often showed a distaste for the abolitionist movement. Henry J. Raymond's *New York Times* was usually described as reasonable, although Raymond himself became a strong supporter of President Lincoln. Greeley and Raymond both became instrumental in the early growth of the Republican Party at this time, as did the publisher of the *Chicago Tribune*, Joseph Medill.

In the years immediately following the Civil War, Charles A. Dana emerged as a great journalist and William Cullen Bryant continued to display a staying power in his life as a newspaperman while creating a body of poetry that was to stand the test of time. Dana took over the *New York Sun* and made it a respectable paper despite its crass, low-brow beginnings. Dana's chief distinction seemed to be the great degree of respect for him expressed by other newspaper leaders of the second half of the 19th century. Bryant was remarkable for his lengthy stewardship of the *New York Post*, serving as its editor from 1829 to 1879.

The 1880s saw the emergence of three journalism giants who appealed to some of the same demographic characteristics in their circulations as did the newspapers of the 1830s and 1840s. Edward Wyllis Scripps left his family's newspaper ventures in the midwest to build an empire on his own, largely by resurrecting the chain idea originated by Ben Franklin. Scripps built the first large chain in the country in conjunction with Milton McRae, who had been business manager of the Cincinnati newspaper owned by Scripps. Their formula for success was to find the best journalists and business managers available and set them up in a community with prospects for growth, a community with no competing newspaper or a weak paper. If the paper succeeded, the employees would share in the profits.

Significantly, the cities that Scripps selected were relatively small when the chain moved in, but eventually attained great population growth. In each instance, Scripps amassed a fortune as a result. Scripps purposely avoided buying or founding newspapers in cities with already established large populations or where there were already strong newspapers. Scripps was known for an editorial policy in his papers that championed the causes of the workingman and criticized what he considered the excessive power of the wealthy.

Yellow Journalism

Some of the same complaints about the plight of laborers and abuses of authority could be found in the pages of newspapers directed by Joseph Pulitzer, an immigrant from Austria and Hungary who came to the United States as a volunteer for the Union army. Pulitzer developed a faculty for the English language very quickly even as he began his newspaper career on a German language newspaper in St. Louis. By 1878, Pulitzer managed to get together enough capital to acquire two failing papers and merge them into the *St. Louis Post-Dispatch*. He made it a profitable paper with a strong appeal to middle class readers. Pulitzer was as talented in the business office as he was at the writing and editing tasks that gave him an outlet for his crusades on behalf of the poor and down-trodden. His profits from the *Post-Dispatch* enabled Pulitzer to buy the nearly bankrupt *New York World*, and gave him a chance to carry his career as champion of the oppressed into the biggest newspaper market in the country. With his entrance into New York, Pulitzer embraced the kind of sensationalism that had been seen in the era of Ben Day and James Gordon Bennett.

The late 19th century was a perfect time for a revival of news devoted to sex, violence, gossip and trivia. This was an age of industrial expansion even greater than the 1830s. This was the age of the use of steel in construction, a growing oil industry, the advent of electricity, a growth of heavy industry, and increasing urbanization. The population of New York City tripled between 1870 and 1900. In that 30-year period, the nation's population doubled largely because of wave after wave of new immigrants. Many of the immigrants and other workers seeking employment in the increasing number of factories would settle in New York's tenements. These conditions made it ideal for the kind of sensationalism embraced by Pulitzer, who said that content gave him an opportunity to reach the very people whose rights he wanted to promote. Pulitzer's *World* crusaded for economic and social reforms and for legislation to benefit the poor and disadvantaged. Pulitzer used the *World* to crusade against sweatshops and in favor of increased education for the children of immigrants. While doing this, his paper reached circulation levels never approached before.

The eventual circulation records came, however, with the advent of competition from William Randolph Hearst and his *New York Journal*. The battles for leadership in the circulation wars of the 1890s were fueled by rampant sensationalism, including crusades, staged stunts, the hiring of celebrity authors to write newspaper articles, and any other tactic that would excite the reader. Hearst's newspapering background was in San Francisco; where, with the backing of the family fortune, Hearst ran a newspaper that had as one of its reasons for existence the promotion of the political future of Hearst's father, a United States Senator.

The younger Hearst had become enamored of sensational techniques while observing the *Boston Globe* and Pulitzer's *World* when he was enrolled at Harvard. Upon his return from Harvard, Hearst found that sensationalism worked for the *San Francisco Examiner*. In his first year running the *Examiner,* at the age of 24, he doubled its circulation. It took six years of generating profits with his father's paper to convince Hearst that he was ready for the big time—ready to compete with Pulitzer. Senator George Hearst died in 1891, leaving his son millions of dollars. With a nearly unlimited supply of money, Hearst was able to buy the *New York Journal* and put himself into direct competition with Pulitzer. Pulitzer's sensationalism was pale in comparison with Hearst's *Journal*, which featured gory stories with colored gory illustrations, while screaming headlines flamboyantly displayed Hearst's showmanship. Phony stories purporting to be science, outright frauds, attempts to solve crimes that police had closed the book on, and so-called campaigns on behalf of the poor were trumpeted in the *Journal* with enormous headlines and outlandish illustrations.

It was a fictional cartoon character that gave a name to this circulation battle between the two disparate newspaper leaders. Pulitzer was a hard-working journalist who knew how to make money. Hearst was the dilettante son of a distinguished multi-millionaire. Pulitzer had striven mightily to make his *World* a success. Hearst inherited a fortune and had a talent for spending that money. Hearst used his financial windfall to buy the best talent he could locate to work for the *Journal,* often pirating away some of Pulitzer's best people. It was the theft of a very popular Pulitzer cartoon strip and its artist that led the competition to be called yellow journalism.

Hearst hired the artist, Richard Outcault, away from Pulitzer and with him came the cartoon strip "The Yellow Kid" from Hogan's Alley. Pulitzer hired another cartoonist, George Luks, to continue the very popular feature. For a number of years both papers had cartoons featuring the grinning youngster and his yellow neck-to-toe shirt. The public associated the intense competition between the *World* and *Journal* with the blatant headlines, gory crime stories, excessive self-promotion, contests, crusades, campaigns and other shameless sensationalism with the label yellow journalism.

The most notorious of the excesses came about during the conflict with Spain over that country's administration of its Cuban territory. It was claimed at the time and believed ever since that both papers, during the period from 1895 to 1898, served to inflame a jingoism in the American public that led to popular support for going to war with Spain. The *World* and *Journal* both reached daily circulations of one million while running stories of purported Spanish atrocities and dirty dealings by a Spain decried as a brutal imperialistic power. Hearst even hired the well-known artist Frederic Remington to illustrate stories that catered to a burgeoning patriotism in the United States and a rebellion by Cubans that appeared consistent with the Monroe Doctrine. Hearst used not only artists' illustrations, but also photographs, many of them faked, to dramatize news content that openly advocated United States military intervention.

The circulation wars supported the rebellious Cuban military junta's propaganda barrage that seemed to justify a need for help from the United States. It was as if Americans felt that it was time to energetically take a leading role in inter-American affairs; an action that could lead to commercial profit for American business through expanded trade and increased opportunities for investment. There was even belief that military support to the rebels could eventually result in the annexation of Cuba. Moral outrage was a frequent theme of both the *World* and the *Journal* right up until the mysterious and still unexplained explosion that sunk the American battleship Maine in Havana Harbor in February, 1898. Many newspapers, not just the big two, made it appear that the Spanish were responsible.

Pulitzer's *World* called for war, arguing that human liberty demanded it. The *Journal* used large headlines and colorful illustrations to promote the war fever. All of this fanned the flames of American enthusiasm for retaliation against those believed responsible for the sinking of the Maine.

United States military forces did intervene and the war ensued. It lasted only four months, with Spain simply pulling out and going home with little actual conflict. The actual hostilities were short-lived, but the newspapers virtually invaded Cuba with a horde of reporters. It was a popular war and, of course, a popular victory, largely because of the impression of glory displayed in the columns, headlines and illustrations, including photographs, in the massive coverage by the sensational press. Hearst spent $500,000 to cover the abbreviated conflict. It is estimated that 500 United States journalists were sent to Cuba. Hearst himself anchored his personal yacht off the Cuba coast and was said to have rode on horseback in the direction of hostilities. A dozen or more vessels were hired by the newspapers to make the run from Havana to the nearest telegraph in Florida with dispatches from the scene of what battles there were.

Your Thoughts

What do you think about the circulation wars between Joseph Pulitzer and William Randolph Hearst? Were they good for journalism or bad? Why?

Muckraking

Following the Spanish-American War, there was a lessening of the worst elements of sensationalism, although many newspapers continued to seek the mass audience. There was still the appeal to the downtrodden and the disenfranchised. One result of this effort in the first two decades of the 20th century was the emergence of muckraking, which was largely a magazine phenomenon, but also appeared in some of the newspapers of the day.

The term muckraking was given to these crusading journalists by President Roosevelt following disclosure of a scandal within the Navy during his administration. Roosevelt coined the term muckraker in an attempt to discredit investigating journalists. He meant it to be a derogatory expression, indicating that the more sensational of such reporters were like the man in the stables in John Bryan's *Pilgrim's Progress* who spent so much time raking up the filth that he was tainted by it. Journalists viewed the practice as an effort to function like private detectives, to perform a public service by ferreting out corruption, misdeeds, crime, malfeasance and misfeasance where law enforcement failed or was itself corrupt or slovenly.

Scripps, Hearst and Pulitzer had thought of the newspapers as champions of the people, an attitude that many journalists carried with them into the early 1900s. Publishers and editors thought of themselves as reformers and viewed the early 20th century as a time when America was in need of reform. Their reporters were often given a mandate to crusade on behalf of social justice. Their task was to search out and expose criminal activities, to embrace an investigative journalism that would fight against big business and uncontrolled corruption. Several newspaper reporters embarked on investigative pieces that became so lengthy that they were better suited for publication in magazines devoted to current affairs. Often the magazine articles were reprints, or lengthier revised versions, of crusading accounts by newspapers in various cities. Many were original works of such prominent investigators as Ida Tarbell, Ray Stannard Baker, Lincoln Steffens, David Graham Phillips, Alfred Henry Lewis, Samuel Hopkins Adams, William Allen White, Finley Peter Dunne, Charles Edward Russell, George Kibbe Turner, and Will Irwin.

Ida Tarbell exposed the unfair business practices of the Standard Oil Company. She discovered monopolistic activities squeezing out competition and collusion with other firms to drive up prices at the expense of the American consumer. Tarbell's carefully documented record of John D. Rockefeller's misdeeds ran from 1902 until 1904 in a series of articles in *McClure's,* the first of the major muckraking magazines. Also in *McClure's,* Lincoln Steffens produced a series on "The Shame of the Cities," which described corrupt governments in St. Louis, New York, Chicago, Minneapolis, Philadelphia, Pittsburgh, and other large municipalities. The series was later continued by George Kibbe Turner to include other cities where favors were exchanged for graft by the city fathers. Ray Stannard Baker's years with *McClure's* resulted in exposure of corruption in the labor unions, including child labor. Business trusts, graft, political machines, and corrupt labor bosses were chief among the hard-hitting revelations in *McClure's*; but similar exposures appeared in some of *McClure's* competitors, including *Harper's, Scribner's, Atlantic Monthly* and other literary journals, as well as journals of opinion like E.L. Godkin's *Nation.*

A regular contributor to *McClure's* was William Allen White, who had already demonstrated with his *Emporia Gazette* in Kansas that newspapering outside New York City merited some attention. White's editorials and his involvement in state and local politics gained him a national reputation as a capable journalist. Much of his work was reprinted widely by other publications, especially magazines. White was a small-town editor with a national constituency and much of that resulted from his articles in *McClure's.* White was also, at various times, an advisor to national political leaders, including Presidents Theodore Roosevelt and Franklin D. Roosevelt.

Newspaper reporter Will Irwin joined *McClure's* in 1906 to serve eventually as managing editor and editor. Irwin was among those who wrote about the greed of newspaper publishers and their inability or unwillingness to stand up to powerful advertisers. Another muckraker who was critical of the press was Upton Sinclair, who noted conflicts of interest and ethical lapses on the part of publishers and editors.

Another early muckraking magazine was *Cosmopolitan,* which in 1906 ran the series, "The Treason of the Senate," by David Graham Phillips. *Cosmopolitan* also carried investigative pieces by Alfred Henry Lewis that examined how the wealthiest millionaires got that way. At the same time, *Everybody's* was exposing the manipulations of Wall Street bankers and bond traders, but it was *Collier's* that eventually took the initiative away from *McClure's* after 1905. Among several investigations into business, politics, and other societal concerns was a series of articles in *Collier's* by Samuel Hopkins Adams that exposed the fraud involved in the sale and advertising of patent medicines.

But most noteworthy, late in the muckraking period, was *American* magazine, a publication operated by reporters rather than businessmen. Some of the *McClure's* writers put together the financing to buy *American* and put themselves on the editorial board. The most respected of the investigative journalists, Lincoln Steffens, Ray Stannard Baker and Ida Tarbell, were directing the magazine and were themselves regular contributors. William Allen White and Finley Peter Dunne joined them on the editorial board.

One of the most effective journalistic efforts by a muckraker appeared in book form. It was the novel, *The Jungle*, appearing in 1906 and written by Upton Sinclair. It revealed the unsanitary conditions in Chicago's packing houses, and led to the passage by Congress of the Pure Food and Drug Act.

During the period from 1900 to 1920, many states and federal laws tightened controls on political patronage, conflict of interests, deceptive advertising, and illegal or unethical business practices, especially those affecting trusts or cartels, or collusion between labor unions and employers that failed to benefit union members. Child labor laws and regulations limiting sweatshops came about at this time. The end result was that the muckrakers ran out of material. Some investigative reporting occurs today, but nothing like the serious documentation and exposure of wrongdoing that dominated an era when major publications were built around the concept of journalism as social reform and consumer protection.

Jazz Journalism

The 1920s saw the emergence of jazz journalism, which was also called tabloid journalism. The tabloid format, the small-sized pages, became popular just as papers moved again toward sensational content and a sensational layout and design. The extensive use of photography marked this period. It was a hedonistic time in America and newspapers reflected the antics of the flappers, the gangsters, and the newly-created celebrities of radio's popular comedy and variety shows and the movies' bigger-than-life entertainment. Much of the newspaper content was about the private lives and scandalous behavior of popular show business figures, or about speakeasies and roadhouses, bathtub gin and rumrunners.

The general spirit of peace and prosperity in the nation after the end of World War I, coupled with the lawlessness associated with prohibition, gave newspapers reason to titillate readers with frothy human interest material for light reading and stories of gore and gangsterism for thrills. By now, Hearst was producing the *New York American* as a sensational paper, but it became difficult to compete with Joseph Patterson's *New York Daily News*. Patterson was a grandson of the prominent publisher of the *Chicago Tribune*, Joseph Medill. Patterson chose not to return to Chicago and the *Tribune* after his military service, leaving that opportunity to his cousin, Robert R.

Your Thoughts

Would you like to see more "muckraking" by today's journalists? Why or why not?

McCormick, who preferred to be called Colonel McCormick. Captain Patterson wanted to operate a newspaper much like the brightly sensational London tabloids he became familiar with during World War I. He and McCormick began to start the tabloid in New York together, but the Colonel quickly returned to take over the *Tribune*. The *Illustrated Daily News*, as it was called for a short time, began in the middle of the summer of 1919. From the outset, the *Daily News* appealed to the barely literate and the still large immigrant population of New York. Within five years, the circulation reached 750,000, the largest total in the United States. By 1928, it reached more than one million readers and 10 years later, it hit the two million mark. Much of its early success resulted because it was placed on newsstands that had sold only foreign language papers before. Its large-sized pictures sold it to that readership. Its tabloid page size helped to sell it, certainly among subway riders who found it convenient.

Its major competition came at first from two Hearst papers, the *Morning American* and the *Evening Journal*. Neither could keep up with the circulation growth of the *Daily News*, so Hearst started a new tabloid, the *Daily Mirror*. The circulation wars of the 1920s in New York were already notable when a newcomer decided to tackle the circulation giants, despite their success and their seemingly unlimited resources. It was Bernarr Macfadden who outdid the already notorious tabloids with a brand of sex, sin, salvation, violence and trivia that depended heavily on pictorial content even greater than that already being offered by his established rivals.

Bernarr Macfadden was a millionaire obsessed with health and fitness. His passion for physical culture resulted in financial reward as he produced and marketed products for bodybuilders, physical culturists, health faddists, and others persuaded by the advertising for food supplements, wheat germ, molasses, vitamins, and exercise equipment. Macfadden got into the magazine business with physical culture magazines, then with the highly successful True Story magazine. His magazine ventures apparently convinced him that he could be a newspaper publisher just as easily as a Hearst or a Patterson could. Macfadden had some success with a picture magazine and it appeared to be virtually a model for his newspaper, the *Daily Graphic*. Graphic it was; not just with a lot of pictures and large ones at that, but also lurid visual content. Macfadden did not bother with a membership in the Associated Press nor a sub-

scription to any other wire service. His news was the gut-wrenching, tear-jerking, scandal-mongering, anger-provoking events that described the pitiful and the pitiless.

It could be called gutter journalism. And it worked. Newsstand sales of the *Graphic* increased as the sleaze in its pages increased. Macfadden's problem, however, was that advertisers never supported his paper the way the readers did. Macfadden lost a lot of his fortune and closed down the *Graphic* in 1932. Hearst too had a difficult time through the 1930s trying to compete with the *News*, which continued to be America's circulation leader into the 1980s.

Contemporary Newspapers

A serious problem developed with the tremendous circulation growth of so many metropolitan newspapers. Their production costs and their circulation costs rose with their circulation numbers. There was only so much advertising revenue to go around and increasing size and complexity of a giant newspaper operation inevitably meant a need for higher advertising rates or more advertisers buying space in the publication, or both.

In the 1920s, consolidations and mergers of many newspapers accompanied the outright demise of others. Costs of production, distribution and labor became so great as to be prohibitive. The number of daily newspapers reached a high point in 1910 with 2,600, was down to 2,300 by 1920, to 1,700 by 1990 and shrinking even more in the 21st century. New York City went from 15 dailies in 1910 to nine by 1930 and four by 1990. The primary trend in 20th century newspapering was the merging and consolidating of newspapers, resulting in the elimination of all but one paper in small- to middle-sized communities and the giant metropolitan paper with a hyphenated name and little or no competition.

By the middle of the 20th century, the successful papers were small, suburban dailies, usually under chain ownership. In the bigger cities, the newspapers that survived were those with little competition. Chicago journalism was significant largely because of the early influence of Joseph Medill, founder of the *Tribune* and the later impact on that paper by his grandson, Colonel Robert McCormick. By the 1950s and '60s, McCormick had continued the *Tribune's* history of successful management in terms of profit and circulation, but had caused it to be criticized for biased approaches to major social issues. The *Tribune* was regarded as conservative, not only in editorial policy, but sometimes even in its news sections. The *Chicago Daily News* emerged from the shakedown of competition and the resultant mergers as the *Tribune's* chief rival.

The *Los Angeles Times*, under the leadership of the Chandler family, for decades topped the advertising income figures in Southern California and outlasted its frequent competitors until it became a lone metropolitan organ for Los Angeles, although surrounded by solid suburban dailies. Typical of highly regarded newspapers to thrive while others were disappearing are the *St. Louis Post-Dispatch* with its origins as a Pulitzer vehicle, and the *Louisville Courier-Journal* (Kentucky) with its legacy derived from Henry Watterson early in the century and Barry Bingham at mid-century. Watterson was editor of the *Courier-Journal* for 50 years, starting shortly after the Civil War. Watterson was a voice of moderation during turbulent racial strife in the South. After his retirement, the Bingham family took over the paper and, especially under Barry Bingham, it earned a reputation for excellence in news coverage and editorial insight. Barry Bingham, Jr., who also became involved in broadcasting, became editor and publisher in 1971 and continued a tradition that eventually led to recognition of Pulitzer prize jurors that cemented its reputation.

Another paper with multiple Pulitzer prizes is the *St. Petersburg Times* (Florida). Much of its prestige is attributed to the highly journalistic principles of Nelson Poynter, who operated the *Times* from 1938 to 1978. Even after Poynter's death the paper continued to win awards for journalistic standards, graphics and color printing.

The *Atlanta Constitution* and the *Atlanta Journal* were both strong newspapers and continued to have separate editorial policies even after coming under the same ownership. A leader among Southern newspapers is the *Miami Herald*, a member of the Knight-Ridder newspapers group. The *Herald's* John S. Knight twice served as president of the American Society of Newspaper Editors. The Knight family took over the *Herald* in 1937 as one of 16 papers in a chain that included such major papers as the *Detroit Free Press* and the *Philadelphia Inquirer* and *Daily News*. In 1974, the Knights merged with Ridder Publications, which owned or had a substantial interest in 19 dailies.

The only newspaper in the country rivaling the *New York Times'* prestige is the *Washington Post*. The *Post* had won numerous awards for independent and public-spirited journalism even before its emergence as a courageous vehicle for investigative reporting of a major political scandal in the Nixon administration. Nixon's White House threatened the newspaper's management with reprisals, but the paper stayed with two police beat reporters who found that a simple burglary was not so simple after all. Reporters Carl Bernstein and Bob Woodward join publisher Katherine Graham and Editor Ben Bradlee as major figures not only in the history of journalism, but also in the history of American politics.

Until the advent of *USA Today*, there were few significant newspapers with national audiences. The *Christian Science Monitor* has always been a specialized daily. Its specialty resulted from its avoidance of stories about disasters and crimes. This allowed the *Monitor* to become a journal of interpretation, able to take a long view of major news from overseas and from the nation's capital. It could also do more than other dailies with cultural events with lengthier features on the arts and literature.

Also thought of as specialized is the *Wall Street Journal*, a comprehensive financial daily. It is known for its tightly written, clear summaries of significant national and world news events and its feature pieces on major business trends and the economy.

It should be noted that of the regular newspapers, only the *New York Times* has had a national circulation of any significance. The largest circulation of these national newspapers belongs to *USA Today*, which emerged in the 1980s to set a trend for other papers with its compelling color photographs and extensive, colorful graphics, including charts and maps. Some newspapers since have used art direction and design specialists to work with editors to make their publications visually appealing. Newspapers that had before used only black and white photographs began to add more color in the wake of *USA Today's* success. *USA Today's* staff has described its approach as an attempt to respond to reader interests. They say the newspaper is designed on the basis of market research, giving the readers what they want. The marketing approach must tell *USA Today* decision-makers that the public wants tight packaging, color photographs and sprightly graphics. It must also indicate a desire for something like a TV newscast in print, a hardcopy version of what broadcast news sends through the air, because the content is, at best, brief.

The Contemporary Magazine

A significant departure in magazine publishing came in 1922 with the *Reader's Digest*, published by DeWitt Wallace. It was intended from the beginning to print condensed versions of articles that had been well received when they first appeared in other magazines. Its circulation grew steadily until the mid 1990s, when it was consistently one of the top three magazines in total readership with a circulation averaging 20 million copies a month.

A magazine demonstrating success on more than one level was the *New Yorker*, founded by Harold Ross in 1925 as a humorous look at the sophistication of metropolitan lifestyles. It developed a more literary and more analytical approach as the humor became less and less in evidence. It remained, however, a symbol of sophistication and has always been known for its celebrity writers, well-written fiction, feature stories and reviews of music and drama. Its influence on other magazines became apparent when after the 1960s, other publications began to emulate its practice of maintaining a close relationship between its content and its advertising, a technique designed to convince potential advertisers that their ads would be read.

This close tie between advertisements, articles and features has always been quite obvious in the pages of *Playboy*. Hugh Hefner's first issue appeared in 1953 and was an instant success. Hefner was always able to attract famous contributors and major writers to ensure quality articles to accompany the centerfolds and other nude photographs and the sex-oriented features in the magazine. *Playboy* can attribute much of its success to the fact that the demographically targeted audience for the magazine's content is also expected to be attracted to the advertisements. Often it is difficult in *Playboy* to see much difference between a feature on men's fashions and an advertisement for men's apparel. It is a technique that ensures considerable interest on the part of potential advertisers.

During the 1960s, many large circulation general magazines disappeared. The competition for advertising income resulted in hard times for magazines aimed at general audiences. Television could reach millions of viewers at a lower cost per contact. Many large, long-established magazines became extinct in the 1960s, unable to compete with television for advertising dollars. Their cost per contact, also called cost per thousand, was too much higher than that offered by television. From about 1960 on there was a proliferation of specialized magazines intended for fairly small circulations. Their formula for success was to deliver a demographically desired narrow set of readers that would appeal at a fairly low cost to a specific advertiser.

There are specialty magazines for just about any narrow interest one can think of. Advertisers can make good use of them because they deliver exactly the type of person who would buy the product. Motorcycle helmet manufacturers would buy space in publications for motorcycle enthusiasts. It made little sense to buy a network television commercial for hundreds of thousands of dollars to reach millions of people if only a few thousand of them would ever buy a safety helmet. The history of the magazine was always a history of specialization, but the need to adapt to television made that narrow focus even more pronounced in the second half of the 20th century.

Books Come of Age

At about the time of World War I and the years immediately following, book publishing was stimulated by the appearance of some strong publishing houses. Many of the most prominent names in the industry began just before or just after 1920 and their firms continued on in one form or another into the 1990s. These giants of book publishing included Alfred A. Knopf, Bennett Cerf, Alfred Harcourt, Donald Brace, Richard Simon, Max Schuster, Stanley Rinehart and Charles Scribner. They joined established firms like Lippincott, Prentice-Hall, Macmillan, Doubleday and Houghton Mifflin, among others, in aggressively marketing some of the most successful authors of the 20th century. In the 1920s and 1930s, Americans were reading the works of F. Scott Fitzgerald, Ernest Hemingway, Thomas Wolfe and, late in the period, William Faulkner.

By the 1940s and 1950s, the success of Random House and the emergence of paperback publishing resulted in a spurt of book publishing activity. Random House published prominent authors like John O'Hara, Irwin Shaw and Truman Capote.

One of the most significant developments in the history of book publishing was the paperback. There had been earlier attempts at softcover printing of books, especially in England and Germany, but not until 1939 was there a real breakthrough. It came with a firm called Pocket Books that concentrated on reprints at a very low cost. The publishing companies that followed the Pocket Books model found that reprinting their titles in paperbacks expanded their markets. Bantam Books came along in the 1940s publishing small-size, softcover books on timely subjects.

A comic book publisher, Dell, also produced a large number of paperbacks. Eventually, some firms began to publish original material in paperback rather than simply reprinting from the hard cover stock. New American Library was founded in 1948 to issue a quality line of paperbacks, including the Signet and Mentor series. In the 1960s, New American Library was purchased by the Times Mirror Company, but only after it had already established itself as the most literary of the softcover publishers. One reason for the phenomenal success of paperback publishing was a marketing strategy that was economically efficient because it featured a distribution agreement with magazine wholesalers. By using an already-existing network of distributors, paperback publishers were able to keep costs down considerably.

In the 1980s and 1990s, the industry was going through changes in ownership of the established publishing houses. The major firms were merging and consolidating in many instances into media conglomerates involving broadcast stations and networks, or newspaper and magazine chains.

The Newer Media: Movies, Radio and Television

The history of radio and of the movies is a chronology of the same era. Both began with inventors, scientists, and eventually hobbyists who worked out the preliminary technology and techniques that led each to flower at about the same time and to flourish together until the advent of television, which has a history severely dependent on both radio and film. The three 20th century media have an interdependent relationship with each other, and to some extent, a symbiotic relationship with the music recording industry. Radio especially both serves and is served by the recording studios.

Setting the stage for all of this was the development of the telegraph in 1844 when instantaneous communication over distance and time was born. The telephone in the 1870s and the demonstration of radio waves in the 1880s led to further development. By 1895, experiments with electromagnetic technology led Guglielmo Marconi to send messages in Morse Code without the need for wires. Reginald Fessenden and Lee de Forest experimented with the vacuum tube and were able to send voices over the airwaves for the first time in 1906. Fessenden combined telephone components with a high frequency generator so that voices could be transmitted. De Forest invented the Audion grid, inside the vacuum tube, making possible a small unit combining transmission and reception.

In 1888, Thomas Edison, who had already been working on and nearly perfecting the phonograph, used a camera to record images on a cylinder, resulting in what many consider, the first actual motion picture film. Edison then developed the Kinetoscope, a device for viewing motion pictures through a peephole. Edison formed a motion picture production company and displayed his product in Kinetoscope parlors, where one person at a time could view the film. By 1895, inventors in the United States and France had come up with a means to project the pictures onto screens so that several people could view films simultaneously. The projection machines meant that the Kinetoscope parlors could be replaced with facilities that would allow viewers to sit in a hall or large room and watch images projected on a sheet functioning like a screen. These were called Nickelodeons and proliferated between 1900 and 1912. The nickel admission gave a customer a half dozen short, silent films—the whole program lasting about an hour. There was little in the way of story in any of these films. The first actual narratives on film came from the Edison Studio because of the work of one of Edison's cameramen, Edwin S. Porter, who eventually became Edison's primary creator of movies. Porter's best-known work, "The Great Train Robbery," is often cited as the first movie to tell a story. It ran eight minutes and simply depicted the holdup of a train, the subsequent formation of a posse, and the pursuit and capture of the gang of robbers. It was the most popular movie in the country until the advent of major changes in movie-making in 1912.

The Nickelodeons were located in the urbanized areas of the Northeast, the slums and tenement neighborhoods where many immigrants lived in industrial cities. Many Nickelodeon customers spoke little or no English. Language was not a barrier for the barely literate audience for the silent, short films of the Nickelodeon. Eventually, movie makers realized there was an audience beyond the urban poor that they could reach. That audience, however, was used to live plays on stage, musical performances like opera or operettas, and, of course, vaudeville. The fledgling movie industry had to offer a product to lure those audiences away. It was not easy, because the new medium was viewed as tasteless, trivial, vulgar and of primary appeal to the lowest elements of society. One attempt to overcome the problems was to build magnificent movie palaces in good neighborhoods, thus creating an image of prestige and sophistication. But that would not have helped without the necessary first step—the makeover of the product. Films had to be made longer and with more complex story lines and more plots of universal appeal.

The earliest movies were one-reelers. By 1912, Europeans were already trying to tell one long story by use of several reels in the same movie. Two-reelers, lasting 20 minutes or more, were already showing up in some of America's Nickelodeons by 1912, so it was inevitable that someone would emerge as a pioneer in the attempt to take movies to the mass audience.

That man was David Wark Griffith. He started his career as a playwright, but ended up as an actor when he offered a script to the Edison Studio. Griffith left acting quickly, learned the directing trade from Porter, and left Edison to go to Biograph. From 1908 to 1915, Griffith made hundreds of short films for Biograph. He then left to join an independent company, where he got the opportunity to make what turned out to be the breakthrough film for the industry. The film, "The Birth of a Nation," was a glorification of the Ku Klux Klan in the years after the Civil War, but it was a cinematic triumph despite its controversial view of reconstruction.

Griffith showed everybody how to tell a story with film, how to use close-ups, how to use camera movements for effect, dollying in and out, trucking left and right. Griffith coached his actors and actresses. He used lights and shadows to create mood. He used fading in and fading out of shots to indicate the passage of time. In short, Griffith virtually invented the cinematography that has changed little, if any, to this day. "Birth of a Nation" was a blockbuster, obviously the first one, and ran for three hours, reel after reel. It earned a great deal of money, so much so that Griffith continued to be ambitious in his productions. An example was his extravagant "Intolerance," produced at a cost of $2 million and running more than three hours.

During this breakthrough period—the years just before 1920—Mack Sennett founded the Keystone Studio and began to produce comedies, usually slapstick with a lot of bumbling police officers and car chases. Charlie Chaplin made several short comedies and by 1920 was the most famous movie star in the world. Between 1915 and 1920, the Hollywood film industry had been accepted by the middle classes and movie theaters were considered respectable. The huge growth in attendance during that period foretold the coming golden age for film.

The Development of Radio

That golden age was to parallel the burgeoning popularity of radio as an entertainment medium. While movie makers perfected their craft in one or two reelers shown in tacky Nickelodeons, physicists and electrical engineers were embracing new electronic gadgetry. Experimentation with electromagnetic waves had led to ship-to-shore communication early on, because vessels at sea could benefit from radio waves transmitted over long distances putting them into contact with distant locations. Early radio operators were enthusiasts who were largely communicating with each other using sets that they had built from kits. There were few assembled sets and they were expensive for hobbyists. Radio was a scientific marvel to many tinkerers who enjoyed building their own sets and would then delight in any audible signals that they could pick up. Even before broadcasting as we know it began, it was a popular hobby and an exciting experiment for Americans who enjoyed an experience much like today's ham radio operators.

By 1920, it was no longer only amateur radio fans who were attracted to broadcasting. Radio sets were being manufactured for use in the home with the price brought down to a reasonable level as more and more of the ready-made sets were purchased. The broadcasting of regularly scheduled programs began giving the general public something to listen to. It was really an amateur effort by an engineer, Frank Conrad, that resulted in radio programming. Conrad, a Westinghouse employee, built a transmitter over his garage and sent music through the air, while asking any listeners to send him postcards to indicate that they received his music or to request a musical selection that he could play for them on his next broadcast. The response was so enthusiastic that Westinghouse decided to get into the business of broadcasting. The obvious plan was to sell Westinghouse receiving equipment to people who would enjoy the entertainment being offered.

Eight months later, in November of 1920, station KDKA was on the air as the first commercially licensed radio station in the United States. KDKA was licensed by the federal government to be a business as opposed to an amateur activity, hobby or experimental activity by an engineer or inventor. Radio operators had already been licensed because of the need to ensure clear reception by avoiding the overlap between signals. There had been voluntary agreements and eventually government licensing to promote a separation of channels.

KDKA was the first station, but it was not alone for long. Other manufacturers of radio equipment rushed to provide content for potential buyers of their products. Retail firms, schools, churches, and others who had messages to deliver or persuasion to offer applied for licenses under a 1912 law that was intended to deal with radio telephony, ship-to-shore broadcasts. By 1924, there were more than 600 radio stations on the air, but the government did not have the power under the 1912 act to ensure enough locations on the frequency spectrum to accommodate all of those who wanted to broadcast.

Many signals overlapped. Many broadcasters edged over onto nearby frequencies. Some would occasionally send out a signal on any arbitrarily chosen frequency desired at the time, then move to another frequency later. The amplitude modulation, or AM, system could carry over great distances and was even more powerful after the sun went down. Especially at night, but to some extent during the day, listeners of local stations would hear a cacophony of competing sounds from distant locations interfering with their reception. The airwaves had become a mess and those in the business for profit went to the federal government for help.

The only legislation available, the 1912 act, did not prescribe a specific frequency for anyone acquiring a license. The licensee could pick any frequency, even one already in use. Overlap and interference had become inevitable, so Congress passed the Radio Act of 1927 to create an orderly allocation of frequencies. Anyone who wanted to transmit had to agree to do so on an assigned frequency, with a specifically allocated level of power and mandated hours of broadcast time. Some were daylight only. Others had reduced power at night and some were allowed 24 hours daily at a specific power level.

The Radio Act of 1927, with its Federal Commission to enforce its provisions, gave government authority to regulate virtually all technical aspects of radio. Significantly, the justification for this power was found in the newly enunciated principle that the airwaves belonged to the people and that the government, in a representative form of democracy, could act for the people in regulating the use of the airwaves in the public interest and convenience.

However, the 1927 act became outdated as experiments with electromagnetic energy indicated that new electronic forms of communication would eventually emerge and would have to be regulated as well. The result was that Congress in 1934 replaced the 1927 act with the Federal Communications Act of 1934 to ensure that AM radio was not the only medium under a form of regulation intended to protect the public's interest in how public property, the air above us, could be used for private profit.

The very first radio stations were financed by various means until advertising became the industry's economic foundation. The first commercials appeared on the air in 1922, but it took two or three more years until advertising was commonplace. Early advertising on radio was rarely about products or about direct sales. It was instead primarily institutional advertising; simple, restrained announcements of a company or institution sponsoring a particular program. The origin of this was no doubt the previous practice of attempting to entice philanthropists to donate the funds to put a station on the air, maintain its operations, and finance its programs. That resulted in on-air recognition of the source of the philanthropy. That idea failed, though. Another plan was a subscription system where set owners paid a fee, much like cable TV instituted years later. The more common practice, one that worked for a short time, was for a department store or automobile dealer, for example, to operate a station that would be a magnet to pull customers into the store. That system began to fade out as commercials clearly made radio financially viable. Even the stations owned and operated by set manufacturers soon found out that advertising was the prime source of profit.

Music was the most popular content of radio in the 1920s, most of it live. Recorded music did not yet have the sound quality or full reproduction of the range of music that the recording industry would later develop. At first, it was classical and semi-classical music, but near the end of the decade, Guy Lombardo and Paul Whiteman and their dance music heralded the big band sounds that were to be the radio fare of the 1930s. The voices of Bing Crosby and Kate Smith were first heard in live broadcasts in the late '20s. It was estimated that 75% of the content of AM radio in the first 10 years was music. As the decade ended, drama was beginning to appear and would become a staple of programming, along with comedy in the 1930s. Radio news was in its infancy in the 1920s and did not really grow until the 1930s when it became a significant force in the decade that began radio's golden age.

The Golden Age for Radio

Some three million radio sets a year were being sold by 1930 and manufacturers had come up with receivers that no longer were so bulky and not so dependent on thick wires and large batteries. Radios ran on ordinary house current and were attractively designed to look like furniture. The network system contributed greatly to radio's popularity with the public and to the economic health of the stations. It was quite expensive for a station to produce live entertainment for several hours a day. Networks made it possible for the sharing of costs as several stations carried the same program at the same time. More than that, the networks eventually paid the stations to carry the network commercials. Stations were supplied free programming and were paid to transmit it. Advertisers liked the network arrangement, because the purchase of one commercial could result in its simultaneous appearance on hundreds of stations across the land. The networks collected the money from the sponsor, took a portion first and distributed the rest as shares to the affiliated stations.

Between 1923 and 1927, a few attempts were made to create small or regional networks, and some temporary networks began operating. Of these, the most successful was made up of stations owned by RCA. It was called the National Broadcasting Company, and it assured itself of a fast start when it took over what was virtually a network of the stations formerly owned by AT&T. These stations became available as a unit when AT&T divested itself of broadcast stations while staying in the business of leasing lines to the networks for station interconnection.

At first, NBC operated as two separate networks, calling them the Red and Blue networks. A third network originated in 1927 when a failing network, United Independent Broadcasters, merged with the Columbia Phonograph Record Company to form the Columbia Broadcasting System. All three networks went coast-to-coast in 1927 and by 1930 were supplying more than 50 hours of programming a week to their affiliates.

Eventually, the FCC forced NBC to sell its Blue network, citing antitrust concerns. The Blue network was bought by Edward Noble in 1943 and he renamed it the American Broadcasting Company in 1945. A fourth radio network had been founded in 1934 as a small, specialized news service to independent stations. It grew greatly in the number of affiliates, especially in smaller markets where the Big Three were not as eager to affiliate with stations their advertisers might not want to pay for because of their smaller audiences. It opened a niche for Mutual as a strong news service for such stations and resulted in Mutual gaining many more total affiliates than CBS, NBC, or later, ABC.

Daytime soap operas and evening presentations of comedy, variety and drama were the network fare. Historians point to the quality of the productions, the talent of the best performers of the day, the attention to good writing, the imaginative sound effects, and the genius of creators like Orson Welles, Arch Oboler, and Norman Corwin, as justification for calling the 1930s and 1940s radio's golden age. Dramatic productions of the era included the acclaimed "Mercury Theater of the Air," "The First Nighter," and many other programs based on radio scripts by the best writing talent of the period. During the same era that movie attendance reached its peak at 90 million tickets sold weekly, the American public embraced radio enthusiastically as its in-home entertainment. Radio was called "the theater of the mind" as millions of people would sit at home in the evening and "watch the radio."

Drama shows included mysteries, westerns, police-action shows and provocative complex presentations appealing to the intelligentsia. Shows concentrating on crime and suspense included "The Shadow," "The Inner Sanctum," "Johnny Dollar," and "Mister District Attorney." Westerns included "Hopalong Cassidy," "The Lone Ranger," and the original "Gunsmoke" in its pre-television setting.

Situation comedies pre-dated television as a primary draw for radio listeners. "Duffy's Tavern," "Fibber McGee and Molly," and "Amos and Andy" attracted huge audiences eager for laughter, especially during the national malaise resulting from the great economic depression. Even into the 1940s, these comedies and variety shows featuring comedians and popular music brought lighthearted entertainment into American homes. Top variety shows included those that featured Jack Benny, Fred Allen, Bob Hope, Bing Crosby and Eddie Cantor, among many others. The variety shows introduced many of the "big band" performers whose music was to dominate not only radio, but also the concert halls, ballrooms, movies, and recording studios of the 1930s and 1940s.

Shows for the youngsters attracted big audiences in the after-school hours including "Jack Armstrong, the All-American Boy," "Dick Tracy," and "Buck Rogers." Earlier daytime programming included quiz shows and game shows, some of which also made the evening schedule. But the bulk of the day was turned over to the Soap Opera. The sponsors of daytime drama about personal crises and family life were usually the manufacturers of soap, detergents, other cleaners and household products. "One Man's Family," "Portia Faces Life," and "Backstage Wife" were most prominent among the 30 to 40 dramas that appeared on the air by 1940.

The Depression Years

The depression years were a time of misery for millions. Unemployment was high, businesses were going bankrupt, unemployment compensation did not exist yet, and many people were without food, clothing or shelter. It was a time when everybody seemed to suffer, even those with some kind of work or some help from family, church or charity. Entertainment was inexpensive via movies and free through radio. Entertainment was a boon to those who needed their spirits lifted. Froth, fun and frivolity experienced vicariously could ease some of the despair and degradation felt by the disadvantaged and downtrodden. A movie theater was a warm and comfortable spot to wile away unwanted free time for the unemployed or underpaid. It was a low-priced amusement, with double and triple features filling the void for many unfortunates for between 10¢ to 25¢. Radio was essentially free once you had a set and the cost of electricity was minimal.

The depression did not hold back the development of the movie industry nor did it hinder radio stations and networks. These media prospered while other businesses failed. There was a need for what they offered and they met that need with continued high quality products, including upbeat escapist movies and radio's varied diversions from the realities of a bad time in the life of America. Advertising revenues for both stations and networks climbed steadily despite the depression and movie audiences continued to range above 80 million a week.

The Golden Age for Movies

The golden age for movies was already underway, certainly by the late 1920s, primarily because of the advent of synchronized sound in films. Going to the movies had already become a prime pursuit of most Americans. It was a popular family activity. The first film with a fully compatible sound system was *The Jazz Singer.* It featured Al Jolson singing "Mammy," "Blue Skies," and "Toot, Toot, Tootsie," all big hit tunes. The movie played to standing room only crowds. Immediately, every major studio began to convert to sound. Theaters all over the country had to be wired for sound. By 1930, the days of silent movies were over and the movie industry was clearly into its golden age.

Between the 1930s and 1950s, film became the most popular form of mass entertainment. Movies reached their peak in that 30-year period, appealing to entire families and drawing them out of their homes. The films were shot in black and white and featured actors and actresses who were so popular that their names on a marquee guaranteed ticket sales no matter what the title of the movie was. The star system guaranteed audiences because of the popularity of the headliners like Judy Garland, Ginger Rogers and Fred Astaire, Bob Hope and Bing Crosby, Cary Grant and Myrna Loy, Nelson Eddy and Jeanette MacDonald. A movie starring Gary Cooper was destined to be a hit, as was any movie that offered Lana Turner, Clark Gable, Spencer Tracy, W.C. Fields, Carole Lombard, Mary Pickford, Gloria Swanson, Tom Mix, and of course, the Barrymores—John, Lionel and Ethel.

There were many others who had adoring fans and it was a system that perpetuated itself as more stars came along to replace those who faded from the screen. By 1945, weekly ticket sales reached 90 million, a figure reached first in the early 1930s. Weekly box office sales were fairly steady from the late 1920s to the late 1940s, generally above 80 million. A major decline set in with the advent of television. Movie attendance dropped dramatically starting in the early 1950s, hitting a low of 17 million in the 1970s and inching up to an average of 18 million weekly in the 1980s. Through the 1990s, the totals were coming close to averaging 20 million weekly. In other words, one-fourth as many tickets are being sold at movie theaters now as there were in the golden age of Hollywood.

In the 1950s, the movie industry finally gave up black and white photography, hoping for an advantage in the competition with television. Color films had been made occasionally since the 1920s, but there was no impetus to convert to color until television came along and was black and white in its early years. The majority of films prior to the advent of television had been shot in black and white only for economic reasons. Those reasons seemed unimportant when attendance figures dropped. Even with the move to color, audiences did not flock back to theaters. To try to draw patrons back, the industry turned to franker themes, more explicit sexual portrayals, increasing levels of violent action, special effects, and other approaches that television was not offering at the time. Still, entire families did not return to theaters. Industry figures show clearly that today, the ticket buyers are young people, generally under the age of 30. Hollywood produces one-third as many titles per year as in the glory days.

The Development of Television

Even before 1930, European inventors managed to transmit some fuzzy images, giving hope that television was quite possible. Numerous tests were being conducted in Europe after 1930, but primarily using mechanical devices rather than electronic to record images and then send them with the illusion of motion. The screens were quite small, there was poor picture definition (a lack of clarity), and the screen was dim.

In the United States, attempts were made occasionally even before 1930 to send a still photograph or a motion picture by wireless, but these experiments failed to overcome the difficulty of scanning all elements of the picture at once. Instead, the picture would roll across the screen bit by bit until finally all of it could be viewed, much like a fax machine feeds line by line until the whole message appears.

Much of the credit for overcoming the early shortcomings of the equipment used to send images by radio waves goes to Vladimir Zworykin, an RCA scientist, who first invented the iconoscope, the initial electronic television camera and, later, the kinescope, a cathode ray tube, that was the key to receiving signals. The iconoscope allowed for a larger screen, brighter imagery and greatly improved clarity.

Competing with RCA to develop a workable television transmitting and receiving system was a smaller operator, Television Laboratories, Inc., with Philo Farnsworth as lead inventor. Farnsworth came up with a fully electronic system that would turn a photograph into electrical charges and transmit them to a receiver that would read them as picture elements. Farnsworth had experimented with a means of scanning that gave better picture definition than seen before. Because of the competition between Farnsworth and RCA's Zworykin, legal disputes arose over rights to the various achievements of each. The result was that RCA, with its resources, agreed to make royalty payments for patents originating with Farnsworth, who agreed then to allow RCA to use his patents. It was a strange agreement, with RCA not buying the patents outright as one would expect. These agreements solidified the research efforts of the most successful of the many experimenters who had been determined to make television a commercial medium.

Despite all of these attempts throughout the 1930s to come up with a workable television system, it was not until 1939 that there was a public display of the system that the industry would follow. By 1941, the first few commercial television stations went on the air, but World War II delayed further development. It was not until the end of World War II that there was an increase in the number of stations.

The FCC actually granted approval for 18 licensees to go on the air as early as 1941, but only seven were in operation by the end of the year and only three more by mid-1942 when construction on new stations stopped because of the war. These stations were on the air from 10 to 15 hours a week and had audiences of only a few thousand. When the war started, there were about 15,000 television sets in the country. When the war ended in 1945, only six stations were still on the air. The war resulted in wholesale conversion of civilian manufacturing into production of military supplies and equipment. Civilian production was cut back as the factories found themselves turning out tanks, planes, bullets, weapons, and military-oriented electronic gear.

Once the war ended and American industry returned to civilian production, the potential for television's growth was obvious. In fact, the potential was too great. In 1946 and 1947, the FCC received so many applications for construction permits from television stations that a concern grew about the ability of the spectrum to handle so many new frequencies. The technology was available, the manufacturing capacity was developing quickly, and there was a vast labor pool of returning servicemen; many having military experience already in electronics. Television set manufacturers were going into production and networks were supplying programming to the few stations on the air when the FCC decided to put a freeze on applications.

In effect, the FCC had come up with a plan for channel assignments that would allow for opening up the airways to television transmissions without having to face the mess that resulted on the AM dial in the 1920s before the 1927 Act. The orderly allocation of television frequencies that came out of the freeze period resulted in specific limits on what communities would have stations, on what channels, and the distance in miles that channels would be separated from each other, as well as the level of power available and the location of the transmitter.

Finally, 13 years after the 1939 demonstration and 11 years after the first seven stations went on the air, television was ready to break through. That 1952 breakthrough brought about a dramatic change in American lifestyle and inevitably impacted the other media, especially radio and movies.

Television's Impact on Movies

As pointed out earlier, America's attachment to television dramatically changed movie making. There were estimates that only 10% of the population in the 1980s were going out to the theaters compared with estimates that 65% attended movies in the 1930s. The ticket prices increased faster than the rate of inflation during that period, because movie production costs were constantly increasing as fewer tickets were being sold. If you cannot make a profit on volume, you have to charge more per unit. From 1980 to 1990, the average cost of producing a movie doubled.

An age polarization has developed in the movie audience since television began to keep adults in their living rooms in front of the home screen. Industry figures have shown that 70% of the audience is under 30 years old and that 50% is between the age of 18 and 24. About two-thirds of movie viewers are between the age of 12 and 29.

The studios tried to combat television with the large screen formats, including cinerama and cinemascope, to emphasize the smallness of the television picture at home. They tried movies that would give the illusion of three dimensions in the short-lived attempt to spice up the theaters with so-called 3-D movies. Most of the big studios simply shut their doors, selling off their property that had become more valuable to real estate developers.

Some finally turned to producing television programs on their sound stages. Although there was reluctance at first, eventually some of the remaining studios made millions of dollars in profit by selling their pre-1948 films for display on television. Studio executives said they did that only because those movies were of such vintage that they had no value for distribution to theaters. The next step was inevitable. If there was money to be made by dealing with the industry that had caused such devastation to the film industry, then the movie people had to give up their resistance. They first began to reap profits by selling the more recent of their productions to television and later got into the business of making feature films especially for television.

Your Thoughts

If you had been involved in the movie industry in the 1950s and 1960s, what would you have done to compete with television? Why?

Television's Impact on Radio

Radio, too, was altered considerably after television's breakthrough in 1952. Network radio began immediately to lose its luster. Its programs and its appeal moved to television, which offered viewers all of the big stars they had earlier sought out on radio. Station owners and managers in the mid-1950s were telling the networks that they no longer wanted their programs. Soap operas, dramas, game shows, comedy and variety were now television content. Television had usurped radio's format and the networks certainly could not offer the same programming on both radio and television.

Radio stations dropped their affiliate relationships and provided their own programming. ABC, CBS and NBC had to drop their long-form entertainment programs and operate much like Mutual. By the late 1950s, radio networks had become suppliers of frequent, short newscasts, leaving their affiliates free to develop their own content. That meant radio became a glorified jukebox. Instead of going head-to-head with television, radio offered an alternative to the tube. The disc jockey concept, with recorded versions of popular songs, became the salvation of the industry. In fact, it resulted in a new prosperity.

Stations found out immediately that playing phonograph records supplied free by recording industry promoters gave them a low overhead, a minimal operation compared to the large staffs and expensively acquired facilities needed before. It did not take station executives long to realize the income potential from such down-sizing. With operating costs so much less now, advertising sales staffers could appeal to potential sponsors by pointing out how little it cost to advertise on radio—10% to 20% of what it cost for comparable time on television. Advertisers were told that radio offered specialized audiences, specific sets of music listeners, who could be identified demographically and appealed to at a low cost. Focused advertising to targeted audiences for sponsors of specific products appealing to identifiable listeners worked for radio. It did not hurt that the music format also allowed for more commercials. The television impact on radio was severe, but it worked out ideally in the long run for the stations, if not for the radio networks.

Each radio station would create an image for itself, a formula for success with a clearly defined audience in mind, an audience not likely to be shared with any other station. The type of music to be played and the personality of the disc jockey would establish an individual identity. Some stations would offer country and western music, some rock music, and others would be considered middle-of-the-road. There were even more specific subsets within each of the general musical formulas. The radio stations became more local and less dependent on national advertising as they gave up the network programs.

In the 1960s, a few radio stations began all-news programming, an attempt to stimulate some of the radio journalism that disappeared when television usurped the old radio format. All-news, or more accurately, news-talk formats are often called "talk radio," "information radio," or some other variation of talk and news. They have long blocks of news programming and many hours of telephone call-in shows, often with flamboyant or controversial hosts talking with and/or berating guests. The format developed as AM radio looked for methods of dealing with the increasing popularity of FM stations. To recover from the losses of their listeners to the FM band, AM stations needed alternative programming. Music was the staple of FM. Music could be reproduced with greater range on FM and FM did not pick up static the way AM did.

Frequency modulation (FM) was developed and patented by Edwin Armstrong in 1933 on the assumption that it would be a better carrier of music than amplitude modulation (AM). The initial disadvantage seemed that FM signals could not reach the distances that AM could. The FM transmissions go only to the horizon; unlike AM, which can bounce off the ionosphere and reflect back to earth over vast distances. Frequency modulation also can be stopped by large buildings and hills. This limitation indicated to broadcast technicians in the 1930s that Armstrong's invention was suited primarily for the audio carrier for television broadcasts. Television, too, was a transmission that could not go beyond the horizon.

Armstrong and RCA fought in the courts over rights to the FM applications when RCA was eager to enter into television research. Armstrong had been supported in his early efforts at creating the FM sound, but RCA's use of his invention for television broadcasts was viewed by him as a violation of their agreement. Eventually, RCA had to pay Armstrong his royalties and give him his recognition as the inventor of a radio system, not just simply an audio carrier for television.

Because FM radio covered a smaller area with better reception, it was at first believed to be a means of confining radio broadcasts to small, local areas. A signal could be confined to a local area and not interfere with other signals coming from greater distances. This would allow for a great many more radio stations to be licensed by the government without competing with each other for channel space. The industry had a tremendous investment in AM equipment and inventory and did not immediately embrace FM as an equal partner. Existing transmitters, receivers and manufacturing equipment would be close to obsolete if the clear, clean signals of FM were to attract large numbers of listeners.

Entrenched AM station owners and operators lobbied the government for protection from what they viewed as a threat to their investments. In the 1940s, the FCC moved the FM band to another part of the spectrum, making the existing FM sets obsolete. The FCC gave the spot on the band to television

where FM had been since the first experimental FM license was granted in 1939. The FCC further hindered FM's development by permitting the practice of simulcasting, which allowed an AM licensee to acquire an FM station and then merely duplicate the same programming on both stations. This meant the listener had little reason to buy a separate FM receiver. In fact, many FM stations in the 1950s and 1960s were owned by AM licensees who were merely hedging their bets just in case FM ever did become competitive. Eventually, the manufacturers turned out sets with FM and AM receivers combined, including AM-FM transistor radios and car radios that finally included the FM receivers. At the same time, in the 1960s, the FCC was awarding licenses almost exclusively for FM stations because the AM band was so crowded, was authorizing the development of FM stereo, and was starting to reduce the amount of simulcasting allowed.

Soon after these developments, FM began to realize its potential and began to show strength in audience ratings figures by the 1970s and was dominating AM in audience size by the 1980s. By 2003, with fewer than half of the total radio stations, FM had 70% of the listeners.

Radio-Television News

The 1930s saw the emergence of journalism via radio. Earlier, operators of radio stations seemed to think of themselves as operating more like vaudeville or musical comedy than like a newspaper. After 1927, many station owners began to think of news as a means of meeting the public service requirement of the 1927 Act. Also, live radio programming was expensive at a time when large studios were filled with audiences who had to be provided for, full orchestras performed on large stages, and large casts of singers, actors, comedians and other performers were aided by several sound effects specialists, audio equipment operators, and many other technicians. The overhead was considerable, especially before the use of audio tape and the emergence of pre-recorded programs. It was less costly for station management to put one person in front of a microphone reading copy prepared by a staff of five or six former newspaper reporters or editors.

By the mid-1930s, radio was seriously committed to journalism. If it was a golden age for the industry, it was also a golden age for broadcast news, especially in the years immediately preceding World War II. It started with the fact that early radio newsgatherers and newswriters came from newspaper backgrounds. An important factor was the radio format in the pre-television years. Programs ran for 30 minutes or a full hour, so a news show would be blocked out for a long enough period of time to allow for extensive coverage, detailed stories, and backgrounding of major events, as well as segments devoted to analysis and commentary.

Through radio's golden age, radio commentators were given large blocks of time because the long-form format allowed for it. H.V. Kaltenborn, John Cameron Swayze, Lowell Thomas, Elmer Davis, Upton Close, and Fulton Lewis had significant impact on politics with their incisive commentary and reasoned analysis. They became household names just like movie stars.

Another type of radio commentator was the spirited, opinionated, controversial commentator on scandals, gossip, show business, and other non-political aspects of society. Chief among these were Walter Winchell and Gabriel Heater. Winchell, more than the other commentators, became a true celebrity. He had the highest audience totals of any of the radio journalists and analysts. Winchell was dynamic and colorful. Heater was less flamboyant, but still so popular with audiences that he got more air time and a higher salary than any of the famous voices on the air. Heater started as a reporter, covering for radio some of the biggest stories of the day. He was so impressive, that he was given his own program of commentary by popular demand.

By the late 1930s, the youngest of the commentators was already gaining some of the recognition that eventually would lead most observers to describe him as the best broadcast journalist ever. That was Edward R. Murrow, who, like H.V. Kaltenborn, carried to the American people much of the news of Europe in the years just before World War II began. Beginning in 1938, Murrow implemented an arrangement that used newspapermen, under his direction, to offer impressions of events from major European capitals about Hitler's war machine. These broadcasts, via shortwave, were arranged for CBS by Murrow and prominently featured William L. Shirer, a former wire service and newspaper reporter who quickly became an outstanding radio reporter. Murrow was European News Chief for CBS when the war broke out. Later, Murrow brought the Battle of Britain into American living rooms with unforgettable descriptions of Nazi air attacks against London. Murrow also was aboard an American plane during an air raid on Berlin.

By the 1950s, Murrow was described by his colleagues as a relentless seeker of truth and as a strong promoter of ethics and responsibility in broadcast reporting. Some called him the conscience of broadcast journalism. He was firmly established as a leader in the early attempts at making television news as serious about good journalism as radio news had already become when he faced his biggest challenge. The McCarthy era resulted in Murrow receiving criticism from elements of society that at first failed to recognize that no matter how justified some of Senator Joseph McCarthy's concerns might have been at the time, there was still no justification for overlooking or even flaunting the Constitution. McCarthy supporters were distressed when Murrow's reporting revealed that McCarthy was a bully, a liar, a demagogue, and had been reckless in making wild, unsubstantiated charges against loyal Americans who disagreed with the senator's paranoid view of patriotism.

Any lingering doubts about the accuracy of Murrow's exposure of McCarthy's evil intent and disgusting tactics were dispelled when, on live television, McCarthy broke down before a national audience. It was during a televised United States Senate hearing into McCarthy's irresponsibility that the senator openly revealed his mental instability. McCarthy was stripped of his power by his colleagues in the Senate and condemned by that body. McCarthy disgraced himself by his conduct during the televised Senate hearing and the Senate's action against him further secured that public disgrace.

Murrow continued to show the same kind of courage in the production and presentation of some of the most highly acclaimed documentaries ever seen on network television. When Murrow, a cigarette smoker, died of lung cancer in 1965, he left behind a legendary reputation. Young broadcast journalists are often offered Murrow as their model for extraordinary reporting, integrity, elocution, courage, and ethical stature.

CBS had emerged as the most honored and most respected radio news organization in the late 1930s, with much of the credit going not only to Murrow, but also to Shirer, Kaltenborn, Paul White, Sig Mickelson, Robert Trout, and other pioneers. Through the war years and into the 1950s, it was still CBS that earned plaudits for journalistic achievement as Winston Burdett, Richard C. Hottelet, Eric Sevareid, Walter Cronkite, Charles Collingwood, and Howard K. Smith made the transition from radio to television reporting. It was Cronkite who followed Murrow as the symbol of stability and integrity for this most respected of the network news organizations. Cronkite became the primary anchor for CBS television news in 1962. Cronkite was the ratings leader until his retirement in 1980. CBS and NBC continued as strong competitors for news audiences and for prestige, but by the 1980s there was a decrease in network management's belief that having outstanding news coverage was of itself intrinsically valuable.

Instead, profitability of news and public affairs programs became the motivating force. The great CBS documentaries became fewer and fewer and the bosses at all of the networks concentrated on competition for the largest possible audiences for their news programs, which were bringing in unheard of amounts of advertising dollars.

As the popularity of television news grew, at both the local station and network levels, the attempts to reach the levels of excellence seen earlier were replaced by a star system with anchors achieving both huge salaries and celebrity status similar to movie stars. Newscasters by the 1980s and 1990s were drawing increasingly larger audiences and the networks and stations both were finding more air time for their news product as they also expanded their news staffs and their equipment and facilities. The end result was a product clearly appealing to and benefiting the audience of mature, high-income viewers strongly desired by advertisers.

Your Thoughts

Why do you think the quality of radio and television news has declined?

What would you suggest be done to improve the quality of radio and television news?

Think Back

1. Why is Johann Gutenberg so important in the history of mass media?

2. What were the major early newspapers and who were the major publishers in the American colonies?

3. Why is Benjamin Franklin considered the "father" of American journalism?

4. What were "viewspapers?"

5. What were the major newspapers and publishers in the pre-Revolutionary War period?

6. What were the most important early magazines and who published them?

7. Who were the major players in the development of the political press?

8. What were the major newspapers and who were the major editors and publishers during the 1800s?

9. Why are Joseph Pulitzer and William Randolph Hearst considered giants in the history of journalism?

10. What is "muckraking?"

11. What were the major newspapers and names associated with "jazz journalism?"

12. What are the major "national" newspapers these days?

13. How are modern magazines categorized?

14. What have been the most significant developments in the history of book publishing?

15. What were the major contributions in the development of movies, radio and television. Who were the big names?

16. What were the major names and developments in the history of radio and television news?

Newspapers

The newspaper industry is hurting. Ad revenue is down, circulation is down and veteran employees are being laid off or taking early retirement offers. Some experts are predicting that the printed newspaper that has been in existence in North America for more than 300 years probably has, at best, about 20 more years before it slips into communication history much like telegrams, 8-track tapes, transistor radios and black-and-white television sets.

In an effort to remain economically viable, some daily newspapers are putting most of their news online and cutting back the production of their printed product to two or three days per week. Other newspapers are consolidating sections, reducing the number of pages per issue, making their pages smaller and depending more on user-generated material.

Most of the problems facing newspapers stem from a troubled economy and competition from new media technologies, but many newspapers have hurt themselves and their peers by practicing sloppy, unethical journalism. The vast majority of newspaper editors and reporters practice their craft with integrity, professional commitment and a dogged effort to discover and report the truth in a fair and balanced manner. A few, however, fail to follow the basic tenets of the profession: don't fabricate and don't plagiarize.

Recent Scandals

The prestigious *New York Times* has been embarrassed by a scandal that made headlines all over the world. Editor Howell Raines and managing editor Gerald Boyd resigned in the wake of a newsroom mutiny and revelations of outright lies by a young reporter believed to be sheltered by Raines and Boyd, despite concerns by *Times* staffers of fabrications and plagiarism. The allegations that reporter Jayson Blair was careless and mistake-prone, as well as emotionally troubled, preceded the eventual disclosures by outside publications that Blair was practicing simulated rather than real journalism. Eventually, senior editors of the *Times* who said they overlooked Blair's problems because he was young and had great promise had to confront a firestorm of criticisms of the venerable *Times* for 36 Blair stories that were either fabricated or plagiarized.

The *Times* continued to suffer from adverse publicity when reporter Rick Bragg resigned, following a reader's complaint about a Bragg story that, upon investigations by the *Times,* turned out to have been someone else's work.

The *Times* was not the only major newspaper to receive adverse publicity about fabrications of quotes or of complete stories and for plagiarizing stories or parts of stories. The *Washington Post* has a history of respected journalism, but lost some of its prestige gained from Watergate coverage when a series of stories about a young heroin addict written by Janet Cooke raised concerns and was disputed by law enforcement investigators who insisted that they would have known of the existence of the 8-year-old dealer.

The Washington police chief was skeptical and demanded that she reveal her sources. Cooke claimed that her source had to remain anonymous. Under constant pressure from her editors and incredulity expressed by police agencies, Cooke finally revealed that the central character in her series was actually a composite of older youngsters and the basic story was a fake.

The *Boston Globe* forced a columnist to resign because some of the individuals mentioned by name in some of her columns were fictitious. Patricia Smith was said by the *Globe's* ombudsman to have fabricated quotes in an attempt to make her writing more stimulating. Smith defended her actions by saying that the non-existent people and the fake quotes helped to drive a point home and actually did a service for her readers. The *Globe* didn't accept her attempt to justify her unethical behavior.

Plagiarism was at the core of another embarrassment for the *Globe.* Columnist Mike Barnicle was fired after a column that appeared under his name was determined by his editors to be a series of jokes by comedian George Carlin. Later the paper rehired Barnicle, leading to 50 or more *Globe* staffers signing a protest. Despite the protest, Barnicle continued with the paper until a number of similar problems came up about another of his columns. Barnicle was then fired again.

The newspaper industry has survived these problems and is maintaining its overall image as a purveyor of responsible journalism. However, there are critics, including prophets of near doom, who say newspapers cannot survive the advent and continued growth of alternative news media. Radio, television, and cable were the early challengers. Now, we also have online media and several news services available via e-mail.

Declining Numbers and Readers

The death of the American newspaper has long been predicted, but it is still with us. In the 1920s, because of mergers and consolidations, the number of dailies was reduced as production and circulation costs made it obvious that there was not enough advertising revenue to support so many large metropolitan papers. As this trend toward fewer big dailies continued through the 1930s, alarmists predicted further decline, despite the continued expansion of the number of weekly papers. The invention and display of the facsimile machine in the 1940s resulted in claims that newspapers would quickly disappear to be replaced by information delivered directly to homes by the facsimile machine. As new technology appeared, so too did dire predictions of the effect on the newspaper's future. Yet, the facsimile machine

took another 40 years to gain any popularity and then not as a delivery system for newspapers.

The advent of radio as a competitor for advertising dollars in the 1920s also brought a gloomy business forecast for the newspaper industry, but it was the emergence in the 1950s of television as a major national preoccupation that fueled more speculation about potential disaster for the newspapers. Not only was television to be competitive in the quest for advertising income, but it was also expected by many to destroy Americans' ability to read, or at least their interest in reading. Big city newspapers continued to die off in the second half of the 20th century, but new, smaller suburban dailies came into existence as a result of population shifts. The number of weekly newspapers never diminished. The newspaper industry was changing even into the 21st century, but change did not mean disaster.

Metropolitan newspapers have declined in number for the last 80 years, but the growth in suburban dailies and in community, or weekly, newspapers has kept total circulation somewhat steady. Factoring in statistics from all forms of newspapers, circulation has held steady at about 60 million a day since the 1920s, but it has not kept pace with the population growth.

Demonstrating that the picture is more one of change than of anything else is the shift away from afternoon publication. The biggest, most prominent metropolitan newspapers are delivered in the morning. Smaller dailies, suburban newspapers and newspapers in small- to medium-market communities, have afternoon delivery. At one time, there were nearly six times as many afternoon newspapers as morning. After newspaper production costs increased greatly in the 1920s and economic problems forced consolidations and group ownership, many of the newspapers that were merged out of existence were afternoon papers. By the 1940s, the ratio was four afternoon newspapers to one morning paper. By the 1990s, the ratio was two to one. Today, there are fewer afternoon daily newspapers than morning daily newspapers. Some of the biggest afternoon newspapers in the country went out of business in the 1980s, including the *Washington Star, Philadelphia Bulletin, Minneapolis Star, Des Moines Tribune, Cleveland Press,* and *San Diego Tribune.*

Many afternoon newspapers have been affected severely by changing transportation habits in metropolitan areas. No longer are as many people riding buses, subways and trains home from work and occupying themselves on the otherwise boring ride with a newspaper. Instead, suburban life and the construction of more and more freeways put commuters into their cars in the late afternoon and evening.

It is easy to note the impact of television news in the late afternoon and early evening, once a time for reading the afternoon newspaper. There is more time given to news on television between 4 P.M. and 7 P.M. than at any other period of the day. In fact, television programming generally attracts millions of viewers through the evening, beginning at the time when many Americans arrive home from work.

The shift from an industrial society to a service-oriented, white-collar society has changed habits of many in the work force. Afternoon newspapers were important to those who arrived home in the mid-afternoon when so many jobs in the urban areas were in manufacturing, where plants and factories had 7 A.M. to 3 P.M. shifts. In the last 20 years, increasingly more city dwellers arrive home from offices, shops and stores after a 9-to-5 shift and are greeted by television news.

It has become more and more difficult to compete with television news when the afternoon newspapers have had difficulty finding news that was not reported in the morning paper. For afternoon distribution, a paper has a mid-morning deadline. Often transportation is difficult in congested urban areas, creating problems.

The Response to Challenge

There is no doubt that newspapers have had to change because of television. The 1950s were somewhat reminiscent of the press-radio war of the 1930s when newspaper publishers and owners feared the competition from radio for the available advertising dollars. Radio never seemed to affect newspaper circulation and the amount of money spent on advertising in all of the media increased over time. Yet the newspaper industry tried to pressure the wire services into keeping radio stations and networks from acquiring any of the news generated by the wire services existing at the time. In the 1950s, newspapers at first tried a technique that failed when used against radio two decades earlier. They refused to publish a television log, would not carry stories about television in their news sections, and would not review television programs in the arts and entertainment columns. That was short-lived. Readers demanded printed television schedules much like the movie listings in their newspapers. Many newspapers today have specialized writers who cover the television industry and their Sunday editions offer magazines devoted to local television schedules that rival *TV Guide.*

In effect, radio, at first, and television, eventually, replaced the hawkers who would stand on the corner stimulating newspaper sales by screaming out the headlines to passersby. Broadcast media, with their short bursts of incomplete fragments of information,

Your Thoughts

What suggestions would you give to the publishers of afternoon newspapers to help them survive?

encourage those interested to turn to the newspaper for full understanding of such abbreviated accounts of possible news. Radio and television are there first with sights and sounds of snippets of news, but the newspaper can be depended upon to amplify and explain in much greater detail. Newspapers offer interpretation and explanation so their readers can gain a comprehension of events.

Since the advent of television, newspapers have offered more features, a greater range and variety than television can provide. Scoops, "extras," and immediate, fast-breaking news are tough to come by in competition with media that are quicker, but extensively researched features elaborating on issues or on lifestyle give newspapers an advantage. Some newspapers are much like magazines in the extensive treatment they give to special features on politics, leisure, art, youth, health, careers, business, the economy, etc.

Despite the best efforts of bright, innovative and committed people, the number of daily newspapers will likely continue to decrease for the next several years. While there may always be some version of a newspaper in most cities, it is clear that the days of multi-newspaper cities are numbered. At the turn of the century, there were just 39 cities with "competing" newspapers. In 13 of those cities, the "competitors" were functioning under what is called a Joint Operating Agreement. The papers have independent news-editorial staffs, but share advertising and production staffs, as well as revenues. In 12 of those cities, the competition was between morning and afternoon newspapers and in just 14 cities was there actually head-to-head competition. In other words, consumers had more than one choice for a morning newspaper in only 14 cities. Everywhere else, it was "buy our newspaper or don't buy any."

Unfortunately, more and more consumers are opting for the latter option.

Many critics point to studies that find the American public has lost a great deal of faith and trust in newspapers. Among the factors cited for this "credibility crisis" are errors and inaccuracies, a loss of connection with the community, bias, sensationalism, and misplaced priorities. Many newspapers are working diligently to address such concerns and some have even set up ombudsman programs. Such programs go by different names—Readers' Representative, Ombudsman, etc.—but the role remains the same. Such staffers serve as liaisons between consumers and the reporters, editors, photographers and publishers. When readers have complaints, the ombudsman investigates and makes a report, both to management and to readers. Occasionally, an ombudsman might notice unfair, unprofessional or inappropriate practices and procedures and call them to the attention of management. In short, an ombudsman can be an important link in the chain that attempts to rebuild and secure public trust in newspapers.

Online Media: Friend or Foe?

While most daily newspapers have extensive online versions, most of the sites do not generate a significant amount of revenue for owners. On average, newspaper-related web sites account for less than 10% of a newspaper's total revenue. Most experts predict that the percentage will continue to grow, but the impressive growth enjoyed for the past several years has begun to slow down and flatten out.

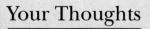

Your Thoughts

What would you suggest newspaper publishers do to improve the revenue generating aspect of their online products?

Why do you think your suggestions would work?

Despite the rather meager economic impact on traditional printed newspapers, online products are prompting changes in newspaper content. As with earlier technological innovations, the competition from online media has forced printed newspapers to do more commentary, analysis, investigative journalism, special features, in-depth examinations of issues and has brought about a "hyper-local" focus. Printed newspapers will never be able to compete with online products in the arenas of speed, adaptability, interactivity, searchability and easy access to varied sources of information. Instead, to survive, they must continue to search for ways to attract and hold the interest of all potential readers, not just those over 50 years-old.

Ownership Patterns

Most American newspapers are owned by groups/ chains and conglomerates. Many own or are owned jointly with radio and television stations, magazines, cable companies or book publishers. The most common arrangement is the group, in which two or more (usually many more) newspapers in different communities have common ownership. The 10 biggest groups have more than one-third of the circulation. Some of the best-known newspaper groups include Gannett, McClatchy, Newhouse, the Tribune Company, News Corp., the New York Times, MediaNews Group, E. W. Scripps and Hearst. Other large groups may not be as well known. For example, Donrey Media owns more than 50 newspapers, but they are not in large population centers. Other newspaper groups are actually part of publishing empires that include magazine and book publishers. There are about 160 groups, whether owned with other media or not, in the United States. They have been buying up the individually owned newspapers so fast that very few remain. Groups even buy other groups and, of course, other media.

There is growing concern about the dangers of so much control in so few hands. A reduction of the number of voices available is worrisome enough without the additional fear of so much power over communication by large corporations. Add to this the lack of variety of viewpoints likely in American media and the ownership's distance from the typical newspaper community. Can we get a newspaper with a management team that is aware of its readers' needs when a distant ownership's demands for profit are more crucial to the management than the local community's interests? Local ownership and local management are rare in the newspaper industry.

Concentration of ownership in a small group of companies has resulted from several factors, with tax laws one of the most obvious. It is advantageous for a corporation, under existing tax laws, to use up its profits in the purchase of other businesses rather than paying out those profits to employees or stockholders. Capital gains taxes are lower than income taxes, therefore media companies avoid paying regular personal or corporate income tax on any gain resulting from taking profit in salary, bonuses or dividends. Instead, they pay no tax on that money in the year they use it to buy another business. Later, when that business is sold, only a capital gains tax is paid, and that's half the rate of personal or corporate income tax. The trend toward giant corporate mergers is seen in many parts of the American economy, not just in the media. It is going to continue as long as it is more profitable to make a conglomerate even larger. The disparity between income taxes and capital gains taxes is so big that it is even an advantage to buy a company for more than it is actually worth.

Another reason then for the trend toward concentration of ownership is the profit to be made by individuals who sell to groups. If you can get more for your newspaper than it is really worth, the inducement to sell is strong. Both buyer and seller do well.

Some family-owned newspapers are sold when the owners' heirs have no interest in the business. Newspapers are becoming larger and more complicated businesses to run, making it difficult for an individual to operate in competition with the giants and all of their resources. Newspaper production costs are becoming prohibitive for all but the conglomerates, who have consolidated purchasing and billing offices, shared marketing expertise, pooled sales forces, and negotiated long-term contracts for supplies and materials bought in bulk, therefore at lower prices. Becoming part of a conglomerate also promises financial stability, partly because of size and partly because of diversity. Size means clout with lending institutions when seeking capital for any of the single parts of the conglomerate in need of new buildings, new presses, computers or advanced technology. Diversity helps the overall profit stay firm even when one or more of the units is struggling.

The Newspaper Organization

The typical newspaper, no matter its size, is usually made up of five departments: editorial, advertising, circulation, production and business. The publisher of a newspaper is the executive in charge of all five departments. Each department has a supervisor who reports to the publisher. Most likely, the publisher has experience in the business office or in advertising and is the representative of the ownership. Individual owners have often named themselves as publishers, but with groups the publishers come from the ranks of professional managers or from those who distinguished themselves first as editors, business managers or advertising directors.

The supervisor of the business or administrative department is often called a controller, or business manager, and has responsibility for the accounting staff and the personnel office. The business department is responsible for billing and expenditures, as well as coordinating with all other departments on matters affecting income, expenses and profits.

Closely related to the accounting and disbursement functions of the business end is the advertising department. This is where the revenue is produced by the sale of advertising space. The advertising department handles display advertising and classified advertising. Display ads are those placed both by national and local advertisers. Display ads can be retail advertising from local merchants and businesses or national advertising from agencies handling brand-name merchandise for manufacturers or major services like various franchise operations, airlines, resorts, oil companies, etc. Classified advertising, the want ads, is the separate section containing announcements of real estate for sale or rent, vehicles for sale, jobs wanted or employment opportunities, and personal announcements.

The circulation director is in charge of subscriptions, renewals and the tasks involved in getting copies out to homes, coin boxes and display racks in stores. The circulation department attempts to generate sufficient numbers of readers to bring in revenue and to increase the value to potential advertisers.

The production department, once called the back shop, is where the typesetting and printing is done. Copy is sent electronically to a photo-composition machine that produces text on photographic paper to be photographed with a large camera. The completed negative is used to make an offset printing plate, which is attached to a printing press and used to make the press run. Many production departments have changed over to desktop publishing with all of the copy being sent over the computer to the composition department where it is plated and sent to press.

On many newspapers, the five departments are structured into two basic divisions—the business and editorial operations. The business side manages the newspaper's financial affairs and its advertising. The editorial side acquires and processes news, comment, entertainment and other non-advertising content. Certainly advertising, circulation and production are separate departments when the newspaper is organized into two separate divisions, but the advertising director, circulation manager and production director report to a business manager rather than directly to the publisher. In this structure there is also a separate business department to take care of maintaining the facilities and handling accounting and personnel matters.

No matter the organization, there is expected to be a strong separation, even a gulf, between the editorial and advertising departments. To maintain objective editorial judgments, the news staff is not supposed to know who is advertising for what products or services or what the advertisements say. The advertising department will let the editorial department know what parts of the pages are reserved for advertisers. This allows the editorial staff to work on content to fill the open spaces. The typical issue of a paper is 65 percent advertising content. Editorial fills the rest of it, with 20 percent of the total devoted to actual news. The other 15 percent is made up of comic strips, crossword puzzles, advice-to-the-lovelorn columns and other non-news material provided by the editorial department. The Sunday edition is an exception, virtually a special issue devoted primarily to undated features and a great amount of special advertising sections. A very small percentage of the Sunday paper is news. Most of the Sunday issue is put together earlier in the week before the news is available.

The editorial department is the news department, which comes up with all of the printed matter in the paper, except for advertising. Heading the editorial staff is the editor, sometimes called editor-in-chief. The editor is in charge of the information content, with overall responsibility for news policy and works directly with the publisher. The editor must coordinate any overlapping activities with each of the other departments, meet with legal staff on problematic stories, see to the efficiency and efficacy of newsroom expenses, and exert leadership in the community. Reporting to the editor is the managing editor, who is responsible for the day-to-day operation of the newsroom, including personnel matters. The managing editor is a leader in the newsroom and the supervisor of certain sub-editors. There are many sub-editors, each responsible for a different section of the paper or a different function of the editorial process. The city editor is responsible for local news coverage, including making the assignments for reporters and supervising copyreaders. Most newspapers also have assistant city editors, or ACEs as they are called. On the biggest newspapers in the country, the title is often metropolitan editor.

Directly under the managing editor is the news editor, who supervises the copy editors and decides where stories will be placed on the pages. Page design is a function of the news editor, whose responsibility for inserting stories into the paper often requires consultation with the section editor or managing editor on important stories. The copy editors do the actual editing of stories for accuracy, grammar, conciseness, etc., and then write the headlines. Many individuals carry a title with the word "editor" in it, but do very little editing of copy. Often the title indicates a supervisory position, a degree of authority, often over those who really do edit stories.

Supervising reporters, writers and copy editors for the sports section will be a sports editor. There could be an arts and entertainment editor. At one time, every newspaper had a society editor. Those sections have been revamped and renamed in recent years, but still have someone with authority over the staff for the section. This could be the "Scene" editor, "View" editor, "Lifestyles" editor, or "Family Living" editor. In San Diego, the name of this section changes almost daily. Names include *Quest, Health, Currents* and *Food*. The business section could have an editor, and might even have a separate real estate editor. A major figure among these section heads is the Sunday editor, who has plenty of work to do well ahead of the publication day for each Sunday issue. More than any other supervisor, the Sunday editor buys freelance material, magazine-like features that can be inserted early in the week.

The wire editor is concerned with national and international news from the major press associations, which at one time sent their copy along landlines, or wires. Now they distribute electronically and use satellite transmissions, but they are still often referred to as wire services, a nickname that stuck even if it is anachronistic. The wire editor selects, edits and determines placement (with consultation) of stories from Associated Press, Reuters and other news services.

Some newspapers have a state editor, especially those with large out-of-town circulations. The state editor works with staff reporters, some of them in distant bureaus, and with correspondents in outlying communities. These correspondents, usually called stringers, often get paid by the story or by the published inch and sometimes submit on speculation rather than by assignments.

One of the most independent of the supervisory editors is the editorial page editor, who often answers only to the editor-in-chief, in other words, not to the managing editor, city editor, or any section editor. The intent is to separate, as much as possible, the opinion section of the editorial department from the news section. The editorial page editor is often called the associate editor, and is in charge of editorial writers and columnists. His or her responsibility is for the editorial page and the "op-ed" page, which is the page opposite the editorial page, one that carries syndicated opinion pieces and/or local commentaries. The Letters to the Editor column is on one of these pages. The editorial page editor designs these two pages, selects and edits the letters, supervises any editorial cartoonists, and sees to the writing of the editorials by specialists in that task. Editorial writers approach their work as the voice of management. The unsigned editorials are not individual opinions as are the offerings by identified columnists on the "op-ed" page.

The word "editor" has different meanings. It can indicate someone who selects copy from sources, one who buys stories from freelancers or stringers, one who assigns general assignment reporters to cover events, and one who supervises personnel, as well as one who checks for grammar, spelling, punctuation and word usage. The word "editorial" also can be used in different ways. As noted already, an editorial is an unsigned essay expressing the opinion of ownership on a major, even controversial, issue. It has no byline, unlike commentaries by columnists that appear on the same or adjoining page. The columnists offer opinions on controversial matters, but are speaking as individuals, so their articles or essays are not editorials. The space on the left-hand side of the page, typically with a wider column, is designated for the editorials.

As an adjective, editorial is used to describe the news and opinion function of the newspaper. The editorial side is the part of the operation that excludes business aspects, circulation, advertising and the backshop. Those who gather, write and edit news and those who handle the editorials and other opinion pieces are members of the editorial staff.

The backbone of the editorial side is the reporter, who has to search out the sources for information and gather the details necessary to write a story. The general assignment reporters must be prepared to write on virtually any topic, unlike beat reporters, who specialize in a specific type of coverage. A beat reporter might cover a police station or law enforcement generally. Another beat reporter might be assigned to the courts, or city council, or local government generally. Some reporters are even more specialized. Examples would be those who cover science, medicine, business and the environment.

Photographers are part of the editorial staff and may draw their assignments from the city editor, often accompanying a general assignment reporter to an event. Sometimes photographers draw assignments from a photography editor. Almost every page of a typical newspaper has one or more photographs. Photographs not taken by the newspaper's staff photographers originate with a wire service. Photographers do not write news stories, but they often have to gather information for the caption that goes with the photograph, certainly in the instances where there is no reporter and the photographer is sent alone because only a photograph is needed. The news judgment and experience needed in visual treatment of news would make it imperative that we call these individuals photojournalists. They need to develop skill not only in techniques of lighting, framing and composition of good pictures but they also must have an instinct or awareness for news values. Photojournalists use increasingly complicated technical equipment to create visual images that are both art and journalism.

While newspapers can be a relatively profitable business, salaries for reporters and editors are nothing to write home about. Beginning newspaper journalists average about $600 per week. Veteran reporters average about $1,000 per week. Editors average about $1,200 per week. Online divisions of newspapers normally pay a bit better, though. It is not unusual for a beginning web site writer/reporter to earn $1,500 per week and experienced online staffers can command about $2,000 per week.

Today's Newspapers

As we've seen, newspapers come in all sizes and styles; however, there are about nine traditional categories of newspapers.

1. International/National Dailies
2. Metropolitan/Regional Dailies
3. Local Dailies
4. General-Interest Non-Dailies (mostly weeklies)

Your Thoughts

If you were going to pursue a career in the newspaper industry, what aspect interests you most? Why?

5. Minority
6. Foreign Language/Ethnic
7. Religious
8. Military
9. Specialty (mostly business, entertainment, sports)

Unlike newspapers in the rest of the world, the typical newspaper in the United States is very local in its coverage of news events. In many nations, the newspaper is a vehicle for news of national and international events. Many can be called national newspapers, both because of their coverage and their distribution well beyond the city of origin.

In the United States there was no true national newspaper until the 1980s, with the emergence of *USA Today*. There are those who claim that the *Christian Science Monitor* and *The Wall Street Journal* are national newspapers because of their national circulations through regionally printed editions. However, each is a specialized publication, making it a close cousin to the kind of national newspaper so common in Europe, for example. On its circulation alone, *The Wall Street Journal* might be considered a national paper.

USA Today is a true national newspaper. It is printed at several points around the nation on the presses of dailies owned by the parent Gannett Company. *USA Today* was started by Gannett in the early 1980s to build a national audience with capsulized news summaries, flashy graphics, and extensive use of color. Gannett calls it "The Nation's Newspaper," and fills it with very brief news stories not much different from television news. Most of the articles run less than 600 words, making it little more than a headline service.

The typical American newspaper serves a specific community with news of interest to its local readers. The orientation is to community and state news primarily, but with some coverage of national and international events. The look of each newspaper is similar. The front page has major local, national and international news, with no advertising. The inside pages of the first section are filled with advertising, often half page and full-page advertisements, with articles of national and international importance. On the front page of the next section is local and state news and no advertising. The rest of that section is heavy with display advertisements and more local, state and regional news. Third, fourth and fifth sections are devoted to sports, arts and entertainment, and financial and business news. The upper half of any page is considered a spot for more important news than is the bottom part of the page. It is assumed that "above the fold" is where the most significant copy goes. In each section, page one is where the biggest story goes.

The appearance of many dailies has changed recently. Changes have involved new sections, new typefaces, more illustrations, more use of color, and increasing use on page two of a section devoted to summaries of the stories to appear in the rest of the paper. In recent years we have seen wider columns of type, more and bigger photographs, fewer stories on the front page, and a tendency toward lifting sections from stories, especially quotations (or pullquotes), and setting them adjacent to the story in larger type and with bold boxes around them. Newspaper publishers are seeking a look or design that will appeal to younger readers or to call attention to a missed reading opportunity.

Some newspapers are more regional than local in their approach to coverage and their identification of their potential circulation. The *Des Moines Register* is certainly a local paper to its metropolitan Des Moines area readers, but it is distinctive as a regional paper also. The *Des Moines Register* is read all over the state of Iowa and its content is a reflection of its readers. From Denison in western Iowa to Muscatine well to the east of Des Moines, events are noted in the pages of the *Des Moines Register* that in other large dailies would be defined as too far away to be newsworthy. Residents of Cedar Rapids read the *Des Moines Register* as well as the *Cedar Rapids Gazette*. The *Des Moines Register* is in the households in Iowa City alongside the *Iowa City Press Citizen*. The *Honolulu Advertiser* is a state-wide newspaper, with local news defined very broadly. *The Boston Globe* is not just a Boston newspaper but is also a service to all of New England.

At the turn of the century, the U.S. had about 1,500 daily newspapers. About 800 of those were morning newspapers and about 700 were afternoon/evening newspapers. Morning newspapers grab the lion's share of the circulation. About 48,000,000 morning newspapers and about 8,000,000 afternoon/evening newspapers are sold each day (Monday–Saturday).

In mid-2008, there were about 1,450 daily newspapers being published in the United States—about 820 morning newspapers and about 630 afternoon/evening newspapers. Total daily circulation dropped to about 55 million—47 million in the morning and about 8 million in the afternoon/evening.

Most daily newspapers have relatively small circulations. More than 40% print fewer than 10,000 copies per day and only about 3% print more than 250,000 copies per day. Just three newspapers have circulations greater than one million per day.

The World of Weeklies

The most local of all newspapers are the weeklies. At one time called the grassroots press, weeklies were thought of as small town newspapers. They were thought of exclusively as rural or suburban, but many are now found in big cities, serving neighborhoods or specific urban communities within the larger metropolis. Anymore, they are referred to as community newspapers, perhaps reaching a beach area only, a neighborhood around a large university, a gentrified section of town with a newly emerging demographic profile, or a youth-oriented market across the whole geographic area. Some tend to be arts-oriented or political in content, while others are alternative newspapers, descendants of the underground newspapers of the 1960s. Of course, there are still country weeklies. The suburbs have their specialized local publications with a weekly roundup of events not likely to be carried in the metropolitan paper. The typical weekly is published on Thursday. Advertisers like to see their messages in print going into the weekend when consumers head to supermarkets, department stores and shopping malls. The weekly is a good advertising vehicle for the small town or neighborhood firm that would find a larger newspaper or television station to be cost inefficient. Small town radio, small dailies and thousands of weeklies offer lower advertising rates to small businesses that do not need to reach audiences beyond their immediate locale.

A common weekly publication is the shopper, or free distribution paper. This type of advertising vehicle has been around for most of this century. Often these are facetiously referred to as "throw-aways,"

because they most often contain nothing but advertisements. In the last 20 years or so, some of them have begun to print public relations news releases, a local calendar of events or community bulletin board, features or entertainment-related material, and anything that is supplied to them free-of-charge and does not require much editing. These free-distribution newspapers do not have editorial departments and are produced by the same staff members who put together the display ads. Late in the 20th century they had become strong competitors for the advertising dollar and forced some newspapers to add free-distribution papers, or shoppers, to their own operations. Weeklies come and go quickly sometimes, but by most estimates, there are approximately 7,000 weeklies in the United States.

Specialized Newspapers

Although we think of the typical paper as an organ that generally reaches out to the full community, some target particular readers. Among the most specialized newspapers are those aimed at a specific minority group, a narrow religious denomination, a targeted special interest, or a non-English speaking audience.

Foreign language newspapers have been part of the American scene since before the Revolution. Colonists, for the most part, were English speaking, but some of them had come from parts of Europe where other languages were spoken. By the 1770s, there was a need for French language papers. German and Scandinavian newspapers flourished in Cincinnati, Milwaukee, Chicago, Minneapolis and elsewhere in the early 1800s. As immigrants from southern and eastern Europe began to arrive later in the 19th century, newspapers began to appear in Slavic languages, among others. Many immigrant groups eventually assimilated and newspapers in their languages, almost all of them weeklies, were disappearing rapidly in the middle of the 20th century. Some small ethnic, foreign language newspapers have survived, however. There are publications for the newest types of immigrants published partly in English and partly in Arabic, Vietnamese, Chinese, etc. By most counts, there are about 160 weekly "ethnic" newspapers in the U.S.

Hispanic Newspapers

Common ethnic newspapers are those intended for the largest of the nation's minority groups. In particular the number of Spanish-language newspapers is increasing greatly because of the huge influx of immigrants from Mexico and other Latin American countries. Some of these are major publications in cities with hundreds of thousands of Spanish-speaking residents.

Most of the approximately 150 Latino newspapers are weeklies, although the 12 dailies being published by the turn of the century have achieved large enough circulations to indicate potential for more dailies to appear.

African-American Newspapers

Newspapers circulating in African-American communities have a long history. The first of them was started in 1827 by the Reverend Samuel Cornish and John B. Russwurm. They called it *Freedom's Journal.* Cornish had edited three different weeklies in New York City and Russwurm was the first African-American to graduate from a college in the United States. Russwurm, an 1826 graduate of Bowdoin College, said *Freedom's Journal* had a mission to plead the cause of black Americans and to agitate against the inhumanity of slavery. Another early black newspaper of significance was *The Ram's Horn,* which gave Frederick Douglass his start in newspapering. Douglass, a freed former slave, had established himself as a writer and orator before publisher Willis A. Hodges named him as editor of *The Ram's Horn* in 1847. The newspaper did not last long and Douglass quickly established his own anti-slavery newspaper, initially titled *North Star,* but later renamed *Frederick Douglass' Paper.* Douglass joined a Washington weekly, the *New Era* after the Civil War. It was intended to support efforts of newly freed blacks. It struggled financially, to the point that Douglass had to put his own money into it and eventually gave it a new name, *The New National Era.* Douglass finally closed it in 1875 because of continued losses. Douglass became a symbol of black achievement through his newspaper career and his autobiographical writings.

It has always been difficult for black newspapers to secure enough advertising income to survive, let alone show a profit. Three newspapers were circulation leaders during the 1930s, '40s and '50s before a decline began in the wake of heavy black migration to industrial cities. The big three were the *Chicago Defender,* the *Pittsburgh Courier* and Baltimore's *Afro-American.* Each had a national readership, especially among blacks in the southern states, but African-American readers eventually favored their local newspapers rather than those of national influence. The big three survived, even with reduced circulations, but from the 1960s on, no paper was more powerful or significant than the *Atlanta World, Los Angeles Sentinel* or *Philadelphia Tribune.*

During the civil rights movement and the turbulence that followed, national circulation was achieved by newspapers published by the growing Black Muslim movement and, for a time, the Black Panther party. By the 1970s and '80s, John Sengstacke had created a chain of black newspapers, with the *Chicago Defender* as its linchpin. The *Michigan Chronicle* became his most successful paper in what was called the Defender group, a set of community-based newspapers. Another chain was that of John H. Murph, III, the Afro-American group, based in Baltimore.

A black newspaper that changed greatly in the 1980s was the *Amsterdam News* of Harlem, which had been quite sensational, devoted to crime and sex as its prime content. As other Harlem weeklies went out of business, it became much more moderate in tone and published solid local news of black accomplishments. It had extensive sports coverage and became recognized for its attention to women's issues.

In the mid-1980s, Robert Maynard became the first black owner of a metropolitan newspaper, the *Oakland Tribune.* Maynard named himself publisher and editor after heading a group that bought the newspaper from Gannett. Maynard had been a reporter in Pennsylvania before earning a Nieman fellowship to Harvard and then a reporting job at the *Washington Post.* Maynard was the editor of the *Oakland Tribune* before becoming its owner.

By the end of the 20th century, there were about 195 newspapers owned and edited by blacks for black readers, most of them weeklies and a few monthlies. More than 3,000 black newspapers had been founded since 1927, but most had a short life span. Those surviving today face competition from standard commercial newspapers that are striving to hire African-American reporters and editors. Many newspaper organizations have developed special programs for recruiting and training minorities, although most fall far short in the effort. There also has been a greater effort to cover news of blacks and other minorities in the mainstream newspapers. This has made it difficult for black newspapers to retain staff members who leave for bigger commercial newspapers once they are experienced.

Native-American Newspapers

Native-American newspapers have been few in number and have never had much financial support. Those that lasted into the 21st century were promoting causes and promoting the welfare of Native Americans. The American Indian Historical Society and the Mohawk nation have both given financial support to newspapers designed to promote the preservation of Indian heritage and encourage self-pride among Native Americans. In South Dakota, the *Indian Country News* has been a voice of rural indians. The *Cherokee Advocate* in Oklahoma has functioned as a voice of Native Americans and has concentrated on news of specific interest to its targeted readers. The *Navajo Times* demonstrated editorial judgment that stressed news items affecting Native Americans directly.

What Is News?

In the newsrooms and city rooms of small and large newspapers, weeklies and dailies, decisions are made about what material in the total newsflow will be selected for inclusion in the local section, sports pages, national and international section, or on the business pages. The typical situation is that more news items are available than can be used in the limited space in the newspaper. Most stories are rejected, others are allowed to move along the selection channel toward the news desk and then on to be printed and distributed.

Studies investigating the behavior of newspaper editors in accepting or rejecting news material, funneling news possibilities into the "news hole" and on to the reader, were based on theories about "gates" that regulate materials passed along channels to a consumer. The theory began with the flow of agricultural products from the farm through the groceries and supermarkets and on to the dinner table. The concept resulted from observers' awareness that inferior tomatoes were not picked, but left to rot, that plums or pears crushed by the weight of boxes in transport were rejected by middlemen, and produce clerks threw out vegetables left too long in the market. Shoppers thump watermelons, squeeze fruit and even sniff some items before selecting and rejecting.

Similarly, the passage of a piece of news along a channel is dependent upon the fact that at certain points along the channel there are "gates" operating to accept some news items and reject others. Manning those gates are city editors, copy editors, news editors, even reporters. This "gatekeeper" construct can be described as a chain with each link carrying a message or messages. The simplest chain is a sender passing a message to a receiver; but in social communication most of these chains are longer than two persons and all persons along the chain are "gatekeepers," opening or closing "gates" to messages that come along.

These "gatekeepers" at the source could be eyewitnesses to news events or police officers taking down information for incident reports or arrest reports. The newspaper's first "gatekeeper" is the reporter, who must decide what to accept from witnesses or from police reports and which to pass on to the desk. Perhaps the key "gatekeepers" are those who make up the pages, or even the wire editors who select from many possibilities, or the city editor who determines what will get coverage. At any rate, it is the "gatekeepers" who define news.

News has been defined in many textbooks and by many working journalists. The "man bites dog" axiom results from the contention that news is the extraordinary event, the unusual, the odd, the different. Others talk of consequence, significant, human interest, etc. But operationally, news is what an editor says is news.

The "gatekeeper" analysis of news flow results in a definition of news that is based on determinants of news studied by researchers from academia and observed by news writers and editors from their experience. These determinants, or elements, of news are also called dimensions of news by some who have tried to come up with a useful definition. The result is that news is defined as that which interests people, is unusual or out-of-the ordinary, a departure from the expected, and contains one or more, in combination of the following elements or dimensions: consequence or significance, conflict, timeliness, proximity, prominence and human interest.

Consequence or significance in a news story is the part that has high impact on the reader. High impact items concern matters likely to have an effect on many members of the audience or a strong, personal effect on individuals in that audience. Tax increases, interest rates, loss of job, change in school schedules, any possible life changes, or effect on social or political relationships could have significance or consequence.

Conflict items involve verbal or physical clashes between principals of the story or between principals and natural forces. Conflict could include heated arguments at a school board meeting, a demonstration at a rally, a labor-management confrontation, a major traffic snarl bringing freeway traffic to a standstill, a volcano eruption, a jetliner crash, a riot, armed conflict leading to potential war.

Prominence is a dimension based on a known principal, that is, a person, institution or issue well known through past publicity or position in society or the community. This is a dimension of news based partly on familiarity but very strongly on notoriety and celebrity.

Proximity has to do with how local a news story is, how close to home. Proximate items are items about people or events in the immediate coverage area.

Timely items are those dealing with recent happenings, updated items with new leads or fresh material never used by other media. Timeliness is a dimension usually indicating that something happened in the last 24 hours.

Human interest is an element of news that editors and writers have a difficult time describing, or putting into words, but they say they know it when they see it. It typically is something that brings to the reader a chuckle, a laugh, a smile, a tendency toward crying a little bit, or a slight tear drop forming and a little sniffle. It can be heart-warming or nearly heart-wrenching. It often has to do with children or pets, hard-luck stories, rags-to-riches stories, or anything that appeals to the heart or emotions of the reader.

No matter how it is defined, those who determine what is news are dependent upon events, or recognizing when a circumstance or occurrence stands out in terms of its specific location or specific time. Happenings that stand out give the news a lot of visibility and the reader a quick awareness of such occurrences. One result of the focus on events is the public relations technique of creating instant visibility through the pseudo event. In recent years there has been a proliferation of events that are not spontaneous but are pre-planned by publicity specialists to get news media attention. News coverage is a virtual certainty when this public relations technique is used by people who are not only aware of the event focus of the media but also have a knowledge of news values. They create these pseudo events to attract news coverage that they hope will help the image of their clients. A pseudo event is planned or artificially contrived for the sole purpose of being reported. It can be a ribbon-cutting ceremony, a grand opening of a shopping mall, a disc jockey broadcasting from a flag

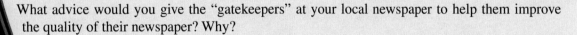

Your Thoughts

What advice would you give the "gatekeepers" at your local newspaper to help them improve the quality of their newspaper? Why?

pole high atop the radio station building, or a local politician taking to a bulldozer to move sand or silt from a streambed when other politicians were delaying the needed disposal by waiting for an environmental impact report.

Press Associations

Newspapers depend heavily on press associations, or wire services, for a great deal of their non-local news. These are national organizations that allow newspapers to have a wide range of coverage from national and international news centers. There were once two dominant American press associations—the Associated Press and United Press International. Most newspaper people and broadcast journalists simply refer to them as wire services. However, news is no longer sent by telegraphic wire but transmitted instead by computer networks linked by telephone lines, optical cables, micro-wave links, and satellites. In addition, there are supplemental wire services, some of them quite small and usually specialized. For a monthly charge that depends on the newspaper's circulation, wire services will send a constant flow of news items, whether local, state, regional, national or international.

Associated Press had its forerunner in 1848 when the *New York Herald* of James Gordon Bennett, the *Courier and Enquirer* of James Watson Webb, Horace Greeley's *Tribune,* and the *Journal of Commerce* began to procure news in common, primarily by sharing telegraph dispatches. The precedent for this had been established during the previous two or three years when a few newspaper publishers were unhappy with the rates they were being charged for telegraph lines used to transmit stories from the Mexican War battlefront. They saved money and improved their coverage of the war by sharing a telegraph line. The use of the telegraph, starting in 1844, spurred cooperative ventures by newspaper publishers who pooled their resources to share costs. In 1846, a group of small newspapers in upstate New York already had formed a press association to get the same news by telegraph as their big city rivals. When smaller newspapers were able to demonstrate the potential for cooperative news it was inevitable that the bigger dailies would develop a large-scale wire service to serve far-flung publications and meet the needs of the biggest newspapers in New York City.

The name Associated Press did not come into general use until after 10 or more years of operation by a group legally founded in 1849 as the Harbor News Association. From its first meetings, though, the group that planned to get a firm grip on cooperative telegraphic news coverage was generally referred to as the New York Associated Press. Seven New York newspapers combined to receive news by the same telegraph line and to also sell that news to outsiders, including newspapers in Philadelphia, Baltimore and other major cities. Before the term Associated Press came into general use in the 1860s, the founders also used the title Telegraphic and General News Association.

Among the founders, the major players were Henry J. Raymond, then an assistant to Webb of the *Courier and Enquirer,* and David Hale of the *Journal of Commerce.* Raymond later was to be the prime force behind the origin of *The New York Times.* Raymond has been described as a leader in negotiating contracts and working out the agreements necessary to establish the cooperative venture. Hale was so impressed with the pooling already attempted during the Mexican War that he's supposed to have initiated the efforts to create this forerunner of the Associated Press by contacting his bitter rival, Bennett at the *Tribune,* and suggesting the cooperative news-gathering that led to the meetings in 1848 that got the groundwork laid.

For a time the Associated Press was largely an Eastern operation linking newspapers in metropolitan centers on the Atlantic seaboard. After the Civil War it increasingly moved westward, covering the whole nation. The completion of a transatlantic cable in 1866 brought quicker and greater access to news from Europe. Early in the 20th century, the Associated Press was reorganized, primarily by consolidating regional AP groups, a move that eliminated a problem created by challenges by other groups of newspapers.

United Press International was formed in 1958 as a result of a merger between William Randolph Hearst's International News Service and the United Press founded by E.W. Scripps in 1907. Hearst had copied the Scripps' effort in 1909. When they merged, the result was vigorous competition for AP through the 1960s, '70s and into the '80s.

Scripps and Hearst started UP and INS for newspapers that could not obtain, or did not care to have,

Associated Press membership. The Associated Press was a cooperative, requiring newspaper owners to join as members. Scripps started United Press to sell news to subscribers on a contract basis, not as a cooperative. Hearst followed with International News Service as an answer to the closed-membership policy of Associated Press, giving INS the opportunity to serve a variety of clients selling news it collected to subscribers at home and abroad.

UPI is a shell of its former self today, with very few employees or customers. It's likely to sail off into the media sunset very soon. The Associated Press and Reuters remain relatively viable and continue to provide quality service to clients around the world.

Press Syndicates

Feature syndicates have their origins in a service during the Civil War era by a Baraboo, Wisconsin, newspaperman, Ansell Kellogg, who offered other editors a chance to avoid clipping interesting material from other newspapers. Kellogg did it for them and mailed them ready-to-print feature items, with an emphasis on entertaining rather than informing readers. Other entrepreneurs soon followed Kellogg's example, forming businesses to procure and distribute opinion columns, fiction, essays, short stories, poetry, cartoons and other non-news content. Eventually, some of the most popular features for newspaper readers were provided by hundreds of syndicates of varying size and influence, including comic strips, puzzles and games, advice-to-the-lovelorn columns, advice columns generally, and horoscopes, among others. The appeal of comic strips has long been noted and reader surveys often indicate that "Dear Abby" and "Ann Landers" are the most-read items in newspapers. The syndicates generally regarded as reaching the most readers with their products are King Features Syndicate, United Media, Universal Press Syndicate, North American Syndicate, and Tribune Media Services.

Most Americans appreciate the comic strip as a consistent feature of every newspaper and note that as they go from one part of the nation to another the same comic strips often are available to them. Comics began in the 1890s and their popularity has spread throughout the world. The first comics were intended for children, but quickly publishers realized that adults also enjoyed them. The first national syndication of comic strips began in 1915, although artists' drawings, usually one panel rather than a strip, had appeared in individual newspapers before the turn of the century. The battle between Hearst and Pulitzer for the right to publish a comic character called the "Yellow Kid" in 1896 displayed the intense battle between the two for Sunday circulation and gave the name yellow journalism to the era.

One of the earliest and longest-lived was the "Katzenjammer Kids," which started in 1897 and was eventually syndicated by King Features. The first regular daily cartoon strip was "Mutt and Jeff," appearing in the *San Francisco Chronicle* in 1907. By the 1920s and '30s, Hearst's King Features Syndicate had acquired such reader favorites as "Barney Google," "Tillie the Toiler," and "Thimble Theater," featuring Popeye, Olive Oyl, Wimpy and Bluto. Hearst also had the most popular comic strip of all, Chic Young's "Blondie." Competing syndicates also came up with long-running comics at that time, including "Gasoline Alley," "Harold Teen," "Little Orphan Annie," "Tarzan," and "Dick Tracy." Adventure themes in some of the strips began to make them more than "funny papers," as they were usually called. "Jerry and the Pirates," "Steve Canyon," "Joe Palooka," and, of course, "Superman" demonstrated that action stories and superhumans could take their place alongside the humor.

More recently, newspaper feature syndicates have supplied us with "Garfield" the cat, "Bloom County," "Peanuts," with Lucy, Linus and Snoopy, "Beetle Bailey," and the always controversial "Doonesbury." Garry Trudeau began drawing "Doonesbury" in 1970 and immediately satirized American politics and culture. Trudeau's creations like Zonker, Duke, B.D. and Joanie Caucus were seen along with Bill Clinton, Al Gore, George Bush, Dan Quayle, Richard Nixon, Ronald Reagan and Jimmy Carter, all cartoon characters to Trudeau.

Newspaper Production

Changes in the way newspapers are produced have altered the appearance of newsrooms and made for drastic adjustments in the way editorial staff members do their jobs. In the last 50 years, newspapers have experienced the most significant technological developments in their history. Formerly, reporters would use typewriters to type their stories on a piece of copy paper, which would then be corrected by a copy editor, who would assign its place on a page by drawing its location on a piece of paper called a dummy. A linotype operator would convert the stories into punched tape. That tape would be used to run the linotype machine, which turned out slugs of type, pieces of metal used to print one row of type one newspaper column wide. The machine would continue to produce slugs until stories were set in type. In the composing room, they would be assembled to make up pages according to the dummies. These would be locked into a metal form the size of a newspaper page and molds of heavy paper would be created called mats, which were used to cast, from molten metal, the stereotype plates. The half cylinder plates were put into a cylindrical printing press. Layout people used to have to work with strips of letters formed from molten lead to arrange stories on a page, laying them out and changing them as changes were made in the planned format of each day's paper. Today, computers handle most, if not all, of the pagination work.

Reporters no longer type stories on paper. Instead they are typed directly into a computer and seen on a video display terminal. As the reporter types, the letters appear on the screen. Editors also work with the keyboard and video display terminal to edit each story, and to set column width, length, typeface and headline. Once it is edited, the story does not have to be sent to a composing room to be typed again by a linotype operator. A button is pushed and the story is sent to be made into a photocopy, a printing plate, electronically. A very fast photocomposition machine prints the story in the selected sizes and styles of type and in the desired column widths. The text is produced on photographic paper, which is then pasted onto a sheet corresponding to a newspaper page. That is photographed with a large camera, resulting in a completed negative to be used to make an offset printing plate.

Reporters are finding that their computers can do some of their work for them. If the writer deletes a portion of a story, the computer rearranges the rest of the story on the page. The computer checks for spelling errors and even decides where to hyphenate words that must be carried over to the next line. In addition, laptop computers allow reporters to send stories from the scene directly to computers in the newsroom.

The next step is the sending of stories to newsroom computers through cellular telephones. Photographers already can send electronically digitized video pictures back to the newsroom for instant use.

The Newspaper of the Future

The current distribution system may eventually disappear, with the newspaper delivered to the home via something like today's fax machine and/or some form of computer-based, digital, electronic system. The cost of newsprint is becoming so great that newspapers are cutting back on page size and number of pages. Some traditional broadsheet newspapers are changing to tabloid size. Already, many readers are scanning the news on home computer video screens and perhaps printing hard copies of the stories they want to take with them. By electronic scans of the newspaper's products, the receiver of the material can pick and choose some of the items and in any length desired. In other words, electronic distribution could mean newspaper readers would not all get the same information, but would instead exercise their own control over content. There would no longer be the same mass-oriented newspaper for everyone on the circulation list.

News would become a specialized commodity, with readers grabbing from the screen only the stories of narrow interest to them leaving alone the other available news. Most Internet versions of daily newspapers are free or available for modest fees. Such in-home delivery systems can be marketed by promoting the potential for each reader to receive, in effect, an individualized newspaper. Readers can be promised the opportunity to select only those items unique to their tastes, reading levels, and special interests, including vocations or avocations. Newspaper publishers might find that they can reduce operating costs by determining the kinds of information readers want and don't want and then increasing the "in-demand" content and eliminating expenditures associated with the "no-demand" content. Digital technology also permits more interactivity and individual searching of archival information sources. In effect, readers can become their own editors. If more information is desired, additional searches can be undertaken. In addition, readers can set their own information-gathering agendas, exploring databases and areas that might not have been included in a hard-copy version of the newspaper. Readers do not have to be satisfied with the daily decisions made by editors and publishers. As long as information is in the system, readers can access it.

One early method of sending newspapers direct to the home was teletext, where pages of text were displayed on a television screen. The subscriber chose only those pages needed or desired. Another early attempt was videotex, where a home computer was used to access a large computer, thereby making available an extensive menu of news items because of the storage capacity of the large computer. Teletext and videotex did not catch on well with the public, even though media companies spent millions researching their cost effectiveness. Of course, such efforts paved the way for the more sophisticated and efficient delivery of electronic information via the Internet. Publishers who experimented with the early forms of electronic delivery learned that the cost of a special computer, added software costs, additional expenses for special terminals, the subscription price to the newspaper, and the telephone company fees all

combined to discourage consumers from choosing the electronic option. But now, with the Internet and increasing computer literacy among consumers, many media experts believe that the electronic delivery of the traditional newspaper soon might be the only economically viable way to survive.

Even if electronic newspapers do make it, some critics fear the loss of community and shared knowledge that might result from such individualized newspapers. The "Daily Me" syndrome might reduce socialization opportunities and give us less to talk about with our family, friends and co-workers. Critics also worry about menu-driven news and information, because it reduces the chances that people will be exposed to new things. If a person asks his or her computer to provide just the information and news that he/she thinks will be interesting, how will people find out about new things to be interested in? In addition, what about people who can't afford to speed along the information highway, have technophobia or simply choose not to spend hours each day in front of a computer screen? Will the proliferation of "Daily Me's" tend to create a society of information have's and have-not's? And what about government's role in ensuring relatively equal access to basic information? Will government have to take a more active role in regulating information content and access? Interesting questions and issues to ponder.

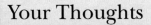

Your Thoughts

If you could design the newspaper of the future, what would you be sure to include? Why?

Do you think the "hardcopy" newspaper will survive much longer? Why or why not?

Revamping the "Gray Lady"

The severe advertising downturn in the newspaper industry was part of the reason that the venerable *Wall Street Journal* transformed itself a bit. A major redesign included the following elements:

1. A new-look, less-imposing front page
2. A new section, Personal Journal, featuring such consumer issues as travel, personal finance, health and safety
3. More color
4. More graphics
5. New segments
6. Teasers for inside pages on the front pages of sections

The publisher of *The Wall Street Journal* said he hoped the new format would bring in new, younger readers, especially women, and new advertisers. He planned to include more news about consumer electronics, up-scale retailing, health care and automobiles in his efforts to snag more 18-to-49-year-olds that advertisers covet. He needed to try something.

The amount of advertising in his paper dropped almost 40% in just one year in the early part of the 21st century.

Recent Research Developments and Issues

Ad revenues for the biggest newspaper groups have been declining for several years. Drops of between 5% and 10% per year have been common, with some newspaper groups losing even more. There are exceptions, of course, but most newspapers and most newspaper groups are not attracting the amount of ad revenue they need to maintain staffing levels and quality newsgathering. Deep staff cuts have been common.

Some good news for alternative newspapers. Readership was up 3% in 2007 compared to 2006. The top three alternative newspapers in reach (ranked by percentage of readership in an area) were the *Isthmus* in Madison, Wisconsin, the *Inlander* in Spokane, Washington, and the *Reader* in San Diego, California. All three newspapers reached a bit more than 35% of the adults in their areas.

Think Back

1. What were some of the major newspaper scandals in the early part of the new millennium and who were the reporters and editors involved?

2. How good is the current "health" of the newspaper industry? Why?

3. What are the differences and similarities between morning and afternoon newspapers?

4. What have been the major changes in the newspaper industry in the last several years?

5. What are the trends associated with ownership of newspapers?

6. How is the typical newspaper organized? What are its major departments?

7. List the various types of newspaper editors and describe what they do.

8. What are the different categories of newspapers?

9. What is the definition of news? What are the major aspects/elements of news?

10. Who are newspaper "gatekeepers" and what do they do?

11. What are the major press associations, wire services and syndicates?

12. What are the major steps in the newspaper production process?

13. What does the future look like for newspapers? How might new technology affect newspapers?

14. Why was *The Wall Street Journal* revamped and what were the major changes?

15. What's been happening to advertising revenues for newspaper groups lately?

16. What are the readership trends for alternative newspapers?

6

Magazines

Magazines best illustrate the fragmentation of American mass media markets. Magazines have a large audience, but that audience is scattered among thousands of specialized publications. Not only is the audience large, but it is growing faster than the population, unlike newspaper readership, which holds steady while the population increases.

Like books, magazines demand active participation. Although coffee table books can attract casual readers, magazine readers appear to be somewhat elite and specialized users in a fragmented market. Many Americans receive several magazines each week in the mail. Professional journals, religious periodicals, hobby magazines, newsweeklies, and entertainment magazines, among others, crowd the mailbox. Some of us engage in impulse buying at the supermarket or convenience store.

Research reports from the Magazine Publishers Association have indicated that one-third of American adults are heavy magazine users. They have been described in some of these studies as much more interested in their magazines than in watching television. They are college-educated professionals with above average incomes. These findings do not contradict the data that show that there are younger, heavy television watchers who read *Glamour* or *Cosmopolitan,* or even younger females, with no or low income, who read *Seventeen.*

Certain magazines have loyal readers with strong ties to their publications. *Popular Mechanics, Playboy, National Geographic,* and *Time* are among those whose subscriptions are consistently renewed. Maintaining subscriptions is crucial to magazine publishers, because buying a year of publications at once is a greater guarantee than dependence on spur of the moment newsstand sales.

Other studies indicate that almost 90% of American adults read an average 10 issues a month.

Although magazines are affordable to most people, the household income of the typical reader is above the national average. In general, the more education a person has, the greater his or her magazine consumption.

Magazines are our most diverse print medium. When television took hold in the 1950s, large circulation magazines had difficulty attracting advertisers, who instead began to buy time on television. Millions of viewers were reached at a cost per thousand viewers lower than for the big general interest magazines. The problem with magazines like *Coronet, Colliers, Look,* and *Saturday Evening Post,* among others, was that they attracted large and diverse audiences, as did television. As advertisers moved to television, magazines with circulation so great that their costs of operation needed high advertising rates to pay the bills were to die off because of their own success. They were too big to survive. The cover price of such magazines was not sufficient to cover the expenses of producing glossy, full-color publications. Distribution costs increased with larger readership and the most prominent magazines of the 1960s and 1970s were losing money with every issue that they sold, so they disappeared.

Advertisers and readers were instead attracted to special-interest magazines, those that could meet the diverse interests of Americans—hobbies, various recreational pursuits, entertainment, religion, cultural and ethnic issues, business and economic concerns, home and garden, lifestyle and fashion. Few specialized magazines were truly impacted by television.

The word magazine originally meant storehouse, borrowed from a French word for store. The word is still used to indicate the cartridge chamber of a gun or the closet or shed where explosives are kept. A similar word was used also in the Middle East to indicate a storehouse or repository for merchants. It figures that once publications came about containing a varied collection of items that they would be called magazines. Today's magazine is a publication that serves as a repository of information, entertainment and advertising. It houses poetry, fiction, photographs, commentary, advice, humor, etc., in a compendium of articles, stories and essays in one printed receptacle.

The most significant feature of the typical magazine today is its specialized content. In fact, there is no typical magazine. The extraordinary variety of specialties demonstrates that each magazine stores material appealing to the interests of a specific segment of society. There are about 15,000 magazines in the United States, but they have little in common with each other. The one characteristic they share is regular publication. It is difficult to determine what is or is not a magazine. The definitional problem makes it virtually impossible to count the number of magazines in the country. The usual estimate of 15,000 has come from various guesses by scholars, publishers, and advertisers who try to account for newsletters, house organs, reviews, journals, and many other difficult-to-label publications in their broad definition.

Is the *Daily Racing Form* a newspaper or magazine? Is the *National Enquirer* a newspaper or magazine? What about the *Wall Street Journal*? Each looks like a newspaper. Each carries news items, although for the *National Enquirer* and its imitators, their frivolous, frothy fluff and attention to celebrities would take them out of the newspaper category. The sleazy, supermarket tabloids are then nearly always defined as magazines, even with a format that looks like a newspaper. The *Daily Racing Form* not only looks like a newspaper but carries news stories and is published just as frequently as a newspaper. However, its content, unlike that of a newspaper, is severely specialized. The *Wall Street Journal* is also a specialized medium, a characteristic of magazines, but carries some general news items as well as news of interest to its specialized, targeted audience. Since they bill themselves as newspapers they are seldom included in the magazine category. But the need to question where they fit demonstrates the ongoing difficulty in first defining what is a magazine and then trying to get an accurate count of such publications.

Various sources have estimated the number of magazines published in the United States at anywhere from 10,000 to 20,000, with the great variation in the range resulting from how a magazine is defined. Small company magazines, for example,

don't always get included in some tabulations. That type of publication is regarded by some observers as too much like a trade, technical or professional journal, a separate category to some. Some newsletters are not regarded as magazines in directories of publications. Others say newsletters and other public relations vehicles fit their definition. Also, some such publications don't last long enough to make a directory listing before being replaced with another, possibly short-lived, publication. The 15,000 figure is arrived at by assuming the fluid nature of such ventures and by defining magazines as bound publications of eight or more pages issued on a regular basis. Magazines are published quarterly, bimonthly, monthly, biweekly or weekly, perhaps even occasionally.

A magazine is most likely to be narrow in both content and audience. The history of the magazine is a history of specialization, although the emergence of television made the specialization even more necessary. The general interest magazines that existed before television had to redefine their content and their audience or face extinction. Magazines with large circulations could not deliver the numbers that television could. Advertisers could get many millions of viewers at a much lower cost than what they paid to get a few million readers. The magazine industry was altered greatly by television. Thousands of narrow interest magazines were not affected, but the few national magazines that had been flourishing before the 1950s found themselves in distress. *Coronet, Life, Look, Literary Digest, Collier's, American* and other mass circulation magazines ceased operations. Some later came back in modified form and made no attempt to attract TV-sized audiences. The problem was that their national circulations were in the four to six million range when network television shows were reaching 20 million households.

Magazine production and distribution costs were so great that their publishers could not reduce their advertising rates to meet or beat the competition from television. A full-page ad in a general circulation magazine cost the same as a commercial on network TV. Throughout the 1950s and into the 1960s, advertisers demonstrated a preference for television for national advertising. As advertising fell off, publishers tried to economize. They spent less on production, partly because postal rates went up at the same time that advertisers were taking their money elsewhere. The magazines grew thinner as they lost advertisers and kept their 60/40 ratio of advertising to editorial content and their quality dropped as they made cutbacks. Circulations began dropping as readers became dissatisfied with the changes.

The end result was more magazines, but each with fewer readers. Readers were willing to buy the magazines for specialized information on topics of strong personal interest. From the 1960s on, there was a proliferation of small circulation magazines in an increasingly segmented readership. There is a specialized magazine for every hobby, profession, or inclination. There are several different specialty publications dealing with each of the several kinds of motorcycles, or motorcycle activities. People who have tattoos on their bodies have choices among the magazines devoted to the tattoo as an art form, or as a political or social statement. Magazines are devoted to differing aspects of gardening, to thoroughbred horse racing, to quilt making, and how to pick numbers in state lotteries. Recent years have seen an increase in the numbers of magazines filled with information for users of computers.

Advertisers seek out specialty magazines because they reach specifically targeted groups of consumers of their products. The manufacturer of a new type of bridle or bit suitable only for race horses would have no interest in buying space in newspapers or time on national radio or television because so few members of those audiences will be interested. The device must be brought to the attention of the individuals who would buy something like that. Instead of an expensive outlay in major media reaching large numbers of people not likely to use the product, the advertiser spends less on small magazines whose readers are expert trainers of race horses in need of the bridle or bit.

Narrowly focused magazines make profits by not competing with television for advertising income. Magazines are at a disadvantage compared with television when they attempt to increase readership. Television can increase the numbers of viewers without an increase in costs of production. Magazines find that their costs for labor, materials, printing, and certainly delivery increase greatly as the circulation goes up. A relatively small circulation keeps costs of operation down, but successful specialty magazines circulate among a large enough segment of the targeted consumers to attract advertisers. Many advertisers are willing to pay the relatively high advertising rates charged by specialty magazines, because

advertisers know that most readers of such publications are likely buyers.

As the specialized magazines found prosperity, and as more of them began to appear, general circulation magazines sought methods of overcoming the impact of television. Their first effort was a failure and resulted in the deaths of some of the best-known magazines. It was the ill-fated competitive drive for added circulation engaged in by the largest magazines that doomed them. Trying to build circulation, they offered long-range subscriptions to readers well below normal subscription costs. This reduced initial revenue but drove up production and distribution costs. Advertising rates went up because they were pegged to audited circulation figures. As magazines closed their doors because of the ruin brought by trying to build circulation, the remaining general interest magazines looked for alternatives. The obvious possibility was cutting circulation. Some went so far as to tell subscribers they didn't want them anymore. During the 1960s, some subscribers received letters telling them they no longer fit the profiles of the kinds of readers desired by a magazine. This did have the effect of reducing costs, but it was a public relations disaster for the magazine industry generally.

Those who survived did so by adjusting in ways that would not only cut operating expenses, but also help them identify demographic characteristics of their readers. They began to gather data and analyze subscribers' activities and interests in terms of advertisers' needs. Socio-economic indicators from information about subscribers helped the magazine publishers to identify for their advertisers where specific sales messages should be placed to reach the targeted consumer. One technique employed by many magazines, especially those already somewhat specialized, was the regional edition. The *Wall Street Journal* had already been publishing four regional editions and a national edition. The editorial content was the same in each, but banks and other financial institutions could buy space at a fairly inexpensive rate in an edition reaching the geographic area where their customers lived. A nationally-circulated publication would have cost such advertisers more and would have delivered too many readers outside their region and not at all likely to be customers.

Several magazines began to allow advertisers to avoid buying the entire national circulation and instead substitute ads for a local or regional audience at a lower rate. This effort was primarily successful for the newsmagazines because of their already special orientation. They had always offered an identifiable type of reader, one with some degree of affluence and a fairly high educational level. Advertisers have always been eager to reach consumers who display an interest in news, so these regional editions had a built-in success factor when local advertisers responded to the lower ad rates. The biggest problem for most publishers with producing regional editions was the added expense of expanding the sales force. Extra sales costs could eventually mean a diminishing return even with the added revenue from regional editions. By the 1970s, the general interest magazines still in existence had been downsized or retrenched as the industry moved away from the national publication of universal interest to more specialized magazines. *Life* magazine, one of the last great universal/general interest magazines, ceased regular monthly publication in May, 2000. Time, Inc. announced that it hopes to put out occasional issues for special events. In its place, Time, Inc. planned to launch at least three, new specialized magazines— *Real Simple* for women, *eCompany Now*, a technology and business publication, and a large print edition of *Time*.

An example of how narrowly based a magazine can be is *ACE Fitness Matters*, a publication for physical fitness professionals. It was introduced in 1995 by the American Council on Exercise, a non-profit organization, as an alternative to magazines like *Muscle and Fitness, Men's Fitness, Flex,* and *Shape. ACE Fitness Matters* was available by mail order only and came in a loose-leaf format, the better for subscribers to read and keep sections that they might want to file in a collection of health and fitness information. *ACE Fitness Matters* started with a subscription list of 30,000 fitness instructors certified by the American Council on Exercise.

The Magazine Industry

Magazines have many characteristics in common with newspapers, but differ initially in that everything in an issue of a magazine, including the advertising, is expected to appeal to every reader. Newspapers, on the other hand, have so many varied items that a typical reader picks and chooses a few from among the total. The newspaper is primarily news with just a small portion of entertainment, including comic strips, crossword puzzles and horoscopes. The general interest magazine offers more entertainment, usually from 20 to 30 percent fiction. Unlike newspapers, magazines often exhibit a personality, usually a reflection of its editor or publisher. Hugh Hefner and *Playboy* are viewed as indistinguishable. There is no denying that *The New Yorker* demonstrates the biases of its staff. Its personality is obvious, as is that of *MAD* magazine.

A magazine is published less frequently than a newspaper, although there are weekly newspapers and weekly magazines. Magazines are packaged and presented differently from newspapers. Typically, the format is different, with the magazine bound rather than folded. The magazine usually has a cover and is on better-quality paper. Magazines are intended for a more leisurely readership, with less concern for immediate events and more attention to interpretation and for a broader view. More than anything, the content reveals the difference. Readers buy magazines for specialized, segmented topics not available generally in the other media.

The initial start-up costs for a magazine are relatively modest, making it fairly easy to get into magazine publishing. Because publishers don't own their own production and printing equipment the big expenses of operation don't come until later. Maintaining publication eventually becomes quite costly. From 300 to 400 new magazines are launched each year. About 10% of them will be successful, usually only the ones produced by firms already publishing established magazines. Anyone engaging in an initial magazine venture must expect to lose money until the necessary advertising and circulation contacts can be established and maintained.

The number of magazines Americans buy each year stays about the same, but publishers are charging more each year. As costs to the consumers go up, circulation in general does not change.

The frequency of publication of magazines has stayed virtually the same for decades. About 20% come out once a week, 7% every two weeks, 42 percent once a month, 11% every two months, and 13% are quarterlies.

The most widely read magazines in the United States are *AARP, The Magazine, Reader's Digest, TV Guide, Better Homes and Gardens,* and *National Geographic. AARP, The Magazine* is a specialized publication in that it is targeted for retired persons. Its circulation is certain to keep increasing because it is read by one of the fastest growing age groups in the country—people over the age of 50. Any magazine aimed at the special needs and interests of the rapidly increasing membership of the American Association of Retired Persons is bound to grow in both circulation and advertising revenue.

Reader's Digest is the largest circulating magazine in the world. It sells millions of copies overseas. At first glance it appears to defy the common logic that a magazine cannot have broad content and serve a broad audience and still take in enough advertising income to overcome production and distribution costs. However, it does have a narrow audience and one that gets ever more narrow as it gets even older and even more conservative. The content too can be thought of as somewhat narrow, because the publisher conducts frequent surveys of its older, conservative readership to determine their interests and assess any possible changes in those interests. *Reader's Digest* also keeps its production costs down by avoiding the "slick" look of other magazines by using cheaper paper stock and less expensive printing and binding techniques. The publisher also, partly because of reprints, has less invested in the content than other publishers, further reducing the overhead.

TV Guide is obviously specialized in content but has a very general audience. However, *TV Guide* actually has more than 100 separate local audiences and serves as the ultimate in regional editions. *TV Guide* offers low ad rates for local advertisers eager to appear in what looks to be a national publication. Only two or three articles appear nationally. The rest is an index of programming for a local television market.

National Geographic is among a few magazines that keep costs down by publishing as arms of nonprofit educational foundations. *Smithsonian* and *Natural History* are others of this type. They get tax and mailing rate advantages that cut publishing costs. *National Geographic* has an advantage resulting from its high renewal rate for subscribers. The renewal rate for *National Geographic* is 86 percent, well ahead of any other publication. Maintaining subscribers is important to a publisher because it demonstrates longevity and staying power. Subscribers sign up for a year at a time. Also, Americans everywhere demonstrate the popularity of *National*

Geographic by refusing to throw it away as they do other magazines after reading them. It is believed that thousands of Americans maintain stacks of *National Geographic* issues that have been saved for 20 to 30 years.

General-interest consumer magazines still account for a large share of total magazine circulation despite the large number of specialized magazines. Others with large circulations, mostly from four to eight million, include *Better Homes and Gardens, Family Circle, Good Housekeeping, Ladies' Home Journal,* and *Woman's Day.* Some of these so-called family magazines depend on sales at newsstands and grocery store checkout counters. This has the advantage of avoiding postal costs, which can be considerable. Others ccept the high postal rates to get the security of annual subscription payments made in advance.

Revenues from magazine advertising and circulation approach $120 billion a year, two thirds of that generated by consumer magazines. Compared to the number of specialized magazines, there aren't many general circulation magazines, but their national distribution gives them great prominence and a large circulation. For a general circulation magazine to make a profit it must contain two-thirds advertising. When its issues are approaching only half advertising, a magazine is approaching failure.

The money that comes in from subscriptions and from advertisers is spent primarily on circulation and production costs. Nearly 70 percent of the revenue dollar goes to circulation costs and the expenses of manufacturing and distribution. Administrative and related expenses, including promotional efforts, account for 15 percent or more. Editorial costs range from 10 to 15 percent, but usually closer to 10. That leaves a profit of from three to six percent, although that figure and the others can vary quite a bit. Two-thirds of magazine sales are through mailed subscriptions. As noted earlier, about half of the total earnings of consumer magazines come from advertising and the other half from newsstand sales and subscriptions.

The amount of advertising carried in each issue is seasonal. For example, after Christmas shopping season is over, advertisers cut back on spending.

Circulation figures are obviously measurable, but readership is another matter. Circulation is the number of copies sold at the newsstand or through subscriptions. Readership is determined by figuring in

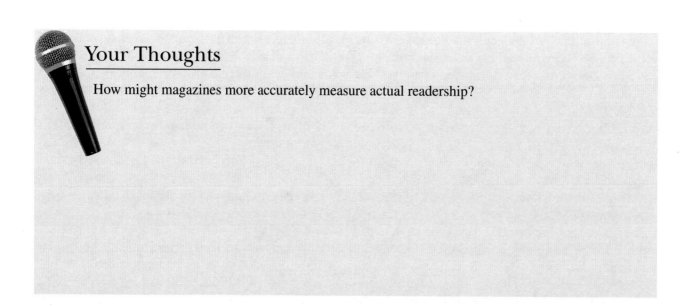
the pass-along factor. The number of people who read at least part of a magazine is greater than the number who purchase magazines. Several members of a household read each issue, or at least are exposed to some of its content. Waiting rooms in many office buildings, especially those for doctors and dentists, increase the available audience considerably. This extra exposure for the typical issue of any magazine, especially national general interest magazines, is far greater than it is for broadcasting or for newspapers and books. Advertising is sold in magazines on estimated readership, as a result, not simply on circulation figures.

Advertisers use data from the Audit Bureau of Circulation to help them determine which magazines are better at reaching the audiences they want. Circulation figures for magazines are verified by the ABC, which publishes them for the convenience of both publishers and advertisers.

Types of Magazines

There are many ways to categorize magazines. Consumer or general interest is one way discussed already in this chapter. Specialized publications could be broken down into groups of specialties, probably to include sports, farm, business, music, photography, health, and many, many others. Another way is to suggest only two categories: entertainment and news/opinion. Another method is to use the source of the publication to develop categories. That

way you get academic and scholarly journals, business and trade journals, non-profit publications, public relations or company publications, among others.

Perhaps the easiest method is to look at two general categories that can be further broken down into identifiable types within each. One has to start with consumer or general interest magazines. Another category could be trade, technical and professional journals, which would include company publications.

Consumer magazines are the ones earning the most money from both advertising income and sales through newsstands or subscriptions. They are marketed generally and each is generally greatly different from the others.

Trade, technical and professional journals are intended for specific careers, industries, businesses, trades or professions and are read by individuals in those fields. Some of these are delivered free and are supported by advertising or by the public relations arm of a business or industry. They can cover a broad range of publications and include many interests, but each is likely to be targeted at leaders in a given profession or calling.

Types of consumer magazines could include newsmagazines, opinion magazines, men's interest and women's interest magazines, sex magazines, city magazines and quality magazines. Sports could fit under men's interest or could be a separate type. What are referred to as farm magazines are difficult to categorize. They seem like part of the business or trade press but have some aspects of general interest publications.

Generally included under trade, technical and professional journals are the following: trade journals, business magazines, sponsored publications, and academic or scholarly journals.

News Magazines

The acknowledged leader of the newsweeklies is *TIME*, with a circulation of nearly four million. *TIME* was founded by Henry Luce in 1923 as an information vehicle, but presented a dose of entertainment in its approach to the news. Its structure was such that rarely would a news story be the work of one reporter or writer. News is assembled by teams of correspondents and editors and is filtered by a final rewrite. Because of pass-along readership, *TIME* is expected to have more than 20 million American readers each week and probably another 10 million overseas readers. *Newsweek* and *U.S. News & World Report* have circulations of nearly two and one-half million. *U.S. News & World Report* tends to have a stronger business news orientation than the other two, and it has fewer, but longer in-depth articles, usually about economic news. All three tend to be influential because of the type of readers they attract. They are thought of, along with newspapers like the *New York Times* and *Wall Street Journal*, as important sources of information for people of influence. The best predictor of newsmagazine readership is education, with well-educated males more likely than anyone else to read *TIME, Newsweek* and *U.S. News & World Report.*

Opinion Magazines

These range from the liberal *New Republic* to the conservative *National Review*. One of the oldest and most respected of these is *The Nation,* founded by E.L. Godkin just after the Civil War. *The Nation* was the prototype for magazines of today that seek reform by offering critical voices on political and social issues. Some of them have done investigations into corruption in business and government. A significant opinion magazine of the 1920s and 1930s was the *American Mercury* of George Jean Nathan and H. L. Mencken. It was highly readable and showcased the cantankerous Mencken, who railed against middle class values and set a standard for opinion writing. Another significant publication no longer with us was *The Reporter*, which went out of

business while it had the highest circulation of any other opinion magazine. It was a liberal magazine, but was anti-communist during the 1950s and 1960s and never moved further to the left when other liberal magazines did. It was losing so much money that it folded in 1968 despite being the circulation leader among its type.

Opinion magazines and their cousins, the quality magazines, have high subscription rates. They get little advertising revenue, much of that from book publishers. They typically contain only 32 pages of letters to the editor, articles, editorials and reviews of books and plays. Most of the articles are written by university professors and moonlighting newspaper people. The editorials are about the only content written by the staff. Most have circulations of 40,000 to 50,000, a few higher and a few lower.

Among the liberal opinion magazines *The Nation* has been notable for devoting full issues to what its editors considered abuses in the FBI, CIA and the military, as well as attacks on the Reagan and Bush administrations. The *New Republic* is strongly liberal but not as strident as others. Its early history was filled with writings from the nation's most famous journalists, including Walter Lippmann, who served as an editor in the 1920s.

Another venerable opinion magazine is *The Progressive*, founded in 1909 by Senator Robert M. LaFollette as a voice of the midwestern progressive movement. In 1969, it devoted a complete issue to "The Power of the Pentagon." It was so well-received that the issue had to go to three printings even though the first press run was for twice the usual number. It was such a significant piece that the Viking Press then reproduced it in book form.

In 1979, *The Progressive* was taken to court by the Pentagon because of an article thought to provide details on how to assemble a thermonuclear bomb. The government sought an injunction in federal court to stop the magazine from publishing the article. The magazine's publisher said the information was from public sources and its publication would provide Americans with the information necessary to make an informed decision on nuclear issues. The government argued that national security was at stake and censorship was justified in this instance because such knowledge in the wrong hands presented immediate, direct and irreparable harm to the people of the United States. A federal judge agreed with the Pentagon that it was not a violation of freedom of the press to restrict publication when the public did not need to know technical details about hydrogen bomb construction to carry on a public debate.

The judge granted the injunction by saying that *The Progressive* article could help some other nations move faster in developing a hydrogen bomb. The editors of *The Progressive* vowed to appeal the injunction all the way to the Supreme Court on Constitutional grounds. The confrontation between the press and government in the Supreme Court was averted when the government had to withdraw its suit because a newspaper published a story containing much of the same information and the legal issue became moot. A blatant case of censorship that fizzled out before it could be heard by the Supreme Court gave the magazine more prominence than any opinion magazine before or since.

The most influential of the conservative opinion magazines is the *National Review*, founded in 1955 by William F. Buckley, Jr. It carries more advertising than other opinion magazines and has one of the largest circulations of its type. It is much better written than other opinion magazines and uses high quality paper stock and better production than others, including original art and full color on the cover.

Other conservative opinion magazines include *Conservative Digest,* a monthly publication, and *Commentary*, also a monthly. A quarterly called *The Public Interest* also offers conservative opinion, as does a tabloid weekly, *Human Events*.

Similar publications also referred to often as quality magazines are *Smithsonian, Harper's* and *Atlantic Monthly.*

Men's Interest Magazines

There is an overlap between sex magazines and sports magazines and the traditional publication aimed at male readers. An early publication of this type was the *Police Gazette,* filled with stories from police blotters and of sporting events. Also in the first half of this century, *True Detective* and several other detective-oriented magazines, often based on true crime accounts, targeted male readers. The diversity in men's interests was demonstrated early on and still is by the success of *Popular Mechanics, Sport, Sports Afield, Field and Stream,* and *Argosy. Esquire* was created for the more sophisticated male, with excellent articles and fictions complemented by illustrations that featured attractive women. Both sex-oriented magazines and sports magazines have proliferated and become more and more specialized.

Leading the way for growth in publishing sex-oriented magazines was Hugh Hefner's *Playboy,* founded in 1953 with a small capital investment. Its phenomenal success has resulted in many imitators, with all of them attempting to exploit the female body even more than Hefner did. None has matched the success of *Playboy*, but none employed some of the most famous writers in the country to do articles and fiction as Hefner did.

One major reason for Hefner's success is the advertising policy that rejects ads for products that are considered sleazy or bizarre and rejects ad copy that is too sexy. The effort is to integrate editorial content and advertising so that subscribers will be as interested in the ads as in the articles and other features. Advertisers like the idea that their material will be of interest to the audience for the publication. *Penthouse, Hustler, Gent* and *Dude* have never been able to match the formula nor the success of *Playboy*. A part of *Playboy's* appeal is an emphasis on men's fashions, a feature that draws advertising from clothing manufacturers. Fashion for men has become the theme in some newer magazines. *Gentleman's Quarterly* and similar publications have caught on in recent years.

Sports is viewed as a male preoccupation and magazines to meet that interest have included *Outdoor Life* as one type and *The Sporting News* as another. *Outdoor Life* stresses conservation as well as hunting and fishing. *The Sporting News* is one of the oldest magazines and for decades was a baseball-only magazine in a tabloid format. It looks much like a newspaper, but is now a statistic-packed record of all major sports. Currently, the major publication for sports enthusiasts is *Sports Illustrated*, a Time, Inc. publication that has been marketed quite successfully. It is a slick, excellently produced weekly that avoids reporting on games or contests and instead offers features and background on behind-the-scenes events or personality profiles of athletes or sports celebrities, especially when there is controversy. *Sports Illustrated* makes news in all of the media once a year when attention is given to its biggest selling issue—the annual swim-suit edition.

Women's Interest Magazines

The typical magazine reader is most likely to be a female, mature, well-educated, and in a household with a well-above-average income. Magazines compete for women readers. Surveys and subscription lists show that women tend to read magazines more than men do. One clear indicator is that magazines that appeal primarily to women far outsell those that appeal primarily to men. Men are more likely, according to the data, to read magazines devoted to sports, mechanics and science, and information about business and finance. Men also are more likely to read the newsmagazines. Women are more likely to read magazines about health, fashion, beauty, glamour, child care, gardening, home decor, and related household information. In all, women are the single most important target audience for magazines and their advertisers.

As early as 1830, a magazine for women, Godey's *Lady's Book*, was part of the first period of magazine expansion. It reached a circulation of 150,000 by the 1850s and was rivaled eventually by *Peterson's*, founded in 1842 to offer women hand-colored engravings of fashions and fiction stories. By the 1880s and 1890s, many women's magazines appeared, helped largely by the cheap postage rates adopted in 1879. Some of the most successful women's magazines of the 20th century were founded in the years just before 1900. Cyrus H.K. Curtis founded the *Ladies' Home Journal* in 1883, and it became the number one publication for women immediately. Not until *McCall's* topped its circulation in the late 1950s did *Ladies' Home Journal* lose its dominance. Competing with these two was *Women's Home Companion*, which carried advice columns and articles on health, fashion, home decorating and child rearing.

In the last half of the 20th century, six women's magazines were consistently among the top 10 circulation leaders. They were *McCall's, Ladies' Home Journal, Better Homes and Gardens, Family Circle, Woman's Day,* and *Good Housekeeping*. Competing with the big six were *Redbook* and *Cosmopolitan*. *Redbook*, like *Woman's Day* and *Ladies' Home Journal*, sold well when positioned at the checkout in the supermarkets. *Redbook* is marketed for the middle-class homemaker. *Cosmopolitan*, however, targets young, single women. Its nearly readers are between 18 and 34, career oriented, and interested in romance. *Cosmopolitan* and the fashion-oriented magazines, *Vogue, Glamour,* and *Mademoiselle*, by the 1980s and 1990s had bitten into the advertising revenue of the long-term circulation leaders among women's magazines. Also gaining strength were magazines targeting the liberated woman. The first of these was *MS*, but *Savvy, Self* and *New Woman* quickly followed. A fur-ther segmentation is seen in *Essence*, aimed at professional African-American women.

Humor Magazines

The first magazine to be noted for its humor and cartoons, especially political satire, was *Puck*, founded in 1877. Judge, founded in 1881, and *Life*, in 1883, were early publications dependent on colorful cartoons. This was not the same *LIFE* as the picture magazine that was so popular in the middle of the 20th century. Humor with a social conscience was the approach taken by both *Puck* and *Life*. *Puck* was initially a Democratic Party organ with its humorous barbs aimed at Republicans. Also among early humor magazines were several on college campuses, beginning with *The Harvard Lampoon* in 1876. *The Harvard Lampoon* built a reputation with its annual issues parodying other publications. By the 1950s, many of the campus humor magazines began to fade away, with almost all disappearing by 1996. College students seemed to find their comic relief in movies, on television, and in *MAD* magazine. *MAD* was founded in 1952, designed for teens and pre-teens and primarily appeals to males. *MAD* has been unique because it did not accept advertising and did not advertise itself. *MAD* is noted for mocking traditional social and political values, and especially for its parodies of advertisements.

For an older audience, *The National Lampoon* parodies social institutions, with its satire directed at the media among its funniest offerings. *The National Lampoon* was founded by some former editors of *The Harvard Lampoon*. One of the newest and most successful is *SPY*, which makes use of cartoon-style artwork to support its humorous commentary.

City Magazines

The first of the breed was *San Diego Magazine*, founded in 1948 by Edwin Self as a rather somewhat irreverent melding of culture and commentary. In 1977, Self and his co-publisher and co-editor, Gloria Self, his wife, were honored at the Annual City Magazine Conference for originating the first independent city magazine in the United States. Other cities had publishers emulating San Diego Magazine by the 1960s, including Los Angeles, Cleveland, Philadelphia and San Francisco. *San Diego Magazine* has always had a solid journalism foundation, exploring local issues in depth, but it is also known for its attention to the glitter and glamour of San Diego and La Jolla social life. Its most prosperous citizens are photographed at benefits and other charitable events for the moneyed and their pictures are jammed into the back of the publication near the reviews for all of the expensive and trendy restaurants whose advertisements fill several pages.

Popular features, in addition to articles and essays on local cultural events, include lists of San Diego's most eligible bachelors and a rundown on the city's most successful lawyers. Readers are surveyed and the results reported in the magazine's description of the best restaurants in the area in each of several categories. San Diegans to watch in the new year is one of its most notable annual features. Self said he started the publication with inspiration from sophisticated and literate magazines like *The New Yorker, Atlantic Monthly* and *Saturday Review*. Not until 1948 did we see the first city magazine, but within 45 years there were more than 100 publishers across the country following Self's lead.

The typical city magazine attempts to critique local politics and the local social scene, especially entertainment and restaurants. In the 1980s, a new form blossomed with the development of business city magazines, including the *San Diego Business Journal*, among others. Some city and regional magazines concentrate on in-depth reporting, such as *Texas Monthly*, which has some national circulation. Other publications in the state of Texas include *San Antonio Monthly, Houston City,* and in Dallas-Fort Worth, one simply called *D.*

The best known of the city magazines is *New York*, which is never to be confused with *The New Yorker*, a national magazine rather than a city magazine. Even though clearly a city magazine, *New York* sells many copies outside the city. It is known for its role in developing the "new journalism" of the 1960s, a type of feature writing that blends fact and fiction. *New York* was created by the staff of the defunct *New York Herald-Tribune* to concentrate on life in Manhattan and problems facing its residents. It is sophisticated and tends to appeal to intellectuals, a social and political elite, and those heavily involved in the city's cultural events.

Celebrities and the glamorous are the centerpieces of *Los Angeles* magazine, one of the strongest financially of this type. Film and television executives and performers are given heavy coverage in each issue. Reader surveys on life-style issues are regular features. A lot of photographs, humor columns, and light news items are complemented by occasional substantive and incisive journalism. *Los Angeles* magazine readers are college-educated, prosperous, urban professionals, who like to travel and dine out, a demographic profile that appeals to advertisers.

The success of this relatively new phenomenon in magazine publishing is credited to the upscale audience delivered by these publications. Merchandisers of many services and products—fashions, entertainment and restaurants—find the well-heeled and well-educated readers to be ideal targets for anything marketed to an elite audience. As a result, such magazines attempt to establish strong local identities, strive for good editorial matter, get readers involved through surveys, and emphasize high-quality graphics.

Business Magazines

In the trade, technical and professional category, the most familiar to the general public would be business magazines. The biggest and most likely to have a broad-based coverage of this type would be *Forbes, Fortune, Business Week, Money,* and *Barron's*. Others include *Nation's Business*, published by the United States Chamber of Commerce, and Dun's *Business Month.*

Forbes is an aggressive voice for the capitalist system. *Fortune* is a bi-weekly appealing to the most literate of the nation's business leaders. *Business Week* is a strongly news-oriented weekly with an appeal to the younger business people. *Nation's Business* covers the nation's capital and interprets government actions and their impact on the business climate. *Money* offers advice on the ups and downs of the stock market and it carries informative material of value to the small investor. In addition to the nationally-published magazines of this type there are also regional and city magazines devoted to business. The city and regional magazines are produced by smaller local publishing firms or by chambers of commerce. Examples include *Kansas Business News, Northwest Investment Review,* and *Mid-South Business*, among others.

Most of the revenue for business magazines comes from advertising, sometimes as high as 90 percent. Subscriptions are rare. Some of them have controlled circulations, which is non-paid circulation. This works because it gives advertisers what they need—a large number of people in a specific field or industry reading their messages.

Trade Journals

Some business-oriented publications are so specialized that they concentrate on a specific product or service. Hundreds of journals aimed at a particular trade or industry include *The American Brewer, Modern Packaging, Sales Management, Data Communications, Modern Machine Shop, Publishers Weekly, Progressive Grocer, Supermarket News,* and *Convenience Store News.* These are sometimes called "professional journals" or "business publications," but such titles do not adequately convey the variety of such "horizontal" publications.

They are "horizontal" because they spread across all companies and related firms in a given industry, as opposed to a "vertical" publication dealing with a single company. Trade magazines are profit makers, carrying a lot of advertising. Some of the ads are institutional (self-promotion by the companies touting themselves to their peers) and others are from suppliers to the particular industry. It has been said that many trade journals are read for their ads. Trade journals are rarely sold at newsstands or by the single copy. They are sold by subscription. The average circulation for a trade journal is about 50,000.

Some of the newest trade journals focused on high technology and electronics. *Byte, Computer World, Wired, PC Magazine, PC Computing,* and *Windows Magazine* are examples. With the increasing popularity of electronic communication came the growth of magazines like Internet World and Net Guide. All of these are filled with advertisements from the manufacturers of both hardware and software.

Company Publications

Unlike trade journals, these vertical magazines are not published for profit, but are produced for public relations purposes. They are often thought of as much like the business or trade magazines, but differ in that they are usually management's effort to communicate with employees and afford employees an opportunity to communicate with each other. They are often referred to as "house organs," although some of their publishers tend to call them "organizational publications." Their publishers are public relations staff members of corporations, businesses, industries, labor unions, government agencies and educational institutions. They range from slickly produced, high-quality publications like *Arizona Highways* to unimpressive, inexpensively printed newsletters or bulletins.

Typically, they contain news and features about activities within the firm or among its employees. They are basically informative, although persuasion is part of the mix because of the internal public relations. Often they go also to stockholders or customers, so external public relations dictates content as well. There are probably up to 9,000 such publications with a total circulation of 200 million, but such figures are estimates because of the difficulty of keeping track across so many firms of varying sizes and complexity. Some companies produce several magazines. A major nation-wide manufacturer might have at least one, maybe more, publications in each of its plants in addition to a major magazine published at the headquarters and distributed to all of the plants. There could be separate publications in a given company for different types of employees. There could be one magazine for upper management, one for middle management, and another for those on the assembly line.

Many companies attempt to keep an active public relations effort by hiring experienced journalists to produce articles on safety, working conditions, pension benefits, investments and recreation that employees might have difficulty finding anywhere else. Probably half or more of the magazines in the country are produced by public relations practitioners. It is estimated that 15,000 people work on company magazines, most of them journalism graduates with prior experience in newspapering or magazine production. Some of these company magazines are often referred to as "sponsored publications." They include those aimed at customers or the external audiences for a trade or industry. University alumni magazines, in-flight magazines, and others that carry some advertising seem to be a special brand of company magazine. Other examples include publications like *American Legion* and *Elks.* The in-flight magazines by appearance and content are much like general circulation magazines. They carry more than the expected travel articles. They have cartoons, crossword puzzles, advice columns, essays and even some occasional fiction. Some of the articles are about social, political and economic issues that are certain to keep the passenger occupied during flight.

Newsletters

Some of the most expensive publications, with subscription costs of as much as $500, are newsletters, which are typically offered as expert advice or opinions. Most editorialize and forecast. Individuals viewed as authorities in specific areas of expertise can charge readers a lot of money to share that expertise. Many such newsletters deal with investing, new technology, or a particular political posture. A newsletter with a $500 a year subscription cost is the *Lundberg Letter*, which reports news of the oil industry and keeps track of trends related to gasoline prices. One of the earliest and most prestigious is the *Kiplinger Report*, a collection of items on personal finance and small business activities that often strays into interesting items far afield from money matters.

Academic Publications

Some professional journals are devoted to reports of research conducted within a field of study. *The New England Journal of Medicine, Psychological Abstracts, Public Opinion Quarterly, Veterinary Practice Management,* and *The Journal of Applied Psychology* are among several publications read by professionals in certain fields who want to learn more about their art, craft or calling. Some are published by universities. Others are published by professional organizations, such as the American Bar Association or The Society of Professional Journalists. An example is *American Medical News,* which is published by the American Medical Association for its members. Technical and professional people can keep up with changing practices and standards through the research reported in such journals. An unusual scholarly journal is a British publication, *Nature*, which blends highly technical scientific research reports with essays on ethical and economic concerns for scientists.

The Business Side of Magazines

The business operation starts with the solicitation of advertising and the acquisition of subscribers. Magazine sales staffs seek out potential advertisers whose interests coincide with those of the readership. They target their content and style to attract specific readers in previously determined demographic profiles. That way the magazines can attract the advertisers seeking readers with already known interests.

For a start-up publication, a business plan is needed that describes the direction the magazine is headed by outlining all of the previously completed market research and the data gathered on potential readership. A staff is hired and contracts are let for production and printing, as well as distribution and circulation. Subscribers can be acquired by buying all or a portion of another magazine's subscription list. This is expensive, but if it brings a response from 12% to 15%, it will pay off. Another technique to acquire new subscribers, even for established magazines, is to purchase ads in other magazines.

To keep advertisers happy and to provide them enough service to keep them from deserting magazines for other media, many magazines offer regional editions. In this way, an advertiser can further target the message by buying space in copies of the issue that go only to certain areas of the country. An example would be an ad for an anti-freeze that would appear in copies in northern parts of the country but not in the warmer areas like Florida or Southern California. Another attractive inducement for advertisers is the split run, which results in helpful information to the advertiser about the effectiveness of specific ads. It is done by running two different ads in a single issue and using something like coupon returns to determine reader response.

The biggest problems for both new and established magazines are the constantly increasing costs of paper and postage. A shortage of wood pulp for making paper has caused some observers to predict a dim future for the magazine business. New technology is seen as a possible recourse. Some publishers are already beginning to prepare for a future that might include electronic delivery of the kinds of content now in trade journals and newsletters. Through telephone and cable lines to personal computers, information is sold and delivered that used to arrive on hard copy in a magazine format. Of course, the relative permanence of the printed publication may ensure print as a form of delivery despite the rising cost of paper.

With postal rates also rising rapidly, the selling of magazines by subscription becomes less desirable. Alternatives can be deliveries by carriers, much as the newspapers do, or by concentrating more on display spaces in supermarkets, convenience stores, newsstands, and the like. It is too soon to assess just how cost-effective some kind of carrier system could eventually become. Competition on display racks is difficult to overcome, with attention-getting photos and cover art needed to overcome all of the other magazines' attractive cover designs. Just getting space in such display areas can be a problem, especially for a new magazine going up against those already allocated premium display space.

Postal regulations were amended in 1794 to allow the mailing of magazines at favorable rates, although the legislation did state that delivery of magazines was not a primary function of the postal service. In 1879, Congress passed a law to encourage the growth of magazines by giving magazines second-class mailing privileges. The result was a reasonably priced delivery system, virtually a subsidy that encouraged and made possible the success of many publications. However, postal rate increases in the 1960s were already reducing the near subsidy when in 1970, the Post Office Department was abolished as a Cabinet-level agency and replaced by the United States Postal Service, a subdivision of the Executive branch. With the passage of the Postal Reorganization Act in 1970 and the rate increases that followed, the impact on printed matter was severe. For some magazines, postal rate increases ate into the profit margin, making it nearly impossible to keep the circulation high enough to attract advertisers. Postal rates for printed matter went up nearly 500 percent during the 1970s.

In recent years, many magazines, for the most part already under group/chain ownership, have been further incorporated into media conglomerates. Most magazines are published by multi-magazine groups. The buying of paper in large quantities reduces the unit cost for each magazine in the group. Printing costs per periodical can be reduced when a printing contract guarantees a full schedule of production jobs, that is, a steady income for the printer. Centralized facilities for circulation and management can reduce the overhead for each publication. One magazine, especially when each typically by design has a limited audience potential, can be strained by too much overhead and can find group ownership as salvation. In the 1980s in particular, large corporations and conglomerates were buying up magazine groups and merging them into their giant empires. Magazines, in many instances, by the 1990s, were portions of large conglomerations of cable companies, broadcast properties, book publishers, and even many non-media businesses.

People magazine, launched in 1974, is a good example of the new-era magazine industry. It is part of the AOL-Time Warner media empire. It's gossipy, abbreviated approach to most issues and events is popular with consumers. Each week, *People* sells about four million copies. Every page of advertising in the magazine costs at least $138,000. That means *People* usually leads the magazine industry with between $625 million–$650 million in advertising revenues per year. Combine that amount with subscriptions and single-copy sales and *People* rakes in about $1 billion per year.

On the other end of the spectrum in the magazine industry is *Life* magazine, another AOL-Time Warner product. *Life* started as a weekly in 1936 and was extremely popular and profitable for a number of years. Time and technology took their tolls, however, and even though *Life* remained "modestly profitable," AOL-Time Warner ended regular, monthly publication

Your Thoughts

Suggest FIVE things that magazines need to do to be more successful.

of the magazine in May, 2000. Poor growth potential and a need to reallocate resources to new magazines were among the reasons given for ending the run of one of the most famous magazines in history. The new magazines born on the corpse of *Life* were Real *Simple*, a women's magazine, *eCompany Now*, a technology and business publication, a large-print edition of *Time* and an Australian edition of *InStyle*, a celebrity gossip magazine.

In a kind of "good magazines never die, they just morph into something new" type of announcement, Time, Inc. decided to reincarnate *Life* magazine as a Sunday newspaper supplement. *Life* was first published in 1936 as a weekly, and its general-interest approach lasted until 1972. It came back as a monthly in 1978 and ceased regular publication in 2000. The Sunday *Life* faces plenty of competition. *Parade*, *USA Weekend* and *American Profile* are already established, proven commodities in the newspaper supplement game. *ife*, the supplement, didn't last very long and despite occasional rumors of its rebirth, it seems the life of *Life* has ended.

The Magazine Operation

Most magazines maintain small offices and are operated by only a few people. Much of the work is contracted out to specialists, especially the printing process. A staff of 10 to 12 would be fairly typical. There are magazines with circulations of close to one million that employ from 25 to 30 people.

The typical magazine's organizational chart is much like that of a newspaper, meaning that there are likely to be five departments: editorial, circulation, advertising, administration or business, and manufacturing/distribution. The editorial department is responsible for content, including articles, essays, features, fiction, photographs, etc. Circulation handles the subscriptions, acquiring new readers and servicing those on the current list. Advertising sells the ads that surround the magazine's content, bringing in the income for the magazine. The business office, or administration, manages the overall operation, keeping track of income and expenses, paying the bills, and assuring fiscal soundness in every department. Manufacturing/distribution is the department that sees to the actual production and the dis-

semination of the final product to newsstands or to the mailing firm that sends it to subscribers.

One reason the number of employees is so low is the dependence on freelancers, who come up with unsolicited manuscripts or can be assigned to special writing tasks on a per-article basis. Of course, magazines can also assign articles to their own staff members. Some freelancers are almost employees, because of the reliance placed on specific individuals' work by a publication over time. They are often described by the magazine as regular contributors. Very few freelancers can make a living at freelance work only, despite the fact that about half of the magazines in the United States depend primarily on freelancers for their copy. Freelancers are paid by the article and most contribute to more than one magazine at a time. The small magazines often pay from $100 to $200 for an article. The general circulation magazines, often called "slicks," might pay $3,000 or more for an article.

The smaller the magazine, the more dependence on freelancers. The big newsmagazines, on the other hand, have hundreds of employees on staff. Newsmagazines are the major exception to the practice of maintaining small staffs. Salaries for full-time magazine staffers are comparable to those in the newspaper industry. Staff writers and photographers average between $600 and $1,500 per week. Editors normally earn between $1,000 and $2,000 per week.

Most freelance writers must work on speculation, meaning an inquiry is first sent to an editor. If it is approved, it means only a go-ahead to submit a finished article for a decision about its possible use. If it is then rejected, there is no income for the writer. If it is accepted, a check is mailed to the writer.

Many magazines, because of the inherent vulnerability in using outside writers, employ fact-checkers as well as copy editors. They go to the sources and attempt to verify the facts in an accepted manuscript.

The editor, or managing editor, is crucial to the magazine's success. The appeal of the content to the desired audience is the editor's responsibility. Selecting the right kind of material and ensuring that it is interesting and well-written are important tasks for the editor, who has to guarantee a final product that strongly appeals to the target reader. A managing editor's responsibilities often extend beyond the editorial department to include liaison with each of the other departments. The bigger magazines will also have an assistant editor in charge of each section. An important job in most magazines is the art director, who is in charge of design. The art director tries to create an attractive appearance, an impact created by blending art with the copy and making the copy visually pleasing by its display, through selection of type for titles and headings. The art director's task is often completed just before the the magazine's pages are sent to an outside printing firm.

Most magazines do not have their own printing facilities, preferring instead to have printing contracted out. Weekly, monthly or quarterly publication usually does not justify the expense of buying and maintaining printing facilities. Plus, many publishers have found that by putting out their printing needs for bid, the competition among printers results in a lower cost per copy than they could achieve on their own.

Electronic Magazines

Desktop publishing, eMagazines and e-zines have changed the magazine industry rather dramatically and promise to create even more changes in the future. Computers make it possible for an individual or relatively small staff to gather information, write copy, edit copy, produce graphics, manipulate photos, lay out pages and provide camera-ready copy for a printer or web site. Combine the ease of production, relatively low-cost production and a ready supply of freelancers and other information providers and you have the formula for magazine mania. Look for a proliferation of specialized magazines at a newsstand or computer terminal near you soon.

To battle an advertising downturn, the e-zine, *Salon,* offered an ad-free version for just $30 per year. Some critics wondered about the message the offer sent to potential advertisers, though: "Advertise with us and reach people too cheap to pay for the content of our magazine." Not a very compelling sales pitch, is it? Still, by increasing revenue streams, *Salon* hoped to cut into its losses of $60 million in its first three years of "publication."

Recent Research, Developments and Issues

Traditional magazines are still relatively popular with consumers. For example, the top 10 female-oriented magazines have a combined circulation of almost 40 million. The "comers" in the magazine industry in the early 21st century included *O, Maxim, Yahoo! Internet Life, ESPN Magazine, Self, Fitness, Health, Parents, InStyle* and *FamilyFun.*

Bidding wars for pictures of celebrities continue to be good news for the paparazzi, but somewhat bad news for magazines. As *People, US Weekly* and tabloids like the *National Enquirer* push to get the latest revealing photo of the celebrity of the moment, prices for such photos skyrocket. For example, the first photographed kiss between Ben Affleck and Jennifer Lopez reportedly sold for about $100,000. The most valued photos are ones that appear to be blatant intrusions into the everyday lives of celebrities, because such photos provide the illusion of intimacy with celebrities. Catch a celebrity off-guard, having a bad-hair day or dressed in some less-than-flattering outfit, and you can get a magazine to shell out BIG.

Customer complaints about the racy language on magazine covers prompted Wal-Mart Stores to partly obscure four women's magazines sold at its checkout aisles. *Redbook, Cosmopolitan, Marie Claire* and *Glamour* were targeted for their "provocative" prose. Wal-Mart did offer full frontal viewing of the magazine covers at the back of its stores, though. Wal-Mart stopped selling three men's magazines, *Maxim, Stuff* and *FHM,* in response to customer concerns about the content and image of the magazines.

A survey in 2007 found that young people actually read more magazines than do people over 45 years old. The total average was 17 different consumer magazines read within the past six months. People younger than 34 read an average of almost 19 different magazines. People older than 45 read an average of about 16 different magazines. Statistics related to the number of issues of magazines read are even more impressive. The overall average was 29 issues in six months. Young people averaged about 31 issues. Older people averaged about 27 issues. Women read more different magazines and more issues than did men. Women averaged 18 different magazines and 32 issues. Men averaged 15 different magazines and 27 issues.

It's not all good news for the magazine industry, though. A Project for Excellence in Journalism study found that news magazines are losing circulation and ad revenue. Magazines also rank below ALL other news media as sources of news and information for national and international issues.

U.S News & World Report is no longer a "weekly" magazine. Instead, it's a biweekly magazine. Times are tough for *Time* and *Newsweek*, too. Ad pages dropped 24% for *Newsweek*, 27% for *Time* and 33% for *U.S. News* in the first half of 2008. Some experts were predicting that since "news" and "weekly" seem a contradiction in terms, especially with so many new media options available to consumers, the traditional news magazines might be out of business by 2015. Editors and owners vowed to remain viable by changing strategies, improving online products and re-designing their printed products. Good luck with that.

Magazine industry leaders are encouraging their colleagues to maximize their use of the Internet. With rising production, personnel and mailing costs, complementary and stand-alone E-zines and web sites likely will receive added attention in the next few years. Everybody in the magazine business will have to think and do digital to survive in a ever-fragmenting contemporary media environment.

Your Thoughts

How many different magazines do you read in a six-month period?

Why do you read the magazines you do?

How many issues of magazines do you read in a six-month period?

Think Back

1. What are some of the recent magazine readership statistics?

2. What are the differences between general-interest and special-interest magazines? Give specific examples of each.

3. What are the major types/subcategories of magazines. Give an example of each category.

4. What are the major steps/processes involved in producing a magazine?

5. What are the major jobs/staff positions in the magazine industry?

6. What or who are "freelancers?"

7. How has desktop publishing and computer technology changed the magazine industry?

8. How many different magazines do people read in a six-month period? How many different issues of magazines do people read in a six-month period?

9. How do magazines rank as sources for news and information about national and international issues?

10. What has happened to the traditional news magazines and what does the future hold for them?

11. What are many magazines trying or planning to do in an attempt to remain economically viable?

7

Books

Whether hand-written or block-printed, books had been available to the most literate and most well-to-do elements of European society for 300 years before Gutenberg, and apparently for quite some time before that in Asia. The origins of the art of printing by mechanical means are not totally clear, but there are indications of some kinds of printing methods in both China and Japan at least 1,000 or more years before Gutenberg. During the 8th and 9th centuries the Japanese and Chinese were known to have produced complete books by printing on hand-carved wood blocks. Soon, similar printing techniques were developed in Egypt and Persia. In Korea, printers were turning out histories using bronze pictographs as movable type only 100 years after such typefaces were first employed in China. These initial efforts in the Orient at attempting a system using movable type were from 300 to 400 years before Gutenberg.

Well before movable type was available in Europe, some of the world's most significant accounts of its history came from epic descriptions in book form, usually hand-written, at least initially. These included the New Testament, the stories telling of the life of Christ and the writing of Hebrew Talmudists who produced copies of the Old Testament and other major religious books. Confucius told of the China of his day. Julius Caesar's commentaries and Plutarch's lives of powerful figures are examples. Included also are Homer's *Iliad* and *Odyssey,* as well as eight volumes of the history of the war between Athens and Sparta written by Thucydides. For nearly three centuries, there were copies being made of Marco Polo's hand-written descriptions of his two trips to China. All of this indicating that development in printing in the Orient eventually spread to Europe and influenced the development of the English language book publishing industry.

Paper was being produced in China shortly after the birth of Christ and was used only in the Orient for 750 years, until Arabs began to meet the Chinese as the Moslem faith began to spread. It was another 500 years before a few European countries felt the impact of Moslem migrations and papermaking reached parts of Europe. By the 1300s, all over Europe there were people grinding up linen and other fibers to create a mulch that could be dried into a product upon which inked marks could be pressed. When Gutenberg began experimenting with printing equipment in the 1440s there was already a thriving papermaking industry on the European continent.

In the early to mid-1400s, much of the book production was done for religious purposes, but a need was developing for books for secular audiences. For centuries, most of the books in Europe resulted from the efforts of monastic orders perceiving a need to preserve and copy ancient Judeo-Christian documents. During the middle ages many monks devoted their lives in a commitment to God to the copying of manuscripts by hand. The universities of the middle ages had no shortage of books because of the proliferation of the hand-copied reproductions of manuscripts and the frequent use of wood block printing, which was introduced to Europe when Marco Polo returned from China in 1295.

Between 1400 and 1450, fewer books were being done by copying in monasteries and an increasing number were produced instead by either block printing from wood or from a metal block. The chiseling or whittling of letters in a large block of wood was painstaking work and each block was useless for anything other than the one page it was designed to stamp onto paper. If you had a 500-page book you needed 500 blocks of wood. In northern Germany and the Netherlands, silversmiths and other metalsmiths developed a less painstaking process. It amounted to a single block or lead plate cast from clay that had metal letters individually pressed into it. It was easier to produce a metal block than a wood carving, but the final appearance of the printed product was not as appealing and not as artistically satisfying as either wood block or Gutenberg's movable type.

The Gutenberg Impact

What Gutenberg did was to bring together the existing printing methods in a revolutionary rather than evolutionary way. Gutenberg came up with metal, multiple dyes of individual letters that could be inserted into type cases to keep them in straight lines. He also designed a form, or matrix to keep the lines justified and to make pages uniform. Most of the attention usually given to his achievement has been to the significance of the efficiency and effectiveness of his technique for using movable pieces of type, including the significance of constantly re-using type faces to ensure uniformity of the final product. A second innovation often given less attention was the borrowing of the type of wine press used by grape growers along the banks of the Rhine, where Gutenberg lived near Mainz, Germany. This wine press gave just the right pressure for ideal reproduction from type to printed page and had a vise that screwed type and paper together perfectly.

The Gutenberg use of the wine press was significant in that it was the primary piece of equipment for the producers of books and other publications until the advent of power-driven presses in the early 1800s. Gutenberg's instrument increased the speed and efficiency of printing and gave impetus to increased publishing activity and eventually a spread of literacy. It was much easier after that to produce books and there was a great increase in book reading. There was little technological change in the production of books for the next 350 years, except for modification of the worm screw vise used by Gutenberg into a multiple thread screw and the substitution of metal for wooden parts. Literacy was developing, but slowly, so there was no great need to strive for improvements. In the 1600s and 1700s, printers continued to operate hand presses producing one page at a time.

Printing did spread quickly in the wake of Gutenberg. Rome had a movable type printing press operating by 1467, Venice in 1469, and Paris by 1470. The first English language press was established in London in 1476 by a businessman with literary interests, William Caxton. Some say it was Caxton, while living in Germany and France, who printed the first book in the English language, a translation of the *Iliad*.

Books in the Colonies

By 1638, printing had come to the American colonies and with it book publishing. At first, the colonists were busy clearing the wilderness and struggling through a frontier existence. There was little leisure time, so not much opportunity for book reading. Much of the early printing in the colonies was of bibles and other religious materials until compulsory public education was established in the 19th century.

A major figure in colonial book publishing was Benjamin Franklin, who produced one of America's first books, *Poor Richard's Almanac*. In fact, almanacs in 18th-century America were the most popular type of book. Ben Franklin also printed in his shop in Philadelphia the first novel in the colonies, *Pamela,* by Samuel Richardson.

Bookstores were social and recreational centers for American colonists. They were gathering places for those interested in literature. They were like coffee shops, restaurants, or pubs where reading could be done leisurely over an ale or a coffee. Food and drink were the accompaniment for discussions of ideas by the highly educated, propertied classes who frequented the bookstores. Often the proprietor was also the printer and publisher of books, no doubt even an author. Even at that, book publishing was slow to develop until after the American Revolution. Before 1800, few Americans knew how to read and few could afford the price of a book. Restrictions on printing implemented by colonial governors, who were agents of the crown, limited book publishing also.

During the Revolution there was a shortage of printing supplies. Most of the paper and ink had been imported from England, a supply that was to be cut off. A few domestic paper mills had begun to operate, but too few to meet the demand in the 1770s. Paper was then made from linen and cloth and was scarce until after the war.

With no international copyright law, colonial printers had frequently reprinted British novels. It was cheaper to reprint and sell those than to publish American writers, who would expect to receive royalties. By 1790, the United States Congress passed a copyright statute to restrict the reprinting or importing of copies of a work without an author's permission. The effect of the laws was to severely restrict those who had quite commonly practiced plagiarism and to ensure that authors would be entitled to the profits from their creative works.

Technological Innovations

By 1811, presses were, for the first time, steam driven and capable of much more speed and efficiency. This made possible the production of a great many more titles because it also happened at a time when the market was developing for mass-produced books. As Americans found themselves with more leisure time, the book became a popular mass medium. Books at that time were also becoming less expensive with the advent of mass production. The steam-powered press was developed by a German printer, Friedrich Koenig, who spent eight years trying to marry the steam engine with the printing press. He was able to demonstrate it successfully in 1811. It could print 1,100 single-sided sheets in one hour. By 1818, Koenig and his partner in manufacturing presses redesigned the press so it could print both sides of a sheet of paper more or less simultaneously.

In 1830, an Englishman, David Napier, modified Koenig's steam-driven press so that its printing speed was tripled. In the United States that same year, Hoe and Company started manufacturing a version of the Napier press that was even a little faster, up to 4,000 pages an hour. Hoe and Company came up with a rotary press in 1844 that further increased the rate of printing and modified the rotary press further in 1849 until it could print 8,000 pages an hour.

The most powerful work of the period, the one with the most impact, was Harriet Beecher Stowe's *Uncle Tom's Cabin,* a book that appeared in 1852 and sold 300,000 copies in the first year. It was serialized in newspapers and performed on the stage. *Uncle Tom's Cabin* instantly reminded Americans that the slavery issue would not go away. Its realistic description in a fictional setting of the oppression and inhumanity inherent in the system gave rise to

support throughout the North for the abolitionist movement that preceded the outbreak of the Civil War. One of the most prominent of the abolitionists was a freed slave, Frederick Douglass, whose first autobiographical book, *Narrative of the Life of Frederick Douglass,* was published in 1846. He followed that with a second autobiographical book, *My Bondage and My Freedom* in 1855. The first two Douglass books were written while he was a newspaper and magazine owner and publisher, and an accomplished orator at a time when oratory was a prized talent. After returning from his career in periodical journalism, Douglass completed volume three, the final volume of his autobiography, *Life and Times of Frederick Douglass,* in 1878.

From 1836 to 1857, William McGuffey wrote six reading books for schoolchildren, each one increasing in difficulty. These were the standard schoolbooks for 50 years and sold more than 120 million copies. Other school books began to appear and were the forerunner of the large quantities of textbooks published in the years immediately following compulsory education. Massachusetts pioneered in 1895 with a statute requiring every child to attend school for a set period of years. By the turn of the century, nearly 80% of the states had such legislation, although it was not until 1918 that every state had compulsory education. This greatly increased the demand for textbooks, as did a growth in popularity of college education near the end of the 19th century.

In 1891, an international copyright law gave further protection to American authors. Following this legislation, all authors, foreign and American, had to give permission before their works could be published or reprinted. The law, in effect, granted royalties to foreign authors whose works had previously been pirated by United States publishing houses. Publishers after 1891 were legally required to pay royalties to all authors, which meant that American writers were helped considerably. No longer would it be advantageous for publishers to choose British writers over Americans.

20th Century Books

The first half of the 20th century could be considered a period of commercialization in book publishing, with a combination of quality literature that was marketed well and a heavy volume of mass appeal. Very early in the century several writers displayed an ability to seek social justice while entertaining and stimulating large numbers of readers with realistic novels. When Upton Sinclair wrote his novel, *The Jungle,* in 1906, it not only portrayed the difficult conditions of those working in packing houses but also demonstrated vividly the unsanitary and unhealthful practices in packing plants. The result was Congressional passage of the Pure Food and Drugs Act.

Historical novels were favorites in this period, as were adventure stories. Superficial and popular works included, in 1920, H.G. Wells' *Outlines of History* and, in 1926, Will Durant's *Story of Philosophy.* More and more people were moving to urban centers as a result of all of the new jobs created by the industrialization just before the turn of the century. This meant that in the biggest cities there was an increasing number of bookstores responding to an increase in the urban population and a rising literacy rate.

A big year for the book industry was 1920 with the publication of Edith Wharton's *The Age of Innocence,* and F. Scott Fitzgerald's first novel, *This Side of Paradise.* In 1926, Ernest Hemingway's *The Sun Also Rises* was a significant event, as was Thomas Wolfe's first novel, *Look Homeward Angel,* in 1929. In 1939, John Steinbeck's *The Grapes of Wrath* was a novel that portrayed the misery of the depression of the 1930s. William Faulkner's novels, from *Sartoris* in 1929 through *Intruder in the Dust* in 1948, earned him the O. Henry Memorial Award in 1939 and a Nobel Prize for Literature in 1950. Although Faulkner's early novels brought him more acclaim than money, his later books appealed to popular taste and earned him a good income.

These and other strongly commercial novels appeared as a number of new and aggressive firms entered the publishing business. Alfred A. Knopf, Simon and Schuster, Stanley Rinehart, Harcourt and Brace, and McGraw and Hill joined Random House as major players immediately in the book industry. McGraw-Hill was founded in 1909, Prentice-Hall in 1913, Simon & Schuster in 1924, and Random House in 1925.

By the 1940s, book publishing had become so commercial that it was much like any other big business. Printing and marketing practices changed to meet the mass demand for new works of fiction. Major publishing houses provided a variety of services to a full stable of authors. They sought out authors, provided them with editing and production help, arranged for the printing and distribution, handling all of the sales and eventual payment of royalties. Disappearing in the middle of the 20th century were the specialty firms handling one type of book.

Significant changes were taking place in the publishing industry in the second half of the 20th century. A resurgence in paperback publishing may have been the single greatest phenomenon in book publishing after World War II. Another major development was a trend toward the business of publishing going public. Labor costs, production expenses reaching unheard of heights, and a need for investment in modern equipment and facilities strained the resources of the owners of independent book publishers. Their salvation was to sell stock in their firms to individual investors. They also found themselves merging with other publishers, creating larger units and pumping more capital into the merged firm to ensure sufficient resources to compete with even larger rivals.

The need for increased capital and for modernization of presses and other production and distribution equipment was primarily a result of growth in the industry. Increased enrollments in universities because of the G.I. Bill after World War II and the Korean War sparked a great demand for textbooks. Enrollments were rising at an even greater rate in elementary and secondary schools, because of the baby boom of the late 1940s and 1950s. During the last five decades of the 20th century, the industry growth rate was from 7% to 10% every year.

Some already prominent authors like Steinbeck, Faulkner and Hemingway were still being published early in the period, but soon they were joined by John O'Hara, John Updike, Tom Wolfe, Joan Didion, James Clavell, E.L. Doctorow, and mystery and adventure writers like Robert Ludlum, John LeCarre, Ken Follett and Jeffrey Archer. Romance and mystery were combined in books by Mary Higgins Clark and Elizabeth George. Stephen King was the acknowledged leader of a corps of writers in the horror genre. Much of the period was marked by best sellers of little substance produced by Danielle Steel, Sidney Sheldon, Judith Krantz, Jackie Collins, Michael Crichton, and John Grisham. An outstanding success and almost one of a type was Tom Clancy, whose sales per title averaged 1.3 million for each techno-military-spy-mystery thriller.

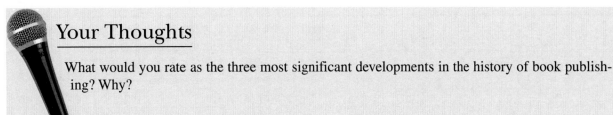

Your Thoughts

What would you rate as the three most significant developments in the history of book publishing? Why?

There were books published during this period that impacted greatly on the political and social climate of the time. In 1962, Rachel Carson's *Silent Spring* was an energizer for those who would initiate and continue the environmental movement that has so altered our thinking in recent years. Significant in the midst of the civil rights movement in the 1960s was the 1965 publication of *The Autobiography of Malcolm X.*

Publishing as an Industry

Book publishing is both a cultural activity and a more complex business than ever before. So-called "bean counters" from giant corporations and professional managers from media conglomerates run things. The mergers of publishing houses has been followed by major corporations moving in to buy publishing firms. Media companies and electronics giants are the new owners of publishing houses. The recognition that new technology meant new means of storing, retrieving and delivering data made information-related businesses into the publishing business a wise investment.

In the Information Age, or at least in an Information Society, a seemingly endless list of communication devices becomes available and those who master those tools profit from the power that accrues to them. Whether a company had been manufacturing television sets or producing television programs, or whether renting landlines or satellite use, or whether it was Xerox or IBM, it was likely to combine with book publishers in a wedding of information partners. CBS, for example, became one of the largest publishing companies in the United States. On the whole, book publishing has become interwoven with other media and media-related industries in a group of a few large conglomerates. About a dozen major corporations are responsible for most of the book titles issued each year.

With publishing companies now subject to foreign investment, buyouts and takeovers, a bottom-line approach to profits might bring into the business a new breed of marketing people and a set of owners whose loyalties lie with stockholders. When book publishers acquire financial resources from profit-oriented investors, even those in other communications industries, they lose autonomy in decision-making. They might find themselves acquiring and producing books on criteria defined more by shrewd business practices than by artistic merit or literary quality. For generations, publishers were able to publish works that were never destined to earn much money, but would lend stature or prestige to the firm. Books of educational, scientific, literary or artistic quality were often published on merit, but the increasing role of market research in determining what would be a profitable publication makes that difficult now.

Where and How Publishing Gets Done

The publishing industry is found primarily in and around New York City, although Boston, Chicago and other cities have publishing firms. Some small towns and medium-sized cities have small or specialized publishing houses. Dubuque, Iowa is one example. Belmont, California is another. All of the activities do not take place at the publisher's headquarters. Typesetting, printing and binding are often, if not nearly always, contracted out. The authors are everywhere, functioning like freelance magazine writers. Their agents and editors are normally based near the firm's headquarters. The graphics department is in-house, but proofreading and the reviewing of potential manuscripts are often done outside the staff.

There are many opportunities for freelancers with special skills to sell themselves to book publishers. Many people in the industry are independent contractors, especially the writers and illustrators. Writers of books depend on agents to work out arrangements for them which will lead to production contracts with publishers. Without an agent, a first-time author is likely to be powerless and frustrated. An unsolicited manuscript is not welcomed. Most publishers simply refuse to open the package containing an unsolicited manuscript. Only the books offered by agents are accepted for review and possible publication. The agent is entitled to a fee that usually amounts to something near 15% of the author's royalty. The royalty for an author can be negotiated, but is likely to range from 10% to 15% of the book's cover price.

Some books are solicited or commissioned. Publishers who have had success with certain authors or certain types of books will often get the idea for a book. Editorial people on the staff have the task of acquiring the manuscript and shaping it into a product for the marketing and sales people. The editorial staff members work with designers and graphics people as well as the author and editor.

If the idea for a book comes from the writer, it is usually presented in a brief prospectus form by the writer's agent. It is then reviewed for potential. If it passes, it goes to an editor who will look at sample chapters, or perhaps even a full manuscript. If the editor feels the idea is a good one, a full manuscript then goes out for evaluation by freelance, well-recognized authorities who can reject it or send it back for revisions and eventual approval. That is typically a conditional approval, meaning that it is one more step in the screening process, although nearly the final one. If the manuscript is still in favor, its last stop is most likely with an editorial board that ultimately decides whether to go ahead with production. All of these steps are possible points for rejection and few manuscripts ever get through the whole screening process.

A publishing firm typically has different types of editors, each responsible for a specialized activity. Some editors analyze and edit manuscripts and others prepare the final copy for the typographer. Others evaluate the quality of the manuscript and its marketability. Some are developmental editors who work closely with writers on each step of the planning and organizing of the manuscript. Others are copy editors who check grammar, spelling, word usage and punctuation.

An editor who is very important in the origins of the manuscript, in the initiation of the project, is the acquisitions editor. This person specializes in generating manuscripts, primarily by seeking out potential authors, checking their ability and availability before recruiting them. And recruit them is what the acquisitions editor does. This is someone who studies the market for possible reader interest and who keeps track of the sales of different types of books. If an acquisitions editor has an idea for a book, a search is started for the right author to do it. The acquisitions editor is expected to know the prior work of various authors, although quite often will simply enlist an agent or agents to find the right person for a specific idea. Literary agents are valuable both to authors and the publishing firms. They generally know the types of books each individual publishing house is likely to look for and maintain relationships with acquisitions editors and other personnel at various publishing companies. The agents have contracted with writers whose track record they know well or whose work they have reviewed and determined as likely to sell.

Once the manuscript is in the hands of a publisher a contract is signed. An advance might be paid to the writer, which is likely to be charged against any eventual royalties. The percentage of the book's sales to be paid as a royalty is specified in the contract. The advance payment varies greatly with the reputation of the author. A famous politician or entertainment figure could get hundreds of thousands of dollars as advance money and will get to keep it even if the book's sales do not meet the costs. A successful author with a record of bestsellers can command a large advance. A first-time author is likely to get very little in the form of advance, because the risk is so great.

Well before the manuscript is completed, the publishing firm's production staff gets to work on trying to develop illustrations, designing the print type, page design, including the length of each line and the overall format of the book. The production crew works on the appearance of the book early in the process and does it in consultation with the marketing chief, the project editor, and others with skills and experiences valued in the design process.

When the manuscript is complete and the production staff has put everything together, it goes outside the publishing house to a compositor. Very few firms own their own equipment for composing and printing. The compositor buys the paper, takes care of the type preparation, and sees to it that printing and binding are done, probably by contracting with another company. Compositors use computer programs to prepare the type and design for the printer. Editorial changes, proofreading corrections, and adjustments in the design can be done much easier with computers than with linotype machines, although some compositors still have linotypes available.

The first printed version to come from the compositor is called the galley proof. Proofreaders and the author, along with the project editor, check for any errors or typos, any mishaps that need correction. Any errors found in the galley proof can be corrected at less expense than later when the book comes out in actual pages instead of long sheets of raw copy. Page proofs will also be checked by the project editor and the author before it goes to the printer. The process of going from final manuscript to bound book may take six months or more.

Categories of Books

There are two broad categories in the publishing world: trade books and text or reference books. The trade book is the type of general book that most of us buy at a bookstore. The trade book category includes the various fiction and non-fiction books sold to the general public. A few trade books become profit-makers for their publishers, but most do not succeed. Each is a risk. The most successful trade books are almost always works of non-fiction.

Self-help books sell in greater volume than any other type. The greatest success and the less risk is for publishers who produce books giving advice on how to have a better marriage, how to be a better parent, how to achieve happiness, how to be healthy, or how to be successful. Books on understanding your emotions, developing your personality, getting to know your feelings or learning to communicate are also among the ones the publishers know will bring them profits. A definite market for self-help books has been identified so there is little or no risk to the publishing firm that produces these books or, for that matter, almost any non-fiction book. Books on how to renovate your attic without hiring a professional, or how to care for your dog or cat, or how to repair your own

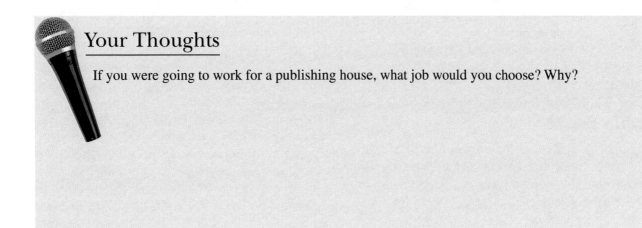

Your Thoughts

If you were going to work for a publishing house, what job would you choose? Why?

car are guaranteed big sellers. Cookbooks do phenomenally well. One reason is that they do not go out-of-date. Their sales do not diminish much over time.

The distinction between fiction and non-fiction is not always clear. In this age of television infotainment and docudrama, we find novels based on fact and we find some novelists turning to non-fiction because it sells better. Some writers use material from the headlines as fodder for fiction plots. Some tell of familiar news events, but with real persons disguised, sometimes barely disguised, as fictional characters.

To further blur the distinction between fact and fiction, there are so-called new journalists who embrace a non-fiction reportage. Truman Capote's *In Cold Blood* is an example of this technique. It avoids the standard information gathering and reporting approach of journalists and tells a real-life story in novel form. Writers such as Norman Mailer and Tom Wolfe focus on writing style and the quality of description rather than on the typical journalistic interview techniques and neutral or objective writing style. Theirs is a personal approach with a demonstration of insight into the participant's behavior and perception of the source's intent while trying to make journalism an art form.

Mailer's *Armies of the Night* was a personal account of his participation in and view of a march and protest against the Pentagon. Wolfe's *Electric Kool-Aid Acid Test* was his personal statement on the drug culture of American youth in the 1960s. Gay Talese re-wrote history in his history of the *New York Times* in his novel, *The Kingdom and the Power*. Another example is a novel by Gore Vidal, *Burr*, in which Aaron Burr and many other individuals who lived during the early 19th century are credited with dialogue that no one living in this century could have heard and related to the author. A book in novel form about actual events, but fictionalized to the point where one could forget that these were once real people is apt to make some of us worry about the ethics of blurring fact and fiction.

Trade Books

Trade books, including fiction and non-fiction, are designed for the general public and are typically sold through bookstores and to libraries. Trade books typically begin as hardcover editions, written for adults or children, and are often later re-published in paperback. Successful print runs of hardcover editions can result in paperback versions that carry the success even further. Americans spend twice as much annually in dollar volume on hardcover trade books as on their paperback reprints. They are sold through retail outlets and marketed through direct-mail advertising, telephone marketing, book clubs, and advertisements in selected magazines and newspapers. The newspaper ads are primarily placed in Sunday supplements carrying reviews of books. Publishers are very dependent on other media, especially the promotion they get from reviews in newspapers and magazines. Books are also promoted by the frequent appearances of authors on radio and television talk shows.

Each year thousands of new titles are published, each one a gamble. Most never return a profit. The industry survives, even thrives, on the few trade books that make so much money that they make up for all of those that lose money or break even. Usually, it is necessary to sell 5,000 or more copies of a given title for a publisher to at least break even, yet only about 5% of all new books sell that many. That helps explain the high cost to the consumer of a hardcover book. It is difficult to predict how well a book will do in competition with other titles. If only a few money-makers compensate for all of the gambles that failed, those few must make huge profits. In actuality, the hardcover editions, even of the successful books, are not going to make up that gap. The big profits come from re-issuing the title in paperback or in selling the rights to a publishing firm that will reprint the book in paperback.

There are several different kinds of trade books, including those intended for a youth market, with both teenage books and younger children's books. These are usually referred to as juvenile books and include everything from books that parents have to read to preschoolers to Nancy Drew mysteries and R.L. Stine novels for older children or young adults. Religious books are a sub-category of trade books. Bibles, prayer books and hymnals are joined by novels with religious themes and books dealing with contemporary social issues from a religious point of view.

There are some bookstores that specialize in carrying only books with religious themes. Biography, including autobiographies, is another type, as is poetry. There are specialties among trade books in music, drama, art, sports and travel, to include both fiction and non-fiction in each of these. Any of these types could also be published in hardcover or paperback. Any of them could be produced as books on tape. Those who prefer to hear their books might be visually impaired or prefer to listen while jogging, driving a car, or casually involved in a non-demanding household chore. Science fiction and horror are types of trade books that take up a lot of shelf space in the nation's bookstores.

A type of book that tends to fit in an overlapping area between trade books and textbooks is the professional book. These are often directly related to occupations or careers. A prime example would be medical books intended for nurses, doctors and other health professionals, although some of these are popular with laypeople and a few are designed to be sold to the general public as guides to diseases and symptoms. Another type is the technical or scientific book, which is intended for readers with a background in or interest in any of the sciences or in the technology. A third type covers many other professions, such as law, business management, sales, insurance, etc. These professional books are quite nearly reference works, books that would be used by students and scholars, or in classroom instruction.

Reference Books and Textbooks

Reference books are typically placed in the same category as textbooks, or as an adjunct form of publishing to the textbook. Dictionaries, atlases and encyclopedias are the most well-known of these, but there are as many reference books as there are topics for inquiry or study. Reference materials are most often published for libraries and are sometimes published by university presses. University presses specialize in publishing scholarly work that would not have mass appeal.

In the publishing house that produces both trade books and textbooks, the two departments are often so completely separate that they seem like different companies. Of course, there are many firms that specialize in publishing only textbooks. The textbook market is an attractive one for publishers. There is less risk. A textbook that sells well can continue for years to make money for a publisher. The mandatory nature of textbook adoptions by elementary and high schools is an advantage. Although adoptions by individual college and university professors are not mandatory, they do offer the possibility of a fairly permanent long-term readership.

The publishers of textbooks for elementary and high schools have the frustration of dealing with screening committees to ensure standardized texts across a school system. The need for approval from selection committees requires extra attention to specific concerns for uniformity in hundreds of classrooms. Indecision is inevitable in committee deliberation and it forces publishers to seek constantly to satisfy every person in the deliberative process.

The elementary and secondary division, despite the potential frustrations, is quite often the most profitable division of many publishing firms. The publishers must follow dictates of the boards or committees that want the broadest, possibly blandest and least offensive content possible to cover a range of students in a variety of schools in the system. This usually means books written by a team of in-house editors experienced and flexible enough to prepare a product that will satisfy disparate interests.

Some states have narrowly restricted state-wide rules on readability that must be followed in the development of any textbooks no matter what the subject matter. There are also state-wide adoption codes listing taboo subjects or treatment of content, largely to avoid controversy and to reduce complaints from parents who naturally have a wide range of political or social values. Publishers accept all of this, because one big adoption could bring in several million dollars in sales.

In higher education, the professor makes the decision about what text to use for a specific class, although occasionally a department committee will choose a text for a multiple section course. College and university bookstores do not select books, they merely stock what professors order from the publisher. The market for each text is not great because of the narrowness of the subject for each course, but the relative permanence of the demand compensates for that. Professors who write these books update them every four to six years as the material becomes dated. This results in a continued permanence from the publisher's ability to keep turning out new editions of the same title.

Sales representatives from publishing firms call on professors to acquaint them with available books. These salespeople are called "travelers" and often perform as recruiters or scouts for new manuscripts. They are usually experienced in the professor's discipline, specializing in only certain subject areas. They must of necessity be familiar with academic institutions and with the disciplines of the professors whom they serve.

A problem for textbook publishers has been the steady drop in the number of books being sold in college bookstores. With only a slight decline in college enrollment in recent years, there has been a 30% decrease in the number of college textbooks sold. Most of the decline in sales of new books has been explained by two interrelated factors. From the mid-1980s to the late 1990s, the price to the student of a typical textbook doubled. Textbook prices have increased at a rate far in excess of inflation during the period. Students are often unable to buy new books and professors are sometimes unwilling to order books that are too costly for their students. Professors who at one time required two or three texts in a given course will order only one or two. If a course can be taught without a text, although not necessarily desirable, a professor will attempt it in the effort to avoid burdening students with excessive costs. The key element in this problem is the used book trade. Students try to save money by buying used copies and, as a result, cause the prices of both used and new books to increase.

Professors naturally adopt newly revised texts to take advantage of the latest knowledge in the subject. Updated books are obviously desired as knowledge advances so both updated versions of established texts and new books need to be published. These are expensive to produce. College bookstores, meanwhile, are buying back books from students at the end of each semester. The next set of students then has the option of buying a used book or a new copy of a required text. Of course, the used copy sells for a little less.

There are even firms that specialize in buying used books from bookstores that failed to sell what they bought back from students. These companies in turn sell them to any of several other bookstores on campuses across the country. What all of this does is drive up the price of both the new and the used copies. Publishers are forced to revise and update texts more frequently to make up for their loss of sales of each edition to the used version of that edition. That is expensive. Also, publishers have to increase the cost of each edition to cover the added costs from the sales of used books wiping out the market so rapidly. Used book prices continue to escalate because the bookstores continue to sell them just below the new book cost.

The Paperbacks

Paperback books were first produced in this country before the Civil War. The dime novel of the 19th century was a form of inexpensive escapist fare, offering stories of romance and adventure, especially with western themes. From the 1840s until the turn of the century, mass produced books at 10¢ a copy guaranteed that books would be a popular mass medium. They experienced a surge shortly after the Civil War when the cost of paper was at its lowest.

In the 1880s, about one-third of the titles published in the United States were paperback. One reason for this was the reprinting of works by foreign writers who were not being paid royalties. The cost of producing such reprints went up greatly with the international copyright law of 1891, which granted royalties to authors from other countries. With no more chance to pirate some writers' work, with publishers killing each other off in price wars, and with costs increasing during the late century industrialization, the paperback activity dwindled. However, in Europe the less expensive paperbacks continued to flourish in the first half of the 20th century. In Germany, paperback success in the 1920s and 1930s gave American publishers a model for the resurrection of paperbacking that began in the United States with Penguin Books in 1939.

When the mass marketing of paperbacks began, readers were offered primarily reprints. A book would first appear in hardcover. About a year or so later, once hardcover sales had tapered off somewhat, the book's rights would be sold to a paperback company. The lower cost of paperbacks made the book more of a mass medium. A major reason for the boom in paperback publishing was the development of perfect binding, which produced great savings when high speed presses and offset printing were used in the production process. Perfect binding is the method of using adhesive to bind books instead of sewing them.

Hardbound books and paperbacks complement each other. The small paperback format made it possible for all kinds of books to reach larger audiences than ever before. It also made possible an expanded audience for authors whose hardcover books were reprinted. Many of the big publishing firms got into paperbacking either to issue reprints of their successful hardcover books or to print original material in paperback form. A publisher might even produce hardcover and softcover editions of a given book simultaneously.

Eventually, the industry divided into two types: mass-market paperbacks and trade paperbacks. Mass-market paperbacks are mainly distributed through chain stores, supermarkets, drug stores, and also in bookstores. They are usually sized to fit supermarket and drug store racks. Harlequin romances are typical of these. Western novels, science fiction, and adventure stories are also typical of mass-market paperbacks. Trade paperbacks are often reprints of hardcover trade books and can be more expensive and better made books. They are generally sold in bookstores and many can be considered to be quality publications. One reason for quality in paperbacking is the publishing of the classics in that format. This is because no royalties have to be paid on works with expired copyright. This means profits can be made on books that sell in relatively small quantities because of the lower costs in producing them in paperback. These can compete with hardcover books in college bookstores and compete for adoption by professors who could require them for their students.

An impetus for original publishing in paperback is the lower royalties paid to authors. Writers of original material for paperback get royalties 25% to 30% of what publishing firms pay for hardback authors. Of course, the potential for a greater number of sales still can make the royalty percentage just as attractive as a higher one with lower projected sales volume.

The distribution system for paperbacks is a significant factor in keeping prices down. It starts with sheer numbers of copies in the print run. The cost per unit, as a result, is reduced greatly. But this means a method of distribution must be used to efficiently handle such large quantities of books. The distribution pattern is essentially the same as that used by the magazine industry. Like magazines, paperbacks are placed in display racks in airports, drug stores, newsstands, convenience stores and supermarkets. These outlets are saturated with copies, many more than are likely to be purchased. Those that do not sell are either returned or destroyed. To get credit for unsold books, the retail store operators are not expected to return the complete books, just the covers, after shredding the insides. Such returns are a problem for publishers and they do everything possible to keep the numbers of returns down.

The retailer can get a full return in cash or credit on every copy that does not get sold. The typical rate of return is between 30% and 50%. The biggest sellers tend to bring in enough money to more than make up for those that do not stay in the racks very long.

The Marketing of Books

Book publishing is a gamble and publishers need to make efforts at reducing the odds. Sometimes a previously successful author comes up with a manuscript that does not meet expectations, despite the publisher's advance investment. Sometimes taking a chance on an unknown, but promising author simply does not work out. It is possible that a well-written, highly entertaining and readable, carefully edited book might not catch on despite its obvious attributes. Often the timing could be wrong and competition from other books can reduce to failure what otherwise could have been a bestseller.

Publishers have had decades of experience with techniques of advertising, promotion and marketing that they hope will reduce the element of chance. By the standards of other major businesses, book publishers' advertising budgets are minimal; however, the total marketing strategy for a book can cost the publisher enough that it will increase considerably the price of the book. Typically, the publisher's marketing expense is about $1 for each book sold. The expense is justified by the need to reach potential readers who would otherwise be unaware of the book.

About 100 new books or reprints are produced each day in the United States. These compete immediately with the thousands of titles already on the shelves of bookstores and retail store racks. The task of the publisher is to create awareness among millions of Americans for a given title. That effort can be very expensive. Complimentary copies are given to book editors of newspapers and magazines in hopes of getting a review published. The most desired review would be one in the *New York Times* Book Review section. All publishers strive mightily to get a review in the highly credible, authoritative *New York Times*.

Another favorite of publishers is the radio or television talk show circuit. An appearance by an author on a popular television show, like ones hosted by Larry King or Jay Leno, will guarantee an increase in sales for any book. Oprah Winfrey even has a regular segment where she asks her viewers to read a certain book and then brings the author on later in the month to discuss it. Such publicity and plugs have made some made some books instant "best sellers."

Authors are assisted by their publishers in junkets or book tours across the country. They appear on local radio and television and visit bookstores, signing autographs and mingling with potential readers. These book tours are planned as valuable tools in an overall public relations effort on behalf of the book. Most publishers believe the book tour is cost-efficient and effective, but only if targeted properly. The problem is the over saturation of book authors on the talk shows. Publishing firms have to be selective about target audiences and which authors to send out to overcome the heavy competition on the talk show circuit. One way to handle the media blitz is to have the author attend autographing parties and make bookstore personal appearances as the primary part of a visit to a city where the appearance on radio or television can be almost incidental. A full package of promotional activities on the tour makes it likely that one or more will reach enough readers to justify the overall expense to the publisher.

One effective technique is to persuade the operators of retail outlets to display a book prominently in the windows of stores, on the counters or special racks in locations of heavy foot traffic in the store. Publishers can also use direct mail to reach the most likely audience for a book. Mailing lists can be purchased that give a publisher a targeted set of readers fitting a demographic profile. A publishing firm might want the subscription list for *Sports Illustrated* or the *Sporting News* if it's trying to market a biography of George Steinbrenner or Michael Jordan.

Book clubs generate predictable sales for a given title and create an opportunity for extra promotion for any title selected. The extra exposure is an asset despite the fact that the book clubs negotiate with considerable leverage for very low prices from the publisher for books that they select. Book clubs dis-tribute to their subscribers through the mail. Most are rather small and cater to special interests, but the two major book clubs are so large that selection by one of them is a guarantee of success for a book. The Book-of-the-Month Club was founded in 1926 and is by far the largest. The next largest is the Literary Guild, founded in 1927. The Literary Guild has nearly two dozen subsidiary, specialized clubs offering titles in mystery, science fiction, adventure, cooking, gardening, and other topics. The third major book club is the Reader's Digest Book Club, which distributes condensed books.

Bookstores

Today's typical American bookstore is most likely part of a large chain, and there are increasingly fewer chains because of mergers. The chains expanded rapidly in recent years, primarily with large outlets in shopping centers and malls. Barnes & Noble is the largest chain in the country, but has competition from the newest, fast-growing chain, Borders. Waldenbooks, B. Dalton and Brentano's are familiar names on the front doors of retail outlets, but are casualties of the mergers and takeovers in the trend toward mega-bookstores, especially Barnes & Noble. These national chains worked to drive many independents or smaller chains out of business by offering huge discounts on bestsellers while carrying a relatively small inventory.

As independents went out of business and the public found it difficult to find some titles, the big

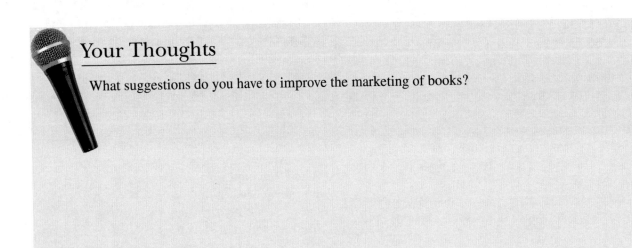

Your Thoughts

What suggestions do you have to improve the marketing of books?

chains responded by opening their superstores, each one stocking seven or eight times as many titles as their original stores. Chain stores are able to keep prices down and profits up through large-scale purchasing and a computerized inventory control that ensures having in stock the very books that buyers want. They can keep their markup on books low, but make up for the lower profit on each book through high sales volume. Barnes & Noble discounts 20% off hardcovers, 30% off *New York Times* current best-sellers, and 20% off *New York Times* paperback best-sellers. Crown built an image as a cut-rate or discount chain with a large selection of titles. Crown did this by keeping prices below other major chains through a practice of buying very cheaply stocks of former best-sellers and other popular titles that the publishers had overstocked and could not move or store.

The biggest change in recent years, apart from Barnes & Noble acquiring some of its primary competitors, has been the phenomenal growth of Borders as a national chain. Borders began in 1971 as a small, independent store in Ann Arbor, Michigan, and had 1,100 stores worldwide in 2008. Borders is competing with the giants by offering a large inventory of books and music, an in-house cafe and a public relations plan that tries to create a literary image for the chain. A typical Borders outlet has 30,000 square feet of floorspace, 140,000 book titles, and 60,000 music titles. The literary image is enhanced by offering primarily classical and jazz music. Listening stations highlight the music section and customers are encouraged to sit and read in the book section. They are encouraged to carry their coffee throughout the store and sip as they read or listen. Borders employees say their stores are like community centers, places to browse and hang out, to meet people, and to spend a family evening.

Many of the few remaining small, independent bookstores are surviving by specializing. Some offer used books, especially older, hard-to-find, or out-of-print titles. Some specialize in mysteries and thrillers, or science fiction, or New Age books. They might also sell greeting cards, stationery and related items. They too are offering coffee and snacks to create a browsing atmosphere. Their future is uncertain because of the strength of the conglomerate-owned superstores. Such superstores could do to the privately owned bookstore what Home Depot has done to hardware stores and what McDonald's has done to independent fast food outlets.

The book industry continues to prosper even in the face of competition from a variety of media, including sophisticated new technology. The Internet, home video, CD-ROMs, and other new delivery systems offer sights, sounds, color and interactivity, but books continue to hold their own. Americans are buying 1.2 billion books a year and that total has increased despite newer media and the continued popularity of movies and television.

An obvious difference is that books are not supported by advertising. Another difference is in the long life of a book, its virtual permanence. Books are collected and maintained and re-read. They are durable and enduring, often lasting long enough to help transmit our cultural heritage. Books educate us, inspire us, and entertain us. Books influence other communication media. The narrative form of the novel has been the model for movies and television's dramatic productions. Books have survived and will likely continue to survive in the 21st century, because they can co-exist with each medium that comes along.

Electronic Books, Book Readers and Bookstores

Books may be with us forever, but the form they take, the way we "read" them and the way we buy them or get them from libraries may change dramatically in the next few years. Amazon.com, Barnesandnoble.com and VarsityBooks.com are a few of the major companies that sell books online. The profit margin for such "virtual bookstores" can be much higher than traditional, "bricks and mortar" bookstores, so many experts are predicting that online bookstores could soon be where most of us will be doing our shopping.

Even online bookstores might eventually be replaced by simple catalogs of "electronic" books. Such books can be delivered in digital form, so the need for retailers and warehouses full of hard-copy books will be eliminated. Publishers, in the traditional sense of the word, might fade into the sunset, too. Author Stephen King and others have experimented with "e-books" and most experts predict that once the expected technical glitches are worked out, the direct delivery of books from author to reader will become commonplace. In March, 2000, King made his 66-page ghost story, *Riding the Bullet,* available exclusively on the Internet for a fee of $2.50. Many of the sites that had been contracted to make the e-book available crashed under the unexpected high demand for the book. King was quoted as saying he hoped the new delivery method would open up new markets and prompt more people to read books.

Digital book projects are underway at several universities in the United States. The University of Pennsylvania Library and Oxford University Press partnered on a five-year project (2000–2005) that involved the online publishing of about 1,500 new history books. In addition to publication, a study will be conducted to determine how such e-books are used, what their impacts are and what cultural changes, if any, they create. Some of the scholars involved in the project believe e-books, especially scholarly books, will likely be used for skimming and for finding specific passages that will be included in research papers and articles. In addition, participants say e-books will likely serve as a sort of "test drive" for potential buyers. Consumers will check out the electronic version to help them decide whether or not to purchase the hard-copy version. The project participants do not believe e-books will soon replace hard-copy books. Instead e-books will likely serve as supplements and provide a different way for people to acquire the information and/or entertainment they desire.

E-books do create a minor problem for consumers, of course. You have to have some way to read the things. Computers and even personal organizers can be used, but electronic book readers will likely be the most convenient method to accomplish the task. Such readers are hand-held devices that display text on a flat-panel screen. NuvoMedia, Inc. and SoftBook Press, Inc. are among the pioneers in this area. E-book readers cost between $300–$600. Sizes vary, but most are about eight inches by six inches. Memory/storage size varies, too, but most can hold up to about a dozen standard-size books. In addition to books, people can also access selected magazines and newspapers and even load personal files into the devices. The fees charged for loading books and other materials into an electronic book reader will likely come down, but initially they were not that much different from the cost of the hard-copy version of the desired material.

With E-books, e-bookstores and e-book readers come new professional, legal and ethical concerns, of course. E-books can greatly reduce the time it takes to get information from an author to consumers. That can mean lost opportunities to verify the accuracy of content. Even in traditional, hard-copy publishing where there is often up to a year between the time a manuscript is completed and a finished book hits the market, unsubstantiated allegations sometimes make it into print. Critics have long complained about the lack of adequate fact-checking in book publishing and e-books can only exacerbate the problem.

Another troubling development is the practice of e-bookstores charging publishers to promote products and not informing consumers about such financial arrangements. Amazon.com apologized and offered refunds to customers for not being more open about the "co-operative advertising" packages offered to publishers. These $10,000 packages included a prominent display on the Amazon.com home page, an author profile or interview and a complete book review. In addition, payments could guarantee placement of a book in Amazon.com's "Destined for Greatness" section and its "What We're Reading" list. Amazon.com pointed out that such deals were not unlike those available at "bricks and mortar" stores. Such stores charge fees for in-store and in-window displays of books. Amazon.com and competitor Barnes&Noble.com have promised to inform customers when publishers have paid for special treatment and consideration by the online retailers.

Read Me a Story

Audio books have been around for a long time and they're still relatively popular. Studies have found that about 90,000,000 Americans drive to work each day and the average commute time is one hour. With so many people spending that much time in a car, the market for audio books remains solid. In 2008, audio books were a $218 million per year industry. Most popular new titles are among 20,000+ titles available.

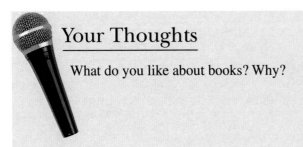
Recent Research, Developments and Issues

Many book publishers have built profitable web sites where customers can buy cyber versions of everything from the most steamy novel to the most upright reference work. E-book sales in 2008 reached $67 million. While that's not much of the $25 billion in income generated by the book industry in 2008, it sure beats the measly $500,000 made from e-books in 2000.

Downloading e-books to personal digital assistants, personal computers, and other hardware is relatively easy. After scanning an online catalog and making selections, customers are e-mailed their books. That doesn't leave many excuses for not reading.

E-book publishers include the following:

e-books.com

simonsays.com

Amazon.com

contentlinkinc.com

Barnes&Noble.com

borders.com

It's been a tough road for independent book stores recently. The market share for independents has dipped from about 33% in 1990 to less than 12% today. Still, independents are fighting the good fight. The American Booksellers Association started a program/service called Book Sense. The collective sales strategy makes it possible for customers to purchase gift certificates that are redeemable at hundreds of independent book stores nationwide. In addition, a web site connects all member stores and their inventories.

Sony and other major manufacturers have developed relatively sophisticated e-book readers. Most of the readers can hold between 80–100 standard-size books. E-book readers cost between $199 and $499 on average. Costs per downloaded book normally run about 20% less than hard-copy versions. Costs may come down as manufacturers and consumers compromise on what might be considered "appropriate" advertising that would be transmitted along with a desired novel or how-to e-book.

Statistics released in mid-2008 listed U.S. books sales holding steady at about $25 billion per year. E-book sales were up 24%, to about $67 million, and audio book sales were up 20%, to about $218 million.

Think Back

1. Who were some of the big names in the development of printing? What did they contribute?

2. What were the highlights in the development of paper?

3. Who were the major players in book publishing in colonial America? What did they contribute? Make note of all the major "firsts."

4. Who were the major authors in the 1800s?

5. What were the major publishing houses in the 1800s?

6. Who are the major authors of the 20th century?

7. What are the major publishing houses of the 20th century?

8. What have been the major effects of media mergers on book publishing?

9. What are the major steps in getting a book published?

10. What are the basic roles and responsibilities of the major staff members in a publishing house? Be specific.

11. What are the major differences between trade books and textbooks/reference books? Give some examples of each type.

12. What percentage of new books end up being successful and what makes a book successful?

13. Why are college textbook sales dropping?

14. Why have paperbacks been described as one of the most significant developments in book publishing?

15. What is "perfect binding" and why is it important?

16. What is the difference between mass-market paperbacks and trade paperbacks?

17. What happens to paperbacks that don't sell?

18. How much does it cost to market a book and what are the major techniques used to market books?

19. How many new books are produced each day?

20. How are bookstores doing these days and what are the major competitive techniques used by such stores?

21. Why have book sales remained rather high even with all the new media competition?

22. What are the elements associated with e-books, e-book readers and e-bookstores? What are the concerns associated with e-publishing?

23. What is the current status of e-book sales, e-book readers and independent book stores?

Radio

When it comes to commercial radio, it appears that everybody has a gripe, except the corporations atop the multi-billion dollar industry. Near the end of the 20th century, radio regulation was eased, opening the door for corporate ownership of hundreds of radio stations. An executive at Clear Channel Communication, which once owned 1,200 stations, responded to listener complaints of sameness by insisting that stations play what the audience wanted to hear. Those doing the griping are mostly young and long the mainstay of the radio audience. The gripes are typically about overdosing on the same songs or artists, with some playlists that are so skimpy that listeners tire of the same 10 or 12 songs day after day.

Arbitron ratings in the early 21st century revealed that the industry's long-time target audience, teenagers, was listening less often. In a 10-year period, overall radio listening dropped from an average of 23 hours a week to 20 hours. Teenage girls are listening only 16 hours a week and teenage boys only 12 hours a week. Untold numbers now download music off the Internet; millions of Americans are dialing into Internet radio every day. For the young, it's all about music. They complain that FM radio is too narrow, appealing to the lowest common denominator with its slimmed down playlist.

Critics of the industry pointed to the absence of "personality" due to disc jockeys restricted by playlists and by research. The industry's research findings direct them to what they believe that the public wants; if they don't provide it, the audience will leave. The days of free-form radio and personalities like Murray the K, Lee "Baby" Sims and other larger-than-life personality jocks are largely over. Some remain, but not with the opportunity to show the energy and creativity of an earlier era.

One result of the industry's bigness is the system used by owners of multiple stations where live, on-air talent has been replaced with prerecorded material. The "voice tracking" is described by its detractors as flat and colorless. Clear Channel, however, claims that it cuts expenses, maximizes the ability to serve the various stations' listeners with major air personalities and gives advertisers a chance to have the best voices available to pitch their products.

If gripes are directed mostly at music selection and primarily at FM radio, what does that mean for AM radio, which in bigger markets does not typically compete against the FM effort to attract the youthful music listeners? Talk radio, news-talk, news and information, all sports, and the like don't show the drop in listening that FM music stations see in their Arbitron numbers. If FM is charged with having sound-alike formats, AM is apparently the alternative. Controversy and audience participation have built a niche for AM radio. If there are gripes about AM radio, they are aimed at what many listeners perceive as a right-wing bias on the part of many talk show hosts and the listeners who call in. The on-air controversy generated by telephone callers clashing with the host is no stronger than the controversy in the public, which owns the airwaves, about whether the licensees of these stations are serving the whole public when they offer one-sided programming so frequently. Again, industry representatives have said that their research and the ratings told them clearly what the public wants to hear.

The Telecommunications Act of 1996 is credited with or blamed for what happened in the radio business. Previously, ownership was limited to 40 stations nationally and four in any market: two AM and two FM. Now there is no cap on how many one company can own nationally. In addition, local ownership limits doubled to eight stations.

Despite complaints about bland disc jockeys, or perhaps because of the complaints, recent years have seen the revival of the once-popular on-air hoax. In the 1970s, a disc jockey once stirred listeners, as well as animal rights activists, by telling the story progressively over several days of his new cat and how he was getting it to co-exist with his dog, which was jealous of the newcomer. He suddenly capped the story by describing how the dog viciously attacked the cat and ate it. Of course, there never was a dog or a cat, but listeners were saddened, appalled, outraged, disgusted and stimulated to see that something was done about the terrible deed. Animal rights activists, law enforcement and others responded, eventually revealing the hoax. Thirty or more years later, hoaxes, pranks, stunts and wild promotional efforts became even more frequent. Listeners everywhere have been bamboozled by one of the oldest stunts of all. This is where a disc jockey supposedly locks himself into the studio because he has been fired and nobody can get him to leave. He says he will play the same song over and over again until his loyal listeners protest enough that the boss will relent and give him his job back. This classic prank and all of the others are designed not only to excite the listeners, but also to get newspaper and television news coverage of the stunt.

Recent hoaxes have included a disc jockey telling his audience that a cat had been tethered to a helium-filled balloon and was floating across the local skies as listeners called into describe the path of the balloon. Finally, one caller told the audience that he saw a man with a gun who shot the balloon and the cat fell to earth. There was no cat, no balloon and no callers. The voices describing the fictitious cat's adventure were all pre-taped. This episode brought on a community outcry, especially with municipal officials incensed about the waste of public resources in the effort to investigate. A station in Kansas warned its listeners that the city's drinking water contained dihydrogen monoxide, resulting in 150 calls to city government and fear of a terrorist plot against the municipal water plant. Dihydrogen monoxide is the scientific name for water. A Denver disc jockey twice faked dropping a live chicken from his station's multi-story office building, contending that there would be an early spring if the bird survived. The most extreme stunt had to be the one that got two disc jockeys fired and their two co-conspirators criminally charged for purportedly having sex in St. Patrick's Cathedral in New York City as the two disc jockeys offered a running commentary. Howard

Stern has made a practice of his fans' attempts to trick network news anchors. Stern plays tapes of those who succeed in pretending to be eyewitnesses to breaking news events.

The renewal of such pranks and the unusual number of them is said by station promotion directors to be a result of increased pressure to stand out in a competitive radio market at a time of shrinking budgets and limited resources for promotional activities.

The Federal Communications Commission has a rule banning hoaxes, but the rule has many loopholes. The Enforcement Bureau of the FCC has been slow to file any hoax cases and equally as slow to look into many of them.

AM and FM radio have been around for years. Traditionally, younger people, between the ages of 15 and 25, listened to FM radio, while older people, between the ages of 45 and 60, listened to AM radio. But now those rules are changing as there is a new, exciting kind of radio—satellite, digital radio.

XM Radio was created by Gary Parsons, Hugh Panero, Greg Cole, Stephen Gavenas, Lee Abrams and Dave Logan who teamed up with programming people and financial partners. Sirius Satellite Radio was created by David Margolese, Joseph Clayton, John Scelfo, Guy Johnson and Patrick Donnelly.

After several years of heated competition for advertisers, program content, big-name celebrity performers and customers, XM and Sirius merged in 2008. Actually, Sirius bought out its rival for about $5 billion. At the time of the merger, the companies had a combined total of 17 million subscribers. The U.S. Justice Department approved the merger despite complaints from consumer groups and traditional broadcasters. Critics feared the loss of competition and increased prices for service. A spokesman for the Justice Department said the evolution of technologies will give satellite radio plenty of competition in the future and will help keep costs down.

In a move to secure FCC approval for the merger, XM and Sirius agreed to do the following:

1. Place price caps on programming and offer "a la carte" pricing so consumers can pick what programs/channels they want without having to buy a bundle of programs/channels.
2. Share their technology with radio receiver manufacturers to increase purchase options for consumers.

3. Provide channels for non-commercial, educational and public safety programming as well as channels for programming produced by minorities, women and under-represented groups.

4. Provide radios for current subscribers that will be able to access programming from either XM or Sirius.

Digital radio is the transmission and reception of sound which has been processed using technology comparable to that used in CD players. In short, a digital radio transmitter processes sounds into patterns of numbers, or digits. At the listeners' end, digital radio receivers provide a standard of sound quality that is significantly better than conventional analog radios, just as CDs sound better than LPs.

Digital radio sounds great. It's better than both AM and FM, but you can't hear it on a regular radio, yet. The problem is the bandwidth. In broadcasting terms, the bandwidth is the radio spectrum or space required for delivering a given signal. Different types of signals require different types of bandwidths. For instance, the current TV signals require 6 MHz of bandwidth per channel, while FM requires 0.25 MHz and AM only requires 0.01 MHz per channel. Digital radio, in contrast, needs up to 1.5 MHz per stereo service, because of the fact that each service requires 1.5 million bits per second of data to reproduce stereo sound. Since digital radio takes up so much bandwidth, it is not available on the radio now. But with the advent of a new technology known as "digital compression" it is possible to reduce the number of bits in a stereo signal from 1.5 million down to less than a quarter of a million per second, without any noticeable difference in the sound quality.

This technology provides listeners the option to purchase satellite digital radio. Digital radio receivers cost about $300, plus you pay a monthly subscription fee. You can have digital radio installed in your car, home office or anywhere you prefer.

Digital technology also makes High Definition radio possible. HD radio enjoys the improved sound quality that the technology brings, but HD also makes it possible for owners to add one or two "side channels" or "side stations" to their primary station. HD2, as it's called in the radio industry, allows stations to create sister/brother stations that can either simulcast the same programming as the original station, or owners can diversify and broadcast a completely different style of programming content on their "side channels." At the end of 2007, there were more than 1,000 U.S. radio stations taking advantage of the HD2 technology. HD receivers cost about $200–$300 dollars, but there is no monthly subscription fee, and, at least initially, most HD2 "side channels" were commercial free. Traditional radio broadcasters are hoping that HD2 will help them compete with satellite radio for listener loyalty.

As the 21st century began, radio moved into cyberspace, with a capability of reaching audiences 10,000 miles away just as easily as ten miles away. An FM station with limited power for over-the-air transmission can use the Internet to be heard anywhere in the world by anyone with a personal computer. An AM station with 1,000 watts of power used to be at a big disadvantage in competing with full-power rivals, especially those 50,000 watt clear-channel signals, but not so much now. The power of Web broadcasting signaled a new era for radio, one in which new listeners could mean new advertising income, especially from sponsors desiring to reach computer users. Radio can now draw new online advertisers who recognize that the Web helps reach listeners who aren't always near a radio, but are quite likely to be at their desktop computers, in their offices, for example. Web radio is already reaching more people in their offices than any of the other traditional media.

In January of 2000, a survey found that 15 percent of the American public had listened to radio online, twice the percentage of a year earlier. Between 1995–2000, there was a tenfold increase in the number of radio stations transmitting their signals over the Internet, with thousands of stations taking old-fashioned broadcasting into the digital age. A 2007 study found that 19% of Americans regularly listen to Web-based radio stations. That's about 57 million listeners. At the time of the study, that number of listeners was greater than the number of satellite radio, HD radio, podcasts and cell-phone radio combined listeners.

The Internet gives radio a low-cost way to reach national or global audiences, because the cost of transmission has nothing to do with distance. The expense of the technology to put radio stations on the Internet has decreased considerably since large numbers of broadcasters began hitching a ride on the Internet in the late 1990s.

Internet radio does present some problems for managers of corporate communications networks, Internet service providers and even many users. For one thing, continuously sending audio over the Internet strains online resources that might otherwise be devoted to Web browsing or sending e-mail. It may add to the distractions available to office workers, who can tune in to news or music programs. It's also impractical for people, who can listen to Web radio only by tying up their home phone lines, possibly at hefty per-minute rates. Easing such concerns are high-speed Web technologies such as cable modems and digital subscriber line service for telephone connections, because they allow Web surfers to stay connected to the Internet without interfering with cable TV or phone service.

Traditional radio station operators might view online radio stations as both a threat and an opportunity. Arbitron studies suggest that online radio does eat away at the local listener base, but also presents the radio industry with the chance to pick up a lot of new listeners. Arbitron suggests local stations can better please online listeners by devising content in conjunction with their normal broadcasts. One way would be to offer alternative streams targeting underserved niche audiences. Stations don't have to limit themselves to merely reproducing what's actually going out over the air. A strong suggestion is that all radio should become more specialized. Arbitron surveys indicate that listeners who visit radio sites want information on community events, concerts, and the titles and artists of the songs currently being played.

When more and more online-only radio stations appear, there will be even more expressed concerns about what the Federal Communications Commission might be able to do to regulate them as it does over-the-air radio. Currently, the courts see online broadcasting as akin to print, something protected by First Amendment rights with no conflict with any public First Amendment rights. Many listeners, however, are likely to think of it as closer to traditional broadcasting. The FCC has no jurisdiction since online broadcasting doesn't use public airwaves. For online to come under the FCC mandate, the courts would have to reverse themselves, and, with the lengthy history of how that regulation has evolved, that simply isn't likely to happen. If anything, the FCC is likely to favor online radio because it would be seen as a way to serve small audiences not served by big-budget radio stations owned by multi-media corporations and conglomerates. When the Communications Decency Act was passed by Congress in 1996, it was almost immediately challenged. The courts looked at the Net and said it was more like newspapers and magazines than the airways. The courts have consistently held that Congress originally charged the FCC with licensing over-the-air radio because the radio dial is very limited, with only so much room on the frequency spectrum for private businesses to use the public's air to send their signals. But on the Internet the possibilities are endless.

Initially, online was having difficulty attracting advertising revenues. Even though start up costs are minimal, eventual growth can create costs. For a company streaming music over 100 or more channels the infrastructure to support that many simultaneous streams would be considerable. Online stations were getting underway on a capitalization as low as $10,000 but quickly found that to attract advertisers, more money was going to be needed for heavy marketing. Early advertisers included technology companies and other Internet companies. Next came consumer product companies that were developing Internet campaigns. Editors of an online magazine devoted to the radio and online radio industries predicted that by 2010, radio on the Net would be attracting advertisers from more than software companies and computer firms. Issues of Webnoize (www.webnoize.com) were looking toward a future in which traditional radio several years down the line would lose some audience share to both Internet radio and satellite radio. The expectation was that for at least the first ten years of the new century, traditional radio would be benefiting greatly from having so many Internet companies advertising with them.

In the early years of the 21st century, radio could be described as a thriving medium serving audiences that were looking for portability and immediacy. Radio was delivering targeted audiences to advertisers at a low cost when compared with advertising rates charged by newspapers, magazines and television. The predominant issue for the industry was the continuing dominance of FM over AM. In the biggest markets, advertisers were more attracted to FM, frequency modulation, than to AM, amplitude modulation. Another major issue early in the 21st century was a rapid consolidation in the radio industry, including multiple purchases of stations in groups and mergers of small group ownerships into larger groups of stations. The pyramiding effect of all of these mergers and consolidations was that eventually Texas-based Clear Channel Communications Inc. became the nation's biggest radio company with more than 1,200 stations across country.

Congress, near the end of the 20th century, had relaxed radio ownership limits to breathe new life into an industry trying to compete for local advertising dollars against newspaper monopolies and a rising number of television stations and national networks. In 1997, no radio group controlled more than 30 stations. By 1999, the top five companies each owned more than 100 stations, and most owned several stations in a single market. The deregulation set off a consolidation frenzy. Clear Channel completed its purchase of third-ranked Jacor Communications and merged with AMFM, a merger that resulted in the largest such acquisition in history. The combination of Clear Channel and AMFM became one of the nation's biggest outlets for advertisers, with 860+ radio stations, 19 television stations, 550,000+ billboards and Katz Media, a firm that represents electronic media. By mid-2000, the combined companies were taking in more than $5 billion in advertising, about the same amount as News Corp. and Walt Disney Co. In all, it underscored a trend among media companies toward offering advertisers packages of commercial space in multiple outlets. Infinity, previously known as a radio group, was drawing in new advertisers and securing higher ad rates through a plan that offered advertisers a combination of radio, billboard, Internet and TV time.

The Radio Signal

When a radio wave is transmitted by varying its volume, audio engineers call that modulating the amplitude. The FM signal results from modulating the pitch, or frequency, of the electromagnetic wave. AM signals will travel greater distances than FM broadcasts, especially at night. The FM signal is line-of-sight, going straight toward the horizon and beyond without a bend or a bounce. The result is, that because of the curvature of the earth, frequency modulation does not reach more than a few miles. An AM signal, on the other hand, could reach hundreds of miles, although not many stations have been given enough power to do so. The AM wave can bounce off electrically charged particles in the ionosphere allowing it to cover a large area, but it also picks up unwanted interference from weather and other atmospheric conditions. Because FM's signal penetrates rather than bounces, it cannot travel as far, but it does not pick up static. By varying the frequency, FM's inventors came up with a carrier wave that was much better than AM at reproducing the full range of sound, a crucial factor for music lovers. Because it is free of static, or any extraneous interference, FM offers a better quality signal than AM.

The AM stations are located between 540 and 1600 kilohertz on the electromagnetic spectrum. Some of them are given the maximum 50,000 watts of power and are placed low on the dial. The lower the spot of the AM dial, the farther the signal will travel. In other words, the weaker frequencies are up near 1400 to 1600 kilohertz and need more power to travel as far as those lower on the dial. The FCC has designated many of the stations on the lower part of the dial as clear-channel stations, intending that they reach large numbers of people over a large geographical area with their 50,000 watts of power. Many other stations are given from 2,500 to 10,000 watts of power while located on the middle of the band, making them regional stations. It is FCC policy to allow a number of such regional broadcasters to reach a whole large state or maybe a group of smaller states, but with a signal that is not so strong that the same channel cannot be assigned to other stations in other parts of the country.

The third class of AM operation allowed by the commission is the local station. These are on higher frequencies, probably above 1200, and are given the minimum 250 watts of power so they can be duplicated many times over all across the country. These stations have signals that carry over a 30- to 40-mile area and serve small communities. An example would be a station in a small town in Nebraska sharing 1480 or 1540 with stations in Illinois, one or both of the Dakotas, Iowa, Ohio and in other scattered locations. There is little chance of any of them ever interfering with each other.

The FCC has also created types of classes, or channels, for FM stations. The most powerful FMs are in class C, with 100,000 watts of power. The higher frequencies allocated by the FCC for FM stations require a bit of power to travel even 20 to 30 miles. The less powerful FM stations are either class B or class A.

Audiences have responded to the better fidelity of FM and overwhelmingly favor it. Industry estimates are that 75% of the radio audience is with the FM stations, although slightly more than half of the stations in the country are on the AM band. FM has been increasingly more favored by listeners since the FCC decided in the 1960s that FM signals were better suited to stereo sound than AM. The FM audience is attracted to music. AM listeners tune to news, sports, call-in shows, and other, usually quite local, non-music offerings.

Automation, the compact disc and computers have given FM stations even more advantages in the last few years. Increasing use of automated equipment has reduced operating costs for stations with the short-range FM signal suitable for a small, local area. A competitive edge for FM results from AM's need for larger transmitters, taller and larger towers, and generally more expensive electronics for the kind of signal that goes a long distance. The lower start-up and operating expenses, plus less maintenance for the FM signal result in a lower financial investment and an on-going economic advantage over AM. One reason listeners give for preferring FM is they believe that they hear fewer commercials. If FM can charge lower commercial rates and still meet expenses, there is no great need for so many commercials. Obviously, the higher the ratings a station has, the more the sponsor is willing to pay for a commercial. That factors well for the FM station because of its dominance over AM in the competition for listeners. The compact disc and computers eliminated needle noise and record wear and added to the already superior sound quality on the FM band.

Radio stations rarely play records any more. Until recently, almost all music was transferred to cartridges for play on the air. The improved sound attributed to the CD, or compact disc, and digital music from computers is a boon to FM because it is primarily a provider of music. Many AMs, particularly in the middle-sized to large markets, have avoided trying to compete with the same type of music or the same music formats that spell success for FM. Instead of disc jockeys, some AM stations offer drive-time hosts who entertain with games, quiz shows, comedy routines, quirky interview guests, listener participation, and some wild stunts. Some of the so-called AM disc jockeys never play music.

The AM format in the larger markets is rarely that of one person playing music. Instead, it is either morning or afternoon drive time, a pair of congenial or zany hosts doing jokes, discussing local topics of major concern and inviting listeners to participate. They usually give away movie tickets, ballgame tickets, memorabilia, etc.

Often, this is an aggregate of three or four persons, each with an area of responsibility. One of them no doubt does voice impressions of celebrities and other comedy bits. Another looks for the human interest and oddity in the day's news and comments on that and even invites calls from listeners on such topics. Another leaves the station and broadcasts intermittently from various locations around the city giving hints as to where he or she is.

Comedy, conversation and conviviality join community as the ingredients of much of AM program content in the effort to find an alternative to the music on FM. The AM stations seek an alternative, mobile audience and try to grab their attention with what they cannot get on television or by listening solely to music. In the periods of the day when radio listening drops, the tendency is for more serious, more political or issue-oriented programs, usually featuring a local host or a syndicated or network talker. These hosts are often controversial, inviting callers and then arguing with them and even insulting them. Rush Limbaugh combines a sense of humor with a clear political slant to generate huge audiences through bombast and controversy. Jim Rome offers a hard edge to his put-downs of many of his callers on his nationally broadcast sports talk show.

In smaller markets, there is little distinction between AM and FM. If you are the only voice in the community, it is difficult to find a specialty. In towns small enough to support one or two radio stations, the approach is likely to be what radio became in the years shortly after television usurped the early network format of radio game shows, drama, soap operas, and other 30-minute to one-hour programs. In smaller markets, AM and FM both provide what was radio's alternative to the competition from television. These stations play the hits, "Jukebox" style, one song after another with occasional network newscasts and even some brief locally-produced news updates. Certainly, the disc jockey approach in AM continues throughout much of the industry, not just in small towns. In the bigger cities some AM stations specialize in some music format not directly competitive with what is on FM stations. Country music comes to mind, as does the oldies format, especially music of the swing or big band era.

A prime reason for the success of the disc jockey style from its very beginning was the very strong and mutually beneficial relationship that developed with the recording industry. Record producers learned as early as the 1950s that disc jockeys provided extensive exposure for their products and were eager to supply records and albums at no cost. This symbiotic relationship came about because the radio station got free product and the record producers got free promotion. Radio airplay helped to sell records and radio stations operators learned from record store sales what audiences wanted to hear.

At the turn of the century, there were about 4,800 commercial AM radio stations operating in the U.S. Commercial FM stations numbered about 6,300 and there were about 2,900 non-commercial FM stations.

Low-Power Radio Stations

As the 21st century began, the FCC, in response to the trend of consolidation within the radio industry, created low-power FM radio stations in an effort to provide access to the airwaves for more diverse voices. Such stations have a limited range—about one mile to no more than 18 miles depending on the height of the broadcast antenna and the terrain of the land in the area—and they have to be non-commercial. About 1,000 such stations were initially created. Underrepresented groups, educational institutions, religious groups and community groups are permitted to apply for a license to operate a low-power radio station. To start the process, two broad categories of stations were created—LP10 (1 watt to 10 watts) and LP100 (50 watts to 100 watts). The FCC said that licenses will be awarded based on the strength of a group's ties to the local community that the station would serve. Established full-power radio station managers are opposed to the creation of low-power stations, because they fear interference in the form of static or distorted signals. The FCC engineers have assured those concerned that low-power stations will be able to coexist with full-power stations and consumers will not be bothered by overlapping signals.

Payola Problems

Major scandals have developed because of the close relationship between disc jockeys and recording companies. Disc jockeys were believed by record promoters to have a strong influence on the musical taste of American youths, the major purchasers of recorded music. The representatives of firms that produced and distributed recordings of popular music began to bribe disc jockeys to ensure that their songs would be played on the air. Disc jockeys, until this scandal developed, had great power over which song would be a hit and which would go nowhere. If records got no air play, they likely got little success on jukeboxes, therefore sales in the stores were not very strong.

In 1960, Congress conducted hearings into charges that bribes had been given to disc jockeys and other station personnel who could control the playing of records on the air. This practice was quickly labeled "payola," a term that resulted from combining the concept of payment with the name of the record player, the Victrola. Sometimes the bribery took the form of giving a music director or program director financial interest in a certain album or single or even in the record company. This practice was well known throughout the industry during the 1950s, with the amount of the bribe usually based on how often the record was played and on the size of the market. Late in the period as more and more program directors began to take the selection of records away from individual disc jockeys and centralize such choices, the competition among the record companies became more intense and the payments got bigger.

During the Congressional hearings, which eventually led to legislation making "payola" illegal, several disc jockeys admitted taking bribes. The Federal Communications Commission was given the power to stop the practice and station licensees cracked down on their employees by careful monitoring of decisions about airplay and putting staff members on notice that they would be prosecuted if caught taking bribes. The station owners were, of course, afraid of losing their licenses and were not about to tolerate any actions that could cause them problems with the FCC. In 1960, a grand jury in New York charged eight broadcasters with participation in bribery for accepting more than $100,000 to play records. Their cases were in the courts for the next five years and were generally handled by the dispensation of fines and probation in exchange for guilty pleas.

Payola did not go away, although it did seem to lessen considerably. In 1974, there were resignations from a handful of radio stations when payola charges surfaced. In 1984, Congress again conducted hearings about the practices, but not much of significance resulted. Investigators were told that payola was difficult to identify when cash and gifts were often given in appreciation and should not be construed as bribery. These hearings bogged down in an inability to determine the significance of gifts given after airplay rather than before and whether it could ever be demonstrated that a gift was related to a specific record.

A year later, newspaper reporters claimed to have uncovered evidence that payola existed in a new form. These charges were that record companies paid a small group of independent record promoters millions of dollars a year to get certain records listed on the charts, the industry's list of week-by-week big hits. *The New York Times* carried accusations that these independent promoters would spend money legitimately promoting hit records but would also spread a small portion of that money around unethically and illegally in under-the-table payments to program directors. The result of a series of newspaper stories was that the six major record companies dropped their relationships with several independent promoters. The allegations in the mid- to late-1980s were about the actions of the independent promoters not the record companies. Part of this period of rumors and allegations of payola was what came to be labeled "drugola." It was contended at the time that the promoters were rewarding radio station executives with cocaine and other popular drugs to encourage them to increase the airplay of certain songs.

These allegations were never actually proved, so "drugola" faded as an issue. A federal statute says payola is a misdemeanor offense punishable by a maximum fine of $10,000 and one year in jail. However, there is no illegality unless a prosecutor can clearly show that any drugs, money or other gifts can be tied specifically and only to one specific record's airplay—a difficult task.

In 2007, four broadcast conglomerates that owned about 1,700 radio stations agreed to pay $12.5 million in fines to settle payola violations. Entercom Communications, Clear Channel Communications, CBS Radio and Citadel Broadcasting also agreed to provide airtime for local artists and independent record label artists. In announcing the payola settlement, FCC Commissioner Michael Copps said "pay-for play" broadcasting cheats consumers and musicians, because it denies consumers their right to choose and deprives musicians of the exposure they need to survive.

Aspects of Radio

Radio requires no special skill on the part of the audience, unlike print media which require the ability to read. Radio is the most pervasive of all of the media. It goes with us wherever we go. It is so portable that we can use it anywhere. The portable radio and the car radio give us flexibility as listeners and give the industry a great opportunity to reach active consumers in a highly mobile society. We listen to the radio as we workout on exercise equipment, as we jog or walk, and even as we wander through the mall.

The radio is an aid to the commuter, bringing company on long drives and offering information about traffic conditions. We hear the radio even by accident, from devices carried by passersby and from speakers in the stores where we shop. Radio is ubiquitous, primarily because of its portability, but also because of its presence in the automobile. Americans spend so much time on the roads, streets, highways and freeways that they come to depend on the radio to keep them in touch with life around them while isolated in their vehicles. There are three times as many radios in the United States than there are people. There are twice as many radio sets in American homes as television sets. Research demonstrates that 96% of Americans over the age of 12 listen to radio each week.

There are about 14,000 radio stations in the United States, each of them carrying information and entertainment through a virtual person-to-person communication. One announcer seems to be talking to one person at a time, yet one station reaches thousands of listeners, and the industry counts millions of listeners at any given moment.

Local advertising accounts for 75% of the typical radio station's income. National and regional spot advertisers generate about 20% of the income. A station affiliated with a network will get from 5 to 10% of its income from the network. For those who are affiliates, the networks supply programming to individual stations and pay money from advertising income to the stations. For both AM and FM, there is so much dependence on local programming that networks are used primarily for occasional newscasts. Also, some AM stations take network feeds of nationally syndicated talk shows. Rush Limbaugh is probably the best known of these, but several others have large national audiences thanks to their affiliations with hundreds of local stations.

Networking began with early radio, but has become more significant in television as nationally produced material became increasingly less valuable to the local audiences of radio. Radio stations function much like magazines in their appeal to advertisers. Local station programmers understand the fragmented special interests that individual advertisers would like to reach at low advertising rates.

This is similar to the specialized content and narrow appeal of so many magazines that keep their production and distribution costs down by targeting a narrowly defined sub-audience. A magazine, like a radio station, can keep its advertising rates down by specializing in target readers, or listeners, identified as very likely to be interested in the specific content. Radio networks were in their glory when national programming was each station's primary content, much like today's television stations. In the years before television, national advertisers realized the potential for reaching more buyers for their products and services by linking several stations together by land lines, resulting in simultaneous broadcasting in several cities. A large number of stations hooked up to these lines allowed the networks to charge high advertising rates. However, that advantage virtually disappeared for the radio stations with the advent of television.

Radio prime time, where the largest audiences are and where the highest advertising rates are, is in the early morning and to a lesser extent, in the late afternoon. Prime time for television is in the evening when viewers are home and the networks and cable channels provide their most attractive programs. Radio, however, has it highest audiences when listeners are not at home. They are on the road. The largest number of listeners are tuned to radio during what is called "drive time." Listeners tune in primarily from 6:00 am to 9:00 am and again from 3:30 pm to 6:30 pm, although the drive time hours vary greatly from one part of the country to another. Radio listening drops off in the middle of the day as most Americans find themselves in the workforce and again at night when television sets are turned on.

Radio listening is often unplanned, a result of a need for background sound or a diversion while doing something else, or a sudden traffic jam causes a driver to search for a traffic report. Word of mouth tells us of a breaking news event, necessitating a check of the radio dial for instant coverage of timely events. Some radio listening is scheduled. The alarm on the clock radio goes off at the same time each workday and music or news is the background through the shower, breakfast and preparation for the day ahead. Often the drive to work or school is at the

Your Thoughts

Do you listen to AM or FM stations more often? Why?

When do you listen to the radio most often? Why?

What could radio station executives do to get you to listen to the radio more often?

same hour each day and for the same length of time. That could mean a certain station is scheduled for that period of drive time, although many of us are button pushers in the car, scanning the dial as we drive.

The extent of radio listening can be appreciated when we learn that 44% of Americans say they listen to the radio between midnight and 6:00 am. That is radio's downtime. Radio rating services have learned that even during odd hours, radio reaches a good-sized audience. The audience between midnight and daylight is young, with a median age of 30 on weekends. Industry figures show 26% of the potential audience listens during radio's prime time and that drive time listeners are a little older than those at night and on weekends. The statistics gathered by those who supply the industry with ratings data indicate that women listen more than men and black Americans listen more than those in other ethnic or racial categories.

Radio Programming Formats

With so many radio stations available to consumers in most areas, especially medium to large cities, stations try to develop programming that will appeal to selected segments or groups of people. Such specialized programming makes it easy for consumers to find the type of music, news and talk that interests them. Traditional radio programming formats include adult contemporary, contemporary hits, album-oriented rock, middle-of-the-road, beautiful music, oldies, country, urban contemporary, jazz, religious, classical, news-talk and specialty.

Adult Contemporary (AC)

Adult contemporary is a format designed to appeal to 25 to 40 year olds and offers adult rock and light rock music. About 20% of the stations in the country program this type of music. It is very prevalent on the FM band. Some of the same music could be a major part also of the contemporary hits format. In fact, rock music in one variation or another is the most common formula in the radio industry. Adult contemporary has been a consistently successful approach with its blend of selected hit singles and

some album cuts. It is sometimes referred to as soft rock, but often it simply features rock performers in some of their ballads or love songs. It also offers some crossover artists doing country-rock or jazz-rock tunes.

Contemporary Hits Radio (CHR)

Top 40 or contemporary hits radio is big with teenagers. The music is usually dependent upon Billboard magazine's list of the current best selling songs. It's a format that closely follows listener preferences. Top 40 could even be top 30 with a disc jockey playing a fairly small number of best-selling singles, with a few songs on that list getting extra play.

Album-Oriented Rock (AOR)

Album-oriented rock is music for those who have just left their teens. It is similar to top 40, but tends to have a play list of the most popular songs over a period of two or three years not just the current hits. In fact, some album-oriented rock formats feature hits from an earlier period similar to an oldies format. Most, however, feature contemporary tunes. Album-oriented rock appeals strongly to young males beyond their teens. This was, in its early years, an FM phenomenon and was called progressive radio. It developed as an alternative to AM radio's repetitive playing of the same contemporary hits.

Middle-of-the-Road (MOR)

Middle-of-the-road is the format aimed at those in their late 20s and early 30s who prefer their music not to rock too much but not very soft either. The music is sometimes contemporary, but often covers a period of five to 10 years of the work of long-time popular artists. The middle-of-the-road format often calls for the disc jockey to do more talking, more interaction with the audience, in what some call personality radio. It can result in comedy bits, stunts, games, contests, calls from listeners, much more conversation and disc jockey activity than the hard rock formats.

The middle-of-the-road format avoids the frenetic rhythms and raucous instrumentation of the heavy rock 'n roll that teenagers prefer. MOR is intended to attract some young adults but tries not to alienate those who find hard rock objectionable. This format avoids extremes. Never will it offer heavy metal or semi-classical. Never will it play show tunes. You can hear rhythm and blues music if it isn't too ethnic. You can get some country and western, as long as it doesn't approach bluegrass and isn't too "down home" or "hillbilly." Jazz is all right if it isn't too innovative. This format delivers a demographic profile of young people with high educational and high income levels. It does that by the personality of the announcers, the audience involvement, and in offering music that won't drive away listeners whose target profile appeals to advertisers.

Beautiful Music

Related to MOR is the beautiful music, easy listening or soft hits format. This depends heavily on the music to carry it with little awareness on the part of the audience of the disc jockey's role. Rock music fans call this "elevator music." It is often referred to as "dentist's office music" or "Muzak radio." It appeals heavily to women, but also generally to large numbers of mature adults. Its smooth-sounding standards, romantic ballads, show tunes and lush instrumentals make this format commercially viable. It is at the top of the ratings in many markets and near the top in others, perhaps because so many competing rock stations combine to share portions of the large rock audience.

When this format evolved in the years following radio's changeover to the playing of recorded music as a response to television's incursion, this style was called "good music" by those in the industry. By the 1970s, it was being called "easy listening," and by the late 1980s and into the 1990s, it was usually referred to as "beautiful music." It got its highest ratings and greatest popularity by the mid-1980s, serving as radio's background function. It is generally conceded that it serves listeners well who need the radio to keep them company as they go about activities that otherwise keep them busy. Some of the smoother, more mellow sounds of contemporary rock performers make it to this format.

Oldies

One of the most difficult formats to describe is the one that depends on music that was popular in an earlier era. The wide diversity of such music indicates a variety of specializations within the specialty. These stations are generally quite unlike each other. Some play the music of the 1970s, some the 1960s, others the 1990s, or a particular type of music during one period or another. What is an old tune to one person is still a new song to another.

These formats, depending on the types of songs played as much as the era selected, are often called "golden oldies," "vintage gold," "classic gold," "gold," or "classic rock." One AM station calls itself "the memory station." A format can be selected to reach a target audience so that advertisers for specific products will know how to reach potential buyers. Stations seek a demographic identity by identifying oldies as the music of Herman's Hermits, Paul Revere and the Raiders, the Beatles or even the Monkees.

Country

Country, or country-western, is one of the most popular types of programming. There are more stations employing this format than any other. Adult contemporary is the second most frequently employed format.

Country gets older listeners and does well with men. Every big metropolitan area has at least one country station and some have two, demonstrating that the rural sound has appeal even in the big cities. Only the various rock formats are more commercially successful than country and western. In the south and parts of the midwest, country stations pull in even bigger numbers of listeners than rock formats. The demographic profile of the country station listener is fairly mature, and heavily male. Significantly, country listeners spend their money at a greater rate than the population generally, and spend it on big-ticket items: boats, recreational vehicles, trucks, jet skis, etc. Advertisers are eager to buy time on such stations.

Many in the industry no longer refer to it as country and western, but instead choose to simply call it country music. Much of this format's growth came in the mid-1980s and it has remained as a staple in the radio business ever since.

Country music has "carried over" to much of the mainstream music audience these days. Many radio stations carry some country songs in their adult contemporary, middle-of-the-road or Top 40 playlists. The crossover has featured numerous instances in the 1990s of rock performers incorporating country influences in their songs. Industry sources say that probably 50% of the stations in the United States play at least some country songs. The best known country artists are known to even larger audiences now.

Urban Contemporary (UC)

Soul music is the usual label for the playlists on the 300+ stations appealing primarily to African-American listeners. Some are actually owned by Blacks, but others are primarily operated by and staffed by Black employees under White ownership. They program for an urban audience and play the music that is considered too ethnic for most of the popular music formats, although much rhythm and blues still can be heard on adult-oriented radio and, especially urban contemporary formats. Most soul music stations are in the largest metropolitan centers and many of them carry playlists very similar to those of the adult contemporary or Top 40 stations. However, some rappers and hip-hop performers are more likely to be featured on stations that appeal primarily to African-American listeners.

Jazz

Jazz stations are few, appear to be diminishing in number, and tend to be near the bottom of the ratings in every market in which they appear. Because the potential audience is so small, they exist only in big cities where they carve out a small niche in the overall audience, one that is thought of as a loyal audience. Listeners of jazz are believed by advertisers to be young, affluent, well-educated, goal-oriented and success driven. Today's jazz music is greatly different from what radio stations programmed in their earlier years, largely because, by its very nature, jazz music is destined to change and evolve. It is a form of innovative music that allows a performer to be creative, to improvise and to offer personal interpretations of the basic idiom. Today's fusion jazz is so different from the origins of jazz that many might have difficulty even making the connection. It is a music that has evolved through changing technology and new instrumentation.

Religious

Religious stations abound in the so-called Bible Belt, the nation's south and lower midwest, but are found also everywhere else. There are about 1,100 stations programming primarily inspirational music, speeches, church services, religious news and promotional material for one denomination or another. It is a format that certain advertisers are eager to embrace because of the clear demographic profile of the listeners. Some of the stations are owned and operated by a sect or denomination that uses the station to spread its faith and to maintain the loyalty and enthusiasm of its members.

Classical

Classical and semi-classical were once staples on the radio band, important in the early years but dwindling in numbers since the 1980s. In fact, semi-classical stations have all but disappeared and only a handful remain playing classical music. These are primarily public stations that tend to offer non-commercial artistic or cultural programs with the classical music only a part of the broadcast day.

Talk Radio

Talk radio has been credited with or blamed for, depending on your political persuasion, the resurgence of political conservatism, and specifically what some observers called the Gingrich Revolution. It is argued that Newt Gingrich and the Contract with America got much of their impetus from this country's talkathon culture. It is estimated that 75% of America's radio talk show hosts are politically conservative, but not all of talk radio is politically conservative, and all of its topics are not political. Rush Limbaugh is probably the best known radio talk show host.

Other talk programs specialize in health, gardening, entertainment, sports, consumerism, and many other topics. A San Diego station with a talk format carries, in addition to Rush Limbaugh and a local political conservative as host, a landscape architect doing a well-received weekend morning show on home gardening and a weekend afternoon show featuring an auto mechanic answering listeners' questions about problems with their cars. The same station had a program called "Ask the Builder," with a contractor answering questions, and one called "Financial Management," with two certified financial planners fielding calls from listeners. It is one of two talk shows on the station devoted to investments.

Another show host is an expert on property management and co-hosts with a lawyer who specializes in representing landlords sued by their tenants.

A competing station offers a talk program hosted by a lawyer who invites other lawyers to join him to answer questions about any legal problems the listeners might have. Both stations offer computer experts as hosts of programs for callers who have trouble with software, hardware or anything else in cyberspace. In a digital world, on-line enthusiasts who get lost on the Internet or face malfunction in their home PCs, can turn to radio for help. Computer gurus have joined the variety of talk show hosts, nearly all of whom dispense information and advice in a call-in format. Some feature studio and phone guests who answer questions from listeners.

Admittedly, this variety is tempered somewhat by the preponderance of politically oriented and politically conservative hosts, and by the tendency of many others to embrace sensational topics. The variety also is limited by the fact that 80% of the nation's radio talk show hosts are male.

All-talk radio makes the listener part of the show, creating an instantaneous two-way interactive communication, with millions of Americans participating in a national discourse each day by telephoning their questions and their opinions to over-the-air chat lines.

All-News

All-news formats have been appearing in greater numbers as AM stations look to avoid direct competition with FM. The all-news format obviously works better in large metropolitan areas where a specialized format can still appeal to sufficiently large numbers of listeners. The demographics of this audience can appeal greatly to advertisers. The all-news audience is well-educated, mature, high income, and loyal to the station. There are about 600 AM stations carrying from 18 to 24 hours of news a day, up from 60 or so just 20 years ago.

News-Talk

News-talk is a format based on the belief that audiences crave information. Many listeners need constant awareness of the world around them, to be aware of what their friends, co-workers and neigh-bors are talking about or concerned with. Demographics weigh heavily in a decision to go to what is often called an "information" format. For advertisers, no format is better at attracting males, especially mature, affluent males, than a combination of all-news and all-talk. The talk shows attract 35- to 65-year olds; all-news programming draws 25- to 45-year olds. Both formats appeal strongly to men. A station's sales staff armed with this information can pitch a presentation to potential advertisers who want their messages to reach adult males.

More than 1,800 stations employ the news-talk, or news and information format, up from only 300 in the late 1980s. By combining two formats into one, a program director adds to flexibility by being able to adjust the on-air content for maximum effect on the targeted demographic groups depending on time of day and the potential numbers of listeners. An all-news format pulls in big audiences during morning and afternoon drive times. In mid-morning, when audiences are smaller, a talk-show aimed at women can offer not only interactivity with telephone call-ins, but also special features on topics that appeal to the primarily female daytime audience. In the afternoon, before returning to a solid block of news, the station can again overcome the potentially small audience by stressing topics related to the political, social and personal issues that dominate the lives of those who are listening.

The station's overhead is minimal on a telephone call-in show, so it is economically worthwhile to seek some rating strength with talk shows at a time when the number of listeners cannot be expected to be very great. The evening and night-time hours are also not expected to produce large audiences, so the flexibility of the news-talk format allows for an adjustment again. This usually means play-by-play sports, a sports-oriented talk show, or some other type of narrowly specialized call-in show, including some that are dating services, advice-to-lovelorn programs, medical advice from physician hosts, and many other possibilities. Call-the-doctor programs, in particular, have been a staple of night and weekend programming on these formats when there is a need to offer another type of information at a time of traditionally low radio listening. The news-talk approach is the third most frequently-employed format behind adult contemporary, the leader, and second-place country music.

All-Sports

All-sports formats are a variation of news-talk. They are few in number and they usually have low ratings, but do have a clear demographic profile for certain types of advertisers. These stations, out of necessity in the biggest markets, generally offer mostly talk with occasional short summaries of sports news. Many of the call-in shows have on-the-air sports celebrities as guests for interviews and to draw the audience into explanation and discussion of events or contests being explored. This gives listeners a chance to go on the air with the host and the guesting sports personality.

Foreign Language (Spanish)

The rapidly growing Spanish-speaking population in this country has aided the growth of Spanish-language broadcasting. Most of it came in the late 1990s as AM stations foundered when their earlier formats could not compete with FM for audiences.

Format Popularity

In general, the following is how the various radio station programming formats stack up based on audience share:

1. News-Talk	18.2%
2. Urban Contemporary	12.4%
3. Adult Contemporary	11.4%
4. Country	11.0%
5. Spanish	7.7%
6. Oldies	6.0%
7. Album-Oriented Rock	5.4%
8. Modern Rock	5.4%
9. Contemporary Hits	4.4%
10. Hot Adult Contemporary	4.0%
11. Classic Rock	3.4%
12. Jazz	3.0%
13. Classical	2.2%
14. Adult Alternative	2.0%

The rest of the audience listens to religion-based stations, ethnic stations and all-sports stations.

Station Operation

The general manager is the executive in charge of all phases of the station's operation. All department heads come under supervision of the general manager. The general manager is responsible for business operations, including billing and payroll. The general manager has ultimate control over engineering and maintenance, as well as the news department, promotional efforts, local and national sales departments, relations with the community and, of course, responsibilities to the public through the Federal Communications Commission and its interpretations of a radio station's obligation to serve the public interest. It is the general manager's job to see that the station's application for license renewal is met with favor by the FCC.

Sales Manager/Account Executives

The sales manager is in charge of the income-producing department, which is typically the largest department in a radio station. It is made up of a section devoted to local sales and one to national

Your Thoughts

What are your THREE most favorite radio programming formats? Why?

accounts. The sales manager's staff is a group of individuals who contact potential advertisers and try to convince them to buy time on the air to sell their products and services. These people are called account executives and are generally among the highest paid people in radio. The general manager, in almost every instance, has come through the ranks of sales to become local sales director then national sales director, and sales manager before becoming general manager. Many of those working in radio view the general manager as a sort of super sales manager.

The account executive must bring in enough advertisers, not only to generate revenue for the station's overhead, but also to be sure the station is profitable. The members of the sales staff work on a commission basis, which is why they are so well-paid in a medium that has consistently generated huge profits for its owners and investors. Salespeople do a lot to create those profits and are rewarded by getting up to a 15% commission on each commercial sold. However, if they fail to bring in advertisers, they do not last long.

Traffic Department

Working closely with sales is the traffic department. Traffic is responsible for creating and then maintaining a daily program log, which is really a method of keeping track of all of the commercials and when they air. The log displays the broadcast day, the flow of programming through a 24-hour period, giving a minute-by-minute account of when each commercial is to go on the air. Every program, every announcement, every newscast, every station identification, and every commercial must run as scheduled according to the log. Disc jockeys, engineers and announcers must follow the log exactly. If a mistake is made, a discrepancy report must be filed with station management. If the mistake is on a commercial, the sponsor is given another commercial, free, in what is known as a "makegood."

Production Department

The production department works closely with sales, although it is aligned with the programming department. In many stations, certainly small stations and those in small markets, production is part of programming. Disc jockeys or announcers, typically assigned to programming, usually spend part of their workday in a production studio. A disc jockey is usually scheduled to work seven hours a day, but only three to four hours on the air. The rest of the day is given to preparation time, personal appearances, and most often, working on the production of commercials. The production director often has disc jockey duties as well. When an announcer comes off an air shift, it is usually time to go into the production studio where the station's jingles, public service announcements, promotions, commercials, and other pre-recorded sounds are prepared. That effort is supervised by the production director.

Engineering Department

Often, engineering is the smallest department in the operation, but it could be argued that it is the most important. The engineers monitor the station's signal, keeping their eyes on the dials that indicate when the carrier wave, antenna current, transmitter output, etc., are all functioning to keep the station on the air and in federal compliance with restrictions that protect stations from interfering with each other while sending a signal with carefully regulated parameters. Engineers maintain a log of their transmitter readings to satisfy federal requirements. The engineers perform maintenance on all of the electronic equipment and do any necessary repairs. Engineers are needed for broadcasts from remote locations, initially to set up and check on the facilities needed and then to handle the production in the field to be sure a good, clean signal gets back to the station control room for eventual broadcast. Some stations get along with as few as two or three engineers, usually a chief engineer and an assistant, maybe a third person shared part-time with another station department.

Program Department

The program department bears ultimate responsibility for the product offered to the listener—the sound of the station. Because the general manager typically has a background in sales and often knows nothing, or very little, of music, production, or program content, program directors quite often end up with virtually full authority over every part of the station's operation except sales. The programming department is so important overall that only the general manager can match the program director in power, responsibility, authority and prestige in the station hierarchy. Sometimes these executives are called program managers or operations managers. In addition, they often assume the additional roles of promotion director, music director or production director.

In the medium-sized and big-market stations, the program director (or program manager) will appoint one of the disc jockeys to be a part-time music director or part-time production director. In some cases, a full-time specialist in production is hired, who, of course, is directly answerable to the program director. Often, program directors are reluctant to give up the role of music director. They control the music choices themselves or hire consulting firms that specialize in creating packages of music guaranteed to appeal strongly to a station's desired target audience. A program director's job security is tied directly to the success or failure of the format in achieving the audience ratings needed either in numbers or demographics, or both. Many program directors, feeling this pressure, attempt to control their own fate by not delegating the responsibility. Others are willing to trust the expertise of consultants. Of course, if the ratings go down, the consulting firm can be blamed and the program director is safe until the next ratings book comes out.

The program director is ultimately responsible not only for the amount and type of music played but also for everything else that goes on the air. It is the program director who hires and fires disc jockeys and assigns them their duties and their schedules. Additional duties include audience analysis and interpretation of ratings data. Many program directors also assume the promotion duties. Others will be willing to hire promotion directors to stage events, contests, stunts and activities involving station personalities, and to market or advertise the station through billboards, newspaper ads or any other means of getting the attention of potential listeners.

The job of program director evolved from the changing system of organizing duties and responsibilities for the very first full-time disc jockeys. Radio's formula for success in the 1950s was to avoid competing directly with television for audiences. Radio began to find fertile ground in morning and afternoon drive time for a mobile audience, one that could be reached through the repetition of popular "jukebox style" music and the personality of the announcers. Initially, these disc jockeys had considerable autonomy in selecting their music and in what they could say on the air between musical selections. Many stations would promote one of them to be chief announcer, a position for someone who would control work schedules, deal with personnel matters, determine music play and regulate the disc jockey's broadcast comments. That position quickly evolved into music director, then to program director. The stations then had someone not only to dictate what records would be played and in what order; but also to assume jurisdiction over most operations and functions identified as crucial to the sound of the station and, thus, to the ratings. That pretty much made this the most powerful, most responsible job in the radio industry.

Disc Jockeys

The disc jockey has been a crucial element in radio programming since the 1950s, although there was some playing of recorded music well before then. Until the 1940s, live music was what radio primarily offered. However, the disc jockey concept was supposed to have begun in the mid-1930s with Al Jarvis in Los Angeles and Martin Block in New York. Each offered a simulation of live broadcasting of dance bands through sound effects and recorded music. Martin Block has been mentioned often as the prototype for the modern disc jockey, but only because he took the Al Jarvis "Make Believe Ballroom" concept to a highly developed level in very polished productions and brought the sound to much larger audiences. Jarvis might have been first, but Block did more to market the spinning of records and make the program of recorded music highly profitable by drawing so many listeners that sponsors were eager to buy air time.

Until 1940, most stations avoided the playing of phonograph records, fearing the wrath of musicians who insisted that recorded music on the air would hurt sales in record stores. The musicians also complained that the use of recorded music on individual stations violated exclusivity agreements in network contracts. The impetus for many stations deciding to follow the model of Al Jarvis and Martin Block came with a 1940 court ruling the radio stations could play records without causing injury to the composers, artists, performers and music producers. In the late 1940s, radio stations were regularly employing people to spin records, read live commercials and give the time and temperature during the periods of the day when they were not carrying network soap operas, quiz shows, or dramas.

By the early 1950s, recording studios realized that radio was good for their business. The record distributors began to send singles and albums to the radio stations, hoping for airplay to give the music great exposure and help generate added sales in the record stores. But it was not until audiences began to desert radio for television, as television growth really broke through in the mid-1950s, that the disc jockey approach became the staple of radio programming. Radio found a way to bring the audiences back and found a way to avoid going head-to-head with television by taking advantage of radio's mobility. With a lone individual playing records, radio programming expenses were minimal compared with the pre-television years. With the disc jockey approach, stations could provide a constant, but interruptible flow of instantly available, but brief segments of entertainment, easy to tune in and to tune out without feeling that something is lost.

Most disc jockeys say they think of themselves as talking with individual listeners rather than a mass of people. They try to establish rapport with the audience and express themselves while not getting in the way of the music. They say they enjoy the feeling of communicating and enjoy the near-celebrity status often given them by listeners. The music might be the reason for many listeners to be loyal to a favorite station, but it is the disc jockey's personality that many of them identify with. When asked about their favorite radio stations, listeners often mention the names of disc jockeys before the call letters or frequency.

The disc jockey follows what is called a "clock," which amounts to dividing each hour of a workshift into segments representing different program elements. The hour usually begins with a brief newscast, followed by a popular song, followed by a current big hit, followed by a potential hit and then a break for commercials concludes the segment. The program director or a consultant has determined each part of the clock for the disc jockey to follow. The second segment might open with a commercially successful tune, then an oldie followed by one moving up on the current charts before concluding with a set of commercials. The next part of the clock's rotation could open with a current hit, then go to a potential hit then to a recent, but no longer hot tune. Within each part of the hourly clock, the disc jockey

will have an opportunity to tell jokes, take phone calls, give time and temperature, do station promotions, or run contests.

News Department

Even though many people turn to radio for news, most stations do not place great emphasis on news. It's rare to find more than one or two people working in news at a given station. As a result, staffers must do a variety of things: report, write, produce and announce. Read more about radio news near the end of this chapter.

Ratings

There is nothing that generates more conversation and more anxiety among radio people than "the books," the compilation of statistical data available to station management (primarily the sales department) from an audience rating firm.

The earliest efforts at attempting to count the number of listeners came with a ratings service for the Association of National Advertisers in the 1930s. These early ratings were called the Crossleys because they were administered by Archibald Crossley. They were immediately followed by the Hooperatings, also in the 1930s, organized by C.E. Hooper. Both were achieved by a random sample of listeners who were called by telephone and asked about their listening habits. Another early rating service, operating by the 1940s, was called Pulse and was based on in-home interviews with listeners. Much later, more sophisticated methods were developed by Arbitron, RAM, Mediastat, and other commercial firms that supplied the stations with audience estimates through listener diaries, meters attached to sets, as well as two types of phone interviews.

The telephone-coincidental is random calling to ask what the person is listening to at that time, if at all. Telephone-recall is asking those called to tell about what stations were listened to and when over the previous 12 to 24 hours. Another technique is to analyze audience response to programming by trying for qualitative assessments of who is listening, when, for how long, and with what intensity. This is done by focus groups, sets of 12 to 20 listeners carefully selected for intensive in-person interviews. The meter method is primarily a television ratings technique, although television ratings services, primarily Nielsen, confirm the accuracy of their data with back-up telephone calls and in-home diaries.

In radio, the diary method has become the most prominent technique. Arbitron is the radio industry's main supplier of audience data. Arbitron came about after broadcasters decided to ensure that ratings information would be accurate by setting up their own industry-supported research bureau. The American Research Bureau was created in 1949 and moved quickly to eliminate the telephone calling and instead asked listeners to fill in diaries and mail them back. Control Data Corporation bought the American Research Bureau and changed its name to Arbitron. A great deal of information can be supplied to each station in a market by Arbitron's method of requesting a sample of listeners to fill out a book that will include not only the whole family's listening habits, but also personal data on each family member. Arbitron can back up the diary with telephone inquiries and meters to verify the accuracy and reliability of the data.

An Arbitron book details a metropolitan area's ratings in numerical breakdowns of audience characteristics and gives estimates of the numbers of people listening to each station in the market, quarter hour by quarter hour. Arbitron provides the stations with three other measurements in addition to the average quarter hour, which is simply the average number of people listening to a station in any given 15-minute period. Of course, Arbitron supplies a basic rating, or the percentage of the total population that a station is reaching. Another significant measurement is the share, which is the percentage of sets tuned to the station out of only the sets that are turned on at that time.

A very important piece of information for the program director is the "cum," or cumulative ratings figures, which are estimates of the total number of people who have tuned in, at least for a little while, during a specific time period. Of these four measurements, the cum is the one that seems to have the most impact on programming decisions. All of the measures of radio listening are obviously of value to the sales staff, which has the task of convincing advertisers that the station's target audience is a cost-effective buy for a potential sponsor. But the cumulative audience estimate tells programmers that some listeners might tune in for a time, leave their sets or listen elsewhere, then tune back in. Program directors, realizing that radio listening is not done over long periods of time, can adjust their commercial breaks, newscasts, specific songs or types of songs, etc., that will generate increasingly large cumulative numbers. Every time someone tunes in, tunes out, tunes back in, that's an extra listener.

Thanks to Arbitron, station owners learn the income level, marital status, age, race, gender, occupation, educational level, and other socio-economic data about the audience. These aspects of audiences and sub-audiences are as important to potential advertisers as the size of a station's audience.

Station management depends on the ratings to set advertising rates. The station commanding the highest advertising rates usually is the one with the most listeners, or the one with the highest numbers in the most desired demographic profile. Certain groups of listeners might be more appealing to advertisers than others, so a format aimed at a target audience delivering more of that type of audience than competitors for that set of listeners can pay off in more revenue.

Arbitron ratings periods are scheduled four times a year in the bigger markets, once or twice a year in smaller markets. The resultant book breaks down the market into ratings, shares, cums, and average quarter-hours for each station. Armed with this information, a station's sales staff can inform potential sponsors of the value of buying advertising messages and at what time of day for what profiled listeners. Success demonstrated by a ratings book can determine the cost of a commercial. A station usually raises or lowers its rates to reflect scores in the Arbitron book. A low-priced commercial on one station might not be the bargain it appears to be if the audience is too young, or its income level too low, etc., so a higher-priced commercial on a competing station could be more cost effective because Arbitron data reveals that the audience will spend money on the advertiser's product.

Ratings have played a central role in determining radio content and radio's advertising rates since the 1930s. The evolution of audience assessment techniques over 60 years has made Arbitron the acknowledged leader in getting reliable information about the consumption of the radio product. Arbitron has had to come up with new methods over time to keep pace with technology, but still uses the basics of survey research to get statistics that chart audience size, characteristics and behavior.

Portable People Meters (PPM) are the latest innovation in radio ratings technologies and audience measurement. PPMs are electronic devices that make it possible to measure the listening habits of people automatically. Electronic codes embedded in radio programming are recorded by the PPMs. At the end of each day's radio listening, the people using the PPMs send the data to a central computer for processing. No diaries, no straining your memory—just carry your PPM and send in the recorded data each day.

Regulation

During the formative days of this nation, men such as Thomas Jefferson fought long and hard to provide constitutional guarantees for a free press. Jefferson realized that where the government is subject to constant surveillance by mass media, it probably can never conceal from the people any anti-democratic plans.

Since opposition to government control of the mass media is so firmly planted, one may logically question the control exercised over the broadcasting media by the Federal Communications Commission. Is such control justified, or is it repugnant to the basic features of American democracy? What is the extent of this control? Why can broadcasting be subjected to it, and why aren't newspapers controlled in the same way?

The answers to most of these questions lie in the essential differences between the print and broadcast media. Courts have consistently held, contrary to popular belief, that the newspaper is not a public utility. Rather, it is simply a private enterprise—a business engaged in selling a product to a consumer. While it is true that most of the financial support for the newspaper comes from the advertising it carries, the newspaper nonetheless does sell its product. A publisher specifically solicits subscriptions to the paper and when you pay your 50¢ for the morning newspaper, you are giving a monetary consideration for a product, just as surely as when you plop down your money for your morning cup of coffee. Furthermore, just like any business, you or your neighbor or anyone else in the United States can go into the business of publishing a newspaper at any time you please—this, of course, subject to the normal business requirement of adequate capital.

In contrast to these points, broadcasting does not sell a service to its consumers. The broadcaster's product is available free of charge to anyone willing to tune in, assuming, of course, that the potential audience member has a radio or television receiver. You may choose to tune away from a radio station any time, and you will be out nothing more than the amount of time you have spent listening. You will have suffered no financial setback.

Also unlike the newspaper, you cannot simply decide to go into the broadcasting business. There are a limited number of frequencies available for broadcasting. From the standpoint of physical restrictions, there is simply not enough room on the broadcast band for everyone who might like to go into the radio or television business. To this extent, broadcasting is not a private enterprise in the sense that the print media are.

The one thing that really distinguishes broadcasting from the print media is that it makes unique use of public property—namely, the atmosphere around us. From a legal standpoint, the air has long been considered as part of the public domain. That is, no one can "own" the atmosphere; rather, it belongs to all of the people. It is reasonable, then, that all of the people should have some kind of say in just how this property is used. Obviously not everyone can be consulted concerning the use of this property. One of the functions of a government is to represent all the people and scrutinize the use of the public's property.

This is rather like any other situation involving public property. The city park in your town is a good example. The park is owned by the public. Through the city government, the public maintains the park. City employees keep the area clean, mow the lawns, take care of the walks and drives through the park, and so on. In many parks, vendors walk about selling hot dogs, balloons or novelties. In some parks, there are amusement rides. As a rule, these enterprises are conducted by private citizens, not by the city itself. In other words, such vendors are trespassing on public property for their own private profit. In order to ensure that these private individuals act in the best interests of the public, which owns the property, the city usually licenses these concession operators. They are given special permits to offer their goods and services for sales in the public park. Usually, the number of such franchises is limited. And should a vendor do something which the city does not believe to be in the public interest, the privilege is taken away.

This vendor could fail in the obligation to the public by becoming apathetic in discharging the duties or by acquiring too much control. If a private citizen were to own all of the vending stands in the park, a lack of competition would reduce the vendor's interest and ability to serve the public. The vendor may become so concerned with personal profit that the obligation to serve the public interest might be overlooked.

In broadcasting, these dangers of monopoly are overcome through regulation. Broadcasters are licensed by the government on behalf of the national public. This government regulation procedure dates back to 1912, when the so-called Marine Radio Act granted the power of issuing broadcast licenses to the Commerce Department. At that time, little thought was given to commercial broadcasting as we understand it today. The prevailing view of radio was a picture of point-to-point communication, such as telephone and ship-to-shore radio. The first radio station in the commercial sense of the term—that is, a station broadcasting to anyone who happened to be listening—was licensed in 1920.

Within a few years, the airwaves were bursting with people who wanted to "talk on the radio." They came on the air irregularly and often switched from one frequency to another. And what's more, the idea of selling their time on the air to people who wanted a commercial message broadcast soon became popular. Like the vendor in the park, these people were—in a sense—trespassing on public property for private profit. And in doing so, they were making a bedlam of the public airwaves.

It was not long before Secretary of Commerce Herbert Hoover was deluged with complaints about the use of the public air—and many of these complaints came from responsible broadcasters. Hoover, who was charged with the responsibility of the Marine Radio Act, admitted that he did not have time, money, staff, or even the authority to resolve many of these complaints.

Thus, in 1925 with the full support of leading broadcasters, Hoover went to Congress to ask that something be done. And as the first permanent radio network was being established in late 1926, legislative leaders in Washington debated a bill which was to become the Federal Radio Act of 1927. This act attempted to settle some of the basic problems facing broadcasting and established a Federal Radio Commission to carry out the provisions of the act. Congress took its authority to impose such legislation on broadcasting from the same grounds discussed earlier in this book: namely, that broadcasting facilities were limited and that it was the government's responsibility to see to it that these facilities would be used only by those individuals who would serve the public interest—especially since they would be using public property for private profit.

Two years after the Radio Act was passed, it became apparent that while the "idea was good" the law was ineffective. Thus, Congress fought for the next five years over ways to improve the law. Eventually they came up with the Federal Communications Act of 1934, which has served broadcasting regulation, with minor changes, ever since that time. The Communications Act replaced the old Radio Commission with the Federal Communication Commission.

Despite major, new legislation in 1996, the organic law of broadcasting is found in the Communications Act of 1934, the organ from which broadcast law springs. The act, passed by both houses of Congress and signed by the president, among other things, created the Federal Communications Commission. Other legislation since then has had the effect of building on the basics of the 1934 statute. The FCC, however, has the power, as a result of its mandate in the Communications Act of 1934, to make policy and to interpret legislation. The FCC can issue rules, regulations, orders, promulgations, and directives affecting any and every broadcast station in the country. It can make decisions based on reviews of station performance, listener or viewer complaints, and applications for license renewal. Its decisions can be appealed through the federal court system.

But even with the Communications Act, broadcasting regulation is sometimes not all that some people would desire. Witness, for example, the television quiz show scandal of the late '50s and the subsequent Congressional investigations. Witness the continuing controversy over too much sex and violence in television programs. Witness the struggle involving the Federal Trade Commission concerning dishonesty and misrepresentation in radio and television commercials.

Some of the weaknesses in present day control of broadcasting can be traced to a simple problem of manpower. The FCC has a very limited staff with which to supervise all the activities of all the broadcasting services, as well as telephone, citizens band, microwave, amateur radio, ship-to-shore radio, and the myriad of other communication services that fall under FCC jurisdiction.

One of the severest limitations on government control of broadcasting, however, is the very principle of public interest which broadcasting regulation supposedly serves. Under the Communications Act, the FCC is charged with seeing to it that broadcasters operate in the public interest, necessity, and convenience. On the surface, this does not seem to be a difficult charge, and in many cases there is no problem. But often the commission and the commission members are at loggerheads with themselves and with various special interest groups, and sometimes with Congressional lawmakers, over the definition of that nebulous substance, the public interest.

It has been said that, in effect, the so-called "public interest" changes every time a new commissioner joins the FCC and certainly what is public interest in my mind, may not be what you conceive of as public interest. Beyond this, public taste—and therefore public interest—is subject to the vagaries of changing times.

Since the 1980s, radio stations have been living with something called deregulation, which does not mean no regulation. It could well mean that licensees have more latitude in determining what is in the public interest. It was part of President Ronald Reagan's administration's overall effort in taking the government out of many private businesses, or at least reducing the government's role in the private sector. Many other industries—trucking, airlines, telephone companies, etc.—found themselves deregulated during the Reagan years and beyond. For radio and television stations, it means that there is still an FCC and the airwaves still belong to the people. But the commission has reinterpreted its role and some of its obligations under the 1934 statute.

For the most part, deregulation has resulted in a reduction of paperwork for both broadcast station owners and the government agency regulating them. For example, among the relaxation of requirements is that detailed program logs, previously required for public and FCC inspection, no longer have to be maintained. Some rules have been eliminated, including one that restricted stations to no more than 18 minutes of commercials in an hour. Also eliminated were many formal requirements demanded of stations detailing their method of ascertaining community interests and the means subsequently of addressing such issues in their programming. Guidelines requiring a certain percentage of non-entertainment program content were eliminated, leaving such public affairs shows to be governed by marketplace considerations. The FCC no longer requires that a licensee keep a station a minimum of three years before selling. Radio stations can now be bought and sold whenever the owner chooses. The commission's recommendations to licensees regarding children's programming have been eliminated.

The justification given for deregulation was that with so many broadcast stations on the air, the marketplace could ensure quite adequately that the public interest would be served. This concept of marketplace would include all of the other competing media—print, cable, films, home video, computer-aided communication, including the Internet and its electronic forum. Some argued that deregulation was necessary because their conception of the First Amendment was such that regulation by government limited broadcasters' opportunity to serve side-by-side with the print media as watchdogs over government. Contemporary radio, except for control of technical standards, is almost totally free of government regulation.

The Telecommunications Act of 1996 promoted immediate and far-reaching change for everyone involved in broadcast and cable television, local stations, cable operators, over-the-air and cable networks, distributors, advertisers, and telephone service providers. Yet, the radio industry was affected even before passage of the federal law, apparently in anticipation of even more than what was covered in the radio section of the bill. Speculation had already started about the possibility that the AM and FM bands would eventually be converted to a single digital band. The prediction was that the Federal Communications Commission would allocate slots on the digital radio spectrum based on the number of AM and FM properties currently in existence. This speculation assumed that all radio stations in existence in 1996 would be created equal on a new band within a few years.

Before the ink was dry on the telecommunications act, radio groups Jacor Communications and

SFX Broadcasting announced major acquisitions, obviously motivated by less stringent radio ownership regulations. The radio-related portion of the bill allowed a company to own as many as eight outlets in a major market—up from a maximum of one AM station and one FM station prior to 1993, and two AM and two FM stations between 1993 and 1996. Of course, between 1996 and today, mergers, buyouts and partnerships have changed the landscape of radio even more.

Radio Stations as Investments

The financial community has become very enamored of radio as an investment. The key to corporate success is thought to be not just the number of stations owned, but also how much they earn and how they are organized within single markets. Because advertisers will pay for market penetration, a cluster of radio stations in a market will be a potent force. A company with multiple stations and a variety of programming can attract varied sets of listeners that can be sold to an advertiser as one huge audience.

In the rush to acquire spots on radio dials, many companies were paying prices two and three times greater than the last time a station had been sold. It was the beginning, and a dramatic one, of a new era in radio station trading and industry-wide consolidation. As the flurry of sales and trades began, there were worries that such massive consolidation would eventually force small market radio operators into bankruptcy because of the pressure of corporate competition.

Of course, new technology could change in ways that could benefit even small station owners and operators. Automation, syndicated program material delivered by satellite transmission, and more dependence on audio networks could reduce some of the pressure on small-market operations. That would mean a move away from radio's long-running practice of localization and specialization to specifically targeted audiences. Syndicated services result in a sameness as does an overdependence on network-originated content. Satellite technology's multi-channel capacity opens up new program possibilities and potential cost-cutting opportunities for the radio industry. In fact, radio could eventually be moved off the frequency spectrum and offer its listeners an interactive form of communication. Radio could end up a broad-band cable service with several channels being delivered at once. If radio embraces emerging technologies, the profit picture, already a promising one, could be greatly increased.

The News Function

The impact of broadcast news on our social, political and cultural life is staggering. Almost effortlessly, the American public is made aware of suicide bombings in Israel, celebrity divorces, gang violence in urban streets, the activities of politicians, both local and federal, and the workings of the United Nations. The

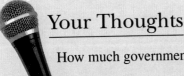

Your Thoughts

How much government regulation should there be over radio? Why?

What form should such regulation take? Why?

instantaneous nature of radio can bring us running accounts of late-breaking developments almost as they happen. We have come to depend on radio news for the basic stories as soon as possible. We want and expect the highlights, the key factors, the featured personalities, the latest break in the case and the outcome of a major trial. These things and more are what we expect from broadcast news, especially radio news.

News was not a major part of radio in its very early years when radio was regarded as show business, much like the vaudeville of the 1920s. After the 1927 Radio Act and its wording that stressed a public service obligation for license holders, many radio station operators increasingly began to convince each other that if they offered some news in their entertainment package, the government would favorably look upon them as striving to meet a public service commitment. In addition to defining news as public service, these owners began to look toward news as a less expensive type of programming. In the days of live musical and dramatic performances on radio, a station or network's capital outlay for building space and large studios was great. The labor costs and other expenses of live, in-studio productions were considerable. By the early to mid-1930s, radio news was finally emerging, largely because it cost the station management much less to produce than other program content.

Some newspaper owners, fearing the competition for advertising from an upstart journalistic medium, began to hedge their bets by getting into the radio business themselves. Some newspaper people saw radio also as a means of promoting their papers. Many newspaper firms began to put their own radio stations on the air. About one-third of the radio stations on air in the 1930s were owned by newspapers.

Many publishers feared the radio competition so much that they began a campaign to stifle radio. Radio income was on the rise despite the Great Depression. Radio was on the air with scoops on major stories before newspapers could come out with their "extras," special editions on major breaking events that are rarely published now because of radio and television.

Many newspapers, in retaliation, stopped printing the radio program logs, which had been published as a service to readers/listeners. Without the newspaper log, listeners had a more difficult time locating their favorite programs. Newspaper publishers and editors pushed hard for Congress to ban radio reporters from having access to the Congressional press galleries. The biggest battle in this press-radio war of the 1930s was over access to news provided by the wire services. The publishers pressured the wire services not to sell news to radio stations, and, in the case of the Associated Press, not to allow broadcasters to become members of that collective news-gathering agency. The lack of membership status meant the AP's news stories were not available to stations.

Eventually, a short-lived and ill-fated agreement was worked out between some broadcasters and major newspaper companies. Not all of radio was involved in working out the agreement, so it was destined not to work. It did demonstrate the feelings of journalistic inferiority of the networks that participated. They agreed to sharply restrict their news efforts. They agreed that no news story of more than 30 words would be aired, making them no more than a headline service. They also agreed that they would do no newsgathering on their own and would broadcast news only twice a day for a total of 10 minutes and that these newscasts would be broadcast well after the sale and delivery of the morning and afternoon newspapers. They also agreed that, in exchange for getting news from the then three major wire services, they would not permit commercial sponsorship of newscasts.

Within a few years, it was becoming clear that radio broadcasts actually stimulated newspaper readership rather than discouraged it. The newspaper industry's own studies showed that readers looked first at stories in print that they had been exposed to earlier by either word-of-mouth or radio coverage. They got only a surface impression from a brief radio treatment and sought out the newspaper for greater detail and more background. In addition, instead of advertisers deserting the newspapers and taking their money to radio, there was a big increase in the amount of money spent nationally by advertisers. The newspaper share of the totals shrank, but dollar amounts spent with newspapers did not diminish from this competition.

The agreement failed primarily because many local stations did not have to honor it and became aggressive newsgatherers on their own instead of depending on their network affiliation. Newspapers that owned radio stations violated the agreement by sharing news with their stations. New services were created to supply news to radio. The fear that one or more of these would become competitive made Associated Press, International News Service, and United Press more and more willing to seek radio clients and less eager to feel intimidated by the newspapers. One of these, Transradio, was becoming so successful that it actually acquired a few newspaper clients.

The war between newspapers and radio ended a few years after the agreement collapsed, largely because the networks had already developed their own newsgathering operations and were fully into the news business when significant events were taking place in Europe. When Hitler's armies were on the march and World War II was looking more and more likely, the networks were already able to transmit live, eyewitness reports on the European war by shortwave. These accounts were then rebroadcast over standard frequencies to American listeners. Radio news coverage of the events preceding America's entry into the war were so extensive and so important to a news-hungry nation that the newspapers could no longer have any hope of stifling radio as a news medium.

Even before this, the newspaper industry lost a battle in the courts over who had proprietary rights to news. Newspapers claimed that copyright laws were being violated by radio stations that used the newspaper as a source for their news. Courts interpreted copyright statutes as allowing for the factual content of news to be in the public domain. Newspaper publishers were told that only the particular expression of a writer, or something creative that no other writer could have come up with, could be copyrighted. Under copyright law, no fact or idea could be protected and no one could own news, or at least the factual elements within a news story. The courts, in effect, told radio stations and networks that newspapers could not stop them from using newspaper stories as material for rewriting and reworking in their own words.

Once Pearl Harbor was bombed and the United States was in the war against Japan and Germany, the reports and interpretations Americans had been getting from the networks in the late 1930s were expanded to include coverage from the Pacific front. The second world war brought radio news to its maturity, to a role as a global news medium. Listeners heard first-hand reports of battles on Pacific islands just as they had listened to stories of Hitler's march into France and Poland or the bombing of London. Americans heard of Bataan, Corregidor, Iwo Jima, Guadalcanal and Okinawa. Today's broadcast journalists provide instantaneous electronic coverage of worldwide events through CNN, NBC, CBS and ABC because we have come to expect it. These expectations were created when radio was the unexcelled and unchallenged news medium in the country during radio's golden age of the 1930s and 1940s. That was to change, of course, with the advent of television.

Today, at large stations and in all-news or news-talk formats, there will be an executive in charge of the news operation. This individual will carry the title of news director and will function as a department head much like the program director does. However, in small markets or in radio stations with formats that allow for little news, the program director often supervises news content.

No matter the station's format, news is usually emphasized on the radio in the early morning and afternoon drive periods. Beginning in the late 1980s, television networks and local television stations began to increase their news offerings to include more news programming in the morning, yet radio continued to hold onto its news audiences from 6 am to 10 am. About half of the adult Americans surveyed in recent years have indicated that they regard radio as their primary source of news in the morning. Television is mentioned by about one-third of those responding to the surveys, with the newspaper mentioned by 15 percent.

Radio news staff size and function vary greatly with the size of the station and the market. The typical news staff in a medium- to large-market station with a music format is made up of three to six people under the supervision of a news director, who might also perform newsroom duties during part of the day. The news director might double as a newscast editor or anchor in addition to performing administrative duties. Often, the news director functions as an assignment editor. Typically, the other members of the staff will work half of the day as writers-newscasters and part of the shift as reporters out in the field with audio tape recorders. At stations with full news staffs, the editors and newscasters write their own copy. They copyedit public relations news releases, wire service stories and scripts used in previous newscasts. They provide four to five minutes of news every hour and half-hour during drive time and only once an hour during the other daytime periods. Usually, at night the local news is replaced by network newscasts, if there is any late night news at all. Radio news in the music station's format is scaled back considerably on the weekends, probably to half of what is produced weekdays.

Small stations in the good-sized markets and stations in small towns usually have only one or two people to share the news duties. These low-budget operations are common in big cities for stations that simply are not competitive in the market and, of course, in smaller communities where the advertising base is not sufficient to generate the revenue to support a major news effort. In fact, in some of these stations, especially FM stations, there might be no news at all. The low-budget news staff could be one person assembling copy from a wire service to read on the air with little revision, or two people sharing the responsibility of newsgathering, writing or editing.

Certainly, in an all-news format or the news-talk format, news is a much bigger department. Most such stations are in the largest cities in the country where a radio station can profit from such a narrow specialty.

There will be a pair of full-time assignment editors, three or four full-time newscast editors or producers, and a managing editor overseeing day-to-day newsroom activities and personnel matters, while serving as liaison to the news director. In an operation this big, the news director will be a full-time administrator, an executive with a sufficient number of duties to preclude actual news reporting, editing or newscasting. The news director will be busy with policy matters, coordinating with other station departments and management, dealing with the community, and representing the station in its relationships with the industry, the public, the station's lawyers, political and governmental functions and the like. The news director in an all-news station has a big budget to work with, but must maintain control over expenditures for equipment and facilities and must be on top of changing technology and any other potential expenses while demonstrating the skills of a good financial manager.

The following is a sample of procedures, guidelines and directives found in newsroom guides or manuals provided to staff members at some of the better local radio news operations:

1. Maintain staff reporters to provide original coverage of local news events.

2. Write or rewrite all local copy for newscasts.

3. Carefully edit and frequently rewrite national and international wire copy.

4. Make wide use of tape recorded interviews and telephone reports.

5. Use mobile units for fast, flexible coverage and for direct broadcasts from the scene.

6. Encourage reporters and writers to contribute new ideas and to be aware that radio is suitable to imaginative, creative and unusual treatment of news.

7. Follow the standards of professional conduct and ethical behavior consistent with the codes of conduct for the Society of Professional Journalists and the Radio Television News Directors Association.

Non-Commercial Radio

When radio was new, there was no immediate consensus of how to pay for the costs of operation, or whether the medium should be a subsidized one or a profit-making venture. Media already in existence in the 1920s paid their own way and even made profits. In many nations around the world, the decision was to have government operated radio broadcasts. Many people in the United States encouraged that system also, but it was a tough sell in a country based on democratic principles that would not allow the content of any medium to be controlled by government. The idea that government intervention in programming and news decision-making was too likely for those fearing a basic conflict in such a system meant that serious consideration was never given to government operation.

The system used by the British was also proposed. That involved a fee system with listeners paying a small sum with each radio receiver purchased and making an annual payment to cover the expenses of programming and transmitting broadcasts.

Eventually, of course, the profit motive became too popular for any other proposal to be considered. However, one of the other ideas had some potential for a type of broadcasting that evolved as an alternative to commercial radio. The method of funding libraries, museums, and universities was offered as a possibility, but it did not develop exactly as proposed. This was the idea that philanthropy could finance the radio industry, specifically through endowments made by wealthy benefactors, whose large gifts of money would allow stations to use the earnings on investments to pay their expenses.

Universities were involved in the experiments with radio even before stations, as we know them, went on the air. Professors of physics and of electrical engineering began with wireless signals and inevitably developed the ability to transmit voice and music. Once radio was beyond the stage of experimentation by university researchers, the professors involved in its earliest years were no longer interested, but their institutions began to think of radio as an educational tool and a means of reaching beyond the Ivory Tower to the greater community beyond. Through the 1920s, universities began to support educational stations, as they were then called, despite efforts by commercial broadcasters to keep the frequencies for themselves.

Advocates of non-commercial radio saw the possibility of a system side-by-side with commercial interests of stations endowed by non-profit organizations such as educational, religious and labor organizations. Commercial broadcasters were quick to lobby Congress and the Federal Radio Commission, and its successor, the FCC, against such an arrangement. Despite such efforts, a few non-commercial stations managed to survive until 1967 when this type of broadcasting was given a tremendous boost. So-called educational stations before 1967 had been supported by various endowments, including contributions from the Ford Foundation and other smaller foundations.

Some cities and states own and support non-commercial radio stations. New York City has been operating WNYC since 1924. The states of Wisconsin and Iowa, through their major universities, have long histories of funding non-commercial radio. Radio station WCFL billed itself as the voice of labor because it was owned and operated by the Chicago Federation of Labor. Some such stations are affiliated with high schools or school districts and depend on taxes for financial support. A few are owned by private foundations, but most are at least partially, if not heavily, supported by colleges and universities.

They are no longer called educational stations, partly as a result of a Carnegie Commission report in the 1960s that recommended a national system of what would be called public stations. As a result, support from the federal government followed. Congress appropriated money to improve existing non-commercial stations and even to create new ones. The Public Broadcasting Act of 1967 made these broadcasters eligible for grants not only from individual listeners, philanthropists, foundations and corporations, but also from the federal government. An independent agency, the Corporation for Public Broadcasting, was created by this legislation to administer the distribution of funds to these newly-designated public stations.

Going on the air in May, 1971 was a network for non-commercial radio stations. This network, National Public Radio, is overseen by the Corporation for Public Broadcasting and provides programs for up to 50 hours a week to member stations. Estimates are that NPR reaches 10 million listeners each week, certainly less than the commercial stations, but still enough to give non-commercial radio its own niche in the industry. Some of NPR's programs are produced by member stations and shared with each other through network distribution. Others are produced at NPR's headquarters. Member stations can secure grants for operating expenses and can broadcast according to Corporation for Public Broadcasting guidelines, but the level of support for many of them may often not be sufficient. An obvious result is the need for stations to use air time to beg for listener subscriptions and to engage in other fund-raising activities, primarily seeking donations from local corporations that can justify a tax write-off through such aid to non-profit institutions.

Many listeners point to a pair of public affairs shows as the most respected of all NPR's offerings. These are "All Things Considered" and "Morning Edition." These two news-oriented programs are sent by satellites from National Public Radio's Washington, D.C. facilities to affiliates all over the country. They have consistently displayed initiative in reporting and extensive coverage of world and national events. Unlike commercial networks, these two NPR programs offer considerable analysis and detail. Where commercial radio stresses fast-breaking straight news accounts, "Morning Edition" and "All Things Considered" concentrate on a public affairs approach that stresses insight and background on more universal concerns than the simple facts of an immediate news event.

The Future of Radio

In one month alone, from February 8, 1996, to March 8, 1996, the industry's biggest corporations paid $2 billion dollars to buy radio stations. They were betting on digital audio broadcasts, a new technology capable of sending music and information in the form of zeros and ones, as in a computer code. The origin of this was in Japanese development of digital audio tape in the late 1980s. This technology was similar to that used for compact discs and was about half the size of conventional audio cassettes, with the quality of sound comparable to compact discs. The result was experimentation with a kind of radio transmission that would eliminate all of the static and hiss in over-the-air radio signals and eliminate the distinctions between AM and FM. A listener would have the ability to dial a given number for a signal from a satellite or a cable feed and the particular selection would be translated by digital codes into a clean, noise-free transmission to the home receiver. This could mean hundreds of radio program choices for listeners, instead of the limits necessitated by the scarcity of channels on the frequency spectrum. Instead of a metropolitan area with 30 or 40 radio stations, there could be an infinite number available. In the small towns with only one AM, or in medium-sized markets with a pair of AMs and a pair of FMs, the future would mean virtually hundreds or thousands of radio programs on demand and from a single digital radio dial for everybody in the land.

As more program choices are made available through technology, each station will have to struggle harder for even a small portion of the large, overall audience. Cable systems and satellites will be bringing into our homes a greater number of audio feeds, increasing the number of musical services, talk shows, direct-to-home programming and such niche or specialty programs as computer help, gardening help, health, fitness, investing, etc.

Previously, radio stations were primarily owned by radio-only companies, but that has been changing. Radio ownership will be found more and more in companies that also own newspapers, television stations, cable firms, plus other communication and non-communication enterprises. As book publishers, magazine production companies, computer firms and media conglomerates move into radio station ownership, management and programming decisions will inevitably move further and further away from the operations end of the station itself.

Local radio advertising revenues should continue to increase, as should profitability. Radio still has the largest cumulative audiences of any medium, despite the obvious popularity of television. With the worth of stations beginning to increase, with its ability to offer low advertising rates, and with its ability to deliver specific subaudiences, radio has a special niche as an advertising medium. All of the factors should ensure profitability in both the short and long-run.

Recent Research, Developments and Issues

Over-the-air radio stations appear to be in need of a way to compete against the constantly increasing popularity of satellite radio. The consumer demand for satellite radio could eventually be matched by the slowly emerging switch from analog to digital, with its stereo separation and wider frequency response. High-definition radio experimentation began before the turn of the 21st century, but system development was not immediate. Once Federal Communications Commission approval was granted, what was expected to be a long-term transition began with 1,800 high-definition stations broadcasting by the beginning of the year 2008.

Stations can use much of their existing equipment, with digital and analog radio occupying the same spectrum. The first of these stations delivered both analog and digital programming by using unused space around the analog frequencies. The changeover to digital can be done quickly and not at great expense by adding an audio processor, some monitoring equipment, a high-definition radio signal generator, and digital transmitter to existing facilities.

The listener does not have to buy new equipment because AM and FM stations can transmit over the same frequencies, whether analog or digital. The expense to the consumer is in the optional extra features, especially for the 75% of users who listen to radio all or part of the time while driving. Car radios cost an average of $300 more when installed with units for the early adopters. Eventually, consumer demand can bring those prices down. Even without extras, like text information showing call letters, song titles and artist information, the listener gets improved reception and better sound quality.

Early adopters said that FM stations sounded like CDs and AM sounded like FM. In bigger markets, many AM stations dropped music programming in the 1970s when 70% of the national audience listened to music on FM. At one point, AM stereo seemed like a possibility but it never took off and AM simply failed to match FM's stereo performance. As high-definition radio gains market strength it could mean a return to music on the AM band, which has been offering a lot of news and talk in recent years. Industry experts were predicting that the AM band will be revitalized at a time when FM stations are commanding higher sales prices than AM. The overall expectation is that AM station investment will possibly be more attractive while over-the-air radio will definitely compete favorably with satellite.

In late 2004, shock jock Howard Stern announced he was abandoning terrestrial radio and joining Sirius Satellite Radio. He said part of the reason for the move was to free himself from FCC "censorship." Although the $500 million he reportedly got from Sirius for himself and his crew might have had something to do with the move, there is no doubt that since satellite radio does not lease the public airwaves as does traditional radio, Stern and his imitators are intrigued by the ability to say and do what they want without fear of oversight and sanctions from the FCC or other governmental agencies.

Sirius hoped Stern's move would help convince millions of subscribers to sign up for its $13 per month satellite radio service. XM Satellite Radio had more than four times the number of subscribers as Sirius at the time of Stern's announcement, so Sirius needed to get serious about attempting to grab more of the satellite radio listening audience. Some media analysts predicted that the aggressive programming moves by both Sirius and XM would force traditional over-the-air radio stations and networks to become more creative and competitive. If that happens, consumers should benefit, because few listeners enjoy long blocks of commercials, limited song playlists, the loss of true "localism," the mega-consolidation of ownership and the lack of diversity that dominated commercial radio in the early part of the 21st century.

XM Radio increased its reach by offering some of its stations to subscribers over the Internet. For about $8 a month, customers got access to about 70 commercial-free stations and about 10 other stations. XM Radio Online cost subscribers to the satellite service an additional $4 per month, creating new revenue streams.

Radio stations in the United States played more than 84,000 different songs in 2003. Of that number, about 3,000 were totally new songs. The number of new artists to get airplay hit nearly 600. Diversity might not be as limited as some critics believe. While there is no doubt that some "cookie-cutter radio" does exist, consolidation has not completely shut the door to new sounds and new musicians.

Copyright and fee questions inhibited the early growth of Internet radio and simulcasting on the Internet by commercial, over-the-air radio stations. In mid-2002, the U.S. Copyright Office ruled that Webcasters had to pay 70 cents for every song heard by 1,000 listeners. The fees were retroactive to 1998. Big money, for sure. No one was really happy with the plan, so Internet broadcasters and the recording industry worked out a new deal that was similar to the formula used to collect fees for songs played on the air. The rate is based on a percentage of the revenue generated by each station. The money is then distributed to musicians and their record labels.

In late 2002, the FCC approved a standard technology for digital radio. Besides improved sound quality, digital radio permits listeners to see the names of songs and artists. In addition, music and information can be stored on a computer hard drive, so radio becomes much more interactive.

Country music is by far the most popular programming format in the United States. More than 2,000 stations play country music, followed by news-talk (1,100), oldies (800), adult contemporary (700), Spanish-language (600), adult standards (550), Top 40 (500), soft adult contemporary (375), hot adult contemporary (375), and religious (350). Rock is being played on about 300 stations.

A study by the Project for Excellence in Journalism found that about 94% of American adults listen to the radio at least occasionally. About 82% reported they would likely continue to listen to traditional radio stations despite the proliferation of new communication technologies. About 22% said radio was their primary source for national and international news and information. About 43% wanted the FCC to have the right to oversee/monitor the content of satellite radio programming.

A study in early 2008 reported that about half of the adults in the United States and Canada said radio was "an important part of their lives." Only 11% said they had no use for radio as a source of information or entertainment. Among the benefits of radio mentioned by the respondents were convenience, portability, localism and free programming.

An economic analysis in 2008 found that free radio airplay was responsible for up to $2.5 billion in annual music sales. The figures covered only album (CDs) and digital track sales. The analysis determined that the more a song is played on the radio, the more sales are generated.

A 2007 study found that radio stations that had more broad-based programming formats enjoyed more ratings stability than did stations that featured more tightly targeted formats. Adult Contemporary, Country, News and News-Talk were among the formats that demonstrated consistent ratings, while Classic Rock, Oldies and other "specialty" formats had much more ratings variability.

Another 2007 study found that despite conventional wisdom, most listeners *do not* tune out during radio commercial breaks. On average, only about 8% of listeners change stations when a commercial airs. The longer the commercial break lasts, of course, the more likely it is that listeners will tune out, but if commercial breaks are kept to a reasonable length, listeners seem willing to stay put.

Think Back

1. What are the listenership statistics and complaints about radio these days?

They are dropping from 23 hours a week to 20 hours. Going to downloading music from the internet, or online radio. They complain that it is too narrow & only appealing to the lowest denominator and it's slimmed down playlist.

2. What are the pros and cons of multi-station ownership of radio stations?

The Cons are that the price / programming will become a la carte, and that both company's have to share technologies w/ radio receiver manufacturers.
The Pros are that channels are provided for non-commercial, educational & public safety programming & programming produced by women & minorities. Also, provide radios for current subscribers to come from either company.

3. What are the major elements of satellite radio and what did XM and Sirius agree to do to win approval for their merger? It sounds great, but you can't hear it on regular radio. & Gives listeners the option to purchase it. It also makes High Definition (HD) possible.

4. List the pros and cons associated with radio webcasting.

Pros: reach more people all over the world & it's a low-cost way to do it.

Cons: ① strains online resources, ② add to distractions to office workers, ③ and impractical for people & ties up the home phone line.

5. What are the ownership trends in the radio industry?

Created a consolidation frenzy. It underscored a trend to offer advertisers packages of commercial space in multiple outlets.

6. What's the difference between AM radio and FM radio?

FM: their signal results in modulating the pitch or frequency of the electro magnetic wave. And it is of line sight.
AM: their signals will travel greater distances than FM, especially at night. It also can reach hundreds of miles.

7. Why is the disc jockey system popular on radio?

Because they are able to offer drive-time hosts who entertain with games, quiz shows, comedy routines, quirky interview guests, listener participation & some wild stunts. They bring personality to the radio.

8. What are low-power radio stations and how are they awarded to groups?

They have a limited range and they have to be non-commercial. They are awarded based on the strengths of a group's ties to the local community that the station would serve.

9. What is "payola" and how does it work in radio?

It is a bribe given to disk jockeys and other station personnel who could control the playing of records on the air. It affected the competition & the bribes got bigger.

10. Why is radio still a very popular medium with consumers?

Because it is a really simple concept & you can do it when you're in your car, so you can keep yourself busy & company.

11. What are the traditional programming formats used by radio stations?

Adult contemporary, contemporary hits, album-oriented rock, middle of the road, beautiful music, oldies, country, urban contemporary, religious, jazz, classical, news-talk & specialty.

12. What are the typical departments in a local radio station?

Traffic department, Production department, ~~Broadcasting~~ Engineering Departme Program department.

13. How are ratings data acquired in radio?

First they called them on the phone, then they used the diary method.

14. What regulations are imposed on local radio station owners?

They can't have a monopoly, broadcasters are licensed by the government on behalf of the national public.

15. What past, present and future problems/issues are associated with the practice of radio journalism?

They stole stories from newspapers, which made newspapers stop publishing radio program logs (which caused problems for listeners). Then the agreement they came to, was violated by newspapers who owned radio stations b/c they shared ~~the~~ their information.

16. What is non-commercial radio?

Main mission is to be a public service. Public broadcasters receive funding from diverse sources including license fees, individual contributions, public financing & commercial financing.

17. What are some of the likely future developments that will affect radio?

Become available in homes, on the television, still going to be making profit through all of the technological advances.

18. What are the elements of "high definition" radio?

It improves sound quality, allows owners to add one/two "side channels" or "side stations".

19. Why did Howard Stern leave terrestrial radio and what were the particulars of his deal with Sirius Satellite Radio? He announced he was leaving and he was able to receive $500 million & free himself from FCC "censorship."

20. What are the recent statistics regarding songs played on the radio listenership the most popular programming formats and music sales related to radio airplay?

Television

The first Super Bowl of the 21st century featured a system trumpeted by ABC as Enhanced TV, with nearly 700,000 viewers opting to access live programming and electronic, computer-based information related to the game. The network called it an affirmation of the coming of age of convergent television, a collaboration of various producers and networks on interactive TV applications. Enhanced TV heightened viewer participation in the content of Super Bowl XXXIV and promises much more, although many such high-tech wonders are still simply promises. After all, nearly 90 million Super Bowl viewers did not watch Enhanced TV. Predictions are that eventually millions of Americans will have set-top boxes, allowing them to select their own camera angles, choose their own sideline shots or overhead views from a blimp, while also choosing one commercial rather than another.

Technology is already beginning to make it possible for viewers to be free of the networks' timetable, working around network decision makers' emphasis on lead-ins and audience flow. A development known as "personal television" can put viewers in charge of setting viewing schedules. They can buy a device about the size of a VCR, called a personal video recorder, and pay a subscription fee. The viewer is then offered a personal television menu, meaning the chance to see what you want whenever you want to watch it. A central computing system is updated daily through a phone line, making possible the transmitting to and from the in-home system of TV listings, choices, and preferred viewing times.

A major selling point is the ability of the system to record programs almost automatically. Once the viewer establishes a pattern, the personal video recorder "learns" and will tape a favorite program with no further prompting and no additional requests. If the viewers' habits are consistently obvious, similar programs or movies will also be taped. If you tend to choose action-adventure movies, more of the same will be provided even without a specific request.

In the first year of the 21st century, this technology was adding thousands of viewers to its lists of subscribers. Personal video recorders give viewers the ability to pause in the middle of a live program and pick up again where you left off, plus you get your own at-home instant replay. The makers of these systems say one big advantage is that software can be upgraded and new features added without needing a new box, with all additions and improvements done on the phone line. Experts predict that in the next few years, millions of viewers will be using such systems to create their own personal television networks.

The TiVo Personal Television Service and its competitors are examples of attempts to create a marriage between video and computers. It's an important part of an emerging effort to graft technological innovations onto television, an attempt to achieve a convergence of computers, the Internet, and television, all interacting through the same box, cable or satellite dish.

Television Is Life

Television is a pervasive force in the lives of most Americans. Most of us rely almost exclusively on television to keep us informed about our community, city, state, region, country and world. Most of us use television as our main source of entertainment and relaxation.

Estimates vary, but it's clear that almost every American household owns at least one color television set and most households have two or more sets.

In fact, a recent census found that there are more television sets in the United States than toilets.

All those sets get plenty of use, too. Researchers estimate that the average household watches about 56 hours of television programming per week. The average person watches about 30 hours per week. That's about two months of continuous viewing per year. In a 65-year life, that works out to be nine years of round-the-clock TV watching. That sounds like a lot, but it's pretty easy to rack up the hours in front of the tube. If you watch a little TV in the morning, watch news in the evening, catch the usual lineup of your favorite prime-time programs, watch late-night news and either Jay Leno, David Letterman or "Nightline." you're well on your way to that 30-hour per week mark. Throw in a sporting event or two on the weekend, plus an entertainment program or two and you've probably broken the 30-hour barrier.

Many experts are concerned about the amount of time that children spend plopped in front of television sets. Children average about four hours of TV viewing per day. Some studies have found that the more TV a child watches, the more likely it is that the child will be overweight and have under-developed social skills. Many critics claim TV is a "thief of time," robbing children and their parents of opportunities to read, talk, play and interact with friends and family members.

Television Outlets

The television system in the United States is comprised of networks, network-affiliated local stations and independent local stations. With the recent start-up of new networks, there aren't many true independent stations left, but there are a few.

The major networks include ABC, CBS, NBC, PBS, FOX and the CW. Of course we have cable networks and specialized programming channels that resemble networks—CNN, CNBC, MSNBC, Fox News Channel, ESPN, Home Shopping Network, etc. When a local station agrees to hook up with a network and air most, if not all, of the network's programs, the local station becomes a network-affiliated station or a network affiliate. In San Diego, KGTV(10) is an ABC affiliate, KFMB(8) is a CBS affiliate, KNSD(39) is an NBC affiliate, KPBS(15) is a PBS affiliate, KSWB(69) is a FOX affiliate, and XETV(6) is a CW affiliate. If a local station is owned by a network, it is known as a network O & O, which means "owned and operated" by the network. In San Diego, NBC owns KNSD, so KNSD is an NBC O & O.

If a local station is not allied with a network, it is known as an independent station. You'll usually find independent stations only in the biggest U.S. cities.

Your Thoughts

How much television do you watch in an average week?

Why do you watch television?

What are your favorite programs? Why?

The major networks all plunged deeper into the red at the turn of the century as they lost audience to cable, home video, and other competition. In 1979, ABC, CBS and NBC attracted 57% of the viewers during prime time. In 2000, ABC, CBS, NBC, plus FOX and the smaller networks combined attracted about 30% of the prime-time audience. In fact, in the summer of 1998, more people were watching programs provided by cable systems than were watching the four major TV networks combined.

Of course, fewer viewers means fewer dollars. NBC was the last one at the end of the century to show a profit, but its successes were dwindling considerably and its ratings falling in the wake of the loss of "Seinfeld" and professional football. NBC also had taken a big hit financially with spiraling costs associated with "ER."

The most profitable networks now are the cable channels, which collect both advertising and subscriber fees. But cable operators could find their earnings under pressure eventually as more choices and the Internet fragment viewership. Cable TV systems hope that by providing digital TV and other digital services, including commercial-free audio programming, they will remain profitable. Using digital technology, cable systems can provide several hundred channels of programming and make the viewing and/or listening experience more interactive. In addition, digital technology allows consumers to send and receive e-mail and surf the Internet without having to miss any of their favorite programs.

Over-the-air broadcast TV stations are joining the digital revolution, too (DTV). Digital technology makes it possible for stations to transmit 6–8 channels simultaneously instead of just one. How such multi-channel capacity will be used is the big question, of course. The FCC has ordered all local stations to begin broadcasting digital signals by mid-February, 2009. Many stations are already doing so and some network programs are simulcast using both analog (the current system) and digital signals. Of course, to enjoy the benefits of digital TV, we're all going to have to buy a new set or use cable or satellite services.

With all the developing technologies creating unlimited possibilities and programming options, many experts predict that television will soon follow the model of radio. Just as radio stations had to change from "something for everybody" content providers and satisfy themselves with serving a certain type of listener, television stations will have to find niches that they can serve. Stations will likely differentiate themselves using the perceived interests and lifestyles of fragmented groups. Typical demographics will be used, too, of course. Ages, income levels, occupations, religions, political concerns and gender will all be used to target certain segments of national, regional and local populations. This concept has been labeled "narrowcasting," by some experts. While such fragmentation of the audience has worked for radio, some critics suggest that as television audiences begin to separate themselves into smaller and smaller groups, the loss of "shared viewing experiences" might have serious deleterious effects on society. Losing the ability to discuss a program or even a news development with friends and co-workers could lead to the creation of a relatively lonely and uncommunicative society.

The FCC has recognized the changing landscape associated with traditional television broadcasting and has given the okay for a single company or network to own two stations in a given city. This will only be permitted in the nation's largest cities, those with at least eight stations, but it is an example of attempts to allow the owners of traditional broadcast properties to remain competitive. The FCC recognizes the possible loss of diverse voices in an area where one company owns more than one TV station, but with all of the other media outlets available in big cities, enough diversity of opinion and content should exist to prevent any single company from dominating the public agenda.

Delivering TV Signals

The wonder of television, whether it is regular TV(525 scanning lines of dots) or high definition TV—HDTV—(1,000 scanning lines of dots and more dots), can be delivered to homes in a variety of ways.

1. **Over the air:** The traditional networks and local stations broadcast and satellite their signals free to homes and central distribution locations (cable systems, etc.).
2. **Cable:** Underground or overhead wires/ cables connected to homes. Program providers send material to cable center and then material sent to homes for a fee.

3. **Digital Cable:** Fiber optic cables used to connect homes so that channel capacity is increased and two-way, interactive communication is possible. Data and other information can be sent using fiber optic cable, too. Fees are increased.

4. **Wireless Cable:** Material sent to homes for a fee using microwaved signals. Limited capacity.

5. **Direct Broadcast Satellite:** Programs sent directly to homes for a fee. Similar to cable, but no wires. DBS companies pay program providers for material.

6. **Internet:** Programs can be streamed live or selected from archived files of current hits and past classics.

7. **Cell Phone:** Programs can be accessed live or from archived files via wireless networks.

8. **Telephone Company:** AT&T and other telephone companies are beginning to offer television services using a combination of satellite and digital technologies.

Types of Stations

There are three basic types of television stations: VHF, UHF and cable. VHF stands for "very high frequency" and UHF stands for "ultra high frequency." The over-the-air VHF stations are channels 2–13. The over-the-air UHF stations are channels 14–83. Cable stations do not broadcast their signals over the air and can be assigned just about any channel number that is not being used by a local station.

Some people get a bit confused about channels for local stations, because many cable television systems do not use the same over-the-air channel for a station on their cable line up. For example, in San Diego, KNSD is a UHF station on channel 39, but the cable television systems in San Diego put KNSD on channel 7 for the convenience of consumers. You wouldn't want to have to punch in 3–9 on the old remote every time you wanted to watch KNSD, would you? Channel 7 is so much more convenient. It's right next to channel 6, XETV, and channel 8, KFMB. If we keep going, we get KUSI(51) on channel 9 and if we go back down, we find KSWB(69) on channel 5. The cable systems even moved KPBS(15) to channel 11 to save us time and trouble. We can just run up and down between channels 5 and 11 to get all the major local stations in San Diego.

Direct Broadcast Satellite (DBS) and low-power television stations are relatively recent entrants into the world of competitive television, but they hold great promise for the future. DBS, as the name implies, makes it possible for a program supplier to transmit directly to individual households without having to go through a network, cable system or some other "clearinghouse." Low-power stations, as the name implies, do not have a strong broadcast signal. They are designed to serve a small, specific geographic area. The signal might not reach much more than a few miles. A large number of such stations could be permitted to operate in a large city, each serving a different part of the city. The possibilities for niche and specialized programming are endless for both DBS and low-power stations.

DBS systems are now permitted to carry and transmit the signals of local television stations. Prior to 2000, such systems were forbidden from doing so, but the government decided DBS could provide competition for cable TV systems. Financial arrangements will have to be worked out, of course,

Your Thoughts

Do you think it's a good idea or a bad idea for local cable systems to change the over-the-air channel assignments of local stations? Why?

but at least now DBS is a viable alternative to cable TV for most consumers and the competition between DBS and cable theoretically should mean more reasonable costs for consumers.

There are about 1,800 local television stations in the U.S. About 600 are commercial VHF stations, 800 are commercial UHF stations, 130 are non-commercial VHF stations and 270 are non-commercial UHF stations. In addition, there are about 2,300 low-power television stations, about 11,000 cable systems and two major DBS systems.

Station Departments

Stations vary, of course, but most have at least five basic departments. If you remember the acronym PEONS, you'll remember the departments. Sometimes employees at local television stations probably feel like peons, but working in television can be an exciting and rewarding career.

Programming/Production
Engineering
Office/Clerical/Traffic
News/Sports
Sales

Programming/Production

People who work in the programming department are responsible for making sure every minute of the broadcast/cablecast day is filled with news-oriented, information-oriented and entertainment-oriented programs. They assist with locally produced programs, network-supplied programs and syndicated programs. More on types of programming later.

Production people run studio cameras, help light studio sets, direct programs and assist with technical aspects—audio, video, graphics. They also assist with the production of commercials, live remotes and other locally originated programming.

Engineering

People who work in the engineering department are responsible for making sure the television signal gets from the station to the transmitter or cable system. They are also in charge of maintaining and monitoring the equipment needed to accomplish the miracle of television.

Office/Clerical/Traffic

Office workers in a local television station include secretaries, receptionists, messengers and switchboard operations. Traffic refers to things that come and go on the air. It involves keeping track of programs and advertisements to be sure that everything aired that was supposed to air and that it all aired at the time it was supposed to air.

News/Sports

People who work in news and sports gather, write, process and produce news and public affairs programming. The news department is usually responsible for most, if not all, of a station's locally originated programming. More on the people who work in news and sports later.

Sales

People who work in the sales department are responsible for selling commercial time to individuals, organizations, companies, businesses and corporations. They deal with the representatives of major manufacturers and with local retailers. Sometimes they just arrange to place already-produced commercials on the air and other times they help local retailers to produce commercials that will eventually air.

Ratings

Ratings are the name of the game for most local television stations and networks. Television is probably one of the last examples of a true mass medium. Most television executives want to attract as large of an audience as possible. It doesn't hurt to attract the right demographics, too, of course, but the more viewers, the better.

Television stations and networks set their advertising rates—what they charge advertisers—based on ratings. Generally, the more viewers a station or network has, the more it can charge for its time. Since every station has about the same amount of time to sell, the more you can get for that time, the more profits you can make. The more profits you can make, the more money you have to hire the best people and produce the best programming. The better people and programming you have, the more viewers you can attract. The more viewers you attract, the more you can charge advertisers. Get the picture?

There are two basic components of ratings. One aspect is called a "rating" and the other is called a "share." A rating is the percentage of households (TVHH) tuned in to a given station based on the total number of households in an area. For example, if there are 100,000 TVHH in an area and 10,000 of those households are tuned in to KTIM-TV, KTIM-TV has a rating of 10.

A share is the percentage of TVHH tuned in to a given station based on the total number of TVHH with their sets in use at a given time (Households Using Television—HUT). For example, if KTIM-TV still has its 10,000 viewers, but only 50,000 of the 100,000 TVHH are actually watching TV, KTIM-TV has a 20 share. The "share" is based on the HUT numbers and the rating is based on the "TVHH" numbers.

Quite often, shares are about twice as large as ratings. That tells you that at any given time, only about half of the TVHH that could be watching TV, actually are watching TV. Sometimes, shares are three or four times larger than ratings. It all depends on how many of those all-important TVHH are actually glued to their TVs. One thing to keep in mind is a "rating" can never be higher than a "share."

Gathering Ratings Data

Nielsen Media Research is the major player in the television ratings data game. Arbitron used to be a major competitor, but Arbitron has decided to put most of its attention toward gathering radio ratings data. Television ratings data can be gathered in a variety of ways. These include diaries, audimeters, people meters and coincidental telephone surveys. All of the methods used to gather television ratings data depend on the careful, scientific selection of a sample of the population upon which to base estimates of the viewing habits of the total population. Many people are skeptical that such samples, which usually range from 400 to 5,000, can accurately represent the actual viewing habits of TVHH across the country. But if such samples are selected randomly, that is, every person in the targeted population has an equal chance to be included in the sample, then we can be reasonably sure that the sample is reasonably representative of the total population.

Stratified random sampling techniques can be used to help ensure that samples truly represent the diversity of people in a population. For example, if we know that a target population has an ethnic makeup of 15% African-American, 30% Latino-American, 10% Asian-American and 45% Caucasian-American, researchers can stratify their random sample to be sure to include approximately equal proportions of such ethnic groups. Of course, statification also can be done, and often is done, using sex, age, educational attainment and other demographic variables.

One of the biggest complaints about ratings services is that too often major subgroups in society are systematically under-sampled. Critics have suggested for many years that minority groups, especially Latinos and Asians, are severely underrepresented in most television ratings efforts. Another group that is often underrepresented is young adults. Since people in the early 20s are often fairly mobile in their living arrangements—they're in college or changing jobs often—it's rather hard to find them and ask them to participate in ratings surveys. As a result of such under-sampling, many stations and networks complain that the ratings misrepresent the size and demographic makeup of their viewership.

Ratings Diaries

Diaries are probably the most common method of gathering television ratings data. Selected TVHH are asked to keep track of their TV viewing habits for a week. The diaries are reasonably comprehensive. After gathering rather complete demographic information about the members of the household, they break each day into 15-minute blocks. For each 15-minute block, respondents are asked to fill in the name of the station, the channel number, the name of the program and how many people of each sex are watching.

Diaries work reasonably well if the respondents take their responsibility seriously; however, as you might guess, not all respondents are as diligent about filling in their diaries as perhaps they should be. Research has found that quite often respondents do not actually watch TV with their ratings diary in hand. Instead, they wait until the day before they're supposed to mail their diaries back to Nielsen and then try to recall what they were watching when and who was watching. Respondents have even been known to lie about their actual viewing patterns. Yes, it's hard to believe, but true. Some people are ashamed to admit that they watch *Inside Edition* instead of *The NewsHour with Jim Lehrer* on PBS, so they write down they were watching PBS. Such imprecision and outright distortions bother many people in the television industry, but there's not much they can do about the situation.

Audimeters

Audimeters are small monitoring devices that are attached to television sets. Audimeters record when a television set is on and what channel it is tuned to. Such automation takes the lying and imprecision out of data gathering, but have you ever left the room or gone off somewhere and left your TV set on? Audimeters really can't determine how many people, if any, are actually watching a program. They can only determine what channel the set is tuned to. Audimeters are used to provide what are called "overnights" in the television industry. Overnights are the ratings of programs that aired yesterday. In most major television markets, the country's biggest cities, local stations find out every morning how their programs fared against every competitor's programs. The data gathered in these "wired markets" also can be used to determine national ratings for network programs.

People Meters

People meters combine the advantages of diaries and the precision of audimeters. Audimeter-like devices are paired with a key pad and respondents are asked periodically to key in a personal code number to let the computer know they're actively watching TV. People meters are a good compromise method to gather TV ratings data, but some research has shown that after a fairly short period of time, people get tired of pushing the buttons on the key pad. Research also has shown that even if people do keep pressing the appropriate buttons, they very often leave the room where the TV is playing and/or they read, play with pets and talk with family members. In short, even though the ratings data might indicate that they were watching a given program, it could very well be that they weren't watching very closely and probably missed at least some of the all-important

commercials. People meters have been used since the mid-1980s to compile national ratings and they are beginning to be used to gather local TV station ratings data.

Coincidental Telephone Surveys

Coincidental telephone surveys are not used as much in the gathering of television ratings data as they are in the gathering of radio ratings data. Still, they can provide a sort of "snapshot" look at what people watch on TV at a selected time. The way it works is researchers call people during a selected time of day or right after a selected time. People are asked what they're watching "right now" or what they just finished watching. Of course, demographic data is collected and sometimes people are asked to answer some "test" questions about the programs watched. Such questions can trip up viewers who aren't really sure about what they've been watching.

Paying for Ratings

The networks and local stations pay fees to Nielsen Media Research to obtain ratings data. Such data do not come cheap. Fees vary, of course, depending on the number of TVHH sampled and how often samples are taken, but they can range from $100,000 a year to more than $1,000,000. In most television markets, ratings data are gathered for an entire month four times each year. These periods are known as "ratings months," "sweeps months," "sweeps weeks" or simply, "sweeps." Typically, the months are February, May, July and November.

Of course, as mentioned earlier, most of the major cities in the United States are "wired markets" and receive ratings data every day. Still, even in wired markets, the sweeps months take on special significance. Networks run all new episodes of their prime-time programs. Blockbuster specials, miniseries productions, made-for-TV movies featuring big stars and popular theatrical films are usually always saved for airing during such months. In addition, the networks and local stations often air their most significant investigative news stories during the "sweeps." It's not unusual to find a bit more emphasis on sex, crime, violence, perversion and other titillating subjects filling up network and local station newscasts. Promotions of such stories and special programming usually are increased, too. Networks

Your Thoughts

Which method of gathering ratings data seems best to you? Why?

What suggestions do you have for improving the accuracy of ratings data?

and stations take out full-page advertisements in newspapers and magazines, plus run seemingly endless commercials for the stories and programs.

Sweeps weeks are hyped so much because it is the ratings during these weeks that are used to set the advertising rates until the next sweeps period. If a network or local station can pull big numbers for a special program or special news report, it can reap the benefits of higher ad rates for the next couple of months. On the other hand, if ratings during sweeps weeks drop, it means a lean couple of months as ad rates have to be discounted.

Sources of Programming

The programming mix at most local television stations is significantly different from that at most local radio stations. Most radio stations create the bulk of their programming, buy some syndicated programming and air very little, if any, network programming. Most local television stations rely on networks to provide the bulk of their programming, buy some syndicated programming and produce very little original programming.

Most local television stations are affiliated with a network. As a result, much of the local station's programming is provided by the network. Early-morning news and information programs, daytime dramas, network newscasts and specials, prime time programs and late-night entertainment or news programs pretty much fill up most of the broadcast day.

Drop in a few sporting events on the weekend and there is not much time left for a local station to fill.

The network usually pays the local station a small fee (about 30% of the local station's advertising rate for the national commercials that are aired) for running the network's programs and commercials. Most local stations make about 10% of their income from network fees. The networks also provide local stations with between six and eight minutes per hour for local commercials during network programs. ABC, CBS, NBC and PBS are the biggest providers of programming, but FOX and the CW are moving up fast.

Local network affiliates also buy programming from syndicated services and companies, although independent stations buy a lot more, because they do not have a network to count on to supply five to eight hours of programming per day. Major syndicators include Paramount, Universal, King World and Viacom.

Syndicated programming comes in two basic types: original syndication and off-net syndication. Original syndication includes programs that are produced specifically for sale to local stations. Such programs include *Judge Judy, Entertainment Tonight, Wheel of Fortune, Jeopardy* and *Oprah*. Off-net syndication includes programs that currently are running on a network or at one time ran on a network. What happens is the producer of the program packages up the old episodes and makes them available to the highest bidder in each television market. It's not unusual for a program to air its new episodes on one local station, the appropriate network affiliate, but have its old episodes running on a different station in the same market. For example, KTIM-TV, an NBC affiliate, would, of course, air the new episodes of *The Office,* but because it got outbid by KBUK-TV, an ABC affiliate, the old episodes of *The Office* air on KBUK at 7:30 every evening.

There's big money in syndication. Oprah Winfrey is usually one of the highest paid entertainers thanks to the millions she makes from syndicating her talk show. A local station pays thousands of dollars per episode for a syndicated program. Multiply that by 200 or more stations in other markets that do the same thing and you can see why producers of television programs are eager to move their network programs into syndication. In fact, for many programs, it is not until they go into syndication that they begin to show a profit. Production costs per episode can run more than $1 million and since networks don't pay anywhere near that for first-run programming, producers must wait for syndication to see the big returns on their investments.

Most local stations do very little production of original programming. News and public affairs programs usually are about it. Occasionally, a local station might produce a children's program. Some stations also have local hosts for old movies, cooking shows, fishing/hunting shows, home fix-up shows and other specialized programming. Producing locally originated programming takes a big commitment of time, energy, creativity, talent and money. Sadly, most local stations simply don't have enough of such things. Most content themselves with producing an hour's worth of local news each day, although many produce two, three, four and even five hours per day of news. A recent study in San Diego found that the six, English-language stations producing newscasts aired a total of 113 hours of local news per week.

Many local stations are partnering up with cable television systems to provide more extensive news coverage. The cable system will dedicate a different channel or a portion of a channel to the local station so newscasts can be replayed several times a day. In some cases, the local station might even place original news programming on the cable channel, especially during coverage of a breaking event or when an issue demands in-depth coverage.

For example, KGTV, channel 10, in San Diego teamed with Cox Communications to program a separate cable news channel. For most of the day, the news channel airs replays of the major newscasts that first aired on KGTV. There are original newscasts,

but only at selected times. Occasionally, however, especially during the coverage of breaking news, the cable news channel continues news programming when KGTV feels the need to offer viewers something other than news. A good example of this occurred in October, 1996, when a major fire ripped through parts of San Diego's north county. The fire reached its most devasting power on a Monday night. It just so happened that the San Diego Chargers were playing on ABC's *Monday Night Football.* KGTV was faced with a dilemma. Leave the football game to provide coverage of the fire or stay with the game and fail to live up to one of its most important responsibilities—provide information and help the community. Luckily for KGTV, it had the option to tell viewers who wanted to stay with the fire coverage to shift over to the cable news channel. Viewers who preferred to watch the football game, stayed with KGTV. Most everyone was well served.

Another example of "partnering up" is when local stations join on-line information providers. KGTV partnered with America Online (AOL) in a project called Digital City San Diego. KGTV provided updated news and information to Digital City San Diego and AOL made it available to its subscribers. Text, sound, pictures and interactivity were all part of the service. It's just another example of the convergence of media and the blurring of the traditional lines separating the media from one another.

Almost all local television stations have reasonably elaborate web sites that offer enhanced coverage of major stories, plus links to more information about the people, places, things and issues reported on during regularly scheduled newscasts. Partnerships with other media—radio stations, newspapers, cable operators and local magazines—are still common, however. The web sites of most stations are prime examples of media convergence. The sites include text (print media), audio (radio), video, graphics and slide shows (television), plus links and interactivity (computers).

Concerns about Violence on Television

Concerns about violence on television, especially in programs that children are likely to see, seem to grow by the day. The major concerns include fears that "copycatism" or imitation of violent acts depicted on television will increase, fears of a growing public desensitization to and acceptance of real-life violence and fears that so much televised violence will lead people to believe that the real world is a very dangerous place and that few people and/or organizations should be trusted.

Such fears and concerns may be well-founded. A major nationwide study of television programming found that about 60% of the entertainment programs on television contained violent acts. About 33% of programs with violent acts had nine or more of such acts. About 60% of the violent acts featured no real pain, 75% did not have any "immediate" punishment associated with the acts, only 16% had any negative consequences and just 15% of the programs provided an "advisory" about violent content.

The American Medical Association has developed a kind of "top 10 list" of things that parents can do to help ensure the quality of the time that children spend watching television. The list includes the following:

1. Know what shows your children are watching.
2. Avoid using television as a babysitter.
3. Limit television viewing to two hours per day.
4. Keep television sets out of children's bedrooms.
5. Do not permit television viewing during meal times.
6. Plan television viewing. Select specific programs to watch. Don't just turn on the set to see what's on.
7. Help children critically evaluate program content and advertisements.
8. Watch television with your children. Discuss program content with them.
9. Limit your own television viewing time. Be a role model.
10. Let your voice be heard by television executives and advertisers. Tell them what you like and don't like.

Some of the expressed concerns about violence on TV may be having an effect on program providers. A study of the first four weeks of prime-time, network TV programs in 1989–90 and 1999–2000 found that depicted acts of violence had actually decreased slightly during the decade; however, there was three times more sexual content and four times more foul language in 1999–2000 than in 1989–90. Critics used the results to urge parents to complain to program providers, take television sets out of kids' bedrooms (about 50% of U.S. kids have a TV set in their rooms), and boycott advertisers who support offensive programs.

Television Program Ratings

As a response to some of the concerns about violent acts, sexual activities and bad language on television and in an effort to provide "parental guidelines," the television industry developed a system for rating program content that is similar to the one used for movies. The categories include the following:

1. **TV-Y:** Material suitable for children of all ages.
2. **TV-7:** Material suitable for children seven years old and up. Content might frighten some children.
3. **TV-G:** Material suitable for all audiences. Program contains little or no violence, strong language or sexual situations.
4. **TV-PG:** Parental guidance suggested. Program may contain some coarse language, some violence and suggestive sexual language and/or situations.
5. **TV-14:** Parents strongly cautioned. Program not suitable for children less than 14 years old. Strong language, violence and sexual content.
. **TV-MA:** Mature audiences only. Program not suitable for children less than 17 years old. Profane language, graphic violence and explicit sexual content.

Producers, broadcast networks, cable channels, syndicators and others who originate programming rate their own programs. Local television stations or cable systems can override a program's original rating and give it a new rating. News and sports programs are not rated. The rating designations appear in the top-left corner of the television screen during the first 15 seconds of a rated program.

Critics complain that the rating system is too general, vague, inconsistent and unregulated. They want a system that provides separate ratings for language, violence and sexual content. They say a rating system should provide parents with more detailed information about the type, amount and intensity of violence, language and sexual activity. They also want an independent panel or panels to rate programs. Such a panel would be very busy. Every day in the United States, we have about 2,000 hours of television programming available to us.

Some program providers add selected letters to the ratings categories. The degree of intensity associated with the letters varies by category. These letters include the following:

1. **FV**—Fantasy Violence
2. **V**—Violence (moderate to graphic)
3. **S**—Sexual Situations (moderate to explicit)
4. **L**—Course Language (moderate and infrequent to crude and frequent)
5. **D**—Suggestive Dialogue (moderate to intense)

The rating system is supposed to be used in conjunction with the federally mandated V-chip that has been installed in most newer television sets. The V-chip makes it possible to block channels and/or selected programs based on rating designations.

Television News

Most people report they get most of their news and information about the world from television. Such findings are a bit disturbing when you think about how little time people probably spend watching television news. Plus, even when people do watch, research shows that about 75% of them do something else in addition to watching. In other words, most people eat, drink, talk, work, read, sew or participate in numerous other activities while they are supposedly "watching" television news. Not exactly a ringing endorsement of the quality of television news, is it? In addition, just how much information about the world are people really getting from television?

Television news does have a few things going for it, of course. The three biggest advantages that television news enjoys are immediacy, visuals and believability and trust. Television news can be as immediate as radio news. Regularly scheduled programming can be interrupted whenever any major news event breaks. Live coverage of such events creates some problems, though. Getting crews to the scenes of the events, getting a signal from the location back to the station so it can be sent to viewers and preempting programs that people really want to see.

The last problem probably presents the biggest obstacle to live coverage of breaking events. Whenever a station or network preempts regular programming, it runs the risk of missing the playing of commercials. Miss a few high-income commercials, some of which might even be worth more than $500,000, and the old bottom line might take a pretty big hit. As a result, even though the technology is in place, it takes a really big, breaking news event to get most stations or networks to break into regular programming to air bulletins or live news coverage.

The visual nature of television news sets it apart from all other news media. Marrying pictures with sound creates the possibility of increasing the impact of news and information on viewers. People like to see things with their own eyes. They like to be able to look into the eyes of a politician to judge for themselves if he or she is lying or telling the truth. They like to see the extent of the damage caused by a major brush fire rather than simply relying on a reporter to tell them how bad things are.

Being able to see things for yourself probably helps explain why television news enjoys a relatively high credibility rating with most viewers. "I know what happened. I saw it with my own two eyes." People trust television. They believe pictures and video don't lie. They're wrong, of course. Pictures and video can and do lie. Your eyes can play tricks on you. So, too, can people in television news. By using creative editing, juxtapositioning, lighting effects, unusual angles, computer imaging and other special effects, reality can be greatly distorted.

Another reason why people trust television news more than most other sources of news and information is the relationship that many form with newscasters. Researchers have found that some people form para-social relationships with newscasters. They begin to think of the newscasters as friends. They trust, admire and respect the newscasters. Such good and trusted friends wouldn't mislead us, would they?

Problems in Television News

Not all is rosy in television news, of course. In fact, the list of problems is quite long. It includes limited time to present news, abbreviated stories, small news staffs, low pay, fierce ratings competition, over dependence on visuals, transitory nature of the product and lack of substance.

Even though many stations now program up to six hours a day of news, comparatively speaking, television news does not really provide that much information. For example, if a script used in a half-hour television news program were printed as newspaper copy, it wouldn't even fill one page. If a station wanted to broadcast every word in a Sunday edition of the *New York Times,* it would have to broadcast 24 hours a day for more than a month.

As a direct result of the limited time available to program television news, most individual stories are relatively brief. Stories without visual enhancement rarely run longer than 15 seconds. Stories with graphics, but no video might run 25–30 seconds. Stories with video, but no reporter voice-over might run 45 seconds. Stories with video, sound bites from sources and reporter narration might run 1:15 or maybe 1:30. Rarely, however, will a television news story run much longer than 1:30. It's pretty difficult to include all the significant information that the public needs when you only have 1:30.

Television news staffs are almost always smaller than the staffs at newspapers. For example, in San Diego, most of the television news departments have staffs of about 50–70 people. The *San Diego Union-Tribune* has about 150 reporters and editors gathering news every day. Such comparisons are common in cities across the United States. A smaller staff means less original news gathering. Less original news gathering means less coverage of the important events and issues in a community.

Few people get rich in television news. Sure, some newscasters can make more than $1 million per year, but most don't and everybody else in the newsroom usually makes quite a bit less than the newscasters. For example, videographers average about $50,000 per year. Newscast producers and reporters earn about $55,000. Newscasters average about $90,000 and news directors earn about $80,000. Such salaries are not bad, of course, but many other pro-

fessionals make a lot more. One major concern related to the relatively low pay is how will the profession continue to attract bright, energetic, fair-minded and talented people when other professions offer salaries that often are twice as high? Good question.

The competition for ratings supremacy is normally quite fierce in most local television markets. Such pressure can lead to compromising journalistic integrity. Instead of going for good, solid journalism, a station might opt for sex, sleaze, crime, violence and entertainment in an effort to win a greater share of the ever-declining audience for television news. Reporters might be tempted to cut a few corners or to stretch the truth a bit. Extra "live shots" might be aired, even though there's really no reason to go live.

Since television is a visual medium, visuals tend to dominate the concerns of many television news executives. They want visuals included with stories and they want as many visuals as possible. If a story isn't all that visual, if it gets aired at all, you can bet it will be brief. On the other hand, if a rather insignificant story has great visuals associated with it, expect it to run 1:00–1:30. The bigger the flames, the more blood on the road, the more tears streaming down the faces of grieving relatives, the more likely it is that a story will run and that it will run for the maximum amount of time.

Despite all the potential to convey important information to people, television news comes up rather short as an effective channel of communication. Research has found that most people do not remember too much about the newscasts they watch. When viewers are asked to recall stories from a newscast they watched no more than 30 minutes previously, out of 20 possible stories, the average number remembered is less than two. Almost half the viewers can't remember even one story. Not exactly a ringing endorsement of the effectiveness of television news, is it?

One reason that so few stories are recalled is that too often on television news programs there is not much worth remembering. There simply is not much substance or nourishment included in newscasts. If nothing much meaningful, interesting, amusing, diverting, disturbing or significant is offered, why remember any of it? Of course, as mentioned earlier, most viewers are doing something else while they "watch" television news, so it's not too surprising that so little content can be recalled. But just 10%? That's a bit depressing.

Jobs in Television News

The head of the television news operation is known as the news director. He or she hires, fires, sets policy, worries about the budget and serves as the liaison for the news department with station management. Being a news director is not an easy gig. The average tenure for a news director at a local station is only about two years. They either get fired because of low ratings or quit to take a job at a bigger station to replace a person who probably got fired because of low ratings.

The person who is responsible for organizing the newscast is the producer. He or she decides what stories are going to be aired, how long stories are going to run, where they're going to run in the newscast, which newscaster will read which stories and what graphics or special effects will be used.

The assignment editor/manager keeps an eye on what's happening in town and assigns reporting crews to cover the stories he or she feels are most likely to attract and interest viewers. The assignment editor/manager reads newspapers, checks wire services, checks emails, reads faxes, pours over news releases and listens to several different scanners—police, fire, airport, etc.—to be sure no big story is missed.

Videographers or photojournalists or "shooters" capture action on video. Most of the time they edit video, too. They also usually drive the news cars/vans/trucks and make suggestions to reporters about how to cover a story. In the good news operations, videographers are considered equal to with reporters. Sadly, there aren't that many good television news operations.

Reporters gather the news, interview sources, write the scripts and narrate the stories. They often appear on camera from the field or in the news studio. The best ones are personable, yet tough, compassionate, and persistent. There are too few good ones.

Newscasters, or news anchors, read the news on the air. They are the "anchors" of the news team. Most have worked their way up from the ranks of reporters, but some have never done much reporting. Many newscasters, especially in the smaller markets,

write at least some of the material that they read. Newscasters in the top 25 markets probably don't write much, if any, of the copy they read.

Sportscasters and weathercasters are "specialized" newscasters. They report sports and/or weather in specifically identified newscast segments. They are supposed to be "experts" in their fields. Quite often, in addition to presenting the news in their areas, they are expected to provide entertainment, especially humor and "personality." Other specialty newscasters/reporters include the following: investigative, consumer, troubleshooter, health, environmental, police beat, city hall and education.

Other staff positions in a television newsroom include assistant producer, writer, production assistant, video editor and camera assistant. Assistant producers help newscast producers. They sort scripts, arrange for graphics and run errands. Writers write, or more accurately rewrite, copy. They write most of the on-camera readers that don't have any video. Production assistants do a little bit of everything. They serve as receptionists, answer phone calls, file, check computer logs, etc. Video editors edit video. They often work with reporters and photographers, but also log and edit video that is sent to a station by satellite or closed circuit feed from a network or syndicator. Camera assistants work with videographers. They carry equipment, help set-up for live shots, run errands and serve as messengers between field shoots and the newsroom.

Television Newscast Formats

Four basic newscast formats dominate television news. They are the Traditional format, Eyewitness format, Magazine format and the Newsroom/Newscenter format. It might be difficult to find a "pure" example of any of the formats. Most stations combine elements of each to create a hybrid format of their own.

In the Traditional format, the pace of the newscast is rather slow. You might get no more than 8–10 stories in a half-hour. The network evening newscasts are good examples of the Traditional format. At the local level, the newscast is often predictably segmented. You can almost set your watch by the segments—local news, national news, international news, weather, sports, good-bye. Usually a mature man serves as the lone newscaster. There is little or no joking and chatting on the air among newscaster, sportscaster, weathercaster and reporters who come onto the news set.

In the Eyewitness format, the pace of the newscast quickens dramatically. It's not unusual to have 20-30 stories in a half-hour. The newcast is free-wheeling. If international news is the big news of the day, it leads the newscast. If sports is the big news, it leads. The father- or grandfather-figure newscaster is out. Instead, we get "Barbie and Ken." They're young, good-looking, energetic, personable and almost always a man and a woman. Joking, chit-chat and good-natured bantering are a big part of the format. Anchors are supposed to come across as friends that viewers can identify with. Video, especially action video, is stressed. Rarely will a story be aired if it doesn't have a strong visual component. The goal is to allow viewers to become "eyewitnesses" to the news. In addition, reporters are encouraged to do "stand-ups" in their stories to prove that they, too, are "eyewitnesses" to the news.

Sex, crime and violence dominate the content of most Eyewitness format newscasts. Catchy names for the news programs are used in an attempt to build station identity. Eyewitness News, Action News, Newswatch, Newscene, Nightcast, Pro News and News Alive are some of the most popular ones. Sometimes things get a bit out of control with the for-mat and that's when some of the following negative-connotation labels/names have been used to describe the format: "Happy Talk;" "Tabloid TV;" "Fuz-Wuz;" "Flash-Crash;" and "If It Bleeds, It Leads."

The Magazine format can be broken down into two types. It can include coverage of two or three major stories in a half-hour. Such network prime-time news programs as *60 Minutes, 20/20,* and *Dateline* are good examples of this format. Some local stations air their own versions, too. The other form of Magazine format is a blend of elements from the Eyewitness format and the Traditional format. A station might add a co-anchor, but keep the pace relatively slow and limit the on-air banter. A station might have just a father-figure anchor, but chat it up and whiz through the newscast at a story per minute. Most local news operations use a variation of the Magazine format.

The Newscenter/Newsroom format is really more of a presentation style rather than a pure format. In it, newscasters deliver the news from the newsroom, NOT a news studio. The goal is to drive home the point with viewers that the station's newscasters and reporters feel most comfortable in a newsroom and news gathering never stops. We'll see people wandering around or dashing around behind the newscasters. We'll see reporters talking on the phone and typing at their computers. Occasionally, a newscaster might turn to a reporter in the newsroom and ask him or her to make a comment or two about the story he or she is

Your Thoughts

Which television newscast format appeals to you the most? Why?

What changes would you make to improve your favorite format? Why?

Design a new format for television news. Give it a name and be specific about its elements.

working on. Much of the orchestrated integration of newsroom resources is more for show than substance, but viewers seem to like it.

Recent Research, Developments and Issues

The average cable TV bill doubled between 1996 and 2004. In an effort to combat skyrocketing prices, some cable TV executives suggested to federal regulators that consumers be permitted to "customize" the set of channels and networks they want and pay for only those channels and networks. Research shows that only about 20% of cable TV customers are interested in sports programming, so why should those folks have to pay for expensive ESPN and Fox Sports offerings that are usually included in "expanded basic packages?"

Prime time programming on broadcast networks is often criticized for not providing a fair representation of various minority groups. For example, in the 2003–2004 season, Latinos made up 6% of the characters portrayed in prime time. That's about half of what the actual percentage of Latinos is in the United States. In addition, researchers found that Latinos were four times more likely than other races to be cast as domestic workers. The same researchers found that 65% of all the characters were male, creating another distorted picture of reality.

A study of the 2002–2003 prime time season found that women made up 22% of the creators of TV programming—executive producers, producers, directors, writers, editors and directors of photography. Behind-the-scenes power can translate into on-screen visibility.

Even the best television news organizations can run into trouble. In late 2004, CBS aired a story about alleged special treatment that George W. Bush received while he was serving in the Texas Air National Guard. CBS based its story, in part, on memos that had been obtained from unnamed sources. As it turned out, the memos were not authentic. After defending its story for a couple of weeks, CBS admitted it was wrong and apologized. CBS appointed outsiders to conduct an investigation of what went wrong and promised to be more vigilant in the future.

The Parents Television Council studied prime time entertainment programming in 1998, 2000 and 2002 and found an increase in profanity on almost every network and in almost every time slot. From 1998 to 2002, during the first hour of prime time, often called the "family hour," foul language increased about 95%. During the second hour, it increased about 109%. During the last hour of prime time, it increased about 40%.

A study in 2008 found that consumers spend more than half of their "media time" watching television (53%). Radio finished second (23%), followed by the Internet (19%), newspapers (4%) and magazines (2%). The same study found that television continues to be the favored source of news and information for consumers. About 55% of the respondents picked television.

Another 2008 study found that, in general, television viewers are more loyal to programs than they are to networks and/or stations. The survey found that about 97% of U.S. adults watch TV during a typical week. About 70% watched four or more programs per week and 71% watched programs on four or more channels per week. Almost 40% of the respondents said they were willing to pay a fee to download TV programs from a digital service. An equal number preferred to get such programs for free and were willing to watch embedded commercials as a trade-off. Commercials were the biggest complaint about "real-time" TV (64%), followed by the inability to pause/rewind (40%), the inability to time-shift (38%) and unappealing content (14%).

The writers' strike of 2007–08 likely contributed to speeding up the decline in ratings for network TV's prime-time programs. In mid-2008, ratings for all of the big networks were down, for some by as much as 20%, with CBS, NBC and the CW the biggest losers. Local television newscasts fared better in the ratings than did their networks. Ratings for late-night newscasts dropped about half as much as did the ratings for the network programs immediately preceding the newscasts.

A study in early 2008 found that 25% of viewers were watching less TV because of the writers' strike. Most indicated they were spending more time on the Internet, watching DVDs and reading books, magazines and newspapers.

A study in late 2007 found that almost 20% of American households that use the Internet watch television programs online. In addition, 73% of online households used the Internet for entertainment purposes and reported that what they liked best about online TV was the convenience and the ability to avoid commercials.

Even with the ability to watch TV online, the viewing of traditional TV remained relatively steady through 2007. The average household watched about eight and a quarter hours per day. Most of the viewing appears to be limited to a relatively small number of stations. While most U.S. adults have about 110 channels to choose from, only about 16 channels are viewed for more than 10 minutes per week. Most U.S. households receive their television programs via cable (62%). Direct broadcast satellite (DBS) delivery is used by about 26%.

Experts are predicting that more households will likely turn to cable or DBS in response to the government-mandated switch from analog broadcasting to digital broadcasting scheduled for February, 2009. The switch was ordered by Congress to make more efficient use of the public's airwaves. The old analog space on the spectrum was to be made available to the providers of wireless communication services. A study in early 2008 found that about 45% of households that received their TV signals over-the-air planned to continue to receive their signals that way after the switch to digital transmission.

Without cable or DBS service, an analog TV set would be unable to receive broadcast signals after February, 2009. Digital converter boxes were made available to people who did not want to buy a new digital set or subscribe to cable or DBS services. In early 2008, about 17 million U.S. households fell into that category. At least 9 million households were predicted to have reception problems even with a digital TV set or converter box, because of "challenging reception areas" in the country. Welcome to the digital world! At least the federal government made $40 subsidy coupons available for those households choosing to purchase converter boxes. A survey in 2008 found that about 60% of Americans were aware of the switch.

A study in 2007 found that portrayals of lesbian, gay, bisexual and transgender (LGBT) people on scripted TV programs declined for the third straight year. About 1% of the series regulars were LGBT characters. The same study looked at race and gender on TV, too. Whites accounted for 77% of the regular characters, African-Americans accounted for 12%, Latinos accounted for 6% and Asian-Americans accounted for 3%. Male characters outnumbered female character 57% to 43%.

In September, 2006, Katie Couric became the first female to serve as the lead newscaster for a network TV nightly news program. Her ratings were impressive for a short time, but began to fade quickly and by mid-2008, CBS and Couric reportedly were both looking for ways to facilitate her honorable departure from the CBS news anchor desk. In April, 2008, the CBS Evening News was mired in third place in the network news ratings race with a record low number of viewers. With a little more than 5 million viewers each night, CBS was about 2 million viewers behind ABC and about 3 million viewers behind NBC.

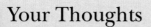

Your Thoughts

How important do you think it is for the demographic composition of characters on network television entertainment programs to be reasonably representative of the U.S. population? Why?

Think Back

1. List the major new technology-based impacts on television.

   Enhanced TV, "personal TV's, personal video recorders and TiVo.

2. How much television do people watch?

   The average person watches 30 hours per week.

3. What are the major concerns associated with excessive TV viewing by children?

   The child will become overweight and have underdeveloped social skills.

4. How can TV signals be delivered to consumers?

   Over the air, through cable, digital cable, wireless cable, direct broadcast satellite, internet, cell phone and the telephone company.

5. What are the major television networks?

   ABC, CBS, NBC, PBS, FOX, and the CW.

6. How can local television stations be categorized?

They can be ~~affiliated~~. known as affiliates to major cable stations.

7. Describe the usual relationship between a network and a local station.

It will either be an affiliate with the networks or it can be fully owned, as in owned and operated (O&O), or it isn't allied with an network, and become an independent station.

8. What are the three basic types of stations?

VHF, UHF & cable.

9. What are the major departments in a typical local television station?

Programming/productions
Engineering
Office/Clerical/Traffic
News/Sports
Sales

10. What's the difference between a rating and a share?

A rating is the percentage of households ~~turn turned~~ tuned in to a given station based on the total number of households in an area.
A share is the percentage of TVHH tuned into a given station based on the total number of TVHH with their sets in use at a given time.

11. What are the major methods used to gather ratings data for television stations and networks?

Rating Diaries, Audimeters, People Meters, Coincidental Telephone Surveys, & Paying for Ratings.

12. What are the major sources of programming for local stations? Give an example of each type.

Networks provide bulk of the programming, buy syndications and produce little original programming.

13. What are the major ratings designations/categories for television programs?

TV-Y, TV-7, TV-G, TV-PG, TV-14, TV-MA.

14. What are the major concerns about the rating system for individual programs?

They feel that the rating system is too general, vague, inconsistent and unregulated.

15. What are the advantages that television news enjoys?

A high credibility rating, people trust it.

16. What are the disadvantages that television news suffers?

There is limited time available to program TV news, stories run shorter, TV news staffs are almost always smaller than the staffs at newspapers $ few people in TV news get rich.

17. What are the typical jobs in a local television news department?

News Director, Producer, Assignment Editor/Manager, Videographers, Reporters, Newscasters, Sports/ Weathercasters, and others.

18. What are the major television newscast formats? Give the basic elements of each one.

Traditional format, Eyewitness format, Magazine format, and Newsroom/ Newscenter format.

19. How fast are cable TV bills rising and what could be done to help consumers reduce their bills?

20. What are some of the most recent statistics associated with how much television people watch and how they seem to prefer to watch it?

21. What are the major issues and problems associated with the switch from analog to digital television broadcasting?

22. What were the major findings of a 2007 content analysis of network scripted programs? Note the sexual preferences of characters, plus race and gender.

23. How did the Katie Couric/CBS news arrangement work out?

The Recording Industry

10

Turmoil

The Internet age generated a popular but illegal application of computer technology: getting music free. At least it was free for awhile. The battle against illegal downloading of music took a strange turn when makers of a computer game based loosely on Robert Louis Stevenson's *Treasure Island* told the Recording Industry Association of America that children could be enlisted in the effort to stop music pirates. The game was intended to take youngsters into the make-believe-world of pirates while also teaching them about music copyright laws. The RIAA, among other efforts, had mounted a few educational programs against bootlegging music and welcomed the interactive computer game and its underlying message against the piracy that had caused CD sales to slide precipitously. Industry efforts at education had concentrated on college students and their participation in file-sharing networks that attracted tens of millions of copyright infringers. However, the computer game targeted the younger music lovers who didn't yet necessarily expect to get music free. The thrust of the fantasy scenarios in the game was to ridicule bootleggers through displaying an evil pirate leader who unfairly manipulates children who love music.

The Napster online music service offered a variety of live tracks, bootlegs, individual songs, and even samples of other users' libraries, all without paying the labels and music publishers for their property. The major record labels shut down the original Napster in 2001 with a federal court injunction that barred its users from violating copyrights. Among the businesses that then began to compete for the defunct Napster's former file sharers were online music stores charging a modest monthly fee to hear or rent an unlimited number of tracks. Most of them offered the subscription service on a monthly basis, but some

also charged one dollar or so to download an individual song. Consumers were thereby able to avoid buying full CDs or only those singles chosen by the record label.

Major record companies tried for years to stifle the online music business with restrictions on what music lovers could do with downloaded songs. Eventually, the recording firms made their licensing terms more favorable to independent companies and even started to accept online partners.

Ironically, the primary reason the music producing companies found themselves in upheaval was the CD itself. When that format was adopted to replace records it initially resulted in huge profits because music fans were ecstatic over the digital quality and the durability of the discs. Many who had been buying music on vinyl quickly realized that they had a technology that would allow them to grab any song they wanted without cost by finding, retrieving and disseminating any piece of music on the Internet. File sharing, at first through Napster, created a system that resulted in lower profits for artists, producers and retail music outlets.

The RIAA reacted with an aggressive and controversial attempt to use the law against thousands of individuals rather than go after companies that were profiting from the rampant piracy on the Internet. Cases were filed in federal court against hundreds of people described in the lawsuits as egregious offenders, defined as those who shared a significant number of songs with a great many others with Internet access. The cases involved charges of large libraries of songs offered for copying on file-sharing networks. Those individuals named by the Recording Industry Association of America allegedly violated the labels' copyrights by downloading or sharing without permission. The defendants were charged with offering for copy an average of 1,000 songs each. The potential penalties could have amounted to hundreds of thousands of dollars per person.

Once many turned themselves in and offered to agree to settlements of much lower sums, the RIAA offered amnesty for file sharers who turned themselves in before they were targeted. Music industry executives said they were not eager to sue, but all of the defendants had been warned that what they were doing was just as illegal as shoplifting, but they still did not stop. The lawsuits drew praise from many artists, composers, independent record labels, recording studios and music retailers, but did not end the drop in CD sales nor ultimately help protect copyright holders.

Early in the 21st century, the music industry began rushing headlong into the technology-driven future. Record companies in the 1990s had been fighting online piracy and complaining about potential damage by the Internet to the traditional structure of album-based music sales. But early in the year 2000, most of the major record companies were following the trend of getting ready to sell music to a new generation that prefers to download music from the Internet rather than buy discs and consumers began to benefit as the recording industry started to distribute some of its music online. For those who want their music sooner and easier, the focus by major labels on the Internet promised more choice, more immediacy, and more control. The Internet was expected to eliminate much of the expense of distribution by recording firms, although some CDs would still be bought in retail stores, despite the online delivery systems.

A move by Time Warner Inc. triggered the radical changes. Time Warner and America Online merged in what was then the largest business transaction in history. It was the first purchase of a major media company by an Internet company. The merger brought together the world's largest entertainment company with the major Internet service provider, and provided America Online with Time Warner's expansive and easy-to-use system of distributing news and entertainment material, making the Internet a mass media industry. Consumers could access telephone, Internet, movies and news over the same system, as AOL acquired the second largest cable system in the country, Time magazine, HBO, CNN, Warner Bros. studio, and WB Television network, along with music labels Elektra, Warner Bros. Records, Atlantic, and Rhino.

The Digital Dilemma

At the center of the storm associated with online music was a company called MP3.com. The online music distributor developed the MP3 technology that compresses large digital files, like those on music CDs, and allows computer users to download files off the Internet. Such files can be listened to using computers or hand-held players. The good news about such technology is that it allows musicians to distribute their music faster and easier. The bad news about such technology is it makes it a lot easier for music piracy to take place. Piracy is the unauthorized use of copyrighted music.

MP3.com started out as a rather minor annoyance to the major music companies, but when MP3.com started its "Instant Listening Service," the industry leaders took more notice. The service provided a way for consumers to acquire digital copies of their personal music CDs. Of course, clever computer users found ways to "swap" files and that's what caused the major problems. The Recording Industry Association of America (RIAA) sued MP3.com for copyright infringement and sought $6.75 billion in damages—$150,000 for each of the 45,000 CDs in the MP3.com database. RIAA alleged that MP3.com had violated the Digital Millennium Copyright Act by illegally archiving copyrighted music online. MP3.com shot back that the RIAA was just angry that a new technology was changing the recording industry and didn't know any other way of trying to control things.

With more than 500,000 music files online, at least 200,000 visitors to MP3.com's web site each day and computer systems at colleges and universities freezing up because of too much use of Napster.com and Gnutella.com, online music sites that used the MP3 technology, online music was obviously popular with consumers. It also grew in popularity with major recording artists who saw the new technology as a way to be more creative with their music and possibly reach new audiences.

The Industry Elements

Records don't dominate the recording industry anymore, but they're still around and some experts predict they may enjoy a comeback. Compact discs (CDs), cassette tapes and, of course, digital recordings are now making a big impact.

The recording industry consists of three major parts. Each part is important in its own right, but it is the integration of the parts that makes the recording industry what it is. The three parts are:

1. Artistic Component
2. Business Component
3. Audience Component

Artistic Component

The artistic component includes the people who create the music and lyrics, the technicians who assist the artists with the technical aspects of production and the producers who oversee/coordinate the creative and technical development of the musical works. Musicians and songwriters are the heart and soul of the music industry, but producers and sound technicians help refine raw products and raw talent into marketable material.

Business Component

The business component includes people who work for recording companies, those who work for individual artists, those who work for organizations that assist recording companies, those who work for companies that assist with the distribution of product and information about the recording industry and those who work for retailers who sell recordings to consumers.

Among those who work within the industry are corporate officers, marketing experts, sales promoters, advertising representatives, public relations practitioners and artist-and-repertoire (A&R) representatives. Corporate officers manage the financial affairs of the companies. Marketing experts attempt to develop markets for the musical products and to package products attractively. Sales promoters attempt to boost sales and radio airplay of songs. Advertising representatives develop strategies for promoting the products, plan advertising campaigns, create the ads themselves and evaluate how effective campaigns have been. Public relations practitioners try to put the companies and their artists in the best possible light. Finally, A&R representatives fan out across the globe looking for and developing talent—new singers, musicians, songwriters and bands.

Among those who work for individual artists are agents, managers and personal publicists. An agent attempts to obtain opportunities (gigs) for an artist and represents an artist in contract negotiations with recording companies, managers of performance venues and heads of production companies. A manager oversees aspects of performance bookings and tours. Where the artist/band eat and what they eat, where the artist/band sleeps and how the artist/band gets from place to place are all part of a manager's job. Personal publicists serve as liaisons between the artist/band and the news media. Publicists also coordinate responses to fan mail and the many public appearances for charity and publicity purposes.

Among those who work for organizations that assist recording companies are representatives of publishing rights organizations and those who work for unions. Publishing rights organizations collect fees from people or businesses that use recordings. Examples include radio stations, television stations, restaurants, bars and jukebox companies. The fees are collected based on either a per-use basis or a percentage of profits basis. The major publishing rights organizations include the American Society of Composers, Authors and Publishers (ASCAP), Broadcast Music Incorporated (BMI) and the Society of European State Authors and Composers (SESAC). ASCAP is the biggest and most powerful of the publishing rights organizations. Unions include the American Federation of Television and Radio Artists (AFTRA) and the American Federation of Musicians (AFM). Quite often artists must be members of the appropriate union in order to perform on the air and/or in certain venues.

Among those who work for companies that assist with the distribution of product and information about the recording industry are trade press journalists, selected radio station personnel and distributors. Trade press journalists provide information about the recording industry, artists and groups. They review new releases, examine trends and speculate on the lasting-power of artists and groups. Among the leading trade press publications are *Billboard, Cashbox, Record World, Radio and Records, Down Beat* and *Rolling Stone*.

Radio station program directors or music directors are in charge of deciding what gets played on the air and what doesn't. Disc jockeys and station "personalities" also can have some influence on what gets played, how often it gets played and what is said about it on the air. Radio airplay is critical to the success of most songs, of course, so station programmers and disc jockeys are in a fairly powerful position. Most music-oriented stations that play contemporary music receive about 300 new releases per week on average. As a result, competition for air time is fierce. Promoters have been known to try to entice preferential treatment for their products/performers by offering money, drugs and other favors to both programmers and disc jockeys. More on "payola" later.

Distributors deliver products to retailers. They set up sales displays, distribute promotional materials—t-shirts, posters, toys, etc.—and are responsible of being sure that there is always enough product available to meet demand.

Retailers include outlets that are devoted to the recording industry, general merchandisers, discount outlets and record clubs/mail order.

About 50% of U.S. record/CD/cassette sales are made by discount stores. Department stores account for about 25%. Record stores contribute 15% and record clubs/direct marketing add 10%.

Audience Component

Consumers play an important role in the recording industry, of course. Recording artists and the companies that represent them are all at the mercy of the traditionally fickle music-loving public, especially teenagers and young adults. One-hit wonders abound in the recording industry. Rare is the singer or band that stays on top for more than a year or two. In fact, about 80% of the millions of recordings produced every year do not achieve enough sales to show a profit. Most experts say for a single to break even, it must sell a minimum of 50,000 copies. For an album to break even, it needs to sell approximately 150,000 copies. Don't feel too sorry for recording artists and executives, though. For the past several years, the recording industry has enjoyed sales in excess of $40 billion.

Selling recordings can be a profitable business for all concerned. As an example, it costs about $4 to produce a CD. That includes fees to artists, production costs and promotions costs. The recording company sells the CD to retailers for about $8. Retailers normally charge consumers anywhere from $12 to $17 for the same CD. Most recordings are purchased by young people. In fact, about half of recording sales are made to people 25 years old or younger.

The money pie in the recording industry is normally cut in a rather unequal way. Traditionally, the producer receives about 45% of the income from a recording. Retailers pocket approximately 25%. The distributor rakes in 20%. The writers and the performers get the remaining 10%.

The Recording Industry Association of America keeps track of sales and awards gold, platinum and multi-platinum records based the number of sales a recording achieves. To earn a gold record, a single must generate one million sales. An album must generate 500,000 sales or $1 million in wholesale revenue. Wholesale equals about one-third the amount of retail sales. For example, if an album sells for $15, only $5 would count toward the $1 million "gold record" target.

To earn a platinum record, a single must generate two million sales. An album must generate one million sales or $2 million in wholesale revenue. To earn a multi-platinum record, a single must generate three million sales. An album must generate two million sales or $4 million in wholesale revenue.

Your Thoughts

Why do you think so few recordings turn a profit?

What would you suggest be done to improve the chances that a recording will become successful?

Recording Companies

The recording industry is dominated by a handful of major companies. Recent mergers have left us with four giant recording industry conglomerates: Universal Music Group, Warner Music Group, EMI Group, and Sony BMG. Each company controls a variety of different "labels." Labels include Capitol, Virgin, Rhino, Columbia, Epic, WTG, Chrysalis, Decca, Kapp, Geffen, UNI, A&M, Island, Mercury, Motown, Arista, Atco, Atlantic, Elektra, Reprise and Warner Brothers.

The so-called "majors" account for about 90% of all the recordings made and marketed every year. Independents or "indies" account for the remaining 10%. Indies usually try to specialize in a specific type of music, sort of "niche" labels, in their efforts to survive.

Issues and Problems

Among the issues and problems associated with the recording industry are:

- Homedubbing
- Piracy
- Payola
- Obtaining accurate sales data
- Retailing shifts
- Obscene lyrics
- Sex, violence, racism and misogyny in music videos
- Performers serving as poor role models
- Consolidation of companies

Homedubbing

As home recording and computer file-sharing equipment has improved in quality and dropped in price, the dubbing of records, CDs, files and tapes has increased dramatically. As a result, sales have dropped. One person buys a recording and then creates copies or loans it to his or her friends who share or dub off copies for themselves. In addition, many radio stations encourage dubbing off the air by playing whole albums and CDs without commercial interruption. The Recording Industry Association of America estimates that homedubbing costs musicians and their recording companies between $1 billion and $2 billion per year.

Piracy

Many of the recordings sold at swap meets, garage sales and on street corners are pirated versions of originals. Pirates take an original and make hundreds, if not thousands, of unauthorized copies. Asia and the Middle East are the hotbeds of such activity. The U.S. government has tried to work out agreements with offending countries to curb the practice, but it continues to flourish. The Recording Industry Association of America estimates that pirated recordings account for about 20% of all recordings sold. Such piracy costs recording companies about $5 billion per year not counting the new, improved digital piracy.

Experts and recording company executives are especially concerned about piracy possibilities associated with the evolution of the digital recording and transmission of music. The ease of recording, copying and sharing online music files might encourage novice "pirates" to join their more professional counterparts and slice into recording company profits even more.

Payola

Payola scandals hit the recording industry on a fairly regular basis. In fact, most radio stations require that employees sign an agreement not to accept money, gifts, drugs or other inducements from recording companies and independent record promoters. Such bribes and inducements are made in the hope that station personnel will give preferential treatment to the works of a certain performer or band. A kind word or two from a disc jockey, extra airplay and/or airplay at the best times of the day—normally morning and afternoon "drive time"—can mean dramatically increased sales and profits for a recording.

Obtaining Accurate Sales Data

Finding out the total number of sales for a recording after an extended period of time is not all that difficult, but trying to measure sales soon after a recording has been released is not an easy task. Retailers must be contacted and they must report sales accurately. In addition, while sales for major releases by major recording companies are reasonably easy to monitor, sometimes the sales for releases by independent recording companies are not as easy to track. Such recordings might be sold primarily at smaller retailers and such retailers might not be sampled as regularly by monitoring organizations. The result: inaccurate and misleading sales data. *Billboard* magazine and others try to accurately "chart" the sales and airplay of recordings, but it is not an easy task. The electronic scanning of bar codes (SoundScan) has helped in obtaining more accurate and more timely sales data, but obtaining such data is still an inexact science.

Retailing Shifts

More people are buying their recordings online, from discount outlets and from record clubs these days. A large number patronize general merchandisers. As a result, record stores are having a tough time surviving. Some experts fear such stores will probably fade away all together in the not-too-distant future. If that happens, consumers likely will miss out on a great deal of expertise and personalized service.

Of course, the online availability of CDs and individual cuts has a major impact on retailing. Again, discount stores, general merchandisers and record clubs probably will continue to sell CDs, but specialty stores might not be able to generate enough sales to remain viable unless they diversify their merchandise and/or service.

Obscene Lyrics

Several years ago, the language used in many recordings got so bad that consumer activists, including the Parents' Music Resource Center, threatened legal action and pressured recording company executives into placing warning labels on their products. They wanted to be sure that parents and everyone else would know that the lyrics contained profane, obscene and/or sexually explicit language. The jury is still out, however, on how well the "Explicit Lyrics—Parental Advisory" labels are doing in the effort to protect innocent ears.

Raunchy Music Videos

Studies have shown that a large percentage of music videos contain violence, reasonably explicit sexual content and a disturbingly high incidence of assault/harassment of women. Such examples don't do much to improve the image young men have of young women, nor the image that young women have of themselves.

Poor Role Models

In addition to the poor examples displayed on video and in lyrics, rock-n-rollers often are poor models in their personal lives. Drugs, booze, fast driving, fast living, promiscuity, failed marriages, trashing hotels, excessive tattoos, body piercing, outrageous hair styles, weird clothes and uncontrollable anger/hatred/rebelliousness are all part of the standard package. Not exactly the boy and girl next door, eh? Also, not exactly the model most of us would want our children and their friends following.

Consolidations

The major record companies dominate the industry already. It's pretty tough for an independent record company to make it these days. As the mega-media mergers continue between giants like Disney and Cap Cities, AOL and Time Warner, etc., the corporate mentality could start to stifle the creative and risk-taking forces of musical artists and their associates. The homogenization of music could result. Alternative rock and experimental music might have a difficult time finding an outlet. We'd all be the worse off should that occur. Perhaps the Internet will help the music visionaries and off-the-wall artists to reach an audience.

Recent Research, Developments and Issues

During the first nine months of 2004, album sales in the United States rose almost 6%. The increase broke a pattern of significant declines over the previous four years. Analysts attributed the increased sales to a renewed interest in music, the introduction of new technologies for recording devices including the iPod, and improved, more-popular music that broke traditional genre barriers.

In April 2003, Apple Computers introduced its iTunes Music Store. For 99 cents, people could legally download a song from the Internet. The effort was an immediate success. In just its first month of operation, iTunes sold 3 million songs; not bad for a "Macintosh-only" service.

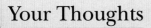

Your Thoughts

What would you suggest be done to deal with the problems facing the recording industry? Be specific for each of the nine problem areas: dubbing, piracy, payola, sales data, retailing shifts, obscene lyrics, raunchy videos, poor role models, consolidation of ownership.

In another example of how success breeds imitation, RealNetworks, Roxio's Napster, America Online, Musicmatch, Sony, Wal-Mart and Microsoft, among others, introduced online music services very similar to Apple's iTunes. Apple's iTunes reported more than 125 million downloaded songs in just its first 18 months of operation. Funny how $125 million can motivate competition.

After successful copyright-infringement lawsuits against Napster and MP3.com, the Recording Industry Association of America (RIAA) got really serious in its fight against online piracy in mid-2003. It launched a campaign of lawsuits against individuals who illegally downloaded and posted copyrighted songs on the Internet. The RIAA used software that scanned peer-to-peer networks to identify offenders. Hundreds of lawsuits were filed in the early months of the search for music pirates.

Early responses to the RIAA's action and threats of even more lawsuits included a report that discovered that in just one month following the filing of RIAA lawsuits, more than one million households deleted all the digital music files that they had saved on their computers. In addition, KaZaA, the most popular file-swapping service in 2003, lost about half of its users in the six months following the RIAA's announcement of its "get-tough" policy. A survey in early 2004 found that the percentage of Americans who downloaded music online dropped from 29% in May 2003, to just 14%.

Sony and Bertelsmann AG officially merged their music businesses in August 2004. Both companies were equal partners, controlling 50% each. Among the labels controlled by Sony BMG are Arista, Columbia, Epic, Jive and RCA. Artists include Beyonce, Britney Spears, Usher, Celine Dion, the Dave Matthews Band, Alicia Keys, Christina Aguilera, Avril Lavigne and Bruce Springsteen. The joint venture pretty much reduced the number of major recording companies to just four—Sony BMG Music Entertainment, Universal, EMI and Warner.

Sony BMG now is the second largest recording company. Universal is first with a market share of about 26%. Sony BMG has about 25%, Warner and EMI have about 12% each and independent labels have a combined 25%.

In an effort to deal with declining revenues associated with piracy, the Recording Industry Association of America proposed in early 2008 to challenge the right of people to transfer songs from their own legally purchased CDs to their personal computers. Consumer rights organizations criticized the RIAA's position and urged the RIAA to join consumers in developing new economic models for the recording industry.

New models are needed because U.S. album sales dropped almost 10% in 2007. The number of digital tracks sold jumped almost 45%, though; however, such tracks sell for considerably less than do complete albums. Concert tours by musicians in

2007 were well received. Ticket revenue jumped about 8% to a record total of almost $4 billion. With average ticket prices consistently rising each year to more than $60 in 2007, it's easy to see why revenues have increased every year for the past decade.

CBS Corp. acquired Last.fm in 2007 and used the community-based music network to develop an ad-supported website devoted to streaming popular music. The free, on-demand music service offered access to songs from the major recording companies and more than 150,000 independent labels and artists. An ad appears on screen while the song plays. Consumers can stream a song up to three times for free. After that, consumers are given an option to purchase the song via a download through iTunes, Amazon and other sources.

The EMI Group in 2007, in an effort to boost sales, agreed to sell its songs via iTunes without anti-piracy software. The absence of digital-rights management (DRM) software that limits the number of computers and devices that a song can be played on makes EMI titles more attractive to many consumers.

Think Back

1. What major changes has the developing technology associated with online music had on the recording industry? *The creation of MP3 and took out the CD's consumers, because it alot of things went digital. Allows the muscians to go distribute their music faster/easier.*

2. What have been the impacts of the mega-company mergers, consolidations and buyouts within the recording industry?

   The mega-mergers account for 90% of the music being made. The Payola's were meant to be banned and new employees had signed a agreement not to accep them. The consolidations make it hard for independent companies to make it on their own.

3. What are MP3 files and what is MP3.com?

   It is able to compress large digital files and allows computers users to download files off the Internet. And MP3.com is an online music company & music distributer.

4. What are the three basic components of the recording industry? List the major aspects of each component.

   Artistic Component

   Business Component
   Audience Component

5. List the "major" companies in the recording industry.

Universal Music Group
Warner Music Group
EMI Group
Sony BMG

6. List the major music "labels."

Capitol, Virgin, Rhino, Columbia, Epic, WTG, Chrysalis, Decca, Kapp, Geffen, UMI, A&M, Island, Mercury, Motown, Arista, Atco, Atlantic, Elektra, Reprise & Warner Brothers.

7. What does it take to get a gold record, a platinum record or a multi-platinum record?

Gold: A single needs 1 million sales.
Platinum: A single needs 2 million sales.
Multi-Platinum: A single needs 3 million sales.

8. What are the major problems facing the recording industry?

Home dubbing; Piracy; Payola; Obtaining accurate sales data; Retailing shifts, Obscene lyrics; Sex, violence, racism & misogyny in music videos, performers serving as poor role models, Consolidation of companies.

9. What are the major online music services?

Real Networks, Roxio's Napster, America Online, Music Match, Sony, Microsoft & Apple.

10. How is the Recording Industry Association of America trying to fight online piracy? How successful has it been?

It has tried many lawsuits, But it hasn't really work unfortunately.

11. What were the 2007 sales statistics for CDs, digital tracks and concerts?

CD's: 10%.
Digital Tracks: 45%.
Concerts: 8%.

12. What are some of the major efforts being made by recording companies and others to boost revenues?

Some agreed to sell alongside the online companies such as iTunes.

The Motion Picture Industry

11

The millennium opened with high costs and tough times for movie makers. Threats from new technologies and a continuing cooling-off of production activity caused suppliers such as camera leasing companies to complain that business had fallen off by half. Sound stages in Southern California were showing vacancies after being booked tight five to ten years earlier. Location shooting on Los Angeles area streets was down. Studios were shelving projects before completion when their budgets simply climbed too high. The industry-wide contraction and belt-tightening in the movie business caused talent agencies to begin retrenching. With the studios making fewer movies and watching costs more closely, even big agencies like William Morris and International Creative Management suffered cutbacks. The agencies lost business when Disney and Warner Brothers began shedding unproductive deals with producers. Disney even consolidated its production operations into one unit to cut overhead.

Earlier, movie makers had come up with a kind of logic that baffled decision makers in other business endeavors. They said they preferred to make several films at $100 million each rather than produce a few at $15 million. Their logic was that there would actually be less risk in the big budget pictures because audiences were eager for spectacular films. The strategy in the movie industry was to spend big even though the potential loss is so much less on a smaller-budget picture. A blockbuster movie was expected to generate profits so great that losses from other films would be more than offset. This counterintuitive thinking has led the industry to cut back on family-oriented movies and movies aimed at children that might be less expensive to produce, but attract smaller audiences and profits. The fact that ticket sales are usually below costs for family fare adds support to movie executives' belief that small budget films are riskier.

A major reason for moving toward more lavish, expensively-produced movies was the success of special-effects movies. Special effects have star power. Special effects can be very expensive production techniques, but also can make a big difference at the box office.

Making movies is obviously a big business. Independent producers must convince the studios, private investors, or conglomerate parent companies of the studios to take huge risks in the production of a film. Most of the studios and their parent companies are bankers more than they are movie producers. They finance films and distribute them. Insurance firms, oil companies, banks and other investment firms are making decisions about public taste and star quality. Accountants at the corporate level make artistic decisions that in Hollywood's earlier years were based on the instincts of directors and studio executives.

Studios like Columbia, Paramount, Universal, Orion, Warner Brothers, United Artists, and Disney no longer control production of their movies from inception to distribution. Instead, independent film makers tend to go it alone, often using studio properties, finding their own stories, hiring actors and crews, and controlling production until the major studios are asked to take over the packaging and distribution. Often, the independent producers are financed by the studios. Some of the independents arrange their own financing through public and private investors.

With the trend toward $80 million to $100 million in production costs being viewed as the most likely avenue for eventual return on investment, feature films have to gross twice that amount to show a profit, largely because print and marketing costs are additional after-production expenses. Foreign rentals, sales to television and home video, and reissuance at later dates bring additional revenue.

Why do you think fewer people are going to the movies these days?

What could theater owners and movie producers do to boost attendance?

Domestic theater attendance dropped in the 1980s and 1990s, forcing movie makers to rely on sales to television and other non-theater markets for as much as half of their revenue. Before the audiences began to stay home and watch television or rent movies from video stores, three-quarters or more of a picture's revenue came from tickets sold at theaters. The problem for the industry is that movie producers and distributors had been sharing the box office gross evenly with the theater owners. With pay cable, like HBO, Cinemax and Showtime, the studios get only about one-fifth of the revenue, not one-half. Added to the lower percentage of revenue because of pay-TV and home DVD and video viewing is the loss from people recording movies off the air without paying a cent.

Even though movie attendance was down, box office revenues increased, but that was attributed to increased ticket prices. Over the years since the competition with television began, movie theater ticket prices have constantly been increased much faster than the rate of inflation. This has been necessary because the industry has failed to control costs.

Technology has become a major expense as film companies try to outdo each other with special effects and realistic action scenes. More capital chasing a small pool of big-name talent sent actors' salaries into the stratosphere. Major stars command salaries greater than the whole production budgets for movies made 20 years ago. A parallel is the increasing cost of tickets to professional football and basketball games to help pay the multi-million dollar salaries of the sports superstars.

Kevin Costner, Bruce Willis, Julia Roberts, Tom Hanks, Jim Carrey and other popular stars have been paid phenomenal amounts when quite capable actors could have performed the same roles for one-tenth,

perhaps one-twentieth, of the amount. Industry figures demonstrate that salaries accounted for 20% to 25% of production expenses in the 1970s, but often reach 60% now. Another factor driving up ticket prices is the cost of marketing a picture, especially with the big increase in the purchase of television air time to promote a film before its release. Marketing is generally handled by the big studios after they pick up and distribute films made by independent producers. That means they also pick up the marketing expenses, which are much greater than ever before because of the spiraling costs of television commercials.

Despite shrinking audiences and burgeoning costs, the movie industry does show an overall profitable picture. In the 1930s and 1940s, before television, Americans bought about 80 million tickets a week to see movies in theaters. Currently, with video stores, pay-TV, network TV, and other competitors available, only 20 million tickets were being sold each week. Despite this, box office gross figures went from the $3 billion in 1981 to $4 billion in 1984 and over $5 billion in the early 1990s before leveling off for a while and then jumping to over $9 billion early in the 21st century.

As noted earlier, the strategy is to create a blockbuster—a movie that sells more than $100 million in tickets—by investing large amounts of money in the making of a film and then further investing heavily in its promotion. Producers have recognized the increasing value of gaining media attention and using extensive marketing techniques to get a return on investment. The general expectation is that it will take half as much to market a motion picture as it does to produce it. The marketing and promotion expenses include a great deal of paid newspaper advertising supported by radio and TV commercials, press releases, publicity junkets for

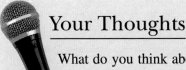
critics and entertainment reporters, and special tie-ins with products or personalities.

Products are given away at music stores where sound tracks from the film are available on compact disc. Fast-food franchises give away movie-related action figures. Toy stores feature a variety of toys patterned after heroes in action films or cute characters from animated features. At one time, a novel could be made into a successful movie, but that practice is now being reversed. A typical tie-in is the release of mass-market paperbacks that were first screenplays. These books created from movie scripts are often filled with photos from the screen version. Even comic books are published from screenplays that were once hit movies, especially if they did well with the youth market.

Much of the marketing cost is the care and feeding of entertainment-related media and their reporters. There are dozens of magazines devoted to stories and photos of movies and movie stars. Movie personalities are interviewed by dozens of reporters under circumstances arranged by the distributor's promotion and public relations department. Newspapers have arts and entertainment sections that are blitzed by studio publicity people in hopes of getting favorable attention to their films. Tie-ins are also forged with television and radio as publicity departments arrange for stars to appear as guests on talk shows and in entertainment news programs. The distributors help with television's so-called documentaries on "The Making of . . ." or "Behind the Scenes of . . ."

Attendance in the theaters also can be improved by arrangements worked out between distributors and theater owners that go beyond publicity and promotion. "Four-walling" is the practice of distributors renting theaters directly from the owners and keeping all of the box office receipts for a limited engagement. It is a practice no longer used by major studios because of anti-trust law, but can still be used by small, independent companies with low-budget films that have a difficult time competing otherwise with the big firms.

"Block-booking" is a technique that is not supposed to be practiced because of legal concerns, but can be modified slightly to avoid monopoly law. It is occasionally employed in modified forms by, in effect, forcing exhibitors to accept mediocre films from a distributor or be denied that distributor's blockbusters. "Blind-bidding" was always a controversial arrangement, one that demands that the theater operators sign contracts for specific movies well before they are released. A less controversial and more likely arrangement is the practice of selective contract adjustments, which simply amounts to preferential treatment for exhibitors who cooperate with distributors in promoting and displaying their films.

The Movie Makers

The free-agent like workers who produce today's movies are constantly banding and disbanding. The pay is good, but the hours are long and the search for work is constant. To get a two-hour long film to the screen it can take from two to four years of effort by roughly 500 people who come together for several months of that period in something akin to a temporary corporation. After the picture is in theaters, they have long since disbanded and moved on to other jobs. They are part of a mobile work force unique to the Southern California entertainment industry. They operate in a system of personal connections that enables thousands of workers to move from temporary project to temporary project. Once a handful of large studios employed everyone from glamorous stars to the carpenters who hammer sets. Today's movie industry workforce is a loose collection of independent contractors with no allegiance to a particular studio.

The process of making a major film is roughly like establishing a manufacturing plant that moves from location to location and is staffed by hundreds of people in jobs that include visual effects, art direction, stunts, sound, production assistants, payroll auditors, props, painters, musicians, sound effects experts and cooks. Workers often travel from film to film in loose confederations, with more senior workers taking along their hand-picked crews as a condition of being hired, in much the same way a building contractor might insist on the same work crews for each housing project. When workers land jobs, the pay is lucrative, but the hours can be as long as 18 hours a day and workers can be gone for months at a time on location. Under constant pressure to deliver on budget and on time, producers, directors and supervisors prefer to surround themselves with people whose work they know. Although that provides for dependable crews, it also makes it harder for outsiders to enter and inhibits diversity.

A list of credits before or after a film, identifies the people who have performed specific tasks in the making of a movie. The title of executive producer often appears before any other in the credits, giving moviegoers reason to believe that it is the name of someone actively involved in an important phase of the production. Actually, it is often an honorary title. The executive producer is typically someone who is a heavy financial backer or the owner of a production company. It's quite likely that it could be someone who owned the rights to the script or has served as business manager for the featured star.

The producer is the active supervisor of the complete project, with responsibility for staying within the budget and on the planned shooting schedule. In fact, the producer comes up with the budget and the shooting schedule in the first place. It is the producer who hires the writers, the director, the actors and other key production personnel. Producers are sometimes stars who have started their own production companies, but most often independent producers rent studio space from the major studios and set out to make movies with money acquired from investors. This is in contrast to the pre-television years when the typical producer was a studio employee.

The director is a creator, someone who takes a script and turns it into a new form. The director is the author of a film just as a writer is the author of a novel. The staging, the cinematography, the locales, the actors' performances, etc., are the work of the director, who expresses his or her vision of the screenplay. Once the producer turns control of the process over to the director, all creative and technical crew members follow the director's wishes and commands. The director has full responsibility for the look and feel of the finished product. The director guides the camera operators through their shots and blocks out the movements of the actors. The director is in charge of those who will later edit the film, determining which scenes stay and which ones are rejected.

The film editor is also called a cutter. Often, directors give film editors a great deal of discretion over the final print. A film editor cuts film on an editing machine and puts it back together, most probably the way the director has prescribed. Sometimes directors show their confidence in film editors by allowing them to omit scenes or to shorten segments on their own. Hundreds of scenes are shot out of time-space sequence and eventually assembled for editing and sound mixing. The film editor can cut to accelerate action or to leave out incidents that weaken dramatic effect. The editor might cut back and forth to simultaneous actions, as when cops chase the bad guys in careening and crashing cars on streets and freeways.

The director and film editor have thousands of feet of film to work with because of the efforts of a team of cinematographers, the camera operators who shoot the picture. They take direction not only from the director, but also from a chief photographer or director of photography. This person frames each camera shot for the most effective visual story-telling and is responsible for the most aesthetically desired lighting for each shot.

The credits of a typical Hollywood movie can list hundreds of titles, most of which are a mystery to the average moviegoer as they scroll by at the end of a film. Here are a few of the jobs and their responsibilities:

- Assistant to (fill in the blank): A personal assistant to actors, directors and producers who has enough clout to negotiate for one of these.
- Boom Operator: A technician who holds a microphone attached to a long arm.
- Dolly Grip: Worker who pushes the dolly that a camera rests on during filming.
- Gaffer: The main electrician in a firm, maintaining the lights.
- Best Boy: The gaffer's assistant.
- Foley Artist: A sound effects specialist, named after sound effects pioneer Jack Foley
- Grip: The equivalent of stagehands, grips move and set up props, scenery, lights, cameras, and other things needed in shooting.
- Key Grip: The chief grip.

- Sound Mixer: Captures all of the sounds during filming. Sounds may be used during the film or as a guide when looping, or dubbing the dialogue.

The Rating System for Movies

During the "Roaring 20s," off-screen misadventures by movie stars became sensationalized in the tabloids, causing a public outrage. Mary Pickford left her husband for costar Douglas Fairbanks. A starlet died during an orgy at a wild party hosted by Fatty Arbuckle, whose career was ended by the scandal. Two popular actresses identified with murder victim William Desmond Taylor, a director, had their careers destroyed. They and Fatty Arbuckle were cleared by juries of any wrongdoing, but the public was appalled. These and other scandals, along with newspaper accounts of high living by several stars, prompted efforts by moralists to "clean up Hollywood."

Nearly half the states in the union were considering film censorship boards when the movie industry embarked on an effort at self-regulation. The industry came up with a trade association, the Motion Picture Producers and Distributors of America, which worked on various proposals for self-regulation until 1930, when it finally adopted a code of conduct. That code had no penalty for noncompliance and did not satisfy those who continued to object to what they perceived in movie scripts as sex, depravity, immorality, and abandonment of good values.

Religious groups especially worked to force the industry to toughen its code. The Catholic Legion of Decency and the Episcopal Committee on Motion Pictures were among those stirring up cries for censorship. Moviemakers responded by creating a new "seal of approval" within the code that made possible the levying of fines. A Production Code Administration of the Motion Picture Producers and Distributors advised filmmakers about how to cut their movies to earn the code's seal. Through the 1930s and 1940s, nudity, profanity and drugs were forbidden as film content.

The code was largely in the hands of its administrator, Will Hays, until 1945 when Eric Johnson took over the administration. The Hays Office, as it was called, inhibited members of the association from using themes related to torture, religion, dance, obscenity, vulgarity, profanity, crime, sex, and any other topics that might offend some segments of the audience. The Hays Office read scripts, looked at final prints, made suggestions for changes, and could veto distribution. No Hollywood movie without the seal of approval played in an American movie house until 1953. By the 1950s, movies had to look for mature subjects and frank themes to compete with television, so sexual and violent content in films reappeared.

A degree of freedom from censorship was achieved in 1952 when the Supreme Court extended freedom of press to include films. The First Amendment protection guaranteed in the Burstyn v. Wilson case did allow prior restraint in regard to obscenity, on the grounds that obscenity is a criminal matter, therefore review boards dealing narrowly and specifically with obscenity are not practicing censorship. In Burstyn v. Wilson, the Court determined that film was a significant medium for the communication of ideas and rejected a claim that the film, *The Miracle,* could be banned on the grounds that it was sacrilegious. Shortly after this, the industry released some films without the seal of approval.

In the early 1950s, there were several official and semi-official boards attempting to censor movies, many of them created by states, municipalities, religious bodies, parent-teacher groups, and professional organizations. By the mid 1960s, most of them had disappeared because of their unconstitutional standards. Because of the First Amendment, states and cities began to look more toward obscenity prosecutions rather than censorship boards for regulating movies.

In 1968, the movie industry devised a rating system designed to give audiences an idea of what they were going to see, in effect, a guide for parents.

G—GENERAL AUDIENCES. For all ages; no nudity or sex, and only a minimal amount of violence. This is a film generally regarded by the Rating Board as accepted for viewing by the whole family.

PG—PARENTAL GUIDANCE SUGGESTED. Some portions may not be suitable for young children. Some mild profanity might be present. Any violence is not to be "excessive." Parents are alerted to the need for inquiry before allowing youngsters to attend.

R—RESTRICTED. Those under 17 must be accompanied by a parent or guardian. There could be rough violence and explicit nudity, even simulated love-making. Parents may wish to view it with their children, because such a film is significantly adult in theme and treatment.

Your Thoughts

What do you think of the MPAA's ratings system for movies? Why do you feel the way you do?

What changes would you suggest to improve the ratings system? Why do you think such changes are necessary?

X—NO ONE UNDER 17 IS ADMITTED, WITH OR WITHOUT A PARENT. This is exclusively an adult film, no doubt openly pornographic. It does allow individual theater operators to make the age limit even higher. (The X rating has been replaced by an NC-17 rating)

Eventually, the X rating was re-labeled because of some serious films by major directors were given the X rating despite their artistic intent and value. The stigma of pornography connoted by the X symbol caused the industry to change the category to NC-17, an easy shorthand for no one under 17 years of age.

Also, a fifth category was adopted to modify the parental guidance standard. PG-13 was meant to let parents know of the need to give special guidance to children under 13. This new category was to cover anything that could be inappropriate for younger children.

This rating system is implemented by a Review Board of the Motion Picture Association of America, an outgrowth of the former Motion Picture Producers and Distributors of America. The MPAA, with the code, places the responsibility for self-regulation upon the audience, rather than upon the filmmaker.

Hollywood Goes International

American-made pictures dominate the world market, with motion pictures more readily available to world-wide viewers than ever before. The widespread distribution of American films in foreign markets demonstrates that film is primarily a visual art form and a visual entertainment vehicle. Language, as such, is not as significant as the mosaic of impressions on the screen that surmounts language barriers, with or without subtitles. American film makers have been marketing their products around the world increasingly since the 1960s.

Most of the sales of movies overseas are made by the members of the Motion Picture Export Association, made up of the biggest firms in domestic movie production and distribution, including Warner Brothers, Columbia, Paramount, MCA, and Metro-Goldwyn-Mayer, among others. Fewer than a dozen nations account for nearly 90 percent of the total dollar income from foreign distribution. Canada, Great Britain, Italy, Australia, Germany and Japan are the primary importers of American films. France, Mexico, Brazil, Hong Kong and Venezuela are also significant markets.

Coinciding with the release of American films abroad is the internationalization of the film industry that has resulted in considerable competition for American products and has brought many foreign films into United States theaters. Australian films have enjoyed successes in many overseas markets and certainly in the United States.

Movies produced by the British have done well critically and financially when shown in the United States, as have several imported from France. Americans have praised the work of Swedish film director Ingmar Bergman and Japan's Akira Kurosawa. Both have used historical settings to display passionate and universal understanding of timeless, yet quite topical themes. The largest film industry in the world is in India, which produces nearly twice as many feature films as the United States each year. Major studios are located in Calcutta, Bombay and Madras, with films produced in a dozen or more dialects for domestic consumption.

Related to the international movie is what the United States film industry once dubbed "the runaway picture." Because of labor costs and problems getting permission from municipal or state governments to use desirable locations or shoot on public property, among other difficulties, some American independent producers took their cameras, crews and actors to Canada, Europe and other foreign locations. They were able to get subsidies from foreign governments, use authentic locales, and improve the profit potential by reducing greatly the cost of production because of much cheaper labor costs. Clint Eastwood and Lee Van Cleef became major American movie stars by first appearing in movies produced in Italy. *A Fistful of Dollars, A Few Dollars More,* and many others are still viewed by millions of Americans in their reissuance on cable television. The term "Spaghetti Western" is used for those low-cost depictions of the American West shot in overseas locales not much different in appearance from southwestern parts of the United States.

The Development of Motion Pictures

The first movies did not need to be much more than scenes of people walking or horses trotting. Audiences at first were just thrilled to see the effect, the gimmickry, but movies could not draw audiences forever on the novelty factor alone. One of the earliest to recognize that audiences would welcome films that told a story was William S. Porter. In 1903, Porter produced *The Great Train Robbery,* generally credited with being the first American movie with a plot, although a very thin one. It was an 8-minute film shot in New Jersey, but intended to be a story of the American West. One of Porter's cameramen, D.W. Griffith, was also an actor and playwright, but chose to work behind the camera on some short films until 1915 when he released a milestone film, one on a scale never attempted before

in the United States. Griffith had been impressed with a novel by Thomas Dixon, *The Klansman,* and wanted to turn it into a full-length movie. A movie was typically shot in two or three days, or at most in a week. Griffith spent six weeks in rehearsal and nine weeks of shooting to create *The Birth of a Nation,* based on Dixon's book. It was a sympathetic portrayal of the Ku Klux Klan, even a glorification of the Klan and its racist actions following the American Civil War. Of course, it resulted in controversy over its portrayal of Blacks during the era of reconstruction in the South. Its showing in some cities resulted in mob violence and race riots.

The Birth of a Nation established David Wark Griffith as a genius in his field, an innovator, so creative that little is new in cinematography or film production since the techniques pioneered by Griffith. He was heralded as a brilliant director for his attention to dramatic flow and his realization of the potential for the camera to capture the emotions of actors.

With Griffith, the camera was no longer simply a witness to a scene. The camera was on the move. It was trucked, dollied, panned, lowered and raised. It created action not just followed it. Griffith added to the story by mixing his close-ups with shots that would cut away to a larger view of the scene.

The Birth of a Nation is still considered a major cinematic achievement, certainly the most influential silent film ever made. It was a huge box office success that helped create a new form with its moving shots, disparate pieces of film joined together, extreme close-ups, grand scale and lavish photography. It was accompanied by a complete score to be performed by a full orchestra.

The Talkies

Experiments with sound had been conducted with the first attempts at showing movies before the turn of the century. However, it was not until 1921 that commercial applications began to show demonstrated success. Lee de Forest's audion tube for radio reception appeared as an amplification system for sound movies. De Forest's phonofilm followed in 1922 and permitted sound to be recorded directly on the film in synchronization with the picture. Quickly competing with phonofilm was Warner Brothers and Western Electric's Vitaphone process, a sound-on-disc system. Vitaphone would not become the standard of the industry, but would lead to great changes. The first feature-length film with the Vitaphone sound system was *Don Juan* in 1926, but it was no more than a crudely synchronized musical score.

The breakthrough film was 1927's Warner Brothers hit, *The Jazz Singer,* with Al Jolson singing "Blue Skies," and "Toot, Toot, Tootsie." The movie drew standing-room-only crowds and ushered in the era of sound. Its impact on audiences was such that every major studio soon began to convert to sound. By 1930, there were 9,000 movie houses wired for sound at an average conversion cost of $20,000. The investment in the new equipment paid off.

Al Jolson's utterance in the middle of *The Jazz Singer,* "Listen! You ain't heard nothin' yet," turned out to be prophetic. By 1930, the silent era was over and the revolution in sound took the industry into its future. Studios that got into sound early flourished, while those few who continued to make silent pictures soon disappeared. By 1930, about 95% of the movies were produced with sound and audiences had simply stopped going to the silent movies. The addition of the sound track doubled average weekly movie audiences within just four years, reaching 90 million by 1930 and staying near that figure even through the depression.

Many of the stars of the silent era could not make the transition to the talkies. Perhaps because of voice quality, regional accents or demands made on staging by the microphone, several well-known performers, including John Gilbert and Clara Bow faded from popularity. Producers looked to the stage and to radio for fresh faces and fresh voices. New stars emerged, some with Broadway or, at least, live theater experience. Spencer Tracy, James Cagney, Edward G. Robinson, Humphrey Bogart, Bette Davis and Katherine Hepburn brought their theatrical backgrounds to the screen. Greta Garbo, Marie Dressler and a few others remained in prominent roles, because their voices were pleasing to audiences. New stars appeared to replace those who had been promoted at great cost by the studios. Mae West, W.C. Fields, Clark Gable, Cary Grant, Myrna Loy, Gary Cooper, John Wayne, and William Powell were among those who emerged in the 1930s as immediate box-office successes. A movie dynasty was begun because of the deep, resonant voice of Lionel Barrymore. Soon John and Ethel Barrymore joined Lionel, as the first cadre of Barrymores to earn both critical and audience recognition for their craft.

Early on, technicians had to improvise methods of overcoming limitations of the single microphone. Actors, for the most part, were limited to working very close to each other and very close to the only microphone. Soon, a second microphone was added through the use of the first sound mixer, which allowed more flexibility in positioning actors. Sound mixing made it possible to do more with sets and scenery, even to go out of the studio on location. The next step was the separation of sound from picture in the original filming. A director could shoot the pictures at one time, the sound later, and mix them in the studio.

Movie makers found that their production costs per movie would almost double with the expense of new technology and the continuing need for research and experimentation to improve their equipment and facilities to keep up with the inevitable changes in the sound technology. An increasing infusion of capital was needed by the studios to meet the costs associated with talking pictures. New equipment, new sound stages and labor costs for all of the technicians and studio helpers did not come cheap. This created a renewed dependence on outside investment, on bankers, insurance companies, investment firms, and Wall Street.

Because of a heavy investment in such equipment, the studios could not afford to have the equipment and technicians idle. It seemed unproductive not to have them operating at full capacity. In an effort to shave production costs, they came up with a two-tiered system of making movies. They put their best scripts, biggest stars, most experienced crews, primary sound stages and best directors into what were called "A" pictures. No expenses were spared to make movies for mass audiences, and those audiences responded at the box office. The same studios produced "B" movies on low budgets to keep their investments working and earning money by having the studios working all of the time. New talent, untried directors, inexperienced crews, and fresh scriptwriters were virtually auditioned in these inexpensively produced "B" pictures. Many directors of major productions and many eventual box office stars got their first work in "B" pictures. John Wayne began his career in a series of low budget "B" westerns.

The theater owners were forced to accept the low budget "B" pictures because they were supplied films in blocks. For a price, theaters were offered a package of perhaps 30 films, but only 10 or 12 of them would be the ones the audiences really loved. Theater owners had to take the "B" pictures with the "A" pictures, because an "A" picture was never sold by itself. This was when the studios also bought movie houses around the country to be sure all of their products, "A" or "B," were displayed.

Movie studios are still in the distribution business. Tri-Star Pictures, Columbia Pictures, the Cannon Group, Warner, MCA and Paramount were buying theater chains either directly or through their corporate parents. In addition, movie makers followed the same practice in their arrangement with television and cable. Distribution was made in groups of films, with good and not so good in a take-it-all-or-leave-it package deal. Some of those distribution companies were owned by studios.

The advent of sound led to the prominence of movie musicals for nearly two decades. The attitude seemed to be if movies could talk, why not have them sing as well. The 1930s was noted for movie musicals, especially those with dance scenes staged by Busby Berkeley. Audiences were awed by aerial scenes shot from cranes high above the dancers in complex and surreal dance numbers. Also drawing large audiences in the 1930s were any of the musicals that featured Fred Astaire and Ginger Rogers. Emphasis was on the dance numbers in their movies, which all seemed to follow the same formula.

The 1930s was a decade of innovation in animation with Walt Disney and his staff of artists creating Mickey Mouse, Donald Duck and other cartoon characters. Child stars were very big during this period. Judy Garland became a star in *The Wizard of Oz* and was teamed with Mickey Rooney in a series of films. Other child stars included Jackie Coogan, Jackie Cooper and Shirley Temple.

The 1940s was the last decade of great financial success for the big studios. It was also an era of great cinematic achievement. Rivaling *Birth of a Nation* for innovation and successful experimentation was *Citizen Kane,* released in 1941. It is on many lists of the best movies ever made. It was produced in only six months at a cost of less than $1 million. *Citizen Kane* was directed by its star, Orson Welles, who was only 26 at the time. Welles had achieved fame as a young genius for his leadership in developing radio's Mercury Theater of the Air, and brought his radio players to Hollywood with him when RKO gave him the artistic freedom and ample budget to film a psychological study of publisher William Randolph Hearst.

Citizen Kane was a fictionalized, unflattering description of the life of the egocentric, sensational newspaper circulation leader, who was a major figure of the American scene at the time. Hearst tried to stop its dis-

tribution, even offering the studio all of the production costs if it would destroy the prints and negatives. Critics loved the movie, giving it great reviews. The public was apparently turned off by its somber tone, experimentation with narration, and its complexities. Welles employed new techniques that are now part of the art of film. He combined animation and live footage to create the impression that a camera was moving across the top of a building, through the roof and down into a room. He employed lighting techniques that created unusual effects with shadows and sound effects that created mood. With its lack of success initially at the box office, it was several years before RKO was able to break even on the cost of an innovative work of art that was actually intended for a mass audience. It was a basic story not unlike other Hollywood plots meant for popular entertainment, but it is remembered more for its stimulating experimentation.

Other major films of the 1940s included *Casablanca,* which almost always joins *Citizen Kane* on the list of best movies ever made or, at least, on the list of most-remembered or most-loved films ever. *Casablanca* was a spy tale set in the era just before the United States entered World War II. It tells the story of an American restaurant proprietor in Nazi-occupied Morocco who tries to stay above the fray. He tells the Germans that he is not political, but is eventually dragged into the conflict by the only woman he ever loved. The movie starred Ingrid Bergman and Humphrey Bogart.

Easy Rider was the 1960s film that captivated the spirit of the youth audience, with its appeal to the subculture of drugs and anti-establishment attitudes. It began a series of youth-oriented protest films. *Easy Rider* may have been the first movie to openly endorse drugs, but it wasn't the last. Its music, like the music on radio in the 1960s, was regarded as provocative and drug-oriented. Many found great significance in the song "Born to be Wild" as a theme for the 1960s and 1970s.

Effects of Television on Movies

Feature films may no longer be as profitable as they were in their early years, but they still do well in the youth market. Movie makers were injured initially when television kept audiences at home, but eventually movies started being made for television and movie production firms became producers of television fare. Theatrical films and made-for-TV movies comprise a significant share of both network programming and the content of non-network stations, as well as the cable channels, especially pay cable. When most Americans preferred to watch a small screen at home in their easy chairs, the movie industry adjusted by making their own contributions to the success of television and by carving out a demographic niche for a movie market.

Several surveys by polling firms and by the Motion Picture Association of America indicated that, even before television, 70% to 75% of moviegoers were under the age of 30 and very, very few were over 50. Various studies demonstrated that movies attracted teenagers, with estimates of possibly 50% of the movie audience between 12 and 21, and 30% under 15. While some adults go to movies only occasionally, almost half of the people in the United States do not go to even one movie a year. Despite this, until the late 1960s, the studios were aiming their movies at a family audience, primarily middle-class and middle-aged.

Hollywood had found its formula by the 1970s. It was the attempt to offer something distinct from what was then being shown on television. It meant frank themes, artistic style, often a counter-cultural tone, sexual suggestion, issue-oriented adventure themes, and any other creative efforts to attract a young, mobile, active audience without driving away their parents. The formula seemed to work immediately because of new, independent film makers who understood and sympathized with the youth culture. Often, such movies appealed also to older moviegoers and television viewers. This approach developed shortly after huge profits were earned by a half dozen movies produced just before 1970 that were youth-oriented, even antiestablishment, that did not drive away older ticket buyers.

The film industry's response to television included a dependence on the freedom of the movie makers to show and say whatever they pleased. Explicit sex scenes in films like *The Fox* and *I Am Curious (Yellow)* showed that movie taboos would soon disappear in the attempt to acquire and maintain the youth market. Film was shifting to treatments of social issues and frank themes that early television avoided.

The decline of the movie business that began in the 1950s was a direct result of the breakthrough for television after the Federal Communications Commission lifted a freeze on station licenses in 1952.

Television, by the end of the 1950s, had replaced movies as America's favorite entertainment. Within 15 years, the annual income from movie ticket sales was half of what it had been before television. Some studios shut down. Monogram and Republic were the first of the big studios to close rather than look for a way to produce something that might be an alternative to television. Other majors simply reduced production. Others, like MGM, sold off large portions of their land, finding that there was more value in real estate. This was when many of them went totally into color production. A few experimented with three-dimensional films because television was limited to the flat, two-dimensional screen. They were referred to as 3-D movies. They required audience members to wear awkward, almost unmanageable and uncomfortable glasses to get the effect. Most people didn't like wearing the glasses and said the first time they saw a 3-D movie was special, even exciting, but after that the novelty was gone. Attendance at 3-D movies declined quickly.

One of the success factors for some movie makers was a tie with television. In the mid-1950s, Warner Brothers began to sell shows to ABC that were produced specifically for television. Several such series vaulted formerly weak ABC to the top of television ratings. Soon other film producers began to produce programs for network television. By the 1960s, it was common for feature films to be produced for television.

The movie theater had become a place for young people to go while their parents stayed home in front of the television set. The new youth audience meant film makers had to respond with movies that young people could identify with. 1954's *The Wild One,* with Marlon Brando, was a success in theaters because of its theme of youthful alienation, complete with rebellion in a motorcycle culture. Also hitting home with the younger generation was *Rebel Without a Cause,* which made James Dean an antiauthority cult figure. His image as a rebellious, youthful antihero carried over long past his death in a car crash in 1955. Dean appeared in only three movies, yet has endured all these years as a symbol of the bored, restless, reckless, confrontational rebel.

Hollywood also embraced technological changes in a response to television. It became easier to make color movies with the invention of Technicolor in the 1920s, but it was an expensive process. Despite the availability of Technicolor, most movies were shot in black and white until the 1960s. With the incredible popularity of television, filmmakers turned to color as an advantage over television. The impetus for color was simply that it was something not offered by early televisions.

The big screen was another bit of technology intended to give the theaters an advantage. Television's small screen could in no way match the wrap-around of Cinerama or the wide screen effect of Cinemascope. Cinerama made possible sweeping panoramas that were not possible on TV screens. The problem was the expense of operating Cinerama systems with their multi-camera set-ups, curved screens and special projectors. Cinemascope was not as costly as Cinerama, requiring much less special equipment, but did require a screen that was 2½ times wider than it was high, giving it the ability to show wide vistas.

Welcome to the Present and the Future

The rating of movies continues to be a controversial subject. Producers and the creative people in the movie industry complain that ratings tend to stifle creativity and can damage profit potential. Parents and media watchdog groups complain that most movies are nothing but smut, violence and dirty language with little or nothing being produced that is consistent with family values. Although, an MPAA survey found that 76% of parents said movie ratings were at least fairly useful.

Some experts believe that "going digital" will help get the movie industry back in the black in a big way. Qualcomm and Hughes-JVC have developed a digital projection system that can deliver films to theaters. CineCom Digital Cinema projectors use computer signals, refracted light and mirrors. Satellites beam the movies to the projectors. The system makes it possible to have multiple audio tracks that can fill the theater and/or permit films to be shown in multiple languages at the same time. Multiplex theaters would be able to increase the number of screens showing a "hot" film with a simple click of a mouse and not have to obtain a pricey print. Digital signals could also be used to trigger devices that would omit odors on cue and/or cause theater seats to shake, rattle and roll. Digital projection systems will be faster, more efficient, more flexible and much cheaper than traditional methods. It can cost up to $60,000 to create a theater-quality, celluloid print of a film and copies can cost about $2,000. When the blockbuster movies need about 5,000 copies, the expenses can add up. With digital systems, millions of dollars in distribution and copying costs can be saved.

Some experiments with digital projection and creation of films have been conducted. In the first successful effort, Lance Weiler and Stefan Avalos, two freelance filmmakers, partnered with some satellite companies to retrofit a few theaters to project their movie, *The Last Broadcast*. While their e-movie was the first to be shown in a traditional theater, others have been mining the potentially lucrative market of "direct-to-computer" filmmaking and distribution. AtomFilms.com, iFilm.com and Sightsound.com are among the companies that specialize in e-movies. Situations vary, but the Metafilmics $3 million movie, *Quantum Project*, is a typical example of how the process works. The movie was released initially on the World Wide web through Sightsound.com. Viewers downloaded the film after paying a fee of about $3. Users needed a high-speed Internet connection, unless they wanted to wait a day or two for the downloading to be completed.

One of the potential drawbacks to digital movies is the ease with which digital video can be copied, pirated and spread. Many traditional movie producers are reluctant to release their films in a digital format for fear of blatant copyright infringement. Producers are working with electronics manufacturers and computer companies in an effort to develop anti-piracy technologies. Until at least some copyright infringement protection can be assured, don't expect to see too many of your favorite, first-run films coming to a computer screen near you.

The MPAA has vowed to pursue and sue anyone who steals product and illegally transmits it via the Internet. The organization has its work cut out for it, though, because the same technology that makes it relatively easy to spread bootlegged music over the Internet can be used to spread bootlegged video. High-speed, high-powered computers are needed to do the dirty work, but that's usually no problem at most colleges and universities. The way most of the current "black-market" for purloined video works is this: A mixing studio employee or theater projectionist steals or makes a copy of a first-run film, possibly even before wide release of the film. The product is then transferred digitally into a computer file. Once it's there, the Internet can become its universe.

Interactivity is one of the advantages of digital signals, but interactivity can be used with more traditional systems, too. In the mid-1990s, *Mr. Payback* became the first commercially released interactive movie. It played in a limited number of theaters for a limited period of time (it wasn't a very good movie), but it did bring some new elements to the experience of going to the movies. Viewers were given keypads and periodically during the 25-minute movie they were asked to choose what they wanted a character to do from a menu of possible actions. For example, the character could leave or stay in a room. Viewers got to choose. Whatever action received the most votes, became part of the plot. With about 30 possible story lines and about 25,000 different choices (viewers made about 12 per showing), things could get a bit complicated. Besides, do you go to the movies to become part of the decision-making process associated with the plot or do you go to relax and be engaged mentally and emotionally, but not physically?

Recent Research, Developments and Issues

Competition from online-based, rent-by-mail businesses, online movie systems and video-on-demand services from cable television were cutting into the profits of bricks-and-mortar video stores by mid-2004.

NetFlix, Blockbuster, Amazon.com and Wal-Mart, among others, were all offering online DVD rental services at the end of 2004. All of the services operated in similar ways. For a monthly fee, a consumer was entitled to unlimited rentals. A person was limited to three DVDs at one time, but once a DVD had been returned, in postage-paid envelopes, another DVD could be shipped.

NetFlix and TiVo hoped to blend their services to pipe DVD-quality movies into homes via high-speed Internet connections. Near the end of 2004, the two companies had a total of more than 4 million subscribers. The joint effort faced stiff, established competition from CinemaNow, MovieLink, and Starz.

The top movies of the 2004 summer provided a snapshot of what might be a trend in the film industry. Four of the top 10 money-making films were sequels. *Shrek 2* led the way with almost $450 million in domestic box-office revenue, followed by *Spider-Man 2, Harry Potter and the Prisoner of Azkaban* and *The Bourne Supremacy*.

Online piracy reared its ugly head in the movie industry in a big way during the early part of the 21st century. The Motion Picture Association of America estimated that about 400,000 illegal movie downloads were occurring every day. As computers improve and broadband Internet connections become commonplace, MPAA officials warned that piracy would become even more of a problem. In an effort to head things off at the pass, movie studios began developing antipiracy measures, suing the most egregious pirates and asking Congress for legislative limits on the technologies used to facilitate piracy.

A study by AT&T Labs in late 2003 found that the prime source of unauthorized copies of new movies on file-sharing online networks was movie industry insiders. Nearly 80% of the "leaked" copies of about 300 movies were traced back to such insiders. Production assistants, people in promotions departments and even Academy Awards screeners/voters were identified as the main culprits in the growing underworld of movie pirates.

In the early part of the 21st century, Qualcomm developed a digital cinema technology to replace the traditional projector used to show movies. Texas Instruments and Boeing were experimenting with digital projectors and compression technologies, too.

Qualcomm's system makes it possible to beam digital versions of movies to theaters via satellite or fiber-optic cables. Among the benefits of digital movies is that the picture quality stays consistent and does not degrade with each showing as does a traditional film print. Of course, with digital technology comes increased opportunities for piracy

In addition to piracy, other problems faced by the pioneers in the digitalization of movie transmission and projecting were trying to standardize the engineering aspects of equipment and signals, plus the cost of the new technologies. The economic problems of the movie industry, especially for theater operators, could delay the adoption of digital technologies for several years.

Apple's iTunes started its online movie service in late 2006. Costs to purchase a film ranged from $10 to $15. Apple also developed a device, dubbed iTV, that made it possible to wirelessly send movies and other digital content stored on a computer to a television set. Big screen TVs are much better for viewing movies and other downloaded content than typical computer screens.

Moviemaking remains pretty much a male-dominated profession. A study found that only 15% of all directors, producers, writers, cinematographers and editors who worked on the 250 top-grossing films in the United States in 2007 were women. Almost a quarter of such films employed no female directors, producers, writers, cinematographers or editors. Broken down by job title, women accounted for 6% of all directors, 22% of producers, 10% of writers, 2% of cinematographers and 17% of editors.

A report on the year 2007 in the film industry included generally favorable results. Domestic ticket sale revenues were up about 5.5% to $9.6 billion. Worldwide ticket sale revenues were up almost 5% to an all-time high of $26.7 billion. Domestic attendance remained relatively steady at about 1.5 million tickets sold. The average ticket price was about $7. About 600 films were released in 2007, and the average cost to produce and market a film was about $107 million.

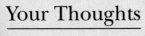

Your Thoughts

Why do you think so few women work as directors, producers, writers, cinematographers and editors on the big Hollywood films?

What changes in policies, procedures and training programs would you recommend to increase the number of women who work as directors, producers, writers, cinematographers and editors in Hollywood?

Think Back

1. What were the major trends in the movie industry in the early part of the 21st century? Some of the trends was to make lavish & expensive movies. Use alot of special effects & to spend between $00 million - $100 million in production costs.

2. What are the apparent trends in movie attendance these days? There are trends like "Four-Walling", & "Blind-bidding" & "Block-booking".

3. Why are "blockbusters" such a big deal now?

4. What are the major roles and responsibilities of an executive producer, producer, director and film editor?

Executive Producer: heavy financial backer or owner of a production company.

Producer: Active supervisor of complete project; they stay within budget & planned shooting schedule (probably makes them). Hires the directors, writers & actors.

Director: creator, takes script & makes it into a new form.

Film Editor: cuts film on an editing machine & puts it the way the director wants.

5. What do the following people do in the movie industry?
   A. boom operator *Technician who holds microphone attached a long arm.*
   B. dolly grip *worker who pushes the dolly that a camera rests on during film.*
   C. gaffer *main electrician in a firm, maintaining the lights.*
   D. best boy *gaffers assistant*
   E. foley artist *A sound effects specialist, named after sound effects pioneer Jack Foley*
   F. grip *Equivalint of stage hands, grips move & set up props, scenery, lights, cameras, etc.*
   G. key grip *chief chief grip*
   H. sound mixer *captures all of the sounds during filming. Sounds may be used during the film or as a guide when looping/dubbing the dialgue.*

6. How and by whom are films rated?
   By the MPAA & like othes; through certain censorship regulations. G & PG, R, PG-13, NC-17.

7. What are the categories used in movie ratings?
   G, PG, PG-13, R, NC-17.

8. What are the "out-of-Hollywood" trends in the film industry?
   Film is more of visual artform and a visual entertainment vehicle. Language is not as significant.

9. Who were the early pioneers in the film industry and what were their major contributions?
   William S. Porter: first to tell an actual story
   D.W. Griffith: Took more time w/ filming, making full-length movies.

10. What major changes/effects did the "talkies" have on the film industry?

Doubled audience attendance. Some of the previous actors couldn't cross over so well, ending their careers. Created a division in types of movies ("A" & "B" movies). Led to more musicals & animation.

11. Who were the big names in the production of movie musicals and what did they contribute?

12. Who were the major actors and actresses in the history of filmmaking?

Spencer Tracy, James Cagney, Edward G. Robinson, Humphrey Bogart, Bette Davis, Katherine Hepburn.
Fred Astaire & Ginger Rogers.

13. Who were the major directors in the history of filmmaking?

Orson Welles, Marlon Brando

14. List several of the major technological developments in filmmaking and discuss their impacts.

15. What are the possibilities and issues associated with digital creation and distribution of movies?

16. What are the major online/mail movie rental services and how do they operate?

Netflix, Blockbuster, Amazon.com & Walmart.

17. How is the Motion Picture Association of America trying to deal with online piracy in the movie industry? Congress Asked Congress to create legislative limits on technologies used to facilitate piracy. They also sued.

18. What is "digital cinema" and what are the major companies involved in the development of the technology for digital cinema?

To be able view movies from online & Netflix, TiVo, CinemaNow, Movie Link & Starz.

19. What were the percentages of female directors, producers, writers, cinematographers and editors who worked on the 250 top-grossing U.S. films in 2007?

Directors: 6%.
Producers: 22%.
Writers: 10%.
Cinematographers: 2%.
Editors: 17%.

20. What were the major statistics associated with the year 2007 in the film industry?

- Domestic ticket sales revenue, up 5.5% to $9.6 billion.
- World-wide ticket sales revenue up 5% to $26.7 billion.
-

Public Relations

The term public relations is used and misused so often that the professional practitioner might be chagrined and the uninitiated quickly confused. Those who practice public relations are not licensed as those in medicine, law or accounting. There is nothing to stop someone from using the title public relations specialist nor public relations counselor.

Even as dedicated, well-educated true professionals come into the field with a knowledge of research techniques, skills in communication, and an awareness of ethical practices, they are confronted by the often mistaken view of public relations generated by the wannabes, the hustlers, the incapable, and those with questionable motives. Over-the-hill, out-of-work former celebrities often tout themselves as public relations specialists as they make themselves available (for a price) as "greeters" at bowling alleys, car washes, supermarket openings, etc. Unemployed journalists who don't call themselves freelance writers might borrow instead the title freelance public relations person, at least until they get back to full-time work in a newsroom. Public relations is an easy and all-encompassing label for many individuals to adopt if they think it will give them some identity, even if it isn't always clear to observers what that identity is.

A public relations specialist's duties include, but are not limited to, the following: writing news releases, booklets, texts, reports, speeches, and copy for all media; editing employee publications, newsletters, shareholder reports, and other management communications; contacting all broadcasting and print media on behalf of the employer; and handling special events such as press parties, convention exhibits, open houses, new facility or anniversary celebrations. In addition, other jobs include making appearances before groups; using a background knowledge of art and layout for developing brochures, booklets and annual reports; determining the goals of the public relations effort and recommending steps to carry out the programs; and working closely with the marketing, advertising and sales departments when announcing new products or services. Above all, a public relations specialist must first and foremost be a businessperson in order to understand how to perform successfully in business and to comprehend the needs and goals of their clients.

It is easy to assume that part of what public relations does is build images, yet sometimes it seems as if public relations has a bad image. Journalists use the term "flack" as at least partly derogatory when referring to public relations people. Often public relations people are portrayed in fiction, whether in print or on the small or big screen, as sycophants. A classic portrayal of the evil public relations person was in the movie, *The China Syndrome*, where the effort to cover up the potential for nuclear disaster made the nuclear plant's public relations man appear to be a callous, fearful toady subservient to the corporate chiefs. All too often that view is presented, one that shows the public relations people as insincere, glad-handing mouthpieces selling themselves to anyone who can afford their manipulative and unethical huckstering. It is ironic that those who try to build trust, win public support, and communicate effectively find their own image so distorted.

Public relations people do set standards for themselves. They do have a code of ethics. They support colleges and universities that offer courses in the theory and practice of public relations. The field is destined to grow in stature as its practitioners continue their efforts at instilling and maintaining professionalism. Respect is building.

Definition of Public Relations

Public relations is a management function. It is the planned and organized effort to identify and analyze public interests and trends, counsel organization leaders, implement programs that help to establish mutually beneficial relationships between organizations and their publics. Many of the activities involve media communications and public relations messages are often carried in the media disguised as news.

This definition is necessarily incomplete, partly because many people simply cannot agree on what public relations is. Also, many contend that it is a great many different things. For example, career guides often point to as many as 40 to 50 disparate careers with wildly different titles as part of the overall field. The term public relations is an umbrella for several of its functions and activities, as well as some ancillary efforts. This umbrella covers promotion, press agency, lobbying, political campaigning, consumer affairs, fund-raising, charitable works, audience analysis, public opinion research, and, of course, publicity.

All too often, casual observers tend to think of publicity as a synonym for public relations. In a broad sense, publicity is just one more part of the picture. In a narrow sense, it can be a visible and significant part. Publicity is one of the aspects of public relations, although not the only one, that makes extensive use of the mass media. In fact, studies have found that much of the news media content is generated by public relations efforts, perhaps as much as 60% to 75%.

There is also confusion about the similarities and differences between advertising and public relations. Both are thought of as persuasive communications. The major distinction is that the material created by public relations is carried free of charge by the media. News organizations and public relations people have a symbiotic relationship. Radio, television, web sites, newspapers and magazines need content, usually news or feature material, and public relations practitioners need conduits for information, persuasive or not, for their clients. Advertising is purchased time or space in the media and is obviously, overtly commercial persuasion.

Public relations is often behind-the-scenes communication and it can be perceived as subtle in its persuasion. Advertising usually deals directly with consumers and almost certainly involves selling goods or services, or possibly promoting or selling ideas. Public relations is more interested in building or maintaining images rather than making sales. It tends to promote institutions or ideas rather than goods and services.

The definition includes those instances of government and industrial groups that have chosen slightly different titles for the public relations function. Some industries, banks in particular, will have what they call communications departments. Others have public affairs offices or public information offices.

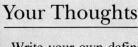

Your Thoughts

Write your own definition of public relations. Be sure to elaborate on the one included in the book.

Why did you include such elements in your definition?

Historical Development of Public Relations

Political campaigning as practiced by contemporary political communication specialists was seen in the 1820s with Andrew Jackson's 1824 campaign, when he won the popular vote, but lost in the electoral college to John Quincy Adams. In 1828, Jackson was elected president, again through heavy populist sentiment. Jackson was a champion of the people, a champion created by public relations techniques. Pseudo events and promotions were staged by Jackson supporters, some of them newspapermen who knew how to build a hero's image.

The campaign that carried this frontiersman to the White House had some of its origins and much of its impetus in rural Tennessee and Kentucky, where small town newspaper editors related the exploits of a brawling, bellowing, larger-than-life, generous and courageous, natural leader whose destiny was to fight against corruption and apathy as effectively as he fought the British and the Indians. The written communications in this campaign were supplemented by torchlight parades, barn dances, brass bands, hoedowns, beer parties and other staged events that rallied the populace behind a natural leader.

Once in the White House, Jackson rewarded some of his public relations people with jobs in his administration. Some of them became so influential, largely because of their ability to keep Jackson's image consistently before the public with their newspaper connections, that they were more powerful than the official cabinet. This "Kitchen Cabinet" was made up of men who were communicators with great political savvy. The Jackson administration's policy and its implementation often got underway in late-night meetings over a bottle or two of bourbon around a table in the White House kitchen.

The prime figures in this early model for what eventually would be a White House communications office were Amos Kendall, Francis Preston Blair and John C. Rives. All three had been brought in from a newspaper in Frankfort, Kentucky. They were initially charged with producing a newspaper in Washington that would be an organ for Jackson and his programs and policies. In effect, they also served as presidential counselors, campaign managers, public opinion pollsters, speech writers, and, of course, publicists. Amos Kendall, although not holding the title, was the first presidential press secretary and congressional liaison.

For the rest of the 19th century, politics was imbued with the techniques of press agency, promotion, and public opinion polling, yet private industry was slow to embrace the idea that communications with the public would have any value. Industrial expansion, prosperity, the business sector creating jobs, and the overall popularity of American business going into the last part of the 19th century seemed to tell corporate and industrial leaders that the less the public knew the better.

That was changed with the increasing role of government in business and the eventual strength of labor unions, which had been around since the 1820s, but were not flourishing until the 1870s and 1880s. Many workers began to see their interests as directly opposed to those of their bosses. The shift in public attitude toward business coincided with government's frequent moves toward regulation of large industries. As the 20th century loomed, big business began to realize the importance of trying to overcome any potential hostility and of courting favor with the public. Although not in common use yet, the term public relations was apparently first heard even before the turn of the century. Its concepts and practices had been around for some time, but its importance and awareness were no doubt heightened by the coining of a name for it.

The first company to establish a corporate public relations department was Westinghouse in 1889 with the hiring of a Pittsburgh newspaperman to direct efforts at influencing various publics. In the 1890s newspaperman George Harvey became a full-time public relations specialist for financiers Harry Payne Whitney and Thomas Fortune Ryan. By this time, other journalists began to make a living in public relations. George V. S. Michaelis established The Publicity Bureau in Boston in 1900, specifically to gather factual information about his clients to be passed on to the newspapers. In 1908, the first publicity office in the nation's capital was opened by William W. Smith on behalf of clients who had business with any members of Congress.

At about the same time, the "father" of modern public relations appeared in the person of Ivy Ledbetter Lee, who contended that the public should be informed by business of both its good news and bad. Lee argued that the propensity for business interests to hide their bad news made them look worse in the long run because when information eventually and inevitably got out it would undermine credibility. Lee was a press agent who was concerned that all too often press agents were whitewashing their clients' activities and it was creating a credibility gap when the truth would come out. Lee contended that the public would make correct assessments and the proper conclusions if given the truth from the very beginning. Lee established his reputation as a pioneer in public relations initially by publishing a declaration of principles that said he dealt in factual information. This set of principles went to newspaper editors, who were told that they were free to check any of his facts independently. A primary point that he made to the newspapers was that if there was anything he offered them about his clients that would be considered by them to be advertising rather than news, then they should simply throw it away.

Among those using public relations in the early part of the 20th century were the railroads, churches, universities, charitable organizations, oil companies and politicians. Partly because Ivy Lee had railroad clients, the term public relations was used in railroad trade publications. It was controversial when Lee revealed complete and factual information about accidents involving his client's trains, but the Pennsylvania Railroad and others led the way in furthering disclosure as better public relations than covering up their disasters. The railroads were among the first industries to stress the need to evaluate and improve customer service as a way to learn of any customer dissatisfaction and eliminate it, a recognition of the value of public relations.

In the decade following 1910, U.S. Steel and AT&T were among corporations advocating truthfulness and avoiding withholding unfavorable information from the public. AT&T's publicity department was given a role in management, initially through the efforts of pioneer public relations specialist James D. Ellsworth, and later by his successor, Arthur W. Page. AT&T made a strong commitment to customer service and a planned program of winning public confidence. Page insisted that his department draw on a systematic diagnosis of public opinion. He wanted data rather than guesswork on the impact on the public of any of AT&T's policies.

Ivy Lee's many contributions to the development of modern public relations include his efforts over several years to help the image of the Rockefeller family.

John D. Rockefeller, Jr., hired Lee at a time when an attempt to break up a strike at the Rockefeller-owned Colorado Fuel and Iron Company had resulted in violence. Lee's advice to the Rockefellers to cooperate with investigators and to participate in the formation of a mediation panel to alleviate workers' grievances was described years later as a public relations outcome of significant value to the Rockefellers. Eventually, with Lee's help, the Rockefellers overcame their unpopularity and became known as one of the nation's most significant philanthropists. By the 1920s, Lee had worked with the airlines to help combat Americans' fear of flying and with the maritime industry to overcome resistance to ocean travel in the wake of the Titanic and Lusitania sinkings, early efforts of crisis management by public relations specialists.

During World War I, journalist George Creel was given a presidential appointment to head the government's Committee on Public Information, an effective means to mobilize public opinion in favor of America's military contributions to the war in Europe and a successful force in stimulating the sales of war bonds. After working with Creel, Carl Byoir launched one of the most successful public relations agencies ever in 1930. Already, John W. Hill and William Knowlton had founded Hill & Knowlton, Inc., which was an even larger firm than Carl Byoir and Associates, Inc. An early public relations counselor was Harold Burson, whose reputation was built on marketing-oriented public relations. His agency, Burson-Marstellar, eventually became as large or larger than Hill & Knowlton.

Another early pioneer in the development of modern public relations practices was Edward Bernays. In his book, *Propaganda*, Bernays wrote that the function of public relations is to persuade and manipulate people for their own good. He saw nothing wrong with "manipulating public opinion" to improve democracy, to achieve desired ends and to balance the fortunes of chance. Bernays is given credit for creating and developing the role of "public relations counsel" to business owners and manufacturers. He preached a doctrine of creating heroes and leaders who could help solve problems and improve society. To achieve this goal, he advocated creating messages that the mass media could share with the public.

By the close of the 20th century, research and communication were at the core of organizational decision-making, planning and managing. Commercial and industrial organizations embraced public opinion research and varied communicative activities, including press agency, publicity, promotion and lobbying. They also used public relations departments internally and agencies externally to conduct fund-raising and membership drives, to manage special events and to coordinate public affairs programs. As the 21st century neared, organizations could identify their policies and procedures with the public interest through the efforts of their public relations staffs. They were then able to evaluate public attitudes and, as a result, plan and execute programs of action to earn public understanding and acceptance.

Modern practitioners vary from those in large agencies and corporate offices to those in small firms. The top public relations agencies have several hundred employees each. They typically have branch offices in several major cities and operate internationally, with offices in major cities around the world. Many large advertising agencies have public relations divisions, with a dozen or more employees in each. These people write speeches, produce annual reports, produce company magazines or newsletters, stage community events, produce video tapes and films, develop political campaigns, train clients in how to meet the public or appear in the media and conduct or evaluate research.

Often, they contract out some specialties. They might use a small agency for a specific task, such as scripting a television program or coordinating a membership drive. Other public relations people are found on the staff of hospitals, schools, labor unions, churches, and a variety of government agencies including each of the armed services. By now, few business policies or agency practices are set without ultimate appraisal of their ultimate effect on the organization's public relations.

The Role of Research in Public Relations

Because the purpose of public relations is to influence public opinion, it is necessary that practitioners begin with the measurement and analysis of public attitude and sentiment. It starts with the assumption that there is two-way communication. Communication must not go in only one direction. The attempt has to be made to understand people before trying to influence them. Public relations must be an active process of pursuing public understanding and acceptance of the communicator's goals or mission. It starts with research techniques that generate an awareness of public perceptions, attitudes and trends concerning subjects of value to a specific community or to society as a whole.

The next step is interpretation of the data to enhance understanding of how common ground can be reached so that effective communication might result in influence or persuasion. This understanding of those to whom information or persuasion might be directed can then lead to conscious efforts to exert influence. By knowing the interests of the public affected by an organization, its management can choose the means by which a consensus can be reached that ensures that both the public's and the firm's interests are being served. Research entails the acquisition of knowledge that allows one to recognize and act on the perceived needs of others, resulting in the ability to position public relations efforts within an overall management plan. Management wants hard facts, not guesswork, before communication messages and strategies are suggested by public relations counselors.

Information gained through studies of potential audiences can be used to forecast future events, pretest messages, and identify audiences as definable, targeted publics rather than undifferentiated masses. Research also can evaluate efforts and demonstrate their effectiveness, allowing for follow-up efforts. If public relations people claim that they contribute to better understanding between publics and organizations, they must be able to substantiate such claims. Research can do that for them. When asked to prove their worth to their clients or their management, they depend upon their ability to conduct research, apply the results to public relations efforts, and measure the effects of such efforts. Public relations departments and agencies need to incorporate data-gathering techniques into every phase of their activities.

The survey method is the most common of the several types of research used in public relations. Surveys are the most effective method for assessing the characteristics of the public in a form that will allow the data to be used in planning and evaluating public relations efforts. Surveys should provide a means to differentiate between subsets of the public rather than measuring a mass response. A survey might be designed to identify what people think of a company or its product. It probably would be an attempt to discover perceptions of a sample of the public impacted by the client. The first step is to determine specifically what is needed from the study. Before defining the study's concepts and terms, it is necessary to look at previous studies that might be related in some way. After unbiased responses are gathered, a reliable basis for recommendations to the client (or to management) can be provided through the analysis of the data and subsequent conclusions.

Many surveys are designed to collect demographic data, which give the researcher the needed information to use in subdividing the responses according to age, sex, educational level, income, occupation, etc. Demographic information makes it possible to measure individual subsets, or specific publics, rather than mass responses. Most surveys are designed to elicit responses to questions an organization wants answered about attitudes, feelings, beliefs, behaviors or perceptions of a specific public on issues crucial to the client. Public opinion polls are used to provide insight into the characteristics of a carefully targeted audience group, and should offer some understanding of why certain opinions exist in a subgroup meaningful to the organization. The primary justification for survey research is to acquire an understanding of the needs and desires of a specific public or publics so that public relations campaigns can be communicated effectively to the right people.

Focus groups are sometimes used in lieu of large surveys or as a preliminary step before conducting a survey. Focus groups are small groups of people, usually selected to represent the demographic makeup of the target population. A researcher or guide meets with the group and asks general questions to get the people talking about their experiences, views, opinions, perceptions, likes and dislikes.

Experimental research is another valuable tool, whether done in the laboratory or in the field. In laboratory experiments, researchers can control any potential outside effects and work to minimize them through a carefully controlled environment. Field experiments allow the researcher to conduct tests in the real world, in a real-life situation. This could mean getting reactions in an authentic setting with the subjects in their normal environment rather than in an artificially created one. Of course, in a field experiment, there is a loss of control over any potential outside variables that might contaminate the

results. You simply cannot hold all of the variables constant in an on-the-job or on-the-spot experiment in a real setting.

No matter whether surveys or experiments are conducted, researchers use three basic means for collecting their data: observations, interviews and questionnaires. The observation method has limitations because the researcher's own experiences and predispositions can easily affect perceptions of what is being observed. Structured observational techniques have been devised to overcome this. Established rules for systematically recording observed data can be made available to observers who are first given considerable training in their use.

Interviews are conducted in person and by telephone. Interviewers, like observers, must be highly trained, primarily to ensure that the interviewers' techniques, posture, non-verbal cues, physical appearance, and the like, do not result in biased responses from the interview subjects. Most interviews are highly structured with a schedule of questions with specific response choices, probably multiple choice or the simple yes/no alternative. Other interviews could be unstructured and would probably allow interviewees to respond to open-ended questions.

The most common form of data collection is the questionnaire, which normally provides anonymity and guarantees a uniform stimulus to each subject, with each respondent asked the same questions in exactly the same way. Questionnaires are inexpensive to administer and are usually sent by mail or e-mail.

A type of research that practitioners believe is most likely to yield data that can be used in planning and evaluating communications efforts is the "audit." The first step in a public relations audit is identifying the public or publics, usually by developing a list of the organization's relevant audiences, including employees, customers, suppliers, stockholders, consumer groups, environmental groups, and any community or local governmental units even tangentially in a position to affect the organization. The second step is to determine the prevailing view of the organization displayed by each public. This can be done by surveys and by content analyses of local media. Image surveys are useful in determining the organization's standing with a given public. These studies start with an attempt to find out how familiar a public is with the organization, its functions, products or services, and its policies.

Then researchers try to determine the characteristics a public or publics attribute to the organization and the extent of positive or negative perceptions. This research effort can often help in planning, because public relations practitioners can compare expressed images in the target audience with the images sought by the organization. The public relations audit finds out what is the overall internal attitude through interviews with management officials, thus learning company strengths and weaknesses. These audits can help identify how closely the attitudes in the public match those of management and can result in an analysis of the disparity between them. Public relations audits provide data for planning future public relations efforts and help to evaluate the effectiveness of previous efforts.

Practitioners also use what they call a communication audit to monitor and evaluate the messages and their conduits in the communications activities in a company. Communication audits can be done internally or externally. A simple part of the audit is a readership survey to learn what articles or sections or publications are being read by which publics. Another part of the communication audit could be a content analysis, often to look for the frequency of favorable or unfavorable news coverage an organization receives in the media that reach targeted publics. In its simplest form, content analysis tells the researchers how often selected topics appear in selected messages in the media under scrutiny.

Readability studies can help determine the potential effectiveness of written messages by assessing how easily they can be understood. The appropriateness of a message for the educational level of the audience can most often be determined by the length of the sentences used in the message. Finally, this audit can be expected to measure public attitudes toward the communication channels used by the organization. Are these channels perceived as biased and self-serving, or as open and trustworthy?

Properly applied research can bolster public relations judgments by basing them on an empirical foundation. Research can confirm assumptions about public opinion on an issue or institution and can corroborate the validity of an organization's public relations effort. Research can clarify issues and can help position communication efforts within an organization's overall plan. Corporate managers need measurable results for defining problems and for evaluating solutions. The task for public relations is to keep management informed of its research results and play a role in management's efforts to accomplish goals set by the objectives ordained by such results.

The Practice of Public Relations

Earlier in this chapter it was noted that public relations differs from marketing and advertising in that it promotes ideas more than products or services and creates favorable attitudes toward organizations. It was also pointed out that it covers a wide variety of objectives and communication tools in a planned effort to influence opinion through two-way communication. Add to this that practitioners believe they are exercising a management function and are guiding an organization's policies, actions, and procedures as they relate to that firm's public or publics. On behalf of the client or management, it is public relations that will execute an action or communication program intended to develop rapport and understanding. Some organizations need public relations campaigns to respond to attacks by competitors or critics. Others want to anticipate difficulty and take into account, in advance, potential negative attitudes or feelings among their publics.

In general, public relations work assignments include the following:

1. Writing and editing
2. Research
3. Media relations and placement
4. Management and administration
5. Counseling
6. Special events planning and coordination
7. Speaking engagements
8. Production of materials
9. Training staffers and executives about media
10. Contact with community members and organizations

A public relations effort can include almost anything that will help advance a particular objective. It could be as simple as publicity or as complex as a long-range community relations endeavor. Publicity could be for a company or for a product. Company publicity involves any activity of a firm that is of interest to the general public. If an organization offers something to the media that is truly newsworthy, it is going to appear in print, online or on the air. General news columns and radio and television newscasts carry stories of the size, location or number of employees of a new plant or planned expansion of an existing facility, especially if it promotes the local economy and creates jobs. Business sections are going to carry articles about promotions within management of a firm, the quarterly earnings of the company, and any specific accomplishment or award earned by the company or one of its management team individually.

Products are often a source of news. The circus arrives in a community and the media look for feature items about the headliners, like the world famous clown or charismatic animal trainer. They know their audiences want to hear about the colorful and unique performers. A newly developed product is always newsworthy, certainly on the business page, but often in the general news section. Research into product improvement or into benefits for consumers can be newsworthy.

Long-range communication strategies include lending executives to the local community chest or other charitable community activities, establishing scholarships and other grants to deserving members of the community, participating in major events like the Fourth of July celebration or Christmas Pageant, and staging open houses or tours of the plant.

Other public relations efforts include detailing the company's side in labor disputes. Unions also have public relations people presenting their side of a labor-management conflict. Public relations staff members are called upon to communicate the company's promotion of or opposition to pending legislation, and outline company policy, or present the firm's point of view on industry activities or positions. Public relations professionals use house organs, newsletters, web sites, seminars, workshops, teleconferences, films or videos and special events to help achieve corporate objectives.

Salaries for beginning public relations practitioners average about $35,000. The median salary of all public relations professionals is about $85,000, but many top-level public relations executives earn $200,000 or more. About 40% of public relations practitioners work for corporations. About 27% work for public relations firms or agencies or act as sole practitioners. About 14% work for associations, foundations or educational institutions. About 8% work within the healthcare professions. About 6% work for government agencies and 5% serve charitable or religious organizations.

Publicity and Promotion

Many confuse public relations with publicity, which is understandable. Publicity, a part of public relations, is an important tool and probably the most visible. The purpose of publicity might be hidden, but its material is seen in print and on television and heard on the air. It is promotional material disguised as news, although often it is inherently newsworthy and carries the ancillary benefit of persuading while informing.

Public relations includes, of course, both information and persuasion. The information aspect makes public relations a legitimate adjunct to journalism, a valuable source for keeping the public aware of topical events and significant issues. Public relations performs a journalistic function when it becomes an auxiliary news source and describes and explains developments in newsletters or the general media. Publicity, in some instances, is the generation of news about an individual, product or industry to appear in commercial media free of charge.

A related aspect is press agentry, which is the planning of activities and the staging of events to

Your Thoughts

What aspects of public relations interest you most? Why?

attract attention or generate publicity. A basic tool in press agentry is the "pseudo-event." There are events that occur naturally—earthquakes, floods, fires, and other disasters. Often, public relations professionals will stage a fabricated occurrence for the exclusive purpose of generating publicity. A disc jockey locks himself in the station's control room and plays only the music he supposedly prefers rather than the program director's playlist. An automobile dealer sits in a car elevated by a crane 100 feet high adjacent to a busy freeway, supposedly refusing to come down until a certain number of cars have been sold.

The media respond to citizens' inquiries by providing reports explaining these strange occurrences. Other pseudo-events are more pedestrian. A supermarket grand opening is staged days or weeks after shoppers have been visiting the store. Waiters and waitresses run through city streets carrying trays of filled wine glasses to see who can finish the route first while spilling the least, in an event sponsored by the wine industry. Many awards and testimonials are conducted only to get news coverage. Public relations practitioners stage media events, because they know that the resultant media content will be more complete and more captivating than if the public relations people simply supplied a news release for media use.

The typical method for informing the media about events and issues is the issuance of a news release. A news release is written much like a news story, but in a form that calls an editor's attention to a possible subject of interest. Some small newspapers, especially weeklies, will print news releases verbatim. Most media gatekeepers use the news release as a source for information about a topic to be developed by assigning a reporter to follow up any leads contained in the public relations material. When the release is sufficient for an editor's needs, it could be printed, copied, linked or broadcast following some editing and/or rewriting. This is fairly typical of what happens, with stories based on publicity releases making up a large part of what appears in news columns or newscasts.

The pseudo-event is a major part of promotional activities, many of which can contribute to sales of products and services as well as enhancing an organization's reputation and building its image. Promotion in public relations must be understood as related to, but different from sales promotion, which includes cents-off deals, premium offers, contests, in-store displays and the like. In the public relations sense, promotion includes those contrived, planned events that lead to publicity. For Example, big city mayors often climb aboard city sanitation trucks to become trash haulers for a day, always accompanied by reporters and photographers.

Movie studios have requested police protection for ticket buyers at theaters showing films with themes related to gang violence. The resultant publicity leads to an increase in ticket sales. Movie makers frequently stage special press screenings of movies that involve expense-paid trips and gifts for reporters. The assumption is that such events help the box office. Other organizations stage lavish press parties, often in connection with a company announcement or anniversary, perhaps a ground-breaking ceremony or corporate merger.

These staged events offer an opportunity for the "press kit" to be used as a valuable publicity tool. It is a packet containing news releases, feature stories, statistical information in an easy-to-read format, biographical data on management leaders, details about the special event, background information on the company, and pens and paper for the reporters' use. The strategy behind a press kit is that most news media will not use a press release word-for-word. The press kit is designed to help editors select the information they need for their inevitable decisions to rewrite it into a story unique to their readers, viewers or listeners. Packaging the press kit attractively can help get the attention of reporters and editors who have many competing news releases and other potential story ideas on their desks.

Public Affairs

There are many aspects to a company's community citizenship that require public relations personnel to work with governmental bodies, regulatory agencies, citizens' groups and other entities outside the organization. These public affairs activities include encouraging employees to participate in community activities, placing the organization in the forefront of civic betterment campaigns, and offering organizational support for charity and philanthropy. Public affairs efforts can make the company a good neighbor and a good citizen, as well as enlist support of community groups for company objectives. The intent is to benefit both the organization and the community through carefully planned, active and continuing participation in community activities. Messages reach communities through employees and their friends and relatives and through fraternal, civic, service and social clubs. Other channels include youth groups, veterans groups, teachers, clergy, union leaders and ethnic or cultural groups. Company officials are encouraged to belong to such groups and to be available for public speeches, for both institutional messages and informal communication.

The interdependence between organizations and communities can be emphasized through an open house. Successful open houses include tours of the company's facilities, displays, product samples or mementos for the guests to take with them, and opportunities for informal talks with the hosts.

Moving into a new community requires preliminary steps toward establishing good relations. A decision about where to locate can depend on early community response to the organization and its objectives. Public relations people attempt in advance to determine community attitudes, awareness, expectations, etc., and to inform their audience of recruitment plans, employee relations, energy use, and appearance of buildings and grounds. The local media are given factual information about the company and its plans.

There is an even greater responsibility when an organization, or one of its facilities, leaves a community, especially if several jobs are wiped out with the departure. Companies have been known to help form development agencies to attract new industry to the community. Reasons for the need to move must be made clear and there must be complete information on all aspects of the plan for departure.

Business and industry have a great stake in local government for two important reasons: they are heavy users of municipal services and they are quite likely to be major taxpayers. Public affairs efforts by corporate public affairs people must of necessity be devoted to building and maintaining good relations with all agencies of local government. Typically, management officials will serve on boards and commissions and the company must support those community leaders who recognize the value of the company's benefits to the local citizens and institutions. Organized, localized grassroots support can be valuable in dealing with state and federal agencies or regulatory bodies.

Government relations with the corporate public relations effort are necessitated by the constant expansion and increasing complexity of local, state and federal regulations affecting wage and hour standards, minority recruitment, zoning, health and safety, insurance, social security, workman's compensation, fees and taxes, and many, many other areas. Corporate political activity is intended to allow an organization to compete with various other interests, all of them seeking political influence, that could result in all pulling in different directions.

Government, at all levels, becomes a referee confounded by competing interests. Another compelling reason for government relations becoming a significant dimension of public relations is that organizations must be prepared to deal with government attempts to seek social goals from business as much or more than economic objectives. Environmental concerns, consumerism, racial and sexual equality and other causes are among the demands made by government that the organization must be prepared for. The result is that no public relations program can ignore provisions for dealing with government bodies.

An organization uses political public relations to oppose or advocate a government proposal or decision or to oppose an action by a special interest group. Also, political public relations enters the fray when a company wants to oppose an action by a labor union or a competing company. The organization will prepare and disseminate research reports, issue news releases, and make experts available for testimonials. Campaign contributions and involvement with political action committees are other useful techniques. Building coalitions with others impacted by the government action can be important.

Letter writing and lobbying are common practices. Lobbying involves any efforts to inform and eventually to persuade government officials to support or oppose decisions in the best interests of the organization. The practice of lobbying has acquired a bad image in the wake of documented instances of graft and influence peddling, but it has a long history as a legitimate tool to compete for the attention of government officials. In fact, the United States Congress is severely dependent upon the work of lobbyists.

The volume of legislation proposed each session is so great that Congressional staff cannot handle all of it. Lobbyists provide the necessary analysis and input needed to demonstrate potential consequences of proposed bills. Lobbyists inform company management of potential developments in the legislative process and on specific measures introduced. They keep track of the progress of bills as they work their way through the Senate or House. They arrange testimony before committees, help draft laws, create personal contacts that can improve communication with officials, and constantly monitor legislative bodies' activities. The lobbyist is the key person in the legislative part of the corporation's political public relations. Electoral and regulatory activities are other parts of the governmental relations process. Electoral activities are seen in the contributions to and support for specific political campaigns, either for issues or candidates. This would include the attempt to elect candidates who are favorable to the interests of the organization or client. More likely, it means working with the elected official after the election is over.

Organizations involve themselves in the political process through political action committees (PACs). These collect money from stockholders, employees, or others who support the company's interests. These committees generate political awareness within the organization and make campaign contributions to those running for office. The hope is that PAC funds going to victors in political races will open doors and provide access to legislators, giving lobbyists an opportunity to do their work as they seek support for a position or opposition to unfavorable legislation.

Public relations personnel often are called upon to attend public hearings to gather information, advise clients or management on opportunities for challenge or intervention, conduct research, develop publicity, oversee presentations before hearings, and generally help management prepare to justify its stance before the regulatory agencies. Many state and federal regulatory bodies greatly affect organizations of all sizes. It has only been since the 1970s that businesses have felt the impact of the Occupational Safety and Health Administration (OSHA) or the Environmental Protection Agency (EPA).

These and other agencies issue rules and regulations that have the force of law. Regulatory agencies like the Federal Communications Commission (FCC), Federal Trade Commission (FTC), a state Fair Employment Practices Commission (FEPC), or any of hundreds of others, will issue rules, orders,

promulgations, guidelines, cease and desist orders, and generally set standards for businesses whose only recourse, other than filing appeals through the courts, is to lobby officials of the agency. These agencies have the power to inspect, review, accept or reject, approve or deny, and generally limit the activities of virtually every facet of business or industry.

Public Relations Counseling

Most definitions of public relations include the notion that social science techniques are used to analyze trends, predict their consequences and counsel organizational leaders on planned programs of action that will benefit the client and the public at the same time. Senior executives are expected to be significantly assisted by public relations counselors in the management of their enterprises, which are almost inevitably confronted with demands for social change. Government intervention, environmentalism, consumerism, community activism, etc., can impact a business more severely than the marketplace. Corporations, whether profit or non-profit, need favorable public opinion while staving off the pressures created by outside forces. The profit picture could be threatened not only by the failure of a product, but also by hostile public opinion.

Public goodwill can go a long way toward reducing the impact of falling sales or other challenges to business. Management, recognizing that good products are not necessarily enough, calls on professional public relations counselors to advise in developing policy and in communicating with the desired audiences. Often these counselors are asked to solve problems related to strike threats by employees, proxy battles with stockholders, or criticism from media, community leaders, or a government agency.

The communications function of a company is generally an unfamiliar area for top management, so public relations professionals counsel them much as a lawyer or accountant would in their specialties. The public relations counselors usually begin with opinion-polling research to determine the actual public reaction. The next step is to analyze the results and to try to determine how best to meet the public interest, how then to frame an appropriate response. This leads to a recommendation to chief executives on a plan of action, probably a communications program to describe in a positive way what the company offers the public in addition to its products or services. Such counseling also can result in long-range, detailed public relations programs, corporate newsletters, company brochures, policy papers, and even help with product promotion or other marketing activities.

Related to this function is an aspect of public relations called crisis management, in which a company seeks to plan in advance for any and all major problems that can be anticipated. Public relations counselors develop a crisis plan that details the actions of all personnel in the event that something goes terribly wrong in the organization. This plan seeks to avoid crisis by foreseeing the possibility. It seeks to plan for the organization's future, evaluate the success or failure of the plan's efforts, and to use the evaluation as updated research for further planning. Public relations personnel advise the organization or client on how to prepare for and manage the unexpected and unwanted when it does occur.

In some instances, the public relations counselor is brought in after a crisis has occurred and is asked to help cope with it. There could be a case of product tampering, an oil spill, the death of animals in a municipal zoo, an industrial fire that released noxious fumes over a neighborhood, and many other possible events that lead to crisis communication. Poor handling of a disaster could result in damage to a company's image at the least and in a lawsuit at the worst. A crisis plan names one person, probably a public relations officer, to be the only source of information about the disaster. It stresses that information released be truthful and accurate. In addition it spells out precisely what is to be shared with news media. Usually, it is better to be partners with news media representatives rather than adversaries during a time of crisis.

Publications

The first job for any new hire in public relations is writing. Obviously, there are many news releases to be prepared for the media, but most casual observers would be surprised to see how many published materials are turned out by public relations practitioners. It is the public relations staff that produces a company's annual report, a formal document issued yearly as a lengthy report to stockholders. An annual report can be an important public relations tool, because it is management's justification for its performance and it gives the company a forum for explaining actions. Any firm that issues stock must prepare and publish an annual report and distribute it to stockholders.

The Securities and Exchange Commission requires disclosure of balance sheets, income statements, statements of the sources of funds, and disclosure of a detailed description of the organization, and a discussion of competitive conditions. The location of important physical properties must be included, along with a list of parent and subsidiary companies and the identities of directors and executive officers. As long as this and other financial information are included, a company can do what it wants in an annual report by way of further content and the layout or design of its document.

Your Thoughts

List FIVE suggestions to help public relations practitioners deal more effectively with crisis communication situations.

The Securities and Exchange Commission and the New York Stock Exchange require also that annual reports be released to the public and the media. The report is directed to stockholders, but is also of interest to potential investors and legislators. The report can have a strong influence on potential investors who want to learn about prospects for the business. Even companies that do not issue stock communicate with their members, employees, boards of directors, or trustees by preparing annual reports. Instead of concentrating on financial matters, they might detail activities, planned programs, new products, recent successes, or anything else that might aid in internal or external public relations. Financial public relations people also prepare quarterly reports and handle preparation and distribution of information about stock splits, stock dividends, and the calling of stockholder meetings.

House organs are published either internally or externally by a company's public relations staff. Internal newsletters, magazines or tabloid newspapers go to employees only while such organs intended for external audiences go to the public, to dealers or customers, or to stockholders. Some firms produce magazines that go to employees and to the outside audience. House organs come out weekly, monthly, quarterly or eight times a year in a variety of formats, ranging from short newsletters on rough newsprint to slick, stylish, four-color magazines intended to create goodwill in a lavish way. House organs are used to inform employees and the public about the organization and its well-being.

Companies often distribute pamphlets, flyers, folders or brochures. These are multi-paneled publications, usually on a single subject. The brochure usually tells its story as the reader unfolds the panels, one after another. Some of these can be used as enclosures, mailed with letters sent to customers, suppliers, government officials, or the media. Some are self-mailers, with space on one of the panels for an address label.

Public relations agencies and PR departments of companies do some of their publications through broadcast media. Printed news releases, press kits, brochures, house organs, quarterly and annual reports are tangible evidence of what public relations is doing to further the communication goals of a client or organization. Each has permanence and can be considered primary carriers of a company message. Publication by PowerPoint slide presentations, video tapes, DVDs, web pages, and computer-generated images are among visual and electronic means available to accomplish the public relations effort.

Electronic methods of delivering information are becoming more and more important, whether for video presentations at seminars and conventions, or for use by public media. Video news releases (VNRs) are sent to television stations in hopes that they will be used to augment the station's footage on newscasts. The public relations person has no control over whether a station will use a video news release or how much it will be edited and rewritten, but television does have a lot more airtime for news than ever before. If the video news release stresses the company too much or hits too hard on a product it may never appear. Those that do get into newscasts should name the source of the VNR.

Television stations are much quicker to run video public service announcements, as long as they don't seem too commercial or too one-sided. A moderate stance with information of an educational nature will usually guarantee some use, especially if the company is barely mentioned. Radio stations use many public service announcements and welcome copy from nonprofit institutions quite warmly. Radio stations also use audio news releases prepared by public relations practitioners.

Most radio stations prefer copy from nonprofit groups like the American Cancer Society, the American Heart Association, the Salvation Army, the American Red Cross, local Blood Bank, etc. They tend to prefer written copy that can then be rewritten to fit the station's format for public service announcements (PSAs). News releases provide a quick, economical means of communicating client spot news or feature material to the public through television and radio and PSAs are even more efficient in terms of cost and probable use.

Agency Public Relations and Corporate Public Relations

Public relations agencies can be large or small and work for clients who can be large or small. Many of them will take on a broad range of clients. Others specialize in a particular area such as political public relations, financial public relations, not-for-profit organizations, or public affairs. A primary reason for the success of the agency concept is the range of services provided. These services might be too expensive if attempted internally by a corporation or non-profit group.

Clients of agencies are also called accounts. The client typically deals with an account executive with the agency, who will be in charge of the effort to accomplish a goal for the client. If the client does not have an internal public relations or public affairs staff, the agency will perform the service and charge the client a fee. If the client does have internal public relations, then the account executive will be leading a team of creative people to deal with a specialized task, one not within the expertise of the internal staff. It could be that the task is so great that the internal staff is not sufficient enough in numbers or experience to handle it. Organizations choose outside public relations counseling in the same way they often turn to external sources for management, legal, or accounting services. Some businesses and industries seek external counseling to get an objective opinion. An in-house staff might be too familiar with internal issues, too loyal to management, and too strongly interested in being team players to provide objectivity in decision-making. An outside consultant can bring a fresh view of the task and offer a different approach to the possible programs of action.

The account executive is the leader of a group of creative people who include copywriters, artists, designers, photographers, graphics specialists, audio and video technicians, and other specialists. This team prepares news releases, press kits, speeches, newsletters, magazines, quarterly and annual reports, radio and television announcements, and videos or other visual presentations. They also arrange for open houses, news conferences, seminars, workshops, public meetings, and other special events.

A public relations plan usually develops from a meeting of the creative team chaired by the account executive. The plan will be taken to the client for approval and the account executive typically suggests a public relations audit of the client's organization to gather data to help solve the problem or meet the task. The audit amounts to a survey of management, employees, customers, providers, or anyone else closely involved with the firm, its products or services. After the audit and the proposed plan are approved, the account executive assigns duties to members of the creative team. As the creative unit is moving along in its efforts, the account executive frequently goes back to the client with examples of completed work to be checked by the client. Once the plan is carried out, it is the account executive who will lead the effort to determine its effectiveness and to determine how well the client liked the project. The account executives in an agency are responsible to senior executives, who run the agency much as executives would in any other business.

Agencies bill clients by a fixed fee, a fee for services, or by a retainer. The fixed fee is set in advance by the client and a senior executive of the agency determining the value of the time spent on the account and the knowledge and experience of the agency's creative people. A fee for services includes a basic cost for time and effort plus reimbursement for special expenses incurred by the agency specifically on behalf of the client. The retainer is a set fee every month to keep the agency and its staff on call and doing tasks on a regular basis for the client. Agency employees are required to keep logs of their activities and to charge billable hours to a specific task to a specific client.

Internal public relations departments may consist of as few as one or two persons or as many as 100. In-house public relations is usually less expensive over the long run than going outside for counsel. An internal public relations or public affairs person has more knowledge and more familiarity with the workings of the organization than outside consultants would. Even with in-house public relations, many companies choose to hire out such tasks as printing, design, video production, and mailing.

In-house public relations departments prepare news releases and handle media relations in virtually every instance. Almost all of them are involved in policy decisions by management about communication practices. At least 80% of them produce newsletters or magazines. Well over half prepare speeches, do publicity and special events, contact public officials, and train their management officials in communication techniques. Some of them prepare financial reports, conduct fund-raising campaigns, or work with labor negotiations, although these are tasks that sometimes are hired out to agencies.

Internal communications generally is one of the in-house department's more valued activities. Information is expected to give employees a desire to do well at their jobs. Management uses internal communication to be sure that employees know where their work fits in relationship to others and to the overall goals of the company. A steady flow of information is expected to reduce the potential for morale problems and to make employees feel that they are treated well.

The most popular method of trying to inform employees is the house organ, probably a newsletter or magazine. It might come out weekly, monthly, or less often, but usually it is the core of any internal communication effort. The house organ should be more than a narrative of births, deaths, company picnics, and employee-of-the-week biographies. It should also tell of external developments influencing the company's practices or potential. It should offer important information regardless of whether it is positive or unfavorable, an indication that management is truly willing to keep open the lines of communication with employees.

Internal communication also can be delivered by the use of bulletin boards, messages in pay envelopes, training manuals, in-house workshops on benefits and seminars on employees' rights or human relations in the workplace. In-house clubs or social units for employees can be encouraged. Athletic teams to represent the company help to instill pride. Social activities can be planned and carried out.

Corporate public relations is often used to respond to outside pressures, to communicate externally with forces in society viewed by some organizations as at least a bit frightening. Many organizations' executives believe they are under pressure from environmentalists or from consumer groups. Others fear the impact of activists in areas like women's rights, civil rights, and, of course, labor unions. Others worry about encroachment by government. Their mandate to an in-house public relations department is to explain corporate actions to the outside world, usually to specific external.

Often, the internal public relations department is working at creating an external image for the company, the way publics view the organization. The time and money spent to develop an internal department for communicating with outside publics is justified as crucial to the corporate image. Techniques for developing and maintaining goodwill include contributions to charity, any other type of philanthropy, involvement in community projects, and open houses to acquaint the public with the organization. Newsletters and magazines are often published for public consumption. Above all, the internal public relations

staff is expected to establish good rapport with the news media. A good corporate department works to get news releases into the media and to create publicity that will get media coverage. Of course, internal public relations staff will prepare annual reports, write speeches, produce brochures and pamphlets, while also staging trade shows and other public events.

Social Responsibility in Public Relations

The practice of public relations had its beginnings in an era when big business was being pressured to be more responsive to the public it served and more responsible to society in general. Public relations quickly evolved into a vehicle for organizational communication with social as well as corporate value. Public relations has always been used by businesses and other organizations to maintain open channels of communication with their various publics in order to be aware of the needs of society and to inform the public about responses to those needs.

This exercise of social responsibility is seen in organizational activities that have a social significance rather than only organizational self-interest. Public relations can demonstrate that social responsibility is consistent with a company's self-interest. During the middle years of the 20th century, the practice of public relations flourished as a new philosophy of social responsibility for business was rapidly emerging. Issues that transcended profit and loss statements faced corporate managers and their public relations staffs.

Public approval was being sought as organizations were led by managers who responded to societal pressures by investing the resources of their companies into social programs, philanthropy, environmental concerns, community activities, etc. By the end of the century, public relations counselors either as consultants or managers were given a voice in corporate decision-making that affected not just the profit picture, but also employees, suppliers, customers, stockholders and even the general public. Underlying the concept of social responsibility is the belief that no matter what happens in the short-range profit picture, over the long haul, profits will be increased.

Public relations practitioners counsel businesses to help fight inflation, practice equal opportunity in hiring and promotion, modify any practices that might pollute the environment, conserve all resources, take extra steps to ensure employee safety, and work toward improving the surrounding community. These are just a few of the practices management acquires from the expertise and knowledge of public relations practitioners that demonstrate to their publics an awareness of their social responsibilities. The role of the public relations counsel or manager is to convince management of the significance or strength of a public need or public attitude that necessitates social change and then to advise on policies that will lead to a desired response.

It follows that public relations as a profession must promote social responsibility within the ranks of its practitioners. The irony of public relations having a poor public image increases the need for public relations embracing a strong commitment to social responsibility for itself. The public relations counsel or manager must be responsible to the client or organization, to society and to the profession of public relations.

Most often, the concern for social responsibility is exemplified in ethical strictures. Responsibility to clients and publics depends upon the ethics of public relations practitioners, both how the profession is practiced and the way it is perceived by society. Professional standards of behavior expected of public relations practitioners stress truth, accuracy, good taste, fairness and responsibility to the public. Counseling management on organizational decisions carries a heavy ethical burden within it. Any corporate public relations policy hinges on significant ethical questions. Answering those questions must be done with an awareness of the responsibility to the profession of public relations and its public image.

Other professions have licensing requirements, boards of examiners, enforced codes of conduct and formal courses of study to define the scope of their ethics and to define their responsibilities. Schools of law, medicine and architecture give a public view of a restricted preparation for each profession. Engineers and accountants are licensed, giving the public a perception of rigorous standards of acceptance into the profession. Lawyers must pass the bar and doctors of medicine can lose the right to practice if their peers find them in violation of ethical procedures. There are many individuals who call themselves public relations practitioners who have no formal training, a limited education, no license, and no board of review to certify them.

Public Relations Society of America

In recognition of the problem, the Public Relations Society of America works to instill ethical practices and values among its members as a major step toward a profession that embraces social responsibility. PRSA has established a voluntary code of ethical standards and a declaration of principles that pledges professionalism. In addition, PRSA has a program of accreditation for its members. Not all public relations people are members and not all members seek accreditation. Those who gain full accreditation are permitted to put the initials APR after their names. That means they have a minimum of five years public relations experience, have passed a discriminating exam in public relations principles, techniques and ethics, and have followed that with successful completion of an oral examination conducted by a jury of peers.

The Declaration of Principles contains a section emphasizing public relations practitioners' principles being based on the fundamental value and dignity of the individual and on the free exercise of human rights, especially freedom of speech, freedom of assembly and freedom of press. It also asks that members commit themselves to understanding and cooperation among diverse individuals, groups and institutions of society.

PRSA's Code of Professional Standards for the Practice of Public Relations includes, among other voluntary guidelines, a section contending that members conduct themselves professionally in accord with the public interest. Another says a member shall not engage in practices that could corrupt the integrity of the channels of communication or the processes of government. In general, sections of the code attempt to promote and maintain high standards of public service. In specific instances, the code lists practices that would be unethical, such as violating a confidence, communicating false or misleading information, conflict of interest, and accepting fees from competing interests or without disclosing the source.

It is expected that potential clients will recognize that PRSA membership and accreditation will indicate competent, responsible professionalism. PRSA membership, at least, should display the needed qualities of experience and knowledge to perform the tasks related to organizational communication, molding public opinion and creating goodwill.

The Public Relations Society of America sponsors student chapters at many universities and colleges. Public relations has been taught in universities since 1923, beginning at New York University. It has been taught in journalism departments, business and marketing or advertising programs, and even in departments of speech communications.

Increasingly, journalism, speech communication and broadcasting departments have been merging into comprehensive schools and colleges, which typically include courses or majors in public relations. PRSA sponsors student organizations in programs that offer at least five courses in public relations. The student group is called the Public Relations Student Society of America (PRSSA).

Another peer group, or trade association, of note for public relations professionals is the International Association of Business Communicators, which also has an accreditation effort. Like PRSA, the IABC tries to promote professional standards. They are the two largest, of perhaps a dozen similar but more specialized associations, of public relations practitioners. Some of these are the National School Public Relations Association, the Chemical Public Relations Association, and the American Society for Hospital Public Relations Directors. PRSA is a result of a merger in 1945 by the American Council of Public Relations and the National Association of Public Relations Council, and in 1961 by the American Public Relations Association.

There are those who argue that professionalism and social responsibility in public relations can only be arrived at through licensing. Others argue that regulation and licensing would be an undesirable form of government control. Self-regulation by organizations like PRSA and IABC is quite possibly an effort to forestall government control. The contention is that if public relations practitioners police themselves through high standards imposed voluntarily there will be no need for licensing regulation by government.

Recent Research, Developments and Issues

Many public relations firms rode the phenomenal success wave of the dot-com companies. Firms specializing in technology enjoyed revenue growth of 47% in 1999. Less than two years later, though, as the dot-com frenzy died down, many public relations firms went out of business or saw flat or single-digit revenue growth. Surviving firms specializing in the Internet shifted focus away from e-commerce to Internet infrastructure and telecommunications companies.

The use and abuse of video news releases (VNRs) has come under much more scrutiny lately. With various federal, state and local governmental agencies and departments cranking out VNRs regularly, while often hiding the source/sponsor of the material, and with local TV stations running the material without mentioning where it came from, critics have had a field day pointing out the ethical breaches by both professions. Consumer watchdog groups have urged both public relations practitioners and local TV news professionals to increase their diligence in dealing with VNRs to ensure that the public is not mislead about who is saying what. The watchdog groups have recommended that whenever any part of a VNR is aired, the source of the VNR should be made clear to audience members and VNRs should not be produced in a way that attempts to hide the public relations purpose of the material.

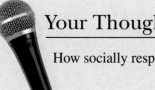

Your Thoughts

How socially responsible do you think most public relations practitioners are? Why?

List FIVE specific ethics code guidelines for public relations practitioners.

Think Back

1. What is a good, modern definition of public relations?

Public Relations is a management function. It is the planned and organized effort to identify and analyze public interests and trends, counsel organization leaders, implement programs that help to establish ~~At~~ mutually beneficial relationships between organizations and their publics.

2. Who were the big names in the development of public relations in the 20th century and what did they contribute?

3. What are the major research techniques employed by public relations practitioners?

4. List all the steps in the public relations process.

5. List the typical work assignments of public relations practitioners.

6. Where do public relations practitioners work and what are their salaries?

7. What are the differences among public relations, publicity and promotion?

8. What are the major roles and responsibilities of public relations practitioners?

9. What are the similarities and differences associated with agency public relations and corporate public relations?

10. What are the major social responsibility and ethical concerns associated with the practice of public relations?

11. What has happened to the public relations firms that chose to specialize in Internet-based companies?

12. What are VNRs and what are some of the major ethical concerns associated with the development and distribution of VNRs?

13

Advertising

We all find information in print advertisements and broadcast commercials, whether it is sought out or acquired unintentionally. Much of what we learn about the goods and services that we buy comes from our exposure to the promotional and marketing techniques of various advertisers. We get impressions of businesses and industries, of brands and types of products, of public servants and political or economic institutions, from the ubiquitous results of the efforts of people who do their advertising and promotion. Promotion in this instance is used as a general term for advertising-related activities like personal selling, publicity (even public relations), exhibitions, contests, displays, premiums or coupons, and anything else reinforcing or supplementing what is said in advertising.

What Is Advertising?

Advertising is the dissemination of persuasive messages in the media, paid for by a clearly identified sponsor, and designed to sell products, services or ideas. Advertising is controlled, in that messages are bought for specific purposes, to achieve specific effects, and to be cost effective. Advertisers seek demographically-identifiable subgroups to receive their messages. They buy space on a specific page or section in a newspaper or on a specific television program. It is controlled because sponsors know exactly what will be said and the message will be perfectly in accord with what the sponsor desires.

Advertising is the economic foundation, the source of income, for most media organizations. The profits for media as businesses depend on advertising. The advertising industry depends on the media

as carriers for its messages. Advertising performs a major role in the American economy. It helps to sell goods and services to consumers, who, in turn, use advertisements to help them choose from competing products and companies. Advertising has become a part of American culture, shaping popular standards and exercising a social influence. It meets society's need for information, goods, services and product development.

Social influence results from both the informative and persuasive aspects of advertising. It informs potential buyers about products, either subtly or directly. It tries to guide the consumer toward a decision about what product or products to acquire. It moves consumers toward one choice rather than another. Persuasive appeals urge consumers toward decisions from several products, toward a set of behaviors dictated by economic and social conditions.

Broadcast station general managers and newspaper publishers most often rise to those executive positions by coming through the sales or advertising departments. It is rare for a broadcast news director or newspaper editor to move up to the top management position. Advertising is the income producer for each medium, except for book publishing, of course. The profit picture often dictates the choice of former sales managers as publishers and general managers.

How Advertising Is Practiced

The three primary levels of activity in the advertising industry are agencies, advertising departments of businesses, and advertising or sales departments of the media.

An advertising agency plans, produces and places advertising for clients. There are two common types of agencies: the full-service agency and the boutique agency. The full-service agency has a large staff of creative people, researchers, writers, photographers, designers, artists, video and film specialists, media buyers and account executives to meet virtually every need that a client has. The boutique agency offers fewer services and is probably a creative group that contracts with other agencies or specialists to provide any additional services for clients. Sometimes a boutique agency is an adjunct to the in-house advertising department of a company.

In the full-service agency, it is the account executive who ramrods the campaign from start to finish. The account executive supervises the team of creative personnel, researchers, writers and artists working on a client's advertising objectives. It is the account executive who coordinates all of the activities that lead to the final print advertisements or broadcast commercials and then sees to their proper placement for effective presentation to the public.

Almost every large company or business has an advertising department to coordinate the firm's advertising. It may also produce some of the advertising, most likely the portion distributed by mail. If the firm does not contract with an agency, the advertising department will handle all of the activities that an agency would be expected to handle. Because its copywriters, graphic artists and production personnel are part of the firm, they can be expected to have an intimate knowledge of the product, the company's goals, and the management strategies. If the firm uses an agency, its advertising department will represent the company in all its dealings with the agency.

Radio stations, television stations, magazines, and newspapers also have their own advertising departments. A radio or television station will have a local sales manager supervising a staff of people who solicit advertising from agencies and from local or regional businesses. A station will also have a national sales manager to solicit advertising from sponsors who buy air time for products or services on many stations across several markets.

A newspaper will have several people in what is called display advertising, which is primarily the sale of space to local retailers, although some national accounts will buy display advertisements. Newspapers also have a classified advertising staff, handling the brief, relatively inexpensive announcements in a separate section of the newspaper.

Types of Advertising

There are seven major types of advertising: national, retail, cooperative, direct mail, institutional, advocacy and trade.

National advertising is sometimes called "brand name" advertising and is typically seen as television commercials on the big networks or as full-page advertisements in major magazines. National advertising, for the most part, is devoted to the selling of products to consumers without much concern about which specific retail outlet consumers use. Examples include Coca-Cola, Pepsi, General Foods, Ford, Toyota, Levi's, Nike, Reebok, Calvin Klein and other major manufacturers.

Retail advertising is more about stores or shops rather than products. It is intended to get consumers into specific retail outlets to buy products that they are no doubt generally aware of. Broadcast stations tend to call it local advertising, as opposed to national advertising. Examples include Vons, Albertson's, Macy's, J.C. Penney's, Discount Tire, Big Five, Sports Authority, Carpeteria, Best Buy, Crazy Eddie's, Home Depot, Drew Ford, El Cajon Toyota, etc.

Cooperative advertising, or co-op, is when retail advertisers and national advertisers get together to share the costs of their advertisements. For example, Ford will share the costs of advertising with local dealers. SONY might offer to pay for part of the advertising costs for Circuit City if SONY products are featured in the ads.

Direct mail advertising is a technique used by many firms. Direct mail advertisers use their own publications rather than mass media in a direct appeal or sales approach to consumers. Leaflets, catalogs, pamphlets and flyers are all used to acquaint consumers with the features of products. A variation of direct mail is direct response advertising. In direct response advertising, companies use the mass media to inform consumers, but the products and services are "not available in any store." Consumers buy directly from manufacturers or suppliers. No retail outlets are visited in connection with the purchases. Examples include special collections of recordings, cookware, floor cleaning products, teeth-whitening systems and get-rich-quick schemes.

Institutional advertising is similar to public relations in that the messages are not outright sales pitches on behalf of products or services, but instead are designed to build images or create goodwill. Examples include Chevron's campaign about environmental safety and campaigns by local television station news departments to position themselves as caring about the community, standing for the community or sponsoring community-oriented events.

Advocacy advertising is similar to institutional advertising. It is intended to promote causes or sway public opinion on controversial issues. A few months before every election, you'll find lots of advocacy ads for propositions, bond proposals, etc. In addition, groups and organizations often use ads to try to convince people to join protests, boycotts, community clean-up efforts, "light the night" campaigns and other activist activities.

Trade advertising is the effort by manufacturers to get retailers to buy their goods and sell them to the public. Trade advertising is often heavily dependent on direct mail. It is a form of advertising that recognizes that retailers are buyers as well as sellers. The brokers, wholesalers and retailers become the customers of the manufacturers. Manufacturers advertise to them stressing the profit potential if they sell the manufacturer's wares. An example would be Rawlings Sporting Goods sending advertising materials to Sportland, a retail sporting goods store, in an effort to get Sportland's owners to sell Rawlings products. Rawlings might also advertise in trade magazines in the hopes of attracting the owners of Sportland and other retail sporting goods stores.

How Advertising Began

The development of movable type was followed quickly by printed advertisements. The first Gutenberg press in London issued an advertisement in 1480 promoting a religious book to be printed on that equipment. In its second year of publication, in 1666, the first English language newspaper, the *London Gazette,* produced a special advertising section.

In the 1690s, an English apothecary was so enamored of advertising that many since have called him the father of modern advertising. He was John Houghton, who advertised more than just his apothecary shop. Houghton sold coffee, tea and chocolate through his energetic advertising efforts. He eventually became a publisher himself and established a newspaper intended for an audience of businessmen. That was the first newspaper to depend heavily on advertising for income. Houghton has been described as very selective in what advertising content he would allow in his newspaper or what products he would accept for advertising. Houghton was quick to reject advertising for anything that he thought to be fraudulent or dishonest.

In pre-Revolutionary America, Ben Franklin was the father of colonial advertising. Franklin was the first American publisher to make huge profits from advertising income. He also excelled at printing and engraving, which resulted in advertisements with great visual appeal to his readers. Other newspapermen who followed Franklin could not match his advertising copywriting and business skill. In fact,

Your Thoughts

Give TWO examples of each type of advertising:

1. National/Brand name—

2. Retail—

3. Co-op—

4. Direct-mail—

5. Institutional—

6. Advocacy—

7. Trade—

although there were advertisements in colonial newspapers, they were not as significant to the economic success of such newspapers until after the Revolution. The next American newspaperman to employ advertising as successfully was Isaiah Thomas, a Boston book publisher, printer, historian, and Revolutionary War figure. Thomas was the second American to depend entirely on advertising income to make his publishing ventures profitable. Other newspapermen of the era depended on stipends, job printing contracts, or financial support from politicians to keep their partisan organs going.

By the 1830s when newspaper circulation numbers were increasing greatly and magazines, heretofore largely unsuccessful, were beginning to proliferate, it was the advertiser who took notice. This was when news rather than views became prevalent in American newspapers. Population growth and urbanization in particular created a greater market for advertisers. The increased circulations made it more cost effective for many manufacturers and retailers who had not advertised before. The increased advertising revenue in the 1830s and 1840s caused newspaper owners to expand their efforts at gathering news and to invest in more advanced printing equipment.

The first of the mass circulation newspapers, Ben Day's *New York Sun,* was the first to employ advertising sales representatives to visit prospects and solicit their advertisements.

Although magazines between 1825 and 1850 were increasing in number and staying in business longer than ever before, they were not carrying as much advertising as they would in the post Civil War era. These were highly specialized publications with low circulation numbers, usually related to religion, music, literature and poetry, or the growing labor movement.

In 1849, Volney B. Palmer opened the first advertising agency. By the end of the Civil War, such agencies were commonplace. They purchased space for their clients, making their profit by getting discounts of 15% to 25% on the stated advertising rates.

Palmer in many ways had already been functioning as an advertising agent before opening his New York office. He had worked in Philadelphia and Boston in the early to mid-1840s, making it a practice of getting a 25% commission on advertising he had solicited for several newspapers. His early success has been credited not only to his salesmanship, but also to his ability as a copywriter. Palmer would often convince clients of his value to them by demonstrating his skill at writing copy, extolling the product. Once the prospect was sold on buying space for Palmer's prose, the newspapers were then his prey as he demanded, and got, hefty discounts off the published rate card.

Another pioneer in the agency business was George P. Rowell, who bought advertising space in large quantities and resold it to advertisers. Rowell primarily acted as a middleman, making it easier for the publishers. One workable technique for him was paying the publishers for advertising space up front, so there was no need for them to wait until the agent got his money from the clients.

A significant factor in generating increased newspaper advertising after the Civil War was the rise of the department store. With the immediate success of these retail stores offering a variety of merchandise, the owners found that newspaper advertising initially created public awareness of such ventures and then continued to stimulate interest in the specific items or brands in the store. This meant a two-tiered approach to advertising. At one level were the advertisements for the store itself (image advertising) and on another level were advertisements for many of the individual products (item and price advertisements) being sold at Carson Pirie Scott, Marshall Field or Wannamaker's. Another factor was the continued growth of Sunday newspapers, which had appeared first in the 1830s, but met opposition on moral grounds by church leaders in the 1840s. Certainly by the 1870s, the Sunday circulations had reached totals that were attractive to advertisers.

The 1880s and 1890s saw an industrial expansion that increased the production of goods and, as a result, stimulated advertising. Markets were expanding greatly and manufacturers turned to advertising to help sell their products. Business expansion and technological development combined with population growth to open an era of increased marketing of more and more quantities and kinds of goods.

This was also the era of great growth in magazines and a greater dependence on advertising income for magazines. New postal rates were helpful to periodicals and increased leisure time helped to increase potential audiences. Women readers became a powerful force. Shelter magazines devoted to home and garden were immediately successful and many continued to be successful well into the 1990s. Fashion magazines prospered. This was the period in which magazines were founded that had long lives. Examples include *Ladies Home Journal, Cosmopolitan, McCall's, Good Housekeeping, Redbook* and *Better Homes and Gardens.* Magazine publishers were now beginning to ensure that advertising revenue would pay for more of the cost of production and readers would pay for less of its actual cost to the publisher than before. This emphasis on the role of advertising increased the publisher's profits while dropping the price paid by the reader.

Much of the modern advertising techniques were founded in the innovations of the 1920s. Research into the effectiveness of persuasive messages, over the air or in print, was stimulated by the advent of radio as a new advertising medium. Art directors were becoming major voices in the agency's decision-making. Among the copywriters, slogan-makers were coming up with memorable identifiers for products. Earning a reputation for copywriting that would endure was Albert Lasker, who would dominate the advertising industry for 50 years. Lasker would become president of the Lord & Thomas agency, which would play a significant role in the push toward national advertising. It was Lasker who strove to convince clients of the need to establish national brand recognition. Lasker was a pioneer in developing fully sponsored radio broadcasts to put his clients' brand names before national audiences.

Coming to the fore in the 1930s were agencies that would continue to be major players in the industry for decades. They included Ted Bates, Leo Burnett, Benton & Bowles, and McCann-Erickson, among others. They joined long-established agencies that shared in the advertising renaissance of the 1920s. These included among others D'Arcy, Campbell-Ewald, J. Walter Thompson, N.W. Ayer, and George P. Rowell. Lasker's Lord & Thomas, founded in 1898, became Foote, Cone and Belding in 1943. Lasker retired from the agency in 1942 but was said to still have considerable influence until 1952.

By the 1950s, television advertising was already firmly established but only for a few major sponsors until the late '50s. DuPont, Alcoa, Lifebouy soap, and General Electric, along with hair care products and detergents, were underwriting the early television programs. By the end of the decade there were 40 million viewers, with advertisers spending nearly $2 billion trying to reach them. That was about one-third of the money spent with advertising media. Television ratings began in 1948 and were taken over by A.C. Nielsen in 1950. Research was initiated, much like the earlier radio studies, to measure the effectiveness of television commercials.

By the 1970s, intensive competition among agencies, creation of new firms, and several consolidations resulted in a period of change. In the 1980s, television viewers were surprised to see commercials that included disparagement of the competitor's product. This comparative advertising was placed in all media, but most heavily in television. There were companies that tried to use the Federal Trade Commission and the courts to challenge those who had criticized their products, but the rulings held consistently that product comparison in advertising was encouraged as long as there were no outright lies and no deception.

The Theory of Advertising

Advertising does serve to inform people, but it is designed to persuade in virtually every instance. Advertisers are persuaders. Their messages are intended to benefit the manufacturer, distributor, or retailer of the products, goods or services promoted in the advertisements. The advertiser is seeking an effect through a carefully coordinated program of specific communications placed in specific media according to a plan. Such planning is dependent upon social science theory. A theory is a set of principles, based on experience and research, that helps to explain reality and predict with some degree of accuracy.

Mass-mediated communication is a complex process. Advertisers start by identifying the important parts of the process. Theorists usually offer the following as the components one must understand to be effective in preparing messages for mass dissemination: source, message, channel, receiver and effect.

Complex though it may be, it is mass communication that most often is most cost efficient for the advertiser. It is not an effective technique for sellers to pay for advertising that does not generate high volume. Using the mass media, one can reach large audiences, but the size and complexity of such communication requires an understanding of the conditions operating that make for success or failure in achieving persuasion. Theory is the starting point.

Theorists tell us that accuracy and reliability in mass communication are dependent upon first the source or communicator, the one sending the message. Second, is a dependence on the message itself and any interference or environmental factors affecting it or its content. Third, is the medium or channel, in other words, the way the message is sent and received, as well as any internal or external forces affecting the transmission or reception. Fourth, is the receiver or audience, those for whom the message is intended. The one part of this theoretical process that the advertiser cannot control is the audience, although the environment in which the message is received can be controlled.

The "Source" in Advertising

The advertiser begins with the strong hope that the source or communicator is credible. A politician, a bureaucrat, a lawyer, or a used car salesman may have a different credibility than a minister or a researcher who cures a terrible disease. Research is available to advertisers demonstrating that source credibility is important in achieving attitude change, for example. Scholars learn that high credibility sources produce more attitude change. Sources are perceived as credible when people believe them to be trustworthy, dynamic, open-minded, knowledgeable and physically attractive.

The "Message" in Advertising

The message often is successful if it appeals to emotions, although other aspects are determinants of the message's effect as well. The message must be clear. Brevity can be an aid to clarity as can the readability of printed material. Readability is largely determined by sentence length and average length of the words used.

Messages can be made more persuasive by the strategy used in preparing and delivering the argument or arguments that an advertiser is trying to present. A one-sided message containing only the side promoting the product or service does not run the risk of putting into the receivers' minds some counter argument that might not otherwise have occurred to them. But such a strategy could backfire and be thought of as unfair if it omits opposing arguments that consumers are already aware of. A two-sided message could overcome this by presenting the sponsor's arguments along with contentions supporting opposing products, goods or services. This strategy could be perceived as fair. One-sided presentations of advertising messages tend to work best for audiences already sympathetic to what is being presented. Two-sided messages are more likely to work when the audience is pre-disposed to be against the proposal or at least not initially supportive of what's being presented.

The "Channel" in Advertising

The channel or conduit through which messages travel can be approached by advertisers as a tool for persuasion. Marshall McLuhan's often-expressed contention that there are hot media and cool media was embraced by many public relations and advertising people as a key to success in persuasion. Simply, their approach was to put hot messages on a hot medium and cool messages on a cool medium. An example of a hot message would be a lengthy, detailed list of figures or prices on several items or products in one advertisement. It would be considered hot in McLuhan terminology, because it would contain a great deal of information and would require little effort on the part of the audience to capture because it would be so clear and extensive in its presentation (item and price advertising). An advertisement, for example, outlining previous home loan rates compared with newer rates and the several advantages to one index over another for the varying price levels of homes in different neighborhoods would be best suited to a hot medium, like a newspaper. To McLuhan, print was hot and television was cool. An advertisement designed to create a feeling, a warm regard, for a company or its product (image advertising) with little content in it, but a lot of emotional pull through working on the senses is supposed to be best on television. The assumption here is that the medium or channel itself is a communicative factor and can be used advantageously by the advertiser. Persuasion can be dependent upon the value of the medium itself to the communication process.

In addition, each medium can appeal to a different type of audience, an audience often demographically identifiable. Newspapers and magazines are often used by people with more education than most and with a generally higher income. Radio reaches the young, the more mobile audience. Television reaches the mass audience more than print. Television audiences cut across age, sex, education level, and income level, but radio audiences are more narrowly separated, more specialized according to music or programming preferences. Magazines, too, appeal to people with narrow, specialized interests.

Print media require literate audiences, at least more so than broadcasting or cable. Advertisers conveying messages that need a lot of copy, a lot of words, are suited for print. Radio messages are processed through the ear and television is a sight and sound medium. Neither requires much literacy skill. Radio and television carry persuasive materials that are processed through much less effort than reading requires.

The "Audience" in Advertising

Conflicting theories abound on the audience's influence on the process of communication, certainly on the persuasive part of the process. There have been suggestions that the media can exercise great influence, because audiences are made up of many isolated individuals, each one highly vulnerable to persuasive appeals. Others have proposed that the members of the mass audience are not all that isolated, but instead tend to congregate in many groups of varying sizes and complexity. As a result, group norms tend to soften the impact of mass-mediated messages.

Social psychologists point to selective exposure as another moderating influence on the power of an advertiser's appeal. An individual or group decision about how much time or attention to give a medium obviously has an impact on how much, if any, of an advertiser's message is received.

Selective retention plays a role, too. It is the inability of members of the audience to remember much of what has been processed. If there is little motivation to process completely a message, or even parts of it, there is minimal engagement of listeners, viewers and readers to the message. Many advertisers seek gimmicks and clever, colorful slogans to establish an identity that is likely to be remembered.

Another concern is that human beings are limited in observational capacity by the influence of family background, educational attainment, class, age, sex, personal relationships and other socio-economic factors. Our attitudes, interests and values alter the way we perceive signals from our environment. Audience members, as a result, practice selective perception. They resist salesmanship and occasionally attend to messages other than the intended ones.

"Effects" of Advertising

If no effect has been achieved, the advertiser has failed to communicate effectively. If the wrong effect results, that too is a failure. One desired effect, of course, is attention to the message. To be ignored or unnoticed by the audience prohibits the attainment of other desired effects. The next necessary effect is to be understood. The message must be comprehended in the manner intended by the advertiser. If there is comprehension, the hope is that members of the audience then learn something. Once there is knowledge of the product or service, it is small step to acknowledging the relationship of what is learned to a need or want in the audience member. Advertising information learned by consumers is an advantage to the communicator because the message can then be accepted and remembered.

The next level in the hierarchy of effects is attitude change, an area in which much of the early research about mass communications was conducted. Early studies tended to reveal that persuasive messages had little effect on changing consumers' attitudes. It is easier to reinforce existing attitudes because audiences tend to ignore any information that is inconsistent with pre-existing beliefs. Advertisers, however, can achieve success in persuading people whose beliefs and attitudes are not very strongly held.

Once attitude change is achieved, even if not easily accomplished, the highest level of intended effects is behavior modification. If the attitude can be directed toward the sponsor's goal, so too can the behavior. Advertising is often aimed at changing buying and voting behavior. Persuasive messages ask us to get up from our easy chairs and do something. More generally, the ubiquity of advertising messages can guide our behavior in dealing with each other and with society's expectations. We get information from the media that directs our behavior in situations similar to what we have seen depicted in newspaper, magazine, radio and television advertisements.

A major problem for advertisers is the difficulty in measuring effects of mass media messages. A significant increase in sales of a product during an advertising campaign may be attributable to many causes. A simple, direct, stimulus-response relationship cannot always be assumed. Media effects generally are difficult to measure, primarily because it is so difficult to hold all of the other variables constant. For an advertising campaign where the desired effect is quite specific and the message carefully directed, such measurement is easier than for other behaviors. Human behavior is quite complex and media are rarely, if ever, the sole, direct cause of an action. Generally, media messages impact on people among a nexus of other factors: home, family, church, educators, political orientation, personality, lifestyle, etc.

The advertising industry overcomes this by using research on which characteristics of advertising are most persuasive for different types of potential consumers of various products. Research is also conducted to determine audience characteristics. This research can lead to targeting sub-audiences on demographic factors at the right time with the right medium. Content can be tailored to meet the needs and wants of consumers identified by age, sex, education, income and interests. The advertising can be supplemented by marketing and promotion techniques, such as new packaging, in-store displays, coupons, refunds, etc.

Advertising Strategies

Planning and strategy start with advertising research. The advertising industry seeks knowledge of what consumers want and how to present their products to potential buyers. Research is also concerned with how to get audiences to buy. Such research is often directed at the barriers that prevent consumers from buying at all or buying more often. Much of the research effort is directed at finding out what type of advertising has worked in the past and why such strategies and techniques were successful. The hope, of course, is that what worked in the past will work again.

Research is limited if studies do not first identify the potential buyers. Once the potential market is identified, researchers try to learn the characteristics of the consumers in that segment of the population. They can be classified demographically, thus establishing the age, sex, income, education, etc., as well as interests and attitudes. This information allows advertisers to target their messages more appropriately.

Tests of visual efficiency are used to see how long a person must attend to an advertisement in order for the product to be recognized later. This also helps to determine how well certain advertisements compete against others for the attention of the listener, viewer or reader.

Other physiological studies of potential consumers are used as well. There are measurements of the effects on the pupil of the eye when exposed to advertisements. There are galvanic skin tests that measure emotional arousal to the sights and sounds associated with an advertisement. Researchers do comprehension and reaction tests to determine whether a message is understood and whether the effect is indifferent or negative.

After a campaign has ended, researchers often step in to find out what should be changed, if anything, on future campaigns. Of course, sales of the product would be an initial indication, but studies are often conducted into association of a slogan with the product or a celebrity endorsement, or which medium was recalled most frequently in regard to the product.

Planning follows research. A series of steps will be planned that are expected to accomplish a specific objective. The first step is to identify the product and analyze what opportunities it presents. This means the campaign starts with preparing to explain the qualities of the product to the consumers you expect would have a need for it. You look for possible emotional appeals the product might offer. This naturally leads to an analysis of the market for the product. You determine who would want the product and why. An objective must be part of the overall planning. The well-developed advertising campaign has aims and goals. An objective creates a framework for decision making and provides a potential for measurement of how close to the goal you come when evaluating the campaign after it has ended.

Advertisers usually think of direct-action objectives as their aims or goals. Direct-action objectives are more easily measured in terms of results. The aim is for sales to go up, or the goal is to get more people to try the product for the first time. Sometimes they come up with indirect-action objectives. These are more concerned with overall communication, with creating awareness or image. Typically, there is no immediate effect attributed to such advertisements.

Typical objectives include getting people to try the product, getting current customers to increase their usage, maintaining product awareness, and changing buying habits. Increasing awareness and increasing sales are common objectives.

Once an objective is determined, the program must be budgeted. Once the budget is set, you can start planning which medium or media to use and how much advertising to place with each. You can estimate the number of people who will be exposed to the campaign. That gives you an opportunity to calculate the cost per thousand. That is the cost of the advertisement divided by the number of thousands of people reached. If an advertisement costs the sponsor $200 and reaches 50,000 people, the cost per thousand (CPM) is $4.00.

Budget and strategy are strongly related. Given a budget, you can determine what media you want to use and how to employ them. Strategy choices start with determining whether to indulge the total market or to go for a market segment. You can create an advertising campaign to sell a product as a mass commodity item or you can position the product instead to a clearly defined portion or sub group. Some cigarette advertisements appeal to smokers generally, but the Marlboro man creates an identity with the male target market and Virginia Slims advertisements do not try to appeal to all smokers.

Another strategy choice is between primary demand and selective demand. This choice is for selling the brand not the generic product. The level of awareness of the product in the marketplace will determine this. When a product is new, primary demand is the strategy used to build a level of awareness. The first advertisements for computer software had to work on primary demand, but eventually were able to shift to individual brand awareness. Selective demand is the strategy employed when the market has become sufficiently competitive that consumers are well aware of the merits of the product generally. Coca-Cola's "It's the real thing" campaign is a good example of the selective demand strategy.

Once the media are selected, the advertisements are created with media, message, strategy and target market in mind. Good copywriting, good presentations and good productions become the foundation of the developed advertising campaign.

The copywriter must decide what to say by determining what will sell the product and how it will be viewed by potential customers. No matter how great the message, if the customer pays no attention to it, it will not be effective. The advertising copy must first get attention and then quickly create interest. After that, the body of the copy can stimulate the desire for the product. The copywriter strives to be understood by using familiar words that are known to the target market. The copywriter's job is to come up with creative problem-solving messages that match what the advertiser believes to be the desires and needs of the target audience.

Good presentation of a well-written advertisement is an absolute necessity. The art director's job is to develop the actual layout of the advertisement and the art used in it. The layout, the appearance or design of the presentation, involves arranging the copy, the size of the illustrations, and the use of color. It is the visual effect of the advertisement that is the key element in the image of the product.

Art is a broad area of concern in advertising. Art can be photographs, computer-generated images or drawings. Art can show the product in use or it can show product features or effects. Art can also show the personality of the product. Photographs can be effective; but often cartoons, images, drawings and diagrams can add some fantasy to the presentation. Color in the art can improve realism and aid in image building, because different colors bring out different emotions for many targeted markets.

Advertising production is the physical creation of the print advertisement or broadcast commercial. Production expenses can be a great problem, but a problem that can be solved in the planning of the campaign. Production requirements must be kept in line with need and budget. Production costs can be excessive, especially in color production and photoengraving in print or animation and location shooting for television. If the advertiser fails to determine in advance the cost effectiveness of production techniques available, a disaster could result for a tight advertising budget.

A remarkably cost-effective means of advertising is "word-of-mouth," or "creating a buzz" advertising. This oldest form of advertising is enjoying a rebirth thanks to the power of the Internet. Companies hire firms to spread the good word about movies, CDs, beauty products, books and concerts. Two of the early leaders in this area were Electric Artists and M80 Interactive Marketing. Such firms hire people, mostly young people, to go online using chat rooms and web pages to promote the activities of their clients. Normally, e-mail trees are used, too. These trees are similar to chain letters and result in the amazingly fast spreading of information. Marketers say they like the new, electronic, word-of-mouth advertising because it is a way to break through the clutter of regular advertising and grab consumer attention and increase brand awareness. Quite often, "swag" is used to cover the cost of hiring young people to get out the good word. Swag is promotional items, including t-shirts, hats, CDs, posters and concert tickets. So, not only is it rather cheap to get a lot of good word-of-mouth advertising, the employees become walking advertising billboards, because they are paid with materials that quite often serve as additional forms of advertising. Such a deal, at least for the promoters, marketers and advertisers.

Most marketers agree that word-of-mouth advertising is more powerful than all other forms of advertising and the efforts of salespeople put together, perhaps as much as 1,000 times more powerful. That is probably especially true for today's young people. Most of the new generation are pretty much immune to conventional advertisements and sales techniques. They see and hear so many commercial plugs and ploys that such efforts are lost on them. But hearing something from a friend or another young person can make a difference. As a result, "buzz" creation and spreading are big in the worlds of advertising and marketing.

The Advertising Industry

The list of advertising media include: newspapers, magazines, radio, television, cable, direct mail, outdoor, theater, online, directory, specialty, transit and point-of-purchase.

Each medium has strong points and weak points. Often a medium is selected because of its appeal to a target audience or because it provides a low cost-per-thousand. A major factor in making a media selection decision is "coverage" or "reach." The advertiser wants to know the circulation figures for a newspaper, the ratings for a radio or television station, or the demographic profile of the targeted readers for a magazine. An outdoor campaign is effective only if the billboards selected are placed at strategic locations guaranteeing a large number of viewers.

Direct-mail advertising is used to arouse interest and to aid customers in their buying practices. Care must be taken to direct such efforts toward qualified, interested prospects to avoid wasting costly mailing pieces.

Point-of-purchase advertising begins when the customer arrives at the place of business. It is there to influence or reinforce the buying decision in favor of the advertiser. All forms of advertising located at or near the point of sale are thought to promote impulse buying while reinforcing persuasion from other advertising media.

Transit advertising includes advertisements on the top or rear of taxis and airport shuttle vans, the signs on the subway terminal wall or side of a bus and the imprinted cards on the inside of the bus. Magnetic signs stuck to cars, trucks and vans are variations, too.

Your Thoughts

Give TWO examples of products or services advertised in the following media:

1. Outdoor—

2. Theaters—

3. Online—

4. Directories—

5. Specialty—

6. Transit—

7. Point-of-purchase—

Specialty advertising is conducted with calendars, matchbooks, pens, pencils, bags, magnets and a great many other items. The intent is to imprint the advertiser's name or logo on a useful article so that each time it gets used, people will see the advertisement.

There are a great many local or specialized directories that carry advertising, but the one nationwide, best-known directory is the *Yellow Pages*. Telephone books are available to almost everyone and have a great degree of permanence since the typical directory is good for a full year.

Movie theater advertising has a captive, well-defined audience. An advertiser can choose theaters that appeal to a particular target market. Some choose theater advertising in the belief that the size of the movie screen has an impact on an audience.

Advertisers are increasingly taking advantage of the Internet's World Wide Web, a system of organizing information on the Internet. The Web allows for presentations that include video, audio and graphics via computer access. Advertisers display their identities and their products in cyberspace with Web homepages.

Another advertising medium is found in the clothes we wear and the signs and notices on our vehicles. The hats we wear carry the names of construction firms, radio stations, trucking companies, farm equipment manufacturers and sports teams. Designer jeans and designer shirts instantly identify the maker. We also become miniature billboards by the T-shirt and sweatshirts that we wear carrying various advertising messages. Our cars and trucks carry not only the manufacturer's names boldly lettered front and back, but also feature bumper stickers promoting the businesses we have patronized. License plate holders tell the drivers behind us the name of the dealership that sold the car. Even the tires have the brand name in raised letters on the side.

Careers in Advertising

More than 100,000 people work in advertising in the United States. A career in the advertising industry typically means working in an agency, the advertising department of a corporation or with a news or entertainment medium that serves as a conduit for advertising.

Many come into advertising with college majors in mass communication, business administration or marketing. Advertising is a business and must be managed on a sound financial basis. Certainly, some business knowledge is important to a successful career, partly because advertising is a problem-solving process. Business schools stress planning and problem-solving. Marketing experience helps one to understand how best to reach potential customers. Marketing uses researchers to pretest messages and to study ongoing advertising campaigns. Marketing is related to merchandising, which involves direct sales and different types of promotions.

The industry needs people who are good communicators, proficient in writing skills or in art, design, or any form of graphic communication. Skill in persuasion can come from clear and communicative copywriting and from the personality or energy of people who enjoy the practice of salesmanship. These are the advertising professionals who can be expected to convince colleagues of an idea, sell a program to a client, or persuade a dramatist or artist of the need for a certain kind of performance, or convince the media representative of the need to convey the message in that medium and in the desired form.

In addition to those who major in advertising, advertising professionals can come from undergraduate majors in journalism, art, psychology, broadcasting and others. Journalism students study advertising as the economic support base for the media and learn the writing, editing, and production skills needed to create print advertisements and broadcast commercials. Often, art departments on campus will offer several advertising courses because of the layout, design and graphics so important to the imagery in persuasion. Psychology students learn about the science of persuasion, how to appeal to various needs and desires.

With a good background in psychology, one can build advertising campaigns on persuasive appeals that are meaningful, believable and distinctive. Understanding that different factors are important when we buy different products can help greatly in reaching and persuading consumers. Psychologists study consumer behavior. The advertiser can use that research to frame appeals that are effective. For example, the cost of a new suit can be a factor for some customers, but others are quick to associate status with the designer label and are willing to spend more for such status.

Preparing for a career in advertising can be done by learning research methodology, whether in psychology and consumer behavior or in other areas of study that assess forms of human behavior. Market research is helpful in nearly all advertising decisions. Consumer motivation studies might be the starting point, but there are also many other tests of consumer habits and attitudes and of advertising messages and their effects.

Computer science and computer engineering experience can be valuable for the advertising professional. Advertising depends on modern technology for research and production. Computers are crucial to the creation, production, distribution, and financial management of all advertising efforts.

With such diverse background and preparation needed, perhaps a generalist is best prepared for an advertising career. This generalist, however, should have one or two strong specialties and should have an entrepreneurial personality and the ability to manage both people and projects.

Goals of Advertising

The specific goals of advertising include the following:

1. Increasing how often a product or service is used.
2. Increasing the ways a product or service is used.
3. Introducing a new product or service.
4. Establishing/reinforcing the credibility of claims about a product or service.
5. Explaining an apparent disadvantage about a product or service.
6. Clearing up misconceptions about a product, service or business.
7. Improving the image of a product, service or business.

Increasing Use

An example of trying to convince people to use a product or service more often would be a mouthwash manufacturer telling us to use mouthwash at least twice a day—once in the morning for yourself and once in the evening for someone you love. Another example would be a shampoo manufacturer who makes sure we all know that it is important to lather, rinse and repeat.

Increasing Uses

An example of trying to convince people to use a product or service in a different way would be a glass cleaner manufacturer telling us to use the cleaner to clean up smudges, dirt and grease on counters, walls and appliances as well as windows and mirrors. Another example would be the orange growers of America reminding us that orange juice is "not just for breakfast anymore."

Introducing New Products/Services

An example of introducing a new product or service would be a company or individual advertising Internet consulting or Web Page design help. Another example would be ads for never-before available cars, beers, soft drinks and cereals.

Establishing Credibility

An example of establishing credibility would be an aspirin manufacturer providing results from a survey of doctors that shows four out of five doctors recommend aspirin as a pain reliever. Another example would be taste tests and other forms of comparisons between the advertised product or service and its competitors.

Explaining a Disadvantage

An example of attempting to explain or justify an apparent disadvantage of a product or service would be a hair color manufacturer admitting that its product is more expensive that its competitors, but "aren't you worth it?" Another example would be a fast food chain telling us that even though its hamburgers had made people sick a few times in the past, it was now using new, improved methods to cook its hamburgers, so they're now the safest in the country.

Clearing up Misconceptions

An example of clearing up a misconception would be the Idaho Potato Growers Association telling us that potatoes by themselves aren't really fattening. It's the butter, sour cream, cheese and bacon bits that add all the calories. Another example would be a ski resort telling us that skiing is really a fairly safe and inexpensive sport even though it appears to be dangerous and costly.

Improving an Image

An example of improving the image of a product, service or company would be the American Bar Association running ads showing how public-spir-ited and generous attorneys actually are. They're really not shysters and chislers out to make a fast buck. Another example would be an oil company telling us it really cares about protecting the environment despite its image as a defiler of nature's beauty.

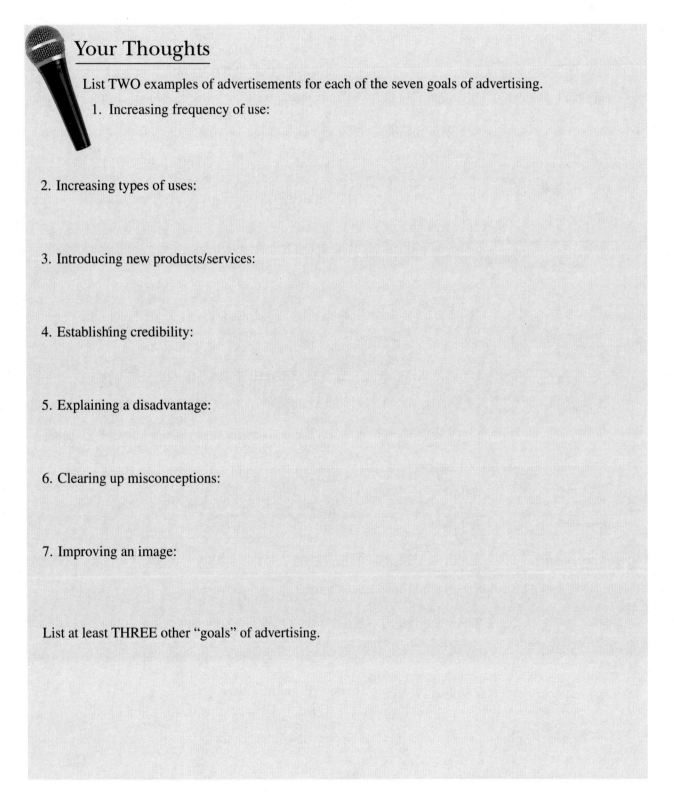

Your Thoughts

List TWO examples of advertisements for each of the seven goals of advertising.

1. Increasing frequency of use:

2. Increasing types of uses:

3. Introducing new products/services:

4. Establishing credibility:

5. Explaining a disadvantage:

6. Clearing up misconceptions:

7. Improving an image:

List at least THREE other "goals" of advertising.

Components of Advertising

Most advertisements have four basic components:

1. The promise of a benefit.
2. A discussion or demonstration of how a product or service works and why it's so much better than its competitors.
3. An effort to support the important claims made about a product or service.
4. Directions to consumers about how to acquire a product or use a service.

Usually, advertisements stress a product's or service's unique selling proposition (USP). In other words, why a product or service is better than and/or different from its competitors or an earlier version of itself. Do the words "new and improved" ring a bell? Such propositions or benefits include quality, performance, price, size, ability to last and quickness of action.

Once the USP has been stressed, advertisements usually deal with showing how well a product or service works and how easy it is to use. Comparisons, statistics and testimonials from satisfied customers or revered celebrities are offered to support important claims. Finally, consumers get specific instructions about what to do—hurry, don't delay, act now, be smart, use it every day, try it for a week, etc.

Approaches in Advertising

A variety of approaches and techniques are used to convince consumers to do whatever it is that advertisers want us to do. Among the most common are:

1. Factual
2. Emotional
3. Comparisons
4. Slogans
5. Spokesperson
6. Slice of life
7. Animation
8. Humor

Factual Approach

The factual approach is basic and direct. It attempts to appeal to the intellect of consumers. Products and services are described and ingredients are mentioned. Sometimes demonstrations are used to show what a product does and how to use it. Interviews with customers can also be used to convince consumers how good a product is.

Emotional Approach

The emotional approach tries to tug at the hearts of consumers. Puppies, babies, kindly grandpas, beautiful sunsets and fun, fun, fun often are used to put a smile on the faces or a tear in the eyes of consumers. Quite often a montage of fun and/or heart-warming activities are put together to show consumers what they're missing by not using the advertised product or service.

Comparisons Approach

The use of comparisons is a common approach. Taste tests, results of performance testing, comparing ingredients and statistical comparisons are used to convince consumers that the advertised product or service tastes better, lasts longer, works faster, has more pain-killing ingredients and is bigger than its competitors.

Slogans Approach

Slogans can be an effective way to get and keep consumers buying an advertised product or service. Often a slogan is put to music, catchy music, and a jingle is born. Both slogans and jingles often get in our heads and it's hard to get them out. We hum and chant our way to the checkout counter with the advertised products in our basket. Don't we all want to buy "The Real Thing?" A company where "Quality is Job One" must be good, right? Who doesn't want to "Be All You Can Be?" Getting that brand name recognition burned into the minds of consumers is an important goal in advertising and slogans and jingles do a good job of that.

Spokesperson Approach

The spokesperson approach can be one of two kinds. Celebrities can extol the virtues of a product or service or "average" people can become spokespeople just from the personas they assume in the advertisements.

Slice of Life Approach

The slice of life approach is a mini-drama or situation comedy. It purports to show a real-life situation in the hope consumers will see themselves in the depiction and be motivated to buy the advertised product or service.

Animation Approach

Using cartoon characters in ads is a popular approach. Traditional animation, computer animation, claymation, puppets and other techniques can be used to depict stunts and situations that would be difficult, if not impossible, for human beings or real animals to do. As a result, many of the animated advertisements are extremely memorable, because they can feature out-of-the-ordinary acts and activities.

Humor Approach

Humor can be a dangerous approach. Sometimes an ad can be so funny that the product or service isn't remembered well. Usually, though, humor is an effective way to begin to build brand recognition. If an advertisement can generate a smile or a laugh, it's a good bet that consumers will likely remember the advertised product or service.

Your Thoughts

List TWO examples of advertisements for each of the eight approaches.

1. Factual:

2. Emotional:

3. Comparisons:

4. Slogans:

5. Spokesperson:

6. Slice-of-life:

7. Animation:

8. Humor:

List FIVE other approaches that you have seen used by advertisers.

Costs of Advertising

A variety of factors affect how much an advertisement costs. In the print media, the size of the ad, the placement of the ad, the number of readers/subscribers that a publication has and the number of times the ad runs are the factors that contribute to setting the "rate" advertisers are charged. In radio and television, the ratings a program has, the length of the commercial, the time of day and the number of times a commercial is aired are the factors used to determine the cost of a commercial or "spot."

Ads in a newspaper might cost as little as $25 and as much as several thousand dollars for a full-page ad. Ads in a magazine might range from several hundred dollars to several thousand dollars. Radio commercials range from $50 to $5,000 or so. Television commercials can cost as little as several hundred dollars to more than two million dollars for a 30-second spot.

Legal Restrictions

Ads, or commercial speech, can be regulated more severely than other forms of speech. The U.S. Supreme Court has ruled that four major factors can be used in the determination of whether commercial speech can be regulated.

1. Is the product illegal or is the ad misleading? If so, regulation is permitted.
2. Does the government have a "substantial interest" in regulating the ad? If it helps society to restrict the ad, regulation is permitted. For example, banning cigarette ads on television might help reduce the number of people who become ill and die from lung cancer.
3. Does the regulation support the government's interest? If the regulation accomplishes what the government wants, regulation is permitted. For example, if banning cigarette ads on television reduces the number of smokers, especially young smokers, the regulation is justified.
4. Is the regulation reasonable? If the regulation is consistently and equitably applied and doesn't go too far or restrict unfairly, regulation is permitted.

Monitoring Advertisements

Many organizations monitor advertising to be sure consumers aren't being misled. The most powerful and influential agency is the Federal Trade Commission. The FTC uses five main factors to judge how truthful and fair an ad is.

1. *Truth and Accuracy.* The claims must be truthful. The product must do what the ad claims it will do. Misleading consumers is not permitted.
2. *Clarity.* The ad must be clear and understandable. Even people with relatively low intelligence must be able to make sense out of the ad.
3. *Opinions vs. Facts.* Facts must be provable. Opinions can be given without proof. A spokesperson or interviewee can claim a product tastes better than a competitor, but if claims are made that a product works faster or lasts longer than a competitor, such claims must be true.
4. *Demonstrations.* If demonstrations are used in an ad, they must be repeatable and the advertised product cannot be manipulated or reinforced. It must be the actual product that consumers can buy off the shelf.
5. *Offensiveness.* Ads should not be in poor taste. They should not sicken or offend consumers.

The FTC can issue a cease and desist order if it judges an advertisement to be misleading. It can also fine a company several thousand dollars for every time a misleading ad is printed or aired.

Ethical Concerns in Advertising

Ethical concerns abound in advertising. Among the most common concerns are:

1. Deception
2. Offensiveness
3. Harmfulness
4. Persuading rather than informing
5. Creating/perpetuating stereotypes

Suggest FIVE things consumers can do to ensure they won't be duped by advertisers.

6. Creating uniformity
7. Creating desires for unnecessary products or services
8. Creating insecurity to sell products or services
9. Distorting the political process
10. Influencing media content

Most people would agree that harming, cheating, lying, bullying and breaking promises are unethical acts. They're simply not right. Obviously, ads that are misleading and deceptive have the real possibility of harming people or cheating them. People might waste hard-earned money and/or be mentally, emotionally or physically injured by misleading, unclear or vague information. Ads that are offensive or in poor taste can be emotionally harmful, too. Of course, ads for products that can be harmful if misused, especially by small children, are problematic. Joe Camel and the Budweiser frogs frequently were criticized for appealing to children. Ads that emphasize persuading more than informing can cheat and mislead consumers.

Creating or perpetuating stereotypes of people, animals, places or things can be harmful to peace and harmony in society. Such actions can inhibit understanding and tolerance. Creating uniformity of thinking and/or action certainly can be harmful to the health and welfare of people and society. Diversity and a respect for different beliefs, attitudes and values are important to ensure that all viewpoints receive a fair hearing in the marketplace of ideas.

Creating desires for unnecessary products or services can lead to violence (the have-nots attempt to take things from the haves) and a general sense of unhappiness and dissatisfaction with life. Creating insecurity to sell products promotes fear, stress and paranoia. Aren't we all afraid to scratch our heads in public? Someone might think we have dandruff. And don't forget the importance of dry underarms, fresh breath and white teeth.

Ads can distort the political process by stressing image over substance and making it possible for elections to be won by the highest and richest bidder. Finally, advertisers can influence media content by placing pressure on writers, editors, publishers, reporters, news announcers, news directors, actors, directors and producers to do or not do something. Advertisers have been known to pull their business from publications or productions that delve into sensitive areas or espouse ideas contrary to those of the advertisers.

Critical Thinking about Advertising

Even though governmental, quasi-governmental and activist groups monitor the wonderful world of advertising reasonably well, illegal and unethical ads still find their way into the mass media on a disturbingly regular basis. Consumers need to develop their own critical thinking and evaluation skills to serve as a last line of defense against such illegal and unethical advertisements. Consumers should take the time to analyze the claims made in ads. What is said, what is not said and how it's said are important considerations. By carefully examining the language and imagery used in advertisements, consumers can cut through the hype and hyperbole and take aim at the truth about products, services and companies.

Among the important things to look and listen for are:

1. Parity claims
2. Definitional wastelands
3. Apples and oranges comparisons
4. Lousy linkages
5. Missing information

Parity Claims

Parity means equal. If a product says "nothing works better" or "nothing lasts longer," what actually is being said? Is the product claiming to be the best? No. It's saying you can't buy anything that's better. Of course, you might be able to buy something else that's just as good for a lot less money, but you'll have to figure that out for yourself. Whenever an advertisement contains strong parity claims, start shopping around. Compare the ingredients, features and price of several competitors. You'll be glad you did.

Definitional Wastelands

Beauty and definitions are in the eyes, minds and hearts of the beholders. How do you define "fast?" If a product promises to provide "fast" relief, what kind of time frame are we talking about? "Fast" to you might be a minute or two. "Fast" to the manufacturer might be 20 minutes. Read labels and check with experts before you buy. And do it "fast."

Another common example of definitional vagueness is when a cereal company shows a picture of a nicely set breakfast table and proudly announces that its cereal is "part" of the displayed nutritional breakfast. Of course, the cereal is PART of the breakfast, but we also see milk, toast, fruit and eggs. How important a "part" is the cereal? Read the nutritional information on the cereal box and decide for yourself BEFORE you buy.

Apples and Oranges Comparisons

You've heard the old saying about comparing apples and oranges, right? It's a technique that involves making an unfair comparison between two things—comparing apples to oranges, get it? Advertisers often use this technique to try to put a positive spin on their product. For example, an ad for an alkaline battery might say "no regular battery looks like it or lasts like it." Sounds like a pretty bold statement, right? But when you analyze what is being said, you discover that when you compare a regular battery with an alkaline battery, the alkaline battery will win every time. It's simply a better battery. The real question is whether the advertised alkaline battery lasts longer than the alkaline batteries of its competitors NOT the regular batteries of its competitors. Tricky, huh?

Lousy Linkages

The old slight of hand trick lives in advertising. It involves linking a relatively desirable quality of a product with a not-so-desirable quality. The hope is that consumers will not be reading, watching or listening very carefully and will get confused about just what is being said. For example, if you hear "Coco Snappies cereal has chocolatey flavor and REAL marshmallows," what actually is being said? The advertiser hopes you'll link REAL marshmallows and "chocolatey" and come up with REAL chocolate, too. Of course, if Coco Snappies had REAL chocolate, don't you think the ad would trumpet that fact? Read, watch and listen carefully.

Missing Information

This technique is sort of the opposite of strong parity claims. Instead of snuggling up to competitors, a product might try to distance itself from its competitors. Not a bad idea, but unfortunately, important information is often left out. For example, an ad for a cleanser might say "E-Z Scrub won't scratch like other cleansers." That's good, right? It's good, but it doesn't mean E-Z Scrub won't scratch at all, does it? It just means E-Z Scrub doesn't scratch as bad as other cleansers. Read, watch and listen between the lines. It will save you grief in the long run.

Effects of Advertising

A one-time popular Honolulu disc jockey had a friend who owned a bakery that produced Portuguese breads and pastries. The disc jockey talked his friend into buying some commercials on his early morning radio show. Not much later the baker telephoned and said, "Lucky! Stop the commercials. I can't handle the new business." Lucky's response was, "Come on Leonard, add more employees. Work harder. Think of the extra money you are making." A few weeks later there was another telephone call with the same complaint. This time the disc jockey suggested getting more ovens and expanding the building. The commercials continued. The telephone calls continued. The bakery eventually expanded until the owner finally had to hire an attendant to direct the traffic through his increasingly larger parking lot.

Advertising works. It can get results, although not always as clearly as in the above examples. The link between an advertising message and the behavior hoped for (usually sales) typically is difficult to determine. Advertising is only one of many variables that can affect behavior.

The family structure, the school system, economic circumstances, the social environment (including peer pressure), religious background and the political structure obviously impinge on behavior. Other factors making it difficult to measure the effects of these persuasive messages include the impact on purchasing behaviors of the packaging of the products, promotion, distribution, the competition, price, and, of course, the product itself. The variety of media and the variety of messages they offer, coupled with the complexity of the needs and wants of a multiplicity of consumers, make it difficult to get easy readings on possible effects of most advertising.

Controversies about the effect of advertising almost invariably focus on broadcast commercials and print media display ads. Direct mail advertising, or junk mail, tends to be more informative, much like classified advertising. Institutional advertising, or industrial advertising, can be a desired communication to a ready audience, much as classified ads tend to offer help to a receptive reader.

Even with newly emerging delivery systems, television advertising continues to receive most of the criticism. Underlying this is the charge that television content generally is not intellectually stimulating, perhaps even deadening to the senses and sensibilities. Because many television programs appeal to the lowest common denominator, the surroundings for persuasive messages are themselves unworthy to those who perceive television viewing as wasteful and mind-numbing. In this context, the commercials are immediately subject to considerable concern. Among the typical charges against television (and cable) advertising are that the messages are simplistic, tasteless, irritating, ubiquitous, and that they perpetuate unfortunate stereotypes.

Advertising is a function of business. Advertising is intended to sell and to persuade. It is dependent on promotion and salesmanship. Some people are not pleased with being exposed to this aspect of business. They find it to be too pervasive, too obtrusive. Billboards, broadcast commercials, skywriting, direct mail, newspaper and magazine advertisements are ever-present. Advertising virtually assaults us from the time the clock radio wakes us through the messages around us all day long until the television set goes off after Letterman or Leno or Conan.

Advertising has changed greatly as a result of the rejection of the old concept of caveat emptor, or "let the buyer beware," a common theme of salesmanship decades ago. Advertising is centuries old. Clay tablets from 4,000 years ago have been unearthed carrying advertising messages. Ancient Egyptians used papyrus to carry sales pitches. In the middle ages, town criers were conveying such announcements. Outdoor advertising and billboards have been around since the Roman Empire. But, concern for the consumer is a relatively new concept.

For most of our history, caveat emptor, "let the buyer beware," was the order of the day. Caveat emptor is a libertarian notion based on the belief that both buyers and sellers should have equal opportunities to make decisions on an equal footing free of government regulation. It is part of the belief that in a free marketplace, both participants should be sufficiently prepared and knowledgeable enough to participate in that marketplace. Caveat emptor assumes that both buyers and sellers can rationally choose from economic alternatives with each bearing the same responsibility and starting with equal awareness of consequences.

Caveat venditor, "let the seller beware," is more at work today. Eventually, it became clear that the marketplace had become overwhelming for one of the participants. The belief now is that the buyer is usually at a disadvantage and cannot hope to have the necessary preparation and acquire the knowledge necessary to make rational decisions about every purchase in an increasingly complex and confusing marketplace of goods and services. At least, there is now an assumption in the marketplace that consumers cannot be expected to be as aware of marketplace factors as those who create and administer the markets. As a result, caveat emptor is no longer the guide. That means controls under law, both statute and commission law, are available to protect the consumer. Specifically, such laws protect the public from fraud, deceit and false or misleading advertising.

Media Portrayals of Advertising and Advertisers

Popular media carry portrayals of advertising as an unethical aspect of business, stereotypically dominated by individuals intent of manipulating consumers. Advertising is viewed as a creation of hucksters who are devoid of ethics, concerned only about the sale of their products and services. The stereotype holds that advertisers make business decisions with little or no regard for ethical or moral considerations, caring only for duping the uncritical buying public.

The influence of advertising is commonly accepted. It can exercise social control and shape popular standards. It not only is credited with social influence but is also believed to dominate American mass media. Advertising is an obtrusive type of communication that calls attention not only to its messages but also to itself. All of us are exposed to advertising. It intervenes in nearly all aspects of our political, cultural, social, economic and recreational activities. Advertising tells us what is in demand and helps to create that demand. Advertising educates public taste while mirroring public taste. Advertising helps us find easily what we need and helps us buy it easily.

Advertising vs. Public Relations, Etc.

Advertising must be distinguished from other forms of communication. There is often confusion about such labels as marketing, promotion, publicity, public relations, sales promotions and advertising.

Advertising is not marketing, nor is it public relations. Marketing is a broad function concerned with determining public needs, developing products to meet those needs, packaging and pricing the products, distributing them, and communicating about them. Public relations establishes a mutually benefi-

cial relationship between organizations and their publics, creating messages that the media carry free of charge because they are disguised as news.

Publicity is just one of the many functions of public relations, one that is often confused with advertising or promotion. Publicity appears in the media, but is not paid for, as advertising is, and often results from the staging of a pseudo event or some promotional effort.

Promotion is the attempt to call favorable attention to a company and its products or services. News conferences announcing a new product, guest appearances by celebrities, grand openings of already opened stores or malls, flag pole sitting, and disc jockeys locking themselves in their studios and playing the same song repetitively are examples of promotions.

Sales promotion includes activities that supplement advertising and personal selling. Sales promotion includes giving out samples in stores and sending samples through direct mail. Sales promotion includes the offer of free coupons, special exhibits set up to display wares at fairs, expositions, or other special events in which exhibitors are invited to participate. An example would be displays or demonstrations set up at a convention of manufacturers by various suppliers to that industry. It would also be demonstrations conducted within a store.

Advertising is impersonal and is bought and paid for by an identified sponsor. It is designed to sell products and services, even ideas. Advertising is a paid, persuasive communication appearing in a mass medium for a specific purpose. The paying sponsor dictates when it will appear on the air and when it will appear in print. Advertisers study their targeted audiences and place their messages where they expect maximum effect for the money expended.

Advertising then must be thought of as part of a marketing framework. Marketing has four parts: product, price, distribution and communication. Advertising is the communications part but it cannot be divorced from the other three.

The Public's Image of Advertising

Public opinion polls have shown the honesty of advertisers to be perceived as just higher than that of used car salesmen! Advertising is often singled out as one of the more unethical areas of business. Some of those who criticize the ethics of advertising are in a subjective area, making judgments based on nebulous values. Others are moderately critical of all forms of salesmanship. Others are offended by advertising's obtrusiveness. Any of us can be concerned about what is deceptive or untruthful in a given advertisement or about the promotion of a product of which we disapprove.

By publicly asking consumers to try their wares, businesses and industries are inviting attacks from the public. Manufacturers and distributors who openly seek public approval through salesmanship are also openly anticipating attacks from those who react with hostility toward advertising. The negativity is partly because some people believe that advertising has the ability to control people against their will. Others contend that advertising appeals to our basic instincts, because its techniques can be highly suggestive of sex or violence. These complainants are appalled at what they consider provocative themes to include nudity, sexism, poor taste and sensationalism.

A grave ethical concern that did not make that list is the complaint that sales staffs of newspapers and broadcast stations influence the news departments. This contention holds that the economic impact of the advertising industry on all of the media, or on a given medium, affects news judgments and alters considerably what the public gets. It is a viewpoint that assumes that the public is hurt by advertiser influence on the content of newspapers and other information conveyors.

Another attack comes from those who believe that television and radio commercials, in particular, are debasing the political process and causing political parties to stress the personalities of their candidates while ignoring the issues. We hear the candidates are packaged and sold to voters much like soap or detergent is marketed. Some Americans are offended by the huge dollar amounts that are expended on the advertising in political campaigns.

Those who complain that advertising slogans make life tough for teachers of grammar should probably worry more about the lyrics in popular music or text-messaging. The so-called purity of the language is threatened enough by daily usage and the assimilation of new cultures into society, without having to worry excessively over the colorful casualness of ad copy. It might be too informal, too breezy and not structured enough for some, but that does not make it improper.

Other criticisms, however, deserve more of our attention. Advertisements for beer featuring prominent athletes and stressing health and fitness are aimed at young audiences when there is evidence that teenage alcoholism is on the rise. Hard liquor manufacturers have decided to end a 60-year ban on advertising their products on radio and television in hopes of attracting more drinkers.

Tobacco products are advertised also in messages aimed at youths attempting to get them hooked on nicotine early. Tobacco products have been cited as a primary cause of death for many Americans. Only in broadcasting do we find a ban on such advertisements. In 1967, Congress amended the 1934 Communications Act to allow the government to forbid advertising cigarettes on radio and television. The rationale behind the ban is that it is not in the public interest for broadcast licensees to promote death. Broadcasters have an obligation to the public interest because the airwaves belong to the people. The license holder has a temporary and conditional permit to transmit signals through the public property and consequently must respect the public's rights. One of these rights could be the opportunity to avoid dangers to public health.

Many tobacco firms have not only continued their print media and billboard advertising, but also have chosen to sponsor major events that get news coverage in both broadcast and print. The hope is that a sponsor's banners and logos will be seen by millions and/or reporters will include the sponsor's name and perhaps even mention a sponsor's products in connection with news coverage. As a result, indirectly, cigarette advertising appears on radio and television. When an auto race, a tennis tournament, or another tobacco industry supported event is aired, quite often banners and logos and even sponsorship identification are prominently featured in the coverage.

There are those who question whether advertising is an appropriate forum for messages about condoms, feminine hygiene products and body-part surgery. Many broadcast stations refuse to accept commercials for hemorrhoid suppositories. To some, these are sensitive areas better left to doctor-patient discussions, family conferences, or other avenues for serious, helpful treatment of such topics. Their contention could well be that some people are offended by a public display through advertising that is not sufficiently targeted. In other words, if you do not want to be confronted by these topics in a media setting there is nothing you can do about it.

Related to this is sexual suggestiveness in some messages, as well as advertisements for sexually-oriented products and services. Should massage parlors be allowed to advertise when some of them might be fronts for prostitution? What about dating services? Should they have to prove they are legitimate before their advertisements are accepted?

Some newspapers have refused to accept motion picture theater advertisements when the film is rated R or NC-17, primarily when it is NC-17. Newspapers have adopted policies on such movie ads, usually related to the graphic imagery of the near nudity or revealing nature of the ad's artwork or the tone or specific wording of the copy.

Calvin Klein Ads

In 1995, an uproar resulted from print ads, largely outdoor advertising and magazines, for Calvin Klein underwear. Youth-oriented underwear ads featured young-looking, presumably teenaged models in what many considered sexually suggestive postures. There were complaints that the copy contained sexually-charged wording hinting at adult seduction of teenagers, even homosexual seduction. In the midst of the criticism, Calvin Klein himself even tried to apologize and explain away the ads as not meant to be as sexual as many perceived them. Klein said they were, after all, underwear ads, not dress suits or other outerwear. Despite Klein's disclaimer, critics called them child pornography, apparently because of the youthful appearance of the models.

Part of the expressed concern was the way a magazine advertisement was done in a center fold-out pictorial similar to those in such publications as *Penthouse, Hustler* and *Playboy*. The blatant sexual nature of the ad coupled with the centerfold format gave the appearance of an attempt to turn adolescents into sexual objects. Sex sells and ads selling sexual images of children resulted in a sudden increase in sales of Calvin Klein jeans. Not to be forgotten is the millions of dollars worth of free publicity that Calvin Klein got in the wake of the news coverage of the public outcry over what many thought was sleazy advertising. Klein did pull the ads after Christian groups protested, but not before the free publicity had generated increased sales.

Ads Aimed at Children

Advertising directed to children draws passionate responses from individuals and organizations. The PTA has directed criticism toward the television networks in particular and has galvanized mothers into teams of monitors of both programs and commercials aimed at youngsters. At one time, it was comic books that were caught in a maelstrom of criticism for their violent-prone story lines, dark themes, and overly violent or sexual drawings. Comic books still get their fair share of criticism, of course, but it is Saturday morning television cartoon shows and their commercials that get most of the heat these days.

One contention is that it is inherently wrong to direct advertising to children. They are too young, too unsophisticated, too malleable, incapable of comprehending or evaluating enticing messages. It can be argued that perhaps it is simply unfair. Proposals to ban or limit television commercials aimed at youngsters, particularly under the age of eight, have been proposed to the Federal Trade Commission, but the FTC has rejected each, instead concentrating on instances of allegations of deception in such commercials.

Complaints result when war toys or weapons are advertised. Some argue that children's values are altered by persuasive messages about products that the complainers contend are harmful. They cite action figures of kickboxers, martial arts stars, super heroes, beastly villains, and the like. In particular, commercials related to violent video games are singled out as representative of inappropriate lessons for kids.

Also singled out are products that are lacking in nutrition or actually contribute to health problems, particularly sugary substances that cause tooth decay and contribute to obesity. Messages that promote consumption of cereals that are primarily made up of sweeteners are called undesirable because the critics consider the products undesirable. Just as undesirable to them as pre-sweetened cereals are the multitude of candy and candy-like products, also primarily because of the potential dental health risks and weight gain. Candy, sugary soft drinks, chewing gum, and other non-nutritious snacks are advertised heavily in youth-oriented magazines and on television, perhaps most frequently on Saturday mornings. Parents are quick to argue that such advertising has an impact on their children and that toy store operators could no doubt attest to increased demand for products advertised in the children's television shows.

Those who support the advertisers right to present their messages and those who believe the individual, adult or child, does not need special protection in a free marketplace can argue that it is up to the parents to help their youngsters to make wise choices, whether from advertised opportunities or from any other decision-making opportunities. Many of these children are dependent upon their parents for the money needed to act on these choices. Isn't that the time for firm parental guidance, for proper handling of the lessons about health, nutrition, aggression, hostility, proper play, and attitudes toward others? Remember, even for children, the effects of advertisements are difficult to measure because of all the variables that influence an individual's consumer behavior.

Deceptive Advertisements

A cigarette was once advertised as it "tastes better." One smoker's reaction was, "Yeah, better than rope." The writer of the slogan would argue with justification that it was vague enough not to be deceptive. Many critics of advertising, or of the tobacco industry, could argue with justification that it is misleading. The crux of this problem is that there is justification for each side on every controversial advertisement when that controversy is generated by charges of deceptive images, deceptive wording, or a resulting deceptive impression about the product or service. To some, such ads may be only innocent exaggerations, or harmless puffery, or perhaps statements of opinion with understandably expressed superlatives. Others might contend that con-

sumers must expect persuasion from a seller and should, with no difficulty, sift through clearly expected grandiose claims as a matter of course.

It comes down to the fact that it is very difficult to pin down the truth in these messages. It would be incredibly rare to find a statement in a broadcast commercial or print advertisement that is clearly true or clearly false. Instead, it is nearly impossible to think of such statements as anything but ambiguous. They are designed to be that way, yet those receiving these assertions and implications often see them in clear terms. They say they feel cheated, that they have been lied to. Are they simply gullible or are the copywriters ingenious? Is truth a personal matter? Is deception a subjective response? Is the consumer capable of deciphering the ambiguities and managing to avoid any attempt to deceive or bamboozle? Is it fair to use the word deceit?

There are some practices that have been determined to be deceptive. The most notorious has been the so-called "bait and switch" tactic. This is when a product has been advertised at a rather low price, but when inquiring at the retail outlet, the buyer is told the item has already sold out. Of course, there is a quick offer to sell a higher-priced substitute for it! The inferior advertised product, if it ever existed, was intended to draw customers in so that they could be switched to the product that was intended for them all along.

Another established instance of clear deception is when an advertiser makes a false promise, similar to the old-time patent medicine huckstering that some snake oil could cure anything. A contemporary example could be a promise that a product advertised would actually cure someone with AIDS, or at least stop the spread of the HIV virus.

The difficulty in defining truth, dishonesty and deception is a major problem for anyone claiming to propose a means to elevate the ethics of the advertising industry. There are some general guidelines that seemed to work for the courts, federal and state regulators and advertising practitioners.

A misrepresentation of fact is considered deception, but a statement may also be deceptive even if it is not technically construed to be a misrepresentation. In fact, it is necessary only to establish the tendency to deceive, not actual deception itself. Substantial test data are needed to support product performance claims, and there must be a "reasonable basis" for making product performance claims.

Some critics accuse advertising of unfairly stereotyping minorities and women, especially women. The contention is that the role of women in society has changed but detergent commercials, among other examples cited, still perpetuate a menial status as housekeeper or homemaker. It may be true that many women, and perhaps some men, choose the homemaker role, but women's rights groups and others charge that the advertisements do not indicate the choices available to women. The argument is that perpetuating 19th century stereotypes keeps women from being recognized in a variety of 21st century roles.

The most universal concern might be that advertising tends to make us buy what we do not really need. This contention seems to be based on the assumption that we do not need much more than basic necessities. A minimalist can easily get through life on a bicycle instead of driving a gas guzzler and can presumably be happy at a formica-topped dinner table instead of enjoying cloth napkins, fine china, and an aged wine. Was it advertising that prompted the gourmet, the oenephile, the sports-car enthusiast, and the first-class airline passenger? Is it possible the demand was created by advertising? Is it possible that wants or demands were there first and advertisers rushed to meet them? Does it matter?

Conspicuous Consumption

Our landfills are spilling over. We are running out of places to put our trash. Do we shoot it into space? Do we bury it at the bottom of the ocean? Is it advertising that directs an economy that seems to create more waste than anything else? Thorsten Veblen's conspicuous consumption has become over-consumption, but is that a function of a multiplicity of social and economic changes, of what we define as progress or of rampant consumer behavior based on wants rather than needs. An individual's values can be expressed in the accumulation of purchases, values that are shaped by, among other things, societal values.

A society can place undue importance on consumption of material goods and an individual can place undue importance on physical appearance or a perception of how one is esteemed by peers. Critics of advertising often contend that such priorities are generated by big businesses trying to promote an expanding economy. The more money spent on advertised products and services, the more profits for the firms that benefit from the expanding economy. The contention is that wants are first created by advertising. The more we want, the more we buy. The more we buy, the greater economic growth. That results in a need for the advertisers to create more for us to want so we will continue to buy. Again, there are others who express the minimalist belief that there is quality of life in simpler pursuits, that we are, in effect, victimized by advertisers leading us into wants and desires that if not harmful, are at least not necessary.

Perhaps it is better to describe the consumer as deserving a certain standard of living rather than seeking something called quality of life. The concept of a standard of living indicates something at least closer to needs than simply wants, even if it can be argued that a standard of living can be defined by what advertisements tell us is needed!

Because giant, established firms have the resources to initiate and maintain very expensive campaigns, advertising might be thought of as a significant contribution to a monopoly. Smaller businesses cannot compete in the advertising arena with the conglomerates that can well afford to control the market through saturation of advertising messages. The smaller firms can be squeezed out. If the situation does not create an absolute monopoly, it might at least be discouraging competition much as any true monopoly might.

Strangely, we do not seem to hear much about the fact that most advertising is aimed at getting us to make choices between and among essentially similar products. We choose from among items that differ in only minor ways. The cost to the consumer of each includes the advertising expense, of course. So much of the advertising that surrounds us is really about product differentiation when there is essentially little or no difference. The result is a need for what might be called excessive advertising, an expensive advertising because of the need to repeat time and again competing claims when there is no real basis for competition. The messages then concentrate on meaningless phrases like "new and improved," or on irrelevant factors like the color or shape of the package. Chief among these factors contributing to increased advertising expenditures and higher costs to the consumer is the perceived need for brand recognition. If you have nothing unique to distinguish you from your competitors, you must stress the reputation that your brand name acquires. The advertiser wants consumers to recognize and value the brand name over all other possible distinctions. Advertisements are successful if they build a reservoir of good feeling and confidence in a brand. The idea is to make the buyer think only of that brand and to maintain a loyalty to it. That takes a lot of repetitive advertising. Of all the efforts at product differentiation, making the brand name distinctive and desirable is what works best. Of course, ultimately, it is consumers who must pay the costs for all of that advertising.

Competition in Advertising

Critics of advertising might be missing the point. Maybe the most severe criticism that can be made is that advertising, despite its ubiquitousness, is not very effective at all. The system negates itself. With counter advertising and advertisements aimed at pushing brand preference, many claims cancel each other out and make it more difficult for each advertiser. Shoppers, because of economic hard times, are often using price not brand name advertising as a determinant. Listeners are punching the buttons on their car radios and tuning out a set of six to eight minutes of commercials when it starts. Of course, they punch the button again when the next station begins its long run of uninterrupted commercials.

Television viewers use the mute on their remote selector or get up from the set and take a break until the string of commercials ends. Perhaps more attention would be paid to the sales messages if there were fewer of them to compete with each other. Perhaps the large amount of advertising and the billions of dollars spent on all of it drives up the cost of products or services to the point where advertising actually decreases what consumers can afford to buy.

Individual media attempt to control their advertising content, usually with in-house codes that spell out standards of acceptable and unacceptable advertising practices. There are also codes of conduct for media trade associations, including the Newspaper Association of America and the National Association of Broadcasters. In addition, the major networks have broadcast standards departments that often ask for substantiation of advertisers' claims before commercials can be aired. The broadcast standards can result in forcing advertisers to change originally submitted copy or visual matter before the networks will allow it to be aired.

Regulation of Advertising

The code of the National Association of Broadcasters was a major force from 1952 to 1982. The code lost some of its provisions when a court ruled that parts of it were in violation of anti-trust laws. No longer could the NAB tell radio and television stations that they were limited in the amount of time they could give to commercials, for example. The 1980s was a period when the Federal Communications Commission was reducing its regulatory power over stations and part of that effort resulted in the virtual elimination of rules limiting the number of commercials permitted each hour.

The advertisers themselves practice a form of self-regulation, described as voluntary and dependent upon management's sense of social responsibility. Many industries say they run the output of their advertising department through the legal department before it goes out. Individual advertisers and representatives of the advertising industry say they need self-regulation to forestall government regulation and to ensure consumer confidence. Critics say such voluntary efforts are largely designed to build goodwill and are really public relations gestures, which quickly make the industry-wide rules and standards, in particular, generally ineffective.

Professor Joel Davis of San Diego State University has studied the role of ethics in advertising decision-making and found that the stereotypical view is that advertisers are devoid of ethics and are uncaring about anything except manipulating the consumer. He adds that there is a near absence of empirical data to support or reject such a stereotype.

The research project was designed to determine to what extent advertising professionals incorporate ethical considerations into their decisions.

The study started with four factors that might influence advertising decision-making: legal, business, peers/others, and ethics. Those four specific considerations were responded to by 206 randomly selected advertising professionals from a variety of agencies. The largest number of those surveyed, almost 40%, said their decisions were primarily influenced by what is legal. A small proportion, only 28%, said ethics was a major factor in decision-making. Relatively few, 15%, said the impact on the agency's business was a major factor. The opinions of peers turned out to be almost non-existent in the determination of these agency professionals.

Those most influenced by ethical considerations were the oldest respondents with the most professional experience, while those influenced by legal considerations were the youngest and least experienced. Another finding was that not only was ethics a primary consideration for relatively few practitioners, but also ethics was not a significant secondary consideration for those primarily influenced by legal or business concerns.

Advertising must have the confidence of potential buyers if it is to work effectively, so it would not be too difficult to get agreement from all parties—critics, consumers, businesses—that advertising should not be dishonest. At issue is whether that can be enforced. Beyond the ethical strictures of voluntary self-regulation are the efforts of government, both state and federal.

A 1911 proposal by a magazine formerly published for advertisers was adapted eventually by several states as a reasonable set of rules for assuring truth in advertising. These state laws, called Printers Ink statutes, did not deal with interstate advertising. *Printers Ink* magazine had called its proposal a model Truth in Advertising law. This statute or variations of it became law in most states. It is difficult, however, to enforce these laws stringently because they are criminal statutes, not civil. Prosecutors hesitate to push for action under such laws because they know how difficult it is to get juries to convict under criminal statutes.

Congress enacted the Federal Trade Commission Act of 1914 to establish an agency to regulate national advertising. That agency, the Federal Trade Commission, was originally intended to control unfair competition in business and to protect such things as brand names while dealing with deceptive business practices. Within five years, the FTC's focus shifted to regulation of advertising. The commission determined that advertising a product falsely took unfair advantage of a competitor and was therefore illegal.

The commission's interpretation was upheld in 1922 when the Supreme Court affirmed its right to regulate false advertising as an unfair method of competition. The greatest support for this interpretation came from the Wheller-Lea amendments to the 1914 act, which extended the FTC's powers. In 1938, the commission was given specific jurisdiction over false advertising of foods, drugs, and cosmetics. The commission was given the right to issue injunctions to halt improper advertising of food, drugs, and cosmetics on the basis that such advertising might be harmful to health. This power depended on a request to the federal district court for such injunctions. The FTC could also use the federal court to issue cease and desist orders that would become final and binding within 60 days of issuance.

Complaints over the years from consumers resulted in an FTC interpretation that the public had a decreasing tolerance for questionable advertising. This caused commissioners to give the highest priority to enforcement of laws regulating advertising, despite its power to cover all phases of unfair competition.

All media, under the law, are considered to be in interstate commerce, which results in the Federal Trade Commission investigating complaints about broadcast commercials. The FTC has a liaison with the Federal Communications Commission to ensure that such complaints are provided to both agencies. Any decisions affecting broadcast advertisers from each agency are to be shared with the other.

The FTC does have its own monitors, but many complaints come from consumers and from competitors. After an investigation has been completed, the complaint might be determined as unjustified or the FTC might determine to conduct a hearing before a trial examiner. If the finding goes against the advertiser, the first step the agency might take is to ensure voluntary compliance. A signed agreement is negotiated that does not constitute an admission of guilt but does demonstrate a recorded public punitive action. The agency can also use what is called a consent order, a settlement based on issuance first of a formal complaint against the advertiser. This, too, does not constitute an admission of guilt.

Another step is the cease and desist order, an injunction that is legally enforceable. The commission also publicizes all such hearings and the orders that result from them. News releases are sent to the media, and the full text of the decision is available to reporters.

The FTC can also order corrective advertising. If a determination has been made that an advertiser deceived the public, the FTC can order a certain percentage of future print advertisements and broadcast commercials to point out the past deceptions and set the record straight.

The most prominent corrective ad decision was in the 1970s when the makers of Listerine were ordered to advertise that their product, contrary to prior advertising, will not help to prevent colds nor sore throats nor lessen their severity. The FTC decision was to stipulate that the corrective ads should continue until $10 million had been spent on them, a sum equal to what was spent on Listerine commercials and print ads over the previous 10 years.

Perhaps the advertising industry's primary self-regulating body is the National Advertising Division of the Council of Better Business Bureaus. It was created to resolve disputes between advertisers and to review complaints from consumers. It is also supposed to monitor advertising practices, primarily concerning itself with the truthfulness of claims and comparisons.

National advertisers actually have a two-tiered approach to self-regulation. The National Advertising Review Board was established in 1971 by the American Association of Advertising Agencies, the American Advertising Federation, the Association of National Advertisers, and the Council of Better Business Bureaus. The National Advertising Review Board acts like a jury of peers and like a review board for the National Advertising Division's decisions. The board includes national advertisers, agency representatives, and laypeople from the public sector. They sit on five-person panels to review decisions appealed by the advertiser.

The National Advertising Division advertises in print media and includes in the ads a complaint form. Most of the resulting complaints are about ads perceived as untruthful or inaccurate. Division investigators, on a voluntary basis, attempt then to field the complaints and to mediate where manufacturers have charged a competitor with making an unfair or unsubstantiated claim. These reviewers will also attempt to serve as judges in instances of consumer complaints about possible misleading promises in advertisements. When their decisions support the complainant, the advertiser will be asked to modify or eliminate the claims that were perceived as offensive or troublesome. That is the point at which the advertiser can appeal to the National Advertising Review Board.

The process described so far has been voluntary, but either the board or the division can refer an advertiser to the Federal Trade Commission if the advertiser refuses to go along with the corrective recommendation.

Recent research has demonstrated, however, that there is little awareness of this two-tiered program for self-regulation. Not only are consumers unaware of the National Advertising Division but also within the advertising industry there is little awareness of the National Advertising Review Board. Two separate surveys, one of which polled the nation's major advertising agencies, found that responsible agency executives knew little about the NARB or NAD. They were more familiar with the guidelines of the American Association of Advertising Agencies and, of course, the government regulatory body, the Federal Trade Commission.

The NAD has a Children's Advertising Review Unit, based on the assumption that children are less sophisticated consumers than adults. The mission is to promote advertising that is responsive to the special circumstances of the younger audience and to display a concern for advertising that could be unacceptable for children even if it were suitable for their parents. For the most part, its activities are concentrated on reviews and evaluations of advertising directed to pre-teens.

Advertising in Cyberspace

Early in the 21st century, cyberspace became the new frontier for advertising and an immediate flashpoint for ethical debate. In particular, the Internet's World Wide Web became a focal point for whether advertising and interactivity should coexist. Commerce on the Internet is becoming increasingly common. It has been predicted that very soon, as much as $600 billion worth of goods and services annually will be bought on the Internet, an estimated 8% of all the goods and services bought in a year.

Online advertising comes in a variety of forms, including pop-ups, pop-unders, floaters, banners and more traditional "display ad-type" offerings. Most

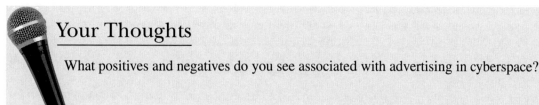

Your Thoughts

What positives and negatives do you see associated with advertising in cyberspace?

List FIVE suggestions for improving advertising in cyberspace. Why do you think your suggestions would succeed?

ads are interactive and include links to more information and sites where consumers can actually buy the products or services advertised. Critics complain about the ease of purchase and the opportunity to embed subtle and not-so-subtle commercial messages into web pages. Critics argue that online ads are too often intrusive, interruptive and can be considered an invasion of an Internet user's privacy. Proponents extol the cost-effectiveness, creative options and the user-friendly aspects of online ads. While online advertising revenues lag far behind advertising revenues for most of the traditional mass media organizations, the revenue-generating potential of online advertising both concerns and intrigues practitioners, regulators and consumers.

Recent Research, Developments and Issues

Product placement or "embedded ads" in movies, television programs and video games raise some interesting ethical issues. Having characters in movies, TV shows and video games use brand-name products can be a lucrative source of revenue for producers,

and advertisers seem eager to pay to have their products seen and talked about in not-so-subtle ways by popular actors and animated characters. Such ads are increasing in number as producers attempt to maximize revenue and deal with growing evidence of consumer avoidance of traditional advertising messages. In 2003, a survey of media planners found that 18% had negotiated a recent product placement deal and 26% said they planned to work on such deals in the near future.

Critics complain that "masked" advertising has no place in contemporary media and that such ads should be clearly identified so consumers know that companies have paid a fee to have their products or services used in a movie, TV program or video game. Critics say consumers have a right to know who is trying to convince them to buy products and services.

Product placement has even crept into the recording industry. In 2002, Jay-Z asked Motorola to two-way page him in one of his songs. Motorola reported a dramatic increase in pager sales as a result of the mention. A consumer group was so concerned that corporate messages were starting to creep into every aspect of our lives that it asked Congress to force recording companies to disclose any product placement deals to consumers.

A global study of product placements in 2007 found that paid product placement accounted for about $5 billion. TV placements accounted for about 70% of the total spending and film placements accounted for about 21%. Placements in video games, music and other media accounted for the remaining 9%. Non-paid product placements—trade outs, bartering, etc.—were even more popular worldwide. Such placements were valued at almost $10 billion in 2007.

The Super Bowl continues to be the super forum for advertising. In 2004, CBS collected an average of $2.3 million for each 30-second TV commercial it aired during the game. That works out to $76,500 per second. With 62 spots for commercials, the cash register fills quickly. The total: $142.6 million.

In 2008, 30-second commercials during the Super Bowl cost an average $2.7 million. The total take: $146 million.

A 2008 study of teenagers found that young people were very receptive and accepting of advertising on social-networking web sites. The teens were most interested in the ads for the following goods and services: financial services (63%), movies in theaters (59%), mobile telephone services/accessories (58%), travel options (57%) and other web sites (53%).

The number of actual commercials during prime-time network television programs has been declining for the past several years. The networks currently air about 11,500 commercials during prime-time. That's about 7% fewer than were aired in 2004. Even though fewer ads are being aired, more time is being devoted to ads. The almost 5,500 minutes of commercials per year now is about 3% more than in 2004. The 30-second commercial is the most often aired (57%), followed by the 15-second commercial (33%) and the 60-second commercial (8%).

Engagement is one of the newest "buzz" words in advertising. The theory is if consumers are "engaged" with the media content, they will be more receptive to the messages contained in the ads associated with the content. Some research supports the theory. It appears that the more relevant content is to audience members, the more ad-related information is recalled.

As advertising continues its march toward ubiquity, cell phones have become an enticing new target. Experts have predicted that cell phone advertising could surpass $11 billion worldwide by 2011. Cell phone ads can come in the form of more-or-less traditional video ads, banner ads, product placement in games and coupons. Early research has found that cell phone users are not overly receptive to being assaulted with ads when they use their phones, but many users have said they'd be willing to tolerate such ads if it meant they could receive "free" TV shows, games, music and other services via their cell phones.

Think Back

1. What is the definition of advertising?

2. What are the major types of advertising?

3. What were the major developments and who were the big names in the history of advertising?

4. How can the SMCR model be used to help explain advertising theory?

5. What are the major strategies and processes in advertising?

6. What are the major elements of the advertising industry?

7. What are the major similarities and differences associated with the various types of advertising agencies?

8. What are the various jobs and/or careers in advertising?

9. List the goals of advertising.

10. List the components of advertising.

11. List the approaches used in advertising.

12. List the legal and ethical concerns associated with advertising.

13. List the things consumers can do to enhance their critical evaluations of advertising messages.

14. What's the difference between caveat emptor and caveat venditor?

15. What are the major effects and/or influences that advertising can have on people?

16. What are the similarities and differences among advertising, marketing, promotions and public relations?

17. What seems to be the prevailing public image of advertising and its practitioners?

18. What are the major concerns associated with the advertising of "sensitive" products and services?

19. Why were advertisements for some Calvin Klein products controversial?

20. What are the major concerns and issues associated with advertising aimed at children?

21. What are some of the major techniques used in deceptive advertising?

22. Define "conspicuous consumption" and explain advertising's role in promoting it.

23. How is advertising regulated and who or what does the regulating?

24. What are the major types of Internet ads and what are the major concerns about them?

25. What are some of the major concerns about "product placement" in TV programs, movies, video games and songs?

26. What have 30-second TV commercials cost during the Super Bowl in the past few years? How much money have networks been making on the ads?

27. How receptive do teenagers appear to be to ads on social-networking web sites?

28. How many commercials are aired by the TV networks during prime-time and how much time is devoted to such commercials?

29. What is "engagement" in advertising and what impact does it seem to have on the recall of advertising messages?

30. What are the major types of ads for cell phones and how receptive to people seem to be toward receiving such ads?

Legal Rights and Limitations

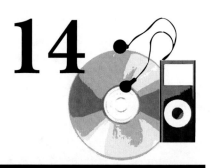

14

The First Amendment is often used to defend the questionable content of mass media messages. When challenged about the appropriateness or truthfulness of their products, many mass media practitioners point to the amendment's reasonably clear provisions.

"Congress shall make no law respecting an establishment of religion, or prohibiting the free exercise thereof; or abridging the freedom of speech, or of the press; or the right of the people peaceably to assemble, and to petition the Government for a redress of grievances."

Taken literally, the First Amendment would seem to prohibit any law that infringes on freedom of speech and freedom of the press. Of course, over time, it has been decided that the First Amendment is not absolute and that reasonable, fair and consistent limitations can be placed on speech and press freedoms. It is the determination of what is reasonable, fair and consistent that makes life and media law interesting.

Obscenity/Pornography

During his tenure as U.S. Attorney General, John Ashcroft promised a crackdown on what he considered a proliferation of adult obscenity. For example, early in the George W. Bush administration, Ashcroft's Justice Department spent $8,000 to cover two partly nude classical statues in the department's Washington offices.

By 2004, Ashcroft had signaled clearly that fighting obscenity was a high priority, initiating a wave of criminal cases against purveyors of pornography. An example was when a sting operation was set up in Pennsylvania. An indictment resulted that charged defendants with selling allegedly obscene materials over the Internet. The indictment said video tapes and DVDs were distributed across state lines through the postal system, a violation of federal law. The sting followed shortly after a Los Angeles police

department obscenity investigation that led detectives to western Pennsylvania. The defendants, based in Northridge, California, operated a triple-X rated entertainment firm with annual sales estimated at up to $50 million. The ten-count federal indictment sent a warning to dozens of adult entertainment companies in the San Fernando valley of Los Angeles, the center of the nation's huge pornography industry. Trade publications estimate that annual rentals and sales of adult videos are close to $5 billion and about 11,000 pornographic titles are produced annually.

The Ashcroft campaign was a renewal of the Reagan administration's war on pornography, when many production companies were put out of business and some of their operators were sent to prison. Attorney General John Meese in 1980 put together a national commission to look at problems of obscenity and pornography. The commission tried to make a connection between extreme adult sex entertainment and child pornography. The commission also tried to link public, antisocial acts of sexual violence with the industry's portrayals of violence and sex together, whether displayed in print or in visual media. Ashcroft followed the Meese commission effort by beginning to focus on online child pornography after first supporting a series of federal and state cases that went after both adult materials and child pornography.

Also in 2004, the Federal Communications Commission put radio shock jocks on notice that they better clean up their air waves. The commission proposed fining Clear Channel Communications $755,000 for alleged violations of indecency laws by talk show host Todd Clem, whose radio name was Bubba the Love Sponge. Also, Clear Channel Communications, the nation's largest radio chain, pulled Howard Stern off its stations in six cities. Stern continued on dozens of other stations, including those owned by Infinity Broadcasting, his syndicator. Clear

Channel said it had a zero-tolerance decency policy, which Stern violated. At the same time, Clear Channel fired Bubba the Love Sponge, contending that his sexually tinged on-air humor was too offensive and approached the limits of broadcast indecency under FCC rules.

Even in a free society, many people contend that the freedom of others must be abridged in order to protect moral standards. Yet, it is difficult, if not impossible, to agree on how far in a free and diverse society we can go in dictating what is morally unacceptable.

One popularly held position is government is obligated to protect all of us from what is dangerous and corruptive. That argument holds that sexually oriented media content is an affront to women, could fall into the hands of children and could result in criminal acts when viewed by those with depraved minds. Those who hold this viewpoint say that individuals who want to read or view pornography must be protected from themselves.

On the other hand, there are supporters of freedom of expression who contend that a free society has no place for arbitrary dictates about moral standards. These people defend the right of others to create, read, hear and/or watch whatever they choose to even if some of the material is repugnant and lacking much artistic or literary value.

Despite continuing disagreement about obscenity and pornography, a legal definition has developed that makes obscenity a crime. Pornography, on the other hand, is not a crime. It may be morally reprehensible material, but it's not criminal. Of course, such material can be offensive to some and acceptable to others, but if a jury finds the content to meet the standards of obscenity that have been set by legal precedent, the material is illegal.

The standard that allows for criminal prosecution while providing safeguards for literary and artistic expression was set in 1957 and modified in 1973. The 1957 precedent came in the Supreme Court decision in Roth v. United States, which reaffirmed the long-standing view that obscenity is not protected by the First Amendment. However, the Roth decision liberalized previous definitions of obscenity and allowed an expansion of literary and artistic freedom.

The Roth test looked to the dominant theme of the work as a whole, so that a work could no longer be determined as obscene because of one, isolated passage. It also judged obscenity by its effect on the average person, not by its effect on children or degenerate adults. In addition, the Roth test used contemporary, community standards, not the standards of some bygone era, to determine what was an affront to public sensibilities. So, in summary, the Supreme Court in Roth defined obscenity as sexually explicit material, that has as its dominant theme, content that offends the average person, applying contemporary community standards, because it appeals to a morbid, unhealthful and unwholesome interest. In decisions that followed Roth, the Court clarified that "community standards" meant those of the "national community."

In a 1973 decision, a Supreme Court with four new judges backed away from the liberalization of Roth and the decisions that followed Roth. In Miller v. California, the Court made it easier to prove that sexually explicit material was obscene. In Miller, the Court rewrote the definition of obscenity to permit local communities to

Your Thoughts

What do you think of the current standards used to determine whether something is obscene or not? Why?

Create a new set of standards for obscenity. Be specific. You can modify existing standards and/or create new ones.

set their own standards. It also ruled that a work only had to lack serious literary, artistic, political or scientific value to be illegal. After the Roth decision, lower courts had interpreted Roth to mean that a work had to be utterly without any redeeming social value to be judged obscene. Since almost anything has at least some redeeming value, obscenity convictions were hard to come by. Miller tightened up the standards considerably and made it much easier for local prosecutors to win their cases, because they could cite local sensibilities and it was much harder for defendants to prove that their works had serious value.

There is a separate standard for works that might be made available to children. In other words, what might be obscene for children, might not be obscene for adults. This concept is called "variable obscenity." It comes from the Supreme Court's determination to ensure the rights of states to adopt different standards for material aimed at children from those aimed at adults. This concept is at work, at least in part, in association with the ratings for movies, indecency on radio or television and with attempts to control indecency and obscenity on the Internet.

Reporter's Privilege

Refusing to identify sources when ordered by a judge can result in contempt citations, despite the presence of laws supposedly guaranteeing journalists the right to protect the anonymity of those who act as whistleblowers. A Los Angeles newspaper reporter, William Farr, served more time under a contempt sentence than any reporter before and since because a judge found a loophole in California law, one that has since been closed by the legislature.

Farr served 46 days in jail, but lived under the threat of jail for eight years: a threat of indeterminate jail time. On more than one occasion, Farr refused to reveal his confidential sources and the judge ordered him to jail, indicating that Farr was not protected by California's source protection law because he had changed jobs. Although he had been a reporter when he wrote his story, he was not working for the newspaper at the time he was asked the question.

Farr spent five years under the threat of being returned to jail following his release pending appeal. During that time, Farr had to fear that if his appeal failed he would be given an unlimited time behind bars because his journalistic ethics required him to keep a con-

fidence. Eventually, Farr was told by the appellate court that because his sentence had been coercive and that he was not likely to give up the information, the sentence had no further purpose. California voters later passed a ballot initiative that placed the state's shield law into the California Constitution, thus giving reporters' source protection added strength. The legislature even amended the statute to include former reporters who had changed jobs since preparing their stories.

The Supreme Court has said that the media are not guaranteed a constitutional right of special access to information not available to the public generally. Although common law has long provided protection against disclosure for doctors and patients, priests and confessors, lawyers and clients, courts have consistently held that such a privilege for journalists is not part of that common law. Journalists have contended that the flow of news is interrupted and news gathering is hindered by legally compelled disclosure. The Supreme Court said it was not convinced that such restrictions are sufficient to damage the news gathering function, but state legislatures and the United States Congress are free to create statutes that would protect reporters from disclosures.

There have been instances where journalists have been afforded First Amendment protection when faced with requests to reveal sources. These cases usually are consistent with a decision of the Supreme Court where it determined that official harassment of the media was the primary reason for most requests for disclosure. Such requests were seen as attempts to disrupt a reporter's relationship with a source rather than for legitimate needs of law enforcement. In the Branzburg case in 1972, the Supreme Court held that journalists are not without First Amendment rights in gathering information for their stories or in protecting confidential sources, but any claim of protection must be judged on a balance between freedom of the press and the general obligation of all citizens to give relevant testimony. The Branzburg case indicated that only where legitimate First Amendment interests require protection will the courts be available to journalists.

It must be stressed that despite the occasional rulings that under certain conditions the First Amendment might provide source protection, often it does not. For example, the Sixth Amendment, designed to guarantee a fair trial, is sometimes viewed by members of the bench and the bar as taking precedence over the First Amendment. It must be remembered also that the

Do you believe that journalists should have the right to refuse to reveal the names of their sources? Why or why not?

Branzburg decision did say that when journalists are called to testify before grand juries that they have no Constitutional protection if they refuse to reveal names of sources or other confidential information. It is only in federal courts of appeal and federal district courts of appeal in very specific decisions since then that some limited First Amendment protections have been applied. Also, when reporters succeed in their requests for such protection in the absence of a state statute, it is most likely to be when they are involved in civil suits.

Most states have enacted statutes supporting the right of reporters to protect their sources and their information. These are usually referred to as shield laws. Even in the absence of a shield law, there could be support for a privilege for journalists in many of the states because of state courts that have sought through the common law or state constitutions some basis for providing journalists an immunity from testifying not available to the public generally. In only a handful of states have there been decisions that journalists have no privilege. Reporters need to check carefully about statutes or precedents because the variations are considerable from state to state.

In addition, there is great variance within the wording of the statutes. Some state shield laws allow reporters to protect only anonymous sources of information. Others protect both sources and information. Some apply only if the information is actually used in print or on the air, excluding notes and background materials. Other shield laws don't help a journalist who is the target of a libel suit. If there is a conflict between the state statute and the concern for the defendant's Sixth Amendment right to a fair trial, the reporter might not be covered. Another possible exception in some states is when the court can find a public interest in the journalist's testimony, it can compel such testimony.

Free Press/Fair Trial

As already mentioned, another issue related to potential citations for contempt in respect to coverage of trials is the conflict between the First and Sixth Amendments. Some observers believe that the right to a free press and the guarantee of a trial before an impartial jury are in conflict. Others believe that there can be a balance between the two rights, a voluntary accommodation worked out cooperatively by the bench, bar and media.

The inherent problem for journalists is that the courts have the final say. All of the media's focus on ethical guidelines and all of their support for the public's so-called right to know don't carry the force of law. The media have influence. The courts have power. It is significant that through the 1970s and 1980s, organizations like the Society of Professional Journalists and the Radio-Television News Directors Association, among others, were working closely with lawyers and judges at the local and state level to locate their limits. By the 1990s, guidelines were clearly evident in most jurisdictions and attempts to curtail trial coverage were less frequent. Journalists today have more latitude before and during trials as long as they observe guidelines about potentially prejudicial information.

It is not against the law to create bias in the minds of potential jury members, but there are many avenues open to the court when extra-judicial information in the media makes it impossible or difficult to guarantee a defendant's rights. Reporters have been found in contempt of court in a few instances, but more often they have been denied cooperation or have been forbidden to have access to information, or have been restricted in their courtroom activities. Direct muzzling of the media could be a violation of the First Amendment, so muzzling of officers of the court indirectly restricts the news gathering process.

Members of the bench and bar have rules they set for themselves that have influenced the voluntary guidelines worked out with the media, who otherwise might feel a need, even a duty, to print or broadcast more than lawyers and law enforcement would want to release to them. Even with the bench-press-bar guidelines so common in most jurisdictions, courts often express concern that prejudicial accounts are carried in the media before and during criminal trials. In effect, the rules of ethics for lawyers are being applied to journalists. Journalists, on the other hand, believe that the claim that news coverage can prejudice jurors is, if not a myth, at least not proven, or provable. Nevertheless, reporters and photographers often follow rules of the court not only to avoid citations for contempt but also to guarantee through their cooperation as much access as possible.

In general, lawyers and law enforcement personnel, as officers of the court, may make public such items as a defendant's name, age, address, employment, marital status and related background information, as well as the substance of the charge and what plea was entered. Journalists can also be told the identity of the arresting agency and the length of the investigation, the circumstances of the arrest and any items seized at the time of arrest.

However, other types of information, believed to create the potential for prejudice in the minds of those who might later be selected for jury duty, are to be kept from reporters. These include confessions, alibis, fingerprint results, lie detector tests, ballistics tests, or any laboratory results. The belief is that some of these might not be allowed into evidence later in many cases and would not be intended for presentation to a jury. Also, journalists are not to be told of the identity or credibility of potential witnesses and are not to be given any information about evidence gathered after the arrest and during the period leading up to trials.

It was the aftermath of the Kennedy assassination that resulted in many calls for media restraint in coverage of sensational crimes and their resultant trials. The Warren Commission was critical of reporters who interfered with police and blamed the media for the circumstances that led to the shooting of Lee Harvey Oswald. Jack Ruby died before his appeal could be heard on the contention that he had been denied a fair trial because of the media. Over the next three decades, much interest centered on the problems created by media coverage of major trials, most efforts being centered on the local level where the previously mentioned guidelines were usually established. Such local agreements between the courts and the media vary widely from place to place and they are often ignored. Often lawyers violate the guidelines and leak information to reporters to help their own cases when they feel there has been too much in the media favoring the other side. Journalists will ignore the voluntary guidelines when they feel unfairly restricted in the performance of their duties. They might feel an obligation to report information that the judge and attorneys don't want released. The rules are voluntary, after all.

Why would reporters refuse in some instances to go along with the agreed-upon guidelines? Aren't they worried about the defendant's rights? Are they violating their own ethics?

In the first place, there is some question about whether news coverage, even of sensational crimes, really influences prospective jurors. It is impossible to conduct scientific research using actual trials. A mock jury would simply not replicate the actual behavior of participants. Research results into potential jury prejudice are inconclusive.

We live in a nation with a high crime rate, indicating that it could be irresponsible for journalists not to keep us fully informed even when some inflammatory information about the accused might not be admissible later at the time of trial. In a free society, one important function expected of journalists is to serve as watchdog over elected and appointed officials, over those who feed at the taxpayers trough. Monitoring the administration of justice, reporting on the system of dispensing justice is part of that watchdog role. Journalists might feel that they are merely lapdogs if they follow too blindly the voluntary guidelines, and lawyers might think of them as a wild pack of vicious dogs if they don't.

It is possible that a truly impartial jury would not serve justice when you consider that it likely would be made up of those who don't or can't read or prefer to watch entertainment fare rather than news or public affairs on television. If a jury is made up of those who have heard nothing of the case in advance is that a jury of fools and losers? Is it a jury of peers? Wouldn't it be better to have a panel of fully-informed citizens, even those who had heard or seen potentially prejudicial information? The jury selection process out of necessity merely seeks out those to serve who can set aside their preconceived ideas and keep an open mind during the adversarial proceeding in the courtroom. They are not required to be totally ignorant or completely unbiased before the trial begins.

The journalist has to decide what is more ethical—following the voluntary guidelines or providing the public with as much information as it deserves. It is a common concern—the rights of the individual who is on trial or the rights of the society to know what takes place in its criminal justice system. Is there a greater danger in a defendant facing some jurors who have advanced knowledge of the case or in the public being kept ignorant of a judicial process in which they have a great deal invested?

The Sixth Amendment also says the accused gets a speedy and public trial. How public is the core of this conflict, but judges and lawyers never appear to worry over the Constitutional requirement that it be a speedy trial. The journalist might ask why the courts attempt to force the media to help them with only one part of the Sixth Amendment mandate, but never seem to do anything about the rest of the defendant's rights. The judicial ethics don't adequately, if at all, deal with the guarantee of a speedy trial, perhaps because it is up to the judges and lawyers themselves to tackle that problem. The bar association's ethics place the burden on the news media to work toward ensuring impartiality, a burden they don't require of themselves in regard to moving trials through the system quickly.

Cameras in Courtrooms

The O.J. Simpson criminal trial really brought to a head the issues of pre-trial publicity and extra-judicial information. At the heart of the controversy, of course, was the presence of cameras in the courtroom. Critics complain that permitting still and video cameras in courtrooms has an influence on participants, a negative influence. Critics claim that lawyers, judges, witnesses, audience members and even jury members play to the cameras. Critics believe that because pictures and video from a trial are made readily available, family members, friends, acquaintances and the public at large can place undo pressure on the trial participants. Everybody has an opinion about the defendant's guilt or innocence.

Supporters of cameras in courtrooms counter such fears by stating that there is little evidence to support such allegations. And they're right about that. Supporters believe that after a short time, most trial partic-

ipants forget that cameras are even in the courtroom, so the presence of cameras in courtrooms really doesn't do much at all, certainly nothing negative. All it does is expand the number of seats in the courtroom. Most of the time anyone who wants to can sit in on a trial. All cameras do is just make it easier for people to "sit in." Supporters also claim that cameras in courtrooms provide a good check on the performance of trial participants. Cameras give the public a chance to see officers of the court in action and make it possible to determine if they're doing their jobs professionally, correctly, fairly and ethically.

Federal courts do not allow cameras, but most states allow at least some trials to have cameras in courtrooms. Most of the time, photographers and videographers must adhere to strict requirements of behavior and access. Limitations might include having the video camera mounted on the wall or in a stationary location on the floor. Only one still photographer might be allowed in the courtroom at a time. Photos or video of jury members might be prohibited. The judge might ask that the faces of witnesses or defendants not be shown. You've probably seen faces blotted out by shimmering electronics.

As we've seen, even if cameras in the courtroom don't have a negative effect on a person's right to a fair trial, it's likely that the out-of-court activity of the news media prior to, during and after a trial will cause some problems, especially in "high-profile" cases. Too often the issue of cameras in the courtroom gets lumped together with more legitimate concerns about the unprofessional, unethical and unfair behavior of the news media during criminal and civil trials.

Judicial Remedies for Prejudicial Publicity

Courts have remedies available to them in case extra-judicial information is overly sensational or unsubstantiated and unprejudiced jurors will be difficult to find. The courts do have measures available when news reports have revealed what the trial procedure would call irrelevant, such as information about a suspect's past or results of a confession or unverified test results that won't hold up in court.

A judge may order a change of venue, the moving of the trial to a distant location in another part of the state where there has been less publicity about the suspect. By moving to another community where the story was not reported on as much, those selected for jury duty likely have been exposed to very little or no coverage. This is difficult in a major criminal case where the publicity is universal and in a small state where you can't move too far away.

The judge also has the power to delay the trial until publicity has died down. A postponement could result in memories of the crime, the arrest and any information about the character of the suspect fading to the point where the people selected for jury duty are more impartial than they would have been earlier. These continuances are routinely granted, but usually for the lawyers' convenience, having little to do with extrajudicial publicity. Lawyers constantly request delays in trial dates when court calendars are backed up because of overcrowding. It's conceivable that some of those called to jury duty when trials are delayed for 18 months were not even living in the community when the publicity first broke. The courts are typically months behind anyway, so a continuance because a defendant's rights are believed in jeopardy because of news coverage could mean a trial 18 months to two years after the arrest. The excessive force trial for four Los Angeles police officers in the videotaped beating of Rodney King got underway almost a year to the day after the incident occurred.

Another remedy available to judges is the sequestration of jurors, isolating them from coverage during the trial itself by keeping them in hotel rooms and having their activities supervised by bailiffs. They take all of their meals together and their access to newspapers, computers, radio and television is restricted and carefully monitored. They are allowed to watch entertainment programs on television, but not the newscasts. They are given newspapers that have had stories about the trial cut from them. The problem with sequestration is that it eliminates only information during the trial coverage not the stories that appeared several months earlier when the jurors had not yet known that they would be selected. It also presents the concern that locking up jury members is treating them like prisoners, denying them access to their homes and their families. Even without sequestration, judges can order jurors to avoid reading newspaper accounts of the trial and insist that they not talk about the evidence presented to them with anybody but fellow jury members.

The most effective and most ubiquitous remedy is what is called voir dire, the careful examination in advance of all prospects for the jury. The jury selection process allows lawyers for both sides to carefully question each person to determine whether bias is obvious or, in some cases, perceived. After some are excused following this examination, only those who have demonstrated to the court an ability or a willingness to keep an open mind are left to serve.

Prosecutors, public defenders and judges should not be overly surprised when some news organizations don't follow totally the voluntary guidelines. Some journalists simply believe that if they practice sufficient restraint, if officers of the court are muzzled by gag orders, and if there are specific remedies for harmful media coverage, then the Sixth Amendment protection is more an obligation of the judiciary than the media. They might somewhat cynically protest that judicial ethics fail greatly in providing for the speedy trial part of the Sixth Amendment, therefore journalistic ethics cannot be expected to bear the burden of providing the impartiality.

The restrictive orders placed on lawyers and law enforcement officers by judges are expected to dry up the sources of damaging information, so reporters feel they are already sufficiently hindered in their trial coverage. Because the guidelines are voluntary and there are no laws forbidding the denial of a suspect's right to an impartial and speedy trial, the punishment for

Your Thoughts

Do you think a person's right to a fair trial should take precedence over the public's right to know? Why or why not?

journalists is a citation for contempt of court. Reporters are apparently willing to risk that when they believe that they have a greater obligation to the public than to the defendant. It usually comes down to a reporter and his or her editor believing that there have been enough safeguards along the way to guarantee that one news story or one element in a story will not be enough to swing the balance against the suspect.

Another recourse for the judge is to declare a mistrial when damaging publicity has been too great. This is an extreme measure and any journalist blamed for a violation of the guidelines that caused a mistrial would be greatly damaged professionally. It would be difficult for a reporter to recover from such a breach of ethics. News organizations are careful to avoid interfering with the orderly administration of justice while also witnessing and evaluating the actions of court officers who are, after all, on the public payroll and accountable for their shortcomings or potential shortcomings. The media are supposed to be free of governmental restrictions and pressures, but freedom does not give license to trample on the system of justice or on the individuals affected by the system.

The Impact of Ethics

Issues like potentially damaging a defendant's right to a fair trial or being cited for contempt are not common in everyday news gathering but they do command a great deal of attention when they occur. Legal problems for journalists are sometimes rare because of ethical constraints in their newsrooms or because of the lessons they learned in the classroom. Newsroom policies and journalism textbooks typically contain rules for reporters to follow that will usually keep them out of legal entanglements.

A typical policy is to avoid the use of anonymous sources. In fact, many media executives and their lawyers require reporters to use information in their stories only if the source is willing to be named. It is common practice for all information to be attributed, at least for the part that actually appears in the final version of the story. In other words, tips from confidential sources can lead you to the people you interview and then identify in the story or can direct you toward the documents or records that you cite. A typical constraint is the need for a second or third source to back up anything given to you anonymously.

The newsroom supervisor will demand that any reporter have at least one, probably two, named sources for every confidential source. Many editors simply don't trust quotes or paraphrases that don't come with a direct attribution. They also believe that the readers, listeners and viewers don't find believable stories that contain phrases like "courthouse observers," "those close to the scene," "informed sources," or "unidentified but knowledgeable observers." The result is that writers often find it difficult to get approval for copy that contains references to anonymous interview subjects or confidential tipsters.

If there is a fear of character assassination from those who secretly and perhaps villainously would plant untrue charges, then why would or should the media ever use anonymous sources? One obvious reason is that many of the informants are in danger. If one talks to a reporter about a crime, there is the risk that revenge will be forthcoming from the criminal. Job security is another good reason. Government employees are especially at risk of losing their jobs if they dare to expose malfeasance, corruption or inefficiency in the bureaucracy. We would like to think they would be rewarded for blowing the whistle on such misdeeds, but we know that quite often the opposite occurs.

Loyalty is another reason that truthful and accurate accounts are provided along with requests for anonymity. It could be loyalty to a labor union that has some bad elements that the source wants cleaned out or loyalty to a political machine that is getting out of control and the source wants back on track. The source wants to stay within the organization to help with the rebuilding, but might not be able to do so effectively if others in the group know of his or her role in the public disclosures.

Because there are some good reasons for individuals in many circumstances to stay out of the limelight, the journalist is often saddled with incomplete but potentially valuable information. Without support from the initial source, the immediate task is to follow-up with other sources. Often it is not a problem. Many bits of information from conversations and anonymous telephone calls lead directly to public records or available documents, which, in effect, become the actual sources for the story. A call comes in carrying a suggestion that perusal of the municipal building inspection department records will indicate that the city allowed five homes to be built on a hillside so unstable that 30 years earlier it had collapsed in a rain-generated landslide that buried homes on the street below. It would be easy enough to look at the city's public records on the construction permits and the newspaper files about the long ago landslide. A story would result with anyone assuming that the sources were newspaper stories, documents and records that the city kept because they were required by law. Who would know that a tip had caused the writer to start such inquiries?

Standard practice is to avoid using anonymous attributions, to get every source to go on record. When someone balks, it means the reporter must use every bit of persuasion possible to be sure that the source is willing to go public. If that fails, the next step is to find others who are willing to speak out and allow their names to be used. If that doesn't work, it is expected that at least one, preferably two, named individuals will be mentioned in the story in support of any anonymously attributed information. Of course, it helps if the source is backed up by public records or official documents available to the public. In addition, quite often the reporter can't be the only one in the news operation who knows the identity of the source. Before someone can be mentioned without the name being used, that person must agree that the reporter's supervisor also be aware of exactly who it is.

These guidelines allow for exceptions where the public interest becomes paramount. An example is seen in the stories in a Seattle newspaper about United States Senator Brock Adams, who was accused by eight women of sexual improprieties. The story in the *Seattle Times* on March 1, 1992, told of accusations over 20 years of persistent physical assaults, sexual harassment and misbehavior, including one woman who claimed to have been drugged and raped and two others who said they had been drugged before being molested. Adams had been a member of the Reagan cabinet, serving as Secretary of Transportation, and was completing a term as United States Senator. The newspaper said it departed from its standard in the use of unnamed sources, because a lengthy investigation revealed a pattern of abuses of power and abuses of women. In a front-page statement accompanying the story, the newspaper's executive editor said the women were determined to be credible and their independent stories of misdeeds fit a pattern. In addition to the women, the newspaper quoted other unnamed sources saying that Adams was known by his staff to aggressively fondle women. Also, five years earlier a woman had publicly accused the senator of rape. The paper said none of the eight accusers would allow their names to be disclosed, but seven of them signed statements for the newspaper and said they were prepared to go to court.

Those circumstances may have been a departure for the *Seattle Times* and its standards on confidential sources, but they are consistent with most newsroom policies. The number of sources, the pattern, the signed statements, and the woman who previously revealed her identity to prosecutors all are within the guidelines that most news organizations would follow.

Invasion of Privacy

Critics of the media and audience members complain often about what they consider invasions of privacy. When we hear charges of recklessness and irresponsibility, they often center on perceptions of intrusion into private matters, exposure of individuals to unwanted publicity. These come from people who don't know the law of privacy and probably don't care. They see it as irresponsible or unethical to put names in news stories even if the practice violates no laws. At the same time, reporters insist that an increasing number of privacy statutes hampers them in their quest to obtain information.

There is a legal right to be left alone. It is found in rulings by judges who have discerned a common law right of privacy evolved primarily in the late 19th century and through the 20th century. You have a legal action available if you contend that your right to privacy has been interfered with and you have been subjected to mental pain much as someone else might have been harmed by bodily injury.

Generally, there are four areas of invasion of privacy that can lead to a possible lawsuit. The first one is usually described as intrusion into a person's physical solitude. This is not about the content of print broadcast media, but about the newsgathering process, the conduct of reporters and photographers. The injured party sues for monetary compensation because of snooping or eavesdropping, probably with high technology devices. Zoom lenses, telephone taps, long-range microphones, hidden recorders or cameras, any devices that improve upon peeking through keyholes, are the instruments of intrusion. Going onto private property without permission, especially anything bordering on illegal entry or trespassing, to get a story could be an invasion of a person's solitude, as would using documents obtained by surreptitiously going through someone's filing cabinet.

The second widely recognized area is the publication of private matters violating ordinary decencies and causing embarrassment. In carrying news stories of private matters, the reporters and editors may think that something is clearly newsworthy, but could be found liable for damages if a person had changed his ways and the story dredged up old news. The resultant embarrassment could be actionable if there was no public interest and no social value in the facts of the story, especially if the complainant was no longer in the public eye and had regained the status of a "private" person. In such cases, truth is NOT a complete defense that journalists can use. The truth must be made public with "good motives."

A third sub-area of privacy law is putting a person before the public in a false light, something that could happen from inaccurate reporting, but that often results from misleading, misinterpreting or misusing a photo or video. Giving a misleading impression of a person's character can prove costly. Creating a false impression is called fictionalization. It often occurs when a reckless untruth is included in a story based on fact.

Another source of privacy lawsuits is the unauthorized taking of a person's name or likeness for commercial or other advantage. The greatest number of these cases of appropriation or misappropriation—the careless use of someone's celebrity for commercial exploitation—has come in cases involving advertising. At times, some of these cases are described as dealing with a right of publicity, a protection from commercial use of a person for gain without consent.

Intrusion

The right of privacy does not forbid the media from carrying accounts of interest to the public even when those named in the stories are unwilling. It is not a violation of seclusion when a person is an object of legitimate public interest because of prominence or because an event or activity pushes the individual into the public arena. When circumstances place a person in the limelight, the right of privacy is relinquished. There are times when one is unwillingly pulled into newsworthy events and involuntarily becomes an actor on the public stage. What is forbidden is the wrongful intrusion in a way that would cause shame or humiliation.

It is not wrongful to take a photograph while on public property and use that picture in a news story. The assumption in the courts is that the photographers and video camera operators are standing in for the public simply taking pictures that you could take if you were there. The problem occurs when the camera operator is in a private place or is displaying annoying intrusive behaviors in a public area. If photographers are not trampling someone's rose bushes or climbing over fences and up trellises, they are not liable. If reporters or photographers gain access by misrepresenting themselves or by bullying individuals, they are very close to trespassing even if they remain on public property. It is that trespass-like action that could prove actionable.

Some journalists might think that concealed electronic devices are indispensable tools for investigative reporting, but courts have told them differently. It is considered intrusion, and therefore an invasion of privacy, to use a miniature camera, a concealed microphone, a long telephoto lens, or other snooping technology to place yourself where you otherwise would not be allowed to go. The courts have held consistently that reporting, even investigative reporting, has been around well before miniature cameras and eavesdropping devices were invented, so any restrictions on harassment of individuals by their use does not hamper newsgathering. ABC-TV learned this lesson in a lawsuit when a North Carolina jury awarded the supermarket chain Food Lion $5.5 billion dollars, almost all of it in punitive damages. Food Lion had sued ABC-TV after the network ran an investigative story about food-handling practices. ABC-TV accused the food chain of selling spoiled meat, tainted chicken and rotten produce and it showed employees performing numerous activities in efforts to repackage and sell the bad food. ABC-TV used hidden cameras to record such actions. The hidden cameras were carried into the workplace by people who used fake résumés at the request of ABC-TV. While appeals later saved ABC-TV, the point remains that not every use of hidden cameras is acceptable.

Journalists must assume that individuals can sue and collect damages for emotional distress even if they are criminal suspects, if their private surroundings have been intruded upon wrongfully, especially if that intrusion is enhanced by electronic or other sophisticated technology. Journalists may not enter private homes surreptitiously, go onto private property without permission, or trespass in an attempt to get a story and expect a judge to say later that the newsworthiness of the story justified such action.

Publication of Private Matters

It is often difficult to figure out in advance what stories will result in lawsuits. In the first place, privacy law is ever-changing and inconsistent, varying from state to state. Secondly, when the facts are accurate, there is a strong tendency to believe that there is no liability even when someone has been embarrassed.

In a case filed against *Sports Illustrated*, reporters were put on notice that people being interviewed had the right to revoke consent to have some of what they said published and that a judge can determine whether standards of a given community might be offended by revealing private facts about an individual. Although the magazine got a reversal on appeal, the case demonstrated how subjective judges could be in determining whether a story was sufficiently newsworthy to justify revealing embarrassing private matters. A successful privacy suit could result even when a truthful report is made if the court holds the public's interest in the story is not legitimate and its publication would be highly offensive to a reasonable person. The truth of the incidents covered in the story would be immaterial to the court's determination as to whether it is a morbid and sensational prying into public lives for its own sake. With this broad language, a judge and jury could decide what is morbid and what are standards of a community or of a reasonable person.

Generally, when the material embarrassing to the complainant came from a public record, the media may use it without fear of losing a privacy suit. Journalists can successfully defend a lawsuit when their information comes from a court record, an official account of the proceedings of a public body, data kept by a county clerk or a similar official discharging a legal duty to keep legally required public documents.

In the absence of a public record, newswriters are in trouble if disclosure of embarrassing details is highly offensive even when the story is newsworthy. An example can be found in a case where *Time* magazine lost a suit because of a story and pictures of a woman in a hospital with a rare eating disorder. The judge said the woman deserved privacy when in a hospital being treated for gluttony. She was losing weight but eating constantly. The judge held that there was no significance to the public in such a disease, it was not contagious, and the magazine's approach to it was almost mocking, making her out to be a freak.

A South Carolina newspaper lost a suit in 1986 because a teenager was identified in a story as the father of an illegitimate child. The youngster was never told that his name would be used in the story about teenage pregnancies, and claimed that the reporter who talked with him indicated only that he was doing a survey. The newspaper's defense was that the young man's name was of legitimate public interest. A jury ruled that it was not of public interest and that it was a matter for a jury to decide and the South Carolina State Supreme Court agreed.

A strong anti-press feeling emanates from many Americans who loudly and with apparent anger insist that journalists recklessly prey upon the private lives of individuals unfortunately captured by events out of their control. The public outcry against the media centers on a perception that there is an unnecessary probing for private information and that citizens are being made victims. Often cited is the ex-Marine who might have saved then-President Gerald Ford from a would-be assassin in 1975. Oliver Sipple was credited with striking the arm of Sara Jane Moore and deflecting her aim. Sipple was quickly regarded as a hero, but within two days, stories began to appear implying that he was a homosexual.

Sipple sued several publications, contending that his sexual preference was not at all related to the news event. The newspapers responded by saying that many elements of Sipple's personal life became matters of public interest because he was swept up into an event of worldwide importance. The basic defense was that individuals who get caught up in public events of transcendent importance give up their rights to privacy. Sipple lost in the trial court but appealed. The Court of Appeal ruled that even if Sipple believed that exposure of his sexual preference had subjected him to ridicule he was still newsworthy because of his heroic act. The appellate court held that the lower court had done the right thing by dismissing his case.

Sometimes it will be considered a private matter if the person was once newsworthy yet reacquired privacy as time lapsed. There is danger to newspapers in the "where are they now" stories or the "20 years ago today" features. The question usually is how much time must lapse before a person had regained anonymity after once being in the public eye. Is prying by the press into a former public figure's past life an invasion denying the individual a sought-after seclusion or is it a legitimate scrutiny of the activities of someone who the public must not forget? Trial courts can be expected in some of these instances to find no justification for news reports that expose a once public individual to an audience that no longer needs to know intimate details of a private life, even if that life was once lived in the spotlight.

False Position in the Public Eye

The publication or broadcast of something false about an individual is likely to lead to a privacy lawsuit if the story could be highly offensive to a reasonable person and if there was negligence or malice in the use of the information. Of course, if the story is not only false, but defamatory, a suit for libel could be brought. In the instance where there is no defamation, only embarrassment or an offensiveness, a privacy action can be initiated even if there is no intrusion and no digging into a shady past.

To succeed in a libel action, a plaintiff must prove a damaged reputation; but in a privacy action claiming false light, one need only prove the story was highly offensive. If a false impression is created about someone because of an error of fact or embellishment of the facts, a court could rule that the complainant had been put in a false position before the public. It would be actionable to say that a hostage was overly friendly toward a captor, to say that someone was a racist, or to try to guess what was going through a crime victim's mind. If you don't have direct quotes from such individuals or have not interviewed them extensively, assumptions about them could result in the highly offensive material that serves as a basis for false-light lawsuits.

Many of these cases result from improper captions with photographs or the use of unrelated photographs to illustrate stories or features. A dignified, conservative businessman could collect damages if a 25-year-old picture of him, long-haired and crazily outfitted, standing with a group of weirdly dressed teenagers, was used to illustrate a story about youthful rebellion. A newspaper would be in trouble if it pulled a file photo of people watching a horse race and used it to supplement an article on compulsive gambling. One or more of those in the photo could collect on a claim that the juxtaposition of the picture and story gives a false impression.

Putting fictional elements into a news story could cause problems for a writer, but even more often lawsuits result from short stories, novels, plays and television or radio dramas in which fiction is based on fact. When fictionalization is the core of the false light privacy action, the best strategy for the defense is to demonstrate that the names of the characters were changed.

Sometimes it takes more than simply changing the name. If the character described in a work of fiction is so well known and can be recognized by an audience, despite a pseudonym, there could be cause for a false light suit. In a situation like that, the writer could include the well-known person as an incidental character somewhere else in the plot. A book that details the life of a hard-drinking baritone, who has hosted a comedy show on television and once was straight man for a zany comedian popular with the French, could be introduced to Dean Martin somewhere in the novel. It has been ruled that it is not invasion of privacy when famous people are portrayed incidentally in fiction on the assumption that readers will know that they are merely to add color to the book.

A newspaper story about a crime that is used as part of an article in a magazine that uses fictionalized accounts of true events could cause the magazine writer some trouble. The courts do hold that it must involve more than mere incidental falsity. Hyping incidents or making the circumstances more entertaining are the kind of intentional efforts that get the media into trouble with stories about even people who are newsworthy. The right to defend oneself by saying that a person is an object of news interest is lost when untrue material is recklessly added to make the story more exciting or more readable. The fictionalization must be irresponsible or sensational for an action to be successful.

Appropriation and Right of Publicity

Privacy lawsuits can result from careless use of a person's name or likeness when it amounts to the appropriation of that person's celebrity for financial gain, most likely for advertising purposes. This area of privacy law includes the use of someone's identity without giving adequate compensation for it.

The very first privacy statute was passed by the New York State legislature in 1903 specifically to prohibit the use of a person's name or likeness for trade purposes or advertising. If no consent had been given, a plaintiff could seek not only money damages but also try for an injunction to stop the use of the name or any picture.

It must be remembered that the right of publicity is available to the famous and celebrated when there is some commercial advantage involved. It does not mean that there is ever any restriction on the use of their identities in news coverage or commentary and analysis of the activities that make them famous. It is not appropriation to use a photograph, sketch, cartoon, or any other likeness, along with a name in news columns or news broadcasts, newspaper or magazine columns or broadcast public affairs shows.

If someone were to attempt to sue for appropriation claiming that their likeness in a sensational news story helped a newspaper to increase its subscription sales, the suit would be rejected. It also would not work if one wanted to claim that an appearance on a radio or television news show helped increase ratings and therefore constituted commercial gain for the station. It is appropriation when used in advertisements or when a promotional display in a store window attracts customers because of the identity of the individual featured.

The individual who wants to sue because his or her personality has been taken for commercial advantage need not be prominent. It could be any person whose name or likeness appears in an advertisement through an innocent error. The simple failure to check the spelling of a name could result in a privacy action. Writing John Johnson of Miller Street when it should have been John Miller of Johnson Street would be the kind of misstep that allowed for no defense.

Defenses in Privacy Lawsuits

Any mass medium sued for invasion of privacy when the plaintiff's case is built on appropriation could be forced to prove that there was "consent." Exceptions are politically-oriented advertisements or public service advertisements or announcements where the likeness of a political leader or prominent activist is used. Publishing the photograph in an advertisement sup-porting or opposing a candidate for office does not require prior authorization. No consent is needed if Native Americans protesting what they consider demeaning names of sports franchises, use the names or likenesses of the owners of the ball clubs.

Typically, advertising agencies, photographers, television and movie production companies, the networks, and publishing firms get written authorization from their subjects. They prepare a standard consent or release form and gain written approval, usually in exchange for some form of compensation. If someone has given consent to privacy invasion, then there is no opportunity to collect damages in a privacy suit later. However, a consent is not valid in perpetuity and the invasion cannot go beyond what is stated in the release.

The consent must be as broad as the invasion, but an individual cannot really be expected to agree to be used for any purpose whatsoever. That means a release form must be both broad and specific. An unlimited consent would not cover a photograph that had been altered after the consent had been granted. If it is not broad enough, however, a plaintiff could contend that consent for one purpose is not consent for another. If a woman agrees to have her photograph used for a promotional piece for a charitable fund-raising fashion show, it does not mean that she agrees to its use as an advertisement for a department store.

Consent is not a particularly common defense when invasion of privacy lawsuits are filed over something that has been included in a news story, documentary or docudrama. Most news organizations do not routinely ask sources to sign consent forms and it is unlikely that a person would give his or her consent to something that would be an invasion of privacy. Consent, usually spoken and recorded, is used more often in connection with obtaining a source's permission to be recorded and/or photographed for a news story.

The more common defense used by the news media and the entertainment media is "newsworthiness." If the media can convince the court that what was printed or broadcast was "newsworthy," the media can get away with invading someone's privacy. Newsworthiness is defined as information that the public is interested in. Since the public, at least part of it, is interested in a great many things, the defense of newsworthiness is pretty broad. It covers both willing and unwilling participants in newsworthy events and issues.

A "public persons/public places" defense can be used in some instances, too. If media content involves well-known people—athletes, movie stars, television personalities, politicians—the public's right to know and the newsworthiness of the content usually can easily be justified. In addition, if information, photos or videos are obtained from news-gathering efforts that take place on public property, it's unlikely that a news organization would lose an invasion of privacy lawsuit.

The defendant losing a privacy action could be assessed punitive damages, meaning that an example could be made of the offender to discourage other media organizations. The plaintiff does not have to prove actual damages to collect in a privacy action. The court can grant assumed damages, or an amount of money assessed because of the general embarrassment suffered, and award it as compensation to the injured person.

Defamation: Libel and Slander

Anyone sued for libel is best served by being able to prove the truth of what was printed or broadcast. If a statement is true, then the person harmed, in effect, had no help from anyone else in creating a sullied reputation. If your own actions cause you to suffer ridicule or embarrassment, lose your job, have your esteem lowered among peers, or cause you to be shunned by society, then you cannot blame the medium that reported those actions. If allegations are false, a person may attempt to collect damages in a libel action. If you collect money from the court to make you feel better about having been defamed, the amount assessed against the defendant will be called "general" or "compensatory"

damages. If you can prove specific monetary losses as a result of defamation—business reverses, clients pulling out, fees and court costs, etc.—you can collect "actual" or "special damages." If the court feels that the defendant was so malicious as to deserve punishment, additional money will be awarded the plaintiff as "punitive" or "exemplary" damages. This attempt to make an example of the worst offenders in libel cases and to punish them can result in the largest amounts of money awarded to those who win libel cases.

There is a general warning to reporters and writers that if they simply follow the ethics of their profession they won't have to defend themselves against libel actions. However, this otherwise good advice presupposes that no mistakes will be made. Various textbooks and followers of the cases that enter the legal system have concluded that most libel suits that are filed have resulted from unintended, accidental errors. Getting a name wrong, transposing pictures, misinterpreting of the charge listed in a police report, misunderstanding a quotation, leaving out a key word, or any of several other honest but unfortunate errors could cost you and your employer damages in a libel case.

Journalists are told that their ethical codes are their best protection against libel suits, because they demand accuracy, verification and confirmation, fair play, balance and objectivity. Despite these strictures, libel is the most common legal problem faced by those who work in the media. The volume of news itself creates the potential for frequent problems.

The very nature of the news process, the writing of instant history under deadline pressure, causes many of the errors that result in the lawsuits that go to trial. Misstatements and misperceptions can result from the pressure of trying to condense great amounts of information into a brief story. The need to get a story into print or on the air in a hurry can result in the haste that fosters errors. Mistakes are almost inevitable in a system that requires its practitioners to process massive amounts of data from sources probably never dealt with before on topics that are unfamiliar and then compress them into the least complicated wording in the fastest possible time span.

The need for objectivity demands that reporters not be very familiar with the content of their stories for fear too much involvement with the subject will result in a loss of objectivity. The general assignment reporter is given opportunities to write about such varied matters as criminology, economics, education, business management, psychology, medicine, the banking system, investment practices, social work, and dozens of others without being expert in any one of them. Even if a reporter has special knowledge on a topic, the need to make it less complicated for the reader, listener or viewer can misshape the story, especially as it goes through the various stages of copy editing and production before it is finally sent to the news consumer. Each person in the chain of checking for spelling, accuracy, libel, brevity, style, and such, is likely to know less about the topic than the preceding person. Each one of the many hands that touch the story can change it and that means more potential for trouble.

Because mistakes do occur, the media are expected to rid themselves of the danger of libel suits by publishing or broadcasting retractions, which by definition must also constitute an admission of error and an apology while correcting the error. If such a retraction is given, it is unlikely that the aggrieved person would file suit. If the lawsuit were pursued, the retraction makes it very unlikely that any damages would be assessed.

Aspects of Libel and Slander

Defamation is the key ingredient in both slander and libel. Defamation is false communication that injures a person's reputation or causes him/her to be ridiculed. Slander is defamation that is delivered orally in a face-to-face setting in interpersonal communication where there is immediate, observable feedback from the audience. Defamation presented through a mass medium is libel.

Libel can be written or spoken. The old distinction between printed defamation being libel and spoken defamation constituting slander died with the advent of radio and television. Since the 1930s, courts have held that defamation presented over radio is libel. Defamation delivered orally over television has been determined as libel not slander since the 1950s. Decisions that followed the 1932 *Sorensen v. Wood* case took up the reasoning that the words written for delivery over broadcast stations constitute libel. In a 1956 case resulting from an ad lib on television, the court said that extemporaneously delivered defamation is libel because of the widespread dissemination. In *Shor v. Billingsley,* a conflict resulting in name-calling between two well-known restaurant owners in New York City resulted in a precedent that television defamation had a great capacity for harm and should be treated as libel even if there were no written script. Because of their reach and impact, broadcast stations can deliver defamatory material with considerable effect, so the libel designation has been favored by most courts.

The 1964 *New York Times v. Sullivan* decision, in bringing defamation cases under the United States Constitution, tended to blur the distinction between slander and libel for broadcast defamation, with Sullivan treating it as libel. The American Law Institute has determined that the more severe penalties, the higher amounts awarded, in libel should be expected from radio and television defamation rather the lesser awards in slander because of the extensive harm to reputations resulting from the vast numbers of people in the potential reach of broadcast communications. The American Law Institute determined that the old distinction between libel and slander was based on the centuries-old belief that there was no enhancement for oral defamation and it could reach only small audiences, which of course, is no longer true.

Libel is considered a greater wrong than is slander, therefore the great potential for dissemination through radio and television dictates that the defamation carried on the airwaves must be treated as libel. There are special circumstances related to ad libs, audience participation, eyewitnesses to news events or other interviewees, that might indicate to the court that a station should not be liable. A newspaper is strictly accountable for anything it publishes, but a radio or television station could end up with someone on the air under live broadcast conditions whose outburst cannot be controlled. If the station is powerless to stop a spontaneous defamation, it might not be held to the rule of strict accountability.

A simple definition for slander would be spoken defamation. Libel is defamation that has the potential for widespread dissemination because it is communicated through a mass medium. Defamation, as indicated earlier, is communication that tends to cause a person to be ridiculed or humiliated, brings about hatred or contempt, a lowering of esteem among peers, injury in business or occupation, and even being shunned or avoided.

In addition to defamation, when a person feels he or she has been libeled or slandered, three other basic elements must be proved—publication, identification and negligence/falsity. Publication is defined as a third disinterested party seeing or hearing the libel. When libel occurs in the mass media, this in not a difficult thing to prove. Identification is defined as people being able to recognize who is being defamed. When a name is used, there is little doubt; however, nicknames, descriptions, demographic profiles, pictures, caricatures and silhouettes also can be used to identify a person. Negligence/falsity is defined as demonstrating that the accusations made about the plaintiff are false. The plaintiff must prove the mass media organization was negligent and printed or broadcast information that is inaccurate, misleading and/or incomplete.

In law, defamation is a tort, a civil wrong for which redress is sought through a lawsuit for monetary damages. When a criminal wrong is committed, the state prosecutes the offender on behalf of society. When there is a tort, the injured person must seek compensation through the civil courts. Although no crime has been committed, society still has a recourse available for damage to one's reputation. Society has an interest in the right to protect an individual's good name and the tort of defamation demonstrates that interest. The aggrieved can become the plaintiff in the filing of an action under civil law to recover money from another. It is the harm to reputation, and the extent of that harm, that determines the amount of money in damages to be assessed against the defendant.

Journalists must exercise great care to avoid harmful words. Jurors are quite likely to value the reputation of a plaintiff very highly and often they go out of their way to compensate the plaintiff for the perceived harm done to his or her reputation. Jurors with no background in writing or reporting are often called upon to make sweeping judgments on journalistic performance. Jury members find themselves intensively examining reporting techniques, editing methods and all of the steps in the processing of news. They can even hear of the plaintiff's inquiry into the state of mind of a journalist in the information-seeking process. With inexperienced people weighing journalistic considerations and passing judgments on media performance, it is possible that juries might be predisposed against the media in libel cases. Despite this, few cases are lost by the media; however, judgments in the hundreds of thousands of dollars do result in the cases that are lost. Add to that the $100,000 and up in court costs in any full trial. There are also the costs of defeating the cases that never come to trial, the ones that are settled out of court, and even the ones that result in victory for the defendant. In sum, there are compelling reasons not to get sued, even if you can win.

Defenses in Libel/ Slander Lawsuits

The defenses available to the target of a libel action demonstrate the methods one can use to avoid a lawsuit. The first defense, sometimes called a complete defense, is provable truth. If what is published or broadcast can be proved as true, there is no libel. Reporters, their editors, the medium's lawyers, and the management will want to assure themselves that the words are true before using them.

The second defense is "privilege." If a story was a fair and accurate report from a public record, an official document, a judicial proceeding or from a public official in the conduct of duty, there is no libel. So, if the writer fairly and accurately quotes or paraphrases from the official documents kept by a county or city, or records of an agency that the law requires must be kept, those are privileged, or immune, from libel action. Reporting from an adversary proceeding in a courtroom also carries this immunity. Prosecutors, defense attorneys, witnesses, and judges all have a primary privilege attached to their words in a trial so that justice can be achieved from a welter of conflicting arguments and impressions. News media that report these words fairly and accurately are given a secondary privilege, which amounts to an immunity from libel even where harm is done. This is sometimes called a conditional privilege. The conditions are that everything must be reported fairly and accurately. If a mistake, a misquote, a misimpression or a biased account appears, the privilege is lost.

School boards, city councils, state legislatures, and other such public bodies must debate without hesitancy or reservation the serious issues before them or we might not get good law. A representative form of government cannot have its officials constrained by a fear of libel laws in their efforts to get honest evaluations of potential legislation before them. If they are to vote on measures without full argument and heated discussion, we might be denied responsible laws. They must have a wide-open, free-wheeling, robust debate before establishing public policy. Their primary privilege results in a secondary privilege attaching to the media that offer those debates to the public for scrutiny. Again, it is conditional on its fairness and accuracy.

A third defense is called "fair comment and criticism." In this defense, truth or falsity are not issues.

Do you think the mass media, especially the news media, get away with too much concerning defamation under existing standards? Why?

If you could rewrite the legal guidelines for libel and slander, how would you do it? Why?

When the media offer reviews, commentaries and editorials, they can defend themselves by demonstrating that their comments were fair and they were simply expressing opinions. Courts have generally protected opinion, holding that differences of opinion should be worked out in debate, not in the courtroom. The media defend themselves by pointing out that an opinion was based on an accurate statement of fact and was directed at those who invite such comment by placing themselves before the public for approval or disapproval. This is based on the assumption that if someone appears in a public performance, that person can expect booing and hissing as well as applause. A politician must expect opposing candidates to comment on his or her fitness for office. A person who provides a service to the public and charges for it has to expect some kind of review of that offering.

The jury will determine if the defendant can prove that the opinion was based on fact and if the comment was fair. The fairness is likely to be determined by whether the comment stayed with the actual public performance or the public life of the office holder rather that into tangential, private, unrelated matters. This defense gives the media protection for their criticism of artists and their art, literary figures and their writings, athletes and their performances, as well as those who sing, dance, play instruments or run for political office. Reviews of movies, plays, exhibits and restaurants are also included.

An additional defense is available to anyone sued for libel by a public official or public figure. To some, this seems like an extension of the fair comment and criticism defense. It does deal with public performances or the seeking of public approval. If the defendant can prove that there was no actual "malice," the plaintiff

can lose even if there has been defamation. Actual malice is defined as publishing or broadcasting a statement knowing that it was false or recklessly disregarding whether it was false. Reckless disregard could be determined by the jury as not following standard journalistic procedures, violating basic rules of fair play and objectivity followed universally by journalists, or someone in the newsroom accepting information from a source who is not at all credible. This defense is available only when a journalist is sued by a public official or a public figure caught up in a controversial issue of major importance.

The intent of this defense is to make it very difficult for government officials to file suit as private citizens and use the libel laws to punish reporters and their news organizations because they disclose the public's business. Any office holder is expected to carry a heavier burden than a private citizen would and should find it more difficult to win a libel suit. This is meant to stop the practice of using libel suits to infringe on the freedom of the press to report on government actions. Those who seek office and put themselves into the middle of significant public issues have to expect searching examinations of their activities and an uninhibited scrutiny of their actions. Therefore, any medium sued for libel by such a plaintiff is held accountable only to defamation resulting from actual malice. An unintended, accidental error would be enough to establish falsity in other libel suits but not when the plaintiff is expected to be under the microscope.

Public officials and public figures are to understand that there is a risk to seeking the spotlight, that the public has a right to investigations into their official conduct and such investigations cannot be thwarted by the chilling effect of libel suits. The Sullivan case set out a Constitutional defense, with the First Amendment supplying a protection for discussion of public matters clearly needed for an informed electorate. An open society needs a free-wheeling, vigorous press so that its citizens can participate in their own government. An unfortunate accidental falsity is not to be allowed to create a climate in which the media are chilled by fear of losing libel suits.

Freedom of Information/Sunshine Laws

Journalists contend that the public's business should be conducted openly and public documents should be readily accessible. To support that contention, journalists often seek such openness through state and federal laws designed to force public officials to meet in public and to open public records and documents for public scrutiny.

Such "open records" laws are called Freedom of Information (FoI) laws and such "open meetings" laws are called "Sunshine Laws." Both types are based on the belief that government in a free society should operate in the open, in the sunshine. These laws are designed either to open public documents to public view or to ensure that meetings of policy-making arms of government agencies are open for all to attend.

All 50 states have laws requiring some public access to government information. Generally, they hold that matters of public record subject to scrutiny are those documents required to be kept by state law. This excludes internal memoranda and files kept by officials for their own convenience. Many records are kept by officials that reporters and the public are not necessarily aware of and most of these probably would not have to be revealed. In addition, there are exceptions and exemptions in each state for personnel matters, medical records, tax information, etc.

Open meetings laws exist in every state, but also allow for some exceptions. Meetings of city councils and school boards generally are required to be open, but members can conduct secret meetings called executive sessions when they consider employee salaries, personnel records, hiring and firing of staff, and anything that might involve a potential invasion of privacy.

There are two federal laws permitting inspection of government records and allowing reporters and the public to attend meetings of federal agencies. Congress passed the federal FoI Act in 1966 and has amended it several times since then. Almost all departments and agencies of the federal bureaucracy are required to comply with requests to provide information about their activities. Exceptions include the CIA and the Internal Revenue Service. Under the act, a reporter, on behalf of the public, must file a request for documents in writing. The agency has 10 working days either to provide the requested information or to deny the request. If the request is denied, a lawsuit can be filed to force the release of the information. The FoI Act contains exceptions for documents related to national security, reports of financial institutions, personnel records, medical records and the investigatory files of law enforcement agencies.

President Clinton signed into law in late 1996 a provision that makes the FoI Act apply to the electronic storage of information. This means that people can request government information that has been stored on computer tapes, files and disks. The guidelines for such information are the same as for hard-copy documents.

The other federal law opens the meetings of dozens of government agencies to public view. Usually, the law is referred to as the Government in the Sunshine Act, it was passed by Congress in 1976. It also contains numerous exceptions, including meetings related to national security, medical and tax issues and discussions of pending lawsuits. This law also says federal agencies must announce the time and place of their meetings in advance so interested parties can attend.

It is not easy to actually use state and federal FoI and sunshine laws. Officials and clerks frequently delay their responses to requests until the last possible moment, require the public to pay "overtime" costs for the people who search for the requested documents and complain that they are short-handed and do not have the budget or the time to help reporters or members of the public with their searches for information. FoI laws make little or no provision for what to do in the case of non-compliance or slow compliance. There are a few criminal sanctions for bureaucrats who violate FoI laws and most really don't fear entrusting their fate to the legal system. Government secrecy is still a problem, of course, and FoI laws and sunshine laws do not guarantee complete and total access to records, documents and meetings. They do, however, guarantee some openness.

Copyright

Copyright law is related to trademarks and patents. It is protection for intellectual property. An author can get protection from infringement by others for creative work, especially literary property. Copyright law prevents others from using the actual literary expression embodied in a poem, song, play, short story, radio program, television program, novel, movie script, etc.

You cannot get copyright protection for an idea, nor for a fact, only for that which is original and creative. You can copyright something that is tangible, including choreographic works, maps, architectural drawings, photographs and works of art. You cannot copyright news, although a description of a news event can be copyrighted. Also, a complete newscast or edition of a newspaper qualifies for copyright protection, because you can copyright the creative layout, design, structure and placement of items in a newscast or on a printed page.

It is not a violation of freedom of the press to limit the use of copyrighted material, because what you may publish or broadcast is specifically limited in this area of law only by the ownership rights of others. Copyright law says literary, artistic and creative works, when original, are transformed into private property. Each of us has the right to control access to our private property, whether real estate, personal property, or literary property.

Applying for Copyright Protection

A copyright notice is placed on a literary or artistic work, stating that it is the protected property of a named author as of a specified date. This tells everyone that it cannot be copied or performed in public without the consent of the copyright owner until the copyright expires. A copyright is in effect for the period of the author's life plus 70 years. Even if the copyright notice is unintentionally omitted, the material is still protected from infringement if the copyright is registered with the federal government.

To gain full protection, the copyright owner must register with the U.S. Copyright Office in Washington, D.C. Authors must submit two copies of the work, a completed application form and a small fee. If infringement occurs after a copyright is registered, the copyright owner may file a lawsuit to collect either statutory damages or actual damages. Statutory damages are determined by the court, and are likely to be an arbitrary sum between $300 and $10,000. Actual damages cover the full amount of the infringer's net profits, if any. For a popular song or book, this could result in an award of millions of dollars.

Courts have always held that some copying of protected works should be allowed under the concept of "fair use." This typically means that a line from a poem, a few words from a song, a paragraph from a short story, etc., could be used without permission in a review. Book reviewers, drama critics and movie reviewers have some latitude in writing about copyrighted material. In general, it is expected that one can quote without permission, up to 250 words from a long work—a short story or novel—and much less from a shorter work. Courts also have ruled that it is not a copyright infringement to use all of a song for a parody. Weird Al Yankovic and others who satirize music are allowed to do so under fair use. Other areas that qualify for the "fair use' protection are legitimate news reports, news-related commentaries and analyses, scholarship and research, plus teaching-related activities. Such use must be in the public's interest, must be limited in scope, must be for nonprofit or educational purposes and must not negatively affect the income-generating potential of the original work. Finally, the Supreme Court has ruled that at-home, non-commercial recording off television for personal use is not a copyright infringement.

Recent Research, Developments and Issues

Janet Jackson's "wardrobe malfunction" during the 2004 Super Bowl halftime show seemed to crystallize efforts to clean up perceived indecent programming on radio and television. The Federal Communications Commission fined CBS a total of $550,000. The amount came from the imposition of a $27,500 fine for each of CBS's 20 owned and operated stations in the United States. The FCC decided not to fine all of the CBS affiliated stations that were not owned by the network's parent company, Viacom, Inc.

The FCC justified the largest fine ever against a television broadcaster based on the 540,000 complaints it received after Jackson's breast was bared when Justin Timberlake removed a portion of her outfit. One FCC commissioner, Jonathan Adelstein, thought the fine should have been more substantial, because CBS made more than $140 million in advertising revenue from the Super Bowl.

About a month after fining CBS, the FCC fined Fox affiliates for airing an "indecent" episode of its reality series, "Married by America." The FCC had received complaints about material that featured male and female strippers in a variety of sexual situations. The commissioners said the material was indecent, patently offensive, and was intended to pander to and titillate the audience.

In June, 2004, Clear Channel Communications agreed to pay a record $1.75 million to settle indecency complaints against Howard Stern and other on-air personalities.

The FCC and federal law prohibit radio stations and over-the-air television stations from airing indecent material between 6:00 A.M. and 10:00 P.M. Material can be judged indecent if it meets a three-pronged test:

1. An average person, applying contemporary community standards, must find that the material, taken as a whole, appeals to prurient interests;

2. The material must depict or describe, in a patently offensive way, sexual conduct specifically defined by law;

3. The material, taken as a whole, must lack serious literary, artistic, political or scientific value.

In the fallout from the Jackson "reveal," major networks and local stations started using slight delays during live programming to avoid the possibility of indecent acts finding their way to the air. CBS used an audio and video delay during the 2004 Grammy Awards.

Viacom and the Walt Disney Co. were fined a total of $1.5 million for violating advertising limits for children's TV programming. Viacom paid $1 million for violations on its Nickelodeon cable network. Disney paid $500,000 for violations on its ABC Family Channel.

For children's TV programs, FCC rules limit commercials to 10.5 minutes per hour on weekends and 12 minutes per hour during weekdays. The rules also bar airing commercials that refer to or offer products related to the program.

Viacom broke the minutes-per-hour limits about 600 times and the product-placement rule about 145 times in 2003. Disney found 31 half-hour episodes where product placement occurred. Both companies blamed human and computer error for the violations.

In August, 2004, a federal judge held a *Time* reporter in contempt of court for refusing to testify before a grand jury investigating the leaking of the name of a covert CIA officer. Matthew Cooper was asked to testify regarding alleged conversations with an executive branch official. The contempt order was lifted about two weeks later when Cooper agreed to testify after his source waived confidentiality.

In early 2008, the Fox TV network decided to challenge the FCC's proposed fine of almost $100,000 for pixilated nudity aired during an episode of *Married by America* in 2003. Fox filed a petition for reconsideration of the FCC's decision to fine the network and some of its affiliated local stations for indecency.

Fox wasn't the only network hit by the FCC in its effort to crack down on indecency on television. ABC and 52 of its affiliate stations were fined a total of $1.4 million for a 2003 episode of *NYPD Blue* that featured shots of a woman's nude buttocks. The FCC claimed the episode depicted sexual or excretory activities in a patently offensive way and was aired between the hours of 6 A.M. and 10 P.M.

Experts noted several interesting aspects associated with the FCC's sanctions against the two television networks and their affiliates:

1. In keeping with its stated intent to deal harshly with perceived indecency, the FCC made it easier to file a complaint by placing a complaint form on its web site.

2. The FCC reiterated its intent to continue to use its contemporary national standard of what is considered patently offensive rather than resort to local standards on a case-by-case basis.

3. The FCC refused to accept pixilation and parental warnings as defenses against charges of indecency.

4. The FCC refused to permit affiliate stations to argue that they should not be held accountable for what their networks put on the air. The FCC said each licensee is responsible for all of the programming that it shares with the public, no matter what the programming source.

In 2006, the FCC fined CBS again for indecency. This time, the $3.6 million fine was for depictions of teenagers engaged in a sexual orgy that aired as part of an episode of *Without a Trace*.

The FCC's "fleeting indecency" policy received new scrutiny after actress Diane Keaton uttered an unbleeped f-word on ABC-TV's "Good Morning America" in early 2008. The FCC received thousands of complaints about the expletive and ABC's failure to keep it off the air.

"Slip of the tongue" indecencies, especially during live broadcasts, used to be sort of "forgiven," but the FCC changed its policies after singer Bono used the f-word during the 2003 Golden Globe Awards. After an appeals court struck down the new, get-tough policy, the FCC appealed the ruling to the U.S. Supreme Court. The Court agreed to hear the case and promised a ruling sometime in the fall of 2008.

Representatives for the major television networks warned that if the FCC were to win its case and be permitted to fine networks and local stations for fleeting expletives and other "spur of the moment" indecencies, it would likely mean the end of live broadcasting. Networks and stations would have to air everything on a delayed basis in order to ensure that no offensive language or acts would make it to the public. With fines as high as $325,000 per profanity or indecency possible, most networks and local stations would not be willing to risk incurring the wrath of the FCC.

The FCC was busy in other areas, too. It issued new rules for newspaper-broadcast cross-ownership arrangements. The new rules removed some of the restrictions on cross-ownership, permitting such consolidation in the country's top 20 markets. Cross-ownership is permitted in smaller markets as long as at least seven hours of news are added to the TV station's programming or either the newspaper and/or the TV station is in financial distress. In the large markets, cross-ownership is permitted only when there are at least eight other independent voices for news and information, plus the cross-owned station cannot be one of the top four in the ratings.

A 2008 study found that cross-owned TV stations actually aired more news than did noncross-owned stations. The cross-owned stations aired about 6% more news on average and up to about 10% more local news than did noncross-owned stations. In addition, cross-owned stations presented 25% more coverage of local and state politics than did noncross-owned stations.

Copyright infringement continues to be a hot topic in Hollywood. In early 2008, leaders in the film and recording industries began lobbying Congressional leaders to pass legislation that would force colleges and universities to filter their computer networks to deter copyright infringement. A study by the Motion Picture Association of America reported that college students, using their schools' high-speed computer networks, were responsible for at least 15% of piracy-related financial losses in the movie industry.

In England, legislation was being developed in early 2008 that would require Internet service providers to cut service to people who illegally download music or films. An estimated six million people per year illegally download music or films in England.

In 2007, Viacom sued YouTube and Google, the owner of YouTube, for copyright infringement. The $1 billion lawsuit claimed YouTube facilitated copyright infringement by its users and did not monitor content closely enough to filter out illegal uses of Viacom's copyrighted material. Viacom was especially concerned about the illegal uses of its MTV and Comedy Central programming content.

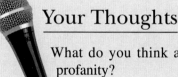

Your Thoughts

What do you think about the government's attempts to control broadcast indecency and profanity?

What do you think about the attempts to reduce copyright infringement?

Think Back

1. What were the major cases in obscenity/pornography law and what was decided?

2. What are the major factors that courts use to determine whether something is obscene or not?

3. What is meant by "reporter's privilege?"

4. What are the basic arguments for and against "cameras in the courtroom?"

5. What are the major issues associated with "free press/fair trial" concerns?

6. How might a judge try to cope with the effects of extra-judicial publicity in the media?

7. What are the major ways in which a person's privacy might be invaded by media organizations?

8. What are the major defenses used in an invasion of privacy case?

9. Define libel and slander.

10. What must a plaintiff in a libel case prove?

11. What are the major defenses that can be used in a libel case?

12. What types of monetary damages can be awarded in a libel case?

13. What are the major precedent-setting cases in libel? What was decided?

14. What is meant by Freedom of Information (FoI)?

15. What is meant by "sunshine laws?"

16. How absolute are FoI laws and sunshine laws? What are some of the major exceptions?

17. What is the definition of "copyright" and how long does a copyright last?

18. What can and cannot be copyrighted?

19. How does someone acquire a legal copyright?

20. What is "fair use" of copyrighted material?

21. What has the FCC been up to concerning "indecency" in radio and television?

22. What are some of the latest developments in the battle over cross-ownership of newspapers and television stations?

23. What's new in the on-going battle over alleged copyright infringement?

15

Ethics

Two thousand years ago in Greece, a philosophy developed that included the concept of ethics, the study of what is good for the individual as well as society. Ethics, to the Greeks, meant patterns of moral behavior that the individual could rationally explain, that could be socially justified, meaning that difficult choices could be made through a critical process, or judgments based on what is good or bad.

Over the centuries, philosophers have identified ethics as a branch of philosophy that is dependent upon making choices not necessarily between good and bad or right and wrong. Often one is faced with equally justifiable actions and is bound by duty or circumstances to decide. It could be equally competing unattractive possibilities that force a dilemma. A knowledge of ethics is supposed to hone the critical faculties that allow a person to make tough choices, to reject part of the conflict rationally.

Ethics is a branch of philosophy that is dependent upon self-imposed conduct based on a consistent set of principles. A basic foundation of broad morality-based principles is necessary before any specific rules can be implemented. Rules of right conduct are general at first and specific only later when an ethical decision is faced. A set of basic principles, as a result, is meaningful to the individual although there is a collective-determined blueprint for morality or responsibility in any society. It is the individual's conduct arrived at individually that is ethics in action. In theory, the individual can learn of broad principles of rational action through the socialization process. In the final analysis, ethics is personal and individual.

Ethics comes from the Greek word ethos, meaning character, but has been used by philosophers over time to indicate a set of standards or responsibilities that we use to guide our behavior toward each other, more like rules of conscience. Ethics deals with the philosophical foundations of making decisions from both good and bad options. One has a good character as a result of making good choices from such options. Philosophers describe ethical choices as moral judgments leading to right rather than wrong behaviors, choices resulting from an understanding of our obligations to others in a collective setting.

It has been more than 2,000 years since Aristotle first lectured on ethics at the Lyceum in Athens, with his rules of conduct and explanations of virtue and goodness. As a teenager, Aristotle began his studies at Plato's Academy, remaining there for nearly 20 years. His earliest written works showed the influence of Plato. Even after leaving Athens for a time and establishing himself as head of his own philosophical school, he continued to display respect for his former teacher, but during those years he decided to rethink his philosophical positions and managed to break from Plato's influence. Upon returning to Athens, Aristotle founded his own center of philosophy at the Lyceum, the so-called "peripatetic" school. This was where Aristotle did most of his writing and teaching of ethics, with his insistence that there are no known absolute moral standards. Aristotle offered instead an ethical theory based on an understanding of human thought, human nature and the realities of daily life.

Aristotle initiated his study of ethics by collecting and analyzing facts, a critical and empirical method that allowed him to generalize from a systemic basis. He is noted for generalizing not only from inductive reasoning but also through the syllogism, a specific form of deductive reasoning. A syllogism proceeds from previously established general rules or facts down to particular instances. A syllogism has a major premise and a minor premise, or a universal premise and a particular premise. The usually offered example looks like this:

Universal (major) Premise:	All men are mortal.
Particular (minor) Premise:	Socrates was a man.
Conclusion:	Socrates was mortal.

A syllogism must start with relevant facts before its conclusions can be expected to determine valid relationships. The underlying rules or principles to be stated from this method are dependent upon the truth and accuracy of the premises, which must also cover all possible cases. One can make a logically correct but untrue conclusion by reasoning correctly from false premises. For example, one could start with the universal premise that all men are mortal, then posit that Max, a dog, is mortal. The false conclusion that Max, the dog, is a man would be incorrect.

Aristotle, through his logical analysis, came up with an ethical philosophy that started with the assumption that the aim of all human action is Good. He said that all human actions and choices aim at some good, with all human activity eventually directed toward happiness. It was his contention that one attains happiness by a virtuous life and the development of reason. The end toward which we are directed for its own sake is absolute good, which motivates all actions and choices. Knowledge of this good gives us an aim for life and a standard for evaluation.

In some instances, the good of the individual and the good of society will coincide, but when they don't, the good of society is to take precedence. It is worthwhile to achieve the good of the individual, but it is even better to achieve the good of the many.

Each of us in different circumstances will define happiness differently, but the nature of happiness is not the issue. The kind of life one leads will determine the type and extent of happiness, and the Good will be derived from that life. The moral life is recommended and is to be acquired through moderation in all things except virtue. Knowledge and self-discipline can lead to moral virtue, which requires conscious choice and moral purpose.

Aristotle believed that a human being's capacity for reasoning was the characteristic that clearly distinguished humans from animals. This ability to reason was, in Aristotle's view, a justification for existence and where inherent goodness can be found in the individual. Moral virtue then is when the human brings appetites and desires under the control of reason. Aristotle did not think of irrational desires and selfish appetites as bad in themselves, but simply as a part of human nature to be brought under rational control. To be lacking in moral virtue is to allow for an excess of animal appetites. Intellectual virtues, on the other hand, cannot have an excess because they are inherently rational and consist of knowledge and understanding. Aristotle believed that intellectual virtue came from learning, but moral virtue was derived from habituation. He contended that one had to practice self-discipline according to a moral principle in a social setting to achieve the motivation necessary to acquire moral virtue.

Aristotle said that choice is closely related to virtue, in that a deliberate choice from possible actions is a key to moral purpose, which he called the most important element in a virtuous act. Choice is a result of one's own initiative and is both voluntary and deliberate, much like a rational wish. According to Aristotle, one can wish for the unattainable, but by definition one can only choose that which is available. Choice then is a result of deliberating about the means to an end that can be met. He said that actions are concerned with means, therefore they are based on choice. This means that each of us is personally responsible for our acts. This concept of personal moral responsibility is particularly important to Aristotle's argument that societies are created so that we can live well and develop our full potentials. If moral purpose is the most important element in a virtuous act, then it finds its zenith in those acts designed to achieve the good in the larger community, because it is composed of many individuals, each of whom will benefit.

Aristotle's ethics include descriptions of individual virtues, such as character, courage and self-control. Much attention is given to different forms of courage. First, is the courage that is between fear and recklessness, with the real test coming in the face of dangers that are within one's ability to control. A courageous person endures fear because of a desire to act with nobility. Aristotle also talks about civic courage, which results from the sake of honor or renown and to escape disgrace. There is also the courage of experience, primarily knowing when danger is real or being familiar with potentially dangerous circumstances. He dismisses as less worthwhile, courage based on blind emotion, optimism or on ignorance. According to Aristotle, courage involves facing what is painful and finding the mean between feelings of fear and feelings of confidence. The end result of courage is pleasant because courage is a virtue, and at its highest level courage makes one even more noble and virtuous.

Aristotle described self-control as a key factor in a person's moral responsibility, with attention to temperance as an adult behavior and self-indulgence as childish. Self-control is a means in regard to sensual pleasures, with a temperate individual enjoying only pleasures that are compatible with nobility and which contribute to health and well-being.

In sum, Aristotle concluded that a virtuous person is one who makes the right choice as a result of free will between alternative courses of action, without yielding to coercion or ignorance. One must anticipate the probable consequences of each course of action and then select the one with the greater amount of good and the lesser amount of evil. If a decision is made based on advance knowledge of the possibilities, it will be a good act if it began with a good motive, used good means, and was followed by good consequences.

Before Aristotle, his mentor Plato had formulated a different ethical view. Plato conceived of a universal good, a single universal ideal. Plato said there is an absolute good which is the source of all goodness in the universe.

Aristotle was not willing to accept the ethical observations from others that the good life was dependent upon obedience to a set of laws imposed on people from without. Instead, he held that the good life consists in the proper development and control of elements within one's own life. Because of this, Aristotle is often referred to as an exponent of self-realization ethics, meaning that organizing all of the elements of one's personality will result in achieving goodness, or a realization of the self. To achieve this, it is necessary to subordinate immediate and short-lived appetites and desires to those pertaining to the whole of life. One must adjust personal interests to the welfare of others, never sacrificing the welfare of a larger group to promote the interests of a smaller one.

Aristotle did not lay down exact rules of conduct because each human being is different from the others, despite some similarities among us, and the circumstances of our lives are constantly changing. Because we need to be prepared for any situation that might arise, what is appropriate for one person in a certain situation will not apply to someone else in a different situation. Instead, according to Aristotle, the good person is one who finds pleasure and satisfaction in doing things that are in harmony with his own good and also the good of others. This is done by acquiring good habits over time, making choices from a sense of duty, and eventually developing a character that makes the right decisions automatic instead of duty-generated.

Traditional Theories of Ethics

Philosophical theories of ethics include the consequentialists, who are results oriented. This means consequences, and consequences only, determine whether an action is right or wrong. There are three important schools of thought in this category: utilitarianism, pragmatism and ethical egoism.

Utilitarians believe that each individual should act in the best interest of everyone concerned. The majority benefit is given the highest priority by anyone faced with an ethical choice, with the individual's needs taking second place. This assumes that each person has a clear awareness of what is best for all and of exactly what is or is not good. The principle of utility has been expressed often in the familiar phrase, "the greatest good for the greatest number." The good of the community, the nation, the collective unit, should be sought and it will include the good of the decision-maker as well.

British philosophers Jeremy Bentham and John Stuart Mill are the originators of utilitarianism as a common ethical view in the modern Western world. Pleasure and happiness were cited by them in the early 19th century as the primary ends of human action. More recently, philosophers have noted that values other than these promoting the pleasurable possess inherent worth.

Happiness, as such, in more recent utilitarian views has been one of the values, not the only one, to be achieved through right decisions. We can distribute the desired results to many more people who might see worth in other attainments, such as home, family, good health, learning, friendship. By producing even more good when we promote values in addition to pleasure or happiness, we reach the greatest number. This wide dissemination of good is an important part of Mills' principle of utility.

Pragmatists believe that truth is what works in practical circumstances. It is successful behavior associated with real-life choices. Pragmatism is to base your conduct on practical means and expedients. There is an element of prediction in this consequentialist theory, because it emphasizes the practical outcomes of events on the assumption that they will replicate themselves later.

The ethical egoist theory holds that we should act in our own self-interests. There are personal ethical egoists and universal ethical egoists. The personal ethical egoist allows others to choose or decide on their own, while operating in his or her own self-interest. The universal ethical egoist believes that in every instance the person's self-interest is the guiding factor in determining ethical conduct.

The traditional philosophical name for consequentialism is teleology theory. It emphasizes the consequences of behavior with the need for an individual to analyze all possible outcomes before taking an action or making a decision. Much attention has been given to what many refer to as situational ethics, which provides an opportunity for individual judgments. Situational ethics is a form of consequentialism.

Non-consequentialism is also called deontological theory and suggests that the propriety of an act, for the most part, ignores outcomes. Three examples of non-consequentialism are: natural law theory, duty ethics and divine command.

In natural law theory the best moral position derives from dictates of reason. The original notion was that we are rational because we are wired that way. Any of us can come to the same answers on questions of ethics. We arrive at our ethical conduct rationally as part of a "It's meant to be" philosophy.

The German philosopher Immanuel Kant formulated duty ethics, which calls on us to act from a sense of obligation. Kant described a fundamental moral law, derived from rationality, that he called the categorical imperative. Through it, each of us knows right from wrong on a moral principle that is binding for everyone. The categorical imperative directs the will of everyone. It is fundamental to all of us. According to duty ethics, we are obligated not because of results but because something is good in and of itself. There are no exceptions to the position that there is always only one correct action, no matter what the circumstances and no matter what the potential consequences. One is law abiding or truthful not because crime victims are injured or people are hurt by lies, but because each of us has a moral duty to follow the law or to be honest.

Divine command theory depends on God. What God commands is right. What God forbids is wrong. This category of non-consequentialism is quite simple for the religious person. For others, it offers the subjective possibility that God commands or forbids something that is already right or wrong rather than it being right or wrong because of God's command. This philosophy emphasizes a clear cut nature of any decision, saying that there are absolutes with no gray areas. Kant's categorical imperative implies that what is right for one is right for all. To Kant, that meant an unconditional, without exceptions, adherence to moral law no matter what the consequences. This is the golden rule in operation, a guide to morally right actions that should be universal law. Kant believed that the conscience was directed by higher truths that must be obeyed within each of us.

According to Kant, one must do what is right under any circumstance and it will be morally right if there are no feelings of guilt because moral law is found in the conscience, not in the human ability to reason. If individuals do not faithfully follow universal duty then societies will be threatened. Obedience to a higher duty will guarantee that all will benefit from individual decisions, that there is a universality to each individual act based on conscience, and that truth and altruism are inherently good for each and for all.

Modern Theories of Ethics

There are newer approaches to ethical behavior that have arisen with mass communication. For example, the justice is blind school of thought, suggests that no biases or prejudices be permitted to influence behavior and no special favors should be granted to anyone. The equal treatment for all is stressed. No special treatment in decision-making is to be given to any individual, group, or institution based on race, creed, color, religion, social position, or financial status.

There is also a theory that requires that the individual seek the middle ground when confronted with extreme possibilities in an ethical decision. This "Golden Mean" school of thought suggests that looking for a possible compromise between widely divergent courses of action could be the most ethical determination.

An extreme possibility, not necessarily acceptable, is one that received considerable attention in the politics of the 1960s—benign neglect. This is the dysfunctional approach that arises when no choice can be made because any alternative is totally undesirable. You do nothing in hopes that the problem will eventually solve itself, or simply go away. The possibility here is that more harm could be done by taking a course of action, therefore if one avoids the dilemma it is more ethical than making a bad situation worse.

General Ethical Concerns

Ethical issues abound in contemporary media. Legal, social, political, economic and moral dilemmas in broadcast, film, recording and print media management, advertising, and public relations occur regularly. Most of the legal concerns center on libel, privacy, copyright, and on the FCC and its rules and regulations. Most political concerns are with coverage of candidates and issues. Social issues are viewed in terms of media effects, or possible impact on the public of content, such as violence or pornography, especially in books and films. Moral issues and ethical issues are virtually synonymous with an apparent assumption that ethical norms are actually rules of moral conduct.

Many definitions of ethics talk about moral choices or moral principles and values as central to an ethical course of action. A typical description of ethics would stress propriety and the moral equality of a course of action. The term ethics refers to applying moral values or to evaluating right from wrong in an individual act but based on societal standards.

Newspapers are seen as unethical by those who decry what they perceive as sensationalism, invasion of personal privacy, bias, and subservience to powerful advertisers. Magazines generate some of the same complaints. Movies and books are described as pandering to the lowest common denominator, to lowering the taste of the masses. Broadcast ethics are cited in such instances as possibly deceptive commercials, invasion of privacy, giving news coverage to terrorists, payola, disc jockeys' indecent language, and any perceived offensive content or bad taste, among many possibilities.

Ethics in Journalism

Discussions, examinations and condemnations of the ethics of politicians and business leaders have been especially "hot" topics lately. Journalists have had a field day exposing the perceived unethical behavior of the rich and powerful. Just about every day some new revelation surfaces about the economic or sexual misdeeds and shenanigans of some public official or public figure.

Such revelations sell newspapers and magazines. Such revelations boost ratings. Many journalists piously denounce the perceived unethical behavior of many of our fallen heroes.

The old saying about throwing stones and living in glass houses pertains here. One of the reasons that journalists have a major image problem is that sometimes journalists don't behave in a very ethical manner. They lie, cheat, fabricate and bully. They have conflicts of interest, they invade people's privacy, they misrepresent themselves, they sensationalize, they overdramatize, they refuse to correct mistakes and they place too much emphasis on "bad" news. They're arrogant, impatient, uncaring and unfeeling. In short, too often too many journalists are too unethical.

Your Thoughts

Write your own definition of ethics.

Why did you include such elements?

Moral Standards

One of the most critical problems associated with ethics in any profession is determining just what is and what is not ethical behavior. This is especially true in journalism, because the issue of "freedom of the press" complicates the process of trying to create guidelines—do's and don'ts—that might restrict news gathering efforts in any way.

There are many definitions of ethics:

1. A system or code of morals of a person, group or profession
2. Moral philosophies
3. Standards of conduct and moral judgment
4. Principles, standards or habits with respect to what is right and wrong in conduct or character

The bottom line, of course, is ethics deals with what is appropriate, fair, right and moral behavior. It's a complicated issue. There are no easy answers. There are no easy prescriptions. The complexities are not overwhelming, though.

Ethics are very personal things. We can have standards, guidelines and codes for groups and professions, but if individuals don't CHOOSE to abide by such standards, guidelines and codes, the system breaks down. Journalists have to make several choices every day—which stories to cover, which sources to interview, which comments and information to include, which angles to stress, how long to make a story, where to place the story—so the opportunities to take the ethical path or the unethical path are almost constantly present.

Ethical Theories in Practice

Traditional theories of ethics can help journalists in their quest to behave in an ethical manner. The "Golden Mean" theory suggests that the best way to determine what is ethical and what is not ethical is to examine the extreme behaviors possible in a situation and then try to take some sort of "middle ground" action.

Example: You're waiting to interview an important businesswoman in her office. She hasn't come in yet. You notice an envelope marked "Confidential" on her desk. You suspect it might contain important information that is critical to the story you're working on.

One extreme behavior would be to steal the envelope (or at least peek inside) before the woman returns. The other extreme would be to ignore the envelope completely and hope to obtain the information in some other way. The middle ground would be to ask the woman if you can read the contents of the envelope.

The "Categorical Imperative" theory suggests that there are universal rights and wrongs. In other words, no matter what the circumstances and no matter what the potential consequences, there is always only one "correct" action. There are no exceptions.

Example: Back to the envelope scenario. If the "right" thing to do is wait until the businesswoman returns and ask her for permission to read the contents of the envelope, then that's what an ethical journalist should do. HOWEVER, if the "right" thing to do is do anything that helps you get a good story, then an ethical journalist should steal and/or peek inside the envelope before the businesswoman returns.

The key to the "Categorical Imperative" theory is who decides what is "right" and "wrong?" Does society decide? Does the government decide? Do national journalistic organizations decide? Do individual news organizations decide? Does each individual reporter, editor or photographer decide?

The "Utilitarian" theory suggests that ethical behavior is that which will cause the greatest benefit for the greatest number of people. An action is ethical if it maximizes value/gain and minimizes loss/pain.

Example: A source tells you some damaging information about one of the biggest suspected drug dealers in town. An hour later, he calls and pleads with you not to print anything he told you. He says his life and the lives of his family members will be in danger if the information gets out.

Using the "Utilitarian" theory, a journalist would have to decide if the greater benefit lies with informing the public and putting the source and his family at risk or in protecting the source and his family by not disclosing the information. In such cases, the public's right to know usually wins out.

The "Veil of Ignorance" theory suggests that ethical behavior is that which is "BLIND." As with justice, equality of treatment is stressed. No special favors are granted. No biases or prejudices are permitted to influence behavior.

Example: You have two main sources for a story you're working on. One is white, rich and powerful. The other is a member of a minority group who is not rich and powerful. Both ask you not to reveal their names.

Your Thoughts

Which theory of ethics appeals most to you? Why?

What theory of ethics do you think most journalists follow? Why?

Using the "Veil of Ignorance" theory, a journalist would either honor both requests or neither request. Race, creed, color, status, power and wealth would not influence the journalist's decision. He or she would not give special treatment to either source. They would be treated equally.

Codes of Ethics

Most codes of ethics in journalism contain principles and some concrete rules, but usually leave plenty of room for individual judgments based on assessments of situations, circumstances and possible consequences. They can help sensitize journalists and make them more aware of what generally is right and wrong. They can provide some steadiness in the rough waters of journalistic decision-making.

All of the major national associations of journalists and many individual news media organizations have codes of ethics. The Society of Professional Journalists (SPJ) has one of the most specific codes of ethics. It's still pretty wimpy, but compared to most of the other codes, it's tough.

Some of the highlights of the SPJ "Code of Ethics:"

1. The duty of journalists is to serve the truth and report the facts.

2. The responsibility of helping the public learn the truth carries obligations that require journalists to do their jobs with intelligence, objectivity, accuracy and fairness.

3. Journalists who misuse their status for selfish or unworthy motives violate a high trust placed in them as protectors of the public's right to know.

4. Journalists should protect the freedom to discuss, question and challenge the actions and utterances of people in government plus other public or private people.

5. Journalists should accept NOTHING OF VALUE. Gifts, favors, free trips and special treatment/considerations can compromise the integrity of journalists AND their employers.

6. Journalists and their employers should conduct their personal lives in a manner that protects them from real or apparent conflicts of interest. A second job, political involvements and service in community organizations can compromise integrity.

7. Stories or information obtained from public relations/public information practitioners should not be published or broadcast without verifying the accuracy of claims, assertions, etc.

8. Journalists will fight to ensure that the public's business is conducted in public and that public records remain just that—PUBLIC.

9. Journalists will protect confidential sources of information.

10. There is NO EXCUSE for inaccuracies or incompleteness.

11. Headlines should not mislead readers.

12. Photographs and telecasts should give an accurate picture of an event. They should not distort reality and/or exaggerate a minor incident taken out of context.

13. Expressions of opinion by journalists should be clearly labeled. Regular news reports should be free of the biases and opinions of journalists.

14. Even partisan comments by journalists should be based on the truth.

15. Journalists will respect the dignity, privacy, rights and well-being of people.

16. Journalists should not communicate unofficial charges against a person withouth giving him or her a chance to reply.

17. Journalists should not pander to people's morbid curiosity about sex, crime and violence.

18. Journalists will make prompt and complete corrections of errors they make.

19. Journalists should encourage their readers, listeners and viewers to voice their opinions about the news media.

20. Journalists should try to prevent violations of code guidelines.

The American Society of Newspaper Editors (ASNE) has a "Statement of Principles." Highlights of the ASNE code include:

1. Journalists have a responsibility to inform people so they can make judgments on the issues of the day.

2. Journalists should not abuse the power of their professional role for selfish or unworthy purposes.

3. Journalists should inform, provide a forum for debate and keep a close watch over all of the sources of power in society, especially government.

4. Freedom of the press belongs to the people. Journalists should not allow anyone to exploit them or their news organizations.

5. Journalists should ensure that the public's business is conducted in public.

6. Journalists should not accept anything nor pursue any activity that might compromise or even appear to compromise their integrity. Journalists should avoid any conflicts of interest.

7. Journalists should ensure that news content is accurate, free from bias, in context and that all sides have been treated fairly.

8. Journalists will make prompt and prominent corrections of significant errors of fact.

9. Journalists will clearly label opinion or personal interpretation.

10. Journalists will respect the rights of people and observe the common standards of decency.

11. Journalists will give persons who have been accused of something a chance to defend themselves at the earliest opportunity.

12. Journalists will honor pledges of confidentiality to sources at all costs. Such pledges should not be given too easily.

The Radio-Television News Directors Association (RTNDA) "Code of Ethics" is relatively short and sweet. Highlights from the RTNDA code include:

1. Journalists have a responsibility to gather and report information of importance and interest to the public.

2. Journalists should report accurately, honestly and impartially.

3. Journalists should present the *source* or *nature* of news material in an accurate, balanced and fair manner.

4. Journalists will reject sensationalism or misleading emphasis in any form.

5. Journalists will not use audio or video material in a way that deceives listeners or viewers.

6. Journalists will not present staged/rehearsed material as spontaneous news.

7. Journalists will identify people by race, creed, nationality or prior status ONLY when it is relevant to do so.

8. Journalists will clearly label opinion and commentary.

9. Journalists will promptly acknowledge and correct errors.

10. Journalists will protect themselves from real or apparent conflicts of interest. They will reject gifts or favors that would influence or appear to influence their judgments.

11. Journalists will respect the dignity, privacy and well-being of people.

12. Journalists will make promises of confidentiality ONLY with the intention of keeping such promises.

13. Journalists will respect a person's right to a fair trial.

14. Journalists will broadcast the private radio or satellite transmissions of other broadcasters ONLY with permission.

15. Journalists will actively encourage their peers to follow the RTNDA "Code of Ethics."

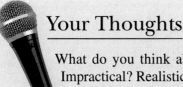

Your Thoughts

What do you think about the content of the codes? Reasonable? Unreasonable? Practical? Impractical? Realistic? Unrealistic? Why do you feel the way you do?

The Society of Professional Journalists conducted a major survey in an effort to determine the views on ethics of members of three prominent professional organizations: the Society of Professional Journalists, the Radio-Television News Directors Association and the Associated Press Managing Editors. Some of the findings demonstrate why it's so difficult to arrive at very many absolutes when it comes to ethics in journalism. About 900 people responded to the survey.

There weren't many significant differences among the groups, but it's clear that there's plenty of disagreement about what is and what is not ethical behavior for journalists. For example, just about all of the respondents agreed that at least some second jobs (moonlighting) were acceptable and just about everyone thought it was a bad idea to reveal the names of rape victims. Other than those two areas, there doesn't seem to be any consistent agreement among journalists.

Take a look at the statistics. You'd think that there would be a lot more agreement about what's appropriate and what's not, but in most cases, a significant number of journalists disagree with the statements. In fact, only rarely did more than 75% of the journalists agree with any statement.

Another complicating factor in trying to get a handle on what's ethical and what's not is the seemingly endless opportunities to go astray and the frequency of apparent ethical transgressions by journalists. Some highlights from another study conducted by Professor Philip Meyer of the University of North Carolina for the American Society of Newspaper Editors found rather regular violations of generally accepted ethical practice. The findings are based on the responses of about 300 newspaper editors.

SPJ Ethics Survey

Statement	Percentage of Agreement		
	SPJ	RTNDA	APME
Some gifts are okay	70%	83%	75%
Holding office is okay	17%	11%	5%
Some moonlighting is okay	99%	98%	99%
Some free trips are okay	65%	65%	49%
Journalistic contests are okay	80%	93%	96%
Commercial contests are okay	69%	80%	64%
Cash prizes are okay	30%	32%	38%
Eavesdropping is not okay	52%	53%	36%
Don't give addresses of crime victims	69%	85%	55%
Don't give names of rape victims	95%	95%	95%
Don't report private suicides	68%	91%	54%
Don't report routine bomb threats	69%	90%	83%

Action/Behavior	Percentage Who See Behavior At Least Several Times a Year
Misrepresentation, eavesdropping, etc.	26%
Granting confidentiality to sources	71%
Invading privacy, hurting feelings	72%
Accepting freebies	33%
Violating government secrecy	39%
Giving publicity to civil disorder	31%
Using "sensationalistic" photos	68%
Getting pressure from advertisers	46%
Having conflicts of interest	30%
Suppressing news to protect community	16%

Lots of "unethical" things going on out there, right? Maybe things aren't as bad as they might seem. Some of the results of another survey of about 100 daily newspaper managing editors by Professor Douglas Anderson might restore your faith a little bit.

About 25% of the editors had posted a code of ethics for staffers to read. About 50% had distributed copies of a code to staffers. The ASNE and SPJ codes were the ones used most often. Almost 50% had developed their own codes to supplement the national codes. Large newspapers were into codes a bit more than small newspapers.

Almost all of the editors thought it was a good idea for staffers to be familiar with the guidelines contained in ethics codes. More than two-thirds said such codes were NOT too vague to be of any practical value.

About 75% of the editors had issued memos to remind staffers of ethical issues. About 66% had held meetings or seminars to discuss ethics.

About 22% of the editors had suspended a staffer and about 25% had fired a staffer for a violation of ethics. Large newspapers had suspended and fired more staffers for such violations than had small newspapers.

About 75% saw some problems with accepting even low-value freebies from news sources. About 90% said special discounts for journalists were not appropriate. About 70% didn't think journalists should accept free trips from news sources.

The editors identified fairness and objectivity, misrepresentation, individual privacy rights vs. public's right to know, conflicts of interest, anonymous sources and compassion for victims vs. the requirements of the profession as the most pressing contemporary ethical issues facing journalists.

Some of my own research shows that while most of the people in charge of radio and television news operations are relatively ethical, there is still plenty of disagreement on just what is acceptable and what is not acceptable behavior for broadcast/electronic journalists.

About 41% of the stations had adopted a formal code of ethics. The RTNDA code was the most often adopted. About 95% of the news directors said electronic journalists should follow the guidelines contained in formal codes of ethics.

The news directors listed FOUR major advantages associated with adopting a formal code of ethics:

1. Provides standards for staffers, especially new staffers
2. Improves the ethics of staffers
3. Improves the social responsibility of staffers
4. Improves credibility and public trust

Gifts/Gratuities	Percentage Who Say Freebie Is Acceptable		
FREEBIE	**ALL**	**RADIO**	**TV**
Tickets to news/sports events	51%	65%	47%
Non-alcoholic beverages at news/sports events	47%	56%	46%
Food at news/sports events	46%	59%	42%
Food at "media/non-news" events/parties	35%	52%	30%
Non-alcoholic beverages at non-news events	33%	49%	29%
Trips to news/sports events	27%	26%	27%
Alcoholic beverages at non-news events	22%	27%	21%
Tickets to news/sports events for PERSONAL use	19%	30%	15%
Alcoholic beverages at news/sports events	14%	17%	13%
Token gifts	10%	6%	8%
Special discounts for being a journalist	8%	11%	8%
Trips for personal pleasure	5%	6%	4%

Moonlighting	Percentage Who Say Opportunity is OK		
OPPORTUNITY	**ALL**	**RADIO**	**TV**
Jobs in fields other than journalism	76%	91%	72%
Announcing sports for a co-owned station	60%	68%	59%
Announcing sports for a competing station	39%	42%	39%
Other jobs in journalism	39%	53%	35%
Narrating commercials in other cities/towns	36%	42%	34%
Public relations for a non-profit organization	36%	42%	34%
Weathercasters narrating local commercials	16%	29%	13%
Sportscasters narrating local commercials	15%	28%	12%
Public relations for a profit-making company	7%	19%	2%
Reporters narrating local commercials	5%	17%	2%
Newscasters narrating local commercials	5%	17%	1%

Conflicts of Interest	Percentage of Agreement		
STATEMENT	**ALL**	**RADIO**	**TV**
At least some freebies are okay	54%	65%	51%
At least some second jobs are okay	81%	94%	78%
Membership in community groups is okay	92%	97%	91%
Holding office in community groups is okay	65%	64%	65%
Journalistic contests are okay	100%	100%	100%
Commercial contests are okay	68%	59%	68%
Self-interests create conflicts too often	27%	68%	24%

Reporting Techniques/Styles	Percentage of Agreement		
STATEMENT	ALL	RADIO	TV
Intruding on private grief is okay	26%	26%	28%
Public people give up many privacy rights	80%	77%	81%
Private lives should be covered only if relevant	75%	70%	76%
Going "undercover" is okay	84%	86%	82%
Hidden cameras/microphones are okay	60%	30%	69%
"Ambush interviews" are okay	47%	52%	47%
Going "live" without a good reason is okay	31%	29%	31%
Reading memos, files, etc. w/o permission is okay	32%	32%	31%
No restrictions on reporting in courts	62%	68%	59%

RADIO-TV NEWS DIRECTORS SURVEY

Reporting Techniques/Styles	Percentage of Agreement		
STATEMENT	ALL	RADIO	TV
"Pooling" should be done if requested by officials	80%	83%	78%
Violating traffic laws is okay	24%	33%	21%
Granting confidentiality to sources is okay	96%	97%	94%
Paying sources for information is okay	14%	17%	11%
Playing "dirty tricks" on competitors is okay	8%	8%	9%
Journalists should help victims in news events	59%	60%	55%

Newscast Production Variables	Percentage of Agreement		
STATEMENT	ALL	RADIO	TV
Too much sensationalism in R-TV news	38%	38%	37%
Too much "fluff" in R-TV news	35%	37%	34%
Too much emphasis on video/sound in R-TV news	19%	20%	19%
Too many unnamed sources in R-TV news	54%	35%	59%
Not enough background information provided	82%	78%	82%
Naming rape victims is okay	9%	5%	12%
Naming victims before families informed is okay	1%	0%	4%
Naming "daredevils" is okay	66%	57%	59%
Naming terrorists is okay	88%	82%	90%
Correcting profane language of sources is okay	51%	50%	49%
Correcting factual mistakes of sources is okay	43%	36%	44%
Correcting grammar mistakes of sources is okay	22%	24%	21%
Holding stories if asked by officials is okay	37%	49%	30%
Reporting suicides of non-public people is okay	15%	21%	14%

The news directors also identified THREE major disadvantages associated with adopting a formal code of ethics:

1. Inhibits flexibility and individual judgment
2. Guidelines are too vague and general
3. Can be used against the station in legal actions

A couple of other findings from the study are kind of interesting, too. The news directors were asked if they thought it was a good idea to require that prospective electronic journalists take a prescribed list of courses while in college, pass a qualifying test and obtain a license BEFORE they are allowed to practice the craft of journalism. In other words, try to make journalism more like other professions—law, medicine, real estate, contracting, cosmetology, etc. The news directors also were asked if they'd like to see some journalistic organization have the power to develop and administer sanctions to punish electronic journalists who violate the guidelines of formal codes of ethics.

About 15% of the news directors thought it would be a good idea to require prospective electronic journalists to take certain courses in college and obtain a license BEFORE being allowed to work in radio or television news. More radio news directors (24%) than television news directors (11%) liked the idea.

About 26% of the news directors thought it would be desirable to have formal sanctions for electronic journalists who violate ethics code guidelines. Again, more radio news directors (33%) than television news directors (26%) supported the idea.

As a summary of the findings from the survey of radio and television news directors, groupings of generally acceptable behaviors, generally unacceptable behaviors and the gray-area behaviors are included below.

Generally Acceptable Behaviors

1. Working at a second job, especially one outside of journalism. Doing play-by-play or "color" sports announcing for a station owned by the same company was also generally acceptable.
2. Joining community groups and even holding office in such groups.
3. Entering contests sponsored by journalistic organizations or commercial entities.
4. Reporting on the private lives of public people, but only if the information is thought to be relevant to how the public person performs his public duties.
5. Using hidden cameras and microphones to gather information.
6. Going "undercover" to gather information. Telling people you're something other than a journalist in order to get them to talk to you or so you can observe people more easily.
7. Agreeing to "pool" equipment, reporters and other resources if asked to do so by government or other officials. This sharing is usually requested when time and/or space is severely limited.
8. Granting confidentiality to sources. Agreeing not to mention their names if they'll provide you with information.

9. Airing quotes from unnamed sources as long as a station news executive knows the names of such sources.
10. Naming the people who do wild and crazy things in an effort to drum up some publicity for themselves or others.
11. Naming terrorists or terrorism organizations.

Generally Unacceptable Behaviors

1. Consuming free food and non-alcoholic beverages at events you've been invited to because you're a journalist even though you're not reporting on the events (non-news events).
2. Taking a free trip to cover some event/issue or for personal pleasure.
3. Consuming alcoholic beverages at news/sports events and at non-news events.
4. Asking for or using free tickets to attend news/sports events or other amusements—zoos, theme parks, concerts, movies, plays, circus performances, ice shows—even though you're not reporting on such events or amusements.
5. Taking free gifts—even small ones—from current or potential news sources.
6. Taking advantage of discounts that are not available to the general public, but are offered to you because you are a journalist.
7. Working at a public relations-related second job.
8. Narrating or acting in commercials.
9. Allowing self-interests to affect news content.
10. Intruding on the private grief of people during times of tragedy.
11. Reading memos, searching through file cabinets and looking through desks to gather information without first obtaining permission from the appropriate people.
12. Naming rape victims.
13. Naming the victims involved in accidents BEFORE the families of such victims have been notified.

14. Reporting on the non-public suicides of non-public people.

15. Paying sources for information.

16. Acquiescing to restrictions placed on how and what can be reported from inside courtrooms.

17. Holding stories when asked to do so by law enforcement or other officials.

18. Playing such "dirty tricks" on competitors as unplugging electrical cords, unplugging microphone cords, providing misinformation and generally attempting to disrupt the news-gathering and news reporting efforts of competitors.

19. Violating traffic laws—speeding, illegal parking or turns—in "hot pursuit" of a story.

20. Sensationalizing stories—hyping them, overplaying the elements of sex, crime and violence in an attempt to boost ratings.

21. Devoting too much time to "fluff" stories—relatively meaningless stories about off-beat people, places and things.

22. Emphasizing video, visuals and natural sound too much in stories. Letting the tail wag the dog so to speak.

23. Correcting the grammar mistakes sources make BEFORE stories are aired.

24. Failing to give enough background information about events and issues so that people have a difficult time understanding the significance of such events and issues.

25. Requiring prospective electronic journalists to take certain courses in college and obtain a license BEFORE they are allowed to work in radio or television news.

26. Imposing sanctions on journalists who violate ethics code guidelines.

Gray-Area Behaviors

1. Accepting freebies from news sources, especially tickets to cover news/sports events and consuming the free food and non-alcoholic beverages available at such events.

2. Doing play-by-play or "color" sports announcing for a station that is not owned by the company that employs you full-time.

3. Working at a second job in some other field of journalism—newspapers, magazines.

4. Conducting "ambush interviews." Showing up unannounced with recorders and cameras rolling in the hope of getting a source's "spontaneous" reaction to a question.

5. Going "live" when you don't really have to.

6. Helping the victims involved in news events and issues.

7. Frequently quoting unnamed sources.

8. Cleaning up profane language used by sources BEFORE quotes and/or "sound bites" are aired.

9. Correcting factual mistakes made by sources BEFORE stories are aired.

Deciding What to Do

Journalists are confronted with ethical issues almost every day. As we've seen, there is not a whole lot of agreement among journalists on just what is and what is not ethical. Codes are vague, situations are different, values are different, people are different and news organizations are different. What's a journalist to do then, when he or she comes face-to-face with a "real-world" ethical dilemma? How is a journalist supposed to figure out what to do? What factors should he or she consider? So many questions and so little time!

Gene Goodwin, in his book, *Groping for Ethics in Journalism,* suggests journalists employ a seven-step method to help them decide what to do.

1. Think about what has been done in the past in similar cases. Past experience and actions can be useful guides for action, especially if we don't repeat the mistakes of the past.

2. Think about what the alternatives are. What different actions COULD be taken? Almost always there are a number of ways to go. Consider as many as possible before taking action.

3. Do a kind of "cost-benefit" analysis. Think about who will be helped and who will be hurt by whatever actions you might take. Again, the best course of action is usually to

try to minimize costs and maximize benefits. No matter what you do, though, it's likely that at least a few people will be harmed in some way. It's unfortunate, but it's a fact of life in journalism.

4. Consider what principles or values might apply. Telling the truth, the public's right to know, fairness, compassion, justice and treating people as you'd like to be treated are just a few of the things to think about. You might also consider some of the traditional theories of ethics and the guidelines/standards contained in codes of ethics.

5. Decide whether an action can be justified to your colleagues, peers, bosses, advertisers, family members, friends, or audience members. Can you persuade people that the action is warranted based on the circumstances and likely outcomes? If you think you'll have difficulty, perhaps you'd better consider another alternative.

6. Decide whether you can live with yourself if you take an action. Will you be able to look at yourself in a mirror and feel proud about what you've done? If not, if you think you might feel guilty, then you'd better come up with another course of action.

7. Decide whether an action fits in with your concept of what good journalism and/or what good citizenship means. Is the action consistent with how you believe journalists should conduct themselves? Is it consistent with how you believe civilized people should treat each other? If you have qualms, take some time and think about other ways to handle the situation.

Model for Action

Joseph Dominick, in his book, *The Dynamics of Mass Communication,* incorporates many of Goodwin's seven steps in a kind of "action plan" for journalists who are confronted with an ethical dilemma.

1. Define the situation. Who's involved? What's involved? What's at stake? What could happen? What are the pros? What are the cons? What are your alternatives?

2. Consider the values present. Is it fair? Is it just? Is it moral? Is it reasonable? Why do you need to do this? Why do you need to do this, this way? Would you want to be treated like this?

3. Think about the ethical principles that apply. Do any of the traditional ethical theories help? Can you find some guidance in a code of ethics? Can you live with yourself if you do this?

4. Decide where your loyalties lie. Should you be true to your news organization, your source, your family, your friends, your audience members, your community, your state, your country, your training or yourself? Why do you have these loyalties? Should you maintain these loyalties? What will happen if you do?

5. Take action. Do something. Make a decision and act on it. Ethical dilemmas have a sort of paralyzing effect on us sometimes, so it is important to analyze the situation, consider the alternatives, think about all the possible outcomes and then ACT! Don't sit around and hope things will get better on their own. Problems and dilemmas have a nasty habit of hanging around unless somebody does something about them. You be that somebody.

Problems and Issues

Clearly, there are serious problems associated with trying to decide what is and what is not ethical journalism. The complicating factors include:

- Situations are different
- People are different
- Communities and societies are different
- News organizations are different
- Journalistic codes of ethics don't offer much help
- "Crime" pays

Just like snowflakes, no two situations are exactly alike. They all have certain unique qualities, so it is difficult to make generalizations about how ethical journalists should act. Difficult does not mean impossible, however.

No two people are exactly alike, either. No two sources. No two journalists. What might be ethical for some, might not be ethical for others.

We are all products of our individual heredities and upbringings. We are who we are and believe what we believe because of what we are born with and what we learn from our family, friends, teachers, acquaintances, co-workers and society in general. We all have our own ideas, opinions, perspectives, backgrounds, attitudes, beliefs and values. This variety makes it difficult to arrive at any consensus about how ethical journalists should conduct themselves.

Do most of the people living in Utah have the same attitudes and values about things that most people living in Southern California have? Of course not. Communities and societies are different, too. Actions that might be acceptable in one community might not necessarily be appropriate in another.

The old saying, "Banned in Boston," is a good example of such differences. Certain books, movies, records, rock groups and even television programs are often banned, pre-empted or censored in some way in certain communities, but allowed to reach people in other areas. Same content. Different communities. It's difficult to find much agreement concerning ethical journalism under such circumstances.

Most news organizations have a "personality" all their own. A socialization process tends to mold staffers into a somewhat cohesive unit. This doesn't mean every staffer thinks alike, of course, but, over time, there is often a sort "coming together" of attitudes and values. Few news organizations are exactly alike, though.

A good example of the differences can often be found in the techniques employed by local television stations in their efforts to be NUMBER ONE in the ratings. At least one station almost always takes the low road and places a heavy emphasis on sleaze—lots of sex, crime, violence, perversion and oddities. At least one station usually tries to stress "quality journalism" and takes the high road. Most stations opt for a sort of middle-of-the-road compromise between all-out sleaze and "just the facts" journalism.

Another good example of news organization differences is the way daily newspapers in New York City report the news. The *Post* and the *Daily News* usually offer sensationalized accounts of events and issues while the *Times* plays things much straighter. With so many different philosophies about what constitutes "good" journalism, is it any wonder that trying to define "ethical" journalism is so fraught with problems?

As we've seen, most of the major codes of ethics in journalism are not as much help as they could or should be. They're too vague. General guidelines are provided, but few, if any, specifics are given. And there's always the loophole wording of "if it compromises" or "if it influences."

Who judges whether a freebie, a second job or some affiliation compromises or influences a journalist's integrity and objectivity? You? Me? The public in general?

We all get to judge a little, but journalists and their bosses make most of those decisions. How likely is it that journalists are going to admit that taking some gift, belonging to some club or working at some part-time job compromises or influences their judgments?

Another problem with the major codes of ethics in journalism is that NONE of them has any teeth. None has any real sanctions that can be imposed on violators. Most mention "encouraging" journalists to act ethically and abide by code guidelines.

There are problems associated with sanctioning violators, of course.

- Who would do the sanctioning?
- What would be the procedures for sanctioning?
- What kind of sanctions should there be?

Perhaps it is such problems and the fear of infringing on a person's freedom of speech/press that prevent journalists from creating stronger codes of ethics. Whatever the reason, the fact remains that the major codes of ethics in journalism don't seem to be doing a very good job of ensuring that journalists practice their craft in an ethical manner.

Gut Check on Ethics for Newsroom Managers

The Poynter Institute, a think tank for those who want to improve journalism, has developed a list of "gut check" questions that newsroom managers/leaders can use to conduct an inventory of their "ethical" readiness in their continuing efforts to improve ethics and deal with difficult issues. The list includes the following:

1. Do you endorse/encourage an atmosphere that puts a premium on identifying ethical problems in their early stages?

Your Thoughts

List four groups/associations that COULD sanction journalists for ethics violations.

List the types of sanctions you think should be imposed on journalists who violate ethics code guidelines.

2. Do you encourage collaborative decision-making and permit multiple and diverse voices to be heard?

3. Do you cultivate the ethical "gadflies" on your staff and encourage them to point out ethical dilemmas and to ask the critical questions?

4. Do you and other managers coach staffers on ethical issues and decision-making procedures?

5. Do you help your staffers develop the abilities to recognize and handle ethical dilemmas on their own?

6. Do you practice what you preach and serve as a model for quality journalism and ethical decision-making?

If more newsroom managers could answer "YES" to these questions, journalism and society would be a lot better off.

One of the biggest problems associated with trying to decide what is ethical and what is not ethical in journalism is the fact that very often a given action will have about as many benefits as drawbacks. Even the most seemingly unethical behavior can often result in many positive developments.

As we've seen, when confronted with an ethical dilemma, journalists should consider such pros and cons before taking action. As you might guess, money, fame, power and influence are among the most common "pros" and it's pretty tough for the "cons" to win out over such formidable competition. The battle must be continually fought, though.

Ethical issues and dilemmas abound in all of the other forms of contemporary media. Various trade organizations have produced guidelines for their members to use when they're confronted with such issues and dilemmas. Most of the codes of ethics,

standards of practice and codes of conduct suffer from the same disease as do the codes of ethics in journalism—they're somewhat vague and lack any real sanctions for code violators. The guidelines are useful, though, in that they provide at least some basis for helping practitioners decide what to do when they're confronted with ethical dilemmas.

The International Chamber of Commerce's Code of Advertising Practice includes the following provisions:

1. All advertising should be legal, decent, honest and truthful.

2. Every advertisment should be prepared with a sense of social responsibility and should conform to the principles of fair competition.

3. No advertisement should impair public confidence in advertising.

4. Advertisements should not contain statements or graphics that offend the prevailing standards of decency.

5. Advertisements should not abuse the trust of consumers or exploit their lack of knowledge or experience.

6. Advertisements should not condone any form of discrimination and should not undermine human dignity.

7. Advertisements should not play on fear without a clear, justifiable reason.

8. Advertisements should not condone or incite violence, nor encourage unlawful or antisocial behavior.

9. Advertisements should not mislead consumers via omissions, ambiguities, or exaggerations.

10. Advertisements should not misuse statistics or scientific terms/procedures.
11. Advertisements should not misuse comparisons. Points of comparisons should be based on facts that can be substantiated.
12. Advertisements should not denigrate any business, profession, activity or product by seeking to arouse public contempt or ridicule.
13. Advertisements should not misuse testimonials or endorsements.
14. Advertisements should be clearly identified/ labeled.

The Public Relations Society of America's Code of Ethics includes the following provisions.

1. Adhere to the highest standards of accuracy and truth.
2. Be faithful to those you represent, but honor your obligation to serve the public interest.
3. Deal fairly with clients, employers, competitors, peers, vendors, the media and the general public.
4. Correct promptly erroneous communications.
5. Reveal the sponsors for causes and interests represented.
6. Avoid real, potential or perceived conflicts of interest.

The International Public Relations Association's Code of Conduct includes the following provisions:

1. Deal fairly with clients and employers.
2. Do not corrupt the channels of public communication.
3. Do not intentionally disseminate false or misleading information.

Recent Research, Developments, and Issues

Even the most respected news organizations can be hit by ethical breaches. The *New York Times* suffered a double whammy of ethical transgressions in mid-2003. Pulitzer Prize-winning reporter Rick Bragg resigned after the newspaper suspended him for a bylined story that turned out to be largely written by a freelancer. No mention of the freelancer's contributions had been revealed to readers.

A few weeks earlier, an even more egregious breach had been discovered. *Times* reporter Jayson Blair was found to have committed "frequent acts of journalistic fraud," including plagiarizing material from other newspapers, making up quotes and lying about where he'd gone to gather information. An internal review discovered problems with about half of the articles Blair had written in the previous eight months.

Blair resigned and apologized for his lapse of journalistic integrity, blaming "personal issues" for his transgressions. The fallout from the incident included the resignations of the top two editors at The New York Times, Howell Raines and Gerald Boyd. A survey of almost 4,000 people found that about 25% trusted the news media less because of the Blair incident. Of course, 55% said the incident really didn't make them trust the news media less, because they didn't trust the news media much to begin with.

Ethical dilemmas increase and intensify during times of war. The Society of Professional Journalists offered the following questions to help journalists resolve, or at least deal with, war-coverage related ethical issues.

1. What's the motivation for publishing or suppressing information, pictures or graphics?
2. What's the government's motivation for requesting publications or suppression of information, pictures or graphics?
3. How reliable and credible is the information obtained and how reliable and credible are the sources of such information?
4. What are the possible/probable consequences of publishing or suppressing information, pictures or graphics? Who will be helped and who will be harmed?
5. What alternative courses of action are available?

Plagiarism reared its ugly head for Katie Couric and CBS in 2007. One of Couric's video essays on the CBS web site turned out to be plagiarized from the *Wall Street Journal*. The essay about library use by young people was reportedly written by a CBS news producer for Couric. Apparently, many of

Ms. Couric's "personal essays" are written by producers and she simply reads them for online delivery. The producer who was guilty of the plagiarism was fired.

Radio shock jock Don Imus joined the CBS producer among the ranks of the fired and disgraced media members. In early 2007, Imus made some racially disparaging remarks about members of the Rutgers University women's basketball team during one of his programs. He weathered the storm of protest for a couple of weeks, but eventually he was suspended and then fired from his morning syndicated radio program. Some experts estimated Imus was making about $10 million a year from his various employment arrangements. He paid a high price for his offensive speech. His absence from the airwaves didn't last too long, though. He was back on the air in less than a year. Sometimes the ability to generate income for owners outweighs concerns about ethics, fairness and propriety.

Air-brushing and other forms of photo/graphics manipulation are practiced regularly in the magazine industry. In early 2008, magazine editors in the United States and England began considering codes of conduct that would provide standards and guidelines for retouching the images and pictures associated with articles in magazines. Images and pictures associated with advertisements in magazines would not be subject to such standards and guidelines, however. Concerns about how the manipulated images of models and celebrities might promote unrealistic perceptions of body and beauty are at the core of the movement to restrict the use of computer-related slimming and anti-aging techniques.

Think Back

1. Define ethics.

2. What are the major traditional theories of ethics and who developed them?

3. What are the major "newer" theories of ethics and what are the major elements of each one?

4. Define and give the basic elements of each of the following ethical theories: Golden Mean, Categorical Imperative, Utilitarian and Veil of Ignorance.

5. List THREE national journalistic organizations that have codes of ethics. Give some of the highlights from each code.

6. What were the general findings of the SPJ ethics survey?

7. What were the general findings of the ASNE ethics survey?

8. What were the general findings of Anderson's ethics survey?

9. What were the general findings of the radio-TV news directors ethics survey?

10. List the SEVEN steps in Goodwin's ethical decision-making model.

11. List the FIVE steps in Dominick's "action plan" for ethics.

12. What are the major complicating factors that make it difficult to create and/or follow codes of ethics?

13. What are some of the shortcomings of the codes of ethics in journalism?

14. What are some of the major advantages of violating codes of ethics?

15. What are some of the major disadvantages of violating codes of ethics?

16. List the "gut check" questions that newsroom managers could ask themselves to determine how well they're facilitating the ethical practice of journalism.

17. What are the major elements of the International Chamber of Commerce's Code of Advertising Practice?

18. What are the major elements of the Public Relations Society of America Code of Ethics?

19. What are the major elements of the International Public Relations Association's Code of Conduct?

20. What were the major ethical breaches committed by reporters for the *New York Times?*

21. What were the questions that the Society of Professional Journalists developed to help journalists deal with war-related ethical dilemmas?

22. How did plagiarism impact Katie Couric and a CBS producer?

23. What happened to radio personality Don Imus when he made some racially charged remarks on air?

24. Why are magazine editors in the United States and England trying to develop some guidelines for digital manipulation of photos and graphics?

Learning Opportunities

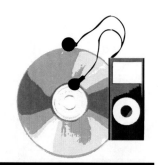

Learning Opportunity One   Due: _____

Learning Opportunity Two   Due: _____

Learning Opportunity Three   Due: _____

Learning Opportunity Four   Due: _____

Learning Opportunity Five   Due: _____

Learning Opportunity Six   Due: _____

Learning Opportunity Seven   Due: _____

Learning Opportunity Eight   Due: _____

Learning Opportunity Nine   Due: _____

Learning Opportunity Ten   Due: _____

Learning Opportunity Eleven   Due: _____

Learning Opportunity Twelve   Due: _____

Learning Opportunity Thirteen   Due: _____

Learning Opportunity Fourteen   Due: _____

Learning Opportunity Fifteen   Due: _____

Learning Opportunity Sixteen   Due: _____

Learning Opportunity Seventeen   Due: _____

Learning
Opportunity

1

Name: _____

Course: _____ Meeting Days/Time: _____

Instructor: _____

Pick FIVE of the most influential figures in the history of the mass media and discuss what you think they'd be doing today if they were involved with a contemporary mass media organization. Explain why you feel the way you do.

Pick one person from each of the following areas: newspapers, books, radio, television and movies.

Learning
Opportunity

2

Name: _____

Course: _____ Meeting Days/Time: _____

Instructor: _____

Ask FIVE friends and FIVE family members how many books they've read for pleasure in the past year. Get a recommendation for a "must-read" book from each of them. Find out what they like about their recommended book.

What's the last book you read for pleasure? What did you like about it?

What book would you like to read? Why?

Learning
Opportunity

3

Name: _____

Course: _____ Meeting Days/Time: _____

Instructor: _____

Examine a copy of the major daily newspaper in your community. Grade it (A+ to F–) on how well it lives up to fulfilling <u>each</u> of its seven major roles and responsibilities. Be sure to cite specific examples to support your seven separate grades.

In a final paragraph, give the newspaper an overall grade and explain why you feel the way you do.

Learning
Opportunity

4

Name: _____

Course: _____ Meeting Days/Time: _____

Instructor: _____

Watch an early evening television newscast on a local station. Grade the station (A+ to F–) on how well it lives up to <u>each</u> of its seven major roles and responsibilities. Be sure to cite specific examples to support your seven separate grades.

In a final paragraph, give the station an overall grade and explain why you feel the way you do.

Learning Opportunity

5

Name: _____

Course: _____ Meeting Days/Time: _____

Instructor: _____

Examine a copy of *Time, Newsweek* or *U.S. News & World Report*. Grade it (A+ to F–) on how well it lives up to <u>each</u> of its seven major roles and responsibilities. Be sure to cite specific examples to support your seven separate grades.

In a final paragraph, give the newsmagazine an overall grade and explain why you feel the way you do.

Learning
Opportunity

6

Name: _____

Course: _____ Meeting Days/Time: _____

Instructor: _____

Start at the beginning of an hour and listen to at least 30 consecutive minutes of an all-news or news-talk radio newscast during morning drive time (6:00 a.m–9:00 a.m.). Grade the station (A+ to F–) on how well it lives up to <u>each</u> of its seven roles and responsibilities. Be sure to cite specific examples to support your seven separate grades.

In a final paragraph, give the station an overall grade and explain why you feel the way you do.

Learning
Opportunity

7

Name: _____

Course: _____ Meeting Days/Time: _____

Instructor: _____

Conduct a mini-survey of 10 of your friends and/or family members to find out what they think about ethics in journalism. What are their biggest complaints? What suggestions do they have to encourage journalists to be more ethical?

After summarizing the findings of your survey, discuss your feelings about the state of ethics in journalism. Do you agree or disagree with the people you interviewed? Why or why not?

What suggestions do you have to encourage journalists to be more ethical?

Learning
Opportunity

8

Name: _____

Course: _____ Meeting Days/Time: _____

Instructor: _____

Think about the ways you've seen journalists depicted in FIVE recent television programs or movies. How were they portrayed? What did they do? How did other characters react to them? Be sure to cite specific examples to support your answers.

Why do you think journalists are depicted in the way they are?

What do you think such depictions do for the image of journalists?

Learning
Opportunity

9

Name: _____

Course: _____ Meeting Days/Time: _____

Instructor: _____

Read a book that deals with ethics in contemporary media. Summarize at least 10 major points/themes in the book. Critique the points/themes. Do you agree or disagree with the author's observations? Why or why not? Be sure to cite specific examples to help explain why you feel the way you do.

BOOK: _____

AUTHOR: _____ YEAR OF PUBLICATION: _____

Learning Opportunity

Name: _____

Course: _____ Meeting Days/Time: _____

Instructor: _____

Pick FIVE specific legal concerns in the mass media. Write a legal statute for each area that improves existing law. Be sure to explain why you think your revisions would make things better.

Learning
Opportunity

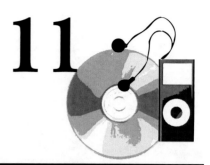

11

Name: _____

Course: _____ Meeting Days/Time: _____

Instructor: _____

Examine an issue of the major daily newspaper in your community and determine what percentage of it is devoted to advertising.

What types of advertisements dominate the newspaper?

Do you see any trends developing? Are certain products advertised in certain sections of the newspaper?

How might newspapers make money besides advertising?

Learning Opportunity

12

Name: _____

Course: _____ Meeting Days/Time: _____

Instructor: _____

Ask 10 friends and/or family members of various ages which theory of mass media message effects makes the most sense to them. Be sure to find out why they feel the way they do. Get them to give you specific examples to support their positions.

Were there differences among the group? What do you make of the differences?

What does your mini-survey tell you about the theories of mass media message effects?

Do you agree or disagree with your interviewees? Why or why not?

Learning
Opportunity

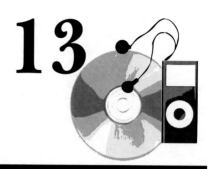

13

Name: _____

Course: _____ Meeting Days/Time: _____

Instructor: _____

Pick FIVE radio stations in your community. Listen to each one for an hour. Listen at the same time of day for five different days. Note the type of programming format for each station. Note the types of products and services advertised on each station.

How much news is aired on each station?

What observations do you have about the target audiences, style, tone, pacing, etc. of each station?

Learning
Opportunity

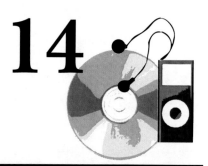

14

Name: _____

Course: _____ Meeting Days/Time: _____

Instructor: _____

Check out a *TV Guide* or a newspaper weekly TV log. Find and list at least FIVE examples of each of the following: network programs, original syndication programs, off-net syndication programs and locally originated programs.

Develop a new program for each source of programming. Be specific. Give plots, themes, locations and main characters.

Learning Opportunity

15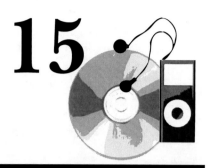

Name: _____

Course: _____   Meeting Days/Time: _____

Instructor: _____

Interview 10 friends and/or family members about their movie-going habits. Select TWO people from each of the following age groups: under 18, 18–25, 26–45, 46–65, 66+.

Find out how often they go. Find out what their favorite type of movie is.

What do they like best about going to the movies? Why?

What do they like least about going to the movies? Why?

Summarize the findings of your mini-survey and discuss your views about going to the movies.

Learning
Opportunity

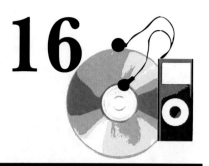

Name: _____

Course: _____ Meeting Days/Time: _____

Instructor: _____

Read a recent issue of a trade magazine for one of the contemporary media. Critique one major article that deals with a current problem/issue in the media. Identify FIVE main points in the article and critique each point.

The majority of your critique should be devoted to your evaluation of the problem/issue and the information contained in the article.

What might the medium or contemporary media in general do to improve the situation?

Learning Opportunity

17

Name: _____

Course: _____ Meeting Days/Time: _____

Instructor: _____

Visit a web site for each of the following:

1. A university
2. A local business
3. A national company
4. A charitable organization

Search for a link to the public relations department and check out a sample of news releases. If releases aren't labeled clearly, they might be found under such labels as "media," "press," "press room," "public affairs," "media relations" or "information."

How "newsworthy" are the releases? Are they written like news stories or are they clearly promotional in nature?

What conclusions about news releases can you draw from your evaluation?

Feedback

Here's your chance to let me know what you think about this edition of *Contemporary Media*. You don't have to include your name, if you'd prefer to remain anonymous. I'm interested in getting your views about the strengths and weaknesses of the book. Thanks for your observations and suggestions.

1. What did you like **best** about the book? Be as specific as possible.

2. What did you like **least** about the book? Be as specific as possible. We can take it.

3. What could be done to improve the book? Be as specific as possible.

4. Rate each chapter on a scale of 1–10 with "10" being excellent.

_____Chapter One: Converging Communications

_____Chapter Two: The Process of Communication

_____Chapter Three: Media Economics

_____Chapter Four: The History of Contemporary Media

_____Chapter Five: Newspapers

_____Chapter Six: Magazines

_____Chapter Seven: Books

_____Chapter Eight: Radio

_____Chapter Nine: Television

_____Chapter Ten: The Recording Industry

_____Chapter Eleven: The Motion Picture Industry

_____Chapter Twelve: Public Relations

_____Chapter Thirteen: Advertising

_____Chapter Fourteen: Legal Rights and Limitations

_____Chapter Fifteen: Ethics

_____Learning Opportunities

5. Any other comments about the book?

Thanks for your comments. Please return the feedback form to:

Professor Tim Wulfemeyer
School of Journalism and Media Studies
San Diego State University
San Diego, CA 92182-4561
twulf@mail.sdsu.edu
(619) 594-2709
(619) 594-6246 (fax)